21ST-CENTURY OXFORD AUTHORS

GENERAL EDITOR

SEAMUS PERRY

This volume in the 21st-Century Oxford Authors series offers students and readers a comprehensive selection of the work of Robert Browning (1812–1889). Accompanied by full scholarly apparatus, this is the first one-volume fully annotated edition of Browning's poetry. It presents work written across the breadth of his career, from the very first poem he published, *Pauline*, to *Asolando*, the volume that was published on the day that he died.

The text chosen is, wherever possible, the text of the poem as it was first published by Browning himself, and as a consequence the volume also constitutes a kind of biography that enables students to understand Browning's development over the course of his life. The edition reveals a poet who began as a bold experimentalist, and who continued to experiment throughout a writing career of more than fifty years. Browning is best known for his dramatic monologues, and the dramatic monologues are fully represented in this volume, but he was also a narrative poet, a poet of philosophical reflection, and a poet who fashioned an extraordinary variety of lyric measures. This volume reveals Browning as a far more versatile poet than he is often taken to be. There are two important prose items, an essay on Shelley and a letter to Ruskin which clarify Browning's intellectual stance. The Notes include brief headnotes to each poem followed by detailed annotation, and they assist the reader in developing a full understanding of these masterful poems.

Explanatory notes and commentary are included, to enhance the study, understanding, and enjoyment of these works, and the edition includes an Introduction to the life and works of Browning, and a Chronology.

Richard Cronin has published very widely on nineteenth-century literature. After teaching for many years at the University of Glasgow, he has recently been appointed to a chair at Oxford Brookes University.

Dorothy McMillan is an Honorary Research Fellow of the University of Glasgow, and has published widely with a particular focus on Scottish literature and poetry by women.

Seamus Perry is the General Editor of the 21st-Century Oxford Authors series. He is Professor of English Literature at the University of Oxford and a Fellow of Balliol College. His publications include *Coleridge and the Uses of Division* and *Coleridge's Notebooks: A Selection*, and, co-edited with Robert Douglas-Fairhurst, *Tennyson Among the Poets* (all OUP).

21st-CENTURY OXFORD AUTHORS

Robert Browning

EDITED BY

RICHARD CRONIN AND
DOROTHY McMILLAN

UNIVERSITY PRESS

OXFORD
UNIVERSITY PRESS

Great Clarendon Street, Oxford, OX2 6DP,
United Kingdom

Oxford University Press is a department of the University of Oxford.
It furthers the University's objective of excellence in research, scholarship,
and education by publishing worldwide. Oxford is a registered trade mark of
Oxford University Press in the UK and in certain other countries

First published 2015
First published in paperback 2018

Published in the United States of America by Oxford University Press
198 Madison Avenue, New York, NY 10016, United States of America

British Library Cataloguing in Publication Data
Data available

Library of Congress Cataloging in Publication Data
Data available

ISBN 978–0–19–959942–4 (Hbk.)
ISBN 978–0–19–879762–3 (Pbk.)

CONTENTS

FROM *HOOD'S MAGAZINE*, vol. 1, June 1844; vol. 2, July 1844; vol. 3, March 1845; vol. 3, April 1845

FROM *BELLS AND POMEGRANATES, NO. VII, DRAMATIC ROMANCES AND LYRICS* (1845)

FROM *LETTERS OF PERCY BYSSHE SHELLEY* (1852)

FROM *MEN AND WOMEN, I AND II* (1855)

FROM *FIFINE AT THE FAIR* (1872)

THE INN ALBUM (1875)

FROM *PACCHIAROTTO AND HOW HE WORKED IN DISTEMPER: WITH OTHER POEMS* (1876)

FROM *LA SAISIAZ* AND *THE TWO POETS OF CROISIC* (1878)

FROM *DRAMATIC IDYLS, 2nd SERIES* (1880)

FROM *JOCOSERIA* (1883)

FROM *FERISHTAH'S FANCIES* (1884)

FROM ANDREW REID, ED., *WHY I AM A LIBERAL* (1885)

FROM *PARLEYINGS WITH CERTAIN PEOPLE OF IMPORTANCE IN THEIR DAY* (1887)

FROM *THE ATHENAEUM*, 13 JULY 1889

FROM *ASOLANDO: FANCIES AND FACTS* (1889)

ACKNOWLEDGEMENTS

We are grateful to the following for permission to reproduce copyright material: the Trustees of the British Museum for *Perseus et Andromède*, Giovanni Volpato after Polidoro da Caravaggio (Fig. 1); Wellesley College, Margaret Clapp Library, Special Collections for the first page of RB's letter to EBB, 1845 (Fig. 3); Glasgow University Library for the title pages of *Men and Women*, vols. 1 and 2, *La Saisiaz*, *Parleyings etc* (Figs. 4, 6, 9, and 11); Galleria Palatina, Palazzo Pitti, Florence for *Doppio Ritratto* (Fig. 7); Balliol College Library for Browning holographs (Figs. 8, 10, and 12); the National Art Library for John Stuart Mill's annotations in *Pauline*.

We thank the librarians of Glasgow University Library, the National Library, Edinburgh, the British Library, Balliol College Library, and the National Art Library who have been unfailingly helpful and informative.

We are greatly indebted to the work of previous editors of Browning, particularly the editors of the Penguin, Oxford, Ohio, and Longman editions of the poems, and to the editors of the various editions of the Brownings' correspondence.

LIST OF ILLUSTRATIONS

LIST OF ABBREVIATIONS

Correspondence	*The Brownings' Correspondence*, ed. Philip Kelley et al. (Winfield, Kan., and London: Wedgestone Press, 1984–)
DeVane, *Handbook*	William Clyde DeVane, *A Browning Handbook*, 2nd edn. (New York: Appleton-Century-Crofts, 1955)
EBB	Elizabeth Barrett Browning
EBB to Arabella	*Letters of Elizabeth Barrett Browning to her Sister Arabella*, ed. Scott Lewis (Waco, Tex.: Wedgestone Press, 2002)
Furnivall	*Browning's Trumpeter: The Correspondence of Robert Browning and Frederick J Furnivall, 1872–1889*, ed. William S. Peterson (Washington: Decatur Press, 1979)
George Barrett	*Letters of the Brownings to George Barrett*, ed. Paul Landis (Urbana: University of Illinois Press, 1958)
Jameson	Anna Jameson, *Memoirs of Early Italian Painters, and of the Progress of Painting in Italy: Cimabue to Bassano*, new edn. (London: John Murray, 1868)
Kelley and Coley	Philip Kelley and Betty A. Coley, *The Browning Collection: A Reconstruction with Other Memorabilia* (London: Armstrong Browning Library of Baylor University, 1984)
Longman	*The Poems of Robert Browning*, Longman Annotated English Poets, ed. John Woolford et al. (London: Longman, 1991–)
RBB	Robert Browning
Ohio	*The Complete Works of Robert Browning, with Variant Readings and Annotations*, vols. i–xvii, ed. Roma A. King, Jr., et al. (Ohio: Ohio University Press, 1969–2011)
Orr, *Handbook*	Mrs Sutherland Orr, *A Handbook to the Works of Robert Browning*, 7th edn. (London: George Bell, 1896)
Orr, *Life*	Mrs Sutherland Orr, *Life and Letters of Robert Browning*, 2nd edn. (London: Elder and Co., 1891)
Oxford	*The Poetical Works of Robert Browning*, Oxford English Poets, ed. Ian Jack et al. (Oxford: Clarendon Press, 1983–)
RB	Robert Browning

Turner	*Men and Women*, ed. Paul Turner (London: Oxford University Press, 1972)
Vasari	*Lives of the Most Eminent Painters, Sculptors and Architects*, 5 vols. trans. from the Italian of Giorgio Vasari with notes etc. by Mrs Jonathan Foster (London: Bohn, 1850–2)
Wedgwood	*Robert Browning and Julia Wedgwood: A Broken Friendship as Revealed in their Letters*, ed. Richard Curle (London: Murray & Cape, 1937)
Wise	*Letters of Robert Browning Collected by Thomas J. Wise*, ed. Thurman L. Hood (London: Murray, 1933)

INTRODUCTION

Robert Browning was born on 7 May 1812, at Camberwell. He was the first child and only son of Robert Browning, a clerk at the Bank of England, and his wife Sarah Anna Wiedemann, ten years older than her husband, who was of Scottish descent. Camberwell was at the time a leafy suburb, and Browning enjoyed a happy, privileged childhood, doted on by parents who early recognized their son's talents. His mother, who was a keen gardener, gave him her love of flowers, and of the garden creatures that appear so often in the poems: newts, slugs, 'the water-beetle with great blind deaf face' ('Sibrandus Schafnaburgensis', 53). His father, still more importantly for the poet he was to become, gave him the run of his library. Robert Browning senior was an inveterate and generously indiscriminate collector of old books. Browning learned little from the local schools he attended, and was disappointed by the newly founded London University where he attended classes for a few months in 1828. But he had his mother's piano lessons, the tutors in music that his parents employed, amongst them a Camberwell neighbour, 'Great John Relfe' ('Parleying With Charles Avison', 81), the composer and musical theorist. He had nearby Dulwich Picture Gallery with its fine collection that he came to know intimately. Best of all he had his father's library and his father's encouragement to explore it. 'Development', a poem first published in *Asolando* on the day of Browning's death, begins proudly, 'My Father was a scholar and knew Greek', and goes on to celebrate the tact with which his father had gone about imparting his love of Greek literature to his son. Browning was amongst the most learned of 19th-century poets, but his learning had the indiscriminate character of his father's library. He retained throughout his life something of the character of the autodidact.

Browning was a precocious youth. His father tried to arrange the publication of a youthful volume of Byronic verse, 'Incondita', inspired perhaps by the news in 1824 of the poet's death. Luckily he failed. The manuscript does not survive. For a time the boy considered becoming a musician, a composer, rather than a poet (he retained throughout his life an interest in other arts, apprenticing himself in the 1850s in Rome to his friend the American sculptor William Wetmore Story, and dreaming, as he records in 'Old Pictures in Florence', of coming across in some dusty shop an undiscovered

Giotto). His course of life was decided in 1826 or 1827 when his cousin James Silverthorne presented him with a copy of Shelley's *Miscellaneous Poems* in William Benbow's pirated edition. It was, as Browning repeatedly acknowledged, under the auspices of Shelley that he became a poet.

In March 1833 Browning inaugurated a poetic career that was to last for more than half a century, until 12 December 1889, when the final volume, *Asolando*, was published. *Pauline*, the poem with which Browning announced himself to the world, is an astonishing performance, a fragmentary blank verse poem in which a young man confesses to the woman who loves him his heady consciousness of his own genius. It is not so much the poem of a 20-year-old as a poem in which the 20-year-old Browning flamboyantly rehearses the kind of poem that a 20-year-old possessed with talents as extraordinary as his own might be expected to write. It is a Shelleyan poem and pauses to pay tribute to Shelley as the 'Sun-treader', but it is already at a remove from its own Shelleyanism. Just as Shelley's *Posthumous Poems* were prepared for publication by his widow, *Pauline* is presented as if edited from the poet's notebooks, presumably after his decease, by the woman to whom the poem is addressed (as if this conceit were not affected enough, the lengthy note by Pauline appended to the poem is written in reasonably accurate French). As John Stuart Mill noted, *Pauline* is the work of a poet possessed of a more intense 'self-consciousness than [he] ever knew in any sane human being'.[1] But he might have added that Browning is not only intensely self-conscious, he is intensely self-conscious about his self-consciousness. Browning was apt to speak of *Pauline* as an aberration and he was persuaded to re-publish the poem only reluctantly. It is often represented as a poem written against the grain of Browning's genius, a confessional poem by a poet whose talent was for the objective and the dramatic. But the intense self-consciousness that Mill recognized in *Pauline* reveals itself all through his career. He follows Shelley, for example ('Less oft is peace in Shelley's mind | Than calm in waters seen' ('The Recollection', 88–9)), in naming himself in poems. He addresses himself in 'A Light Woman' (1855), 'Robert Browning, you writer of plays', mimics in *The Inn Album* (1875) the charge most often brought against him by the critics,

[1] Mill's annotated copy of the poem is now in the National Art Library in the Victoria and Albert Museum, London; a number of Mill's annotations are quoted in the Notes in this volume.

'That Bard's a Browning; he neglects the form', and observes in 'Development', 'But then "No dream's worth waking"—Browning says' (84). Pauline was reviewed respectfully, but in a letter of 1886 to T. J. Wise Browning recalled, 'To the best of my belief, no single copy of the original edition of *Pauline* found a buyer' (*Wise*, 251).

The publication of *Pauline* inaugurated a period of neglect by reviewers and readers that was to persist for thirty years. It was bitterly resented by Browning. As late as 1868, in the first book of his murder epic, *The Ring and the Book*, Browning paused to address his detractors, 'Well, British Public, ye who like me not' (410). Various explanations occur. Browning had the misfortune to begin his publishing career in a decade, the 1830s, in which the market for poetry had collapsed. Only Edward Moxon of the major publishers remained willing to bring out volumes by individual poets, and then only on condition that the poets covered his costs. Browning lacked too the purchase on the literary world that his major contemporary, Tennyson, was able to command. Browning's friends as a young man formed themselves into a loose club known as 'The Set' or 'The Colloquials', and they included in their number distinguished men, some of them poets themselves such as Joseph Arnould who went on to become judge of the Supreme Court of Bombay and Alfred Domett who was to become the first prime minister of New Zealand. But they lacked the access to the major reviews and magazines that allowed Tennyson's Cambridge friends to manage his career so deftly that the publication of the two-volume *Poems* in 1842 established him as the first poet of his generation, and the likely successor to Wordsworth as Poet Laureate when the grand old man should finally die. Browning believed, no doubt mistakenly, that it might all have been different had John Stuart Mill succeeded in placing the review of *Pauline* that he had agreed to write. Browning's career was nurtured by W. J. Fox, editor of the *Monthly Repository*, whom Browning named his 'literary godfather', by friends such as John Forster and Thomas Carlyle, and, up to a point, by the foremost actor manager of the day, William Macready, but they failed to persuade the literary world to share their own respect for the poet and his work. The *Edinburgh Review* in its notice of his play, *Strafford*, categorized him as a member of 'the "Cockney School" of dramatic authorship'.[2] In his early years Browning seemed to invite social condescension. Even some of Elizabeth Barrett's friends formed

[2] *Edinburgh Review*, 66 (1837), 132–51, 147.

the impression that she had introduced him into social circles that were a little above him. Finally, there was the unusual difficulty of poems that made demands on their readers that few were willing or able to accept.

Browning's second publication, *Paracelsus* (1835), a study like *Pauline* of thwarted genius, but far more ambitious both in length and scope, did not sell, but it established Browning as a coming man. Elizabeth Barrett reported that her brother had thought it worthwhile to attend an evening party given by Thomas Noon Talfourd 'just to see the author of "Paracelsus" dance the polka' (*Correspondence*, xi. 228). But the fillip to Browning's reputation did not survive the publication of the third major poem, *Sordello*, 1840, which achieved at once and maintained for many years its reputation as a byword for obscurity. Even Browning's friend Carlyle reported, 'My wife has read through "Sordello" without being able to make out whether "Sordello" was a man, or a city, or a book.'[3] Browning had already embarked on another, longer-lasting experiment that also ended in failure. In 1837 he published his historical tragedy, *Strafford*, to coincide with its production at Covent Garden, with Macready in the title role. Despite Macready's assistance there were only five performances. For much of the next decade, Browning devoted himself to the drama, publishing in that period eight plays, only one of which, *A Blot in the 'Scutcheon*, was ever performed, for just three nights at Drury Lane. Of all this effort, the only trace in this volume is *Pippa Passes* (1841), formally the most original of Browning's plays, and a play which, perhaps for that reason, he never offered for performance, and also, if we grant it the status of play accorded to it in 1884 by the Browning Society when they organized a performance, *In the Balcony* from *Men and Women*, 1855.[4]

The decade in which Browning occupied himself principally with the drama was nevertheless crucial in establishing his character as a poet. It persuaded him that the cast of his talent was essentially dramatic (although he might have deduced as much from *Pauline*, which is a dramatic poem even if the character that it dramatizes is closely modelled on Browning's own), and it convinced him that if he was to embrace the profession of poetry he must do so without the expectation of being read. It was a predicament with practical

[3] DeVane, *Handbook*, 80.

[4] *In a Balcony* was staged at the Prince's Hall, Piccadilly, on the evening of Friday, 28 November 1884. The performance received several reviews, notably one by Frederick Wedmore in *The Academy* (6 December 1884), 383–4.

consequences that Browning met by publishing his work in the years from 1841 to 1846 in a series to which he gave the name *Bells and Pomegranates*, a characteristically obscure title that puzzled even Elizabeth Barrett, until Browning explained that it was a biblical reference chosen to indicate the duty of the poet both to instruct and delight (*Correspondence*, xi. 129). There were eventually eight volumes in the series, if volumes is the right word for paper-bound pamphlets, the first of which, *Pippa Passes*, sold for sixpence. It was the stratagem of a poet determined to reduce to the minimum production costs that he had no expectation of recouping. In the Advertisement to the third volume in the series, *Dramatic Lyrics*, 1842, Browning advised that his poems should be thought of as '"Dramatic Pieces"; being, though often Lyric in expression, always Dramatic in principle, and so many utterances of so many imaginary persons, not mine'. The same volume included Browning's earliest dramatic monologues, two of which, 'Johannes Agricola' and 'Porphyria', had already appeared six years earlier in the *Monthly Repository*. The dramatic monologue, the form with which Browning has remained most closely associated, perfectly suited him at this stage in his career. It allowed expression to his thwarted dramatic ambitions, even if it cemented his reputation for obscurity amongst readers who were unused to first-person poems in which the speaker was not identified with the poet. In Browning's dramatic monologues the speaker often addresses a silent auditor, and in this the form faithfully reflects the predicament of a poet who published his poems without any assurance that they would be read, or, if read, that they would be understood.

On 10 January 1845, Browning wrote his first letter to Elizabeth Barrett. It is an awkward, self-conscious performance, reproduced in this volume, an address by one poet to another who was his senior not only in years but reputation. Elizabeth Barrett's *Poems* of 1844 had established her as a poet second only to Tennyson. Until they met for the first time on 20 May theirs was a purely literary relationship, but the following year, on 12 September 1846, they married secretly, aware that Elizabeth Barrett's father would never consent to the marriage of any of his children. A week later the 40-year-old Elizabeth Barrett eloped with her husband. The two travelled to Paris, and then on to Italy. In 1847 they set up house in 'Casa Guidi' in Florence, which remained their permanent home until 1861. Elizabeth died on 29 June, and Browning left Florence a month later, accompanied by his 12-year-old son, Pen. He was never to return. Browning remains the most famously married poet in all of English literature, a status given him by Elizabeth Barrett Browning's *Sonnets from the Portuguese*, which were recognized almost as soon as she published them in 1850 as an account of her own courtship and marriage. Browning wore that 'strange, heavy crown' (*Wedgwood*, 114) for the rest of his life, but he embellished it too by the poems both before his wife's death and after it in which he wrote his own celebrations of the marriage, poems such as 'One Word More', 'By the Fireside', 'The Householder', and his address in *The Ring and the Book* to his 'lyric Love, half-angel and half-bird' (I. 1391). Within a decade of his death his son published his parents' courtship correspondence, and in 1930 Rudolf Besier's play *The Barretts of Wimpole Street* (filmed versions were produced in 1934 and 1957) confirmed the centrality of the courtship and the subsequent elopement for a new century.

Some later commentators have doubted the happiness of the marriage, but their case rests largely on a tendentious reading of poems that Browning insisted were dramatic as expressions of personal feeling. It is a method of reading that he mocks in 'Master Hugues of Saxe-Gotha' when the organist tries to dissipate the strangeness of the score that he is playing by imagining it as a portrait of the old composer, 'eyes buried in pits on each cheek, | Like two great breves, as they wrote them of yore, | Each side that bar, your straight beak!' (43–5). At the beginning of the relationship at any rate it seems that life imitated art rather than vice versa. The elopement had an origin in the print of Polidoro da Caravaggio's 'Perseus and Andromeda' that Browning kept above his desk, in which Perseus rescued the maiden about to be sacrificed to the sea-monster, and an origin too in Browning's poem 'The Flight of the Duchess'. In his courtship correspondence he discussed 'The Flight' more often with Elizabeth Barrett than any other poem. In January 1845, in only his second letter to his future wife, he represented the two of them as poets of antithetical type: 'you speak out, *you*,—I only make men & women speak, and fear the pure white light, even if it is in me' (*Correspondence*, x. 22). It remained for him a crucial distinction. A poem published in 1876, 'Numpholeptos', hinges on a similar contrast, between the nymph who shines with a cold white light, and the lover who can find her only when her light is refracted into its prismatic colours. He understands himself and his wife as poets of two quite different kinds, and yet he does not quite abandon the notion that they might be revealed at last not as incompatible but complementary. Even in the early letter he added that, though he might not as yet speak his poems in his own person, 'I mean to try.' A month later he was still more explicit. The poems he had published thus far might only have demonstrated his capacity for 'dramatic sympathy', but he hopes still to embark on the great work, 'what I hope I was born to begin and end,—"R. B. a poem"' (*Correspondence*, x. 69). The remark might seem out of character, produced by his anxiety to pay court to his new correspondent, except that near the end of his life, in 1887, in a letter to a young admirer, Margaret Keep, he claimed that he had at last fulfilled that youthful ambition: 'When you speak of "Paracelsus"—written fifty years or more ago—as "Christmas-Eve" was, almost forty—you should understand that they contain only partial endeavours at the truth,—and that only in the whole of my work may be expected to appear a general impression of the truth.'[5] He seems to have believed of his poems what the Pope in *The Ring and the Book* believes of the various depositions submitted in the trial of Guido for the murder of his wife: 'truth nowhere lies yet everywhere in these— | Not absolutely in a portion, yet | Evolvible from the whole' (10. 229–31). The 'truth' that Browning believed himself to have arrived at, not in any one poem, but in his poems taken as a whole, was not simply the truth about himself, but it does seem to have included that truth. In his essay on Shelley Browning distinguishes between the objective and the subjective poet, but goes on to wonder why 'these two modes of poetic faculty may not issue hereafter from the same poet in successive perfect works'. It is noteworthy that he chose to end his greatest volume, *Men and Women*, with a poem 'One Word More' in which he contrived at once to celebrate his achievement as a dramatic poet, and write a tenderly private love lyric to his wife, speaking 'this once in [his] true person' (137):

Love, you saw me gather men and women,
Live or dead or fashioned by my fancy,
Enter each and all, and use their service,
Speak from every mouth,—the speech, a poem.
Hardly shall I tell my joys and sorrows,
Hopes and fears, belief and disbelieving:
I am mine and yours—the rest be all men's. (129–35)

Browning has been almost always celebrated as a dramatic poet, but we hope to indicate in this volume that he is better thought of as a poet preoccupied by the relationship between dramatic and lyric voices,

[5] Quoted in *Poetic Works of Robert Browning*, xv: *Parleyings* and *Asolando*, ed. Stefan Hawlin and Michael Meredith (Oxford: Oxford University Press, 2010), 294.

between speaking in his own voice and allowing men and women to speak through him. He allows in the essay on Shelley that the same poet might contrive to be perfectly subjective and perfectly objective in successive works, but he seems haunted throughout his career by the still more extravagant possibility that the two impulses might both find perfect expression in the one work.

Men and Women was the finest product of the Italian years, years spent largely in Florence, but with summers in the hills, winters in Rome, and longer trips to France and to England. In March 1849, Elizabeth Barrett Browning gave birth to their son Robert Wiedeman Browning, early nicknamed Penini, and known to his father for the rest of his life as Pen. Husband and wife lived a social life, he more than she, a life spent principally amongst the expatriate community, both British and American. Their enthusiasm for Italian nationhood never fully translated itself into an enthusiasm for Italian people. But most of their time was spent with each other. It is surely not a coincidence that it was in these years that Browning made himself into the great poet of marriage in a century remarkable for marriage poetry (think, for example, of Patmore, Meredith, and Hardy). He had always been preoccupied by the relationship between men and women, but the most impressive poems of the early years most often display Browning's unsettling ability to find in the most sociopathic of his speakers a perverse echo of his own subjectivity. Porphyria's lover strangles her, but Browning finds in him a version of the lyric poet, a character evident not just in his elegant five-line stanzas but in the impulse to freeze the moment that prompts him to kill. In 'My Last Duchess' the gusto with which Browning displays the Duke to his reader's appalled fascination has an eerie kinship with the pleasure that the Duke himself takes in displaying to chosen guests the portrait of his murdered wife. It is a talent that he retained throughout his career. The five-line stanza of 'Mesmerism', included in *Men and Women*, is silkier and still more sinister than the stanza of 'Porphyria's Lover'. The mesmerist gloats in his power to summon the phantom image of a woman so powerfully that at the last she must obey 'flesh and all' (73). Not content with summoning her spirit, he continues to exert his power until he gains control of her body too. The poem is suffused by Browning's suspicion of the paranormal arts to which his wife was so attracted, but suffused too by an uneasy recognition that his own dramatic method might entail not a surrender of self but a triumphant demonstration of his own uncanny ability to enter the minds of his characters and usurp their will. His dramatic imagination, the poems often intimate, feeds the urge to exercise power over others that many of his characters display so ruthlessly. None of those characters is held in fiercer contempt than Mr Sludge, the medium, in *Dramatis Personæ*, but the contempt does not obstruct Browning's recognition that Sludge's practices constitute, as Sludge himself more than once claims, a kind of bastard poetry. Poets, too, as Browning acknowledges (most forcefully in *The Ring and the Book*), bring the dead back to life, and the achievements of poets are as dependent on their deployment of rhetorical skills as are Sludge's on his own, more disreputable stratagems. But in the Italian years Browning began to supplement poems of this type with another kind of poem, in which the effort is not to achieve an intimacy with characters that threaten to defeat any such attempt, but to achieve a dispassionate understanding of behaviour much closer home.

Spiritualism prompted the most serious of Browning's disagreements with his wife, other notable causes of dissension being Elizabeth Barrett Browning's admiration of Napoleon III, and her opium addiction. The two first figure in 'A Lover's Quarrel', in which the speaker retains Browning's opinion of Napoleon's wedding—'The Emperor deep and cold' has 'taken a bride | To his gruesome side' (30–2)—but regards his wife's other enthusiasm more emolliently:

> Try, will our table turn?
> Lay your hand there light, and yearn
> 'Till the yearning slips
> Through the finger-tips
> In a fire which few discern,
> And a very few feel burn,
> And the rest, they may live and learn! (43–9)

The poem charts the man's regret for a hasty word that has interrupted an intimacy that he tries to recapture in the delicate movement of his stanzas. It is hard to resist the suspicion that it was prompted by a marital dissension in the Browning household. But just as Browning can recognize a version of himself even in a man as despised as Sludge, he can examine what seems to be a version of himself with a strange dispassion, as intent on analysing the economy of the man's emotions as in giving voice to them.

Elizabeth Barrett Browning held that poets were distinguished by their capacity for seeing double:

> poets should
> Exert a double vision; should have eyes
> To see near things as comprehensively
> As if afar they took their point of sight,
> And distant things as intimately deep
> As if they touched them. (*Aurora Leigh*, 5. 183–8)

Browning had always recognized that capacity in himself, but from the moment that he introduced himself by letter to Elizabeth Barrett and recognized in her a way of seeing that complemented his own he seems to have associated double vision with the institution of marriage. It is as if marriage consecrated his belief that the world is best looked at through two pairs of eyes.

Browning characteristically keeps his own feelings at arm's length, and he treats his own ideas rather similarly. When Andrea del Sarto exclaims, 'Ah, but a man's reach should exceed his grasp, | Or what's a heaven for?' (97–8) the thought has rightly been identified as a favourite of Browning's, the most compressed statement of his belief that only through imperfection can a finite art intimate the matter of infinite moment that is the artist's true concern. But in Andrea's mouth the thought is contaminated by the lassitude evident in the rhythm of the lines. Fra Lippo Lippi is commonly credited with an exuberant vitality that brings his voice rather close to Browning's, but Lippo Lippi's aesthetics are surely compromised by a coarse materialism that can understand the spiritual only by seeking out bodily analogies:

> Why can't a painter lift each foot in turn,
> Left foot and right foot, go a double step,
> Make his flesh liker and his soul more like,
> Both in their order? (205–8)

Lippo Lippi's way of thinking allows scarcely any difference between souls and soles. Some of Browning's most delicate effects are produced by his refusal to bring into perfect accord the character of his speakers and the character of their ideas. The relationship between them is shifting, not fixed, like the relationship between two individuals joined in a marriage.

The technique is most obviously displayed in Browning's political poems. Browning, like his wife, was a steadfast supporter of the Italian nationalist movement, but quite unlike her in the manner in which he treats the issue in his poems. Luigi, the principled assassin of *Pippa*

Passes, disquiets by his deep sense that his work is sanctioned by God (*Pippa Passes*, III. 147–50). His deafness to his mother's entreaties is as likely to appal readers as to win their admiration. Mazzini thanked Browning for 'Italy in England'. He clearly thought of the poem as Browning's contribution to the cause, but the poem seems at least as concerned to reveal the human cost of allowing political commitment precedence over human attachment. Browning is suspicious of political idealists, and just as suspicious of pragmatists (see, for example, 'Respectability'). In his political poems, as in all his poems, he seems scarcely capable of advancing a view without putting that view into question. The late sonnet 'Why I Am a Liberal', written in support of the Liberal Party's 1885 election campaign, works only to prove the rule. Browning seems discomforted not just by the form of the Petrarchan sonnet but by the obligation he has placed himself under to speak with a single mind.

Browning found himself as a poet in Italy, in the years of his marriage. On 29 June 1861, his wife died, and Browning and his young son returned to England. We include one of the letters in which he describes the circumstances of the death. Browning survived his wife for more than twenty-eight years, a prolonged widowhood, complicated by a refusal to remarry despite his seeming inability to live contentedly as a single man. For twenty-five of these years Browning lived at 19 Warwick Crescent, overlooking the Regent's Canal. He was a clumsily solicitous father to his son (who would have had a happier life if his mother's other pregnancies had not all terminated in miscarriages), he took long holidays at home and abroad, usually in France, he took up swimming and smoking cigarettes, and became an inveterate diner out. These were the years in which Browning at last achieved the literary reputation that had eluded him for so long, and won too the reputation that Henry James has done most to preserve of the writer who 'disappoints every one who looks in him for the genius that created the pages they adore' ('The Private Life', 1892). The contrast that James insists on between the public man of 'loud and cheerful and copious conversation' and the writer of genius is not one that would have struck Browning's friends in his flamboyant youth. The London years, the years given over to dining out, have been the despair of even Browning's best biographers, and yet all through these years Browning continued to write. He wrote irregularly, as he had always done, but he wrote still in convulsive spurts of energy.

We have chosen to represent more of this late work than many previous editors, and not just because it is necessary if the work that it was Browning's ambition to write as a young man, the work that he entitled 'R.B. a poem', is to be fairly represented. The decision that will most surprise is to include the whole of a poem for which even Browning's admirer Henry James could summon little enthusiasm. Of *The Inn Album* he was prepared to allow that a 'great poem might perhaps have been made of it', while insisting that, as it was, it could not claim to be 'any poem whatsoever'.[6] We choose it as the last and perhaps the best of the four long poems of the 1870s in which Browning energetically set himself to address the contemporary world. For most writers in their sixties the world that they live in is much less vivid than the world of their youth that they remember, but it was not so for Browning. All four poems deserve to be read more widely, but of *Prince Hohenstiel-Schwangau* (1871), *Fifine at the Fair* (1872), *Red Cotton Night-Cap Country* (1873), and *The Inn Album* (1875), we have chosen the most uncompromisingly modern of all. It is a poem that demands a literary reader, but a reader who is just as conversant with the newspapers, who knows what horse won the Derby in 1875, who knows that Psidium is the fragrance of the season, and that the recent fashion for roller-skating has made 'rink' one of the words of the year. Browning launched his career with the dazzlingly experimental *Pauline*, and forty-three years later in *The Inn Album* he is still conducting restless generic experiments. The poem is, like most of his poems, dramatic, but the speeches of its four unnamed characters are punctuated by laconic third-person interruptions, and regularly disregard the limits that even the most tolerant audience would set to the speeches of characters on stage. Browning compares his poem with a sensation novel, with a tragedy (it does after all end in a murder and suicide), with a comedy (it also ends in a marriage), with an opera (in its closing lines it invokes *Lohengrin* and *La clemenza di Tito*), and with a Shakespearian problem play. 'All's well that ends well!' says the older man (4. 544) in a poem that concludes with a marriage that makes the match between Bertram and Helena seem innocently idealistic. The poem represents a world so fractured that no single genre can contain it.

Our principal aim has been to represent Browning as a poet. There were those amongst his contemporaries who denied that he was one. Browning particularly disliked Alfred Austin, the 'Banjo-Byron' ('Of Pachiarotto, and How He Worked in Distemper', 530), one reason for

[6] *The Nation*, 20 January 1876.

which no doubt was Austin's insistence that Browning 'thinks in prose': the poems consist of 'prose thoughts . . . gratuitously turned by some arbitrary whim, which we confess completely puzzles us, into metre'.[7] Oscar Wilde sharpened the thought into wit ('Meredith is a prose Browning, but so is Browning', 'The Critic as Artist'), and it has retained some currency, but nothing could be further from the truth. Browning as a letter writer is eclipsed by his wife (even in the letters that passed between them in their courtship). He rarely published writing in prose, and when he did the results are unhappy. His essay on Shelley is interesting as the fullest and most considered expression of his views on poetry, but its prose is awkward and affected. Carlyle's description, 'a *little* too elaborate here and there',[8] is one of his rare ventures into understatement. Monsignor's prose in the fourth scene of *Pippa Passes* is, it is true, silkily ruthless, but when he is writing in his own voice, Browning supplies powerful confirmation of Hazlitt's view that 'poets are in general bad prose-writers' ('On Poetry in General'). His verse by contrast, from his very first publication, *Pauline*, is direct, supple, and startlingly his own, as in the glimpse of Andromeda,

> As she awaits the snake on the wet beach,
> By the dark rock, and the white wave just breaking
> At her feet; quite naked and alone. (663–5)

Browning developed mannerisms as he grew older. When the young woman in *The Inn Album* identifies her 'block | Of stumbling' (III. 53–4), few will think the expression an improvement on stumbling block. But the older Browning continued to write perfect lines, as when he notices 'Splintered in the slab, this pink perfection of the cyclamen' (*La Saisiaz*, 40). That is a line that draws attention to itself, but if the occasion demands it, he can be startlingly casual. Few poems end so insouciantly as 'Dis Aliter Visum', 'Now comes my husband from his whist' (150). And there are lines, very many of them, that are wholly Browningian, lines that none but Browning could have written:

> *Bang-whang-whang* goes the drum, *tootle-te-tootle* the fife;
> No keeping one's haunches still: it's the greatest pleasure in life.
> ('Up at a Villa—Down in the City', 53–4)

[7] *Temple Bar Magazine*, 26 (June 1869), 320.

[8] *Collected Letters of Thomas and Jane Welsh Carlyle*, ed. C. A. Sanders et al. (Durham, NC: Duke University Press, 1970–), xxvii. 65.

These lines may be spoken by an Italian nobleman obliged by reason of his poverty to retire from the city to spend some months each year at his country villa, but Browning lends the Italian as he lends most of his characters his own knack for finding the expressive word and the expressive cadence.

The six-beat line that Browning moulds for his Italian has all the vulgar energy of the fife and drum music that the Italian enjoys and it is an enjoyment that Browning for all his musical sophistication evidently shares. He often opens up his poems to the music of the streets. He is heir to Thomas Hood, who was the most sympathetic of all the major Victorian poets to the tradition of comic verse that was so vital in the 19th century, and to the tumbling doggerel metres that the comic poets preferred. As Browning acknowledges in a poem not selected here he had a penchant for 'a grave tale told in crambo' ('Pambo', 2). But his rhythms, like his diction, are remarkably flexible. He had in his youth considered music as a profession. He took lessons in piano, cello, and violin, and later learned to play the organ, and he studied composition with his distinguished Camberwell neighbour John Relfe. His tastes were eclectic, ranging from the music of the Florentine streets to 'Bach's fiddle-fugues', as Mr Sludge calls them (*Mr. Sludge, the Medium*, 1224) (Sludge seems improbably to share Browning's advanced taste for a composer who had only recently been rediscovered). Browning, like the older woman of *The Inn Album*, '[c]ould play both Bach and Brahms' (IV. 415), and he could play lighter music too, a toccata by the fashionable Venetian Baldassare Galuppi, for example. His eclectic taste in music echoes, and perhaps helped to produce, the metrical virtuosity for which Browning is remarkable even amongst his contemporaries, so many of whom were remarkable metrists. He is, for example, the English master of the cretic foot, a foot in which two stressed flank an unstressed syllable. In 'Love Among the Ruins' the poem's rocking rhythm is produced by the alternation between the long and short lines. The short lines, made up of a single cretic foot, so wonderfully attenuate the sentiments that the speaker seems dwarfed by the expanses of time and space from within which he speaks. But a less well-known poem from *Men and Women* 'In a Year' uses cretics just as wonderfully. 'Bitterly we re-embrace, | Single still' (7–8), the woman speaker remarks, and the short line echoes the sentiment, at once completing and repelling the line that precedes it. Browning's metres are not simply decorative. The jaunty rhythm of the student's marching song in 'A Grammarian's Funeral', for example, offers an oblique commentary on the reverence for the life of the mind that the students proclaim. Its rhythms are not those of young men content to live their life 'Dead from the waist down' (132). Browning's metres are often emphatic, but even when they are, they are handled flexibly. The speaker of 'A Toccata of Galuppi's' admires Galuppi's music as being 'good alike at grave and gay!' (26), and Browning searches out metres that are similarly adaptable, not least the metre of 'A Toccata' itself. The four-beat breathlessly rapid line renders Galuppi's Venice as a city of the young, a city given over to the pursuit of pleasure, until the speaker remembers that all those young people have been dead this hundred years, and the metre so perfectly fitted to pleasure-seeking proves itself just as able to mark a catch in the throat, and the desolation of old age: 'what's become of all the gold | Used to hang and brush their bosoms? I feel chilly and grown old' (44–5).

Browning is a poet in the close attention he pays to the sound of his words, but he is a poet, too, in his attention to their look on the page. Browning was never, even as much as poets of the recent past such as Wordsworth and Coleridge, a manuscript poet. Poems for him were completed only when translated into print, which is one reason why he continued to publish throughout the long years in which he found scarcely any readers. 'Saul' first appeared in 1845 in *Dramatic Romances and Lyrics*, in the text that we prefer, as a fragment. It was set out on the page in quatrains in which trimeter and dimeter lines alternate. In *Men and Women* the poem is completed by the addition of a lengthy sermon in which David tries to rouse Saul from his depression, and, as if to register the change, the springy quatrains are rewritten as long, anapaestic, five-beat lines, better adapted to the weighty sentiments that David voices in the later version of the poem, as when he urges 'The submission of Man's nothing-perfect to God's All-Complete' (253). In 'Porphyria', both in its original magazine appearance, and in its re-publication in *Dramatic Lyrics*, the lineation is continuous, disregarding the five-line stanzas in which the poem is composed, and the effect is to call attention to the speaker's capacity for self-deception. The lineation obscures without quite hiding his fear of temporal process, his need to freeze the moment lest he lose it. But similar ploys produce a wide range of effects. In 'My Last Duchess' the couplets are hidden, like the stanzas of 'Porphyria', but from the ear rather than the eye. Browning's enjambments are so extreme that it is possible to hear the whole poem recited and conclude that it is written in blank verse. But once again the device is powerfully expressive. It undercuts the Duke's sang-froid, the easy urbanity of his address,

'Nay, we'll go | Together down, Sir!' (53–4), by reminding the reader that the Duke, who prizes the portrait of his late wife so much more than her person, has himself sat for a portrait, and has become the object of a gaze almost as chillingly detached as his own, almost as willing to look on the Duke as an object of merely aesthetic interest.

Browning is happier in verse than in prose in part because verse accommodates more easily Browning's figurative vivacity. His figures are characteristically abrupt, the word he chooses to evoke the sudden transition between shade and shine in a city of narrow lanes and broad squares such as Madrid, 'abrupt as when there's slid | Its stiff gold blazing pall | From some black coffin-lid' ('Waring', 139–41). The simile catches the moment that the cloth slips with unexpected and even unnecessary energy. Browning loves the vivid: his tulips, for example, are as vivid as Plath's: 'The wild tulip, at end of its tube, blows out its great red bell | Like a thin clear bubble of blood, for the children to pick and sell' ('Up at a Villa—Down in the City', 24–5). The flower, the Murano glass-blower's globe of glass, and the drop of blood share their bright redness, but the energy of Browning's description is produced by bringing together scarlets of such different texture.

These similes of Browning's describe the Madrid streets and the wild flower. They are interested in bringing objects suddenly, with shocking clarity, before the eye. But Browning's figures more often carry his argument, like the figures in the dramatic verse of Shakespeare and the Jacobeans, although Browning's love of Donne's poetry may be just as pertinent—the tulip flower opening like a bubble of glass is itself a Donnean figure. Browning's sophisticated and unsophisticated speakers are alike energetically figurative. The urbane Bishop Blougram, once he starts the notion that this is a 'cabin of a life' in which every passenger is limited to six cubic feet of luggage, develops the figure with a reckless energy. Gigadibs is cast as the naive passenger outraged that he cannot bring with him his favourite Correggio, his marble bath, pianoforte, India screen, and Balzac's novels in the 'new edition fifty volumes long' (100–17). The Bishop is at a far remove from Browning's Caliban, except that Caliban too thinks in figures. When he surmises that Setebos's creation of the world 'came of being ill at ease' (31), he thinks of a fish swept out in the 'crystal spike' of fresh water that a river thrusts out into the sea. The fish longs to enter the warm sea water, 'green-dense and dim-delicious, bred o' the sun', but cannot do so because it is a freshwater fish, and the salt water cannot support its life (33–43). Caliban's figurative imagination succeeds in rendering even Setebos an object of pathos.

Blougram's figures have a harsh, mocking, intellectual clarity, Caliban's are sensual and exploratory, but they are equally idiosyncratic. Browning's figures, his metres, and his characters are all strongly marked, all of them are very often, to use the term that Walter Bagehot famously applied to Browning, 'grotesque'.[9] Every one of Browning's many volumes can seem rather like the basket of seafood proudly displayed by the Amalfi fisherman in 'England in Italy':

> All trembling alive
> With pink and grey jellies, your sea-fruit;
> You touch the strange lumps,
> And mouths gape there, eyes open, all manner
> Of horns and of humps,
> Which only the fisher looks grave at. (56–61)

Bagehot is appalled by the refusal to idealize, but other readers will delight in it. The poems seem to buck against the flat uniformity of the type faces in which the reader meets them, as if Browning has an urge to treat all books like the volume in 'Sibrandus Schafnaburgensis' that he tosses into a crevice in a plum tree where its pages are colonized by bugs 'frisking and twisting and coupling' (58).

Browning was an opinionated man, and could be bluffly uncompromising in the expression of his opinions, but in verse it is rarely so. Verse form (he was not in thrall to the organicist principles of his Romantic predecessors) worked to preserve a distinction between the poem and its sentiments, even when those sentiments display Browning at his bluffest. Verse releases Browning into irresponsibility of a kind in which he rarely if ever allowed himself to indulge in his life. He was on most occasions rather more strait-laced than his wife. He did not, for example, share his wife's inclination to go down on her knees before George Sand. Instead, as Mrs Sutherland Orr records, he treated her with a 'studied courtesy' which was 'felt by her as a rebuke to the latitude which she granted to other men' (Orr, *Life*, 179). But in the verse he is less constrained. In 'Respectability', to take just one example, the speaker and his mistress celebrate the freedom from bourgeois codes that they find in Paris. They walk the city streets by night and 'feel the Boulevart break again | To warmth and light and

[9] *National Review*, 19 (1864), 27–67.

bliss' (15–16). Browning could not have walked the streets of Paris that way in life, but he could in verse. His ideas, like his metres, like his choice of stanza form and diction, have, when he is at his best, a fine unpredictability, which is why his poetry retains its vitality still, a century and a quarter since his death. He wrote to Ruskin, in a letter included here, after Ruskin had complained of Browning's difficulty, 'You ought, I think, to keep pace with the thought tripping from ledge to ledge of my "glaciers", as you call them; not stand poking your alpenstock into the holes, and demonstrating that no foot could have stood there;—suppose it sprang over there?' He is trying to persuade Ruskin that reading might be a riskier, a more exhilarating activity than he had supposed. His poems still have the power to teach that lesson to their readers.

CHRONOLOGY

1806 Elizabeth Barrett born 6 March at Coxhoe Hall, Co. Durham, eldest child of Edward Moulton-Barrett and Mary Graham-Clarke.

1812 Robert Browning born 7 May in Camberwell, London SE, to Robert Browning, clerk in the Bank of England, and Sarah Anna Wiedemann. Robert Browning senior was an amateur scholar with an extensive library.

1814 Sister Sarianna born 7 January.

*c.*1819 Attends lower school at Peckham run by the Misses Ready, sisters to the master the Reverend Thomas Martin Ready. RB went on to study under Thomas Ready from about 10 years old. He spoke of the school with dislike, even contempt, in later years. Most of his real education took place informally at home, although he did have professional tutors.

1824 RB's parents make an unsuccessful attempt to have his poem 'Incondita' published.

1826 Leaves Ready's school and is educated at home. Later that year or early in 1827 James Silverthorne his maternal cousin gives RB a copy of Shelley's *Miscellaneous Poems* and under their influence RB becomes for a period both vegetarian and atheist.

1828 RB enters the newly founded London University and begins study of German, Latin, and Greek. He dislikes student life and finds the lectures inadequate.

1829 In May at the end of the university term RB withdraws from the university and is henceforth self-educated.

1833 *Pauline* published anonymously by Saunders and Otley. Probably no copies are sold.

1834 End February RB travels to Russia with a Russian embassy to St Petersburg. Considers career in diplomacy.

1835 RB's father pays for the publication of *Paracelsus*.

1835 Applies unsuccessfully for appointment to government mission to Persia.

1836 Publishes *Porphyria*, afterwards called *Porphyria's Lover*, and *Johannes*, afterwards called *Johannes Agricola in Meditation*, in the *Monthly Repository*.

1837 RB's play *Strafford* staged 1 May at Covent Garden, after some dispute with Macready about its suitability for the stage. It had only five performances. *Strafford*, printed the day of its first performance, was the only one of RB's early works to appear at the publisher's expense.

1838 RB makes his first journey to Italy in part to research *Sordello*. He arrives in Venice on 1 June and his trip takes in Treviso, Bassano, Asolo, San Zenone, and Possagno; he returns to Venice via Vicenza and Padua, also following Shelley and Byron into the Euganean Hills. EBB's *The Seraphim, and Other Poems* published (June).

1840 *Sordello* published . It is famously and sometimes wittily found obscure.

1841 Publishes *Pippa Passes*, the first in a series of poetry pamphlets, *Bells and Pomegranates*, intended to reach a wider audience than his previous works.

1842 *Bells and Pomegranates*, II (*King Victor* and *King Charles*) and III (*Dramatic Lyrics*).

1843 Publishes *The Return of the Druses* (*Bells and Pomegranates*, IV) and *A Blot in the 'Scutcheon* (*Bells and Pomegranates*, V).

1844 Second Italian journey: arrives Naples towards end of September, sightseeing in the Sorrento peninsula, visiting Vesuvius and Pompeii before going north to Rome, Florence, Pisa, and Livorno where he meets Trelawny, who had known Shelley and Byron. Publishes *The Laboratory* and *Garden Fancies* in *Hood's Magazine*, and *Bells and Pomegranates*, VI (*Colombe's Birthday*). EBB's *Poems* in 2 volumes published (August).

1845 Publishes in *Hood's Magazine*, *The Tomb at St Praxed's* (March), and *The Flight of the Duchess*, 1–9 (April); and *Bells and Pomegranates*, VII (*Dramatic Romances and Lyrics*). On 10 January RB writes his first letter to EBB. 20 May RB visits EBB for the first time, beginning their courtship.

1846 RB publishes *Bells and Pomegranates*, VII (*Luria* and *A Soul's Tragedy*). RB and EBB secretly marry in St Marylebone church on 12 September with RB's cousin, James Silverthorne, and EBB's maid, Wilson, as witnesses. On 19 September the couple leave England for Italy. Travelling by boat and train via Paris, Avignon, and Marseilles, they reach Pisa in October and winter there.

1847 EBB miscarries in March. In the late spring the Brownings settle in Florence in the *piano nobile* or principal floor of 'Casa Guidi', a 15th-century *palazzo* near the Pitti Palace. This is their main residence until EBB's death in 1861.

1849 First collected edition of *Poems* published in 2 volumes by Chapman & Hall. The Brownings' son Robert Weidemann Barrett Browning (Pen, Peni, Penini) born 9 March. Illness and death of RB's mother.

1850 *Christmas-Eve and Easter-Day* published by Chapman & Hall; about 200 copies are sold. EBB's *Poems* in 2 volumes, published in the autumn, sells well and is widely reviewed. In July EBB suffers 4th miscarriage. For the sake of her health the Brownings rent a villa above Siena until November.

1851 July–September the Brownings in London visiting friends and relatives. September they visit Paris where they stay until July 1852 and where they meet George Sand and Joseph Milsand, who becomes RB's trusted reader. Browning is commissioned by Moxon to write an introductory essay to a volume of Shelley letters.

1852 'Essay on Shelley' published but the volume soon withdrawn when letters are found to be spurious. Summer in London where a breach of promise suit has been brought successfully against RB's father; RB assists him and Sarianna to remove to Paris to escape the damages awarded against him. The Brownings return to London in July where they improve their acquaintance with the Tennysons. They return to Florence in November.

1853 In Bagni di Lucca for summer. RB and EBB meet the American sculptor William Wetmore Story: the families become close friends and together move to Florence and then Rome. Rome proves expensive and bad for health of both families: Story's son dies and Pen is ill.

1854–5 In Florence, Paris, London, and Paris.

1855 10 November *Men and Women* in 2 volumes published by Chapman and Hall. Despite RB's expectations it is not very well received and is charged with obscurity.

1856 November EBB's *Aurora Leigh* is published and does so well that the couple expect an alleviation of their financial problems.

1857 John Kenyon leaves the Brownings £11,000 which makes them financially secure. In April EBB's father dies.

1860 In Florence, Siena, and winter in Rome. In Florence in a market Browning comes across the 'square old yellow book' containing documents relating to the Franceschini case of 1698, the story of which forms the basis of *The Ring and the Book*.

1861 Back in Florence in the spring. In June EBB catches a cold which worsens and 29 June she dies in RB's arms. 1 July she is buried in the Protestant Cemetery. RB and Pen leave Florence never to return, initially for Paris with Isa Blagden. Browning and Pen spend time in Paris and Brittany with RB's father and Sarianna; they move finally to London, renting a house at 19 Warwick Crescent where RB lives until 1887.

1862 EBB's *Last Poems* and a volume of her essays published.

1863 *The Poetical Works* in 3 volumes published by Chapman & Hall. Respectful reviews and good sales.

1864 *Dramatis Personæ*, published by Chapman and Hall, is so successful critically and popularly that a second edition is published within the year. RB begins to be a celebrity.

1866 RB's father dies and Sarianna comes to live with RB.

1867 June awarded an Oxford MA by convocation, followed by an honorary fellowship of Balliol College.

1868 *The Poetical Works* in 6 volumes.

1868–9 *The Ring and the Book* published in 4 instalments from November to February by a new publisher Smith & Elder.

1869 In April RB is offered and refuses the Rectorship of St Andrews University.

1871 *Balaustion's Adventure* (August); *Prince Hohenstiel-Schwangau* (December).

1871 Acrimonious split with Lady Ashburton, probably as a result of his clumsy response to her proposal of marriage.

1872 *Fifine at the Fair* (June).

1873 *Red Cotton Night-Cap Country* (May).

1875 *Aristophanes' Apology* (April); *Inn Album* (November).

1876 *Pacchiarotto and How He Worked in Distemper* (July).

1877 *The Agamemnon of Aeschylus* (October).

1878 *La Saisiaz* and *Two Poets of Croisic* (May); in late summer travels with Sarianna via Switzerland to Italy, visiting Asolo and Venice. This successful trip results in seven of the following eleven autumns being spent in Italy.

1879 *Dramatic Idyls* (April). Awarded LLD by Cambridge.

1880 *Dramatic Idyls*, 2nd series (June).

1881 Browning Society founded (October).

1882 Awarded DCL by Oxford. In this and succeeding years his fame spreads and more Browning societies are founded around the world.

1883 *Jocoseria* (March).

1884 Awarded LLD by Edinburgh; *Ferishtah's Fancies* (November).

1886 Joseph Milsand dies (September).

1887 *Parleyings with Certain People of Importance in their Day* (January) is dedicated to the memory of Joseph Milsand. In April RB buys a quite grand house at 29 De Vere Gardens, Kensington; he and Sarianna move there in June.

On 4 October Pen Browning, who has, in part due to the efforts of his father, become quite a well-known portrait painter, and the heiress Fannie Coddington marry.

1888–9 *The Poetical Works* issued in 16 volumes, monthly between April 1888 and July 1889.

1889 *Asolando* published 12 December; Browning dies in Venice at Palazzo Rezzonico later in the day. Browning is buried in Poets' Corner, Westminster Abbey, on 31 December.

1903 Sarianna dies.

1912 Pen dies of a heart attack at Asolo.

1913 The Browning estate is auctioned at Sotheby's, London.

A NOTE ON THE SELECTION AND ITS ORDERING

This selection of Browning's work aims to present to its 21st-century readers a Browning at once familiar and surprising. We offer as a general rule only complete poems, avoiding even whole sections extracted from long poems. Browning's long poems are denatured by being represented by extracts, even although this may seem tempting especially in the case of *The Ring and the Book*. It is certainly with regret that we omit that poem, along with a number of other long poems. In our choice of *The Inn Album* of Browning's later long poems we hope, however, to introduce a 21st-century audience to a little-read and shockingly modern work. Two decisions may seem inconsistent with the rule of choosing whole poems: only the first nine sections of 'The Flight of the Duchess' are offered. These sections were first published in *Hood's Magazine*, 3 (April 1845), 313–18, headed 'Part the First', the long continuation of the poem being added in the version published in 'Dramatic Romances and Lyrics', *Bells and Pomegranates*, VII. 1842; as we explain more fully in the headnote to the poem, there is good reason for regarding the poem in its first published form as a 'fragment', as the earlier and much longer *Pauline* is declared to be in its subtitle, that is, as a poem designed to be incomplete. We believe that a similar case can be made for 'Saul', which we give in the version first published in 'Dramatic Romances and Lyrics', 1842, rather than the longer version published in *Men and Women*, 1855. A third decision might be alleged to involve sleight of hand since we do give the Epilogue—'Amphibian'—and the Prologue—'The Householder'—to *Fifine at the Fair*; on the ground that these are independent poems, albeit poems which chime with the concerns of the long poem.

The copy texts are generally those of the first version in book form—this is to be understood as including the pamphlets *Bells and Pomegranates*, I, III, and VII. We wish to show Browning as he appeared to his reading public throughout the course of his long writing life. Not many poems will be made strange by this choice, although none will be identical with editions which take as their copy texts the *Poetical Works* of 1888–9, holding to the principle that the last edition which the author has overseen must be his preferred text. But corrections made by an elderly man to his youthful work are not necessarily to be preferred. From time to time the energy of the earlier poetry is vitiated, if in tiny ways, by later archaisms: in line 4 of 'Fra Lippo Lippi' and line 234 of 'In the Balcony' 'it's' becomes ''tis' and in line 367 of the latter 'indeed' becomes 'forsooth'. Elsewhere vigorous phrases are toned down: in ['Soliloquy of the Spanish Cloister'] 'Or, the Devil!—one might venture | Pledge one's soul yet slily leave . . .' is livelier than 'Or there's Satan!—one might venture | Pledge one's soul to him, yet leave . . .'. In 'A Light Woman' the grammar of 'And she,—she lies in my hand as tame | As a pear hung basking over a wall' may be improved when 'hung' is replaced by 'late' but the poetry is not; the change from 'hour's feat' to 'moment's feat' at line 252 of 'A Light Woman' undermines the line's authenticity. In 'The Statue and the Bust' the change from 'indolence' which aspires to strive to 'idleness' seems a mistake.

The poems are arranged in the chronological order of book publication and in the order in which they appear in these books. There are a few exceptions in the early work to our general choice of first version in book form as copy text. We have taken as copy texts for 'Porphyria' (now known as 'Porphyria's Lover'), and 'Johannes Agricola' (now known as 'Johannes Agricola in Meditation') the versions first published in the *Monthly Repository*, 1836. Neither of these poems was much revised before their publication in *Dramatic Lyrics*, *Bells and Pomegranates*, III, 1842. But these two magazine poems are Browning's first essays at the dramatic monologue, the genre for which he has become most renowned, and we have chosen to highlight their early publication by choosing the magazine versions. It is also the case that, at least until the 1860s, the poems that Browning published in magazines would have been far more widely read than those published in his own volumes, which is another reason for preserving the magazine text.

The other exceptions to the rule of first version in book form are a group of poems that appeared in *Hood's Magazine* between June 1844 and April 1845: 'The Laboratory', 'Garden Fancies I and II', 'The Tomb at St. Praxed's' (later 'The Bishop Orders his Tomb at St Praxed's'), and 'The Flight of the Duchess', sections 1–9. We have explained above our decision with respect to 'The Flight of the Duchess', the others have been conditioned by our sense that Browning's earliest public text is the superior version. 'The Laboratory', for example, was altered in part because Elizabeth complained about its 'uncertain rhythm'. There are a number of fiddly disimprovements but on the alteration at lines 30–1 of 'this never will free | The soul from those strong, great eyes' to 'this never will free | The soul from those masculine eyes' we rest our case.

There is very little prose in our selection. We choose three letters: one marks the beginning of the celebrated love affair with Elizabeth Barrett in Browning's first letter to her, another its end with a letter to Fanny Haworth in which Browning gives an account of Elizabeth's death. A third letter, one of a number written to John Ruskin, is included because in this letter Browning not only responds to specific charges of obscurity, charges which were by no means confined to Ruskin nor to these poems, but also makes his most robust defence of his practice as a poet. Browning left very little critical prose, nor does he display much talent for it. In the Introductory Essay on Shelley, which we include, he is dealing with a writer whom he greatly admired, yet even here his prose is more distinguished for earnestness than elegance or lucidity.

Browning's *Strafford* was produced at Covent Garden on 1 May 1837 but ran for only five performances; the other drama actually produced in the theatre was *A Blot in the 'Scutcheon* which ran for three nights. We include neither work. It is in the preface to the published version of *Strafford* that Browning speaks of aiming at 'Action in Character rather than Character in Action', but it is a principle better exemplified in the dramatic work that he did not intend for the stage, represented in this selection by *Pippa Passes* and *In a Balcony*, both of which did in fact receive dramatic performances in the 19th century (the latter in Browning's lifetime), and afterwards.

Throughout, obvious errors are silently corrected, but often with Browning what seem to be obvious errors are not certainly so and in these cases (for example at line 76 of 'Old Pictures in Florence') we have indicated why we retain a reading that others have changed.

PAULINE: A FRAGMENT OF A CONFESSION (1833)

Plus ne suis ce que j'ai été,
Et ne le sçaurois jamais être.

MAROT.

Non dubito, quin titulus libri nostri raritate suâ quamplurimos alliciat ad legendum: inter quos nonnulli obliquæ opinionis, mente languidi, multi etiam maligni, et in ingenium nostrum ingrati accedent, qui temerariâ suâ ignorantiâ, vix conspecto titulo clamabunt: Nos vetita docere, hæresium semina jacere: piis auribus offendiculo, præclaris ingeniis scandalo esse: . . . . adeò conscientiæ suæ consulentes, ut nec Apollo, nec Musæ omnes, neque Angelus de cœlo me ab illorum execratione vindicare queant: quibus et ego nunc consulo, ne scripta nostra legant, nec intelligant, nec meminerint: nam noxia sunt, venenosa sunt: Acherontis ostium est in hoc libro, lapides loquitur, caveant, ne cerebrum illis excutiat. Vos autem, qui æquâ mente ad legendum venitis, si tantam prudentiæ discretionem adhibueritis, quantam in melle legendo apes, jam securi legite. Puto namque vos et utilitatis haud parùm et voluptatis plurimùm accepturos. Quod si qua repereritis, quæ vobis non placeant, mittite illa, nec utimini. NAM ET EGO VOBIS ILLA NON PROBO, SED NARRO. Cætera tamen propterea non respuite . . . . Ideo, si quid liberius dictum sit, ignoscite adolescentiæ nostræ, qui minor quam adolescens hoc opus composui.—

H. Cor. Agrippa, De Occult. Phil.

London, January, 1833.

V.A. XX.

Pauline

Pauline, mine own, bend o'er me—thy soft breast
Shall pant to mine—bend o'er me—thy sweet eyes,
And loosened hair, and breathing lips, and arms
Drawing me to thee—these build up a screen
To shut me in with thee, and from all fear,
So that I might unlock the sleepless brood
Of fancies from my soul, their lurking place,
Nor doubt that each would pass, ne'er to return
To one so watched, so loved and so secured.
But what can guard thee but thy naked love?

Ah, dearest! whoso sucks a poisoned wound
Envenoms his own veins,—thou art so good,
So calm—if thou should'st wear a brow less light
For some wild thought which, but for me, were kept
From out thy soul, as from a sacred star.
Yet till I have unlocked them it were vain
To hope to sing; some woe would light on me;
Nature would point at one, whose quivering lip
Was bathed in her enchantments—whose brow burned
Beneath the crown, to which her secrets knelt;
Who learned the spell which can call up the dead,
And then departed, smiling like a fiend
Who has deceived God. If such one should seek
Again her altars, and stand robed and crowned
Amid the faithful: sad confession first,
Remorse and pardon, and old claims renewed,
Ere I can be—as I shall be no more.

I had been spared this shame, if I had sate
By thee for ever, from the first, in place
Of my wild dreams of beauty and of good,
Or with them, as an earnest of their truth.
No thought nor hope, having been shut from thee,
No vague wish unexplained—no wandering aim
Sent back to bind on Fancy's wings, and seek
Some strange fair world, where it might be a law;
But doubting nothing, had been led by thee,
Thro' youth, and saved, as one at length awaked,
Who has slept thro' a peril. Ah! vain, vain!

Thou lovest me—the past is in its grave,
Tho' its ghost haunts us—still this much is ours,
To cast away restraint, lest a worse thing
Wait for us in the darkness. Thou lovest me,
And thou art to receive not love, but faith,
For which thou wilt be mine, and smile, and take
All shapes, and shames, and veil without a fear
That form which music follows like a slave;
And I look to thee, and I trust in thee,

As in a Northern night one looks alway
Unto the East for morn, and spring and joy.
Thou seest then my aimless, hopeless state,
And resting on some few old feelings, won
Back by thy beauty, would'st that I essay
The task, which was to me what now thou art:
And why should I conceal one weakness more?

Thou wilt remember one warm morn, when Winter
Crept aged from the earth, and Spring's first breath
Blew soft from the moist hills—the black-thorn boughs,
So dark in the bare wood; when glistening
In the sunshine were white with coming buds,
Like the bright side of a sorrow—and the banks
Had violets opening from sleep like eyes—
I walked with thee, who knew not a deep shame
Lurked beneath smiles and careless words, which sought
To hide it—till they wandered and were mute;
As we stood listening on a sunny mound
To the wind murmuring in the damp copse,
Like heavy breathings of some hidden thing
Betrayed by sleep—until the feeling rushed
That I was low indeed, yet not so low
As to endure the calmness of thine eyes;
And so I told thee all, while the cool breast
I leaned on altered not its quiet beating;
And long ere words, like a hurt bird's complaint,
Bade me look up and be what I had been,
I felt despair could never live by thee.
Thou wilt remember:—thou art not more dear
Than song was once to me; and I ne'er sung
But as one entering bright halls, where all
Will rise and shout for him. Sure I must own
That I am fallen—having chosen gifts
Distinct from theirs—that I am sad—and fain
Would give up all to be but where I was;
Not high as I had been, if faithful found—
But low and weak, yet full of hope, and sure
Of goodness as of life—that I would lose
All this gay mastery of mind, to sit
Once more with them, trusting in truth and love,

And with an aim—not being what I am.
Oh, Pauline! I am ruined! who believed
That tho' my soul had floated from its sphere
Of wild dominion into the dim orb
Of self—that it was strong and free as ever:—
It has conformed itself to that dim orb,
Reflecting all its shades and shapes, and now
Must stay where it alone can be adored.
I have felt this in dreams—in dreams in which
I seemed the fate from which I fled; I felt
A strange delight in causing my decay;
I was a fiend, in darkness chained for ever
Within some ocean-cave; and ages rolled,
Till thro' the cleft rock, like a moonbeam, came
A white swan to remain with me; and ages
Rolled, yet I tired not of my first joy
In gazing on the peace of its pure wings.
And then I said, "It is most fair to me,
"Yet its soft wings must sure have suffered change
"From the thick darkness—sure its eyes are dim—
"Its silver pinions must be cramped and numbed
"With sleeping ages here; it cannot leave me,
"For it would seem, in light, beside its kind,
"Withered—tho' here to me most beautiful."
And then I was a young witch, whose blue eyes,
As she stood naked by the river springs,
Drew down a god—I watched his radiant form
Growing less radiant—and it gladdened me;
Till one morn, as he sat in the sunshine
Upon my knees, singing to me of heaven,
He turned to look at me, ere I could lose
The grin with which I viewed his perishing.
And he shrieked and departed, and sat long
By his deserted throne—but sunk at last,
Murmuring, as I kissed his lips and curled
Around him, "I am still a god—to thee."
Still I can lay my soul bare in its fall,
For all the wandering and all the weakness
Will be a saddest comment on the song.
And if, that done, I can be young again,
I will give up all gained as willingly

As one gives up a charm which shuts him out
From hope, or part, or care, in human kind.
As life wanes, all its cares, and strife, and toil,
Seem strangely valueless, while the old trees
Which grew by our youth's home—the waving mass
Of climbing plants, heavy with bloom and dew—
The morning swallows with their songs like words,—
All these seem clear and only worth our thoughts.
So aught connected with my early life——
My rude songs or my wild imaginings,
How I look on them—most distinct amid
The fever and the stir of after years!

I ne'er had ventured e'en to hope for this,
Had not the glow I felt at HIS award,
Assured me all was not extinct within.
HIM whom all honor—whose renown springs up
Like sunlight which will visit all the world;
So that e'en they who sneered at him at first,
Come out to it, as some dark spider crawls
From his foul nets, which some lit torch invades,
Yet spinning still new films for his retreat.—
Thou didst smile, poet,—but, can *we* forgive?

Sun-treader—life and light be thine for ever;
Thou art gone from us—years go by—and spring
Gladdens, and the young earth is beautiful,
Yet thy songs come not—other bards arise,
But none like thee—they stand—thy majesties,
Like mighty works which tell some Spirit there
Hath sat regardless of neglect and scorn,
Till, its long task completed, it hath risen
And left us, never to return: and all
Rush in to peer and praise when all in vain.
The air seems bright with thy past presence yet,
But thou art still for me, as thou hast been
When I have stood with thee, as on a throne
With all thy dim creations gathered round
Like mountains,—and I felt of mould like them,
And creatures of my own were mixed with them,

Like things half-lived, catching and giving life.
But thou art still for me, who have adored,
Tho' single, panting but to hear thy name,
Which I believed a spell to me alone,
Scarce deeming thou wert as a star to men—
As one should worship long a sacred spring
Scarce worth a moth's flitting, which long grasses cross,
And one small tree embowers droopingly,
Joying to see some wandering insect won,
To live in its few rushes—or some locust
To pasture on its boughs—or some wild bird
Stoop for its freshness from the trackless air,
And then should find it but the fountain-head,
Long lost, of some great river—washing towns
And towers, and seeing old woods which will live
But by its banks, untrod of human foot,
Which, when the great sun sinks, lie quivering
In light as some thing lieth half of life
Before God's foot—waiting a wondrous change
—Then girt with rocks which seek to turn or stay
Its course in vain, for it does ever spread
Like a sea's arm as it goes rolling on,
Being the pulse of some great country—so
Wast thou to me—and art thou to the world.
And I, perchance, half feel a strange regret,
That I am not what I have been to thee:
Like a girl one has loved long silently,
In her first loveliness, in some retreat,
When first emerged, all gaze and glow to view
Her fresh eyes, and soft hair, and lips which bleed
Like a mountain berry. Doubtless it is sweet
To see her thus adored—but there have been
Moments, when all the world was in his praise,
Sweeter than all the pride of after hours.
Yet, Sun-treader, all hail!—from my heart's heart
I bid thee hail!—e'en in my wildest dreams,
I am proud to feel I would have thrown up all
The wreathes of fame which seemed o'erhanging me,
To have seen thee, for a moment, as thou art.

And if thou livest—if thou lovest, spirit!
Remember me, who set this final seal
To wandering thought—that one so pure as thou
Could never die. Remember me, who flung
All honor from my soul—yet paused and said,
"There is one spark of love remaining yet,
"For I have nought in common with him—shapes
"Which followed him avoid me, and foul forms
"Seek me, which ne'er could fasten on his mind;
"And tho' I feel how low I am to him,
"Yet I aim not even to catch a tone
"Of all the harmonies which he called up,
"So one gleam still remains, altho' the last."
Remember me—who praise thee e'en with tears,
For never more shall I walk calm with thee;
Thy sweet imaginings are as an air,
A melody, some wond'rous singer sings,
Which, though it haunt men oft in the still eve,
They dream not to essay; yet it no less,
But more is honored. I was thine in shame,
And now when all thy proud renown is out,
I am a watcher, whose eyes have grown dim
With looking for some star—which breaks on him,
Altered, and worn, and weak, and full of tears.

Autumn has come—like Spring returned to us,
Won from her girlishness—like one returned
A friend that was a lover—nor forgets
The first warm love, but full of sober thoughts
Of fading years; whose soft mouth quivers yet
With the old smile—but yet so changed and still!
And here am I the scoffer, who have probed
Life's vanity, won by a word again
Into my old life—for one little word
Of this sweet friend, who lives in loving me,
Lives strangely on my thoughts, and looks, and words,
As fathoms down some nameless ocean thing
Its silent course of quietness and joy.
O dearest, if, indeed, I tell the past,
May'st thou forget it as a sad sick dream;
Or if it linger—my lost soul too soon

Sinks to itself, and whispers, we shall be
But closer linked—two creatures whom the earth
Bears singly—with strange feelings, unrevealed
But to each other; or two lonely things
Created by some Power, whose reign is done,
Having no part in God, or his bright world,
I am to sing; whilst ebbing day dies soft,
As a lean scholar dies, worn o'er his book,
And in the heaven stars steal out one by one,
As hunted men steal to their mountain watch.
I must not think—lest this new impulse die
In which I trust. I have no confidence,
So I will sing on—fast as fancies come
Rudely—the verse being as the mood it paints.

I strip my mind bare—whose first elements
I shall unveil—not as they struggled forth
In infancy, nor as they now exist,
That I am grown above them, and can rule them,
But in that middle stage, when they were full,
Yet ere I had disposed them to my will;
And then I shall show how these elements
Produced my present state, and what it is.

I am made up of an intensest life,
Of a most clear idea of consciousness
Of self—distinct from all its qualities,
From all affections, passions, feelings, powers;
And thus far it exists, if tracked in all,
But linked in me, to self-supremacy,
Existing as a centre to all things,
Most potent to create, and rule, and call
Upon all things to minister to it;
And to a principle of restlessness
Which would be all, have, see, know, taste, feel, all—
This is myself; and I should thus have been,
Though gifted lower than the meanest soul.

And of my powers, one springs up to save
From utter death a soul with such desires
Confined to clay—which is the only one
Which marks me—an imagination which

Has been an angel to me—coming not
In fitful visions, but beside me ever,
And never failing me; so tho' my mind
Forgets not—not a shred of life forgets—
Yet I can take a secret pride in calling
The dark past up—to quell it regally.

A mind like this must dissipate itself,
But I have always had one lode-star; now,
As I look back, I see that I have wasted,
Or progressed as I looked toward that star—
A need, a trust, a yearning after God,
A feeling I have analysed but late,
But it existed, and was reconciled
With a neglect of all I deemed his laws,
Which yet, when seen in others, I abhorred.
I felt as one beloved, and so shut in
From fear—and thence I date my trust in signs
And omens—for I saw God every where;
And I can only lay it to the fruit
Of a sad after-time that I could doubt
Even his being—having always felt
His presence—never acted from myself,
Still trusting in a hand that leads me through
All danger; and this feeling still has fought
Against my weakest reason and resolves.

And I can love nothing—and this dull truth
Has come the last—but sense supplies a love
Encircling me and mingling with my life.

These make myself—for I have sought in vain
To trace how they were formed by circumstance,
For I still find them—turning my wild youth
Where they alone displayed themselves, converting
All objects to their use—now see their course!

They came to me in my first dawn of life,
Which passed alone with wisest ancient books,
All halo-girt with fancies of my own,
And I myself went with the tale—a god,
Wandering after beauty—or a giant,

Standing vast in the sunset—an old hunter,
Talking with gods—or a high-crested chief,
Sailing with troops of friends to Tenedos;—
I tell you, nought has ever been so clear
As the place, the time, the fashion of those lives,
I had not seen a work of lofty art,
Nor woman's beauty, nor sweet nature's face,
Yet, I say, never morn broke clear as those
On the dim clustered isles in the blue sea:
The deep groves, and white temples, and wet caves—
And nothing ever will surprise me now—
Who stood beside the naked Swift-footed,
Who bound my forehead with Proserpine's hair.

An' strange it is, that I who could so dream,
Should e'er have stooped to aim at aught beneath—
Aught low, or painful, but I never doubted;
So as I grew, I rudely shaped my life
To my immediate wants, yet strong beneath
Was a vague sense of powers folded up—
A sense that tho' those shadowy times were past,
Their spirit dwelt in me, and I should rule.

Then came a pause, and long restraint chained down
My soul, till it was changed. I lost myself,
And were it not that I so loathe that time,
I could recall how first I learned to turn
My mind against itself; and the effects,
In deeds for which remorse were vain, as for
The wanderings of delirious dream; yet thence
Came cunning, envy, falsehood, which so long
Have spotted me—at length I was restored,
Yet long the influence remained; and nought
But the still life I led, apart from all,
Which left my soul to seek its old delights,
Could e'er have brought me thus far back to peace.
As peace returned, I sought out some pursuit:
And song rose—no new impulse—but the one
With which all others best could be combined.
My life has not been that of those whose heaven
Was lampless, save where poesy shone out;

But as a clime, where glittering mountain-tops,
And glancing sea, and forests steeped in light
Give back reflected the far-flashing sun;
For music, (which is earnest of a heaven,
Seeing we know emotions strange by it,
Not else to be revealed,) is as a voice,
A low voice calling Fancy, as a friend,
To the green woods in the gay summer time.
And she fills all the way with dancing shapes,
Which have made painters pale; and they go on
While stars look at them, and winds call to them,
As they leave life's path for the twilight world,
Where the dead gather. This was not at first,
For I scarce knew what I would do. I had
No wish to paint, no yearning—but I sang.

And first I sang, as I in dream have seen,
Music wait on a lyrist for some thought,
Yet singing to herself until it came.
I turned to those old times and scenes, where all
That's beautiful had birth for me, and made
Rude verses on them all; and then I paused—
I had done nothing, so I sought to know
What mind had yet achieved. No fear was mine
As I gazed on the works of mighty bards,
In the first joy at finding my own thoughts
Recorded, and my powers exemplified,
And feeling their aspirings were my own.
And then I first explored passion and mind;
And I began afresh; I rather sought
To rival what I wondered at, than form
Creations of my own; so much was light
Lent back by others, yet much was my own.

I paused again—a change was coming on,
I was no more a boy—the past was breaking
Before the coming, and like fever worked.
I first thought on myself—and here my powers
Burst out. I dreamed not of restraint, but gazed
On all things: schemes and systems went and came,
And I was proud (being vainest of the weak),

In wandering o'er them, to seek out some one
To be my own; as one should wander o'er
The white way for a star.

* * * *

On one, whom praise of mine would not offend,
Who was as calm as beauty—being such
Unto mankind as thou to me, Pauline,
Believing in them, and devoting all
His soul's strength to their winning back to peace;
Who sent forth hopes and longings for their sake,
Clothed in all passion's melodies, which first
Caught me, and set me, as to a sweet task,
To gather every breathing of his songs.
And woven with them there were words, which seemed
A key to a new world; the muttering
Of angels, something yet unguessed by man.
How my heart beat, as I went on, and found
Much there! I felt my own mind had conceived,
But there living and burning; soon the whole
Of his conceptions dawned on me; their praise
Is in the tongues of men; men's brows are high
When his name means a triumph and a pride;
So my weak hands may well forbear to dim
What then seemed my bright fate: I threw myself
To meet it. I was vowed to liberty,
Men were to be as gods, and earth as heaven.
And I—ah! what a life was mine to be,
My whole soul rose to meet it. Now, Pauline,
I shall go mad, if I recall that time.

* * * *

O let me look back, e'er I leave for ever
The time, which was an hour, that one waits
For a fair girl, that comes a withered hag.
And I was lonely,—far from woods and fields,
And amid dullest sights, who should be loose
As a stag—yet I was full of joy—who lived
With Plato—and who had the key to life.
And I had dimly shaped my first attempt,
And many a thought did I build up on thought,
As the wild bee hangs cell to cell—in vain;
For I must still go on: my mind rests not.

'Twas in my plan to look on real life,
Which was all new to me; my theories
Were firm, so them I left, to look upon
Men, and their cares, and hopes, and fears, and joys;
And, as I pondered on them all, I sought
How best life's end might be attained—an end
Comprising every joy. I deeply mused.

And suddenly, without heart-wreck, I awoke
As from a dream—I said 'twas beautiful,
Yet but a dream; and so adieu to it.
As some world-wanderer sees in a far meadow
Strange towers, and walled gardens, thick with trees,
Where singing goes on, and delicious mirth,
And laughing fairy creatures peeping over,
And on the morrow, when he comes to live
For ever by those springs, and trees, fruit-flushed
And fairy bowers—all his search is vain.
Well I remember * * * *
First went my hopes of perfecting mankind,
And faith in them—then freedom in itself,
And virtue in itself—and then my motives' ends,
And powers and loves; and human love went last.
I felt this no decay, because new powers
Rose as old feelings left—wit, mockery,
And happiness; for I had oft been sad,
Mistrusting my resolves: but now I cast
Hope joyously away—I laughed and said,
"No more of this"—I must not think; at length
I look'd again to see how all went on.

My powers were greater—as some temple seemed
My soul, where nought is changed, and incense rolls
Around the altar—only God is gone,
And some dark spirit sitteth in his seat!
So I passed through the temple; and to me
Knelt troops of shadows; and they cried, "Hail, king!
"We serve thee now, and thou shalt serve no more!
"Call on us, prove us, let us worship thee!"
And I said, "Are ye strong—let fancy bear me

"Far from the past."—And I was borne away
As Arab birds float sleeping in the wind,
O'er deserts, towers and forests, I being calm;
And I said, "I have nursed up energies,
"They will prey on me." And a band knelt low,
And cried, "Lord, we are here, and we will make
"A way for thee—in thine appointed life
"O look on us!" And I said, "Ye will worship
"Me; but my heart must worship too." They shouted,
"Thyself—thou art our king!" So, I stood there
Smiling * * * * * *

And buoyant and rejoicing was the spirit
With which I looked out how to end my days;
I felt once more myself—my powers were mine;
I found that youth or health so lifted me,
That, spite of all life's vanity, no grief
Came nigh me—I must ever be light-hearted;
And that this feeling was the only veil
Betwixt me and despair: so if age came,
I should be as a wreck linked to a soul
Yet fluttering, or mind-broken, and aware
Of my decay. So a long summer morn
Found me; and ere noon came, I had resolved
No age should come on me, ere youth's hopes went,
For I would wear myself out—like that morn
Which wasted not a sunbeam—every joy
I would make mine, and die; and thus I sought
To chain my spirit down, which I had fed
With thoughts of fame. I said, the troubled life
Of genius seen so bright when working forth
Some trusted end, seems sad, when all in vain—
Most sad, when men have parted with all joy
For their wild fancy's sake, which waited first,
As an obedient spirit, when delight
Came not with her alone, but alters soon,
Coming darkened, seldom, hasting to depart,
Leaving a heavy darkness and warm tears.

But I shall never lose her; she will live
Brighter for such seclusion—I but catch
A hue, a glance of what I sing, so pain
Is linked with pleasure, for I ne'er may tell
The radiant sights which dazzle me; but now
They shall be all my own, and let them fade
Untold—others shall rise as fair, as fast.
And when all's done, the few dim gleams transferred,—
(For a new thought sprung up—that it were well
To leave all shadowy hopes, and weave such lays
As would encircle me with praise and love;
So I should not die utterly—I should bring
One branch from the gold forest, like the knight
Of old tales, witnessing I had been there,)—
And when all's done, how vain seems e'en success,
And all the influence poets have o'er men!
'Tis a fine thing that one, weak as myself,
Should sit in his lone room, knowing the words
He utters in his solitude shall move
Men like a swift wind—that tho' he be forgotten,
Fair eyes shall glisten when his beauteous dreams
Of love come true in happier frames than his.
Ay, the still night brought thoughts like these, but morn
Came, and the mockery again laughed out
At hollow praises, and smiles, almost sneers;
And my soul's idol seemed to whisper me
To dwell with him and his unhonoured name—
And I well knew my spirit, that would be
First in the struggle, and again would make
All bow to it; and I would sink again.

* * * * *

And then know that this curse will come on us,
To see our idols perish—we may wither,
No marvel—we are clay; but our low fate
Should not extend to them, whom trustingly
We sent before into Time's yawning gulf,
To face what e'er may lurk in darkness there—
To see the painter's glory pass, and feel
Sweet music move us not as once, or worst,

To see decaying wits ere the frail body
Decays. Nought makes me trust in love so really,
As the delight of the contented lowness
With which I gaze on souls I'd keep for ever
In beauty—I'd be sad to equal them;
I'd feed their fame e'en from my heart's best blood,
Withering unseen, that they might flourish still.

* * * * *

Pauline, my sweet friend, thou dost not forget
How this mood swayed me, when thou first wert mine,
When I had set myself to live this life,
Defying all opinion. Ere thou camest
I was most happy, sweet, for old delights
Had come like birds again; music, my life,
I nourished more than ever, and old lore
Loved for itself, and all it shows—the king
Treading the purple calmly to his death,
—While round him, like the clouds of eve, all dusk,
The giant shades of fate, silently flitting,
Pile the dim outline of the coming doom,
—And him sitting alone in blood, while friends
Are hunting far in the sunshine; and the boy,
With his white breast and brow and clustering curls
Streaked with his mother's blood, and striving hard
To tell his story ere his reason goes.
And when I loved thee, as I've loved so oft,
Thou lovedst me, and I wondered, and looked in
My heart to find some feeling like such love,
Believing I was still what I had been;
And soon I found all faith gone from me,
And the late glow of life—changing like clouds,
'Twas not the morn-blush widening into day,
But evening, coloured by the dying sun
While darkness is quick hastening:—I will tell
My state as though 'twere none of mine—despair
Cannot come near me—thus it is with me.
Souls alter not, and mine must progress still;
And this I knew not when I flung away
My youth's chief aims. I ne'er supposed the loss

Of what few I retained; for no resource
Awaits me—now behold the change of all.
I cannot chain my soul, it will not rest
In its clay prison, this most narrow sphere—
It has strange powers, and feelings, and desires,
Which I cannot account for, nor explain,
But which I stifle not, being bound to trust
All feelings equally—to hear all sides:
Yet I cannot indulge them, and they live,
Referring to some state or life unknown...

My selfishness is satiated not,
It wears me like a flame; my hunger for
All pleasure, howsoe'er minute, is pain;
I envy—how I envy him whose mind
Turns with its energies to some one end!
To elevate a sect, or a pursuit,
However mean—so my still baffled hopes
Seek out abstractions; I would have but one
Delight on earth, so it were wholly mine;
One rapture all my soul could fill—and this
Wild feeling places me in dream afar,
In some wide country, where the eye can see
No end to the far hills and dales bestrewn
With shining towers and dwellings. I grow mad
Well-nigh, to know not one abode but holds
Some pleasure—for my soul could grasp them all,
But must remain with this vile form. I look
With hope to age at last, which quenching much,
May let me concentrate the sparks it spares.

This restlessness of passion meets in me
A craving after knowledge: the sole proof
Of a commanding will is in that power
Repressed; for I beheld it in its dawn,
That sleepless harpy, with its budding wings,
And I considered whether I should yield
All hopes and fears, to live alone with it,
Finding a recompense in its wild eyes;
And when I found that I should perish so,
I bade its wild eyes close from me for ever;—

And I am left alone with my delights,—
So it lies in me a chained thing—still ready
To serve me, if I loose its slightest bond—
I cannot but be proud of my bright slave.

And thus I know this earth is not my sphere,
For I cannot so narrow me, but that
I still exceed it; in their elements
My love would pass my reason—but since here
Love must receive its objects from this earth,
While reason will be chainless, the few truths
Caught from its wanderings have sufficed to quell
All love below;—then what must be that love
Which, with the object it demands, would quell
Reason, tho' it soared with the seraphim?
No—what I feel may pass all human love,
Yet fall far short of what my love should be;
And yet I seem more warped in this than aught
For here myself stands out more hideously.
I can forget myself in friendship, fame,
Or liberty, or love of mighty souls.

* * * *

But I begin to know what thing hate is—
To sicken, and to quiver, and grow white,
And I myself have furnished its first prey.
All my sad weaknesses, this wavering will,
This selfishness, this still-decaying frame . . .
But I must never grieve while I can pass
Far from such thoughts—as now—Andromeda!
And she is with me—years roll, I shall change,
But change can touch her not—so beautiful
With her dark eyes, earnest and still, and hair
Lifted and spread by the salt-sweeping breeze;
And one red beam, all the storm leaves in heaven,
Resting upon her eyes and hair and hair,
As she awaits the snake on the wet beach,
By the dark rock, and the white wave just breaking

FIG. 1 Giovanni Volpato, *Perseus et Andromède* after Polidoro da Caravaggio.

At her feet; quite naked and alone,—a thing
You doubt not, nor fear for, secure that God
Will come in thunder from the stars to save her.
Let it pass—I will call another change.
I will be gifted with a wond'rous soul,
Yet sunk by error to men's sympathy,
And in the wane of life; yet only so
As to call up their fears, and there shall come
A time requiring youth's best energies;
And strait I fling age, sorrow, sickness off,
And rise triumphing over my decay.

* * * *

And thus it is that I supply the chasm
'Twixt what I am and all that I would be.
But then to know nothing—to hope for nothing—

To seize on life's dull joys from a strange fear,
Lest, losing them, all's lost and nought remains.

* * * *

There's some vile juggle with my reason here—
I feel I but explain to my own loss
These impulses—they live no less the same.
Liberty! what though I despair—my blood
Rose not at a slave's name proudlier than now.
And sympathy obscured by sophistries.
Why have I not sought refuge in myself,
But for the woes I saw and could not stay—
And love!—do I not love thee, my Pauline?

* * * *

I cherish prejudice, lest I be left
Utterly loveless—witness this belief
In poets, tho' sad change has come there too;
No more I leave myself to follow them:
Unconsciously I measure me by them.
Let me forget it; and I cherish most
My love of England—how her name—a word
Of her's in a strange tongue makes my heart beat! . .

* * * *

Pauline, I could do any thing—not now—
All's fever—but when calm shall come again—
I am prepared—I have made life my own—
I would not be content with all the change
One frame should feel—but I have gone in thought
Thro' all conjuncture—I have lived all life
When it is most alive—where strangest fate
New shapes it past surmise—the tales of men
Bit by some curse—or in the grasps of doom
Half-visible and still increasing round,
Or crowning their wide being's general aim. . . .

* * * *

These are wild fancies, but I feel, sweet friend,
As one breathing his weakness to the ear
Of pitying angel—dear as a winter flower;
A slight flower growing alone, and offering
Its frail cup of three leaves to the cold sun,

Yet joyous and confiding, like the triumph
Of a child—and why am I not worthy thee?

* * * *

I can live all the life of plants, and gaze
Drowsily on the bees that flit and play,
Or bare my breast for sunbeams which will kill,
Or open in the night of sounds, to look
For the dim stars; I can mount with the bird,
Leaping airily his pyramid of leaves
And twisted boughs of some tall mountain tree,
Or rise cheerfully springing to the heavens—
Or like a fish breathe in the morning air
In the misty sun-warm water—or with flowers
And trees can smile in light at the sinking sun,
Just as the storm comes, as a girl would look
On a departing lover—most serene.

Pauline, come with me—see how I could build
A home for us, out of the world; in thought—
I am inspired—come with me, Pauline!

Night, and one single ridge of narrow path
Between the sullen river and the woods
Waving and muttering—for the moonless night
Has shaped them into images of life,
Like the upraising of the giant-ghosts,
Looking on earth to know how their sons fare.
Thou art so close by me, the roughest swell
Of wind in the tree-tops hides not the panting
Of thy soft breasts; no—we will pass to morning—
Morning—the rocks, and vallies and old woods.
How the sun brightens in the mist, and here,—
Half in the air, like creatures of the place,
Trusting the element—living on high boughs
That swing in the wind—look at the golden spray,
Flung from the foam-sheet of the cataract,
Amid the broken rocks—shall we stay here
With the wild hawks?—no, ere the hot noon come
Dive we down—safe;—see this our new retreat
Walled in with a sloped mound of matted shrubs,
Dark, tangled, old and green—still sloping down

To a small pool whose waters lie asleep
Amid the trailing boughs turned water-plants
And tall trees over-arch to keep us in,
Breaking the sunbeams into emerald shafts,
And in the dreamy water one small group
Of two or three strange trees are got together,
Wondering at all around—as strange beasts herd
Together far from their own land—all wildness—
No turf nor moss, for boughs and plants pave all,
And tongues of bank go shelving in the waters,
Where the pale-throated snake reclines his head,
And old grey stones lie making eddies there;
The wild mice cross them dry-shod—deeper in—
Shut thy soft eyes—now look—still deeper in:
This is the very heart of the woods—all round,
Mountain-like, heaped above us; yet even here
One pond of water gleams—far off the river
Sweeps like a sea, barred out from land; but one—
One thin clear sheet has over-leaped and wound
Into this silent depth, which gained, it lies
Still, as but let by sufferance; the trees bend
O'er it as wild men watch a sleeping girl,
And thro' their roots long creeping plants stretch out
Their twined hair, steeped and sparkling; farther on,
Tall rushes and thick flag-knots have combined
To narrow it; so, at length a silver thread
It winds, all noiselessly, thro' the deep wood,
Till thro' a cleft way, thro' the moss and stone,
It joins its parent-river with a shout.
Up for the glowing day—leave the old woods:
See, they part, like a ruined arch, the sky!
Nothing but sky appears, so close the root
And grass of the hill-top level with the air—
Blue sunny air, where a great cloud floats, laden
With light, like a dead whale that white birds pick,
Floating away in the sun in some north sea.
Air, air—fresh life-blood,—thin and searching air—
The clear, dear breath of God, that loveth us:
Where small birds reel and winds take their delight.
Water is beautiful, but not like air.
See, where the solid azure waters lie,

Made as of thickened air, and down below,
The fern-ranks, like a forest spread themselves,
As tho' each pore could feel the element;
Where the quick glancing serpent winds his way—
Float with me there, Pauline, but not like air.
Down the hill—stop—a clump of trees, see, set
On a heap of rocks, which look o'er the far plains,
And envious climbing shrubs would mount to rest,
And peer from their spread boughs. There they wave, looking
At the muleteers, who whistle as they go
To the merry chime of their morning bells, and all
The little smoking cots, and fields, and banks,
And copses, bright in the sun; my spirit wanders.
Hedge-rows for me—still, living, hedge-rows, where
The bushes close, and clasp above, and keep
Thought in—I am concentrated—I feel;—
But my soul saddens when it looks beyond;
I cannot be immortal, nor taste all.
O God, where does this tend—these struggling aims!*

* Je crains bien que mon pauvre ami ne soit pas toujours parfaitement compris dans ce qui reste à lire de cet étrange fragment—mais il est moins propre que tout autre à éclaircir ce qui de sa nature ne peut jamais être que songe et confusion. D'ailleurs je ne sais trop si en cherchant à mieux co-ordonner certaines parties l'on ne courrait pas le risque de nuire au seul mérite auquel une production si singuliere peut prétendre—celui de donner une idée assez précise du genre qu'elle n'a fait que'ébaucher.—Ce début sans prétention, ce remuement des passions qui va d'abord en accroissant et puis s'appaise par degrés, ces élans de l'âme, ce retour soudain sur soi-même.—Et par dessus tout, la tournure d'esprit toute particulière de mon ami rendent les changemens presque impossibles. Les raisons qu'il fait valoir ailleurs, et d'autres encore plus puissantes, ont fait trouver grâce à mes yeux pour cet écrit qu'autrement je lui eusse conseillé de jeter au feu—Je n'en crois pas moins au grand principe de toute composition—à ce principe de Shakspeare, de Raffaelle, de Beethoven, d'où il suit que la concentration des idées est dûe bien plus à leur conception, qu'à leur mise en execution . . . j'ai tout lieu de craindre que la première de ces qualités ne soit encore étrangère à mon ami—et je doute fort qu'un redoublement de travail lui fasse acquérir la seconde. Le mieux serait de bruler ceci; mais que faire?

Je crois que dans ce qui suit il fait allusion à un certain examen qu'il fit autrefois de l'âme ou plutot de son âme, pour découvrir la suite des objets auxquels il lui serait possible d'attèndre, et dont chacun une fois obtenu devait former une espèce de plateau d'où l'on pouvait apercevoir d'autres buts, d'autres projets, d'autres jouissances qui, à leur tour, devaient être surmontés. Il en résultait que l'oubli et le sommeil devaient tout terminer. Cette idée que je ne saisis pas parfaitement lui est peutêtre aussi intelligible qu'á moi.

PAULINE.

What would I have? What is this "sleep", which seems
To bound all? can there be a "waking" point
Of crowning life? The soul would never rule—
It would be first in all things—it would have
Its utmost pleasure filled,—but that complete
Commanding for commanding sickens it.
The last point that I can trace is, rest beneath
Some better essence than itself—in weakness;
This is "myself"— not what I think should be,
And what is that I hunger for but God?
My God, my God! let me for once look on thee
As tho' nought else existed: we alone.
And as creation crumbles, my soul's spark
Expands till I can say, "Even from myself
"I need thee, and I feel thee, and I love thee;
"I do not plead my rapture in thy works
"For love of thee—or that I feel as one
"Who cannot die—but there is that in me
"Which turns to thee, which loves, or which should love."

Why have I girt myself with this hell-dress?
Why have I laboured to put out my life?
Is it not in my nature to adore,
And e'en for all my reason do I not
Feel him, and thank him, and pray to him—*Now*.
Can I forego the trust that he loves me?
Do I not feel a love which only ONE . . . . .
O thou pale form, so dimly seen, deep-eyed,
I have denied thee calmly—do I not
Pant when I read of thy consummate deeds,
And burn to see thy calm, pure truths out-flash
The brightest gleams of earth's philosophy?
Do I not shake to hear aught question thee? . . . .

If I am erring save me, madden me,
Take from me powers, and pleasures—let me die
Ages, so I see thee: I am knit round
As with a charm, by sin and lust and pride,
Yet tho' my wandering dreams have seen all shapes
Of strange delight, oft have I stood by thee—
Have I been keeping lonely watch with thee,

In the damp night by weeping Olivet,
Or leaning on thy bosom, proudly less—
Or dying with thee on the lonely cross—
Or witnessing thine outburst from the tomb!

A mortal, sin's familiar friend doth here
Avow that he will give all earth's reward,
But to believe and humbly teach the faith,
In suffering, and poverty, and shame,
Only believing he is not unloved ....

And now, my Pauline, I am thine for ever!
I feel the spirit which has buoyed me up
Deserting me: and old shades gathering on;
Yet while its last light waits, I would say much,
This chiefly, I am glad that I have said
That love which I have ever felt for thee,
But seldom told; our hearts so beat together,
That speech is mockery, but when dark hours come;
And I feel sad; and thou, sweet, deem'st it strange;
A sorrow moves me, thou canst not remove.
Look on this lay I dedicate to thee,
Which thro' thee I began, and which I end,
Collecting the last gleams to strive to tell
That I am thine, and more than ever now—
That I am sinking fast—yet tho' I sink,
No less I feel that thou hast brought me bliss,
And that I still may hope to win it back.
Thou know'st, dear friend, I could not think all calm,
For wild dreams followed me, and bore me off,
And all was indistinct. Ere one was caught
Another glanced: so dazzled by my wealth,
Knowing not which to leave nor which to choose,
For all my thoughts so floated, nought was fixed—
And then thou said'st a perfect bard was one
Who shadowed out the stages of all life,
And so thou badest me tell this my first stage;—
'Tis done: and even now I feel all dim the shift
Of thought. These are my last thoughts; I discern
Faintly immortal life, and truth, and good.
And why thou must be mine is, that e'en now,

In the dim hush of night—that I have done—
With fears and sad forebodings: I look thro'
And say—"E'en at the last I have her still,
"With her delicious eyes as clear as heaven,
"When rain in a quick shower has beat down mist,
"And clouds float white in the sun like broods of swans."
How the blood lies upon her cheek, all spread
As thinned by kisses; only in her lips
It wells and pulses like a living thing,
And her neck looks, like marble misted o'er
With love-breath,—a dear thing to kiss and love,
Standing beneath me—looking out to me,
As I might kill her and be loved for it.

Love me—love me, Pauline, love nought but me;
Leave me not. All these words are wild and weak,
Believe them not, Pauline. I stooped so low
But to behold thee purer by my side,
To show thou art my breath—my life—a last
Resource—an extreme want: never believe
Aught better could so look to thee, nor seek
Again the world of good thoughts left for me.
There were bright troops of undiscovered suns,
Each equal in their radiant course. There were
Clusters of far fair isles, which ocean kept
For his own joy, and his waves broke on them
Without a choice. And there was a dim crowd
Of visions, each a part of the dim whole.
And a star left his peers and came with peace
Upon a storm, and all eyes pined for him.
And one isle harboured a sea-beaten ship,
And the crew wandered in its bowers, and plucked
Its fruits, and gave up all their hopes for home.
And one dream came to a pale poet's sleep,
And he said, "I am singled out by God,
"No sin must touch me." I am very weak,
But what I would express is,—Leave me not,
Still sit by me—with beating breast, and hair
Loosened—watching earnest by my side,
Turning my books, or kissing me when I
Look up—like summer wind. Be still to me

A key to music's mystery, when mind fails,
A reason, a solution and a clue.
You see I have thrown off my prescribed rules:
I hope in myself—and hope, and pant, and love—
You'll find me better—know me more than when
You loved me as I was. Smile not; I have
Much yet to gladden you—to dawn on you.

No more of the past—I'll look within no more—
I have too trusted to my own wild wants—
Too trusted to myself—to intuition.
Draining the wine alone in the still night,
And seeing how—as gathering films arose,
As by an inspiration life seemed bare
And grinning in its vanity, and ends
Hard to be dreamed of, stared at me as fixed,
And others suddenly became all foul,
As a fair witch turned an old hag at night.
No more of this—we will go hand in hand,
I will go with thee, even as a child,
Looking no further than thy sweet commands.
And thou hast chosen where this life shall be—
The land which gave me thee shall be our home,
Where nature lies all wild amid her lakes
And snow-swathed mountains, and vast pines all girt
With ropes of snow—where nature lies all bare,
Suffering none to view her but a race
Most stinted and deformed—like the mute dwarfs
Which wait upon a naked Indian queen.
And there (the time being when the heavens are thick
With storms) I'll sit with thee while thou dost sing
Thy native songs, gay as a desert bird
Who crieth as he flies for perfect joy,
Or telling me old stories of dead knights.
Or I will read old lays to thee—how she,
The fair pale sister, went to her chill grave
With power to love, and to be loved, and live.
Or we will go together, like twin gods
Of the infernal world, with scented lamp
Over the dead—to call and to awake—
Over the unshaped images which lie

Within my mind's cave—only leaving all
That tells of the past doubts. So, when spring comes,
And sunshine comes again like an old smile,
And the fresh waters, and awakened birds,
And budding woods await us—I shall be
Prepared, and we will go and think again,
And old loves shall come to us—but changed
As some sweet thought which harsh words veiled before;
Feeling God loves us, and that all that errs,
Is a strange dream which death will dissipate;
And then when I am firm we'll seek again
My own land, and again I will approach
My old designs, and calmly look on all
The works of my past weakness, as one views
Some scene where danger met him long before.
Ah! that such pleasant life should be but dreamed!

But whate'er come of it—and tho' it fade,
And tho' ere the cold morning all be gone
As it will be;—tho' music wait for me,
And fair eyes and bright wine, laughing like sin,
Which steals back softly on a soul half saved;
And I be first to deny, and despise
This verse, and those intents which seem so fair;
Still this is all my own, this moment's pride,
No less I make an end in perfect joy.
E'en in my brightest time, a lurking fear
Possessed me. I well knew my weak resolves,
I felt the witchery that makes mind sleep
Over its treasures—as one half afraid
To make his riches definite—but now
These feelings shall not utterly be lost,
I shall not know again that nameless care,
Lest leaving all undone in youth, some new
And undreamed end reveal itself too late:
For this song shall remain to tell for ever,
That when I lost all hope of such a change,
Suddenly Beauty rose on me again.
No less I make an end in perfect joy,
For I, having thus again been visited,
Shall doubt not many another bliss awaits,

And tho' this weak soul sink, and darkness come,
Some little word shall light it up again,
And I shall see all clearer and love better;
I shall again go o'er the tracts of thought,
As one who has a right; and I shall live
With poets—calmer—purer still each time,
And beauteous shapes will come to me again,
And unknown secrets will be trusted me,
Which were not mine when wavering—but now
I shall be priest and lover, as of old.

Sun-treader, I believe in God, and truth,
And love; and as one just escaped from death
Would bind himself in bands of friends to feel
He lives indeed—so, I would lean on thee;
Thou must be ever with me—most in gloom
When such shall come—but chiefly when I die,
For I seem dying, as one going in the dark
To fight a giant—and live thou for ever,
And be to all what thou hast been to me—
All in whom this wakes pleasant thoughts of me,
Know my last state is happy—free from doubt,
Or touch of fear. Love me and wish me well!

RICHMOND,
October 22, 1832.

FROM *THE MONTHLY REPOSITORY*, VOL. 10, NS 1836, 43–6

[*Porphyria's Lover*] *Porphyria*

The rain set early in to-night:
   The sullen wind was soon awake—
It tore the elm-tops down for spite,
   And did its worst to vex the lake:
I listened, with heart fit to break,
When glided in Porphyria: straight
   She shut the cold out and the storm,
And kneeled and made the cheerless grate
   Blaze up, and all the cottage warm;
Which done, she rose, and from her form
Withdrew the dripping cloak and shawl,
   And laid her soiled gloves by; untied
Her hat and let the damp hair fall,
   And, last, she sate down by my side
And called me. When no voice replied,
She put my arm about her waist,
   And made her smooth white shoulder bare,
And all her yellow hair displaced,
   And, stooping, made my cheek lie there
And spread o'er all her yellow hair,
Murmuring how she loved me—she
   Too weak, for all her heart's endeavour,
To set its struggling passion free
   From pride, and vainer ties dissever,
And give herself to me for ever:
But passion sometimes would prevail;
   Nor could to-night's gay feast restrain
A sudden thought of one so pale
   For love of her—and all in vain;
And she was come through wind and rain.
Be sure I looked up at her eyes
   Proud—very proud—at last I knew
Porphyria worshipped me: surprise
   Made my heart swell, and still it grew
While I debated what to do.
That moment she was mine,—mine, fair
   Perfectly pure and good: I found
A thing to do, and all her hair

In one long yellow string I wound
Three times her little throat around
And strangled her. No pain felt she—
I am quite sure she felt no pain.
As a shut bud that holds a bee
I warily oped her lids—again
Laughed the blue eyes without a stain.
And I untightened next the tress
About her neck—her cheek once more
Blushed bright beneath my burning kiss:
I propped her head up as before,
Only, this time *my* shoulder bore
Her head—which droops upon it still:
The smiling rosy little head!
So glad it has its utmost will;
That all it scorned at once is fled,
And I, its love, am gained instead,
Porphyria's love: she guessed not how
Her darling, one wish would be heard.
And thus we sit together now:
And all night long we have not stirred,—
And yet God has not said a word!

[*Johannes Agricola in Meditation*] *Johannes Agricola*

"ANTINOMIANS, so denominated for rejecting the Law as a thing of no use under the Gospel dispensation: they say, that good works do not further, nor evil works hinder salvation: that the child of God cannot sin, that God never chastiseth him, that murder, drunkenness, &c. are sins in the wicked but not in him, that the child of grace being once assured of salvation, afterwards never doubteth...... that God doth not love any man for his holiness, that sanctification is no evidence of justification, &c. Pontanus, in his Catalogue of Heresies, says John Agricola was the author of this sect, A. D. 1535,"—*Dictionary of all Religions*, 1704.

There's Heaven above: and night by night
  I look right through its gorgeous roof—
No suns and moons though e'er so bright
  Avail to stop me:—splendor-proof
I keep the broods of stars aloof:
For I intend to get to God . . .
  For 'tis to God I speed so fast!
For in God's breast, my own abode,
  Those shoals of dazzling glory past,
I lay my spirit down at last.
I lie—where I have always lain,
  God smiles—as he has always smiled;—
Ere suns and moons could wax and wane,
  Ere stars were thundergirt, or piled
The heavens . . . God thought on me his child,
Ordained a life for me—arrayed
  Its circumstances, every one
To the minutest . . . ay, God said
  This head this hand should rest upon
Thus,—ere he fashioned star or sun!
And having thus created me,
  Thus rooted me, he bade me grow—
Guiltless for ever, like a tree
  That buds and blooms, nor seeks to know
  A law by which it prospers so:
But sure that thought and word and deed
  All go to swell his love for me—
Me—made because that love had need
  Of something irrevocably
Pledged solely its content to be.
Yes, yes,—a tree which must ascend—
  No poison-gourd foredoomed to stoop:
I have God's warrant, could I blend
  All hideous sins, as in a cup,—
To drink the mingled venoms up,
Secure my nature will convert
  The draught to blossoming gladness fast:
While sweet dews turn to the gourd's hurt,
  And bloat, and while they bloat it, blast—
As from the first its lot was cast.

For as I lie, smiled on, full fed
  By unexhausted blessedness,—
I gaze below on Hell's fierce bed,
  And those its waves of flame oppress,
Swarming in ghastly wretchedness,
Whose life on earth aspired to be
  One altar-smoke,—so pure!—to win
If not love like God's love to me,
  At least to keep his anger in . . .
And all their striving turned to sin!
  Priest, doctor, hermit, monk grown white
With prayer: the broken hearted nun,
  The martyr, the wan acolyte,
The incense-swinging child . . . undone
Before God fashioned star or sun!
God—whom I praise . . . how could I praise
  If such as I might understand,
Make out, and reckon on his ways,
  And bargain for his love, and stand,
Paying a price, at his right hand?

BELLS AND POMEGRANATES, NO. I, PIPPA PASSES (1841)

BELLS AND POMEGRANATES.

Nº. I.—PIPPA PASSES.

BY ROBERT BROWNING,

AUTHOR OF "PARACELSUS."

LONDON:
EDWARD MOXON, DOVER STREET.
MDCCCXLI.

FIG 2. Title-page of *Bells and Pomegranates. No. 1—Pippa Passes* (1841).

Pippa Passes

New Year's Day at Asolo in the Trevisan. A large, mean, airy Chamber. A girl, PIPPA, *from the silk-mills, springing out of bed.*

Day!
Faster and more fast
O'er night's brim day boils at last;
Boils, pure gold, o'er the cloud-cup's brim
Where spurting and supprest it lay—
For not a froth-flake touched the rim
Of yonder gap in the solid gray
Of the eastern cloud an hour away—
But forth one wavelet then another curled,
Till the whole sunrise, not to be suppress,
Rose-reddened, and its seething breast
Flickered in bounds, grew gold, then overflowed the world.
Day, if I waste a wavelet of thee,
Aught of my twelve-hours' treasure—
One of thy gazes, one of thy glances,
(Grants thou art bound to, gifts above measure,)
One of thy choices, one of thy chances,
(Tasks God imposed thee, freaks at thy pleasure,)
Day, if I waste such labour or leisure
Shame betide Asolo, mischief to me!
But in turn, Day, treat me not
As happy tribes—so happy tribes! who live
At hand—the common, other creatures' lot—
Ready to take when thou wilt give,
Prepared to pass what thou refusest;
Day, 'tis but Pippa thou ill-usest
If thou prove sullen, me, whose old year's sorrow
Who except thee can chase before to-morrow,
Sees thou, my day? Pippa's—who mean to borrow
Only of thee strength against new year's sorrow:
For let thy morning scowl on that superb
Great haughty Ottima—can scowl disturb
Her Sebald's homage? And if noon shed gloom
O'er Jules and Phene—what care bride and groom
Save for their dear selves? Then, obscure thy eve
With mist—will Luigi and Madonna grieve

—The mother and the child—unmatched, forsooth,
She in her age as Luigi in his youth,
For true content? And once again, outbreak
In storm at night on Monsignor they make
Such stir to-day about, who foregoes Rome
To visit Asolo, his brother's home,
And say there masses proper to release
The soul from pain—what storm dares hurt that peace?
But Pippa—just one such mischance would spoil,
Bethink thee, utterly next twelvemonth's toil
At wearisome silk-winding, coil on coil!

And here am I letting time slip for nought
You fool-hardy sunbeam—caught
With a single splash from my ewer!
You that mocked the best pursuer,
Was my basin over-deep?
One splash of water ruins you asleep
And up, up, fleet your brilliant bits
Wheeling and counterwheeling,
Reeling, crippled beyond healing—
Grow together on the ceiling,
That will task your wits!
Whoever it was first quenched fire hoped to see
Morsel after morsel flee
As merrily,
As giddily . . . what lights he on—
Where settles himself the cripple?
Oh never surely blown, my martagon?
New-blown, though!—ruddy as a nipple,
Plump as the flesh bunch on some Turk bird's poll!
Be sure if corals, branching 'neath the ripple
Of ocean, bud there,—fairies watch unroll
Such turban flowers . . I say, such lamps disperse
Thick red flame thro' that dusk green universe!
Queen of thee, floweret,
Each fleshy blossom
Keep I not, safer
Than leaves that embower it
Or shells that embosom,
From weevil and chafer?

Laugh thro' my pane then, solicit the bee,
Gibe him, be sure, and in midst of thy glee
Worship me!

Worship whom else? for am I not this Day,
Whate'er I please? Who shall I seem to-day?
Morn, Noon, Eve, Night—how must I spend my Day?

Up the hill-side, thro' the morning,
Love me as I love!
I am Ottima, take warning,
And the gardens, and stone house above,
And other house for shrubs, all glass in front,
Are mine, and Sebald steals as he is wont
To court me, and old Luca yet reposes,
And therefore till the shrub-house door uncloses
I... what now? give abundant cause for prate
Of me (that's Ottima)—too bold of late,
By far too confident she'll still face down
The spitefullest of talkers in our town—
How we talk in the little town below!

But love, love, love, there's better love I know!
This love's only day's first offer—
Next love shall defy the scoffer:
For do not our bride and bridegroom sally
Out of Possagno church at noon?
Their house looks over Orcana valley—
Why not be the bride as soon
As Ottima? I saw, myself, beside,
Arrive last night that bride—
Saw, if you call it seeing her, one flash
Of the pale snow-pure cheek and blacker tresses
Than... not the black eyelash;
A wonder she contrives those lids no dresses
—So strict was she the veil
Should cover close her pale
Pure cheeks—a bride to look at and scarce touch,
Remember Jules!—for are not such
Used to be tended, flower-like, every feature,
As if one's breath would fray the lily of a creature?
Oh, save that brow its virgin dimness,

Keep that foot its lady primness,
Let those ancles never swerve
From their exquisite reserve,
Yet have to trip along the streets like me
All but naked to the knee!
How will she ever grant her Jules a bliss
So startling as her real first infant kiss?
Oh—no—not envy this!
Not envy sure, for, if you gave me
Leave to take or to refuse
In earnest, do you think I'd choose
That sort of new love to enslave me?
Mine should have lapped me round from the beginning
As little fear of losing it as winning—
Why look you! when at eve the pair
Commune inside our turret, what prevents
My being Luigi?—While that mossy lair
Of lizards thro' the winter-time, is stirred
With each to each imparting sweet intents
For this new year, as brooding bird to bird—
I will be cared about, kept out of harm
And schemed for, safe in love as with a charm,
I will be Luigi . . . if I only knew
What was my father like . . . my mother too!

Nay, if you come to that, the greatest love of all
Is God's: well then, to have God's love befall
Oneself as in the palace by the dome
Where Monsignor to-night will bless the home
Of his dead brother! I, to-night at least,
Will be that holy and beloved priest.

Now wait—even I myself already ought to share
In that—why else should new year's hymn declare

All service ranks the same with God:
If now, as formerly he trod
Paradise, God's presence fills
Our earth, each only as God wills
Can work—God's puppets, best and worst,
Are we; there is no last nor first.

Say not, a small event! Why small?
Costs it more pain this thing ye call
A great event should come to pass
Than that? Untwine me, from the mass
Of deeds which make up life, one deed
Power shall fall short in or exceed!

And more of it, and more of it—oh, yes!
So that my passing and each happiness
I pass, will be alike important—prove
That true! Oh yes—the brother,
The bride, the lover, and the mother,—
Only to pass whom will remove—
Whom a mere look at half will cure
The Past, and help me to endure
The Coming . . . I am just as great, no doubt,
As they!
A pretty thing to care about
So mightily—this single holiday!
Why repine?
With thee to lead me, Day of mine,
Down the grass path gray with dew,
'Neath the pine-wood, blind with boughs,
Where the swallow never flew
As yet, nor cicale dared carouse:
No, dared carouse! [*She enters the Street.*

I.—*Morning. Up the Hill-side. The Shrub House.* LUCA'S *Wife* OTTIMA, *and her Paramour, the German* SEBALD.

Seb. (Sings.) *Let the watching lids wink!*
Day's a-blaze with eyes, think,—
Deep into the night drink!
Otti. Night? What, a Rhineland night, then? How these tall
Naked geraniums straggle! Push the lattice—
Behind that frame.—Nay, do I bid you?—Sebald,
It shakes the dust down on me! Why, of course
The slide-bolt catches—Well, are you content,
Or must I find you something else to spoil?
Kiss and be friends, my Sebald. Is it full morning?
Oh, don't speak then!
Seb. Ay, thus it used to be!

Ever your house was, I remember, shut
Till mid-day—I observed that, as I strolled
On mornings thro' the vale here: country girls
Were noisy, washing garments in the brook—
Herds drove the slow white oxen up the hills—
But no, your house was mute, would ope no eye—
And wisely—you were plotting one thing there,
Nature another outside: I looked up—
Rough white wooden shutters, rusty iron bars,
Silent as death, blind in a flood of light,
Oh, I remember!—and the peasants laughed
And said, "The old man sleeps with the young wife!"
This house was his, this chair, this window—his.
Otti. Ah, the clear morning! I can see St. Mark's:
That black streak is the belfry—stop: Vicenza
Should lie—there's Padua, plain enough, that blue.
Look o'er my shoulder—follow my finger—
Seb. Morning?
It seems to me a night with a sun added:
Where's dew, where's freshness? That bruised plant I bruised
In getting thro' the lattice yestereve,
Droops as it did. See, here's my elbow's mark
In the dust on the sill.
Otti. Oh, shut the lattice, pray!
Seb. Let me lean out. I cannot scent blood here
Foul as the morn may be—
There, shut the world out!
How do you feel now, Ottima? There—curse
The world, and all outside! Let us throw off
This mask: how do you bear yourself? Let's out
With all of it!
Otti. Best never speak of it.
Seb. Best speak again and yet again of it,
Till words cease to be more than words. "His blood,"
For instance—let those two words mean "His blood"
And nothing more. Notice—I'll say them now,
"His blood."
Otti. Assuredly if I repented
The deed—
Seb. Repent? Who should repent, or why?
What puts that in your head? Did I once say

That I repented?
Otti. No—I said the deed—
Seb. "The deed" and "the event"—and just now it was
"Our passion's fruit!"—the devil take such cant!
Say, once and always, Luca was a wittol,
I am his cut-throat, you are—
Ott. Here is the wine—
I brought it when we left the house above—
And glasses too—wine of both sorts. Black? white, then?
Seb. But am not I his cut-throat? What are you?
Otti. There trudges on his business from the Duomo,
Benet the Capuchin, with his brown hood
And bare feet—always in one place at church,
Close under the stone wall by the south entry
I used to take him for a brown cold piece
Of the wall's self, as out of it he rose
To let me pass—at first, I say, I used—
Now—so has that dumb figure fastened on me—
I rather should account the plastered wall
A piece of him, so chilly does it strike.
This, Sebald?
Seb. No—the white wine—the white wine!
Well, Ottima, I promised no new year
Should rise on us the ancient shameful way,
Nor does it rise—pour on—To your black eyes!
Do you remember last damned New Year's day?
Otti. You brought those foreign prints. We looked at them
Over the wine and fruit. I had to scheme
To get him from the fire. Nothing but saying
His own set wants the proof-mark roused him up
To hunt them out.
Seb. Faith, he is not alive
To fondle you before my face.
Otti. Do you
Fondle me then: who means to take your life
For that, my Sebald?
Seb. Hark you, Ottima,
One thing's to guard against. We'll not make much
One of the other—that is, not make more
Parade of warmth, childish officious coil,
Than yesterday—as if, sweet, I supposed

Proof upon proof were needed now, now first,
To show I love you—still love you—love you
In spite of Luca and what's come to him.
—Sure sign we had him ever in our thoughts,
White sneering old reproachful face and all—
We'll even quarrel, love, at times, as if
We still could lose each other—were not tied
By this—conceive you?
Otti. Love—
Seb. Not tied so sure—
Because tho' I was wrought upon—have struck
His insolence back into him—am I
So surely yours?—therefore, forever yours?
Otti. Love, to be wise, (one counsel pays another)
Should we have—months ago—when first we loved,
For instance that May morning we two stole
Under the green ascent of sycamores—
If we had come upon a thing like that
Suddenly—
Seb. "A thing" . . there again—"a thing!"
Otti. Then, Venus' body, had we come upon
My husband Luca Gaddi's murdered corpse
Within there, at his couch-foot, covered close—
Would you have pored upon it? Why persist
In poring now upon it? For 'tis here—
As much as there in the deserted house—
You cannot rid your eyes of it: for me,
Now he is dead I hate him worse—I hate—
Dare you stay here? I would go back and hold
His two dead hands, and say, I hate you worse
Luca, than—
Seb. Off, off; take your hands off mine!
'Tis the hot evening—off! oh, morning, is it?
Otti. There's one thing must be done—you know what thing.
Come in and help to carry. We may sleep
Anywhere in the whole wide house to-night.
Seb. What would come, think you, if we let him lie
Just as he is? Let him lie there until
The angels take him: he is turned by this
Off from his face, beside, as you will see.
Otti. This dusty pane might serve for looking-glass.

Three, four—four grey hairs! is it so you said
A plait of hair should wave across my neck?
No—this way!
Seb. Ottima, I would give your neck,
Each splendid shoulder, both those breasts of yours,
This were undone! Killing?—Let the world die
So Luca lives again!—Ay, lives to sputter
His fulsome dotage on you—yes, and feign
Surprise that I returned at eve to sup,
When all the morning I was loitering here—
Bid me dispatch my business and begone.
I would—
Otti. See!
Seb. No, I'll finish. Do you think
I fear to speak the bare truth once for all?
All we have talked of is at bottom fine
To suffer—there's a recompense in that:
One must be venturous and fortunate—
What is one young for else? In age we'll sigh
O'er the wild, reckless, wicked days flown over:
But to have eaten Luca's bread—have worn
His clothes, have felt his money swell my purse—
Why, I was starving when I used to call
And teach you music—starving while you pluck'd
Me flowers to smell!
Otti. My poor lost friend!
Seb. He gave me
Life—nothing less: what if he did reproach
My perfidy, and threaten, and do more—
Had he no right? What was to wonder at?
Why must you lean across till our cheeks touch'd?
Could he do less than make pretence to strike me?
'Tis not the crime's sake—I'd commit ten crimes
Greater, to have this crime wiped out—undone!
And you—O, how feel you? feel you for me?
Otti. Well, then—I love you better now than ever—
And best (look at me while I speak to you)—
Best for the crime—nor do I grieve in truth
This mask, this simulated ignorance,
This affectation of simplicity
Falls off our crime; this naked crime of ours

May not now be looked over—look it down, then!
Great? let it be great—but the joys it brought
Pay they or no its price? Come—they or it!
Speak not! The past, would you give up the past
Such as it is, pleasure and crime together?
Give up that noon I owned my love for you—
The garden's silence—even the single bee
Persisting in his toil, suddenly stopt,
And where he hid you only could surmise
By some campanula's chalice set a-swing.
As he clung there—"Yes, I love you?"
Seb. And I drew
Back: put far back your face with both my hands
Lest you should grow too full of me—your face
So seemed athirst for my whole soul and body!
Otti. And when I ventured to receive you here,
Made you steal hither in the mornings—
Seb. When
I used to look up 'neath the shrub-house here
Till the red fire on its glazed windows spread
To a yellow haze?
Otti. Ah—my sign was, the sun
Inflamed the sere side of yon chestnut-tree
Nipt by the first frost—
Seb. You would always laugh
At my wet boots—I had to stride thro' grass
Over my ancles.
Otti. Then our crowning night—
Seb. The July night?
Otti. The day of it too, Sebald!
When heaven's pillars seemed o'erbowed with heat,
Its black-blue canopy seemed let descend
Close on us both, to weigh down each to each,
And smother up all life except our life.
So lay we till the storm came.
Seb. How it came!
Otti. Buried in woods we lay, you recollect;
Swift ran the searching tempest overhead;
And ever and anon some bright white shaft
Burned thro' the pine-tree roof—here burnt and there,
As if God's messenger thro' the close wood screen

Plunged and replunged his weapon at a venture,
Feeling for guilty thee and me—then broke
The thunder like a whole sea overhead—
Seb. Yes.
Otti. While I stretched myself upon you, hands
To hands, my mouth to your hot mouth, and shook
All my locks loose, and covered you with them.
You, Sebald, the same you—
Seb. Slower, Ottima—
Otti. And as we lay—
Seb. Less vehemently—Love me—
Forgive me—take not words—mere words—to heart—
Your breath is worse than wine—breathe slow, speak slow—
Do not lean on me—
Otti. Sebald, as we lay,
Rising and falling only with our pants,
Who said, "Let death come now—'tis right to die!
Right to be punished—nought completes such bliss
But woe!" Who said that?
Seb. How did we ever rise?
Was't that we slept? Why did it end?
Otti. I felt
You tapering to a point the ruffled ends
Of my loose locks 'twixt both your humid lips—
(My hair is fallen now—knot it again).
Seb. I kiss you now, dear Ottima, now and now;
This way? will you forgive me—be once more
My great queen?
Otti. Bind it thrice about my brow;
Crown me your queen, your spirit's arbitress,
Magnificent in sin. Say that!
Seb. I crown you
My great white queen, my spirit's arbitress,
Magnificent—

[*Without.*] The year's at the spring,
And day's at the morn:
Morning's at seven;
The hill-side's dew-pearled:
The lark's on the wing,
The snail's on the thorn;

God's in his heaven—
All's right with the world! [PIPPA *passes.*

Seb. God's in his heaven! Do you hear that? Who spoke?
You, you spoke!
Otti. Oh—that little ragged girl:
She must have rested on the step—we give
Them but one holiday the whole year round—
Did you ever see our silk-mills—their inside?
There are ten silk-mills now belong to you.
She stoops to pick my double heartsease . . . Sh!
She does not hear—call you out louder!
Seb. Leave me!
Go, get your clothes on—dress those shoulders.
Otti. Sebald?
Seb. Wipe off that paint! I hate you!
Otti. Miserable!
Seb. My God! and she is emptied of it now!
Outright now!—how miraculously gone
All of the grace—had she not strange grace once?
Why, the blank cheek hangs listless as it likes,
No purpose holds the features up together,
Only the cloven brow and puckered chin
Stay in their places—and the very hair,
That seemed to have a sort of life in it,
Drops a dead web!
Otti. Speak to me—not of me!
Seb. That round great full-orbed face, where not an angle
Broke the delicious indolence—all broken!
Otti. Ungrateful!—to me—not of me—perjured cheat—
A coward too—but ingrate's worse than all:
Beggar—my slave—a fawning, cringing lie!
Leave me!—betray me!—I can see your drift—
A lie that walks, and eats, and drinks!
Seb. My God!
Those morbid, olive, faultless shoulder-blades—
I should have known there was no blood beneath!
Otti. You hate me then? you hate me then?
Seb. To think
She would succeed in her absurd attempt,
And fascinate with sin! and show herself

Superior—Guilt from its excess, superior
To Innocence. That little peasant's voice
Has righted all again. Though I be lost,
I know which is the better, never fear,
Of vice or virtue, purity or lust,
Nature, or trick—I see what I have done
Entirely now. Oh, I am proud to feel
Such torments—let the world take credit that
I, having done my deed, pay too its price!
I hate, hate—curse you! God's in his heaven!
Otti. Me!
Me! no, no, Sebald—not yourself—kill me!
Mine is the whole crime—do but kill me—then
Yourself—then—presently—first hear me speak—
I always meant to kill myself—wait you!
Lean on my breast . . not as a breast; don't love me
The more because you lean on me, my own
Heart's Sebald. There—there—both deaths presently!
Seb. My brain is drowned now—quite drowned: all I feel
Is . . . is at swift-recurring intervals,
A hurrying-down within me, as of waters
Loosened to smother up some ghastly pit—
There they go—whirls from a black, fiery sea.
Otti. Not me—to him oh God be merciful!

Talk by the way in the mean time. Foreign Students *of Painting and Sculpture, from Venice, assembled opposite the house of* JULES, *a young French Statuary.*

1 *Stu.* Attention: my own post is beneath this window, but the pomegranate-clump yonder will hide three or four of you with a little squeezing, and Schramm and his pipe must lie flat in the balcony. Four, five—who's a defaulter? Jules must not be suffered to hurt his bride.

2 *Stu.* The poet's away—never having much meant to be here, moonstrike him! He was in love with himself, and had a fair prospect of thriving in his suit, when suddenly a woman fell in love with him too, and out of pure jealousy, he takes himself off to Trieste, immortal poem and all—whereto is this prophetical epitaph appended already, as Bluphocks assured me: —"*The author on the author. Here so and so, the mammoth, lies, Fouled to death by butterflies.*" His own fault, the simpleton! Instead of cramp couplets, each like a knife in your entrails,

he should write, says Bluphocks, both classically and intelligibly.—*Æsculapius, an epic. Catalogue of the drugs:—Hebe's plaister—One strip Cools your lip; Phoebus' emulsion—One bottle Clears your throttle: Mercury's bolus—One box Cures* . . .

3 *Stu.* Subside, my fine fellow; if the marriage was over by ten o'clock, Jules will certainly be here in a minute with his bride.

2 *Stu.* So should the poet's muse have been acceptable, says Bluphocks, and Delia not better known to our dogs than the boy.

1 *Stu.* To the point, now. Where's Gottlieb? Oh, listen, Gottlieb—What called down this piece of friendly vengeance on Jules, of which we now assemble to witness the winding-up. We are all in a tale, observe, when Jules bursts out on us by and bye: I shall be spokesman, but each professes himself alike insulted by this strutting stone-squarer, who came singly from Paris to Munich, thence with a crowd of us to Venice and Possagno here, but proceeds in a day or two alone,—oh! alone, indubitably—to Rome and Florence. He take up his portion with these dissolute, brutalized, heartless bunglers! (Is Schramm brutalized? Am I heartless?).

Gott. Why, somewhat heartless; for, coxcomb as much as you choose, you will have brushed off—what do folks style it?—the bloom of his life. Is it too late to alter? These letters, now, you call his. I can't laugh at them.

4 *Stu.* Because you never read the sham letters of our inditing which drew forth these.

Gott. His discovery of the truth will be frightful.

4 *Stu.* That's the joke. But you should have joined us at the beginning; there's no doubt he loves the girl.

Gott. See here: "He has been accustomed," he writes, "to have Canova's women about him, in stone, and the world's women beside him, in flesh, these being as much below, as those above, his soul's aspiration; but now he is to have" . . . There you laugh again! You wipe off the very dew of his youth.

1 *Stu.* Schramm (take the pipe out of his mouth, somebody), will Jules lose the bloom of his youth?

Schramm. Nothing worth keeping is ever lost in this world: look at a blossom—it drops presently and fruits succeed; as well affirm that your eye is no longer in your body because its earliest favourite is dead and done with, as that any affection is lost to the soul when its first object is superseded in due course. Has a man done wondering at women? There follow men, dead and alive, to wonder at. Has he done wondering at men? There's God to wonder at: and the faculty of wonder may be at the same time grey enough with respect to its last object, and yet green sufficiently so far as concerns its novel one: thus...

1 *Stu.* Put Schramm's pipe into his mouth again—There, you see! well, this Jules . . a wretched fribble—oh, I watched his disportings at Possagno the other day! The Model-Gallery—you know: he marches first resolvedly past great works by the dozen without vouchsafing an eye: all at once he stops full at the *Psiche-fanciulla*—cannot pass that old acquaintance without a nod of encouragement—"In your new place, beauty? Then behave yourself as well here as at Munich—I see you!"—Next posts himself deliberately before the unfinished *Pietà* for half an hour without moving, till up he starts of a sudden and thrusts his very nose into... I say into—the group—by which you are informed that precisely the sole point he had not fully mastered in Canova was a certain method of using the drill in the articulation of the knee-joint—and that, even, has he mastered at length! Good bye, therefore, to Canova—whose gallery no longer contains Jules the predestinated thinker in marble!

5 *Stu.* Tell him about the women—go on to the women.

1 *Stu.* Why, on that matter he could never be supercilious enough. How should we be other than the poor devils you see, with those debasing habits we cherish? He was not to wallow in that mire, at least: he would love at the proper time, and meanwhile put up with the *Psiche-fanciulla*. Now I happened to hear of a young Greek—real Greek girl at Malamocco, a true Islander, do you see, with Alciphron hair like sea-moss—you know! White and quiet as an apparition, and fourteen years old at farthest; daughter, so she swears, of that hag Natalia, who helps us to models at three *lire* an hour. So first Jules received a scented letter—somebody had seen his Tydeus at the Academy, and my picture was nothing to it—bade him persevere—would make herself known to him ere long—(Paolina, my little friend, transcribes divinely.) Now think of Jules finding himself distinguished from the herd of us by such a creature! In his very first answer he proposed marrying his monitress; and fancy us over these letters two, three times a day to receive and dispatch! I concocted the main of it: relations were in the way—secrecy must be observed—would he wed her on trust and only speak to her when they were indissolubly united? St—St!

6 *Stu.* Both of them! Heaven's love, speak softly! speak within yourselves!

5 *Stu.* Look at the Bridegroom—half his hair in storm and half in calm—patted down over the left temple, like a frothy cup one blows on to cool it; and the same old blouse that he murders the marble in!

2 *Stu.* Not a rich vest like yours, Hannibal Scratchy, rich, that your face may the better set it off.

6 *Stu.* And the bride—and the bride—how magnificently pale!

Gott. She does not also take it for earnest, I hope?

1 *Stu.* Oh, Natalia's concern, that is; we settle with Natalia.

6 *Stu.* She does not speak—has evidently let out no word.

Gott. How he gazes on her!

1 *Stu.* They go in—now, silence!

II.—*Noon. Over Orcana. The House of* JULES, *who crosses its threshold with* PHENE—*she is silent, on which* JULES *begins*—

Do not die, Phene—I am yours now—you
Are mine now—let fate reach me how she likes
If you'll not die—so never die! Sit here—
My work-room's single seat—I do lean over
This length of hair and lustrous front—they turn
Like an entire flower upward—eyes—lips—last
Your chin—no, last your throat turns—'tis their scent
Pulls down my face upon you. Nay, look ever
That one way till I change, grow you—I could
Change into you, beloved!
                                        Thou by me,
And I by thee—this is thy hand in mine—
And side by side we sit—all's true. Thank God!
I have spoken—speak thou!
                                        —O, my life to come!
My Tydeus must be carved that's there in clay,
And how be carved with you about the chamber?
Where must I place you? When I think that once
This room-full of rough block-work seemed my heaven
Without you! Shall I ever work again—
Get fairly into my old ways again—
Bid each conception stand while trait by trait
My hand transfers its lineaments to stone?
Will they, my fancies, live near you, my truth—
The live truth—passing and repassing me—
Sitting beside me?

Now speak!
Only, first,
Your letters to me—was't not well contrived?
A hiding-place in Psyche's robe—there lie
Next to her skin your letters: which comes foremost?
Good—this that swam down like a first moonbeam
Into my world.
Those? Books I told you of.
Let your first word to me rejoice them, too,—
This minion of Coluthus, writ in red
Bistre and azure by Bessarion's scribe—
Read this line . . no, shame—Homer's be the Greek!
My Odyssey in coarse black vivid type
With faded yellow blossoms 'twixt page and page;
"He said, and on Antinous directed
A bitter shaft"—then blots a flower the rest!
—Ah, do not mind that—better that will look
When cast in bronze . . an Almaign Kaiser that,
Swart-green and gold with truncheon based on hip—
This rather, turn to . . but a check already—
Or you had recognized that here you sit
As I imagined you, Hippolyta
Naked upon her bright Numidian horse!
—Forget you this then? "carve in bold relief" . . .
So you command me—"carve against I come
A Greek, bay-filleted and thunder-free,
Rising beneath the lifted myrtle-branch,
Whose turn arrives to praise Harmodius."—Praise him!
Quite round, a cluster of mere hands and arms
Thrust in all senses, all ways, from all sides,
Only consenting at the branches' end
They strain towards, serves for frame to a sole face—
(Place your own face)—the Praiser's, who with eyes
Sightless, so bend they back to light inside
His brain where visionary forms throng up,
(Gaze—I am your Harmodius dead and gone,)
Sings, minding not that palpitating arch
Of hands and arms, nor the quick drip of wine
From the drenched leaves o'erhead, nor who cast off
Their violet crowns for him to trample on—
Sings, pausing as the patron-ghosts approve,

Devoutly their unconquerable hymn—
But you must say a "well" to that—say "well"
Because you gaze—am I fantastic, sweet?
Gaze like my very life's-stuff, marble—marbly
Even to the silence—and before I found
The real flesh Phene, I inured myself
To see throughout all nature varied stuff
For better nature's birth by means of art:
With me, each substance tended to one form
Of beauty—to the human Archetype—
And every side occurred suggestive germs
Of that—the tree, the flower—why, take the fruit,
Some rosy shape, continuing the peach,
Curved beewise o'er its bough, as rosy limbs
Depending nestled in the leaves—and just
From a cleft rose-peach the whole Dryad sprung!
But of the stuffs one can be master of,
How I divined their capabilities
From the soft-rinded smoothening facile chalk
That yields your outline to the air's embrace,
Down to the crisp imperious steel, so sure
To cut its one confided thought clean out
Of all the world: but marble!—'neath my tools
More pliable than jelly—as it were
Some clear primordial creature dug from deep
In the Earth's heart where itself breeds itself
And whence all baser substance may be worked;
Refine it off to air you may—condense it
Down to the diamond;—is not metal there
When o'er the sudden specks my chisel trips?
—Not flesh—as flake off flake I scale, approach,
Lay bare those bluish veins of blood asleep?
Lurks flame in no strange windings where, surprised
By the swift implement sent home at once,
Flushes and glowings radiate and hover
About its track?—
Phene? what—why is this?
Ah, you will die—I knew that you would die!

PHENE *begins, on his having long remained silent.*

Now the end's coming—to be sure it must
Have ended sometime!—Tush—I will not speak
Their foolish speech—I cannot bring to mind
Half—so the whole were best unsaid—what care
I for Natalia now, or all of them?
Oh, you . . what are you?—I do not attempt
To say the words Natalia bade me learn
To please your friends, that I may keep myself
Where your voice lifted me—by letting you
Proceed . . but can you?—even you perhaps
Cannot take up, now you have once let fall,
The music's life, and me along with it?
No—or you would . . we'll stay then as we are
Above the world—
                    Now you sink—for your eyes
Are altered . . altering—stay—"I love you, love you,"—
I could prevent it if I understood
More of your words to me . . was't in the tone
Of the voice, your power?
                    Stay, stay, I will repeat
Their speech, if that affects you! only change
No more and I shall find it presently—
Far back here in the brain yourself filled up:
Natalia said (like Lutwyche) harm would follow
Unless I spoke their lesson to the end,
But harm to me, I thought, not you: and so
I'll speak it,—"Do not die, Phene, I am yours" . .
Stop—is not that, or like that, part of what
You spoke? 'Tis not my fault—that I should lose
What cost such pains acquiring! is this right?
  The Bard said, do one thing I can—
  Love a man and hate a man
  Supremely: thus my lore began.
  Thro' the Valley of Love I went,
  In the lovingest spot to abide;
  And just on the verge where I pitched my tent
  Dwelt Hate beside—
  (And the bridegroom asked what the bard's smile meant
  Of his bride.)
  Next Hate I traversed, the Grove,

In its hatefullest nook to dwell—
And lo, where I flung myself prone, couched Love
Next cell.
(For not I, said the bard, but those black bride's eyes above Should tell!)
(Then Lutwyche said you probably would ask,
"You have black eyes, love,—you are sure enough
My beautiful bride—do you, as he sings, tell
What needs some exposition—what is this?"
... And I am to go on, without a word,)
Once when I loved I would enlace
Breast, eyelids, hands, feet, form and face
Of her I loved in one embrace—
And, when I hated, I would plunge
My sword, and wipe with the first lunge
My foe's whole life out like a sponge:
—But if I would love and hate more
Than ever man hated or loved before—
Would seek in the Valley of Love
The spot, or in Hatred's grove
The spot where my soul may reach
The essence, nought less, of each ...
(Here, he said, if you interrupted me
With, "There must be some error,—who induced you
To speak this jargon?"—I was to reply
Simply—"Await till ... until . ." I must say
Last rhyme again—)
. . The essence, nought less, of each—
The Hate of all Hates, or the Love
Of all Loves in its glen or its grove,
—I find them the very warders
Each of the other's borders.
So most I love when Love's disguised
In Hate's garb—'tis when Hate's surprised
In Love's weed that I hate most; ask
How Love can smile thro' Hate's barren iron casque
Hate grin thro' Love's rose-braided mask,
Of thy bride, Giulio!
(Then you, "Oh, not mine—
Preserve the real name of the foolish song!"
But I must answer, "Giulio—Jules—'tis Jules!)

Thus I, Jules, hating thee,
Sought long and painfully . . .

[JULES *interposes.*

Lutwyche—who else? But all of them, no doubt,
Hated me—them at Venice—presently
For them, however! You I shall not meet—
If I dreamed, saying this would wake me. Keep
What's here—this too—we cannot meet again
Consider and the money was but meant
For two years' travel, which is over now
All chance, or hope, or care, or need of it!
This—and what comes from selling these—my casts
And books, and medals, except . . . let them go
Together—so the produce keeps you safe
Out of Natalia's clutches! If by chance
(For all's chance here) I should survive the gang
At Venice, root out all fifteen of them,
We might meet somewhere since the world is wide.

1.

[*Without.*] Give her but a least excuse to love me!
When—where—
How—can this arm establish her above me
If fortune fixed my lady there—
—There already, to eternally reprove me?
(Hist, said Kate the queen:
—Only a page who carols unseen
Crumbling your hounds their messes!)

2.

She's wronged?—To the rescue of her honour,
My heart!
She's poor?—What costs it to be styled a donor?
An earth's to cleave, a sea's to part!
—But that fortune should have thrust all this upon her!
(Nay, list, bade Kate the queen:
Only a page that carols unseen,
Fitting your hawks their jesses!)—

[PIPPA *passes.*

Kate? Queen Cornaro doubtless, who renounced
Cyprus to live and die the lady here
At Asolo—and whosoever loves
Must be in some sort god or worshipper,
The blessing, or the blest one—queen or page—
I find myself queen here it seems!
How strange!
Shall to produce form out of shapelessness
Be art—and, further, to evoke a soul
From form be nothing? This new soul is mine—
Now to kill Lutwyche, what would that do?—Save
A wretched dauber men will hoot to death
Without me.
To Ancona—Greece—some isle!
I wanted silence only—there is clay
Every where. One may do whate'er one likes
In Art—the only thing is, to be sure
That one does like it—which takes pains to know.
Scatter all this, my Phene—this mad dream!
Who—what is Lutwyche—what Natalia—
What the whole world except our love—my own
Own Phene? But I told you, did I not,
Ere night we travel for your land—some isle
With the sea's silence on it? Stand aside—
I do but break these paltry models up
To begin art afresh. Shall I meet Lutwyche,
And save him from my statue's meeting him?
Some unsuspected isle in the far seas!
Like a god going thro' his world I trace
One mountain for a moment in the dusk,
Whole brotherhoods of cedars on its brow—
And you are ever by me while I trace
—Are in my arms as now—as now—as now!
Some unsuspected isle in the far seas!
Some unsuspected isle in far off seas!

Talk by the way in the mean time. Two or three of the Austrian Police loitering with BLUPHOCKS, *an English vagabond, just in view of the Turret.*

Bluphocks.* *Oh! were but every worm a maggot, Every fly a grig, Every bough a Christmas faggot, Every tune a jig!* In fact, I have abjured all religions,—but the last I inclined to was the Armenian—for I have travelled, do you see, and at Koenigsberg, Prussia Improper (so styled because there's a sort of bleak hungry sun there,) you might remark over a venerable house-porch, a certain Chaldee inscription; and brief as it is, a mere glance at it used absolutely to change the mood of every bearded passenger. In they turned, one and all, the young and lightsome, with no irreverent pause, the aged and decrepit, with a sensible alacrity,—'twas the grand Rabbi's abode, in short. I lost no time in learning Syriac—(vowels, you dogs, follow my stick's end in the mud—*Celarent, Darii, Ferio!*) and one morning presented myself spelling-book in hand, a, b, c,—what was the purport of this miraculous posy? Some cherished legend of the past, you'll say—"*How Moses hocus-pocust Egypt's land with fly and locust*,"—or, "*How to Jonah sounded harshish, Get thee up and go to Tarshish*,"—or, "*How the angel meeting Balaam, Straight his ass returned a salaam*,"—in no wise! "*Shackabrach—Boach—somebody or other—Isaach, Re-cei-ver, Pur-cha-ser and Ex-chan-ger of—Stolen goods.*" So talk to me of obliging a bishop! I have renounced all bishops save Bishop Beveridge—mean to live so—and die—*As some Greek dog-sage, dead and merry, Hellward bound in Charon's ferry—With food for both worlds, under and upper, Lupine-seed and Hecate's supper, And never an obolus* . . (it might be got in somehow) *Tho' Cerberus should gobble us—To pay the Stygian ferry*—or you might say, *Never an obol To pay for the coble*. . . . Though thanks to you, or this Intendant thro' you, or this Bishop thro' his Intendant—I possess a burning pocket-full of *zwanzigers*.

1 *Pol.* I have been noticing a house yonder this long while—not a shutter unclosed since morning.

2 *Pol.* Old Luca Gaddi's, that owns the silk-mills here: he dozes by the hour—wakes up, sighs deeply, says he should like to be Prince Metternich, and then dozes again after having bidden young Sebald, the foreigner, set his wife to playing draughts: never molest such a household, they mean well.

Blup. Only tell me who this little Pippa is I must have to do with—one could make something of that name. Pippa—that is, short for

* "He maketh his sun to rise on the evil and on the good, and sendeth rain on the just and on the unjust."

Felippa—*Panurge consults Hertrippa—Believ'st thou, King Agrippa?* Something might be done with that name.

2 *Pol.* Your head and a ripe musk-melon would not be dear at half a *zwanziger!* Leave this fool, and look out—the afternoon's over or nearly so.

3 *Pol.* Where in this passport of Signor Luigi does the principal instruct you to watch him so narrowly? There? what's there beside a simple signature? That English fool's busy watching.

2 *Pol.* Flourish all round—"put all possible obstacles in his way;" oblong dot at the end—"Detain him till further advices reach you;" scratch at bottom—"send him back on pretence of some informality in the above." Ink-spirt on right-hand side, (which is the case here)—"Arrest him at once," why and wherefore, I don't concern myself, but my instructions amount to this: if Signor Luigi leaves home to-night for Vienna, well and good—the passport deposed with us for our *visa* is really for his own use, they have misinformed the Office, and he means well; but, let him stay over to-night—there has been the pretence we suspect—the accounts of his corresponding and holding intelligence with the Carbonari are correct—we arrest him at once—to-morrow comes Venice—and presently, Spielberg. Bluphocks makes the signal, sure enough!

III.—*Evening. Inside the Turret.* LUIGI *and his Mother entering.*

Mother. If there blew wind you'd hear a long sigh, easing
The utmost heaviness of music's heart.
Luigi. Here in the archway?
Mother. Oh no, no—in further,
Where the echo is made—on the ridge.
Luigi. Here surely, then!
How plain the tap of my heel as I leaped up:
Aristogeiton! "ristogeiton"—plain
Was't not? Lucius Junius! The very ghost of a voice—
Whose flesh is caught and kept by those withered wall-flowers,
Or by the elvish group with thin bleached hair
Who lean out of their topmost fortress—look
And listen, mountain men and women, to what
We say—chins under each grave earthy face:
Up and show faces all of you!—"All of you!"
That's the king with the scarlet comb: come down!—"Come down."
Mother. Do not kill that Man, my Luigi—do not

Go to the City! putting crime aside,
Half of these ills of Italy are feigned—
Your Pellicos and writers for effect
Write for effect.
Luigi. Hush! Say A writes, and B.
Mother. These A's and B's write for effect I say.
Then evil is in its nature loud, while good
Is silent—you hear each petty injury—
None of his daily virtues; he is old,
Quiet, and kind, and densely stupid—why
Do A and B not kill him themselves?
Luigi. They teach
Others to kill him—me—and if I fail,
Others to succeed; now if A tried and failed,
I could not do that: mine's the *lesser* task.
Mother, they visit night by night...
Mother. You, Luigi?
Ah will you let me tell you what you are?
Luigi. Why not? Oh the one thing you fear to hint
You may assure yourself I say and say
Often to myself; at times—nay, now—as now
We sit, I think my mind is touched—suspect
All is not sound—but is not knowing that
What constitutes one sane or otherwise?
I know I am thus—so all is right again!
I laugh at myself as thro' the town I walk
And see the world merry as if no Italy
Were suffering—then I ponder—I am rich,
Young, healthy, happy, why should this fact trouble me...
More than it troubles these? But it does trouble me
No—trouble's a bad word—for as I walk
There's springing and melody and giddiness,
And old quaint turns and passages of my youth—
Dreams long forgotten, little in themselves—
Return to me—whatever may recreate me,
And earth seems in a truce with me, and heaven
Accords with me, all things suspend their strife,
The very cicales laugh "There goes he and there—
"Feast him, the time is short—he is on his way
"For the world's sake—feast him this once, our friend!"
And in return for all this, I can trip

Cheerfully up the scaffold-steps: I go
This evening, mother.
Mother. But mistrust yourself—
Mistrust the judgment you pronounce on him.
Luigi. Oh, there I feel—am sure that I am right.
Mother. Mistrust your judgment then of the mere means
To this wild enterprise: say you are right,—
How should one in your state e'er bring to pass
What would require a cool head, a cold heart,
And a calm hand? You never will escape.
Luigi. Escape—to wish that even would spoil all!
The dying is best part of it—I have
Enjoyed these fifteen years of mine too much
To leave myself excuse for longer life—
Was not life pressed down, running o'er with joy,
That I might finish with it ere my fellows
Who sparelier feasted make a longer stay?
I was put at the board head, helped to all
At first: I rise up happy and content.
God must be glad one loves his world so much—
I can give news of earth to all the dead
Who ask me:—last year's sunsets and great stars
That had a right to come first and see ebb
The crimson wave that drifts the sun away—
Those crescent moons with notched and burning rims
That strengthened into sharp fire and there stood
Impatient of the azure—and that day
In March a double rainbow stopped the storm—
May's warm, slow, yellow moonlit summer nights—
Gone are they—but I have them in my soul!
Mother. (He will not go!)
Luigi. You smile at me—I know
Voluptuousness, grotesqueness, ghastliness,
Environ my devotedness as quaintly
As round about some antique altar wreathe
The rose festoons, goats' horns, and oxen's skulls.
Mother. See now—you reach the city—you must cross
His threshold—how?
Luigi. Oh, that's if we conspire!
Then come the pains in plenty you foresee
—Who guess not how the qualities required

For such an office—qualities I have—
Would little stead us otherwise employed,
Yet prove of rarest merit here—here only.
Every one knows for what his excellences
Will serve, but no one ever will consider
For what his worst defects might serve; and yet
Have you not seen me range our coppice yonder
In search of a distorted ash?—it happens
The wry spoilt branch's a natural perfect bow:
Fancy the thrice sage, thrice precautioned man
Arriving at the city on my errand!
No, no—I have a handsome dress packed up—
White satin here to set off my black hair—
In I shall march—for you may watch your life out
Behind thick walls—binding friends to betray you;
More than one man spoils everything—March straight—
Only no clumsy knife to fumble for—
Take the great gate, and walk (not saunter) on
Thro' guards and guards——I have rehearsed it all
Inside the Turret here a hundred times—
Don't ask the way of whom you meet, observe,
But where they cluster thickliest is the door
Of doors: they'll let you pass . . they'll never blab
Each to the other, he knows not the favourite,
Whence he is bound and what's his business now—
Walk in—straight up to him—you have no knife—
Be prompt, how should he scream? Then, out with you!
Italy, Italy, my Italy!
You're free, you're free—Oh mother, I believed
They got about me—Andrea from his exile,
Pier from his dungeon, Gualtier from his grave!
Mother. Well you shall go. If patriotism were not
The easiest virtue for a selfish man
To acquire! he loves himself—and then, the world—
If he must love beyond, but nought between:
As a short-sighted man sees nought midway
His body and the sun above. But you
Are my adored Luigi—ever obedient
To my least wish, and running o'er with love—
I could not call you cruel or unkind!
Once more, your ground for killing him!—then go!

Luigi. Now do you ask me, or make sport of me?
How first the Austrians got these provinces—
(If that is all, I'll satisfy you soon)
. . . Never by warfare but by treaty, for
That treaty whereby . . .
Mother. Well?
Luigi. (Sure, he's arrived—
The tell-tale cuckoo—spring's his confidant,
And he lets out her April purposes!)
Or . . better go at once to modern times—
He has . . they have . . in fact I understand
But can't restate the matter; that's my boast;
Others could reason it out to you, and prove
Things they have made me feel.
Mother. Why go to-night?
Morn's for adventure. Jupiter is now
A morning-star . . . . I cannot hear you, Luigi!
Luigi. "I am the bright and morning-star," God saith—
And, "such an one I give the morning-star!"
The gift of the morning-star—have I God's gift
Of the morning-star?
Mother. Chiara will love to see
That Jupiter an evening-star next June.
Luigi. True, mother. Well for those who live June over.
Great noontides—thunder storms—all glaring pomps
Which triumph at the heels of June the God
Leading his revel thro' our leafy world.
Yes, Chiara will be here—
Mother. In June—remember
Yourself appointed that month for her coming—
Luigi. Was that low noise the echo?
Mother. The night-wind.
She must be grown—with her blue eyes upturned
As if life were one long and sweet surprise—
In June she comes.
Luigi. We are to see together
The Titian at Treviso—there, again!

[*Without.*] A king lived long ago,
In the morning of the world,
When earth was nigher heaven than now:

And the king's locks curled
Disparting o'er a forehead full
As the milk-white space 'twixt horn and horn
Of some sacrificial bull—
Only calm as a babe new-born:
For he was got to a sleepy mood,
So safe from all decrepitude,
Age with its bane so sure gone by,
(The Gods so loved him while he dreamed,)
That, having lived thus long, there seemed
No need the king should ever die.

Luigi. No need that sort of king should ever die.

[*Without.*] Among the rocks his city was:
Before his palace, in the sun,
He sate to see his people pass,
And judge them every one
From its threshold of smooth stone.
They haled him many a valley-thief
Caught in the sheep-pens—robber-chief,
Swarthy and shameless—beggar-cheat—
Spy-prowler—or some pirate found
On the sea-sand left aground;
Sometimes there clung about his feet
With bleeding lip and burning cheek
A woman, bitterest wrong to speak
Of one with sullen, thickset brows:
Sometimes from out the prison-house
The angry priests a pale wretch brought,
Who through some chink had pushed and pressed,
On knees and elbows, belly and breast,
Worm-like into the temple,—caught
He was by the very God,
Who ever in the darkness strode
Backward and forward, keeping watch
O'er his brazen bowls, such rogues to catch:
These, all and every one,
The king judged, sitting in the sun.

Luigi. That king should still judge sitting in the sun.

[*Without.*] His councillors, on left and right,
Looked anxious up,—but no surprise
Disturbed the king's old smiling eyes,
Where the very blue had turned to white.
A python passed one day
The silent streets—until he came,
With forky tongue and eyes on flame,
Where the old king judged alway;
But when he saw the sweepy hair,
Girt with a crown of berries rare
The God will hardly give to wear
To the maiden who singeth, dancing bare
In the altar-smoke by the pine-torch lights,
At his wondrous forest rites,—
But which the God's self granted him
For setting free each felon limb
Because of earthly murder done
Faded till other hope was none;—
Seeing this, he did not dare
Approach that threshold in the sun,
Assault the old king smiling there.
[PIPPA *passes.*
Luigi. Farewell, farewell—how could I stay? Farewell!

Talk by the way in the mean time. Poor Girls *sitting on the steps of* MONSIGNOR'S *brother's house, close to the Duomo S. Maria.*

1 *Girl.* There goes a swallow to Venice—the stout seafarer!
Let us all wish; you wish first.
2 *Girl.* I? This sunset
To finish.
3 *Girl.* That old . . . somebody I know,
To give me the same treat he gave last week—
Feeding me on his knee with fig-peckers,
Lampreys, and red Breganze-wine, and mumbling
The while some folly about how well I fare—
Since had he not himself been late this morning
Detained at—never mind where—had he not . .
Eh, baggage, had I not!—
2 *Girl.* How she can lie!
3 *Girl.* Look there—by the nails—
2 *Girl.* What makes your fingers red?

3 *Girl.* Dipping them into wine to write bad words with
On the bright table—how he laughed!
1 *Girl.* My turn:
Spring's come and summer's coming: I would wear
A long loose gown—down to the feet and hands—
With plaits here, close about the throat, all day:
And all night lie, the cool long nights, in bed—
And have new milk to drink—apples to eat,
Deuzans and junetings, leather-coats . . ah, I should say
This is away in the fields—miles!
3 *Girl.* Say at once
You'd be at home—she'd always be at home!
Now comes the story of the farm among
The cherry orchards, and how April snowed
White blossoms on her as she ran: why fool,
They've rubbed the chalk-mark out how tall you were,
Twisted your starling's neck, broken his cage,
Made a dung-hill of your garden—
1 *Girl.* They destroy
My garden since I left them? well—perhaps!
I would have done so—so I hope they have!
A fig-tree curled out of our cottage wall—
They called it mine, I have forgotten why,
It must have been there long ere I was born,
Criq—criq—I think I hear the wasps o'erhead
Pricking the papers strung to flutter there
And keep off birds in fruit-time—coarse long papers
And the wasps eat them, prick them through and through.
3 *Girl.* How her mouth twitches! Where was I before
She broke in with her wishes and long gowns
And wasps—would I be such a fool!—Oh, here!
This is my way—I answer every one
Who asks me why I make so much of him—
(Say, you love him—he'll not be gulled, he'll say)
"He that seduced me when I was a girl
Thus high—had eyes like yours, or hair like yours,
Brown, red, white,"—as the case may be—that pleases!
(See how that beetle burnishes in the path—
There sparkles he along the dust—and there—
Your journey to that maize tuft's spoilt at least!

1 *Girl.* When I was young they said if you killed one
Of those sunshiny beetles, that his friend
Up there would shine no more that day or next.
2 *Girl.* When you were young? Nor are you young, that's true!
How your plump arms, that were, have dropped away!
Why I can span them! Cecco beats you still?
No matter so you keep your curious hair.
I wish they'd find a way to dye our hair
Your colour—any lighter tint, indeed,
Than black—the men say they are sick of black,
Black eyes, black hair!
4 *Girl.* Sick of yours, like enough,
Do you pretend you ever tasted lampreys
And ortolans? Giovita, of the palace,
Engaged (but there's no trusting him) to slice me
Polenta with a knife that had cut up
An ortolan.
2 *Girl.* Why—there! is not that Pippa
We are to talk to, under the window, quick
Where the lights are?
1 *Girl.* No—or she would sing
For the Intendant said . . .
3 *Girl.* Oh, you sing first—
Then, if she listens and comes close . . I'll tell you,
Sing that song the young English noble made,
Who took you for the purest of the pure
And meant to leave the world for you—what fun!
2 *Girl.* [*Sings.*]

You'll love me yet!—and I can tarry
Your love's protracted growing:
June reared that bunch of flowers you carry
From seeds of April's sowing.

I plant a heartful now—some seed
At least is sure to strike
And yield—what you'll not care, indeed,
To pluck, but, may be like.

To look upon . . my whole remains,
A grave's one violet:
Your look?—that pays a thousand pains.
What's death? You'll love me yet!

3 *Girl.* [*To* PIPPA, *who approaches.*] Oh, you may come closer—we shall not eat you!

IV.—*Night. The Palace by the Duomo.* MONSIGNOR, *dismissing his* Attendants.

Mon. Thanks, friends, many thanks. I desire life now chiefly that I may recompense every one of you. Most I know something of already. *Benedicto benedicatur* . . ugh . . ugh! Where was I? Oh, as you were remarking, Ugo, the weather is mild, very unlike winter-weather,—but I am a Sicilian, you know, and shiver in your Julys here: To be sure, when 'twas full summer at Messina, as we priests used to cross in procession the great square on Assumption Day, you might see our thickest yellow tapers twist suddenly in two, each like a falling star, or sink down on themselves in a gore of wax. But go, my friends, but go! [*To the* Intendant] Not you, Ugo! [*The others leave the apartment, where a table with refreshments is prepared.*] I have long wanted to converse with you, Ugo!

Inten. Uguccio—

Mon...'guccio Stefani, man! of Ascoli, Fermo and Fossombruno:—what I do need instructing about are these accounts of your administration of my poor brother's affairs. Ugh! I shall never get through a third part of your accounts: take some of these dainties before we attempt it, however: are you bashful to that degree? For me, a crust and water suffice.

Inten. Do you choose this especial night to question me?

Mon. This night, Ugo. You have managed my late brother's affairs since the death of our elder brother—fourteen years and a month, all but three days. The 3rd of December, I find him...

Inten. If you have so intimate an acquaintance with your brother's affairs, you will be tender of turning so far back—they will hardly bear looking into, so far back.

Mon. Ay, ay, ugh, ugh,—nothing but disappointments here below! I remark a considerable payment made to yourself on this 3rd of December. Talk of disappointments! There was a young fellow here, Jules, a foreign sculptor, I did my utmost to advance, that the Church might be a gainer by us both: he was going on hopefully enough, and of a sudden he notifies to me some marvellous change that has happened in his notions of art; here's his letter,—"He never had a clearly conceived Ideal within his brain till to-day. Yet since his hand could manage a chisel he has practised expressing other men's Ideals—and in the very perfection he has attained to he foresees an ultimate failure—

his unconscious hand will pursue its prescribed course of old years, and will reproduce with a fatal expertness the ancient types, let the novel one appear never so palpably to his spirit: there is but one method of escape—confiding the virgin type to as chaste a hand, he will paint, not carve, its characteristics,"—strike out, I dare say, a school like Correggio: how think you, Ugo?

Inten. Is Correggio a painter?

Mon. Foolish Jules! and yet, after all, why foolish? He may—probably will, fail egregiously; but if there should arise a new painter, will it not be in some such way—a poet, now, or a musician, spirits who have conceived and perfected an Ideal through some other channel, transferring it to this, and escaping our conventional roads by pure ignorance of them, eh, Ugo? If you have no appetite, talk at least, Ugo!

Inten. Sir, I can submit no longer to this course of yours: first, you select the group of which I formed one,—next you thin it gradually,—always retaining me with your smile,—and so do you proceed till you have fairly got me alone with you between four stone walls: and now then? Let this farce, this chatter end now—what is it you want with me?

Mon. Ugo . . .

Inten. From the instant you arrived I felt your smile on me as you questioned me about this and the other article in those papers—why, your brother should have given me this manor, that liberty,—and your nod at the end meant,—what?

Mon. Possibly that I wished for no loud talk here—if once you set me coughing, Ugo!

Inten. I have your brother's hand and seal to all I possess: now ask me what for! what service I did him—ask me!

Mon. I had better not—I should rip up old disgraces—let out my poor brother's weaknesses. By the way, Maffeo of Forli, (which, I forgot to observe, is your true name) was the interdict ever taken off you for robbing that church at Cesena?

Inten. No, nor needs be—for when I murdered your brother's friend, Pasquale, for him . . .

Mon. Ah, he employed you in that matter, did he? Well, I must let you keep, as you say, this manor and that liberty, for fear the world should find out my relations were of so indifferent a stamp: Maffeo, my family is the oldest in Messina, and century after century have my progenitors gone on polluting themselves with every wickedness under Heaven: my own father . . . rest his soul!—I have, I know, a chapel to support that it may: my dear two dead brothers were,—what you know tolerably well; I, the youngest, might have rivalled them in vice, if not in wealth, but from my boyhood I came out from among them, and so am not partaker of their plagues. My glory springs from another source, or if from this, by contrast only,—for I, the bishop, am the brother of your employers, Ugo. I hope to repair some of their wrong, however; so far as my brother's ill-gotten treasure reverts to me, I can stop the consequences of his crime, and not one *soldo* shall escape me. Maffeo, the sword we quiet men spurn away, you shrewd knaves pick up and commit murders with; what opportunities the virtuous forego, the villanous seize. Because, to pleasure myself, apart from other considerations, my food would be millet-cake, my dress sackcloth, and my couch straw, am I therefore to let the off-scouring of the earth seduce the ignorant by appropriating a pomp these will be sure to think lessens the abominations so unaccountably and exclusively associated with it? Must I let manors and liberties go to you, a murderer and thief, that you may beget by means of them other murderers and thieves? No . . . if my cough would but allow me to speak!

Inten. What am I to expect? You are going to punish me?

Mon. Must punish you, Maffeo. I cannot afford to cast away a chance. I have whole centuries of sin to redeem, and only a month or two of life to do it in! How should I dare to say . . .

Inten. "Forgive us our trespasses."

Mon. My friend, it is because I avow myself a very worm, sinful beyond measure, that I reject a line of conduct you would applaud, perhaps: shall I proceed, as it were, a-pardoning?—I?—who have no symptom of reason to assume that aught less than my strenuousest efforts will keep myself out of mortal sin, much less, keep others out. No—I do trespass, but will not double that by allowing you to trespass.

Inten. And suppose the manors are not your brother's to give, or yours to take? Oh, you are hasty enough just now!

Mon. 1, 2—No. 3!—ay, can you read the substance of a letter, No. 3, I have received from Rome? It is on the ground I there mention of the suspicion I have that a certain child of my late elder brother, who would have succeeded to his estates, was murdered in infancy by you, Maffeo, at the instigation of my late brother—that the pontiff enjoins on me not merely the bringing that Maffeo to condign punishment, but the taking all pains, as guardian of the infant's heritage for the church, to recover it parcel by parcel, howsoever, whensoever, and wheresoever. While you are now gnawing those fingers, the police are engaged in sealing up your papers, Maffeo, and the mere raising my voice brings my people from the next room to dispose of yourself. But I want you to confess quietly, and save me raising my voice. Why, man, do I not know the old story? The heir between the succeeding heir, and this heir's ruffianly instrument, and their complot's effect, and the life of fear and bribes, and ominous smiling silence? Did you throttle or stab my brother's infant? Come now!

Inten. So old a story, and tell it no better? When did such an instrument ever produce such an effect? Either the child smiles in his face, or, most likely, he is not fool enough to put himself in the employer's power so thoroughly—the child is always ready to produce—as you say—howsoever, wheresoever, and whensoever.

Mon. Liar!

Inten. Strike me? Ah, so might a father chastise! I shall sleep soundly to-night at least, though the gallows await me to-morrow; for what a life did I lead? Carlo of Cesena reminds me of his connivance every time I pay his annuity (which happens commonly thrice a year). If I remonstrate, he will confess all to the good bishop—you!

Mon. I see thro' the trick, caitiff! I would you spoke truth for once; all shall be sifted, however—seven times sifted.

Inten. And how my absurd riches encumbered me! I dared not lay claim to above half my possessions. Let me but once unbosom myself, glorify Heaven, and die!

Sir, you are no brutal, dastardly idiot like your brother I frightened to death . . . let us understand one another. Sir, I will make away with her for you—the girl—here close at hand; not the stupid obvious kind of killing; do not speak—know nothing of her or me. I see her every day—saw her this morning—of course there is no killing; but at Rome the courtesans perish off every three years, and I can entice her thither—have, indeed, begun operations already—there's a certain lusty, blue-eyed, florid-complexioned, English knave I employ occasionally.—You assent, I perceive—no, that's not it—assent I do not say—but you will let me convert my present havings and holdings into cash, and give me time to cross the Alps? 'Tis but a little black-eyed, pretty singing Felippa, gay silk-winding girl! I have kept her out of harm's way up to this present; for I always intended to make your life a plague to you with her! 'Tis as well settled once and forever: some women I have procured will pass Bluphocks, my handsome scoundrel, off for somebody, and once Pippa entangled!—you conceive?

Mon. Why, if she sings, one might . . .

[*Without*] Over-head the tree-tops meet—
Flowers and grass spring 'neath one's feet—
What are the voices of birds
—Ay, and beasts,—but words—our words,
Only so much more sweet?
That knowledge with my life begun!
But I had so near made out the sun—
Could count your stars, the Seven and One!
Like the fingers of my hand—
Nay, I could all but understand
How and wherefore the moon ranges—
And just when out of her soft fifty changes
No unfamiliar face might overlook me—
Suddenly God took me. [PIPPA *passes.*

Mon. [*Springing up.*] My people—one and all—all—within there! Gag this villain—tie him hand and foot: he dares—I know not half he dares—but remove him—quick! *Miserere mei, Domine!* quick, I say.

PIPPA'S *Chamber again. She enters it.*

The bee with his comb,
The mouse at her dray,
The grub in his tomb
Wile winter away;
But the fire-fly and hedge-shrew and lob-worm, I pray,
Where be they?
Ha, ha, thanks my Zanze—
"Feast on lampreys, quaff Breganze"—
The summer of life's so easy to spend!
But winter hastens at summer's end,
And fire-fly, hedge-shrew, lob-worm, pray,
Where be they?
No bidding you then to . . what did Zanze say?
"Pare your nails pearlwise, get your small feet shoes
"More like . . (what said she?)—and less like canoes—"
Pert as a sparrow . . . would I be those pert
Impudent staring wretches! it had done me,
However, surely no such mighty hurt
To learn his name who passed that jest upon me.—
No foreigner, that I can recollect,
Came, as she says, a month since to inspect

Our silk-mills—none with blue eyes and thick rings
Of English-coloured hair, at all events.
Well—if old Luca keep his good intents
We shall do better—see what next year brings—
I may buy shoes, my Zanze, not appear
So destitute, perhaps, next year!
Bluf—something—I had caught the uncouth name
But for Monsignor's people's sudden clatter
Above us—bound to spoil such idle chatter,
The pious man, the man devoid of blame,
The . . . ah, but—ah, but, all the same,
No mere mortal has a right
To carry that exalted air;
Best people are not angels quite—
While—not the worst of people's doings scare
The devils; so there's that regard to spare!
Mere counsel to myself, mind! for
I have just been Monsignor!
And I was you too, mother,
And you too, Luigi!—how that Luigi started
Out of the Turret—doubtlessly departed
On some love-errand or another—
And I was Jules the sculptor's bride,
And I was Ottima beside,
And now what am I?—tired of fooling!
Day for folly, night for schooling—
New year's day is over—over!
Even my lily's asleep, I vow:
Wake up—here's a friend I pluckt you.
See—call this a heart's-ease now!
Something rare, let me instruct you,
Is this—with petals triply swollen,
Three times spotted, thrice the pollen,
While the leaves and parts that witness
Old proportions and their fitness
Here remain, unchanged unmoved now—
Call this pampered thing improved now!
Suppose there's a king of the flowers
And a girl-show held in his bowers—
"Look ye, buds, this growth of ours,"
Says he, "Zanze from the Brenta,

I have made her gorge polenta
Till both cheeks are near as bouncing
As her . . . name there's no pronouncing!
See this heightened colour too—
For she swilled Breganze wine
Till her nose turned deep carmine—
'Twas but white when wild she grew!
And only by this Zanze's eyes
Of which we could not change the size,
The magnitude of what's achieved
Elsewhere may be perceived!"

Oh what a drear, dark close to my poor day!
How could that red sun drop in that black cloud!
Ah, Pippa, morning's rule is moved away,
Dispensed with, never more to be allowed.
Day's turn's over—now's the night's—
Oh Lark be day's apostle
To mavis, merle and throstle,
Bid them their betters jostle
From day and its delights!
But at night, brother Howlet, over the woods,
Toll the world to thy chantry—
Sing to the bats' sleek sisterhoods
Full complines with galantry—
Then, owls and bats, cowls and twats,
Monks and nuns, in a cloister's moods,
Adjourn to the oak-stump pantry!
[*After she has begun to undress herself.*
Now one thing I should like to really know:
How near I ever might approach all these
I only fancied being this long day—
. . . Approach, I mean, so as to touch them—so
As to . . in some way . . move them—if you please,
Do good or evil to them some slight way.
For instance, if I wind
Silk to-morrow, silk may bind [*Sitting on the bedside.*
And broider Ottima's cloak's hem—
Ah, me and my important passing them
This morning's hymn half promised when I rose!
True in some sense or other, I suppose.
[*As she lies down.*

God bless me tho' I cannot pray to-night.
No doubt, some way or other, hymns say right.
All service is the same with God—
Whose puppets, best and worst,
Are we . . . . . . [*She sleeps.*

FROM *BELLS AND POMEGRANATES, NO. III: DRAMATIC LYRICS* (1842)

[*My Last Duchess*
FERRARA]
Italy and France. I. Italy

That's my last Duchess painted on the wall,
Looking as if she were alive; I call
That piece a wonder, now: Frà Pandolf's hands
Worked busily a day, and there she stands.
Will't please you sit and look at her? I said
"Frà Pandolf," by design, for never read
Strangers like you that pictured countenance,
The depth and passion of its earnest glance,
But to myself they turned (since none puts by
The curtain I have drawn for you, but I)
And seemed as they would ask me, if they durst,
How such a glance came there; so not the first
Are you to turn and ask thus. Sir, 'twas not
Her husband's presence only, called that spot
Of joy into the Duchess' cheek: perhaps
Frà Pandolf chanced to say "Her mantle laps
"Over my lady's wrist too much," or "Paint
"Must never hope to reproduce the faint
"Half-flush that dies along her throat;" such stuff
Was courtesy, she thought, and cause enough
For calling up that spot of joy. She had
A heart . . how shall I say? . . too soon made glad,
Too easily impressed; she liked whate'er
She looked on, and her looks went everywhere.
Sir, 'twas all one! My favour at her breast,
The dropping of the daylight in the West,
The bough of cherries some officious fool
Broke in the orchard for her, the white mule
She rode with round the terrace—all and each
Would draw from her alike the forward speech,
Or blush, at least. She thanked men,—good; but thanked
Somehow . . I know not how . . as if she ranked
My gift of a nine hundred years old name
With anybody's gift. Who'd stoop to blame
This sort of trifling? Even had you skill
In speech—(which I have not)—could make your will

Quite clear to such an one, and say, "Just this
"Or that in you disgusts me; here you miss,
"Or there exceed the mark"—and if she let
Herself be lessoned so, nor plainly set
Her wits to yours, forsooth, and made excuse,
—E'en then would be some stooping, and I chuse
Never to stoop. Oh, Sir, she smiled, no doubt,
Whene'er I passed her; but who passed without
Much the same smile? This grew; I gave commands;
Then all smiles stopped together. There she stands
As if alive. Will't please you rise? We'll meet
The company below then. I repeat,
The Count your Master's known munificence
Is ample warrant that no just pretence
Of mine for dowry will be disallowed;
Though his fair daughter's self, as I avowed
At starting, is my object. Nay, we'll go
Together down, Sir! Notice Neptune, tho',
Taming a sea-horse, thought a rarity,
Which Claus of Innsbruck cast in bronze for me.

[*Soliloquy of the Spanish Cloister*]
Camp and Cloister. II. Cloister (Spanish)

I.

Gr-r-r—there go, my heart's abhorrence!
  Water your damned flower-pots, do!
If hate killed men, Brother Lawrence,
  God's blood, would not mine kill you!
What? your myrtle-bush wants trimming?
  Oh, that rose has prior claims—
Needs its leaden vase filled brimming?
  Hell dry you up with its flames!

II.

At the meal we sit together:
  Salve tibi! I must hear
Wise talk of the kind of weather,

Sort of season, time of year:
Not a plenteous cork-crop: scarcely
Dare we hope oak-galls, I doubt:
What's the Latin name for "parsley"?
What's the Greek name for Swine's Snout?

III.

Phew! We'll have our platter burnished,
Laid with care on our own shelf!
With a fire-new spoon we're furnished,
And a goblet for ourself,
Rinsed like something sacrificial
Ere 'tis fit to touch our chaps—
Marked with L. for our initial!
(He-he! There his lily snaps!)

IV.

Saint, forsooth! While brown Dolores
Squats outside the Convent bank,
With Sanchicha, telling stories,
Steeping tresses in the tank,
Blue-black, lustrous, thick like horsehairs
—Can't I see his dead eye grow
Bright, as 'twere a Barbary corsair's?
That is, if he'd let it show.

V.

When he finishes refection,
Knife and fork across he lays
Never, to my recollection,
As do I, in Jesu's praise.
I, the Trinity illustrate,
Drinking watered orange-pulp;
In three sips the Arian frustrate;
While he drains his at one gulp!

VI.

Oh, those melons! If he's able
We're to have a feast; so nice!
One goes to the Abbot's table,
All of us get each a slice.
How go on your flowers? None double?
Not one fruit-sort can you spy?
Strange!—And I, too, at such trouble,
Keep 'em close-nipped on the sly!

VII.

There's a great text in Galatians,
Once you trip on it, entails
Twenty-nine distinct damnations,
One sure, if another fails.
If I trip him just a-dying,
Sure of heaven as sure can be,
Spin him round and send him flying
Off to hell a Manichee?

VIII.

Or, my scrofulous French novel
On grey paper with blunt type!
Simply glance at it, you grovel
Hand and foot in Belial's gripe.
If I double down its pages
At the woeful sixteenth print,
When he gathers his greengages,
Ope a sieve and slip it in't?

IX.

Or, the Devil!—one might venture
Pledge one's soul yet slily leave
Such a flaw in the indenture
As he'd miss till, past retrieve,
Blasted lay that rose-acacia
We're so proud of! *Hy, Zy, Hine* . . .
St, there's Vespers! *Plena gratiâ*
Ave, Virgo ! Gr-r-r—you swine!

In a Gondola

I.

I send my heart up to thee, all my heart
   In this my singing!
For the stars help me, and the sea bears part;
   The very night is clinging
Closer to Venice' streets to leave one space
   Above me, whence thy face
May light my joyous heart to thee its dwelling-place.

II.

Say after me, and try to say
My words as if each word
Came from you of your own accord,
In your own voice, in your own way:
This woman's heart, and soul, and brain
Are mine as much as this gold chain
She bids me wear; which (say again)
I choose to make by cherishing
A precious thing, or choose to fling
Over the boat-side, ring by ring;
And yet once more say . . . no word more!—
Since words are only words. Give o'er!
Unless you call me, all the same,
Familiarly by my pet-name
Which if the Three should hear you call
And me reply to, would proclaim
At once our secret to them all:
Ask of me, too, command me, blame—
Do break down the partition-wall
'Twixt us the daylight world beholds
Curtained in dusk and splendid folds.

III.

What's left but—all of me to take?
I am the Three's, prevent them, slake
Your thirst! 'Tis said the Arab sage
In practising with gems can loose
Their subtle spirit in his cruce

And leave but ashes: so, sweet mage,
Leave them my ashes when thy use
Sucks out my soul, thy heritage!

IV.

1.

Past we glide, and past, and past!
What's that poor Agnese doing
Where they make the shutters fast?
Grey Zanobi's just a-wooing
To his couch the purchased bride:
Past we glide!

2.

Past we glide, and past, and past!
Why's the Pucci Palace flaring
Like a beacon to the blast?
Guests by hundreds—not one caring
If the dear host's neck were wried:
Past we glide!

V.

1.

The Moth's kiss, first!
Kiss me as if you made believe
You were not sure this eve,
How my face, your flower, had pursed
Its petals up; so here and there
Brush it, till I grow aware
Who wants me, and wide ope I burst.

2.

The Bee's kiss, now!
Kiss me as if you entered gay
My heart at some noonday,
A bud that dares not disallow
The claim, so all is rendered up,
And passively its shattered cup
Over your head to sleep I bow.

VI.

1.

What are we two?
I am a Jew,
And carry thee, farther than friends can pursue,
To a feast of our tribe,
Where they need thee to bribe
The devil that blasts them unless he imbibe
Thy . . . Shatter the vision for ever! And now,
As of old, I am I, Thou art Thou!

2.

But again, what we are?
The sprite of a star,
I lure thee above where the Destinies bar
My plumes their full play
Till a ruddier ray
Than my pale one announce there is withering away
Some . . . Scatter the vision for ever! And now.
As of old, I am I, Thou art Thou!

VII.

Oh, which were best, to roam or rest?
The land's lap or the water's breast?
To sleep on yellow millet-sheaves,
Or swim in lucid shallows, just
Eluding water-lily leaves,
An inch from Death's black fingers, thrust
To lock you, whom release he must;
Which life were best on Summer eves?

VIII.

Lie back; could I improve you?
From this shoulder let there spring
A wing; from this, another wing;
Wings, not legs and feet, shall move you!
Snow-white must they spring, to blend
With your flesh, but I intend
They shall deepen to the end,

Broader, into burning gold,
Till both wings crescent-wise enfold
Your perfect self, from 'neath your feet
To o'er your head, where, lo, they meet
As if a million sword-blades hurled
Defiance from you to the world!

Rescue me thou, the only real!
And scare away this mad Ideal
That came, nor motions to depart!
Thanks! Now, stay ever as thou art!

IX.

1.

He and the Couple catch at last
Thy serenader; while there's cast
Paul's cloak about my head, and fast
Gian pinions me, Himself has past
His stylet thro' my back; I reel;
And . . . is it Thee I feel?

2.

They trail me, do these godless knaves,
Past every church that sains and saves,
Nor stop till, where the cold sea raves
By Lido's wet accursed graves,
They scoop mine, roll me to its brink,
And . . . on Thy breast I sink!

X.

Dip your arm o'er the boat-side elbow-deep,
As I do: thus: were Death so unlike Sleep
Caught this way? Death's to fear from flame or steel
Or poison doubtless, but from water—feel!

Go find the bottom! Would you stay me? There!
Now pluck a great blade of that ribbon-grass
To plait in where the foolish jewel was,
I flung away: since you have praised my hair
'Tis proper to be choice in what I wear.

XI.

Must we, must we *Home*? Too surely
Know I where its front's demurely
Over the Giudecca piled;
Window just with window mating,
Door on door exactly waiting,
All's the set face of a child:
But behind it, where's a trace
Of the staidness and reserve,
Formal lines without a curve,
In the same child's playing-face?
No two windows look one way
O'er the small sea-water thread
Below them. Ah, the autumn day
I, passing, saw you overhead!
First out a cloud of curtain blew,
Then, a sweet cry, and last came you—
To catch your loory that must needs
Escape just then, of all times then,
To peck a tall plant's fleecy seeds,
And make me happiest of men.
I scarce could breathe to see you reach
So far back o'er the balcony,
To catch him ere he climbed too high
Above you in the Smyrna peach,
That quick the round smooth cord of gold,
This coiled hair on your head, unrolled,
Fell down you like a gorgeous snake
The Roman girls were wont, of old
When Rome there was, for coolness' sake
To place within their bosoms.
Dear loory, may his beak retain
Ever its delicate rose stain
As if the wounded lotus-blossoms
Had marked their thief to know again!

XII.

Stay longer yet, for others' sake
Than mine! what should your chamber do?
—With all its rarities that ache

In silence while day lasts, but wake
At night-time and their life renew,
Suspended just to pleasure you
Who brought reluctantly together
These objects and, while day lasts, weave
Round them such a magic tether
That dumb they look: your harp, believe,
With all the sensitive tight strings
Which dare not speak, now to itself
Breathes slumbrously as if some elf
Went in and out tall chords his wings
Get murmurs from whene'er they graze,
As may an angel thro' the maze
Of pillars on God's quest have gone
At guilty glorious Babylon.
And while such murmurs flow, the nymph
Bends o'er the harp-top from her shell,
As the dry limpet for the lymph
Come with a tune he knows so well.
And how the statues' hearts must swell!
And how the pictures must descend
To see each other, friend with friend!
Oh, could you take them by surprise,
You'd find Schidone's eager Duke
Doing the quaintest courtesies
To that prim saint by Haste-thee-Luke:
And deeper into her rock den
Bold Castelfranco's Magdalen
You'd find retreated from the ken
Of that robed counsel-keeping Ser—
As if the Tizian thinks of her!
And if he is not rather bent
On trying for himself what toys
Are these his progeny invent,
What litter now the board employs
Whereon he signed a document
That got him murdered! Each enjoys
Its night so well, you cannot break
The sport up, so, for others' sake
Than mine, your stay must longer make!

XIII.

1.

To-morrow, if a harp-string, say,
Is used to tie the jasmine back
That overfloods my room with sweets,
Be sure your Zorzi somehow meets
My Zanze: if the ribbon's black
I use, they're watching; keep away.

2.

Your gondola—let Zorzi wreathe
A mesh of water-weeds about
Its prow, as if he unaware
Had struck some quay or bridge-foot stair;
That I may throw a paper out
As you and he go underneath.

XIV.

There's Zanze's vigilant taper; safe are we!
Only one minute more to-night with me?
Resume your past self of a month ago!
Be you the bashful gallant, I will be
The lady with the colder breast than snow:
Now bow you, as becomes, nor touch my hand
More than I touch yours when I step to land,
And say, All thanks, Siora...
Heart to heart
And lips to lips! Once, ere we part,
Make me thine as mine thou art!

XV.

It was to be so, Sweet, and best
Comes 'neath thine eyes, and on thy breast.
Still kiss me! Care not for the cowards! Care
Only to put aside thy beauteous hair
My blood will hurt. The Three I do not scorn
To death, because they never lived: but I
Have lived indeed, and so—(yet one more kiss)—can die.

Artemis Prologuizes

I am a Goddess of the ambrosial courts,
And save by Here, Queen of Pride, surpassed
By none whose temples whiten this the world.
Thro' Heaven I roll its lucid moon along;
In Hades shed o'er my pale people peace;
On Earth, I, caring for the creatures, guard
Each pregnant yellow wolf and fox-bitch sleek,
And every feathered mother's callow brood,
And all that love green haunts and loneliness.
Of men, the chaste adore me, hanging crowns
Of poppies red to blackness, bell and stem,
Upon my image at Athenai here;
Of such this Youth, Asclepios bends above,
Was dearest to me, and my buskined step
To follow thro' the wild-wood leafy ways,
And chase the panting stag, or swift with darts
Stop the swift ounce, or lay the leopard low,
He paid not homage to another God:
Whence Aphrodite, by no midnight smoke
Of tapers lulled, in jealousy despatched
A noisome lust that, as the gadbee stings,
Possessed his stepdame Phaidra for the child
Of Theseus her great husband then afar.
But when Hippolutos exclaimed with rage
Against the miserable Queen, she judged
Intolerable life, and, pricked at heart
An Amazonian stranger's race had right
To scorn her, perished by the murderous cord:
Yet, ere she perished, blasted in a scroll
The fame of him her swerving made not swerve,
Which Theseus saw, returning, and believed,
So, in the blindness of his wrath, exiled
The man without a crime, who, last as first,
Loyal, divulged not to his sire the truth.
But Theseus from Poseidon had obtained
That of his wishes should be granted Three,
And this one imprecated now—alive
May ne'er Hippolutos reach other lands!
Poseidon heard, ai ai! And scarce the prince

Had stepped into the fixed boots of the car,
That give the feet a stay against the strength
Of the Henetian horses, and around
His body flung the reins, and urged their speed
Along the rocks and shingles of the shore,
When from the gaping wave a monster flung
His obscene body in the coursers' path:
These, mad with terror as the sea-bull sprawled
Wallowing about their feet, lost care of him
That reared them; and the master-chariot-pole
Snapping beneath their plunges like a reed,
Hippolutos, whose feet were trammelled sure,
Was yet dragged forward by the circling rein
Which either hand directed; nor they quenched
The frenzy of their flight before each trace,
Wheel-spoke and splinter of the woeful car,
And boulder-stone, sharp stub, and spiny shell,
Huge fish-bone wrecked and wreathed amid the sands
On that detested beach, was bright with blood
And morsels of his flesh: then fell the steeds
Head-foremost, crashing in their mooned fronts,
Shivering with sweat, each white eye horror fixed
His people, who had witnessed all afar,
Bore back the ruins of Hippolutos.
But when his sire, too swoln with pride, rejoiced,
Indomitable as a man foredoomed,
That vast Poseidon had fulfilled his prayer,
I, in a flood of glory visible,
Stood o'er my dying votary, and deed
By deed revealed, as all took place, the truth.
Then Theseus lay the woefullest of men,
And worthily, but ere the death-veils hid
His face, the murdered prince full pardon breathed
To his rash sire. Whence now Athenai wails.
But I, who ne'er forsake my votaries,
Lest in the cross-way none the honey-cake
Should tender, nor pour out the dog's hot life;
Lest at my fane disconsolate the priests
Should dress my image with some faded poor
Few crowns, made favours of, nor dare object
Such slackness to my worshippers who turn

Elsewhere the trusting heart and loaded hand,
As they had climbed Olumpos to report
Of Artemis and nowhere found her throne—
I interposed: and, this eventful night,
While round the funeral pyre the populace
Stand with fierce light on their black robes that blind
Each sobbing head, while yet their hair they clip
O'er the dead body of their withered prince,
And, in his palace, Theseus prostrated
On the cold hearth, his brow cold as the slab
'Tis bruised on, groans away the heavy grief—
As the pyre fell, and down the cross logs crashed,
Sending a crowd of sparkles thro' the night,
And the gay fire, elate with mastery,
Towered like a serpent o'er the clotted jars
Of wine, dissolving oils and frankincense,
And splendid gums like gold,—my potency
Conveyed the perished man to my retreat
In the thrice venerable forest here.
And this white-bearded Sage who squeezes now
The berried plant is Phoibos' son of fame,
Asclepios, whom my radiant brother taught
The doctrine of each herb and flower and root,
To know their secret'st virtue and express
The saving soul of all—who so has soothed
With lavers the torn brow and murdered cheeks,
Composed the hair and brought its gloss again,
And called the red bloom to the pale skin back,
And laid the strips and jagged ends of flesh
Even once more, and slacked the sinew's knot
Of every tortured limb—that now he lies
As if mere sleep possessed him underneath
These interwoven oaks and pines. Oh, cheer,
Divine presenter of the healing rod
Thy snake, with ardent throat and lulling eye,
Twines his lithe spires around! I say, much cheer!
Proceed thou with thy wisest pharmacies!
And ye, white crowd of woodland sister-nymphs,
Ply, as the Sage directs, these buds and leaves
That strew the turf around the Twain! While I
In fitting silence, the event await.

Waring

I.

1.

What's become of Waring
Since he gave us all the slip,
Chose land-travel or seafaring,
Boots and chest, or staff and scrip,
Rather than pace up and down
Any longer London-town?

2.

Who'd have guessed it from his lip,
Or his brow's accustomed bearing,
On the night he thus took ship,
Or started landward, little caring
For us, it seems, who supped together,
(Friends of his too, I remember)
And walked home thro' the merry weather,
Snowiest in all December;
I left his arm that night myself
For what's-his-name's, the new prose-poet,
Who wrote the book there, on the shelf—
How, forsooth, was I to know it
If Waring meant to glide away
Like a ghost at break of day!
Never looked he half so gay!

3.

He was prouder than the Devil:
How he must have cursed our revel!
Ay, and many other meetings,
Indoor visits, outdoor greetings,
As up and down he paced this London,
With no work done, but great works undone,
Where scarce twenty knew his name.
Why not, then, have earlier spoken,
Written, bustled? Who's to blame

If your silence kept unbroken?
True, but there were sundry jottings,
Stray-leaves, fragments, blurrs and blottings,
Certain first-steps were achieved
Already which—(is that your meaning?)
Had well borne out whoe'er believed
In more to come: but who goes gleaning
Hedge-side chance-blades, while full-sheaved
Stand cornfields by him? Pride, o'erweening
Pride alone, puts forth such claims
O'er the day's distinguished names.

4.

Meantime, how much I loved him,
I find out now I've lost him:
I, who cared not if I moved him,
—Could so carelessly accost him,
Never shall get free
Of his ghostly company,
His eyes that just a little wink
As deep I go into the merit
Of this and that distinguished spirit—
His cheeks' raised colour, soon to sink,
As long I dwell on some stupendous
And tremendous (God defend us!)
Monstr'-inform'-ingens-horrend-ous
Demoniaco-seraphic
Penman's latest piece of graphic.
Nay, my very wrist grows warm
With his dragging weight of arm!
E'en so, swimmingly appears,
Thro' one's after-supper musings,
Some lost Lady of old years,
With her beauteous vain endeavour,
And goodness unrepaid as ever;
The face, accustomed to refusings,
We, puppies that we were . . . Oh never
Surely, nice of conscience, scrupled
Being aught like false, forsooth, to?
Telling aught but honest truth to?

What a sin had we centupled
Its possessor's grace and sweetness!
No! she heard in its completeness
Truth, for truth's a weighty matter,
And, truth at issue, we can't flatter!
Well, 'tis done with: she's exempt
From damning us thro' such a sally;
And so she glides, as down a valley,
Taking up with her contempt,
Past our reach; and in, the flowers
Shut her unregarded hours.

5.

Oh, could I have him back once more,
This Waring, but one half-day more!
Back, with the quiet face of yore,
So hungry for acknowledgment
Like mine! I'd fool him to his bent!
Feed, should not he, to heart's content?
I'd say, "to only have conceived
"Your great works, tho' they never progress,
"Surpasses all we've yet achieved!"
I'd lie so, I should be believed.
I'd make such havoc of the claims
Of the day's distinguished names
To feast him with, as feasts an ogress
Her sharp-toothed gold-crowned child!
Or, as one feasts a creature rarely
Captured here, unreconciled
To capture; and completely gives
Its pettish humours licence, barely
Requiring that it lives.

6.

Ichabod, Ichabod,
The glory is departed!
Travels Waring East away?
Who, of knowledge, by hearsay,
Reports a man upstarted

Somewhere as a God,
Hordes grown European-hearted,
Millions of the wild made tame
On a sudden at his fame?
In Vishnu-land what Avatar?
Or, North in Moscow, toward the Czar,
Who, with the gentlest of footfalls
Over the Kremlin's pavement, bright
With serpentine and siennite,
Steps, with five other Generals,
Who simultaneously take snuff,
That each may have pretext enough
To kerchiefwise unfurl his sash
Which, softness' self, is yet the stuff
To hold fast where a steel chain snaps,
And leave the grand white neck no gash?
In Moscow, Waring, to those rough
Cold natures borne, perhaps,
Like the lambwhite maiden, (clear
Thro' the circle of mute kings,
Unable to repress the tear,
Each as his sceptre down he flings),
To the Dome at Taurica,
Where now a priestess, she alway
Mingles her tender grave Hellenic speech
With theirs, tuned to the hailstone-beaten beach,
As pours some pigeon, from the myrrhy lands
Rapt by the whirlblast to fierce Scythian strands
Where breed the swallows, her melodious cry
Amid their barbarous twitter!
In Russia? Never! Spain were fitter!
Ay, most likely 'tis in Spain
That we and Waring meet again—
Now, while he turns down that cool narrow lane
Into the blackness, out of grave Madrid
All fire and shine—abrupt as when there's slid
Its stiff gold blazing pall
From some black coffin-lid.
Or, best of all,
I love to think
The leaving us was just a feint;

Back here to London did he slink;
And now works on without a wink
Of sleep, and we are on the brink
Of something great in fresco-paint:
Some garret's ceiling, walls and floor,
Up and down and o'er and o'er
He splashes, as none splashed before
Since great Caldara Polidore:
Then down he creeps and out he steals
Only when the night conceals
His face—in Kent 'tis cherry-time,
Or, hops are picking; or, at prime
Of March, he steals as when, too happy,
Years ago when he was young,
Some mild eve when woods were sappy,
And the early moths had sprung
To life from many a trembling sheath
Woven the warm boughs beneath,
While small birds said to themselves
What should soon be actual song,
And young gnats, by tens and twelves,
Made as if they were the throng
That crowd around and carry aloft
The sound they have nursed, so sweet and pure,
Out of a myriad noises soft,
Into a tone that can endure
Amid the noise of a July noon,
When all God's creatures crave their boon,
All at once and all in tune,
And get it, happy as Waring then,
Having first within his ken
What a man might do with men,
And far too glad, in the even-glow,
To mix with the world he meant to take
Into his hand, he told you, so—
And out of it his world to make,
To contract and to expand
As he shut or oped his hand.
Oh, Waring, what's to really be?
A clear stage and a crowd to see!
Some Garrick—say—out shall not he

The heart of Hamlet's mystery pluck?
Or, where most unclean beasts are rife,
Some Junius—am I right?—shall tuck
His sleeve, and forth with flaying-knife!
Some Chatterton shall have the luck
Of calling Rowley into life!
Some one shall somehow run a muck
With this old world, for want of strife
Sound asleep: contrive, contrive
To rouse us, Waring! Who's alive?
Our men scarce seem in earnest now:
Distinguished names, but 'tis, somehow,
As if they played at being names
Still more distinguished, like the games
Of children. Turn our sport to earnest
With a visage of the sternest!
Bring the real times back, confessed
Still better than the very best!

II.

1.

"When I last saw Waring . . ."
(How all turned to him who spoke—
You saw Waring? Truth or joke?
In land-travel or sea-faring?)

2.

"We were sailing by Triest,
"Where a day or two we harboured:
"A sunset was in the West,
"When, looking over the vessel's side,
"One of our company espied
"A sudden speck to larboard.
"And, as a sea-duck flies and swims
"At once, so came the light craft up,
"With its sole lateen sail that trims
"And turns (the water round its rims
"Dancing as round a sinking cup)
"And by us like a fish it curled,

"And drew itself up close beside,
"Its great sail on the instant furled,
"And o'er its planks, a shrill voice cried,
"(A neck as bronzed as a Lascar's)
"'Buy wine of us, you English Brig?
"'Or fruit, tobacco and cigars?
"'A Pilot for you to Triest?
"'Without one, look you ne'er so big,
"'They'll never let you up the bay!
"'We natives should know best.'
"I turned, and 'just those fellows' way,'
"Our captain said, 'The 'long-shore thieves,
"'Are laughing at us in their sleeves.'

3.

"In truth, the boy leaned laughing back;
"And one, half-hidden by his side
"Under the furled sail, soon I spied,
"With great grass hat, and kerchief black,
"Who looked up, with his kingly throat,
"Said somewhat while the other shook
"His hair back from his eyes to look
"Their longest at us; and the boat,
"I know not how, turned sharply round,
"Laying her whole side on the sea
"As a leaping fish does; from the lee
"Into the weather cut somehow
"Her sparkling path beneath our bow;
"And so went off, as with a bound,
"Into the rose and golden half
"Of the sky, to overtake the sun,
"And reach the shore like the sea-calf
"Its singing cave; yet I caught one
"Glance ere away the boat quite passed,
"And neither time nor toil could mar
"Those features: so I saw the last
"Of Waring!"—You? Oh, never star
Was lost here, but it rose afar!
Look East, where whole new thousands are!
In Vishnu-land what Avatar?

The Pied Piper of Hamelin; A Child's Story

(WRITTEN FOR, AND INSCRIBED TO, W. M. THE YOUNGER.)

I.

Hamelin Town's in Brunswick,
By famous Hanover city;
The river Weser, deep and wide,
Washes its wall on the southern side;
A pleasanter spot you never spied;
But, when begins my ditty,
Almost five hundred years ago,
To see the townsfolk suffer so
From vermin, 'twas a pity.

II.

Rats!
They fought the dogs and killed the cats,
And bit the babies in the cradles,
And eat the cheeses out of the vats,
And licked the soup from the cooks' own ladles,
Split open the kegs of salted sprats,
Made nests inside men's Sunday hats,
And even spoiled the women's chats,
By drowning their speaking
With shrieking and squeaking
In fifty different sharps and flats.

III.

At last the people in a body
To the Town Hall came flocking:
'Tis clear, cried they, our Mayor's a noddy;
And as for our Corporation—shocking
To think we buy gowns lined with ermine
For dolts that can't or won't determine
What's like to rid us of our vermin!
Rouse up, Sirs! Give your brains a racking
To find the remedy we're lacking,
Or, sure as fate, we'll send you packing!

At this the Mayor and Corporation
Quaked with a mighty consternation

IV.

An hour they sate in council,
At length the Mayor broke silence:
For a guilder I'd my ermine gown sell;
I wish I were a mile hence!
It's easy to bid one rack one's brain—
I'm sure my poor head aches again
I've scratched it so, and all in vain.
Oh for a trap, a trap, a trap!
Just as he said this, what should hap
At the chamber door but a gentle tap?
Bless us, cried the Mayor, what's that?
(With the Corporation as he sate,
Looking little though wondrous fat)
Only a scraping of shoes on the mat?
Any thing like the sound of a rat
Makes my heart go pit-a-pat!

V.

Come in!—the Mayor cried, looking bigger:
And in did come the strangest figure!
His queer long coat from heel to head
Was half of yellow and half of red;
And he himself was tall and thin,
With sharp blue eyes, each like a pin,
And light loose hair, yet swarthy skin,
No tuft on cheek nor beard on chin,
But lips where smiles went out and in—
There was no guessing his kith and kin!
And nobody could enough admire
The tall man and his quaint attire:
Quoth one: It's as my great-grandsire,
Starting up at the Trump of Doom's tone,
Had walked this way from his painted tomb-stone!

VI.

He advanced to the council-table:
And, Please your honours, said he, I'm able,

By means of a secret charm, to draw
All creatures living beneath the sun,
That creep, or swim, or fly, or run,
After me so as you never saw!
And I chiefly use my charm
On creatures that do people harm,
The mole, and toad, and newt, and viper;
And people call me the Pied Piper.
(And here they noticed round his neck
A scarf of red and yellow stripe,
To match with his coat of the self same cheque;
And at the scarf's end hung a pipe;
And his fingers, they noticed, were ever straying
As if impatient to be playing
Upon this pipe, as low it dangled
Over his vesture so old-fangled.)
Yet, said he, poor piper as I am,
In Tartary I freed the Cham,
Last June, from his huge swarms of gnats;
I eased in Asia the Nizam
Of a monstrous brood of vampyre-bats:
And as for what your brain bewilders,
If I can rid your town of rats
Will you give me a thousand guilders?
One? fifty thousand!—was the exclamation
Of the astonished Mayor and Corporation.

VII.

Into the street the Piper stept,
  Smiling first a little smile,
As if he knew what magic slept
  In his quiet pipe the while;
Then, like a musical adept,
To blow the pipe his lips he wrinkled,
And green and blue his sharp eyes twinkled
Like a candle flame where salt is sprinkled;
And ere three shrill notes the pipe uttered,
You heard as if an army muttered;
And the muttering grew to a grumbling;
And the grumbling grew to a mighty rumbling;

And out of the houses the rats came tumbling.
Great rats, small rats, lean rats, brawny rats,
Brown rats, black rats, grey rats, tawny rats,
Grave old plodders, gay young friskers,
  Fathers, mothers, uncles, cousins,
Cocking tails and pricking whiskers,
  Families by tens and dozens,
Brothers, sisters, husbands, wives—
Followed the Piper for their lives.
From street to street he piped advancing,
And step for step they followed dancing,
Until they came to the river Weser
Wherein all plunged and perished
—Save one who, stout as Julius Cæsar,
Swam across and lived to carry
(As he the manuscript he cherished)
To Rat-land home his commentary,
Which was, At the first shrill notes of the pipe,
I heard a sound as of scraping tripe,
And putting apples, wondrous ripe,
Into a cider-press's gripe:
And a moving away of pickle-tub-boards,
And a leaving ajar of conserve-cupboards,
And a drawing the corks of train-oil-flasks,
And a breaking the hoops of butter-casks;
And it seemed as if a voice
(Sweeter than by harp or by psaltery
Is breathed) called out, Oh rats, rejoice!
The world is grown to one vast drysaltery!
So munch on, crunch on, take your nuncheon,
Breakfast, supper, dinner, luncheon!
And just as one bulky sugar puncheon,
Ready staved, like a great sun shone
Glorious scarce an inch before me,
Just as methought it said, Come, bore me!
—I found the Weser rolling o'er me.

VIII.

You should have heard the Hamelin people
Ringing the bells till they rocked the steeple;
Go, cried the Mayor, and get long poles!

Poke out the nests and block up the holes!
Consult with carpenters and builders,
And leave in our town not even a trace
Of the rats!—when suddenly, up the face
Of the Piper perked in the market-place,
With a, First, if you please, my thousand guilders!

IX.

A thousand guilders! The Mayor looked blue;
So did the Corporation too.
For council dinners made rare havock
With Claret, Moselle, Vin-de-Grave, Hock;
And half the money would replenish
Their cellar's biggest butt with Rhenish;
To pay this sum to a wandering fellow
With a gipsy coat of red and yellow!
Beside, quoth the Mayor with a knowing wink,
Our business was done at the river's brink;
We saw with our eyes the vermin sink,
And what's dead can't come to life, I think.
So, friend, we're not the folks to shrink
From the duty of giving you something for drink,
And a matter of money to put in your poke;
But, as for the guilders, what we spoke
Of them, as you very well know, was in joke.
Besides, our losses have made us thrifty;
A thousand guilders! Come, take fifty!

X.

The Piper's face fell, and he cried,
No trifling! I can't wait, beside!
I've promised to visit by dinner time
Bagdat, and accept the prime
Of the Head-Cook's pottage, all he's rich in,
For having left, in the Caliph's kitchen,
Of a nest of scorpions no survivor—
With him I proved no bargain-driver,
With you, don't think I'll bate a stiver!
And folks who put me in a passion
May find me pipe after another fashion.

XI.

How? cried the Mayor, d'ye think I'll brook
Being worse treated than a Cook?
Insulted by a lazy ribald
With idle pipe and vesture piebald?
You threaten us, fellow? Do your worst,
Blow your pipe there till you burst!

XII.

Once more he stept into the street;
And to his lips again
Laid his long pipe of smooth straight cane;
And ere he blew three notes (such sweet
Soft notes as yet musician's cunning
Never gave th'enraptured air)
There was a rustling that seemed like a bustling
Of merry crowds justling at pitching and hustling,
Small feet were pattering, wooden shoes clattering,
Little hands clapping and little tongues chattering,
And, like fowls in a farm-yard when barley is scattering,
Out came the children running.
All the little boys and girls,
With rosy cheeks and flaxen curls,
And sparkling eyes and teeth like pearls,
Tripping and skipping, ran merrily after
The wonderful music with shouting and laughter.

XIII.

The Mayor was dumb, and the Council stood
As if they were changed into blocks of wood,
Unable to move a step, or cry
To the children merrily skipping by—
Could only follow with the eye
That joyous crowd at the Piper's back.
But how the Mayor was on the rack,
And the wretched Council's bosoms beat,
As the Piper turned from the High Street
To where the Weser rolled its waters
Right in the way of their sons and daughters!
However he turned from South to West,
And to Coppelberg Hill his steps addressed,

And after him the children pressed;
Great was the joy in every breast.
He never can cross that mighty top!
He's forced to let the piping drop,
And we shall see our children stop!
When, lo, as they reached the mountain's side,
A wondrous portal opened wide,
As if a cavern was suddenly hollowed;
And the Piper advanced and the children follow'd,
And when all were in to the very last,
The door in the mountain side shut fast.
Did I say, all? No! One was lame,
And could not dance the whole of the way;
And in after years, if you would blame
His sadness, he was used to say,—
It's dull in our town since my playmates left!
I can't forget that I'm bereft
Of all the pleasant sights they see,
Which the Piper also promised me;
For he led us, he said, to a joyous land,
Joining the town and just at hand,
Where waters gushed and fruit-trees grew
And flowers put forth a fairer hue,
And everything was strange and new;
The sparrows were brighter than peacocks here,
And their dogs outran our fallow deer,
And honey-bees had lost their stings,
And horses were born with eagles' wings:
And just as I became assured
My lame foot would be speedily cured,
The music stopped and I stood still,
And found myself outside the Hill,
Left alone against my will,
To go now limping as before,
And never hear of that country more!

XIV.

Alas, alas for Hamelin!
  There came into many a burgher's pate
  A text which says that Heaven's Gate
  Opes to the Rich at as easy rate

As the needle's eye takes a camel in!
The Mayor sent East, West, North and South,
To offer the Piper by word of mouth,
  Wherever it was men's lot to find him,
Silver and gold to his heart's content,
If he'd only return the way he went,
  And bring the children behind him.
But when they saw 'twas a lost endeavour,
And Piper and dancers were gone for ever,
They made a decree that lawyers never
  Should think their records dated duly
If, after the day of the month and year,
These words did not as well appear,
"And so long after what happened here
  "On the Twenty-second of July,
"Thirteen hundred and Seventy-six:"
And the better in memory to fix
The place of the Children's last retreat,
They called it, the Pied Piper's Street—
Where any one playing on pipe or tabor
Was sure for the future to lose his labour.
Nor suffered they Hostelry or Tavern
  To shock with mirth a street so solemn;
But opposite the place of the cavern
  They wrote the story on a column,
And on the Great Church Window painted
The same, to make the world acquainted
How their children were stolen away;
And there it stands to this very day.
And I must not omit to say
That in Transylvania there's a tribe
Of alien people that ascribe
The outlandish ways and dress
On which their neighbours lay such stress
To their fathers and mothers having risen
Out of some subterraneous prison
Into which they were trepanned
Long time ago in a mighty band
Out of Hamelin town in Brunswick land,
But how or why they don't understand.

XV.

So, Willy, let me and you be wipers
Of scores out with all men—especially pipers:
And, whether they rid us from rats or from mice,
If we've promised them aught, let us keep our promise.

POEMS FROM *HOOD'S MAGAZINE*, vol. 1, June 1844, 513–14; vol. 2, July 1844, 45–8; vol. 3, March 1845, 237–9; vol. 3, April 1845, 313–18

The Laboratory

(ANCIEN RÉGIME)

Now I have tied thy glass mask on tightly,
May gaze thro' these faint smokes curling whitely,
As thou pliest thy trade in this devil's-smithy,
Which is the poison to poison her, prithee?

He is with her; and they know that I know
Where they are—what they do: they believe my tears flow
While they laugh—laugh at me—at me fled to the drear
Empty church to pray God in for them!—I am here.

Grind away, moisten and mash up thy paste,
Pound at thy powder—am I in haste?
Better sit thus, and observe thy strange things,
Than go where men wait me, and dance at the king's.

That in the mortar—call you a gum?
Ah, the brave tree whence such gold oozings come!
And yon soft phial, the exquisite blue,
Sure to taste sweetly—is that poison too?

Had I but all of them, thee and thy treasures—
What a wild crowd of invisible pleasures—
To carry pure death in a earring, a casket
A signet, a fan-mount, a filagree-basket!

Soon, at the king's, but a lozenge to give,
And Pauline should have just thirty minutes to live!
But to light a pastille, and Elise, with her head,
And her breast, and her arms, and her hands, should drop dead!

Quick—is it finished? The colour's too grim;
Why not like the phial's, enticing and dim?
Let it brighten her drink, let her turn it and stir,
And try it and taste, ere she fix and prefer!

What a drop! She's not little—no minion like me;
That's why she ensnared him: this never will free
The soul from those strong, great eyes: say, "No!"
To that pulse's magnificent come-and-go.

For only last night, as they whispered, I brought
My own eyes to bear on her so, that I thought,
Could I keep them one half minute fixed, she'd fall
Shrivelled: she fell not; yet this does it all!

Not that I bid you spare her pain!
Let death be felt and the proof remain;
Brand, burn up, bite into its grace—
He is sure to remember her dying face!

Is it done? Take my mask off! Be not morose!
It kills her, and this prevents seeing it close—
The delicate droplet, my whole fortune's fee—
If it hurts her, beside, can it ever hurt me?

Now, take all my jewels, gorge gold to your fill,
You may kiss me, old man, on my mouth, if you will!
But brush this dust off me, lest horror there springs
Ere I know it—next moment I dance at the king's.

Garden Fancies

I. THE FLOWER'S NAME

Here's the garden she walked across,
   Arm in my arm, such a short while since:
Hark, now I push its wicket, the moss
   Hinders the hinges and makes them wince!
She must have reached this shrub ere she turned,
   As back with that murmur the wicket swung;
For she laid the poor snail, my chance foot spurned,
   To feed and forget it the leaves among.

Down this side of the gravel-walk
   She went while her robe's edge brushed the box:
And here she paused in her gracious talk
   To point me a moth on the milk-white flox.
Roses, ranged in valiant row,
   Think I will never she passed you by!
She loves you noble roses, I know;
   But this—so surely this met her eye!

This flower she stopped at, finger on lip;
  Stooped over, in doubt, as settling its claim,
Till she gave me, with pride to make no slip,
  Its soft meandering Spanish name:
What a name! Was it love or praise?
  Speech half-asleep, or song half-awake?
I must learn Spanish one of these days,
Only for that slow sweet name's sake.

Roses, if I live and do well,
  I may bring her, one of these days,
To fix you fast with as fine a spell,
  Fit you each with his Spanish phrase!
But do not detain me now; for she lingers
  There, like sunshine over the ground,
And ever I see her soft white fingers
  Searching after the bud she found.

Flower, you Spaniard, look you grow not,
  Stay as you are and be loved for ever!
Bud, if I kiss you, 'tis that you blow not,
  Mind the pink shut mouth opens never!
For while it pouts thus, her fingers wrestle,
  Twinkling the audacious leaves between,
Till round they turn and down they nestle—
  Is not the dear mark still to be seen?

Where I find her not, beauties vanish;
  Whither I follow her, beauties flee;
Is there no method to tell her in Spanish
  June's twice June since she breathed it with me?
Come, bud, show me the least of her traces,
  Tread in my lady's lightest foot-fall.
  —Ah, you may flout and turn up your faces!
  Roses, are you so fair after all?

2. SIBRANDUS SCHAFNABURGENSIS

Plague take all your pedants, say I!
  He who wrote what I hold in my hand,
Centuries back was so good as to die,
  Leaving this rubbish to bother the land;
This, that was a book in its time,

Printed on paper and bound in leather,
Last month in the white of a matin-prime
Just when the birds sang all together.

Into the garden I brought it to read;
And under these arbutes and laurustine
Read it, so help me grace in my need,
From title-page to closing line.
Chapter on chapter did I count,
As a curious traveller counts Stonehenge;
Added up the mortal amount;
And then proceeded to my revenge.

Yonder's a plum-tree, with a crevice
An owl would build in, were he but sage;
For a lap of moss, like a fine pont-levis
In a castle of the middle age,
Joins to a lip of gum, pure amber;
When he'd be private, there might he spend
Hours alone in his lady's chamber:
Into this crevice I dropped our friend.

Splash, went he, as under he ducked,
—I knew at the bottom rain-drippings stagnate:
Next a handful of blossoms I plucked
To bury him with, my book-shelf's magnate:
Then I went in-doors, brought out a loaf,
Half a cheese, and a bottle of Chablis;
Lay on the grass and forgot the oaf
Over a jolly chapter of Rabelais.

Now, this morning, betwixt the moss
And gum that locked our friend in limbo,
A spider had spun his web across,
And sat in the midst with arms a-kimbo:
So I took pity, for learning's sake,
And, *de profundis, accentibus lætis,*
Cantate, quoth I, as I got a rake;
And up I fished his delectable treatise.

Here you have it, dry in the sun,
With all the binding all of a blister,
And great blue spots where the ink has run,

And reddish streaks that wink and glister
O'er the page so beautifully yellow—
Oh, the droppings have played their tricks!
Did he guess how toadstools grow, this fellow?
Here's one stuck in his chapter six!

How did he like it when the live creatures
Tickled and toused and browsed him all over,
And worm, slug, eft, with serious features,
Came in, each one, for his right of trover;
When the water-beetle with great blind deaf face
Made of her eggs the stately deposit,
And the newt borrowed just so much of the preface
As tiled in the top of his black wife's closet.

All that life, and fun, and romping,
All that frisking, and twisting, and coupling,
While slowly our poor friend's leaves were swamping,
Clasps cracking, and covers suppling!
As if you had carried sour John Knox
To the play at Paris, Vienna, or Munich,
Fastened him into a front-row box,
And danced off the Ballet in trowsers and tunic.

Come, old martyr! what, torment enough is it?
Back to my room shall you take your sweet self!
Good bye, mother-beetle; husband-eft, *sufficit* !
See the snug niche I have made on my shelf.
A's book shall prop you up, B's shall cover you,
Here's C to be grave with, or D to be gay,
And with E on each side, and F right over you,
Dry-rot at ease till the judgment-day!

[*The Bishop Orders His Tomb at Saint Praxed's Church* (Rome, 15—)] *The Tomb at Saint Praxed's* (Rome, 15—)

Vanity, saith the Preacher, vanity!
Draw round my bed: is Anselm keeping back?

Nephews—sons mine . . . ah God, I know not! Well—
She, men would have to be your mother once,
Old Gandolf envied me, so fair she was!
What's done is done, and she is dead beside,
And long ago, and I am Bishop since,
And as she died so must we die ourselves,
And thence ye may perceive the world's a dream.
Life, how and what is it? As here I lie
In this state-chamber, dying by degrees,
Hours and long hours in the dead night, I ask
"Do I live, am I dead?" Peace, peace seems all:
St. Praxed's ever was the church for peace;
And so, about this tomb of mine. I fought
With tooth and nail to save my niche, ye know:
—Old Gandolf came me in, despite my care,
For a shrewd snatch out the corner south
To grace his carrion with, God curse the same!
Yet still my niche is not so cramp'd but thence
One sees the pulpit o' the epistle-side,
And somewhat of the choir, those silent seats,
And up into the aery dome where live
The angels, and a sunbeam's sure to lurk:
And I shall fill my slab of basalt there,
And 'neath my tabernacle take my rest
With those nine columns round me, two and two,
The odd one at my feet where Anselm stands:
Peachblossom-marble all, the rare, the ripe
As fresh-pour'd red wine of a mighty pulse
—Old Gandolf with his paltry onion-stone,
Put me where I may look at him! True peach,
Rosy and flawless: how I earn'd the prize!
Draw close: that conflagration of my church
—What then? So much was sav'd if aught were miss'd!
My sons, ye would not be my death? Go dig
The white-grape vineyard where the oil-press stood,
Drop water gently till the surface sinks,
And if ye find . . Ah, God I know not, I! . . .
Bedded in store of rotten figleaves soft,
And corded up in a tight olive-frail,
Some lump, ah God, of *lapis lazuli*,
Big as a Jew's head cut off at the nape,

Blue as a vein o'er the Madonna's breast...
Sons, all have I bequeath'd you, villas, all,
That brave Frascati villa with its bath,
So let the blue lump poise between my knees,
Like God the Father's globe on both his hands
Ye worship in the Jesu Church so gay,
For Gandolf shall not choose but see and burst!
Swift as a weaver's shuttle fleet our years:
Man goeth to the grave, and where is he?
Did I say basalt for my slab, sons? Black—
'Twas ever antique-black I meant! How else
Shall ye contrast my frieze to come beneath?
The bas-relief in bronze ye promis'd me,
Those Pans and Nymphs ye wot of, and perchance
Some tripod, thyrsus, with a vase or so,
The Saviour at his sermon on the mount,
St. Praxed in a glory, and one Pan
Ready to twitch the nymph's last garment off,
And Moses with the tables... but I know
Ye mark me not! What do they whisper thee,
Child of my bowels, Anselm? Ah, ye hope
To revel down my villas while I gasp
Brick'd o'er with beggar's mouldy travertine
Which Gandolf from his tomb-top chuckles at!
Nay, boys, ye love me—all of jasper, then!
'Tis jasper ye stand pledged to, lest I grieve
My bath must needs be left behind, alas!
One block, pure green as a pistachio-nut,
There's plenty jasper somewhere in the world—
And I shall have St. Praxed's ear to pray
Horses for ye, and brown Greek manuscripts,
And mistresses with great smooth marbly limbs
—That's if ye carve my epitaph aright,
Choice Latin, picked phrase, Tully's every word,
No gaudy ware like Gandolf's second line
—Tully, my masters? Ulpian serves his need!
And then how I shall lie through centuries
And hear the blessed mutter of the mass,
And see God made and eaten all day long,
And feel the steady candle-flame, and taste
Good strong thick stupifying incense-smoke!

For as I lie here, hours of the dead night,
Dying in state and by such slow degrees,
I fold my arms as if they clasp'd a crook,
And stretch my feet forth straight as stone can point,
And let the bed-clothes, for a mortcloth drop
Into great laps and folds of sculptors'-work:
And as yon tapers dwindle, and strange thoughts
Grow, with a certain humming in my ears,
About the life before this life I liv'd,
And this life too, Popes, Cardinals and Priests,
St. Praxed at his sermon on the mount,
Your tall pale mother with her talking eyes,
And new-found agate urns as fresh as day,
And marble's language, Latin pure, discreet,
—Aha, ELUCESCEBAT, quoth our friend?
No Tully, said I, Ulpian at the best!
Evil and brief hath been my pilgrimage.
All *lapis*, all, sons! Else I give the Pope
My villas: will ye ever eat my heart?
Ever your eyes were as a lizard's quick,
They glitter like your mother's for my soul,
Or to the tripod ye would tie a lynx
That in his struggle throws the thyrsus down,
To comfort me on my entablature
Whereon I am to lie till I must ask
"Do I live, am I dead?" There, leave me, there!
For ye have stabb'd me with ingratitude
To death—ye wish it—God, ye wish it! Stone—
Gritstone, a-crumble! Clammy squares which sweat
As if the corpse they keep were oozing through—
And no more *lapis* to delight the world!
Well go! I bless ye. Fewer tapers there,
But in a row: and, going, turn your backs
—Ay, like departing altar-ministrants,
And leave me in my church, the church for peace,
That I may watch at leisure if he leers—
Old Gandolf, at me, from his onion-stone,
As still he envied me, so fair she was!

The Flight of the Duchess

PART THE FIRST

You're my friend:
I was the man the Duke spoke to;
I help'd the Duchess to cast off his yoke, too;
So here's the tale from beginning to end,
My friend!

Ours is a great wild country:
If you climb to our castle's top,
I don't see where your eye can stop;
For when you've pass'd the cornfield-country,
Where vineyards leave off, flocks are pack'd,
And sheep-range leads to cattle-tract,
And cattle-tract to open-chase,
And open-chase to the very base
Of the mountain where, at a funeral pace,
Round about, solemn and slow,
One by one, row upon row,
Up and up the pine-trees go,
So like black priests up, and so
Down the other side again
To another greater, wilder country,
That's one vast red drear burnt-up plain,
Branch'd thro' and thro' with many a vein
Whence iron's dug, and copper's dealt;
Look right, look left, look straight before,
Beneath they mine, above they smelt,
Copper-ore and iron-ore,
And forge and furnace mould and melt,
And so on, more and ever more,
Till at the last, for a bounding belt,
Comes the salt sand hoar of the great sea shore,—
And the whole is our Duke's country!

I was born the day this present Duke was—
(And O, says the song, ere I was old!)
In the castle where the other Duke was—
(When I was happy and young, not old!)
I in the kennel, he in the bower:

We are of like age to an hour.
My father was huntsman in that day;
Who has not heard my father say
That when a boar was brought to bay,
Three, four times out of five,
With his hunt-spear he'd contrive
To get the killing-place transfix'd,
And pin him true, both eyes betwixt?
And that's why the old Duke had rather
He lost a salt-pit than my father,
And lov'd to have him ever in call:
That's why my father stood in the hall
When the old Duke brought his infant out
To show the people, and while they pass'd
The wondrous bantling round about,
Was first to start at the outside blast
As the Kaiser's courier blew his horn,
Just one month after the babe was born:
"And," quoth the Kaiser's courier, "since
"The Duke has got an heir, our Prince
"Needs the Duke's self at his side:"
The Duke look'd down and seem'd to wince,
But he thought of wars o'er the world wide,
Castles a-fire, men on their march,
The toppling tower, the crashing arch;
And up he look'd, and awhile he eyed
The row of crests and shields, and banners,
Of all achievements after all manners,
And "ay," said the Duke with a surly pride:
The more was his comfort when he died
At next year's end, in a velvet suit,
With a gilt glove on his hand, and his foot
In a silk shoe for a leather boot,
Petticoated like a herald,
In a chamber next to an anteroom,
Where he breath'd the breath of page and groom,
What he call'd stink, and they perfume:
—They should have set him on red Berold,
Mad with pride, like fire to manage!
They should have got his cheek fresh tannage
Such a day as to-day in the merry sunshine!

Had they stuck on his fist a rough-foot merlin!
—Hark, the wind's on the heath at its game—
Oh! for a noble falcon-lanner
To flap each broad wing like a banner,
And turn in the wind, and dance like flame!
Had they broach'd a cask of white beer from Berlin
—Or if you incline to prescribe mere wine
Put to his lips when they saw him pine,
A cup of our own Moldavia fine,
Cotnar, for instance, green as May sorrel,
And ropy with sweet,—we shall not quarrel.

So at home the sick tall yellow Duchess
Was left with the infant in her clutches,
She being the daughter of God knows who:
And now was the time to revisit her tribe,
So abroad and afar they went, the two,
And let our people curse and gibe
At the empty hall and extinguish'd fire,
Loud as we lik'd, but ever in vain;
Till after long years we had our desire,
And back came the Duke and his mother again.

And he came back the pertest ape
That ever affronted human shape;
Full of his travel, struck at himself—
You'd say, he despis'd our bluff old ways
—Not he! For in Paris they told the elf
Our rough North land was the Land of Lays,
The one good thing left in evil days;
For the Mid-Age was the Heroic Time,
And only in wild nooks like ours
Could you taste of it yet as in its prime,
True castles, with proper towers,
Young-hearted women, old-minded men,
And manners now as manners were then.
So, all that the old dukes had been, without knowing it,
This Duke would fain know he was, without being it;
'Twas not for the joy's self, but the joy of his showing it,
Nor for the pride's self, but the pride of our seeing it.
He reviv'd all usages thoroughly worn out,

The souls of them fum'd forth, the hearts of them torn out:
And chief in the chase his neck he perill'd,
On a lathy horse, all legs and length,
With blood for bone, all speed, no strength;
They should have set him on red Berold
With the red eye slow consuming in fire,
And the thin stiff ear like an abbey-spire!

Well, such as he was, he must marry, we heard:
And out of a convent, at the word,
Came the lady, in time of spring.
—Oh, old thoughts they cling, they cling!
That day, I know, with a dozen oaths
I clad myself in thick hunting-clothes
Fit for the chase of urox or buffle
In winter-time, when you need to muffle;
But the Duke had a mind we should cut a figure,
And so we saw the lady arrive:
My friend, I have seen a white crane bigger!
She was the smallest lady alive,
Made, in a piece of nature's madness,
Too small, almost, for the life and gladness
That over-fill'd her, as some hive
Out of the bears' reach on the high trees
Is crowded with its safe merry bees—
In truth she was not hard to please!
Up she look'd, down she look'd, round at the mead,
Straight at the castle, that's best indeed
To look at from outside the walls:
As for us, styled the "serfs and thralls,"
She as much thank'd me as if she had said it,
(With her eyes, do you understand?)
Because I patted her horse while I led it;
And Max, who went on her other hand,
Said, no bird flew past but she enquir'd
What its true name was, nor ever seem'd tir'd—
If that was an eagle she saw hover,
And the green and grey bird on the field was the plover?
When suddenly appear'd the Duke,
And as down she sprung, the small foot pointed
On to my hand,—as with a rebuke,

And as if his back-bone were not jointed,
The Duke stepp'd rather aside than forward,
And welcom'd her with his grandest smile;
And, mind you, his mother all the while
Chill'd in the rear, like a wind to nor'ward;
And up, like a weary yawn, with its pullies
Went, in a shriek, the rusty portcullis,
And, like a glad sky the north-wind sullies,
The lady's face stopp'd its play,
As if her first hair had grown grey—
For such things must begin some one day!

In a day or two she was well again;
As who should say, "You labour in vain!
"This is all a jest against God, who meant
"I should ever be, as I am, content
"And glad in his sight; therefore, glad I will be!"
So smiling as at first went she.

She was active, stirring, all fire—
Could not rest, could not tire—
To a stone she had given life!
(I myself lov'd once, in my day),
—For a shepherd's, miner's, huntsman's wife,
(I had a wife, I know what I say,)
Never in all the world such an one!
And here was plenty to be done,
And she that could do it, great or small,
She was to do nothing at all.
There was already this man in his post,
This in his station, and that in his office,
And the Duke's plan admitted a wife, at most,
To meet his eye, with the other trophies,
Now outside the hall, now in it,
To sit thus, stand thus, see and be seen,
At the proper place in the proper minute,
And die away the life between:
And it was amusing enough, each infraction
Of rule—(but for after-sadness that came)—
To hear the consummate self-satisfaction
With which the young Duke and the old dame

Would let her advise, and criticise,
And, being a fool, instruct the wise;
And, child-like, parcel out praise or blame.
They bore it all in complacent guise,
As tho' an artificer, having contriv'd
A wheel-work image as if it liv'd,
Should find with delight it could motion to strike him!
So found the Duke, and his mother like him—
The lady hardly got a rebuff—
That had not been contemptuous enough,
With his cursed smirk, as he nodded applause,
And kept off the old mother-cat's claws.

So, the little lady grew silent and thin,
  Paling and ever paling,
As the way is with a hid chagrin;
  And the Duke perceiv'd that she was ailing,
And said in his heart, "'Tis done to spite me,
"But I shall find in my power to right me!"
Don't swear, friend,—the old one, many a year,
Is in hell, and the Duke's self... you shall hear.

END OF PART THE FIRST

First Letter To Elizabeth Barrett, 10 January 1845

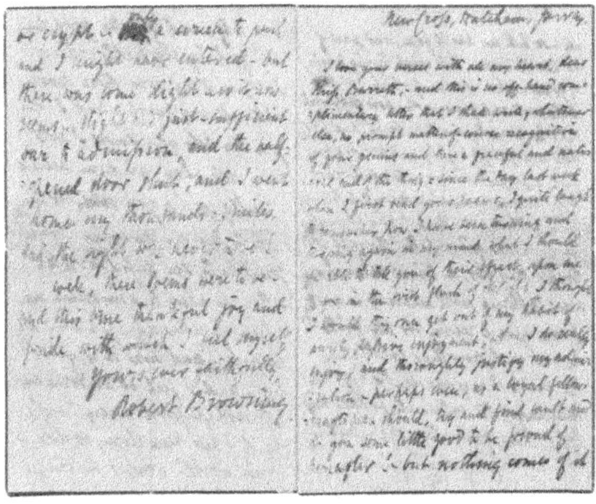

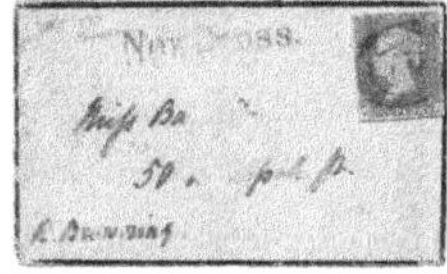

FIG. 3 R.B.'s first letter to E.B.B. (1845), Wellesley College Library, Margaret Clapp Library, Special Collections.

New Cross, Hatcham, Surrey.

I love your verses with all my heart, dear Miss Barrett,—and this is no off-hand complimentary letter that I shall write,—whatever else, no prompt matter-of-course recognition of your genius, and there a graceful and natural end of the thing: since the day last week when I first read your poems, I quite laugh to remember how I have been turning and turning again in my mind what I should be able to tell you of their effect upon me—for in the first flush of delight I thought I would this once get out of my habit of purely passive enjoyment, when I do really enjoy, and thoroughly justify my admiration—perhaps even, as a loyal fellow-craftsman should, try and find fault and do you some little good to be proud of hereafter!—but nothing comes of it all—so into me has it gone, and part of me has it become, this great living poetry of yours, not a flower of which but took root and grew—oh, how different that is from lying to be dried and pressed flat, and prized highly and put in a book with a proper account at top and bottom, and shut up and put away . . and the book called a "Flora," besides! After all, I need not give up the thought of doing that, too, in time; because even now, talking with whoever is worthy, I can give a reason for my faith in one and another excellence, the fresh strange music, the affluent language, the exquisite pathos and true new brave thought—but in this addressing myself to you—your own self, and for the first time, my feeling rises altogether. I do, as I say, love these books with all my heart—and I love you too: do you know I was once not very far from seeing—really seeing you? Mr. Kenyon said to me one morning "would you like to see Miss Barrett?"—then he went to announce me,—then he returned . . you were too unwell, and now it is years ago, and I feel as at some untoward passage in my travels—as if I had been close, so close, to some world's-wonder in chapel or crypt, only a screen to push and I might have entered, but there was some slight . . so it now seems . . slight and just sufficient bar to admission; and the half-opened door shut, and I went home my thousands of miles, and the sight was never to be!

Well, these Poems were to be—and this true thankful joy and pride with which I feel myself

Yours ever faithfully,
Robert Browning

FROM *BELLS AND POMEGRANATES, NO. VII, DRAMATIC ROMANCES AND LYRICS* (1845)

"How They Brought the Good News from Ghent to Aix" (16—)

I.

I sprang to the stirrup, and Joris, and He;
I galloped, Dirck galloped, we galloped all Three;
"Good speed!" cried the watch, as the gate-bolts undrew;
"Speed!" echoed the wall to us galloping through;
Behind shut the postern, the lights sank to rest,
And into the midnight we galloped abreast.

II.

Not a word to each other; we kept the great pace
Neck by neck, stride for stride, never changing our place;
I turned in my saddle and made its girths tight,
Then shortened each stirrup, and set the pique right,
Rebuckled the cheek-strap, chained slacker the bit,
Nor galloped less steadily Roland a whit.

III.

'Twas moonset at starting; but while we drew near
Lokeren, the cocks crew and twilight dawned clear;
At Boom, a great yellow star came out to see;
At Düffeld, 'twas morning as plain as could be;
And from Mecheln church-steeple we heard the half-chime,
So Joris broke silence with, "Yet there is time!"

IV.

At Aerschot, up leaped of a sudden the sun,
And against him the cattle stood black every one,
To stare thro' the mist at us galloping past,
And I saw my stout galloper Roland at last,
With resolute shoulders, each butting away
The haze as some bluff river headland its spray.

V.

And his low head and crest, just one sharp ear bent back
For my voice, and the other pricked out on his track;

And one eye's black intelligence,—ever that glance
O'er its white edge at me, his own master, askance!
And the thick heavy spume-flakes which aye and anon
His fierce lips shook upwards in galloping on.

VI.

By Hasselt, Dirck groaned; and cried Joris, "Stay spur!
"Your Roos galloped bravely, the fault's not in her,
"We'll remember at Aix"—for one heard the quick wheeze
Of her chest, saw the stretched neck and staggering knees,
And sunk tail, and horrible heave of the flank,
As down on her haunches she shuddered and sank.

VII.

So we were left galloping, Joris and I,
Past Looz and past Tongres, no cloud in the sky;
The broad sun above laughed a pitiless laugh,
'Neath our feet broke the brittle bright stubble like chaff;
Till over by Dalhem a dome-spire sprang white,
And "Gallop," gasped Joris, "for Aix is in sight!"

VIII.

"How they'll greet us!"—and all in a moment his roan
Rolled neck and croup over, lay dead as a stone;
And there was my Roland to bear the whole weight
Of the news which alone could save Aix from her fate,
With his nostrils like pits full of blood to the brim,
And with circles of red for his eye-sockets' rim.

IX.

Then I cast loose my buffcoat, each holster let fall,
Shook off both my jack-boots, let go belt and all,
Stood up in the stirrup, leaned, patted his ear,
Called my Roland his pet-name, my horse without peer;
Clapped my hands, laughed and sang, any noise, bad or good,
Till at length into Aix Roland galloped and stood.

X.

And all I remember is, friends flocking round
As I sat with his head 'twixt my knees on the ground,
And no voice but was praising this Roland of mine,
As I poured down his throat our last measure of wine
Which (the burgesses voted by common consent)
Was no more than his due who brought good news from Ghent.

Pictor Ignotus

FLORENCE, 15—.

I could have painted pictures like that youth's
  Ye praise so. How my soul springs up! No bar
Stayed me—ah, thought which saddens while it soothes!
  Never did fate forbid me, star by star,
To outburst on your night with all my gift
  Of fires from God: nor would my flesh have shrunk
From seconding that soul, with eyes uplift
  And wide to Heaven, or, straight like thunder, sunk
To the centre of an instant, or around
  Sent calmly and inquisitive to scan
The license and the limit, space and bound,
  Allowed to Truth made visible in Man.
And, like that youth ye praise so, all I saw,
  Over the canvas could my hand have flung,
Each face obedient to its passion's law,
  Each passion clear proclaimed without a tongue;
Whether Hope rose at once in all the blood,
  A-tiptoe for the blessing of embrace,
Or Rapture drooped the eyes as when her brood
  Pull down the nesting dove's heart to its place,
Or Confidence lit swift the forehead up,
  And locked the mouth fast, like a castle braved,—
Men, women, children, hath it spilt, my cup?
  What did ye give me that I have not saved?
Nor will I say I have not dreamed (how well!)
  Of going—I, in each new picture,—forth,
And making new hearts beat and bosoms swell,

As still to Pope or Kaiser, South and North,
Bound for the calmly-satisfied great State,
Or glad aspiring little burgh, it went,
Flowers cast upon the car which bore the freight
Through old streets named afresh from its event,
—Of reaching thus my home, where Age should greet
My face, and Youth, the star not yet distinct
Above his hair, lie learning at my feet,—
Oh, thus to live, I and my pictures, linked
With love about, and praise, till life should end,
And then not go to Heaven, but linger here,
Here on my earth, its every man my friend,—
Oh, that grows frightful, 'tis so wildly dear!
But a voice changed it! Glimpses of such sights
Have scared me, like the revels thro' a door
Of some strange House of Idols at its rites;
This world seemed not the world it was before!
Mixed with my loving ones there trooped—for what?
Who summoned those cold faces which begun
To press on me and judge me? As asquat
And shrinking from the soldiery a nun,
They drew me forth, and spite of me . . enough!
These buy and sell our pictures, take and give,
Count them for garniture and household-stuff,
And where they live needs must our pictures live,
And see their faces, listen to their prate,
Partakers of their daily pettiness,
Discussed of,—"This I love or this I hate,
"This likes me more and this affects me less!"
Wherefore I chose my portion. If at whiles
My heart sinks, as monotonous I paint
These endless cloisters and eternal aisles
With the same series, Virgin, Babe and Saint,
With the same cold, calm, beautiful regard,
At least no merchant traffics in my heart;
The sanctuary's gloom at least shall ward
Vain tongues from where my pictures stand apart;
Only prayer breaks the silence of the shrine
While, blackening in the daily candle smoke,
They moulder on the damp wall's travertine,
'Mid echoes the light footstep never woke.

So die, my pictures; surely, gently die!
  O youth men praise so, holds their praise its worth?
Blown harshly, keeps the trump its golden cry?
  Tastes sweet the water with such specks of earth?

[*The Italian in England*]
Italy in England

That second time they hunted me
From hill to plain, from shore to sea,
And Austria, hounding far and wide
Her blood-hounds thro' the country-side,
Breathed hot and instant on my trace,
I made six days a hiding-place
Of that dry green old aqueduct
Where I and Charles, when boys, have plucked
The fire-flies from the roof above,
Bright creeping thro' the moss they love.
—How long it seems since Charles was lost!
Six days the soldiers crossed and crossed
The country in my very sight;
And when that peril ceased at night,
The sky broke out in red dismay
With signal fires; well, there I lay
Close covered o'er in my recess,
Up to the neck in ferns and cress,
Thinking on Metternich our friend,
And Charles's miserable end,
And much beside, two days; the third,
Hunger o'ercame me when I heard
The peasants from the village go
To work among the maize; you know,
With us, in Lombardy, they bring
Provisions packed on mules, a string
With little bells that cheer their task,
And casks, and boughs on every cask
To keep the sun's heat from the wine;
These I let pass in jingling line,
And, close on them, dear noisy crew,

The peasants from the village, too;
For at the very rear would troop
Their wives and sisters in a group
To help, I knew; when these had passed,
I threw my glove to strike the last,
Taking the chance: she did not start,
Much less cry out, but stooped apart
One instant, rapidly glanced round,
And saw me beckon from the ground:
A wild bush grows and hides my crypt;
She picked my glove up while she stripped
A branch off, then rejoined the rest
With that; my glove lay in her breast:
Then I drew breath: they disappeared:
It was for Italy I feared.

An hour, and she returned alone
Exactly where my glove was thrown.
Meanwhile came many thoughts; on me
Rested the hopes of Italy;
I had devised a certain tale
Which, when 'twas told her, could not fail
Persuade a peasant of its truth;
This hiding was a freak of youth;
I meant to give her hopes of pay,
And no temptation to betray.
But when I saw that woman's face,
Its calm simplicity of grace,
Our Italy's own attitude
In which she walked thus far, and stood,
Planting each naked foot so firm,
To crush the snake and spare the worm—
At first sight of her eyes, I said,
"I am that person on whose head
"They fix the price because I hate
"The Austrians over us: the State
"Will give you gold—oh, gold so much,
"If you betray me to their clutch!
"And be your death, for aught I know,
"If once they find you saved their foe.
"Now, you must bring me food and drink,

"And also paper, pen and ink,
"And carry safe what I shall write
"To Padua, which you'll reach at night
"Before the Duomo shuts; go in,
"And wait till Tenebræ begin;
"Walk to the Third Confessional,
"Between the pillar and the wall,
"And kneeling whisper *whence comes peace*?
"Say it a second time; then cease;
"And if the voice inside returns,
"*From Christ and Freedom; what concerns*
"*The cause of Peace*?—for answer, slip
"My letter where you placed your lip;
"Then come back happy we have done
"Our mother service—I, the son,
"As you the daughter of our land!"

Three mornings more, she took her stand
In the same place, with the same eyes:
I was no surer of sun-rise
Than of her coming: we conferred
Of her own prospects, and I heard
She had a lover—stout and tall,
She said—then let her eyelids fall,
"He could do much"—as if some doubt
Entered her heart,—then, passing out,
"She could not speak for others—who
"Had other thoughts; herself she knew:"
And so she brought me drink and food.
After four days the scouts pursued
Another path: at last arrived
The help my Paduan friends contrived
To furnish me: she brought the news:
For the first time I could not choose
But kiss her hand and lay my own
Upon her head—"This faith was shown
"To Italy, our mother;—she
"Uses my hand and blesses thee!"
She followed down to the sea-shore;
I left and never saw her more.

How very long since I have thought
Concerning—much less wished for—aught
Beside the good of Italy
For which I live and mean to die!
In love I never was; and since
Charles proved false, nothing could convince
My inmost heart I had a friend;
However, if I pleased to spend
Real wishes on myself—say, Three—
I know at least what one should be;
I would grasp Metternich until
I felt his red wet throat distil
In blood thro' these two hands: and next,
—Nor much for that am I perplexed—
Charles, perjured traitor, for his part,
Should die slow of a broken heart
Under his new employers—last
—Ah, there, what should I wish? For fast
Do I grow old and out of strength;
If I resolved to seek at length
My father's house again, how scared
They all would look, and unprepared!
My brothers live in Austria's pay
—Disowned me long ago, men say;
And all my early mates who used
To praise me so—perhaps induced
More than one early step of mine—
Are turning wise; while part opine
"Freedom grows License," part suspect
"Haste breeds Delay," and recollect
They always said such premature
Beginnings never could endure:
So, with a sullen "All's for best,"
The land seems settling to its rest.
I think, then, I should wish to stand
This evening in that dear, lost land,
Over the sea the thousand miles,
And know if yet that woman smiles
With the calm smile—some little farm
She lives in there, no doubt—what harm
If I sate on the door-side bench,

And, while her spindle made a trench
Fantastically in the dust,
Inquired of all her fortunes—just
Her children's ages and their names,
And what may be the husband's aims
For each of them—I'd talk this out,
And sit there, for an hour about,
Then kiss her hand once more, and lay
Mine on her head, and go my way.

So much for idle wishing—how
It steals the time! To business now!

[*The Englishman in Italy*]
England in Italy

(PIANO DI SORRENTO).

Fortù, Fortù, my loved one,
Sit by my side,
On my knees put up both little feet!
I was sure, if I tried,
I could make you laugh spite of Scirocco:
Now, open your eyes—
Let me keep you amused till he vanish
In black from the skies,
With telling my memories over
As you tell your beads;
All the Plain saw me gather, I garland
—Flowers prove they, or weeds.

'Twas time, for your long hot dry Autumn
Had net-worked with brown
The white skin of each grape on the bunches,
Marked like a quail's crown,
Those creatures you make such account of,
Whose heads,—specked with white
Over brown like a great spider's back,
As I told you last night,—
Your mother bites off for her supper;

Red-ripe as could be,
Pomegranates were chapping and splitting
In halves on the tree:
And 'twixt the loose walls of great flintstone,
Or in the thick dust
On the path, or straight out of the rock side,
Wherever could thrust
Some starved sprig of bold hardy rock-flower
Its yellow face up,
For the prize were great butterflies fighting,
Some five for one cup:
So I guessed, ere I got up this morning,
What change was in store,
By the quick rustle-down of the quail-nets
Which woke me before
I could open my shutter, made fast
With a bough and a stone,
And look thro' the twisted dead vine-twigs,
Sole lattice that's known;
Sharp rang the rings down the bird-poles
While, busy beneath,
Your priest and his brother were working,
The rain in their teeth.
And out upon all the flat house-roofs
Where split figs lay drying,
The girls took the frails under cover:
Nor use seemed in trying
To get out the boats and go fishing,
For under the cliff,
Fierce the black water frothed o'er the blind-rock—
No seeing our skiff
Arrive about noon from Amalfi,
—Our fisher arrive,
And pitch down his basket before us,
All trembling alive
With pink and grey jellies, your sea-fruit,
—Touch the strange lumps,
And mouths gape there, eyes open, all manner
Of horns and of humps,
Which only the fisher looks grave at,
While round him like imps

Cling screaming the children as naked
  And brown as his shrimps,
Himself too as bare to the middle
  —You see round his neck
The string and its brass coin suspended,
  That saves him from wreck.
But to-day not a boat reached Salerno,
  So back to a man
Came our friends, with whose help in the vineyards
  Grape-harvest began:
In the vat half-way up in our house-side,
  Like blood the juice spins
While your brother all bare-legged is dancing
  Till breathless he grins
Dead-beaten, in effort on effort
  To keep the grapes under,
For still when he seems all but master
  In pours the fresh plunder
From girls who keep coming and going
  With basket on shoulder,
And eyes shut against the rain's driving,
  Your girls that are older,—
For under the hedges of aloe,
  And where, on its bed
Of the orchard's black mould, the love-apple
  Lies pulpy and red,
All the young ones are kneeling and filling
  Their laps with the snails
Tempted out by this first rainy weather,—
  Your best of regales,
As to-night will be proved to my sorrow,
  When, supping in state,
We shall feast our grape-gleaners—two dozen,
  Three over one plate,—
Maccaroni so tempting to swallow
  In slippery strings,
And gourds fried in great purple slices,
  That colour of kings,—
Meantime, see the grape-bunch they've brought you,—
  The rain-water slips
O'er the heavy blue bloom on each globe

Which the wasp to your lips
Still follows with fretful persistence—
Nay, taste while awake,
This half of a curd-white smooth cheese-ball
That peels, flake by flake,
Like an onion's, each smoother and whiter—
Next sip this weak wine
From the thin green glass flask, with its stopper,
A leaf of the vine,—
And end with the prickly-pear's red flesh
That leaves thro' its juice
The stony black seeds on your pearl-teeth.
. . . Scirocco is loose!
Hark! the quick pelt of the olives
Which, thick in one's track,
Tempt the stranger to pick up and bite them
Tho' not yet half black!
And how their old twisted trunks shudder!
The medlars let fall
Their hard fruit—and brittle great fig-trees
Snap off, figs and all,
For here comes the whole of the tempest!
No refuge but creep
Back again to my side and my shoulder,
And listen or sleep.

O how will your country show next week,
When all the vine-boughs
Have been stripped of their foliage to pasture
The mules and the cows?
Last eve I rode over the mountains—
Your brother, my guide,
Soon left me to feast on the myrtles
That offered, each side,
Their fruit-balls, black, glossy and luscious,
Or strip from the sorbs
A treasure, so rosy and wondrous,
Those hairy gold orbs!
But my mule picked his sure, sober path out,
Just stopping to neigh
When he recognised down in the valley

His mates on their way
With the faggots, and barrels of water;
And soon we emerged
From the plain where the woods could scarce follow
And still as we urged
Our way, the woods wondered, and left us,
As up still we trudged
Though the wild path grew wilder each instant,
And place was e'en grudged
'Mid the rock-chasms, and piles of loose stones
Like the loose broken teeth
Of some monster, which climbed there to die
From the ocean beneath—
Place was grudged to the silver-grey fume-weed
That clung to the path,
And dark rosemary ever a-dying,
That, 'spite the wind's wrath,
So loves the salt rock's face to seaward,—
And lentisks as staunch
To the stone where they root and bear berries,
And—what shows a branch
Coral-coloured, transparent, with circlets
Of pale seagreen leaves—
Over all trod my mule with the caution
Of gleaners o'er sheaves:
Foot after foot like a lady—
So, round after round,
He climbed to the top of Calvano,
And God's own profound
Was above me, and round me the mountains,
And under, the sea,
And with me, my heart to bear witness
What was and shall be!
Oh heaven, and the terrible crystal!
No rampart excludes
Your eye from the life to be lived
In the blue solitudes!
Oh, those mountains, their infinite movement!
Still moving with you—
For ever some new head and breast of them
Thrusts into view

To observe the intruder—you see it
  If quickly you turn
And, before they escape you, surprise them—
  They grudge you should learn
How the soft plains they look on, lean over,
  And love, they pretend,
—Cower beneath them—the flat sea-pine crouches,
  The wild fruit-trees bend,
E'en the myrtle-leaves curl, shrink and shut—
  All is silent and grave—
'Tis a sensual and timorous beauty—
  How fair, but a slave!
So I turned to the sea,—and there slumbered
  As greenly as ever
Those isles of the syren, your Galli;
  No ages can sever
The Three—nor enable their sister
  To join them,—half way
On the voyage, she looked at Ulysses—
  No farther to-day,
Tho' the small one, just launched in the wave,
  Watches breast-high and steady
From under the rock, her bold sister
  Swum half-way already.
Oh when shall we sail there together
  And see from the sides
Quite new rocks show their faces—new haunts
  Where the syren abides?
Oh, to sail round and round them, close over
  The rocks, tho' unseen,
That ruffle the grey glassy water
  To glorious green,—
Then scramble from splinter to splinter,
  Reach land and explore
On the largest, the strange square black turret
  With never a door—
Just a loop to admit the quick lizards;
  —To stand there and hear
The birds' quiet singing, that tells us
  What life is, so clear;
The secret they sang to Ulysses,

When ages ago
He heard and he knew this life's secret
I hear and I know!

Ah see! O'er Calvano the sun breaks:
He strikes the great gloom
And flutters it over his summit
In airy gold fume!
All is over. Look out, see the gypsy,
Our tinker and smith,
Has arrived, set up bellows and forge,
And down-squatted forthwith
To his hammering, under the wall there;
One eye keeps aloof
The urchins that itch to be putting
His jews'-harps to proof,
While the other thro' locks of curled wire
Is watching how sleek
Shines the hog, come to share in the windfalls
—An abbot's own cheek!
All is over! wake up and come out now,
And down let us go,
And see all the fine things set in order
At church for the show
Of the Sacrament, set forth this evening;
To-morrow's the Feast
Of the Rosary's virgin, by no means
Of virgins the least—
As we'll hear in the off-hand discourse
Which (all nature, no art)
The Dominican brother these three weeks
Was getting by heart.
Not a post nor a pillar but's dizened
With red and blue papers;
All the roof waves with ribbons, each altar's
A-blaze with long tapers;
But the great masterpiece is the scaffold
Rigged glorious to hold
All the fiddlers and fifers and drummers,
And trumpeters bold,
Not afraid of Bellini nor Auber,

Who, when the priest's hoarse,
Will strike us up something that's brisk
For the feast's second course.
And then will the flaxen-wigged Image
Be carried in pomp
Thro' the plain, while in gallant procession
The priests mean to stomp.
All round the glad church stand old bottles
With gunpowder stopped,
Which will be, when the Image re-enters,
Religiously popped.
And at night from the crest of Calvano
Great bonfires will hang,
On the plain will the trumpets join chorus,
And more poppers bang!
At all events, come—to the garden,
As far as the wall,
See me tap with a hoe on the plaster
Till out there shall fall
A scorpion with wide angry nippers!

. . . "Such trifles!" you say?
Fortù, in my England at home,
Men meet gravely to-day
And debate, if abolishing Corn-laws
Be righteous and wise
—If 'tis proper Scirocco should vanish
In black from the skies!

The Lost Leader

I.

Just for a handful of silver he left us,
Just for a riband to stick in his coat—
Got the one gift of which fortune bereft us,
Lost all the others she lets us devote;
They, with the gold to give, doled him out silver,
So much was their's who so little allowed:
How all our copper had gone for his service!
Rags—were they purple his heart had been proud!

We that had loved him so, followed him, honoured him,
  Lived in his mild and magnificent eye,
Learned his great language, caught his clear accents,
  Made him our pattern to live and to die!
Shakespeare was of us, Milton was for us,
  Burns, Shelley, were with us,—they watch from their graves!
He alone breaks from the van and the freemen,
  He alone sinks to the rear and the slaves!

II.

We shall march prospering,—not thro' his presence;
  Songs may excite us,—not from his lyre;
Deeds will be done,—while he boasts his quiescence,
  Still bidding crouch whom the rest bade aspire:
Blot out his name, then,—record one lost soul more,
  One task unaccepted, one footpath untrod,
One more devils'-triumph and sorrow to angels,
  One wrong more to man, one more insult to God!
Life's night begins: let him never come back to us!
  There would be doubt, hesitation and pain,
Forced praise on our part—the glimmer of twilight,
  Never glad confident morning again!
Best fight on well, for we taught him,—come gallantly,
  Strike our face hard ere we shatter his own;
Then let him get the new knowledge and wait us,
  Pardoned in Heaven, the first by the throne!

Home-Thoughts, from Abroad

I.

Oh, to be in England
Now that April's there,
And who wakes in England
Sees, some morning, unaware,
That the lowest boughs and the brush-wood sheaf
Round the elm-tree bole are in tiny leaf,
While the chaffinch sings on the orchard bough
In England—now!

And after April, when May follows,
And the whitethroat builds, and all the swallows—
Hark! where my blossomed pear-tree in the hedge
Leans to the field and scatters on the clover
Blossoms and dewdrops—at the bent spray's edge—
That's the wise thrush; he sings each song twice over
Lest you should think he never could recapture
The first fine careless rapture!
And though the fields look rough with hoary dew,
All will be gay when noontide wakes anew
The buttercups, the little children's dower,
—Far brighter than this gaudy melon-flower!

III.

[*Home-Thoughts, from the Sea*]

Nobly Cape Saint Vincent to the north-west died away;
Sunset ran, one glorious blood-red, reeking into Cadiz Bay;
Bluish mid the burning water, full in face Trafalgar lay;
In the dimmest north-east distance, dawned Gibralter grand and gray;
"Here and here did England help me,—how can I help England?"—say,
Whoso turns as I, this evening, turn to God to praise and pray,
Yonder where Jove's planet rises silent over Africa.

Saul [sections 1–9]

Said Abner, "At last thou art come!
"Ere I tell, ere thou speak,—
"Kiss my cheek, wish me well!" Then I wished it,
And did kiss his cheek:
And he, "Since the King, oh my friend,
"For thy countenance sent,
"Nor drunken nor eaten have we;
"Nor, until from his tent
"Thou return with the joyful assurance
"The king liveth yet,
"Shall our lip with the honey be brightened,
"—The water, be wet.

"For out of the black mid-tent's silence,
  "A space of three days,
"No sound hath escaped to thy servants,
  "Of prayer nor of praise,
"To betoken that Saul and the Spirit
  "Have gone their dread ways.

"Yet now my heart leaps, O beloved!
  "God's child with his dew
"On thy gracious gold hair, and those lilies
  "Still living and blue
"As thou brak'st them to twine round thy harp-strings,
  "As if no wild heat
"Were raging to torture the desert!"
  Then I, as was meet,
Knelt down to the God of my fathers,
  And rose on my feet,
And ran o'er the sand burnt to powder.
  The tent was unlooped;
I pulled up the spear that obstructed,
  And under I stooped;
Hands and knees o'er the slippery grass-patch—
  All withered and gone—
That leads to the second enclosure,
  I groped my way on,
Till I felt where the foldskirts fly open;
  Then once more I prayed,
And opened the foldskirts and entered,
  And was not afraid;
And spoke, "Here is David, thy servant!"
  And no voice replied;
And first I saw nought but the blackness;
  But soon I descried
A something more black than the blackness
  —The vast, the upright
Main prop which sustains the pavilion,—
  And slow into sight
Grew a figure, gigantic, against it,
  And blackest of all;—
Then a sunbeam, that burst thro' the tent-roof,
  Showed Saul.

He stood as erect as that tent-prop;
  Both arms stretched out wide
On the great cross-support in the centre
  That goes to each side:
So he bent not a muscle but hung there
  As, caught in his pangs
And waiting his change the king-serpent
  All heavily hangs,
Far away from his kind, in the Pine,
  Till deliverance come
With the Spring-time,—so agonized Saul,
  Drear and stark, blind and dumb.

Then I tuned my harp,—took off the lilies
  We twine round its chords
Lest they snap 'neath the stress of the noontide
  —Those sunbeams like swords!
And I first played the tune all our sheep know,
  As, one after one,
So docile they come to the pen-door
  Till folding be done.
—They are white and untorn by the bushes
  For lo, they have fed
Where the long grasses stifle the water
  Within the stream's bed;
How one after one seeks its lodging,
  As star follows star
Into eve and the blue far above us,
  —So blue and so far!

Then the tune for which quails on the cornland
  Will each leave his mate
To follow the player; then, what makes
  The crickets elate,
Till for boldness they fight one another:
  And then, what has weight
To set the quick jerboa a-musing
  Outside his sand house
—There are none such as he for a wonder—
  Half bird and half mouse!—
—God made all the creatures and gave them

Our love and our fear,
To show, we and they are his children,
One family here.

Then I played the help-tune of our Reapers,
Their wine-song, when hand
Grasps hand, eye lights eye in good friendship,
And great hearts expand,
And grow one in the sense of this world's life;
And then, the low song
When the dead man is praised on his journey—
"Bear, bear him along
"With his few faults shut up like dead flowrets;
"Are balm-seeds not here
"To console us? The land has got none such
"As he on the bier—
Oh, would we might keep thee, my brother!"
And then, the glad chaunt
Of the marriage,—first go the young maidens—
Next, she whom we vaunt
As the beauty, the pride of our dwelling:
And then, the great march
When man runs to man to assist him
And buttress an arch
Nought can break . . who shall harm them, our brothers?
Then, the chorus intoned
As the Levites go up to the altar
In glory enthroned—
But I stopped here—for here in the darkness,
Saul groaned:

And I paused, held my breath in such silence!
And listened apart—
And the tent shook, for mighty Saul shuddered,—
And sparkles 'gan dart
From the jewels that woke in his turban
—At once with a start
All its lordly male-sapphires, and rubies
Courageous at heart;
So the head, but the body still moved not,—
Still hung there erect.

And I bent once again to my playing,
  Pursued it unchecked,
As I sang, "Oh, our manhood's prime vigour!
  "—No spirit feels waste,
"No muscle is stopped in its playing
  "No sinew unbraced.—
"And the wild joys of living! The leaping
  "From rock up to rock—
"The rending their boughs from the palm-trees,—
  "The cool silver shock
"Of the plunge in a pool's living water,—
  "The hunt of the bear,
"And the sultriness showing the lion
  "Is couched in his lair:
"And the meal—the rich dates—yellowed over
  "With gold dust divine,
"And the locust's-flesh steeped in the pitcher—
  "The full draught of wine,
"And the sleep in the dried river channel
  "Where tall rushes tell
"The water was wont to go warbling
  "So softly and well,—
"How good is man's life, mere living!
  "How fit to employ
"The heart and the soul and the senses
  "For ever in joy!
"Hast thou loved the white locks of thy father
  "Whose sword thou didst guard
"When he trusted thee forth to the wolf hunt
  "For glorious reward?
"Didst thou see the thin hands of thy mother
  "Held up, as men sung
"The song of the nearly-departed,
  "And heard her faint tongue
"Joining in while it could to the witness
  ""Let one more attest,
""I have lived, seen God's hand thro' that life-time,
  ""And all was for best…"
"Then they sung thro' their tears, in strong triumph,
  "Not much,—but the rest!
"And thy brothers—the help and the contest,

"The working whence grew
"Such result, as from seething grape-bundles
"The spirit so true—
"And the friends of thy boyhood—that boyhood
"With wonder and hope,
"And the promise and wealth in the future,—
"The eye's eagle scope,—
"Till lo, thou art grown to a monarch,
"A people is thine!
"Oh all, all the world offers singly,
"On one head combine,
"On one head the joy and the pride,
"Even rage like the throe
"That opes the rock, helps its glad labour,
"And lets the gold go—
"And ambition that sees a sun lead it
"Oh, all of these—all
"Combine to unite in one creature
"—Saul!"

(*End of Part the First.*)

FROM *LETTERS OF PERCY BYSSHE SHELLEY* (1852)

Introductory Essay [*Dec.* 1851]

An opportunity having presented itself for the acquisition of a series of unedited letters by Shelley, all more or less directly supplementary to and illustrative of the collection already published by Mr. Moxon, that gentleman has decided on securing them. They will prove an acceptable addition to a body of correspondence, the value of which towards a right understanding of its author's purpose and work, may be said to exceed that of any similar contribution exhibiting the worldly relations of a poet whose genius has operated by a different law.

Doubtless we accept gladly the biography of an objective poet, as the phrase now goes; one whose endeavour has been to reproduce things external (whether the phenomena of the scenic universe, or the manifested action of the human heart and brain) with an immediate reference, in every case, to the common eye and apprehension of his fellow men, assumed capable of receiving and profiting by this reproduction. It has been obtained through the poet's double faculty of seeing external objects more clearly, widely, and deeply, than is possible to the average mind, at the same time that he is so acquainted and in sympathy with its narrower comprehension as to be careful to supply it with no other materials than it can combine into an intelligible whole. The auditory of such a poet will include, not only the intelligences which, save for such assistance, would have missed the deeper meaning and enjoyment of the original objects, but also the spirits of a like endowment with his own, who, by means of his abstract, can forthwith pass to the reality it was made from, and either corroborate their impressions of things known already, or supply themselves with new from whatever shows in the inexhaustible variety of existence may have hitherto escaped their knowledge. Such a poet is properly the ποιητης, the fashioner; and the thing fashioned, his poetry, will of necessity be substantive, projected from himself and distinct. We are ignorant what the inventor of "Othello" conceived of that fact as he beheld it in completeness, how he accounted for it, under what known law he registered its nature, or to what unknown law he traced its coincidence. We learn only what he intended we should learn by that particular exercise of his power,—the fact itself,—which, with its infinite significances, each of us receives for the first time as a creation, and is hereafter left to deal with, as, in proportion to his own intelligence, he best may. We are ignorant, and would fain be otherwise.

Doubtless, with respect to such a poet, we covet his biography. We desire to look back upon the process of gathering together in a lifetime, the materials of the work we behold entire; of elaborating, perhaps under difficulty and with hindrance, all that is familiar to our admiration in the apparent facility of success. And the inner impulse of this effort and operation, what induced it? Did a soul's delight in its own extended sphere of vision set it, for the gratification of an insuppressible power, on labour, as other men are set on rest? Or did a sense of duty or of love lead it to communicate its own sensations to mankind? Did an irresistible sympathy with men compel it to bring down and suit its own provision of knowledge and beauty to their narrow scope ? Did the personality of such an one stand like an open watch-tower in the midst of the territory it is erected to gaze on, and were the storms and calms, the stars and meteors, its watchman was wont to report of, the habitual variegation of his every-day life, as they glanced across its open roof or lay reflected on its four-square parapet? Or did some sunken and darkened chamber of imagery witness, in the artificial illumination of every storied compartment we are permitted to contemplate, how rare and precious were the outlooks through here and there an embrasure upon a world beyond, and how blankly would have pressed on the artificer the boundary of his daily life, except for the amorous diligence with which he had rendered permanent by art whatever came to diversify the gloom? Still, fraught with instruction and interest as such details undoubtedly are, we can, if needs be, dispense with them. The man passes, the work remains. The work speaks for itself, as we say: and the biography of the worker is no more necessary to an understanding or enjoyment of it, than is a model or anatomy of some tropical tree, to the right tasting of the fruit we are familiar with on the market-stall,—or a geologist's map and stratification, to the prompt recognition of the hill-top, our land-mark of every day.

We turn with stronger needs to the genius of an opposite tendency—the subjective poet of modern classification. He, gifted like the objective poet with the fuller perception of nature and man, is impelled to embody the thing he perceives, not so much with reference to the many below as to the one above him, the supreme Intelligence which apprehends all things in their absolute truth,—an ultimate view ever aspired to, if but partially attained, by the poet's own soul. Not what man sees, but what God sees—the *Ideas* of Plato, seeds of creation lying burningly on the Divine Hand—it is toward these that he struggles. Not with the combination of humanity in action, but with the primal elements of humanity he has to do; and he digs where he stands,—preferring to seek them in his own soul as the nearest reflex of that absolute Mind, according to the intuitions of which he desires to perceive and speak. Such a poet does not deal habitually with the picturesque groupings and tempestuous tossings of the forest-trees, but with their roots and fibres naked to the chalk and stone. He does not paint pictures and hang them on the walls, but rather carries them on the retina of his own eyes: we must look deep into his human eyes, to see those pictures on them. He is rather a seer, accordingly, than a fashioner, and what he produces will be less a work than an effluence. That effluence cannot be easily considered in abstraction from his personality,—being indeed the very radiance and aroma of his personality, projected from it but not separated. Therefore, in our approach to the poetry, we necessarily approach the personality of the poet; in apprehending it we apprehend him, and certainly we cannot love it without loving him. Both for love's and for understanding's sake we desire to know him, and as readers of his poetry must be readers of his biography also.

I shall observe, in passing, that it seems not so much from any essential distinction in the faculty of the two poets or in the nature of the objects contemplated by either, as in the more immediate adaptability of these objects to the distinct purpose of each, that the objective poet, in his appeal to the aggregate human mind, chooses to deal with the doings of men, (the result of which dealing, in its pure form, when even description, as suggesting a describer, is dispensed with, is what we call dramatic poetry), while the subjective poet, whose study has been himself, appealing through himself to the absolute Divine mind, prefers to dwell upon those external scenic appearances which strike out most abundantly and uninterruptedly his inner light and power, selects that silence of the earth and sea in which he can best hear the beating of his individual heart, and leaves the noisy, complex, yet imperfect exhibitions of nature in the manifold experience of man around him, which serve only to distract and suppress the working of his brain. These opposite tendencies of genius will be more readily descried in their artistic effect than in their moral spring and cause. Pushed to an extreme and manifested as a deformity, they will be seen plainest of all in the fault of either artist, when subsidiarily to the human interest of his work his occasional illustrations from scenic nature are introduced as in the earlier works of the originative painters—men and women filling the foreground with consummate mastery, while mountain, grove and rivulet show like an anticipatory revenge on that succeeding race of landscape-painters whose "figures" disturb the perfection of their earth and sky. It would be idle to inquire, of these two kinds of poetic faculty in operation, which is the higher or even rarer endowment. If the subjective might seem to be the ultimate requirement of every age, the objective, in the strictest state, must still retain its original value. For it is with this world, as starting point and basis alike, that we shall always have to concern ourselves: the world is not to be learned and thrown aside, but reverted to and relearned. The spiritual comprehension may be infinitely subtilised, but the raw material it operates upon, must remain. There may be no end of the poets who communicate to us what they see in an object with reference to their own individuality; what it was before they saw it, in reference to the aggregate human mind, will be as desirable to know as ever. Nor is there any reason why these two modes of poetic faculty may not issue hereafter from the same poet in successive perfect works, examples of which, according to what are now considered the exigences of art, we have hitherto possessed in distinct individuals only. A mere running-in of the one faculty upon the other, is, of course, the ordinary circumstance. Far more rarely it happens that either is found so decidedly prominent and superior, as to be pronounced comparatively pure: while of the perfect shield, with the gold and the silver side set up for all comers to challenge, there has yet been no instance. Either faculty in its eminent state is doubtless conceded by Providence as a best gift to men, according to their especial want. There is a time when the general eye has, so to speak, absorbed its fill of the phenomena around it, whether spiritual or material, and desires rather to learn the exacter significance of what it possesses, than to receive any augmentation of what is possessed. Then is the opportunity for the poet of loftier vision, to lift his fellows, with their half-apprehensions, up to his own sphere, by intensifying the import of details and rounding the universal meaning. The influence of such an achievement will not soon die out. A tribe of successors (Homerides) working more or less in the same spirit, dwell on his discoveries and reinforce his doctrine; till, at unawares, the world is found to be subsisting wholly on the shadow of a reality, on sentiments diluted from passions, on the tradition of a fact, the convention of a moral, the straw of last year's harvest. Then is the imperative call for the appearance of another sort of poet, who shall at once replace this intellectual rumination of food swallowed long ago, by a supply of the fresh and living swathe; getting at new substance by breaking the assumed wholes into parts of independent and unclassed value, careless of the unknown laws for recombining them (it will be the business of yet another poet to suggest those hereafter), prodigal of objects for men's outer and not inner sight, shaping for their uses a new and different creation from the last, which it displaces by the right of life over death,—to endure until, in the inevitable process, its very sufficiency to itself shall require, at length, an exposition of its affinity to something higher,—when the positive yet conflicting facts shall again precipitate themselves under a harmonising law, and one more degree will be apparent for a poet to climb in that mighty ladder, of which, however cloud-involved and undefined may glimmer the topmost step, the world dares no longer doubt that its gradations ascend.

Such being the two kinds of artists, it is naturally, as I have shown, with the biography of the subjective poet that we have the deeper concern. Apart from his recorded life altogether, we might fail to determine with satisfactory precision to what class his productions belong, and what amount of praise is assignable to the producer. Certainly, in the face of any conspicuous achievement of genius, philosophy, no less than sympathetic instinct, warrants our belief in a great moral purpose having mainly inspired even where it does not visibly look out of the same. Greatness in a work suggests an adequate instrumentality; and none of the lower incitements, however they may avail to initiate or even effect many considerable displays of power, simulating the nobler inspiration to which they are mistakenly referred, have been found able, under the ordinary conditions of humanity, to task themselves to the end of so exacting a performance as a poet's complete work. As soon will the galvanism, that provokes to violent action the muscles of a corpse, induce it to cross the chamber steadily: sooner. The love of displaying power for the display's sake, the love of riches, of distinction, of notoriety,—the desire of a triumph over rivals, and the vanity in the applause of friends,—each and all of such whetted appetites grow intenser by exercise and increasingly sagacious as to the best and readiest means of self-appeasement,—while for any of their ends, whether the money or the pointed finger of the crowd, or the flattery and hate to heart's content, there are cheaper prices to pay, they will all find soon enough, than the bestowment of a life upon a labour, hard, slow, and not sure. Also, assuming the proper moral aim to have produced a work, there are many and various states of an aim: it may be more intense than clear-sighted, or too easily satisfied with a lower field of activity than a steadier aspiration would reach. All the bad poetry in the world (accounted poetry, that is, by its affinities) will be found to result from some one of the infinite degrees of discrepancy between the attributes of the poet's soul, occasioning a want of correspondency between his work and the verities of nature,—issuing in poetry, false under whatever form, which shows a thing not as it is to mankind generally, nor as it is to the particular describer, but as it is supposed to be for some unreal neutral mood, midway between both and of value to neither, and living its brief minute simply through the indolence of whoever accepts it or his incapacity to denounce a cheat. Although of such depths of failure there can be no question here, we must in every case betake ourselves to the review of a poet's life ere we determine some of the nicer questions concerning his poetry,—more especially if the performance we seek to estimate aright, has been obstructed and cut short of completion by circumstances,—a disastrous youth or a premature death. We may learn from the biography whether his spirit invariably saw and spoke from the last height to which it had attained. An absolute vision is not for this world, but we are permitted a continual approximation to it, every degree of which in the individual, provided it exceed the attainment of the masses, must procure him a clear advantage. Did the poet ever attain to a higher platform than where he rested and exhibited a result? Did he know more than he spoke of ?

I concede however, in respect to the subject of our study as well as some few other illustrious examples, that the unmistakeable quality of the verse would be evidence enough, under usual circumstances, not only of the kind and degree of the intellectual but of the moral constitution of Shelley: the whole personality of the poet shining forward from the poems, without much need of going further to seek it. The "Remains"—produced within a period of ten years, and at a season of life when other men of at all comparable genius have hardly done more than prepare the eye for future sight and the tongue for speech—present us with the complete enginery of a poet, as signal in the excellence of its several adaptitudes as transcendent in the combination of effects,—examples, in fact, of the whole poet's function of beholding with an understanding keenness the universe, nature and man, in their actual state of perfection in imperfection,—of the whole poet's virtue of being untempted by the manifold partial developments of beauty and good on every side, into leaving them the ultimates he found them,—induced by the facility of the gratification of his own sense of those qualities, or by the pleasure of acquiescence in the shortcomings of his predecessors in art, and the pain of disturbing their conventionalisms,—the whole poet's virtue, I repeat, of looking higher than any manifestation yet made of both beauty and good, in order to suggest from the utmost actual realisation of the one a corresponding capability in the other, and out of the calm, purity and energy of nature, to reconstitute and store up for the forthcoming stage of man's being, a gift in repayment of that former gift, in which man's own thought and passion had been lavished by the poet on the else-incompleted magnificence of the sunrise, the else-uninterpreted mystery of the lake,—so drawing out, lifting up, and assimilating this ideal of a future man, thus descried as possible, to the present reality of the poet's soul already arrived at the higher state of development, and still aspirant to elevate and extend itself in conformity with its still-improving perceptions of, no longer the eventual Human, but the actual Divine. In conjunction with which noble and rare powers, came the subordinate power of delivering these attained results to the world in an embodiment of verse more closely answering to and indicative of the process of the informing spirit, (failing as it occasionally does, in art, only to succeed in highest art),—with a diction more adequate to the task in its natural and acquired richness, its material colour and spiritual transparency,—the whole being moved by and suffused with a music at once of the soul and the sense, expressive both of an external might of sincere passion and an internal fitness and consonancy,—than can be attributed to any other writer whose record is among us. Such was the spheric poetical faculty of Shelley, as its own self-sufficing central light, radiating equally through immaturity and accomplishment, through many fragments and occasional completion, reveals it to a competent judgment.

But the acceptance of this truth by the public, has been retarded by certain objections which cast us back on the evidence of biography, even with Shelley's poetry in our hands. Except for the particular character of these objections, indeed, the non-appreciation of his contemporaries would simply class, now that it is over, with a series of experiences which have necessarily happened and needlessly been wondered at, ever since the world began, and concerning which any present anger may well be moderated, no less in justice to our forerunners than in policy to ourselves. For the misapprehensiveness of his age is exactly what a poet is sent to remedy; and the interval between his operation and the generally perceptible effect of it, is no greater, less indeed, than in many other departments of the great human effort. The "E pur si muove" of the astronomer was as bitter a word as any uttered before or since by a poet over his rejected living work, in that depth of conviction which is so like despair.

But in this respect was the experience of Shelley peculiarly unfortunate—that the disbelief in him as a man, even preceded the disbelief in him as a writer; the misconstruction of his moral nature preparing the way for the misappreciation of his intellectual labours. There existed from the beginning,—simultaneous with, indeed anterior to his earliest noticeable works, and not brought forward to counteract any impression they had succeeded in making,—certain charges against his private character and life, which, if substantiated to their whole breadth, would materially disturb, I do not attempt to deny, our reception and enjoyment of his works, however wonderful the artistic qualities of these. For we are not sufficiently supplied with instances of genius of his order, to be able to pronounce certainly how many of its constituent parts have been tasked and strained to the production of a given lie, and how high and pure a mood of the creative mind may be dramatically simulated as the poet's habitual and exclusive one. The doubts, therefore, arising from such a question, required to be set at rest, as they were effectually, by those early authentic notices of Shelley's career and the corroborative accompaniment of his letters, in which not only the main tenor and principal result of his life, but the purity and beauty of many of the processes which had conduced to them, were made apparent enough for the general reader's purpose,—whoever lightly condemned Shelley first, on the evidence of reviews and gossip, as lightly acquitting him now, on that of memoirs and correspondence. Still, it is advisable to lose no opportunity of strengthening and completing the chain of biographical testimony; much more, of course, for the sake of the poet's original lovers, whose volunteered sacrifice of particular principle in favour of absorbing sympathy we might desire to dispense with, than for the sake of his foolish haters, who have long since diverted upon other objects their obtuseness or malignancy. A full life of Shelley should be written at once, while the materials for it continue in reach; not to minister to the curiosity of the public, but to obliterate the last stain of that false life which was forced on the public's attention before it had any curiosity on the matter,—a biography, composed in harmony with the present general disposition to have faith in him, yet not shrinking from a candid statement of all ambiguous passages, through a reasonable confidence that the most doubtful of them will be found consistent with a belief in the eventual perfection of his character, according to the poor limits of our humanity. Nor will men persist in confounding, any more than God confounds, with genuine infidelity and an atheism of the heart, those passionate, impatient struggles of a boy towards distant truth and love, made in the dark, and ended by one sweep of the natural seas before the full moral sunrise could shine out on him. Crude convictions of boyhood, conveyed in imperfect and inapt forms of speech,—for such things all boys have been pardoned. There are growing-pains, accompanied by temporary distortion, of the soul also. And it would be hard indeed upon this young Titan of genius, murmuring in divine music his human ignorances, through his very thirst for knowledge, and his rebellion, in mere aspiration to law, if the melody itself substantiated the error, and the tragic cutting short of life perpetuated into sins, such faults as, under happier circumstances, would have been left behind by the consent of the most arrogant moralist, forgotten on the lowest steps of youth.

The responsibility of presenting to the public a biography of Shelley, does not, however, lie with me: I have only to make it a little easier by arranging these few supplementary letters, with a recognition of the value of the whole collection. This value I take to consist in a most truthful conformity of the Correspondence, in its limited degree, with the moral and intellectual character of the writer as displayed in the highest manifestations of his genius. Letters and poems are obviously an act of the same mind, produced by the same law, only differing in the application to the individual or collective understanding. Letters and poems may be used indifferently as the basement of our opinion upon the writer's character; the finished expression of a sentiment in the poems, giving light and significance to the rudiments of the same in the letters, and these, again, in their incipiency and unripeness, authenticating the exalted mood and reattaching it to the personality of the writer. The musician speaks on the note he sings with; there is no change in the scale, as he diminishes the volume into familiar intercourse. There is nothing of that jarring between the man and the author, which has been found so amusing or so melancholy; no dropping of the tragic mask, as the crowd melts away; no mean discovery of the real motives of a life's achievement, often, in other lives, laid bare as pitifully as when, at the close of a holiday, we catch sight of the internal lead-pipes and wood-valves, to which, and not to the ostensible conch and dominant Triton of the fountain, we have owed our admired waterwork. No breaking out, in household privacy, of hatred, anger and scorn, incongruous with the higher mood and suppressed artistically in the book: no brutal return to self-delighting, when the audience of philanthropic schemes is out of hearing: no indecent stripping off the grander feeling and rule of life as too costly and cumbrous for every-day wear. Whatever Shelley was, he was with an admirable sincerity. It was not always truth that he thought and spoke; but in the purity of truth he spoke and thought always. Everywhere is apparent his belief in the existence of Good, to which Evil is an accident; his faithful holding by what he assumed to be the former, going everywhere in company with the tenderest pity for those acting or suffering on the opposite hypothesis. For he was tender, though tenderness is not always the characteristic of very sincere natures; he was eminently both tender and sincere. And not only do the same affection and yearning after the well-being of his kind, appear in the letters as in the poems, but they express themselves by the same theories and plans, however crude and unsound. There is no reservation of a subtler, less costly, more serviceable remedy for his own ill, than he has proposed for the general one; nor does he ever contemplate an object on his own account, from a less elevation than he uses in exhibiting it to the world. How shall we help believing Shelley to have been, in his ultimate attainment, the splendid spirit of his own best poetry, when we find even his carnal speech to agree faithfully, at faintest as at strongest, with the tone and rhythm of his most oracular utterances?

For the rest, these new letters are not offered as presenting any new feature of the poet's character. Regarded in themselves, and as the substantive productions of a man, their importance would be slight. But they possess interest beyond their limits, in confirming the evidence just dwelt on, of the poetical mood of Shelley being only the intensification of his habitual mood; the same tongue only speaking, for want of the special excitement to sing. The very first letter, as one instance for all, strikes the key-note of the predominating sentiment of Shelley throughout his whole life—his sympathy with the oppressed. And when we see him at so early an age, casting out, under the influence of such a sympathy, letters and pamphlets on every side, we accept it as the simple exemplification of the sincerity, with which, at the close of his life, he spoke of himself, as—

> "One whose heart a stranger's tear might wear
> As water-drops the sandy fountain stone;
> Who loved and pitied all things, and could moan
> For woes which others hear not, and could see
> The absent with the glass of phantasy,
> And near the poor and trampled sit and weep,
> Following the captive to his dungeon deep—
> One who was as a nerve o'er which do creep
> The else-unfelt oppressions of this earth."

Such sympathy with his kind was evidently developed in him to an extraordinary and even morbid degree, at a period when the general intellectual powers it was impatient to put in motion, were immature or deficient.

I conjecture, from a review of the various publications of Shelley's youth, that one of the causes of his failure at the outset, was the peculiar *practicalness* of his mind, which was not without a determinate effect on his progress in theorising. An ordinary youth, who turns his attention to similar subjects, discovers falsities, incongruities, and various points for amendment, and, in the natural advance of the purely critical spirit unchecked by considerations of remedy, keeps up before his young eyes so many instances of the same error and wrong, that he finds himself unawares arrived at the startling conclusion, that all must be changed—or nothing: in the face of which plainly impossible achievement, he is apt (looking perhaps a little more serious by the time he touches at the decisive issue) to feel, either carelessly or considerately, that his own attempting a single piece of service would be worse than useless even, and to refer the whole task to another age and person—safe in proportion to his incapacity. Wanting words to speak, he has never made a fool of himself by speaking. But, in Shelley's case, the early fervour and power to *see*, was accompanied by as precocious a fertility to *contrive*: he endeavoured to realise as he went on idealising; every wrong had simultaneously its remedy, and, out of the strength of his hatred for the former, he took the strength of his confidence in the latter—till suddenly he stood pledged to the defence of a set of miserable little expedients, just as if they represented great principles, and to an attack upon various great principles, really so, without leaving himself time to examine whether, because they were antagonistical to the remedy he had suggested, they must therefore be identical or even essentially connected with the wrong he sought to cure,—playing with blind passion into the hands of his enemies, and dashing at whatever red cloak was held forth to him, as the cause of the fireball he had last been stung with—mistaking Churchdom for Christianity, and for marriage, "the sale of love" and the law of sexual oppression.

Gradually, however, he was leaving behind him this low practical dexterity, unable to keep up with his widening intellectual perception; and, in exact proportion as he did so, his true power strengthened and proved itself. Gradually he was raised above the contemplation of spots and the attempt at effacing them, to the great Abstract Light, and, through the discrepancy of the creation, to the sufficiency of the First

Cause. Gradually he was learning that the best way of removing abuses is to stand fast by truth. Truth is one, as they are manifold; and innumerable negative effects are produced by the upholding of one positive principle. I shall say what I think,—had Shelley lived he would have finally ranged himself with the Christians; his very instinct for helping the weaker side (if numbers make strength), his very "hate of hate," which at first mistranslated itself into delirious Queen Mab notes and the like, would have got clearer-sighted by exercise. The preliminary step to following Christ, is the leaving the dead to bury their dead—not clamouring on his doctrine for an especial solution of difficulties which are referable to the general problem of the universe. Already he had attained to a profession of "a worship to the Spirit of good within, which requires (before it sends that inspiration forth, which impresses its likeness upon all it creates) devoted and disinterested homage, *as Coleridge says*,"—and Paul likewise. And we find in one of his last exquisite fragments, avowedly a record of one of his own mornings and its experience, as it dawned on him at his soul and body's best in his boat on the Serchio—that as surely as

"The stars burnt out in the pale blue air,
And the thin white moon lay withering there—
Day had kindled the dewy woods,
And the rocks above, and the stream below,
And the vapours in their multitudes,
And the Apennine's shroud of summer snow—
Day had awakened all things that be;"

just so surely, he tells us (stepping forward from this delicious dance-music, choragus-like, into the grander measure befitting the final enunciation),

"All rose to do the task He set to each,
Who shaped us to his ends and not our own;
The million rose to learn, and One to teach
What none yet ever knew or can be known."

No more difference than this, from David's pregnant conclusion so long ago!

Meantime, as I call Shelley a moral man, because he was true, simple-hearted, and brave, and because what he acted corresponded to what he knew, so I call him a man of religious mind, because every audacious negative cast up by him against the Divine, was interpenetrated with a mood of reverence and adoration,—and because I find him everywhere taking for granted some of the capital dogmas of Christianity, while most vehemently denying their historical basement. There is such a thing as an efficacious knowledge of and belief in the politics of Junius, or the poetry of Rowley, though a man should at the same time dispute the title of Chatterton to the one, and consider the author of the other, as Byron wittily did, "really, truly, nobody at all."* There is even such a thing, we come to learn wonderingly in these very letters, as a profound sensibility and adaptitude for art, while the science of the percipient is so little advanced as to admit of his stronger admiration for Guido (and Carlo Dolce!) than for Michael Angelo. A Divine Being has Himself said, that "a word against the Son of man shall be forgiven to a man," while "a word against the Spirit of God" (implying a general deliberate preference of perceived evil to perceived good) "shall not be forgiven to a man." Also, in religion, one earnest and unextorted assertion of belief should outweigh, as a matter of testimony, many assertions of unbelief. The fact that there is a gold-region is established by the finding of one lump, though you miss the vein never so often.

Shelley died before his youth ended. In taking the measure of him as a man, he must be considered on the whole and at his ultimate spiritual stature, and not be judged of at the immaturity and by the mistakes of ten years before: that, indeed, would be to judge of the author of "Julian and Maddalo" by "Zastrozzi". Let the whole truth be told of his worst mistake. I believe, for my own part, that if anything could now shame or grieve Shelley, it would be an attempt to vindicate him at the expense of another.

In forming a judgment, I would, however, press on the reader the simple justice of considering tenderly his constitution of body as well as mind, and how unfavourable it was to the steady symmetries of conventional life; the body, in the torture of incurable disease, refusing to give repose to the bewildered soul, tossing in its hot fever of the

* Or, to take our illustrations from the writings of Shelley himself, there is such a thing as admirably appreciating a work by Andrea Verocchio,—and fancifully characterising the Pisan Torre Guelfa by the Ponte a Mare, black against the sunsets,—and consummately painting the islet of San Clemente with its penitentiary for rebellious priests, to the west between Venice and the Lido—while you believe the first to be a fragment of an antique sarcophagus—the second, Ugolino's Tower of Famine (the vestiges of which should be sought for in the Piazza de' Cavalieri)—and the third (as I convinced myself last summer at Venice), San Servolo with its madhouse—which, far from being "windowless", is as full of windows as a barrack.

fancy,—and the laudanum-bottle making but a perilous and pitiful truce between these two. He was constantly subject to "that state of mind" (I quote his own note to "Hellas") "in which ideas may be supposed to assume the force of sensation, through the confusion of thought with the objects of thought, and excess of passion animating the creations of the imagination:" in other words, he was liable to remarkable delusions and hallucinations. The nocturnal attack in Wales, for instance, was assuredly a delusion; and I venture to express my own conviction, derived from a little attention to the circumstances of either story, that the idea of the enamoured lady following him to Naples, and of the "man in the cloak" who struck him at the Pisan post-office, were equally illusory,—the mere projection, in fact, from himself, of the image of his own love and hate.

> "To thirst and find no fill—to wail and wander
> With short unsteady steps—to pause and ponder—
> To feel the blood run through the veins and tingle
> What busy thought and blind sensation mingle,—
> To nurse the image of *unfelt caresses*
> Till dim imagination just possesses
> The half-created shadow"—

of unfelt caresses,—and of unfelt blows as well: to such conditions was his genius subject. It was not at Rome only (where he heard a mystic voice exclaiming, "Cenci, Cenci," in reference to the tragic theme which occupied him at the time),—it was not at Rome only that he mistook the cry of "old rags". The habit of somnambulism is said to have extended to the very last days of his life.

Let me conclude with a thought of Shelley as a poet. In the hierarchy of creative minds, it is the presence of the highest faculty that gives first rank, in virtue of its kind, not degree; no pretension of a lower nature, whatever the completeness of development or variety of effect, impeding the precedency of the rarer endowment though only in the germ. The contrary is sometimes maintained; it is attempted to make the lower gifts (which are potentially included in the higher faculty) of independent value, and equal to some exercise of the special function. For instance, should not a poet possess common sense? Then the possession of abundant common sense implies a step towards becoming a poet. Yes; such a step as the lapidary's, when, strong in the fact of carbon entering largely into the composition of the diamond, he heaps up a sack of charcoal in order to compete with the

Koh-i-noor. I pass at once, therefore, from Shelley's minor excellences to his noblest and predominating characteristic.

This I call his simultaneous perception of Power and Love in the absolute, and of Beauty and Good in the concrete, while he throws, from his poet's station between both, swifter, subtler, and more numerous films for the connexion of each with each, than have been thrown by any modern artificer of whom I have knowledge; proving how, as he says,

> "The spirit of the worm within the sod,
> In love and worship blends itself with God."

I would rather consider Shelley's poetry as a sublime fragmentary essay towards a presentment of the correspondency of the universe to Deity, of the natural to the spiritual, and of the actual to the ideal, than I would isolate and separately appraise the worth of many detachable portions which might be acknowledged as utterly perfect in a lower moral point of view, under the mere conditions of art. It would be easy to take my stand on successful instances of objectivity in Shelley: there is the unrivalled "Cenci"; there is the "Julian and Maddalo" too; there is the magnificent "Ode to Naples": why not regard, it may be said, the less organised matter as the radiant elemental foam and solution, out of which would have been evolved, eventually, creations as perfect even as those? But I prefer to look for the highest attainment, not simply the high,—and, seeing it, I hold by it. There is surely enough of the work "Shelley" to be known enduringly among men, and, I believe, to be accepted of God, as human work may; and around the imperfect proportions of such, the most elaborated productions of ordinary art must arrange themselves as inferior illustrations.

It is because I have long held these opinions in assurance and gratitude, that I catch at the opportunity offered to me of expressing them here; knowing that the alacrity to fulfil an humble office conveys more love than the acceptance of the honour of a higher one, and that better, therefore, than the signal service it was the dream of my boyhood to render to his name and memory, may be the saying of a few, inadequate words upon these scarcely more important supplementary letters of SHELLEY.

Paris, *Dec. 4*[th], 1851.

FROM *MEN AND WOMEN*, VOL. I (1855)

MEN AND WOMEN.

BY

ROBERT BROWNING.

IN TWO VOLUMES.

VOL. I.

LONDON:

CHAPMAN AND HALL, 193, PICCADILLY.

1855.

FIG. 4 Title-page of *Men and Women*, Vol. I (1855).

Love Among the Ruins

1.

Where the quiet-coloured end of evening smiles,
        Miles and miles
On the solitary pastures where our sheep
        Half-asleep
Tinkle homeward thro' the twilight, stray or stop
        As they crop—

2.

Was the site once of a city great and gay,
        (So they say)
Of our country's very capital, its prince
        Ages since
Held his court in, gathered councils, wielding far
        Peace or war.

3.

Now—the country does not even boast a tree,
        As you see,
To distinguish slopes of verdure, certain rills
        From the hills
Intersect and give a name to, (else they run
        Into one)

4.

Where the domed and daring palace shot its spires
        Up like fires
O'er the hundred-gated circuit of a wall
        Bounding all,
Made of marble, men might march on nor be prest,
        Twelve abreast.

5.

And such plenty and perfection, see, of grass
        Never was!
Such a carpet as, this summer-time, o'erspreads
        And embeds
Every vestige of the city, guessed alone,
        Stock or stone—

6.

Where a multitude of men breathed joy and woe
        Long ago;
Lust of glory pricked their hearts up, dread of shame
        Struck them tame;
And that glory and that shame alike, the gold
        Bought and sold.

7.

Now,—the single little turret that remains
        On the plains,
By the caper overrooted, by the gourd
        Overscored,
While the patching houseleek's head of blossom winks
        Through the chinks—

8.

Marks the basement whence a tower in ancient time
        Sprang sublime,
And a burning ring all round, the chariots traced
        As they raced,
And the monarch and his minions and his dames
        Viewed the games.

9.

And I know, while thus the quiet-coloured eve
        Smiles to leave
To their folding, all our many-tinkling fleece
        In such peace,
And the slopes and rills in undistinguished grey
        Melt away—

10.

That a girl with eager eyes and yellow hair
        Waits me there
In the turret, whence the charioteers caught soul
        For the goal,
When the king looked, where she looks now, breathless, dumb
        Till I come.

11.

But he looked upon the city, every side,
        Far and wide,
All the mountains topped with temples, all the glades'
        Colonnades,
All the causeys, bridges, aqueducts,—and then,
        All the men!

12.

When I do come, she will speak not, she will stand,
        Either hand
On my shoulder, give her eyes the first embrace
        Of my face,
Ere we rush, ere we extinguish sight and speech
        Each on each.

13.

In one year they sent a million fighters forth
        South and north,
And they built their gods a brazen pillar high
        As the sky,
Yet reserved a thousand chariots in full force—
        Gold, of course.

14.

Oh, heart! oh, blood that freezes, blood that burns!
        Earth's returns
For whole centuries of folly, noise and sin!
        Shut them in,
With their triumphs and their glories and the rest.
        Love is best!

A Lover's Quarrel

1.

Oh, what a dawn of day!
How the March sun feels like May!
    All is blue again
    After last night's rain,

And the South dries the hawthorn-spray.
    Only, my Love's away!
I'd as lief that the blue were grey.

2.

Runnels, which rillets swell,
Must be dancing down the dell
    With a foamy head
    On the beryl bed
Paven smooth as a hermit's cell;
    Each with a tale to tell,
Could my Love but attend as well.

3.

Dearest, three months ago!
When we lived blocked-up with snow,—
    When the wind would edge
    In and in his wedge,
In, as far as the point could go—
    Not to our ingle, though,
Where we loved each the other so!

4.

Laughs with so little cause!
We devised games out of straws.
    We would try and trace
    One another's face
In the ash, as an artist draws;
    Free on each other's flaws,
How we chattered like two church daws!

5.

What's in the "Times?"—a scold
At the emperor deep and cold;
    He has taken a bride
    To his gruesome side,
That's as fair as himself is bold:
    There they sit ermine-stoled,
And she powders her hair with gold.

6.

Fancy the Pampas' sheen!
Miles and miles of gold and green
    Where the sun-flowers blow
    In a solid glow,
And to break now and then the screen—
    Black neck and eyeballs keen,
Up a wild horse leaps between!

7.

Try, will our table turn?
Lay your hands there light, and yearn
    Till the yearning slips
    Thro' the finger-tips
In a fire which a few discern,
    And a very few feel burn,
And the rest, they may live and learn!

8.

Then we would up and pace,
For a change, about the place,
    Each with arm o'er neck:
    'Tis our quarter-deck,
We are seamen in woeful case.
    Help in the ocean-space!
Or, if no help, we'll embrace.

9.

See, how she looks now, drest
In a sledging-cap and vest.
    'Tis a huge fur cloak—
    Like a reindeer's yoke
Falls the lappet along the breast:
    Sleeves for her arms to rest,
Or to hang, as my Love likes best.

10.

Teach me to flirt a fan
As the Spanish ladies can,
    Or I tint your lip
    With a burnt stick's tip
And you turn into such a man!

Just the two spots that span
Half the bill of the young male swan.

11.

Dearest, three months ago
When the mesmerizer Snow
With his hand's first sweep
Put the earth to sleep,
'Twas a time when the heart could show
All—how was earth to know,
'Neath the mute hand's to-and-fro!

12.

Dearest, three months ago
When we loved each other so,
Lived and loved the same
Till an evening came
When a shaft from the Devil's bow
Pierced to our ingle-glow,
And the friends were friend and foe!

13.

Not from the heart beneath—
'Twas a bubble born of breath,
Neither sneer nor vaunt,
Nor reproach nor taunt.
See a word, how it severeth!
Oh, power of life and death
In the tongue, as the Preacher saith!

14.

Woman, and will you cast
For a word, quite off at last
Me, your own, your you,—
Since, as Truth is true,
I was you all the happy past—
Me do you leave aghast
With the memories we amassed?

15.

Love, if you knew the light
That your soul casts in my sight,
How I look to you
For the pure and true,
And the beauteous and the right,—
Bear with a moment's spite
When a mere mote threats the white!

16.

What of a hasty word?
Is the fleshly heart not stirred
By a worm's pin-prick
Where its roots are quick?
See the eye, by a fly's foot blurred—
Ear, when a straw is heard
Scratch the brain's coat of curd!

17.

Foul be the world or fair,
More or less, how can I care?
'Tis the world the same
For my praise or blame,
And endurance is easy there.
Wrong in the one thing rare—
Oh, it is hard to bear!

18.

Here's the spring back or close,
When the almond-blossom blows;
We shall have the word
In that minor third
There is none but the cuckoo knows—
Heaps of the guelder-rose!
I must bear with it, I suppose.

19.

Could but November come,
Were the noisy birds struck dumb
At the warning slash
Of his driver's-lash—

I would laugh like the valiant Thumb
Facing the castle glum
And the giant's fee-faw-fum!

20.

Then, were the world well stript
Of the gear wherein equipped
We can stand apart,
Heart dispense with heart
In the sun, with the flowers unnipped,—
Oh, the world's hangings ripped,
We were both in a bare-walled crypt!

21.

Each in the crypt would cry
"But one freezes here! and why?
When a heart, as chill,
At my own would thrill
Back to life, and its fires out-fly?
Heart, shall we live or die?
The rest, . . . settle it by-and-by!"

22.

So, she'd efface the score,
And forgive me as before.
Just at twelve o'clock
I shall hear her knock
In the worst of a storm's uproar—
I shall pull her through the door—
I shall have her for evermore!

Evelyn Hope

I.

Beautiful Evelyn Hope is dead
Sit and watch by her side an hour.
That is her book-shelf, this her bed;
She plucked that piece of geranium-flower,
Beginning to die too, in the glass.
Little has yet been changed, I think—

The shutters are shut, no light may pass
  Save two long rays thro' the hinge's chink.

2.

Sixteen years old when she died!
  Perhaps she had scarcely heard my name—
It was not her time to love: beside,
  Her life had many a hope and aim,
Duties enough and little cares,
  And now was quiet, now astir—
Till God's hand beckoned unawares,
  And the sweet white brow is all of her.

3.

Is it too late then, Evelyn Hope?
  What, your soul was pure and true,
The good stars met in your horoscope,
  Made you of spirit, fire and dew—
And just because I was thrice as old,
  And our paths in the world diverged so wide,
Each was nought to each, must I be told?
  We were fellow mortals, nought beside?

4.

No, indeed! for God above
  Is great to grant, as mighty to make,
And creates the love to reward the love,—
  I claim you still, for my own love's sake!
Delayed it may be for more lives yet,
  Through worlds I shall traverse, not a few—
Much is to learn and much to forget
  Ere the time be come for taking you.

5.

But the time will come,—at last it will,
  When, Evelyn Hope, what meant, I shall say,
In the lower earth, in the years long still,
  That body and soul so pure and gay?
Why your hair was amber, I shall divine,
  And your mouth of your own geranium's red—

And what you would do with me, in fine,
  In the new life come in the old one's stead.

6.

I have lived, I shall say, so much since then,
  Given up myself so many times,
Gained me the gains of various men,
  Ransacked the ages, spoiled the climes;
Yet one thing, one, in my soul's full scope,
  Either I missed or itself missed me—
And I want and find you, Evelyn Hope!
  What is the issue? let us see!

7.

I loved you, Evelyn, all the while;
  My heart seemed full as it could hold—
There was place and to spare for the frank young smile
  And the red young mouth and the hair's young gold.
So, hush,—I will give you this leaf to keep—
  See, I shut it inside the sweet cold hand.
There, that is our secret! go to sleep;
  You will wake, and remember, and understand.

Up at a Villa—Down in the City

(AS DISTINGUISHED BY AN ITALIAN PERSON OF QUALITY.)

1.

Had I but plenty of money, money enough and to spare,
The house for me, no doubt, were a house in the city-square.
Ah, such a life, such a life, as one leads at the window there!

2.

Something to see, by Bacchus, something to hear, at least!
There, the whole day long, one's life is a perfect feast;
While up at a villa one lives, I maintain it, no more than a beast.

3.

Well now, look at our villa! stuck like the horn of a bull
Just on a mountain's edge as bare as the creature's skull,

Save a mere shag of a bush with hardly a leaf to pull!
—I scratch my own, sometimes, to see if the hair's turned wool.

4.

But the city, oh the city—the square with the houses! Why?
They are stone-faced, white as a curd, there's something to take
the eye!
Houses in four straight lines, not a single front awry!
You watch who crosses and gossips, who saunters, who hurries by:
Green blinds, as a matter of course, to draw when the
sun gets high;
And the shops with fanciful signs which are painted properly.

5.

What of a villa? Though winter be over in March by rights,
'Tis May perhaps ere the snow shall have withered well off the
heights:
You've the brown ploughed land before, where the oxen steam
and wheeze,
And the hills over-smoked behind by the faint grey olive trees.

6.

Is it better in May I ask you? you've summer all at once;
In a day he leaps complete with a few strong April suns!
'Mid the sharp short emerald wheat, scarce risen three fingers well,
The wild tulip, at end of its tube, blows out its great red bell,
Like a thin clear bubble of blood, for the children to pick and sell.

7.

Is it ever hot in the square? There's a fountain to spout and splash!
In the shade it sings and springs; in the shine such
foam-bows flash
On the horses with curling fish-tails, that prance and paddle and pash
Round the lady atop in the conch—fifty gazers do not abash,
Though all that she wears is some weeds round her waist
in a sort of sash!

8.

All the year long at the villa, nothing's to see though you linger,
Except yon cypress that points like Death's lean lifted forefinger.

Some think fireflies pretty, when they mix in the corn and mingle,
Or thrid the stinking hemp till the stalks of it seem a-tingle.
Late August or early September, the stunning cicala is shrill,
And the bees keep their tiresome whine round the resinous firs on the hill.
Enough of the seasons,—I spare you the months of the fever and chill.

9.

Ere opening your eyes in the city, the blessed churchbells begin:
No sooner the bells leave off, than the diligence rattles in:
You get the pick of the news, and it costs you never a pin.
By and by there's the travelling doctor gives pills, lets blood, draws teeth;
Or the Pulcinello-trumpet breaks up the market beneath.
At the post-office such a scene-picture—the new play, piping hot!
And a notice how, only this morning, three liberal thieves were shot.
Above it, behold the archbishop's most fatherly of rebukes,
And beneath, with his crown and his lion, some little new law of the Duke's!
Or a sonnet with flowery marge, to the Reverend Don So-and-so
Who is Dante, Boccaccio, Petrarca, Saint Jerome and Cicero,
"And moreover," (the sonnet goes rhyming,) "the skirts of St. Paul has reached,
"Having preached us those six Lent-lectures more unctuous than ever he preached."
Noon strikes,—here sweeps the procession! our Lady borne smiling and smart
With a pink gauze gown all spangles, and seven swords stuck in her heart!
Bang, *whang*, *whang*, goes the drum, *tootle-te-tootle* the fife;
No keeping one's haunches still: it's the greatest pleasure in life.

10.

But bless you, it's dear—it's dear! fowls, wine, at double the rate.
They have clapped a new tax upon salt, and what oil pays passing the gate

It's a horror to think of. And so, the villa for me, not the city!
Beggars can scarcely be choosers—but still—ah, the pity, the pity!
Look, two and two go the priests, then the monks with cowls and sandals,
And the penitents dressed in white shirts, a-holding the yellow candles;
One, he carries a flag up straight, and another a cross with handles,
And the Duke's guard brings up the rear, for the better prevention of scandals.
Bang, *whang*, *whang*, goes the drum, *tootle-te-tootle* the fife.
Oh, a day in the city-square, there is no such pleasure in life!

A Woman's Last Word

1.

Let's contend no more, Love,
Strive nor weep—
All be as before, Love,
—Only sleep!

2.

What so wild as words are?
—I and thou
In debate, as birds are,
Hawk on bough!

3.

See the creature stalking
While we speak—
Hush and hide the talking,
Cheek on cheek!

4.

What so false as truth is,
False to thee?
Where the serpent's tooth is
Shun the tree—

5.

Where the apple reddens
   Never pry—
Lest we lose our Edens,
   Eve and I!

6.

Be a god and hold me
   With a charm—
Be a man and fold me
   With thine arm!

7.

Teach me, only teach, Love!
   As I ought
I will speak thy speech, Love,
   Think thy thought—

8.

Meet, if thou require it,
   Both demands,
Laying flesh and spirit
   In thy hands!

9.

That shall be to-morrow
   Not to-night:
I must bury sorrow
   Out of sight:

10.

—Must a little weep, Love,
   —Foolish me!
And so fall asleep, Love,
   Loved by thee.

Fra Lippo Lippi

I am poor brother Lippo, by your leave!
You need not clap your torches to my face.
Zooks, what's to blame? you think you see a monk!
What, it's past midnight, and you go the rounds,
And here you catch me at an alley's end
Where sportive ladies leave their doors ajar.
The Carmine's my cloister: hunt it up,
Do,—harry out, if you must show your zeal,
Whatever rat, there, haps on his wrong hole,
And nip each softling of a wee white mouse,
Weke, weke, that's crept to keep him company!
Aha, you know your betters? Then, you'll take
Your hand away that's fiddling on my throat,
And please to know me likewise. Who am I?
Why, one, sir, who is lodging with a friend
Three streets off—he's a certain . . . how d' ye call?
Master—a . . . Cosimo of the Medici,
In the house that caps the corner. Boh! you were best!
Remember and tell me, the day you're hanged,
How you affected such a gullet's-gripe!
But you, sir, it concerns you that your knaves
Pick up a manner nor discredit you.
Zooks, are we pilchards, that they sweep the streets
And count fair prize what comes into their net?
He's Judas to a tittle, that man is!
Just such a face! why, sir, you make amends.
Lord, I'm not angry! Bid your hangdogs go
Drink out this quarter-florin to the health
Of the munificent House that harbours me
(And many more beside, lads! more beside!)
And all's come square again. I'd like his face—
His, elbowing on his comrade in the door
With the pike and lantern,—for the slave that holds
John Baptist's head a-dangle by the hair
With one hand ("look you, now," as who should say)
And his weapon in the other, yet unwiped!
It's not your chance to have a bit of chalk,
A wood-coal or the like? or you should see!
Yes, I'm the painter, since you style me so.
What, brother Lippo's doings, up and down,

You know them and they take you? like enough!
I saw the proper twinkle in your eye—
'Tell you, I liked your looks at very first.
Let's sit and set things straight now, hip to haunch.
Here's spring come, and the nights one makes up bands
To roam the town and sing out carnival,
And I've been three weeks shut within my mew,
A-painting for the great man, saints and saints
And saints again. I could not paint all night—
Ouf! I leaned out of window for fresh air.
There came a hurry of feet and little feet,
A sweep of lute-strings, laughs, and whifts of song,—
Flower o' the broom,
Take away love, and our earth is a tomb!
Flower o' the quince,
I let Lisa go, and what good's in life since?
Flower o' the thyme—and so on. Round they went.
Scarce had they turned the corner when a titter,
Like the skipping of rabbits by moonlight,—three slim shapes,
And a face that looked up . . . zooks, sir, flesh and blood,
That's all I'm made of! Into shreds it went,
Curtain and counterpane and coverlet,
All the bed furniture—a dozen knots,
There was a ladder! down I let myself,
Hands and feet, scrambling somehow, and so dropped,
And after them. I came up with the fun
Hard by St. Laurence, hail fellow, well met,—
Flower o' the rose,
If I've been merry, what matter who knows?
And so as I was stealing back again
To get to bed and have a bit of sleep
Ere I rise up to-morrow and go work
On Jerome knocking at his poor old breast
With his great round stone to subdue the flesh,
You snap me of the sudden. Ah, I see!
Though your eye twinkles still, you shake your head—
Mine's shaved—a monk, you say—the sting's in that!
If Master Cosimo announced himself,
Mum's the word naturally; but a monk!
Come, what am I a beast for? tell us, now!
I was a baby when my mother died
And father died and left me in the street.

I starved there, God knows how, a year or two
On fig-skins, melon-parings, rinds and shucks,
Refuse and rubbish. One fine frosty day,
My stomach being empty as your hat,
The wind doubled me up and down I went.
Old Aunt Lapaccia trussed me with one hand,
(Its fellow was a stinger as I knew)
And so along the wall, over the bridge,
By the straight cut to the convent. Six words, there,
While I stood munching my first bread that month:
"So, boy, you're minded," quoth the good fat father
Wiping his own mouth, 'twas refection-time,—
"To quit this very miserable world?
Will you renounce" ... The mouthful of bread? thought I;
By no means! Brief, they made a monk of me;
I did renounce the world, its pride and greed,
Palace, farm, villa, shop and banking-house,
Trash, such as these poor devils of Medici
Have given their hearts to—all at eight years old.
Well, sir, I found in time, you may be sure,
'Twas not for nothing—the good bellyful,
The warm serge and the rope that goes all round,
And day-long blessed idleness beside!
"Let's see what the urchin's fit for"—that came next.
Not overmuch their way, I must confess.
Such a to-do! they tried me with their books.
Lord, they'd have taught me Latin in pure waste!
Flower o' the clove,
All the Latin I construe is, "amo" I love!
But, mind you, when a boy starves in the streets
Eight years together, as my fortune was,
Watching folk's faces to know who will fling
The bit of half-stripped grape-bunch he desires,
And who will curse or kick him for his pains—
Which gentleman processional and fine,
Holding a candle to the Sacrament
Will wink and let him lift a plate and catch
The droppings of the wax to sell again,
Or holla for the Eight and have him whipped,—
How say I?—nay, which dog bites, which lets drop
His bone from the heap of offal in the street!
—The soul and sense of him grow sharp alike,

He learns the look of things, and none the less
For admonitions from the hunger-pinch.
I had a store of such remarks, be sure,
Which, after I found leisure, turned to use:
I drew men's faces on my copy-books,
Scrawled them within the antiphonary's marge,
Joined legs and arms to the long music-notes,
Found nose and eyes and chin for A.s and B.s,
And made a string of pictures of the world
Betwixt the ins and outs of verb and noun,
On the wall, the bench, the door. The monks looked black.
"Nay," quoth the Prior, "turn him out, d'ye say?
In no wise. Lose a crow and catch a lark.
What if at last we get our man of parts,
We Carmelites, like those Camaldolese
And Preaching Friars, to do our church up fine
And put the front on it that ought to be!"
And hereupon he bade me daub away.
Thank you! my head being crammed, the walls a blank,
Never was such prompt disemburdening.
First, every sort of monk, the black and white,
I drew them, fat and lean: then, folks at church,
From good old gossips waiting to confess
Their cribs of barrel-droppings, candle-ends,—
To the breathless fellow at the altar-foot,
Fresh from his murder, safe and sitting there
With the little children round him in a row
Of admiration, half for his beard and half
For that white anger of his victim's son
Shaking a fist at him with one fierce arm,
Signing himself with the other because of Christ
(Whose sad face on the cross sees only this
After the passion of a thousand years)
Till some poor girl, her apron o'er her head
Which the intense eyes looked through, came at eve
On tip-toe, said a word, dropped in a loaf,
Her pair of ear-rings and a bunch of flowers
The brute took growling, prayed, and then was gone.
I painted all, then cried "'tis ask and have—
Choose, for more's ready!"—laid the ladder flat,
And showed my covered bit of cloister-wall.
The monks closed in a circle and praised loud

Till checked, (taught what to see and not to see,
Being simple bodies)—"that's the very man!
Look at the boy who stoops to pat the dog!
That woman's like the Prior's niece who comes
To care about his asthma: it's the life!"
But there my triumph's straw-fire flared and funked—
Their betters took their turn to see and say:
The Prior and the learned pulled a face
And stopped all that in no time. "How? what's here?
Quite from the mark of painting, bless us all!
Faces, arms, legs and bodies like the true
As much as pea and pea! it's devil's-game!
Your business is not to catch men with show,
With homage to the perishable clay,
But lift them over it, ignore it all,
Make them forget there's such a thing as flesh.
Your business is to paint the souls of men—
Man's soul, and it's a fire, smoke . . no, it's not . .
It's vapour done up like a new-born babe—
(In that shape when you die it leaves your mouth)
It's . . well, what matters talking, it's the soul.
Give us no more of body than shows soul.
Here's Giotto, with his Saint a-praising God!
That sets you praising,—why not stop with him?
Why put all thoughts of praise out of our heads
With wonder at lines, colours, and what not?
Paint the soul, never mind the legs and arms!
Rub all out, try at it a second time.
Oh, that white smallish female with the breasts,
She's just my niece . . . Herodias, I would say,—
Who went and danced and got men's heads cut off—
Have it all out!" Now, is this sense, I ask?
A fine way to paint soul, by painting body
So ill, the eye can't stop there, must go further
And can't fare worse! Thus, yellow does for white
When what you put for yellow's simply black,
And any sort of meaning looks intense
When all beside itself means and looks nought.
Why can't a painter lift each foot in turn,
Left foot and right foot, go a double step,
Make his flesh liker and his soul more like,
Both in their order? Take the prettiest face,

The Prior's niece . . . patron-saint—is it so pretty
You can't discover if it means hope, fear,
Sorrow or joy? won't beauty go with these?
Suppose I've made her eyes all right and blue,
Can't I take breath and try to add life's flash,
And then add soul and heighten them threefold?
Or say there's beauty with no soul at all—
(I never saw it—put the case the same—)
If you get simple beauty and nought else,
You get about the best thing God invents,—
That's somewhat. And you'll find the soul you have missed,
Within yourself when you return Him thanks!
"Rub all out!" well, well, there's my life, in short,
And so the thing has gone on ever since.
I'm grown a man no doubt, I've broken bounds—
You should not take a fellow eight years old
And make him swear to never kiss the girls—
I'm my own master, paint now as I please—
Having a friend, you see, in the Corner-house!
Lord, it's fast holding by the rings in front—
Those great rings serve more purposes than just
To plant a flag in, or tie up a horse!
And yet the old schooling sticks—the old grave eyes
Are peeping o'er my shoulder as I work,
The heads shake still—"It's Art's decline, my son!
You're not of the true painters, great and old:
Brother Angelico's the man, you'll find:
Brother Lorenzo stands his single peer.
Fag on at flesh, you'll never make the third!"
Flower o' the pine,
You keep your mistr . . . manners, and I'll stick to mine!
I'm not the third, then: bless us, they must know!
Don't you think they're the likeliest to know,
They, with their Latin? so I swallow my rage,
Clench my teeth, suck my lips in tight, and paint
To please them—sometimes do, and sometimes don't,
For, doing most, there's pretty sure to come
A turn—some warm eve finds me at my saints—
A laugh, a cry, the business of the world—
(Flower o' the peach,
Death for us all, and his own life for each!)

And my whole soul revolves, the cup runs o'er,
The world and life's too big to pass for a dream,
And I do these wild things in sheer despite,
And play the fooleries you catch me at,
In pure rage! the old mill-horse, out at grass
After hard years, throws up his stiff heels so,
Although the miller does not preach to him
The only good of grass is to make chaff.
What would men have? Do they like grass or no—
May they or mayn't they? all I want's the thing
Settled for ever one way: as it is,
You tell too many lies and hurt yourself.
You don't like what you only like too much,
You do like what, if given you at your word,
You find abundantly detestable.
For me, I think I speak as I was taught—
I always see the Garden and God there
A-making man's wife—and, my lesson learned,
The value and significance of flesh,
I can't unlearn ten minutes afterward.
   You understand me: I'm a beast, I know.
But see, now—why, I see as certainly
As that the morning-star's about to shine,
What will hap some day. We've a youngster here
Comes to our convent, studies what I do,
Slouches and stares and lets no atom drop—
His name is Guidi—he'll not mind the monks—
They call him Hulking Tom, he lets them talk—
He picks my practice up—he'll paint apace,
I hope so—though I never live so long,
I know what's sure to follow. You be judge!
You speak no Latin more than I, belike—
However, you're my man, you've seen the world
—The beauty and the wonder and the power,
The shapes of things, their colours, lights and shades,
Changes, surprises,—and God made it all!
—For what? do you feel thankful, ay or no,
For this fair town's face, yonder river's line,
The mountain round it and the sky above,
Much more the figures of man, woman, child,
These are the frame to? What's it all about?

To be passed o'er, despised? or dwelt upon,
Wondered at? oh, this last of course, you say.
But why not do as well as say,—paint these
Just as they are, careless what comes of it?
God's works—paint anyone, and count it crime
To let a truth slip. Don't object, "His works
Are here already—nature is complete:
Suppose you reproduce her—(which you can't)
There's no advantage! you must beat her, then."
For, don't you mark, we're made so that we love
First when we see them painted, things we have passed
Perhaps a hundred times nor cared to see;
And so they are better, painted—better to us,
Which is the same thing. Art was given for that—
God uses us to help each other so,
Lending our minds out. Have you noticed, now,
Your cullion's hanging face? A bit of chalk,
And trust me but you should, though! How much more,
If I drew higher things with the same truth!
That were to take the Prior's pulpit-place,
Interpret God to all of you! oh, oh,
It makes me mad to see what men shall do
And we in our graves! This world's no blot for us,
Nor blank—it means intensely, and means good:
To find its meaning is my meat and drink.
"Ay, but you don't so instigate to prayer"
Strikes in the Prior! "when your meaning's plain
It does not say to folks—remember matins—
Or, mind you fast next Friday!" Why, for this
What need of art at all? A skull and bones,
Two bits of stick nailed cross-wise, or, what's best,
A bell to chime the hour with, does as well.
I painted a St. Laurence six months since
At Prato, splashed the fresco in fine style.
"How looks my painting, now the scaffold's down?"
I ask a brother: "Hugely," he returns—
"Already not one phiz of your three slaves
That turn the Deacon off his toasted side,
But's scratched and prodded to our heart's content,
The pious people have so eased their own
When coming to say prayers there in a rage.

We get on fast to see the bricks beneath.
Expect another job this time next year,
For pity and religion grow i' the crowd—
Your painting serves its purpose!" Hang the fools!

—That is—you'll not mistake an idle word
Spoke in a huff by a poor monk, Got wot,
Tasting the air this spicy night which turns
The unaccustomed head like Chianti wine!
Oh, the church knows! don't misreport me, now!
It's natural a poor monk out of bounds
Should have his apt word to excuse himself:
And hearken how I plot to make amends.
I have bethought me: I shall paint a piece
. . . There's for you! Give me six months, then go, see
Something in Sant' Ambrogio's . . . (bless the nuns!
They want a cast of my office) I shall paint
God in the midst, Madonna and her babe,
Ringed by a bowery, flowery angel-brood,
Lilies and vestments and white faces, sweet
As puff on puff of grated orris-root
When ladies crowd to church at midsummer.
And then in the front, of course a saint or two—
Saint John, because he saves the Florentines,
Saint Ambrose, who puts down in black and white
The convent's friends and gives them a long day,
And Job, I must have him there past mistake,
The man of Uz, (and Us without the z,
Painters who need his patience). Well, all these
Secured at their devotion, up shall come
Out of a corner when you least expect,
As one by a dark stair into a great light
Music and talking, who but Lippo! I!—
Mazed, motionless and moon-struck—I'm the man!
Back I shrink—what is this I see and hear?
I, caught up with my monk's things by mistake,
My old serge gown and rope that goes all round,
I, in this presence, this pure company!
Where's a hole, where's a corner for escape?
Then steps a sweet angelic slip of a thing
Forward, puts out a soft palm—"Not so fast!"

—Addresses the celestial presence, "nay—
He made you and devised you, after all,
Though he's none of you! Could Saint John there, draw—
His camel-hair make up a painting-brush?
We come to brother Lippo for all that,
Iste perfecit opus!" So, all smile—
I shuffle sideways with my blushing face
Under the cover of a hundred wings
Thrown like a spread of kirtles when you're gay
And play hot cockles, all the doors being shut,
Till, wholly unexpected, in there pops
The hothead husband! Thus I scuttle off
To some safe bench behind, not letting go
The palm of her, the little lily thing
That spoke the good word for me in the nick,
Like the Prior's niece . . . Saint Lucy, I would say.
And so all's saved for me, and for the church
A pretty picture gained. Go, six months hence!
Your hand, sir, and good bye: no lights, no lights!
The street's hushed, and I know my own way back—
Don't fear me! There's the grey beginning. Zooks!

A Toccata of Galuppi's

1.

Oh, Galuppi, Baldassaro, this is very sad to find!
I can hardly misconceive you; it would prove me deaf and blind;
But although I give you credit, 'tis with such a heavy mind!

2.

Here you come with your old music, and here's all the good
it brings.
What, they lived once thus at Venice, where the merchants were
the kings,
Where St. Mark's is, where the Doges used to wed the sea
with rings?

3.

Ay, because the sea's the street there; and 'tis arched by . . . what you call
. . . Shylock's bridge with houses on it, where they kept the carnival!
I was never out of England—it's as if I saw it all!

4.

Did young people take their pleasure when the sea was warm in May?
Balls and masks begun at midnight, burning ever to mid-day,
When they made up fresh adventures for the morrow, do you say?

5.

Was a lady such a lady, cheeks so round and lips so red,—
On her neck the small face buoyant, like a bell-flower on its bed,
O'er the breast's superb abundance where a man might base his head?

6.

Well (and it was graceful of them) they'd break talk off and afford
—She, to bite her mask's black velvet, he to finger on his sword,
While you sat and played Toccatas, stately at the clavichord?

7.

What? Those lesser thirds so plaintive, sixths diminished, sigh on sigh,
Told them something? Those suspensions, those solutions—"Must we die?"
Those commiserating sevenths—"Life might last! we can but try!"

8.

"Were you happy?"—"Yes."—"And are you still as happy?"—"Yes—And you?"
—"Then, more kisses!"—"Did *I* stop them, when a million seemed so few?"
Hark—the dominant's persistence, till it must be answered to!

9.

So an octave struck the answer. Oh, they praised you, I dare say!
"Brave Galuppi! that was music! good alike at grave and gay!
I can always leave off talking when I hear a master play?"

10.

Then they left you for their pleasure: till in due time, one by one,
Some with lives that came to nothing, some with deeds as well undone,
Death came tacitly and took them where they never see the sun.

11.

But when I sit down to reason,—think to take my stand nor swerve
Till I triumph o'er a secret wrung from nature's close reserve,
In you come with your cold music, till I creep thro' every nerve.

12.

Yes, you, like a ghostly cricket, creaking where a house was burned—
"Dust and ashes, dead and done with, Venice spent what Venice earned!
The soul, doubtless, is immortal—where a soul can be discerned.

13.

"Yours for instance: you know physics, something of geology,
Mathematics are your pastime; souls shall rise in their degree;
Butterflies may dread extinction,—you'll not die, it cannot be!

14.

"As for Venice and its people, merely born to bloom and drop,
Here on earth they bore their fruitage, mirth and folly were the crop.
What of soul was left, I wonder, when the kissing had to stop?

15.

"Dust and ashes!" So you creak it, and I want the heart to scold.
Dear dead women, with such hair, too—what's become of all the gold
Used to hang and brush their bosoms? I feel chilly and grown old.

By the Fire-side

1.

How well I know what I mean to do
   When the long dark Autumn evenings come,
And where, my soul, is thy pleasant hue?
   With the music of all thy voices, dumb
In life's November too!

2.

I shall be found by the fire, suppose,
   O'er a great wise book as beseemeth age,
While the shutters flap as the cross-wind blows,
   And I turn the page, and I turn the page,
Not verse now, only prose!

3.

Till the young ones whisper, finger on lip,
   "There he is at it, deep in Greek—
Now or never, then, out we slip
   To cut from the hazels by the creek
A mainmast for our ship."

4.

I shall be at it indeed, my friends!
   Greek puts already on either side
Such a branch-work forth, as soon extends
   To a vista opening far and wide,
And I pass out where it ends.

5.

The outside-frame like your hazel-trees—
   But the inside-archway narrows fast,
And a rarer sort succeeds to these,
   And we slope to Italy at last
And youth, by green degrees.

6.

I follow wherever I am led,
   Knowing so well the leader's hand—

Oh, woman-country, wooed, not wed,
  Loved all the more by earth's male-lands,
Laid to their hearts instead!

7.

Look at the ruined chapel again
  Half-way up in the Alpine gorge.
Is that a tower, I point you plain,
  Or is it a mill or an iron-forge
Breaks solitude in vain?

8.

A turn, and we stand in the heart of things;
  The woods are round us, heaped and dim;
From slab to slab how it slips and springs,
  The thread of water single and slim,
Thro' the ravage some torrent brings!

9.

Does it feed the little lake below?
  That speck of white just on its marge
Is Pella; see, in the evening glow,
  How sharp the silver spear-heads charge
When Alp meets heaven in snow.

10.

On our other side is the straight-up rock;
  And a path is kept 'twixt the gorge and it
By boulder-stones where lichens mock
  The marks on a moth, and small ferns fit
Their teeth to the polished block.

11.

Oh, the sense of the yellow mountain flowers,
  And the thorny balls, each three in one,
The chestnuts throw on our path in showers,
  For the drop of the woodland fruit's begun,
These early November hours—

12.

That crimson the creeper's leaf across
  Like a splash of blood, intense, abrupt,
O'er a shield, else gold from rim to boss,
  And lay it for show on the fairy-cupped
Elf-needled mat of moss,

13.

By the rose-flesh mushrooms, undivulged
  Last evening—nay, in to-day's first dew
Yon sudden coral nipple bulged
  Where a freaked, fawn-coloured, flaky crew
Of toad-stools peep indulged.

14.

And yonder, at foot of the fronting ridge
  That takes the turn to a range beyond,
Is the chapel reached by the one-arched bridge
  Where the water is stopped in a stagnant pond
Danced over by the midge.

15.

The chapel and bridge are of stone alike,
  Blackish grey and mostly wet;
Cut hemp-stalks steep in the narrow dyke.
  See here again, how the lichens fret
And the roots of the ivy strike!

16.

Poor little place, where its one priest comes
  On a festa-day, if he comes at all,
To the dozen folk from their scattered homes,
  Gathered within that precinct small
By the dozen ways one roams

17.

To drop from the charcoal-burners' huts,
  Or climb from the hemp-dressers' low shed,
Leave the grange where the woodman stores his nuts,
  Or the wattled cote where the fowlers spread
Their gear on the rock's bare juts.

18.

It has some pretension too, this front,
With its bit of fresco half-moon-wise
Set over the porch, art's early wont—
'Tis John in the Desert, I surmise,
But has borne the weather's brunt—

19.

Not from the fault of the builder, though,
For a pent-house properly projects
Where three carved beams make a certain show,
Dating—good thought of our architect's—
'Five, six, nine, he lets you know.

20.

And all day long a bird sings there,
And a stray sheep drinks at the pond at times:
The place is silent and aware;
It has had its scenes, its joys and crimes,
But that is its own affair.

21.

My perfect wife, my Leonor,
Oh, heart my own, oh eyes, mine too,
Whom else could I dare look backward for,
With whom beside should I dare pursue
The path grey heads abhor?

22.

For it leads to a crag's sheer edge with them;
Youth, flowery all the way, there stops—
Not they; age threatens and they contemn,
Till they reach the gulf wherein youth drops,
One inch from life's safe hem!

23.

With me, youth led—I will speak now,
No longer watch you as you sit
Reading by fire-light, that great brow
And the spirit-small hand propping it,
Mutely—my heart knows how—

24.

When, if I think but deep enough,
  You are wont to answer, prompt as rhyme;
And you, too, find without a rebuff
  The response your soul seeks many a time
Piercing its fine flesh-stuff—

25.

My own, confirm me! If I tread
  This path back, is it not in pride
To think how little I dreamed it led
  To an age so blest that by its side
Youth seems the waste instead!

26.

My own, see where the years conduct!
  At first, 'twas something our two souls
Should mix as mists do: each is sucked
  In each now; on, the new stream rolls,
Whatever rocks obstruct.

27.

Think, when our one soul understands
  The great Word which makes all things new—
When earth breaks up and Heaven expands—
  How will the change strike me and you
In the House not made with hands?

28.

Oh, I must feel your brain prompt mine,
  Your heart anticipate my heart,
You must be just before, in fine,
  See and make me see, for your part,
New depths of the Divine!

29.

But who could have expected this,
  When we two drew together first
Just for the obvious human bliss,
  To satisfy life's daily thirst
With a thing men seldom miss?

30.

Come back with me to the first of all,
Let us lean and love it over again—
Let us now forget and then recall,
Break the rosary in a pearly rain,
And gather what we let fall!

31.

What did I say?—that a small bird sings
All day long, save when a brown pair
Of hawks from the wood float with wide wings
Strained to a bell: 'gainst the noon-day glare
You count the streaks and rings.

32.

But at afternoon or almost eve
'Tis better; then the silence grows
To that degree, you half believe
It must get rid of what it knows,
Its bosom does so heave.

33.

Hither we walked, then, side by side,
Arm in arm and cheek to cheek,
And still I questioned or replied,
While my heart, convulsed to really speak,
Lay choking in its pride.

34.

Silent the crumbling bridge we cross,
And pity and praise the chapel sweet,
And care about the fresco's loss,
And wish for our souls a like retreat,
And wonder at the moss.

35.

Stoop and kneel on the settle under—
Look through the window's grated square:
Nothing to see! for fear of plunder,
The cross is down and the altar bare,
As if thieves don't fear thunder.

36.

We stoop and look in through the grate,
  See the little porch and rustic door,
Read duly the dead builder's date,
  Then cross the bridge that we crossed before,
Take the path again—but wait!

37.

Oh moment, one and infinite!
  The water slips o'er stock and stone;
The west is tender, hardly bright.
  How grey at once is the evening grown—
One star, the chrysolite!

38.

We two stood there with never a third,
  But each by each, as each knew well.
The sights we saw and the sounds we heard,
  The lights and the shades made up a spell
Till the trouble grew and stirred.

39.

Oh, the little more, and how much it is!
  And the little less, and what worlds away!
How a sound shall quicken content to bliss,
  Or a breath suspend the blood's best play,
And life be a proof of this!

40.

Had she willed it, still had stood the screen
  So slight, so sure, 'twixt my love and her.
I could fix her face with a guard between,
  And find her soul as when friends confer,
Friends—lovers that might have been.

41.

For my heart had a touch of the woodland time,
  Wanting to sleep now over its best.
Shake the whole tree in the summer-prime,
  But bring to the last leaf no such test.
"Hold the last fast!" says the rhyme.

42.

For a chance to make your little much,
   To gain a lover and lose a friend,
Venture the tree and a myriad such,
   When nothing you mar but the year can mend!
But a last leaf—fear to touch!

43.

Yet should it unfasten itself and fall
   Eddying down till it find your face
At some slight wind—(best chance of all!)
   Be your heart henceforth its dwelling-place
You trembled to forestal!

44.

Worth how well, those dark grey eyes,
   —That hair so dark and dear, how worth
That a man should strive and agonise,
   And taste a very hell on earth
For the hope of such a prize!

45.

Oh, you might have turned and tried a man,
   Set him a space to weary and wear,
And prove which suited more your plan,
   His best of hope or his worst despair,
Yet end as he began.

46.

But you spared me this, like the heart you are,
   And filled my empty heart at a word.
If you join two lives, there is oft a scar,
   They are one and one, with a shadowy third;
One near one is too far.

47.

A moment after, and hands unseen
   Were hanging the night around us fast.
But we knew that a bar was broken between
   Life and life: we were mixed at last
In spite of the mortal screen.

48.

The forests had done it; there they stood—
  We caught for a second the powers at play:
They had mingled us so, for once and for good,
  Their work was done—we might go or stay,
They relapsed to their ancient mood.

49.

How the world is made for each of us!
  How all we perceive and know in it
Tends to some moment's product thus,
  When a soul declares itself—to wit,
By its fruit—the thing it does!

50.

Be Hate that fruit or Love that fruit,
  It forwards the General Deed of Man,
And each of the Many helps to recruit
  The life of the race by a general plan,
Each living his own, to boot.

51.

I am named and known by that hour's feat,
  There took my station and degree.
So grew my own small life complete
  As nature obtained her best of me—
One born to love you, sweet!

52.

And to watch you sink by the fire-side now
  Back again, as you mutely sit
Musing by fire-light, that great brow
  And the spirit-small hand propping it,
Yonder, my heart knows how!

53.

So the earth has gained by one man more,
  And the gain of earth must be Heaven's gain too,
And the whole is well worth thinking o'er
  When autumn comes: which I mean to do
One day, as I said before.

Any Wife to Any Husband

1.

My love, this is the bitterest, that thou
Who art all truth and who dost love me now
  As thine eyes say, as thy voice breaks to say—
Should'st love so truly, and could'st love me still
A whole long life through, had but love its will,
  Would death that leads me from thee brook delay!

2.

I have but to be by thee, and thy hand
Would never let mine go, thy heart withstand
  The beating of my heart to reach its place.
When should I look for thee and feel thee gone?
When cry for the old comfort and find none?
  Never, I know! Thy soul is in thy face.

3.

Oh, I should fade—'tis willed so! might I save,
Gladly I would, whatever beauty gave
  Joy to thy sense, for that was precious too.
It is not to be granted. But the soul
Whence the love comes, all ravage leaves that whole;
  Vainly the flesh fades—soul makes all things new.

4.

And 'twould not be because my eye grew dim
Thou could'st not find the love there, thanks to Him
  Who never is dishonoured in the spark
He gave us from his fire of fires, and bade
Remember whence it sprang nor be afraid
  While that burns on, though all the rest grow dark.

5.

So, how thou woulds't be perfect, white and clean
Outside as inside, soul and soul's demesne
  Alike, this body given to show it by!
Oh, three-parts through the worst of life's abyss,
What plaudits from the next world after this,
  Could'st thou repeat a stroke and gain the sky!

6.

And is it not the bitterer to think
That, disengage our hands and thou wilt sink
  Although thy love was love in very deed?
I know that nature! Pass a festive day
Thou dost not throw its relic-flower away
  Nor bid its music's loitering echo speed.

7.

Thou let'st the stranger's glove lie where it fell;
If old things remain old things all is well,
  For thou art grateful as becomes man best:
And hadst thou only heard me play one tune,
Or viewed me from a window, not so soon
  With thee would such things fade as with the rest.

8.

I seem to see! we meet and part: 'tis brief:
The book I opened keeps a folded leaf,
  The very chair I sat on, breaks the rank;
That is a portrait of me on the wall—
Three lines, my face comes at so slight a call;
  And for all this, one little hour's to thank!

9.

But now, because the hour through years was fixed,
Because our inmost beings met and mixed,
  Because thou once hast loved me—wilt thou dare
Say to thy soul and Who may list beside,
"Therefore she is immortally my bride,
  Chance cannot change that love, nor time impair.

10.

"So, what if in the dusk of life that's left,
I, a tired traveller, of my sun bereft,
  Look from my path when, mimicking the same,
The fire-fly glimpses past me, come and gone?
—Where was it till the sunset? where anon
  It will be at the sunrise! what's to blame?"

11.

Is it so helpful to thee? canst thou take
The mimic up, nor, for the true thing's sake,
Put gently by such efforts at a beam?
Is the remainder of the way so long
Thou need'st the little solace, thou the strong?
Watch out thy watch, let weak ones doze and dream!

12.

"—Ah, but the fresher faces! Is it true,"
Thou'lt ask, "some eyes are beautiful and new?
Some hair,—how can one choose but grasp such wealth?
And if a man would press his lips to lips
Fresh as the wilding hedge-rose-cup there slips
The dew-drop out of, must it be by stealth?

13.

"It cannot change the love kept still for Her,
Much more than, such a picture to prefer
Passing a day with, to a room's bare side.
The painted form takes nothing she possessed,
Yet while the Titian's Venus lies at rest
A man looks. Once more, what is there to chide?"

14.

So must I see, from where I sit and watch,
My own self sell myself, my hand attach
Its warrant to the very thefts from me—
Thy singleness of soul that made me proud,
Thy purity of heart I loved aloud,
Thy man's truth I was bold to bid God see!

15.

Love so, then, if thou wilt! Give all thou canst
Away to the new faces—disentranced—
(Say it and think it) obdurate no more,
Re-issue looks and words from the old mint—
Pass them afresh, no matter whose the print
Image and superscription once they bore!

16.

Re-coin thyself and give it them to spend,—
It all comes to the same thing at the end,
  Since mine thou wast, mine art, and mine shalt be,
Faithful or faithless, sealing up the sum
Or lavish of my treasure, thou must come
  Back to the heart's place here I keep for thee!

17.

Only, why should it be with stain at all?
Why must I, 'twixt the leaves of coronal,
  Put any kiss of pardon on thy brow?
Why need the other women know so much,
And talk together, "Such the look and such
  The smile he used to love with, then as now!"

18.

Might I die last and shew thee! Should I find
Such hardship in the few years left behind,
  If free to take and light my lamp, and go
Into thy tomb, and shut the door and sit
Seeing thy face on those four sides of it
  The better that they are so blank, I know!

19.

Why, time was what I wanted, to turn o'er
Within my mind each look, get more and more
  By heart each word, too much to learn at first,
And join thee all the fitter for the pause
'Neath the low door-way's lintel. That were cause
  For lingering, though thou calledst, if I durst!

20.

And yet thou art the nobler of us two.
What dare I dream of, that thou canst not do,
  Outstripping my ten small steps with one stride?
I'll say then, here's a trial and a task—
Is it to bear?—if easy, I'll not ask—
  Though love fail, I can trust on in thy pride.

21.

Pride?—when those eyes forestal the life behind
The death I have to go through!—when I find,
  Now that I want thy help most, all of thee!
What did I fear? Thy love shall hold me fast
Until the little minute's sleep is past
  And I wake saved.—And yet it will not be!

An Epistle Containing the Strange Medical Experience of Karshish, the Arab Physician

Karshish, the picker-up of learning's crumbs,
The not-incurious in God's handiwork
(This man's-flesh He hath admirably made,
Blown like a bubble, kneaded like a paste,
To coop up and keep down on earth a space
That puff of vapour from His mouth, man's soul)
—To Abib, all-sagacious in our art,
Breeder in me of what poor skill I boast,
Like me inquisitive how pricks and cracks
Befall the flesh through too much stress and strain,
Whereby the wily vapour fain would slip
Back and rejoin its source before the term,—
And aptest in contrivance, under God,
To baffle it by deftly stopping such:—
The vagrant Scholar to his Sage at home
Sends greeting (health and knowledge, fame with peace)
Three samples of true snake-stone—rarer still,
One of the other sort, the melon-shaped,
(But fitter, pounded fine, for charms than drugs)
And writeth now the twenty-second time.

  My journeyings were brought to Jericho,
Thus I resume. Who studious in our art
Shall count a little labour unrepaid?
I have shed sweat enough, left flesh and bone
On many a flinty furlong of this land.
Also the country-side is all on fire
With rumours of a marching hitherward—
Some say Vespasian cometh, some, his son.

A black lynx snarled and pricked a tufted ear;
Lust of my blood inflamed his yellow balls:
I cried and threw my staff and he was gone.
Twice have the robbers stripped and beaten me,
And once a town declared me for a spy,
But at the end, I reach Jerusalem,
Since this poor covert where I pass the night,
This Bethany, lies scarce the distance thence
A man with plague-sores at the third degree
Runs till he drops down dead. Thou laughest here!
'Sooth, it elates me, thus reposed and safe,
To void the stuffing of my travel-scrip
And share with thee whatever Jewry yields.
A viscid choler is observable
In tertians, I was nearly bold to say,
And falling-sickness hath a happier cure
Than our school wots of: there's a spider here
Weaves no web, watches on the ledge of tombs,
Sprinkled with mottles on an ash-grey back;
Take five and drop them . . . but who knows his mind,
The Syrian run-a-gate I trust this to?
His service payeth me a sublimate
Blown up his nose to help the ailing eye.
Best wait: I reach Jerusalem at morn,
There set in order my experiences,
Gather what most deserves, and give thee all—
Or I might add, Judea's gum-tragacanth
Scales off in purer flakes, shines clearer-grained,
Cracks 'twixt the pestle and the porphyry,
In fine exceeds our produce. Scalp-disease
Confounds me, crossing so with leprosy—
Thou hadst admired one sort I gained at Zoar—
But zeal outruns discretion. Here I end.

Yet stay: my Syrian blinketh gratefully,
Protesteth his devotion is my price—
Suppose I write what harms not, though he steal?
I half resolve to tell thee, yet I blush,
What set me off a-writing first of all.
An itch I had, a sting to write, a tang!
For, be it this town's barrenness—or else

The Man had something in the look of him—
His case has struck me far more than 'tis worth.
So, pardon if—(lest presently I lose
In the great press of novelty at hand
The care and pains this somehow stole from me)
I bid thee take the thing while fresh in mind,
Almost in sight—for, wilt thou have the truth?
The very man is gone from me but now,
Whose ailment is the subject of discourse.
Thus then, and let thy better wit help all.

'Tis but a case of mania—subinduced
By epilepsy, at the turning-point
Of trance prolonged unduly some three days,
When by the exhibition of some drug
Or spell, exorcisation, stroke of art
Unknown to me and which 'twere well to know
The evil thing out-breaking all at once
Left the man whole and sound of body indeed,—
But, flinging, so to speak, life's gates too wide,
Making a clear house of it too suddenly,
The first conceit that entered pleased to write
Whatever it was minded on the wall
So plainly at that vantage, as it were,
(First come, first served) that nothing subsequent
Attaineth to erase the fancy-scrawls
Which the returned and new-established soul
Hath gotten now so thoroughly by heart
That henceforth she will read or these or none.
And first—the man's own firm conviction rests
That he was dead (in fact they buried him)
That he was dead and then restored to life
By a Nazarene physician of his tribe:
—'Sayeth, the same bade "Rise," and he did rise.
"Such cases are diurnal," thou wilt cry.
Not so this figment!—not, that such a fume,
Instead of giving way to time and health,
Should eat itself into the life of life,
As saffron tingeth flesh, blood, bones and all!
For see, how he takes up the after-life.
The man—it is one Lazarus a Jew,

Sanguine, proportioned, fifty years of age,
The body's habit wholly laudable,
As much, indeed, beyond the common health
As he were made and put aside to shew.
Think, could we penetrate by any drug
And bathe the wearied soul and worried flesh,
And bring it clear and fair, by three days sleep!
Whence has the man the balm that brightens all?
This grown man eyes the world now like a child.
Some elders of his tribe, I should premise,
Led in their friend, obedient as a sheep,
To bear my inquisition. While they spoke,
Now sharply, now with sorrow,—told the case,—
He listened not except I spoke to him,
But folded his two hands and let them talk,
Watching the flies that buzzed: and yet no fool.
And that's a sample how his years must go.
Look if a beggar, in fixed middle-life,
Should find a treasure, can he use the same
With straightened habits and with tastes starved small,
And take at once to his impoverished brain
The sudden element that changes things,
—That sets the undreamed-of rapture at his hand,
And puts the cheap old joy in the scorned dust?
Is he not such an one as moves to mirth—
Warily parsimonious, when's no need,
Wasteful as drunkenness at undue times?
All prudent counsel as to what befits
The golden mean, is lost on such an one.
The man's fantastic will is the man's law.
So here—we'll call the treasure knowledge, say—
Increased beyond the fleshly faculty—
Heaven opened to a soul while yet on earth,
Earth forced on a soul's use while seeing Heaven.
The man is witless of the size, the sum,
The value in proportion of all things,
Or whether it be little or be much.
Discourse to him of prodigious armaments
Assembled to besiege his city now,
And of the passing of a mule with gourds—
'Tis one! Then take it on the other side,

Speak of some trifling fact—he will gaze rapt
With stupor at its very littleness—
(Far as I see) as if in that indeed
He caught prodigious import, whole results;
And so will turn to us the bystanders
In ever the same stupor (note this point)
That we too see not with his opened eyes!
Wonder and doubt come wrongly into play,
Preposterously, at cross purposes.
Should his child sicken unto death,—why, look
For scarce abatement of his cheerfulness,
Or pretermission of the daily craft—
While a word, gesture, glance from that same child
At play or in the school or laid asleep,
Will startle him to an agony of fear,
Exasperation, just as like! demand
The reason why—"'tis but a word," object—
"A gesture"—he regards thee as our lord
Who lived there in the pyramid alone,
Looked at us, dost thou mind, when being young,
We both would unadvisedly recite
Some charm's beginning, from that book of his,
Able to bid the sun throb wide and burst
All into stars, as suns grown old are wont.
Thou and the child have each a veil alike
Thrown o'er your heads, from under which ye both
Stretch your blind hands and trifle with a match
Over a mine of Greek fire, did ye know!
He holds on firmly to some thread of life—
(It is the life to lead perforcedly)
Which runs across some vast distracting orb
Of glory on either side that meagre thread,
Which, conscious of, he must not enter yet—
The spiritual life around the earthly life!
The law of that is known to him as this—
His heart and brain move there, his feet stay here.
So is the man perplext with impulses
Sudden to start off crosswise, not straight on,
Proclaiming what is Right and Wrong across—
And not along—this black thread through the blaze—
"It should be" balked by "here it cannot be."

And oft the man's soul springs into his face
As if he saw again and heard again
His sage that bade him "Rise" and he did rise.
Something—a word, a tick of the blood within
Admonishes—then back he sinks at once
To ashes, that was very fire before,
In sedulous recurrence to his trade
Whereby he earneth him the daily bread—
And studiously the humbler for that pride,
Professedly the faultier that he knows
God's secret, while he holds the thread of life.
Indeed the especial marking of the man
Is prone submission to the Heavenly will—
Seeing it, what it is, and why it is.
'Sayeth, he will wait patient to the last
For that same death which must restore his being
To equilibrium, body loosening soul
Divorced even now by premature full growth:
He will live, nay, it pleaseth him to live
So long as God please, and just how God please.
He even seeketh not to please God more
(Which meaneth, otherwise) than as God please.
Hence I perceive not he affects to preach
The doctrine of his sect whate'er it be—
Make proselytes as madmen thirst to do.
How can he give his neighbour the real ground,
His own conviction? ardent as he is—
Call his great truth a lie, why still the old
"Be it as God please" reassureth him.
I probed the sore as thy disciple should—
"How, beast," said I, "this stolid carelessness
Sufficeth thee, when Rome is on her march
To stamp out like a little spark thy town,
Thy tribe, thy crazy tale and thee at once?"
He merely looked with his large eyes on me.
The man is apathetic, you deduce?
Contrariwise he loves both old and young,
Able and weak—affects the very brutes
And birds—how say I? flowers of the field—
As a wise workman recognises tools
In a master's workshop, loving what they make.

Thus is the man as harmless as a lamb:
Only impatient, let him do his best,
At ignorance and carelessness and sin—
An indignation which is promptly curbed.
As when in certain travels I have feigned
To be an ignoramus in our art
According to some preconceived design,
And happed to hear the land's practitioners
Steeped in conceit sublimed by ignorance,
Prattle fantastically on disease,
Its cause and cure—and I must hold my peace!

Thou wilt object—why have I not ere this
Sought out the sage himself, the Nazarene
Who wrought this cure, enquiring at the source,
Conferring with the frankness that befits?
Alas! it grieveth me, the learned leech
Perished in a tumult many years ago,
Accused,—our learning's fate,—of wizardry,
Rebellion, to the setting up a rule
And creed prodigious as described to me.
His death, which happened when the earthquake fell
(Prefiguring, as soon appeared, the loss
To occult learning in our lord the sage
Who lived there in the pyramid alone)
Was wrought by the mad people—that's their wont—
On vain recourse, as I conjecture it,
To his tried virtue, for miraculous help—
How could he stop the earthquake? That's their way!
The other imputations must be lies:
But take one—though I loathe to give it thee,
In mere respect for any good man's fame!
(And after all, our patient Lazarus
Is stark mad—should we count on what he says?
Perhaps not—though in writing to a leech
'Tis well to keep back nothing of a case.)
This man so cured regards the curer, then,
As—God forgive me—who but God himself,
Creator and Sustainer of the world,
That came and dwelt in flesh on it awhile!
—'Sayeth that such an One was born and lived,

Taught, healed the sick, broke bread at his own house,
Then died, with Lazarus by, for aught I know,
And yet was . . . what I said nor choose repeat,
And must have so avouched himself, in fact,
In hearing of this very Lazarus
Who saith—but why all this of what he saith?
Why write of trivial matters, things of price
Calling at every moment for remark?
I noticed on the margin of a pool
Blue-flowering borage, the Aleppo sort,
Aboundeth, very nitrous. It is strange!

Thy pardon for this long and tedious case,
Which, now that I review it, needs must seem
Unduly dwelt on, prolixly set forth.
Nor I myself discern in what is writ
Good cause for the peculiar interest
And awe indeed this man has touched me with.
Perhaps the journey's end, the weariness
Had wrought upon me first. I met him thus—
I crossed a ridge of short sharp broken hills
Like an old lion's cheek-teeth. Out there came
A moon made like a face with certain spots
Multiform, manifold and menacing:
Then a wind rose behind me. So we met
In this old sleepy town at unaware,
The man and I. I send thee what is writ.
Regard it as a chance, a matter risked
To this ambiguous Syrian—he may lose,
Or steal, or give it thee with equal good.
Jerusalem's repose shall make amends
For time this letter wastes, thy time and mine,
Till when, once more thy pardon and farewell!

The very God! think, Abib; dost thou think?
So, the All-Great, were the All-Loving too—
So, through the thunder comes a human voice
Saying, "O heart I made, a heart beats here!
Face, my hands fashioned, see it in myself.
Thou hast no power nor may'st conceive of mine,
But love I gave thee, with Myself to love,

And thou must love me who have died for thee!"
The madman saith He said so: it is strange.

Mesmerism

1.

All I believed is true!
  I am able yet
  All I want to get
By a method as strange as new:
Dare I trust the same to you?

2.

If at night, when doors are shut,
  And the wood-worm picks,
  And the death-watch ticks,
And the bar has a flag of smut,
And a cat's in the water-butt—

3.

And the socket floats and flares,
  And the house-beams groan,
  And a foot unknown
Is surmised on the garret-stairs,
And the locks slip unawares—

4.

And the spider, to serve his ends,
  By a sudden thread,
  Arms and legs outspread,
On the table's midst descends,
Comes to find, God knows what friends!—

5.

If since eve drew in, I say,
  I have sat and brought
  (So to speak) my thought
To bear on the woman away,
Till I felt my hair turn grey—

6.

Till I seemed to have and hold,
   In the vacancy
   'Twixt the wall and me,
From the hair-plait's chestnut gold
To the foot in its muslin fold—

7.

Have and hold, then and there,
   Her, from head to foot,
   Breathing and mute,
Passive and yet aware,
In the grasp of my steady stare—

8.

Hold and have, there and then,
   All her body and soul
   That completes my Whole,
All that women add to men,
In the clutch of my steady ken—

9.

Having and holding, till
   I imprint her fast
   On the void at last
As the sun does whom he will
By the calotypist's skill—

10.

Then,—if my heart's strength serve,
   And through all and each
   Of the veils I reach
To her soul and never swerve,
Knitting an iron nerve—

11.

Commanding that to advance
   And inform the shape
   Which has made escape
And before my countenance
Answers me glance for glance—

12.

I, still with a gesture fit
Of my hands that best
Do my soul's behest,
Pointing the power from it,
While myself do steadfast sit—

13.

Steadfast and still the same
On my object bent,
While the hands give vent
To my ardour and my aim
And break into very flame—

14.

Then, I reach, I must believe,
Not her soul in vain,
For to me again
It reaches, and past retrieve
Is wound in the toils I weave—

15.

And must follow as I require,
As befits a thrall,
Bringing flesh and all,
Essence and earth-attire,
To the source of the tractile fire—

16.

Till the house called hers, not mine,
With a growing weight
Seems to suffocate
If she break not its leaden line
And escape from its close confine—

17.

Out of doors into the night!
On to the maze
Of the wild wood-ways,
Not turning to left or right
From the pathway, blind with sight—

18.

Making thro' rain and wind
  O'er the broken shrubs,
  'Twixt the stems and stubs,
With a still composed strong mind,
Nor a care for the world behind—

19.

Swifter and still more swift,
  As the crowding peace
  Doth to joy increase
In the wide blind eyes uplift,
Thro' the darkness and the drift!

20.

While I—to the shape, I too
  Feel my soul dilate
  Nor a whit abate
And relax not a gesture due,
As I see my belief come true—

21.

For there! have I drawn or no
  Life to that lip?
  Do my fingers dip
In a flame which again they throw
On the cheek that breaks a-glow?

22.

Ha! was the hair so first?
  What, unfilleted,
  Made alive, and spread
Through the void with a rich outburst,
Chestnut gold-interspersed!

23.

Like the doors of a casket-shrine,
  See, on either side,
  Her two arms divide
Till the heart betwixt makes sign,
Take me, for I am thine!

24.

Now—now—the door is heard!
  Hark! the stairs and near—
  Nearer—and here—
Now! and at call the third
She enters without a word

25.

On doth she march and on
  To the fancied shape—
  It is past escape,
Herself, now—the dream is done
And the shadow and she are one.

26.

First I will pray. Do Thou
  That ownest the soul,
  Yet wilt grant controul
To another nor disallow
For a time, restrain me now!

27.

I admonish me while I may,
  Not to squander guilt,
  Since require Thou wilt
At my hand its price one day!
What the price is, who can say?

A Serenade at the Villa

1.

That was I, you heard last night
  When there rose no moon at all,
Nor, to pierce the strained and tight
  Tent of heaven, a planet small:
Life was dead, and so was light.

2.

Not a twinkle from the fly,
  Not a glimmer from the worm.
When the crickets stopped their cry,
  When the owls forbore a term,
You heard music; that was I.

3.

Earth turned in her sleep with pain,
  Sultrily suspired for proof:
In at heaven and out again,
  Lightning!—where it broke the roof,
Bloodlike, some few drops of rain.

4.

What they could my words expressed,
  O my love, my all, my one!
Singing helped the verses best,
  And when singing's best was done,
To my lute I left the rest.

5.

So wore night; the east was grey,
  White the broad-faced hemlock flowers;
There would be another day;
  Ere its first of heavy hours
Found me, I had past away.

6.

What became of all the hopes,
  Words and song and lute as well?
Say, this struck you—"When life gropes
Feebly for the path where fell
Light last on the evening slopes,

7.

"One friend in that path shall be,
  To secure my step from wrong;
One to count night day for me,

  Patient through the watches long,
Serving most with none to see."

8.

Never say—as something bodes—
  "So, the worst has yet a worse!
When life halts 'neath double loads,
  Better the task-master's curse
Than such music on the roads!

9.

"When no moon succeeds the sun,
  Nor can pierce the midnight's tent
Any star, the smallest one,
  While some drops, where lightning went,
Show the final storm begun—

10.

"When the fire-fly hides its spot,
  When the garden-voices fail
In the darkness thick and hot,—
  Shall another voice avail,
That shape be where those are not?

11.

"Has some plague a longer lease,
  Proffering its help uncouth?
Can't one even die in peace?
  As one shuts one's eyes on youth,
Is that face the last one sees?"

12.

Oh, how dark your villa was,
  Windows fast and obdurate!
How the garden grudged me grass
  Where I stood—the iron gate
Ground its teeth to let me pass!

My Star

All that I know
  Of a certain star
Is, it can throw
  (Like the angled spar)
Now a dart of red,
  Now a dart of blue,
Till my friends have said
  They would fain see, too,
My star that dartles the red and the blue!
Then it stops like a bird,—like a flower, hangs furled;
  They must solace themselves with the Saturn above it.
What matter to me if their star is a world?
  Mine has opened its soul to me; therefore I love it.

"Childe Roland to the Dark Tower Came"

(See Edgar's Song in "Lear.")

1.

My first thought was, he lied in every word,
  That hoary cripple, with malicious eye
  Askance to watch the working of his lie
On mine, and mouth scarce able to afford
Suppression of the glee that pursed and scored
  Its edge at one more victim gained thereby.

2.

What else should he be set for, with his staff?
  What, save to waylay with his lies, ensnare
  All travellers who might find him posted there,
And ask the road? I guessed what skull-like laugh
Would break, what crutch 'gin write my epitaph
  For pastime in the dusty thoroughfare,

3.

If at his counsel I should turn aside
  Into that ominous tract which, all agree,
  Hides the Dark Tower. Yet acquiescingly

I did turn as he pointed; neither pride
Nor hope rekindling at the end descried,
   So much as gladness that some end should be

4.

For, what with my whole world-wide wandering,
   What with my search drawn out thro' years, my hope
   Dwindled into a ghost not fit to cope
With that obstreperous joy success would bring,—
I hardly tried now to rebuke the spring
   My heart made, finding failure in its scope.

5.

As when a sick man very near to death
   Seems dead indeed, and feels begin and end
   The tears and takes the farewell of each friend,
And hears one bid the other go, draw breath
Freelier outside, ("since all is o'er," he saith,
"And the blow fall'n no grieving can amend")

6.

While some discuss if near the other graves
   Be room enough for this, and when a day
   Suits best for carrying the corpse away,
With care about the banners, scarves and staves,—
And still the man hears all, and only craves
   He may not shame such tender love and stay.

7.

Thus, I had so long suffered in this quest,
   Heard failure prophesied so oft, been writ
   So many times among "The Band"—to wit,
The knights who to the Dark Tower's search addressed
Their steps—that just to fail as they, seemed best,
   And all the doubt was now—should I be fit.

8.

So, quiet as despair, I turned from him,
   That hateful cripple, out of his highway
   Into the path he pointed. All the day

Had been a dreary one at best, and dim
Was settling to its close, yet shot one grim
  Red leer to see the plain catch its estray.

9.

For mark! no sooner was I fairly found
  Pledged to the plain, after a pace or two,
  Than pausing to throw backward a last view
To the safe road, 'twas gone! grey plain all round!
Nothing but plain to the horizon's bound.
  I might go on; nought else remained to do.

10.

So on I went. I think I never saw
  Such starved ignoble nature; nothing throve:
  For flowers—as well expect a cedar grove!
But cockle, spurge, according to their law
Might propagate their kind, with none to awe,
  You'd think: a burr had been a treasure-trove.

11.

No! penury, inertness, and grimace,
  In some strange sort, were the land's portion. "See
  Or shut your eyes"—said Nature peevishly—
"It nothing skills: I cannot help my case:
The Judgment's fire alone can cure this place,
  Calcine its clods and set my prisoners free."

12.

If there pushed any ragged thistle-stalk
  Above its mates, the head was chopped—the bents
  Were jealous else. What made those holes and rents
In the dock's harsh swarth leaves—bruised as to baulk
All hope of greenness? 'tis a brute must walk
  Pashing their life out, with a brute's intents.

13.

As for the grass, it grew as scant as hair
  In leprosy—thin dry blades pricked the mud
  Which underneath looked kneaded up with blood.

One stiff blind horse, his every bone a-stare,
Stood stupefied, however he came there—
  Thrust out past service from the devil's stud!

14.

Alive? he might be dead for all I know,
  With that red gaunt and colloped neck a-strain,
  And shut eyes underneath the rusty mane.
Seldom went such grotesqueness with such woe:
I never saw a brute I hated so—
  He must be wicked to deserve such pain.

15.

I shut my eyes and turned them on my heart.
  As a man calls for wine before he fights,
  I asked one draught of earlier, happier sights,
Ere fitly I could hope to play my part.
Think first, fight afterwards—the soldier's art:
  One taste of the old time sets all to rights!

16.

Not it! I fancied Cuthbert's reddening face
  Beneath its garniture of curly gold,
  Dear fellow, till I almost felt him fold
An arm in mine to fix me to the place,
That way he used. Alas! one night's disgrace!
  Out went my heart's new fire and left it cold.

17.

Giles, then, the soul of honour—there he stands
  Frank as ten years ago when knighted first.
  What honest man should dare (he said) he durst.
Good—but the scene shifts—faugh! what hangman's hands
Pin to his breast a parchment? his own bands
  Read it. Poor traitor, spit upon and curst!

18.

Better this present than a past like that—
  Back therefore to my darkening path again.

No sound, no sight as far as eye could strain.
Will the night send a howlet or a bat?
I asked: when something on the dismal flat
Came to arrest my thoughts and change their train.

19.

A sudden little river crossed my path
As unexpected as a serpent comes.
No sluggish tide congenial to the glooms—
This, as it frothed by, might have been a bath
For the fiend's glowing hoof—to see the wrath
Of its black eddy bespate with flakes and spumes.

20.

So petty yet so spiteful! all along,
Low scrubby alders kneeled down over it;
Drenched willows flung them headlong in a fit
Of mute despair, a suicidal throng:
The river which had done them all the wrong,
Whate'er that was, rolled by, deterred no whit.

21.

Which, while I forded,—good saints, how I feared
To set my foot upon a dead man's cheek,
Each step, or feel the spear I thrust to seek
For hollows, tangled in his hair or beard!
—It may have been a water-rat I speared,
But, ugh! it sounded like a baby's shriek.

22.

Glad was I when I reached the other bank.
Now for a better country. Vain presage!
Who were the strugglers, what war did they wage,
Whose savage trample thus could pad the dank
Soil to a plash? toads in a poisoned tank,
Or wild cats in a red-hot iron cage—

23.

The fight must so have seemed in that fell cirque.
What kept them there, with all the plain to choose?

No foot-print leading to that horrid mews,
None out of it: mad brewage set to work
Their brains, no doubt, like galley-slaves the Turk
Pits for his pastime, Christians against Jews.

24.

And more than that—a furlong on—why, there!
What bad use was that engine for, that wheel,
Or brake, not wheel—that harrow fit to reel
Men's bodies out like silk? with all the air
Of Tophet's tool, on earth left unaware,
Or brought to sharpen its rusty teeth of steel.

25.

Then came a bit of stubbed ground, once a wood,
Next a marsh, it would seem, and now mere earth
Desperate and done with; (so a fool finds mirth,
Makes a thing and then mars it, till his mood
Changes and off he goes!) within a rood
Bog, clay and rubble, sand and stark black dearth.

26.

Now blotches rankling, coloured gay and grim,
Now patches where some leanness of the soil's
Broke into moss or substances like boils;
Then came some palsied oak, a cleft in him
Like a distorted mouth that splits its rim
Gaping at death, and dies while it recoils.

27.

And just as far as ever from the end!
Nought in the distance but the evening, nought
To point my footstep further! At the thought,
A great black bird, Apollyon's bosom-friend,
Sailed past, nor beat his wide wing dragon-penned
That brushed my cap—perchance the guide I sought.

28.

For looking up, aware I somehow grew,
'Spite of the dusk, the plain had given place

All round to mountains—with such name to grace
Mere ugly heights and heaps now stol'n in view.
How thus they had surprised me,—solve it, you!
How to get from them was no plainer case.

29.

Yet half I seemed to recognise some trick
Of mischief happened to me, God knows when—
In a bad dream perhaps. Here ended, then,
Progress this way. When, in the very nick
Of giving up, one time more, came a click
As when a trap shuts—you're inside the den!

30.

Burningly it came on me all at once,
This was the place! those two hills on the right
Crouched like two bulls locked horn in horn in fight—
While to the left, a tall scalped mountain . . . Dunce,
Fool, to be dozing at the very nonce,
After a life spent training for the sight!

31.

What in the midst lay but the Tower itself?
The round squat turret, blind as the fool's heart,
Built of brown stone, without a counterpart
In the whole world. The tempest's mocking elf
Points to the shipman thus the unseen shelf
He strikes on, only when the timbers start.

32.

Not see? because of night perhaps?—Why, day
Came back again for that! before it left,
The dying sunset kindled through a cleft:
The hills, like giants at a hunting, lay—
Chin upon hand, to see the game at bay,—
"Now stab and end the creature—to the heft!"

33.

Not hear? when noise was everywhere? it tolled
Increasing like a bell. Names in my ears

Of all the lost adventurers my peers,—
How such a one was strong, and such was bold,
And such was fortunate, yet each of old
Lost, lost! one moment knelled the woe of years.

34.

There they stood, ranged along the hill-sides—met
To view the last of me, a living frame
For one more picture! in a sheet of flame
I saw them and I knew them all. And yet
Dauntless the slug-horn to my lips I set,
And blew. "*Childe Roland to the Dark Tower came.*"

Respectability

1.

Dear, had the world in its caprice
Deigned to proclaim "I know you both,
Have recognised your plighted troth,
Am sponsor for you—live in peace!"—
How many precious months and years
Of youth had passed, that speed so fast,
Before we found it out at last,
The world, and what it fears?

2.

How much of priceless life were spent
With men that every virtue decks,
And women models of their sex,
Society's true ornament,—
Ere we dared wander, nights like this,
Thro' wind and rain, and watch the Seine,
And feel the Boulevart break again
To warmth and light and bliss?

3.

I know! the world proscribes not love;
Allows my finger to caress
Your lips' contour and downiness,

Provided it supply a glove.
The world's good word!—the Institute!
Guizot receives Montalembert!
Eh? Down the court three lampions flare—
Put forward your best foot!

A Light Woman

1.

So far as our story approaches the end,
Which do you pity the most of us three?—
My friend, or the mistress of my friend
With her wanton eyes, or me?

2.

My friend was already too good to lose,
And seemed in the way of improvement yet,
When she crossed his path with her hunting-noose
And over him drew her net.

3.

When I saw him tangled in her toils,
A shame, said I, if she adds just him
To her nine-and-ninety other spoils,
The hundredth, for a whim!

4.

And before my friend be wholly hers,
How easy to prove to him, I said,
An eagle's the game her pride prefers,
Though she snaps at a wren instead!

5.

So I gave her eyes my own eyes to take,
My hand sought hers as in earnest need,
And round she turned for my noble sake,
And gave me herself indeed.

6.

The eagle am I, with my fame in the world,
The wren is he, with his maiden face.
—You look away and your lip is curled?
Patience, a moment's space!

7.

For see—my friend goes shaking and white;
He eyes me as the basilisk:
I have turned, it appears, his day to night,
Eclipsing his sun's disc.

8.

And I did it, he thinks, as a very thief:
"Though I love her—that, he comprehends—
One should master one's passions, (love, in chief)
And be loyal to one's friends!"

9.

And she,—she lies in my hand as tame
As a pear hung basking over a wall;
Just a touch to try and off it came;
'Tis mine,—can I let it fall?

10.

With no mind to eat it, that's the worst!
Were it thrown in the road, would the case assist?
'Twas quenching a dozen blue-flies' thirst
When I gave its stalk a twist.

11.

And I,—what I seem to my friend, you see—
What I soon shall seem to his love, you guess.
What I seem to myself, do you ask of me?
No hero, I confess.

12.

'Tis an awkward thing to play with souls,
And matter enough to save one's own.
Yet think of my friend, and the burning coals
He played with for bits of stone!

13.

One likes to show the truth for the truth;
That the woman was light is very true:
But suppose she says,—never mind that youth—
What wrong have I done to you?

14.

Well, any how, here the story stays,
So far at least as I understand;
And, Robert Browning, you writer of plays,
Here's a subject made to your hand!

The Statue and the Bust

There's a palace in Florence, the world knows well,
And a statue watches it from the square,
And this story of both do the townsmen tell.

Ages ago, a lady there,
At the farthest window facing the east
Asked, "Who rides by with the royal air?"

The brides-maids' prattle around her ceased;
She leaned forth, one on either hand;
They saw how the blush of the bride increased—

They felt by its beats her heart expand—
As one at each ear and both in a breath
Whispered, "The Great-Duke Ferdinand."

That selfsame instant, underneath,
The Duke rode past in his idle way,
Empty and fine like a swordless sheath.

Gay he rode, with a friend as gay,
Till he threw his head back—"Who is she?"
—"A Bride the Riccardi brings home to-day."

Hair in heaps lay heavily
Over a pale brow spirit-pure—
Carved like the heart of the coal-black tree,

FIG. 5 Giovanni da Bologna, Equestrian Statue of Ferdinand de Medici, with Ospedale degli innocenti, with roundels by Andrea della Robbia, Piazza SS. Annunziata, Florence.

Crisped like a war-steed's encolure—
Which vainly sought to dissemble her eyes
Of the blackest black our eyes endure.

And lo, a blade for a knight's emprise
Filled the fine empty sheath of a man,—
The Duke grew straightway brave and wise.

He looked at her, as a lover can;
She looked at him, as one who awakes,—
The past was a sleep, and her life began.

As love so ordered for both their sakes,
A feast was held that selfsame night
In the pile which the mighty shadow makes.

(For Via Larga is three-parts light,
But the Palace overshadows one,
Because of a crime which may God requite!

To Florence and God the wrong was done,
Through the first republic's murder there
By Cosimo and his cursed son.)

The Duke (with the statue's face in the square)
Turned in the midst of his multitude
At the bright approach of the bridal pair.

Face to face the lovers stood
A single minute and no more,
While the bridegroom bent as a man subdued—

Bowed till his bonnet brushed the floor—
For the Duke on the lady a kiss conferred,
As the courtly custom was of yore.

In a minute can lovers exchange a word?
If a word did pass, which I do not think,
Only one out of the thousand heard.

That was the bridegroom. At day's brink
He and his bride were alone at last
In a bedchamber by a taper's blink.

Calmly he said that her lot was cast,
That the door she had passed was shut on her
Till the final catafalk repassed.

The world meanwhile, its noise and stir,
Through a certain window facing the east
She might watch like a convent's chronicler.

Since passing the door might lead to a feast,
And a feast might lead to so much beside,
He, of many evils, chose the least.

"Freely I choose too," said the bride—
"Your window and its world suffice,"
So replied the tongue, while the heart replied—

"If I spend the night with that devil twice,
May his window serve as my loop of hell
Whence a damned soul looks on Paradise!

"I fly to the Duke who loves me well,
Sit by his side and laugh at sorrow
Ere I count another ave-bell.

"'Tis only the coat of a page to borrow,
And tie my hair in a horse-boy's trim,
And I save my soul—but not to-morrow"—

(She checked herself and her eye grew dim)
"My father tarries to bless my state:
I must keep it one day more for him.

"Is one day more so long to wait?
Moreover the Duke rides past, I know—
We shall see each other, sure as fate."

She turned on her side and slept. Just so!
So we resolve on a thing and sleep.
So did the lady, ages ago.

That night the Duke said, "Dear or cheap
As the cost of this cup of bliss may prove
To body or soul, I will drain it deep."

And on the morrow, bold with love,
He beckoned the bridegroom (close on call,
As his duty bade, by the Duke's alcove)

And smiled "'Twas a very funeral,
Your lady will think, this feast of ours,—
A shame to efface, whate'er befall!

"What if we break from the Arno bowers,
And try if Petraja, cool and green,
Cure last night's fault with this morning's flowers?"

The bridegroom, not a thought to be seen
On his steady brow and quiet mouth,
Said, "Too much favour for me so mean!

"Alas! my lady leaves the south.
Each wind that comes from the Apennine
Is a menace to her tender youth.

"No way exists, the wise opine,
If she quits her palace twice this year,
To avert the flower of life's decline."

Quoth the Duke, "A sage and a kindly fear.
Moreover Petraja is cold this spring—
Be our feast to-night as usual here!"

And then to himself—"Which night shall bring
Thy bride to her lover's embraces, fool—
Or I am the fool, and thou art his king!

"Yet my passion must wait a night, nor cool—
For to-night the Envoy arrives from France
Whose heart I unlock with thyself, my tool.

"I need thee still and might miss perchance.
To-day is not wholly lost, beside,
With its hope of my lady's countenance—

"For I ride—what should I do but ride?
And passing her palace, if I list,
May glance at its window—well betide!"

So said, so done: nor the lady missed
One ray that broke from the ardent brow,
Nor a curl of the lips where the spirit kissed.

Be sure that each renewed the vow,
No morrow's sun should arise and set
And leave them then as it left them now.

But next day passed, and next day yet,
With still fresh cause to wait one more
Ere each leaped over the parapet.

And still, as love's brief morning wore,
With a gentle start, half smile, half sigh,
They found love not as it seemed before.

They thought it would work infallibly,
But not in despite of heaven and earth—
The rose would blow when the storm passed by.

Meantime they could profit in winter's dearth
By winter's fruits that supplant the rose:
The world and its ways have a certain worth!

And to press a point while these oppose
Were a simple policy—better wait,
And lose no friends and gain no foes.

Meantime, worse fates than a lover's fate,
Who daily may ride and lean and look
Where his lady watches behind the grate!

And she—she watched the square like a book
Holding one picture and only one,
Which daily to find she undertook.

When the picture was reached the book was done,
And she turned from it all night to scheme
Of tearing it out for herself next sun.

Weeks grew months, years—gleam by gleam
The glory dropped from their youth and love,
And both perceived they had dreamed a dream,

Which hovered as dreams do, still above—
But who can take a dream for a truth?
Oh, hide our eyes from the next remove!

One day as the lady saw her youth
Depart, and the silver thread that streaked
Her hair, and, worn by the serpent's tooth,

The brow so puckered, the chin so peaked,—
And wondered who the woman was,
So hollow-eyed and haggard-cheeked,

Fronting her silent in the glass—
"Summon here," she suddenly said,
"Before the rest of my old self pass,

"Him, the Carver, a hand to aid,
Who moulds the clay no love will change,
And fixes a beauty never to fade.

"Let Robbia's craft so apt and strange
Arrest the remains of young and fair,
And rivet them while the seasons range.

"Make me a face on the window there
Waiting as ever, mute the while,
My love to pass below in the square!

"And let me think that it may beguile
Dreary days which the dead must spend
Down in their darkness under the aisle—

"To say,—'What matters it at the end?
I did no more while my heart was warm
Than does that image, my pale-faced friend.'

"Where is the use of the lip's red charm,
The heaven of hair, the pride of the brow,
And the blood that blues the inside arm—

Unless we turn, as the soul knows how,
The earthly gift to an end divine?
A lady of clay is as good, I trow."

But long ere Robbia's cornice, fine
With flowers and fruits which leaves enlace,
Was set where now is the empty shrine—

(With, leaning out of a bright blue space,
As a ghost might lean from a chink of sky,
The passionate pale lady's face—

Eyeing ever with earnest eye
And quick-turned neck at its breathless stretch,
Some one who ever passes by—)

The Duke sighed like the simplest wretch
In Florence, "So, my dream escapes!
Will its record stay?" And he bade them fetch

Some subtle fashioner of shapes—
"Can the soul, the will, die out of a man
Ere his body find the grave that gapes?

"John of Douay shall work my plan,
Mould me on horseback here aloft,
Alive—(the subtle artisan!)

"In the very square I cross so oft!
That men may admire, when future suns
Shall touch the eyes to a purpose soft,

"While the mouth and the brow are brave in bronze—
Admire and say, 'When he was alive
How he would take his pleasure once!'

"And it shall go hard but I contrive
To listen meanwhile and laugh in my tomb
At indolence which aspires to strive."

So! while these wait the trump of doom,
How do their spirits pass, I wonder,
Nights and days in the narrow room?

Still, I suppose, they sit and ponder
What a gift life was, ages ago,
Six steps out of the chapel yonder.

Surely they see not God, I know,
Nor all that chivalry of His,
The soldier-saints who, row on row,

Burn upward each to his point of bliss—
Since, the end of life being manifest,
He had cut his way thro' the world to this.

I hear your reproach—"But delay was best,
"For their end was a crime!"—Oh, a crime will do
As well, I reply, to serve for a test,

As a virtue golden through and through,
Sufficient to vindicate itself
And prove its worth at a moment's view.

Must a game be played for the sake of pelf?
Where a button goes, 'twere an epigram
To offer the stamp of the very Guelph.

The true has no value beyond the sham.
As well the counter as coin, I submit,
When your table's a hat, and your prize, a dram.

Stake your counter as boldly every whit,
Venture as truly, use the same skill,
Do your best, whether winning or losing it,

If you choose to play—is my principle!
Let a man contend to the uttermost
For his life's set prize, be it what it will!

The counter our lovers staked was lost
As surely as if it were lawful coin:
And the sin I impute to each frustrate ghost

Was, the unlit lamp and the ungirt loin,
Though the end in sight was a crime, I say.
You of the virtue, (we issue join)
How strive you? *De te, fabula!*

Love in a Life

1.

Room after room,
I hunt the house through
We inhabit together.
Heart, fear nothing, for, heart, thou shalt find her,
Next time, herself!—not the trouble behind her
Left in the curtain, the couch's perfume!
As she brushed it, the cornice-wreath blossomed anew,—
Yon looking-glass gleamed at the wave of her feather.

2.

Yet the day wears,
And door succeeds door;
I try the fresh fortune—
Range the wide house from the wing to the centre.
Still the same chance! she goes out as I enter.
Spend my whole day in the quest,—who cares?
But 'tis twilight, you see,—with such suites to explore,
Such closets to search, such alcoves to importune!

Life in a Love

Escape me?
Never—
Beloved!
While I am I, and you are you,
So long as the world contains us both,
Me the loving and you the loth,
While the one eludes, must the other pursue.
My life is a fault at last, I fear—
It seems too much like a fate, indeed!
Though I do my best I shall scarce succeed—
But what if I fail of my purpose here?
It is but to keep the nerves at strain,
To dry one's eyes and laugh at a fall,
And baffled, get up and begin again,—
So the chace takes up one's life, that's all.
While, look but once from your farthest bound,
At me so deep in the dust and dark,
No sooner the old hope drops to ground
Than a new one, straight to the self-same mark,
I shape me—
Ever
Removed!

How It Strikes a Contemporary

I only knew one poet in my life:
And this, or something like it, was his way.

You saw go up and down Valladolid,
A man of mark, to know next time you saw.
His very serviceable suit of black
Was courtly once and conscientious still,
And many might have worn it, though none did:
The cloak that somewhat shone and shewed the threads
Had purpose, and the ruff, significance.
He walked and tapped the pavement with his cane,
Scenting the world, looking it full in face,
An old dog, bald and blindish, at his heels.
They turned up, now, the alley by the church,

That leads no whither; now, they breathed themselves
On the main promenade just at the wrong time.
You'd come upon his scrutinising hat,
Making a peaked shade blacker than itself
Against the single window spared some house
Intact yet with its mouldered Moorish work,—
Or else surprise the ferrel of his stick
Trying the mortar's temper 'tween the chinks
Of some new shop a-building, French and fine.
He stood and watched the cobbler at his trade,
The man who slices lemons into drink,
The coffee-roaster's brazier, and the boys
That volunteer to help him turn its winch.
He glanced o'er books on stalls with half an eye,
And fly-leaf ballads on the vendor's string,
And broad-edge bold-print posters by the wall.
He took such cognisance of men and things,
If any beat a horse, you felt he saw;
If any cursed a woman, he took note;
Yet stared at nobody,—they stared at him,
And found, less to their pleasure than surprise,
He seemed to know them and expect as much.
So, next time that a neighbour's tongue was loosed,
It marked the shameful and notorious fact,
We had among us, not so much a spy,
As a recording chief-inquisitor,
The town's true master if the town but knew!
We merely kept a Governor for form,
While this man walked about and took account
Of all thought, said, and acted, then went home,
And wrote it fully to our Lord the King
Who has an itch to know things, He knows why,
And reads them in His bed-room of a night.
Oh, you might smile! there wanted not a touch,
A tang of... well, it was not wholly ease
As back into your mind the man's look came—
Stricken in years a little,—such a brow
His eyes had to live under!—clear as flint
On either side the formidable nose
Curved, cut, and coloured like an eagle's claw.
Had he to do with A.'s surprising fate?

When altogether old B. disappeared
And young C. got his mistress,—was't our friend,
His letter to the King, that did it all?
What paid the bloodless man for so much pains?
Our Lord the King has favourites manifold,
And shifts his ministry some once a month;
Our city gets new Governors at whiles,—
But never word or sign, that I could hear,
Notified to this man about the streets
The King's approval of those letters conned
The last thing duly at the dead of night.
Did the man love his office? frowned our Lord,
Exhorting when none heard—"Beseech me not!
Too far above my people,—beneath Me!
I set the watch,—how should the people know?
Forget them, keep Me all the more in mind!"
Was some such understanding 'twixt the Two?

I found no truth in one report at least—
That if you tracked him to his home, down lanes
Beyond the Jewry, and as clean to pace,
You found he ate his supper in a room
Blazing with lights, four Titians on the wall,
And twenty naked girls to change his plate!
Poor man, he lived another kind of life
In that new, stuccoed, third house by the bridge,
Fresh-painted, rather smart than otherwise!
The whole street might o'erlook him as he sat,
Leg crossing leg, one foot on the dog's back,
Playing a decent cribbage with his maid
(Jacynth, you're sure her name was) o'er the cheese
And fruit, three red halves of starved winter-pears,
Or treat of radishes in April! nine—
Ten, struck the church clock, straight to bed went he.

My father, like the man of sense he was,
Would point him out to me a dozen times;
"St—St," he'd whisper, "the Corregidor!"
I had been used to think that personage
Was one with lacquered breeches, lustrous belt,
And feathers like a forest in his hat,
Who blew a trumpet and proclaimed the news,

Announced the bull-fights, gave each church its turn,
And memorized the miracle in vogue!
He had a great observance from us boys—
I was in error; that was not the man.

I'd like now, yet had haply been afraid,
To have just looked, when this man came to die,
And seen who lined the clean gay garret's sides
And stood about the neat low truckle-bed,
With the heavenly manner of relieving guard.
Here had been, mark, the general-in-chief,
Thro' a whole campaign of the world's life and death,
Doing the King's work all the dim day long,
In his old coat, and up to knees in mud,
Smoked like a herring, dining on a crust,—
And now the day was won, relieved at once!
No further show or need for that old coat,
You are sure, for one thing! Bless us, all the while
How sprucely we are dressed out, you and I!
A second, and the angels alter that.
Well, I could never write a verse,—could you?
Let's to the Prado and make the most of time.

The Last Ride Together

I.

I said—Then, dearest, since 'tis so,
Since now at length my fate I know,
Since nothing all my love avails,
Since all my life seemed meant for, fails,
Since this was written and needs must be—
My whole heart rises up to bless
Your name in pride and thankfulness!
Take back the hope you gave,—I claim
Only a memory of the same,
—And this beside, if you will not blame,
Your leave for one more last ride with me.

2.

My mistress bent that brow of hers,
Those deep dark eyes where pride demurs
When pity would be softening through,
Fixed me a breathing-while or two
   With life or death in the balance—Right!
The blood replenished me again:
My last thought was at least not vain.
I and my mistress, side by side
Shall be together, breathe and ride,
So, one day more am I deified.
   Who knows but the world may end to-night?

3.

Hush! if you saw some western cloud
All billowy-bosomed, over-bowed
By many benedictions—sun's
And moon's and evening-star's at once—
   And so, you, looking and loving best,
Conscious grew, your passion drew
Cloud, sunset, moonrise, star-shine too
Down on you, near and yet more near,
Till flesh must fade for heaven was here!—
Thus leant she and lingered—joy and fear!
   Thus lay she a moment on my breast

4.

Then we began to ride. My soul
Smoothed itself out, a long-cramped scroll
Freshening and fluttering in the wind.
Past hopes already lay behind.
   What need to strive with a life awry?
Had I said that, had I done this,
So might I gain, so might I miss.
Might she have loved me? just as well
She might have hated,—who can tell!
Where had I been now if the worst befell?
   And here we are riding, she and I.

5.

Fail I alone, in words and deeds?
Why, all men strive and who succeeds?
We rode; it seemed my spirit flew,
Saw other regions, cities new,
   As the world rushed by on either side.
I thought, All labour, yet no less
Bear up beneath their unsuccess.
Look at the end of work, contrast
The petty Done the Undone vast,
This present of theirs with the hopeful past!
   I hoped she would love me. Here we ride.

6.

What hand and brain went ever paired?
What heart alike conceived and dared?
What act proved all its thought had been?
What will but felt the fleshly screen?
   We ride and I see her bosom heave.
There's many a crown for who can reach.
Ten lines, a statesman's life in each!
The flag stuck on a heap of bones,
A soldier's doing! what atones?
They scratch his name on the Abbey-stones.
   My riding is better, by their leave.

7.

What does it all mean, poet? well,
Your brain's beat into rhythm—you tell
What we felt only; you expressed
You hold things beautiful the best,
   And pace them in rhyme so, side by side.
'Tis something, nay 'tis much—but then,
Have you yourself what's best for men?
Are you—poor, sick, old ere your time—
Nearer one whit your own sublime
Than we who never have turned a rhyme?
   Sing, riding's a joy! For me, I ride.

8.

And you, great sculptor—so you gave
A score of years to art, her slave,
And that's your Venus—whence we turn
To yonder girl that fords the burn!
  You acquiesce and shall I repine?
What, man of music, you, grown grey
With notes and nothing else to say,
Is this your sole praise from a friend,
"Greatly his opera's strains intend,
"But in music we know how fashions end!"
  I gave my youth—but we ride, in fine

9.

Who knows what's fit for us? Had fate
Proposed bliss here should sublimate
My being; had I signed the bond—
Still one must lead some life beyond,
  —Have a bliss to die with, dim-descried.
This foot once planted on the goal,
This glory-garland round my soul,
Could I descry such? Try and test!
I sink back shuddering from the quest—
Earth being so good, would Heaven seem best?
  Now, Heaven and she are beyond this ride.

10.

And yet—she has not spoke so long!
What if Heaven be, that, fair and strong
At life's best, with our eyes upturned
Whither life's flower is first discerned,
  We, fixed so, ever should so abide?
What if we still ride on, we two
With life for ever old yet new,
Changed not in kind but in degree,
The instant made eternity,—
And Heaven just prove that I and she
  Ride, ride together, for ever ride?

The Patriot

AN OLD STORY

1.

It was roses, roses, all the way,
With myrtle mixed in my path like mad.
The house-roofs seemed to heave and sway,
The church-spires flamed, such flags they had,
A year ago on this very day!

2.

The air broke into a mist with bells,
The old walls rocked with the crowd and cries.
Had I said, "Good folk, mere noise repels—
But give me your sun from yonder skies!"
They had answered, "And afterward, what else?"

3.

Alack, it was I who leaped at the sun,
To give it my loving friends to keep.
Nought man could do, have I left undone
And you see my harvest, what I reap
This very day, now a year is run.

4.

There's nobody on the house-tops now—
Just a palsied few at the windows set—
For the best of the sight is, all allow,
At the Shambles' Gate—or, better yet,
By the very scaffold's foot, I trow.

5.

I go in the rain, and, more than needs,
A rope cuts both my wrists behind,
And I think, by the feel, my forehead bleeds,
For they fling, whoever has a mind,
Stones at me for my year's misdeeds.

6.

Thus I entered Brescia, and thus I go!
  In such triumphs, people have dropped down dead.
"Thou paid by the World,—what dost thou owe
  Me?" God might have questioned: but now instead
'Tis God shall requite! I am safer so.

Master Hugues of Saxe-Gotha

1.

Hist, but a word, fair and soft!
  Forth and be judged, Master Hugues!
Answer the question I've put you so oft—
  What do you mean by your mountainous fugues?
See, we're alone in the loft,

2.

I, the poor organist here,
  Hugues, the composer of note—
Dead though, and done with, this many a year—
  Let's have a colloquy, something to quote,
Make the world prick up its ear!

3.

See, the church empties a-pace.
  Fast they extinguish the lights—
Hallo there, sacristan! five minutes' grace!
  Here's a crank pedal wants setting to rights,
Baulks one of holding the base.

4.

See, our huge house of the sounds
  Hushing its hundreds at once,
Bids the last loiterer back to his bounds
  —Oh, you may challenge them, not a response
Get the church saints on their rounds!

5.

(Saints go their rounds, who shall doubt?
 —March, with the moon to admire,
Up nave, down chancel, turn transept about,
 Supervise all betwixt pavement and spire,
Put rats and mice to the rout—

6.

Aloys and Jurien and Just—
 Order things back to their place,
Have a sharp eye lest the candlesticks rust,
 Rub the church plate, darn the sacrament lace,
Clear the desk velvet of dust.)

7.

Here's your book, younger folks shelve!
 Played I not off-hand and runningly,
Just now, your masterpiece, hard number twelve?
 Here's what should strike,—could one handle it cunningly,
Help the axe, give it a helve!

8.

Page after page as I played,
 Every bar's rest where one wipes
Sweat from one's brow, I looked up and surveyed
 O'er my three claviers, yon forest of pipes
Whence you still peeped in the shade.

9.

Sure you were wishful to speak,
 You, with brow ruled like a score,
Yes, and eyes buried in pits on each cheek,
 Like two great breves as they wrote them of yore
Each side that bar, your straight beak!

10.

Sure you said—"Good, the mere notes!
 Still, couldst thou take my intent,
Know what procured me our Company's votes—
 Masters being lauded and sciolists shent,
Parted the sheep from the goats!"

11.

Well then, speak up, never flinch!
  Quick, ere my candle's a snuff
—Burnt, do you see? to its uttermost inch—
  I believe in you, but that's not enough.
Give my conviction a clinch!

12.

First you deliver your phrase
  —Nothing propound, that I see,
Fit in itself for much blame or much praise—
  Answered no less, where no answer needs be:
Off start the Two on their ways!

13.

Straight must a Third interpose,
  Volunteer needlessly help—
In strikes a Fourth, a Fifth thrusts in his nose,
  So the cry's open, the kennel's a-yelp,
Argument's hot to the close!

14.

One disertates, he is candid—
  Two must discept,—has distinguished!
Three helps the couple, if ever yet man did:
  Four protests, Five makes a dart at the thing wished—
Back to One, goes the case bandied!

15.

One says his say with a difference—
  More of expounding, explaining!
All now is wrangle, abuse, and vociferance—
  Now there's a truce, all's subdued, self-restraining—
Five, though, stands out all the stiffer hence.

16.

One is incisive, corrosive—
  Two retorts, nettled, curt, crepitant—
Three makes rejoinder, expansive, explosive—
  Four overbears them all, strident and strepitant—
Five . . . O Danaides, O Sieve!

17.

Now, they ply axes and crowbars—
  Now, they prick pins at a tissue
Fine as a skein of the casuist Escobar's
  Worked on the bone of a lie. To what issue?
Where is our gain at the Two-bars?

18.

Est fuga, volvitur rota!
  On we drift. Where looms the dim port?
One, Two, Three, Four, Five, contribute their quota—
  Something is gained, if one caught but the import—
Show it us, Hugues of Saxe-Gotha!

19.

What with affirming, denying,
  Holding, risposting, subjoining,
All's like . . . it's like . . . for an instance I'm trying . . .
  There! See our roof, its gilt moulding and groining
Under those spider-webs lying!

20.

So your fugue broadens and thickens,
  Greatens and deepens and lengthens,
Till we exclaim—"But where's music, the dickens?
  Blot ye the gold, while your spider-web strengthens,
—Blacked to the stoutest of tickens?"

21.

I for man's effort am zealous.
  Prove me such censure unfounded!
Seems it surprising a lover grows jealous—
  Hopes 'twas for something his organ-pipes sounded,
Tiring three boys at the bellows?

22.

Is it your moral of Life?
  Such a web, simple and subtle,
Weave we on earth here in impotent strife,
  Backward and forward each throwing his shuttle,
Death ending all with a knife?

23.

Over our heads Truth and Nature—
   Still our life's zigzags and dodges,
Ins and outs weaving a new legislature—
   God's gold just shining its last where that lodges,
Palled beneath Man's usurpature!

24.

So we o'ershroud stars and roses,
   Cherub and trophy and garland.
Nothings grow something which quietly closes
   Heaven's earnest eye,—not a glimpse of the far land
Gets through our comments and glozes.

25.

Ah, but traditions, inventions,
   (Say we and make up a visage)
So many men with such various intentions
   Down the past ages, must know more than this age!
Leave the web all its dimensions!

26.

Who thinks Hugues wrote for the deaf?
   Proved a mere mountain in labour?
Better submit—try again—what's the clef?
   'Faith, it's no trifle for pipe and for tabor—
Four flats—the minor in F.

27.

Friend, your fugue taxes the finger.
   Learning it once, who would lose it?
Yet all the while a misgiving will linger—
   Truth's golden o'er us although we refuse it—
Nature, thro' dust-clouds we fling her!

28.

Hugues! I advise *meâ poenâ*
   (Counterpoint glares like a Gorgon)
Bid One, Two, Three, Four, Five, clear the arena!
   Say the word, straight I unstop the Full-Organ,
Blare out the *mode Palestrina*.

29.

While in the roof, if I'm right there—
   . . . Lo, you, the wick in the socket!
Hallo, you sacristan, show us a light there!
   Down it dips, gone like a rocket!
What, you want, do you, to come unawares,
Sweeping the church up for first morning-prayers,
And find a poor devil has ended his cares
At the foot of your rotten-planked rat-riddled stairs?
   Do I carry the moon in my pocket?

Bishop Blougram's Apology

   No more wine? then we'll push back chairs and talk.
A final glass for me, tho': cool, i' faith!
We ought to have our Abbey back, you see.
It's different, preaching in basilicas,
And doing duty in some masterpiece
Like this of brother Pugin's, bless his heart!
I doubt if they're half baked, those chalk rosettes,
Ciphers and stucco-twiddlings everywhere;
It's just like breathing in a lime-kiln: eh?
These hot long ceremonies of our church
Cost us a little—oh, they pay the price,
You take me—amply pay it! Now, we'll talk.

   So, you despise me, Mr. Gigadibs.
No deprecation,—nay, I beg you, sir!
Beside 'tis our engagement: don't you know,
I promised, if you'd watch a dinner out,
We'd see truth dawn together?—truth that peeps
Over the glass's edge when dinner's done,
And body gets its sop and holds its noise
And leaves soul free a little. Now's the time—
'Tis break of day! You do despise me then.
And if I say, "despise me,"—never fear—
I know you do not in a certain sense—
Not in my arm-chair for example: here,
I well imagine you respect my place
(Status, *entourage*, worldly circumstance)

Quite to its value—very much indeed
—Are up to the protesting eyes of you
In pride at being seated here for once—
You'll turn it to such capital account!
When somebody, through years and years to come,
Hints of the bishop,—names me—that's enough—
"Blougram? I knew him"—(into it you slide)
"Dined with him once, a Corpus Christi Day,
All alone, we two—he's a clever man—
And after dinner,—why, the wine you know,—
Oh, there was wine, and good!—what with the wine...
'Faith, we began upon all sorts of talk!
He's no bad fellow, Blougram—he had seen
Something of mine he relished—some review—
He's quite above their humbug in his heart,
Half-said as much, indeed—the thing's his trade—
I warrant, Blougram's sceptical at times—
How otherwise? I liked him, I confess!"
Che ch'é, my dear sir, as we say at Rome,
Don't you protest now! It's fair give and take;
You have had your turn and spoken your home-truths—
The hand's mine now, and here you follow suit.

Thus much conceded, still the first fact stays—
You do despise me; your ideal of life
Is not the bishop's—you would not be I—
You would like better to be Goethe, now,
Or Buonaparte—or, bless me, lower still,
Count D'Orsay,—so you did what you preferred,
Spoke as you thought, and, as you cannot help,
Believed or disbelieved, no matter what,
So long as on that point, whate'er it was,
You loosed your mind, were whole and sole yourself.
—That, my ideal never can include,
Upon that element of truth and worth
Never be based! for say they make me Pope
(They can't—suppose it for our argument)
Why, there I'm at my tether's end—I've reached
My height, and not a height which pleases you.
An unbelieving Pope won't do, you say.
It's like those eerie stories nurses tell,

Of how some actor played Death on a stage
With pasteboard crown, sham orb, and tinselled dart,
And called himself the monarch of the world,
Then going in the tire-room afterward
Because the play was done, to shift himself,
Got touched upon the sleeve familiarly
The moment he had shut the closet door
By Death himself. Thus God might touch a Pope
At unawares, ask what his baubles mean,
And whose part he presumed to play just now?
Best be yourself, imperial, plain and true!

So, drawing comfortable breath again,
You weigh and find, whatever more or less
I boast of my ideal realised
Is nothing in the balance when opposed
To your ideal, your grand simple life,
Of which you will not realise one jot.
I am much, you are nothing; you would be all,
I would be merely much—you beat me there.

No, friend, you do not beat me,—hearken why.
The common problem, yours, mine, every one's,
Is not to fancy what were fair in life
Provided it could be,—but, finding first
What may be, then find how to make it fair
Up to our means—a very different thing!
No abstract intellectual plan of life
Quite irrespective of life's plainest laws,
But one, a man, who is man and nothing more,
May lead within a world which (by your leave)
Is Rome or London—not Fool's-paradise.
Embellish Rome, idealise away,
Make Paradise of London if you can,
You're welcome, nay, you're wise.

A simile!
We mortals cross the ocean of this world
Each in his average cabin of a life—
The best's not big, the worst yields elbow-room.
Now for our six months' voyage—how prepare?
You come on shipboard with a landsman's list

Of things he calls convenient—so they are!
An India screen is pretty furniture,
A piano-forte is a fine resource,
All Balzac's novels occupy one shelf,
The new edition fifty volumes long;
And little Greek books with the funny type
They get up well at Leipsic, fill the next—
Go on! slabbed marble, what a bath it makes!
And Parma's pride, the Jerome, let us add!
'Twere pleasant could Correggio's fleeting glow
Hang full in face of one where'er one roams,
Since he more than the others brings with him
Italy's self,—the marvellous Modenese!—
Yet 'twas not on your list before, perhaps.
—Alas! friend, here's the agent . . . is't the name?
The captain, or whoever's master here—
You see him screw his face up; what's his cry
Ere you set foot on shipboard? "Six feet square!"
If you won't understand what six feet mean,
Compute and purchase stores accordingly—
And if in pique because he overhauls
Your Jerome, piano and bath, you come on board
Bare—why, you cut a figure at the first
While sympathetic landsmen see you off;
Not afterwards, when, long ere half seas o'er,
You peep up from your utterly naked boards
Into some snug and well-appointed berth
Like mine, for instance (try the cooler jug—
Put back the other, but don't jog the ice)
And mortified you mutter "Well and good—
He sits enjoying his sea-furniture—
'Tis stout and proper, and there's store of it,
Though I've the better notion, all agree,
Of fitting rooms up! hang the carpenter,
Neat ship-shape fixings and contrivances—
I would have brought my Jerome, frame and all!"
And meantime you bring nothing: never mind—
You've proved your artist-nature: what you don't,
You might bring, so despise me, as I say.

Now come, let's backward to the starting place.
See my way: we're two college friends, suppose—
Prepare together for our voyage, then,
Each note and check the other in his work,—
Here's mine, a bishop's outfit; criticise!
What's wrong? why won't you be a bishop too?

Why first, you don't believe, you don't and can't,
(Not statedly, that is, and fixedly
And absolutely and exclusively)
In any revelation called divine.
No dogmas nail your faith—and what remains
But say so, like the honest man you are?
First, therefore, overhaul theology!
Nay, I too, not a fool, you please to think,
Must find believing every whit as hard,
And if I do not frankly say as much,
The ugly consequence is clear enough.

Now, wait, my friend: well, I do not believe—
If you'll accept no faith that is not fixed,
Absolute and exclusive, as you say.
(You're wrong—I mean to prove it in due time)
Meanwhile, I know where difficulties lie
I could not, cannot solve, nor ever shall,
So give up hope accordingly to solve—
(To you, and over the wine). Our dogmas then
With both of us, tho' in unlike degree,
Missing full credence—overboard with them!
I mean to meet you on your own premise—
Good, there go mine in company with yours!

And now what are we? unbelievers both,
Calm and complete, determinately fixed
To-day, to-morrow, and for ever, pray?
You'll guarantee me that? Not so, I think.
In no-wise! all we've gained is, that belief,
As unbelief before, shakes us by fits,
Confounds us like its predecessor. Where's
The gain? how can we guard our unbelief,
Make it bear fruit to us?—the problem here.
Just when we are safest, there's a sunset-touch,
A fancy from a flower-bell, some one's death,

A chorus-ending from Euripides,—
And that's enough for fifty hopes and fears
As old and new at once as Nature's self,
To rap and knock and enter in our soul,
Take hands and dance there, a fantastic ring,
Round the ancient idol, on his base again,—
The grand Perhaps! We look on helplessly,—
There the old misgivings, crooked questions are—
This good God,—what he could do, if he would,
Would, if he could—then must have done long since:
If so, when, where and how? some way must be,—
Once feel about, and soon or late you hit
Some sense, in which it might be, after all.
Why not, "The Way, the Truth, the Life?"

—That way
Over the mountain, which who stands upon
Is apt to doubt if it's indeed a road;
While if he views it from the waste itself,
Up goes the line there, plain from base to brow,
Not vague, mistakeable! what's a break or two
Seen from the unbroken desert either side?
And then (to bring in fresh philosophy)
What if the breaks themselves should prove at last
The most consummate of contrivances
To train a man's eye, teach him what is faith,—
And so we stumble at truth's very test?
What have we gained then by our unbelief
But a life of doubt diversified by faith,
For one of faith diversified by doubt.
We called the chess-board white,—we call it black.

"Well," you rejoin, "the end's no worse, at least,
We've reason for both colours on the board.
Why not confess, then, where I drop the faith
And you the doubt, that I'm as right as you?"

Because, friend, in the next place, this being so,
And both things even,—faith and unbelief
Left to a man's choice,—we'll proceed a step,
Returning to our image, which I like.

A man's choice, yes—but a cabin-passenger's—
The man made for the special life of the world—
Do you forget him? I remember though!
Consult our ship's conditions and you find
One and but one choice suitable to all,
The choice that you unluckily prefer,
Turning things topsy-turvy—they or it
Going to the ground. Belief or unbelief
Bears upon life, determines its whole course,
Begins at its beginning. See the world
Such as it is,—you made it not, nor I;
I mean to take it as it is,—and you
Not so you'll take it,—though you get nought else.
I know the special kind of life I like,
What suits the most my idiosyncrasy,
Brings out the best of me and bears me fruit
In power, peace, pleasantness, and length of days.
I find that positive belief does this
For me, and unbelief, no whit of this.
—For you, it does, however—that we'll try!
'Tis clear, I cannot lead my life, at least
Induce the world to let me peaceably,
Without declaring at the outset, "Friends,
I absolutely and peremptorily
Believe!"—I say, faith is my waking life.
One sleeps, indeed, and dreams at intervals,
We know, but waking's the main point with us,
And my provision's for life's waking part.
Accordingly, I use heart, head and hands
All day, I build, scheme, study, and make friends;
And when night overtakes me, down I lie,
Sleep, dream a little, and get done with it,
The sooner the better, to begin afresh.
What's midnight's doubt before the dayspring's faith?
You, the philosopher, that disbelieve,
That recognise the night, give dreams their weight—
To be consistent you should keep your bed,
Abstain from healthy acts that prove you a man,
For fear you drowse perhaps at unawares!
And certainly at night you'll sleep and dream,
Live through the day and bustle as you please.

And so you live to sleep as I to wake,
To unbelieve as I to still believe?
Well, and the common sense of the world calls you
Bed-ridden,—and its good things come to me.
Its estimation, which is half the fight,
That's the first cabin-comfort I secure—
The next . . . but you perceive with half an eye!
Come, come, it's best believing, if we can—
You can't but own that.

Next, concede again—
If once we choose belief, on all accounts
We can't be too decisive in our faith,
Conclusive and exclusive in its terms,
To suit the world which gives us the good things.
In every man's career are certain points
Whereon he dares not be indifferent;
The world detects him clearly, if he is,
As baffled at the game, and losing life.
He may care little or he may care much
For riches, honour, pleasure, work, repose,
Since various theories of life and life's
Success are extant which might easily
Comport with either estimate of these,
And whoso chooses wealth or poverty,
Labour or quiet, is not judged a fool
Because his fellows would choose otherwise.
We let him choose upon his own account
So long as he's consistent with his choice.
But certain points, left wholly to himself,
When once a man has arbitrated on,
We say he must succeed there or go hang.
Thus, he should wed the woman he loves most
Or needs most, whatsoe'er the love or need—
For he can't wed twice. Then, he must avouch,
Or follow, at the least, sufficiently,
The form of faith his conscience holds the best,
Whate'er the process of conviction was.
For nothing can compensate his mistake
On such a point, the man himself being judge—
He cannot wed twice, nor twice lose his soul.

Well now—there's one great form of Christian faith
I happened to be born in—which to teach
Was given me as I grew up, on all hands,
As best and readiest means of living by;
The same on examination being proved
The most pronounced, moreover, fixed, precise
And absolute form of faith in the whole world—
Accordingly, most potent of all forms
For working on the world. Observe, my friend,
Such as you know me, I am free to say,
In these hard latter days which hamper one,
Myself, by no immoderate exercise
Of intellect and learning, and the tact
To let external forces work for me,
Bid the street's stones be bread and they are bread,
Bid Peter's creed, or, rather, Hildebrand's,
Exalt me o'er my fellows in the world
And make my life an ease and joy and pride,
It does so,—which for me's a great point gained,
Who have a soul and body that exact
A comfortable care in many ways.
There's power in me and will to dominate
Which I must exercise, they hurt me else:
In many ways I need mankind's respect,
Obedience, and the love that's born of fear:
While at the same time, there's a taste I have,
A toy of soul, a titillating thing,
Refuses to digest these dainties crude.
The naked life is gross till clothed upon:
I must take what men offer, with a grace
As though I would not, could I help it, take!
An uniform I wear though over-rich—
Something imposed on me, no choice of mine;
No fancy-dress worn for pure fashion's sake
And despicable therefore! now men kneel
And kiss my hand—of course the Church's hand.
Thus I am made, thus life is best for me,
And thus that it should be I have procured;
And thus it could not be another way,
I venture to imagine.

You'll reply—

So far my choice, no doubt, is a success;
But were I made of better elements,
With nobler instincts, purer tastes, like you,
I hardly would account the thing success
Though it do all for me I say.
                                        But, friend,
We speak of what is—not of what might be,
And how 'twere better if 'twere otherwise.
I am the man you see here plain enough—
Grant I'm a beast, why, beasts must lead beasts' lives!
Suppose I own at once to tail and claws—
The tailless man exceeds me; but being tailed
I'll lash out lion-fashion, and leave apes
To dock their stump and dress their haunches up.
My business is not to remake myself,
But make the absolute best of what God made.
Or—our first simile—though you prove me doomed
To a viler berth still, to the steerage-hole,
The sheep-pen or the pig-stye, I should strive
To make what use of each were possible;
And as this cabin gets upholstery,
That hutch should rustle with sufficient straw.

But, friend, I don't acknowledge quite so fast
I fail of all your manhood's lofty tastes
Enumerated so complacently,
On the mere ground that you forsooth can find
In this particular life I choose to lead
No fit provision for them. Can you not?
Say you, my fault is I address myself
To grosser estimators than I need,
And that's no way of holding up the soul—
Which, nobler, needs men's praise perhaps, yet knows
One wise man's verdict outweighs all the fools',—
Would like the two, but, forced to choose, takes that?
I pine among my million imbeciles
(You think) aware some dozen men of sense
Eye me and know me, whether I believe
In the last winking Virgin, as I vow,
And am a fool, or disbelieve in her
And am a knave,—approve in neither case,

Withhold their voices though I look their way:
Like Verdi when, at his worst opera's end
(The thing they gave at Florence,—what's its name?)
While the mad houseful's plaudits near out-bang
His orchestra of salt-box, tongs and bones,
He looks through all the roaring and the wreaths
Where sits Rossini patient in his stall.

Nay, friend, I meet you with an answer here—
For even your prime men who appraise their kind
Are men still, catch a thing within a thing,
See more in a truth than the truth's simple self,
Confuse themselves. You see lads walk the street
Sixty the minute; what's to note in that?
You see one lad o'erstride a chimney-stack;
Him you must watch—he's sure to fall, yet stands!
Our interest's on the dangerous edge of things.
The honest thief, the tender murderer,
The superstitious atheist, demireps
That love and save their souls in new French books—
We watch while these in equilibrium keep
The giddy line midway: one step aside,
They're classed and done with. I, then, keep the line
Before your sages,—just the men to shrink
From the gross weights, coarse scales, and labels broad
You offer their refinement. Fool or knave?
Why needs a bishop be a fool or knave
When there's a thousand diamond weights between?
So I enlist them. Your picked Twelve, you'll find,
Profess themselves indignant, scandalised
At thus being held unable to explain
How a superior man who disbelieves
May not believe as well: that's Schelling's way!
It's through my coming in the tail of time,
Nicking the minute with a happy tact.
Had I been born three hundred years ago
They'd say, "What's strange? Blougram of course believes;"
And, seventy years since, "disbelieves of course."
But now, "He may believe; and yet, and yet
How can he?"—All eyes turn with interest.

Whereas, step off the line on either side—
You, for example, clever to a fault,
The rough and ready man that write apace,
Read somewhat seldomer, think perhaps even less—
You disbelieve! Who wonders and who cares?
Lord So-and-So—his coat bedropt with wax,
All Peter's chains about his waist, his back
Brave with the needlework of Noodledom,
Believes! Again, who wonders and who cares?
But I, the man of sense and learning too,
The able to think yet act, the this, the that,
I, to believe at this late time of day!
Enough; you see, I need not fear contempt.

—Except it's yours! Admire me as these may,
You don't. But what at least do you admire?
Present your own perfection, your ideal,
Your pattern man for a minute—oh, make haste!
Is it Napoleon you would have us grow?
Concede the means; allow his head and hand,
(A large concession, clever as you are)
Good!—In our common primal element
Of unbelief (we can't believe, you know—
We're still at that admission, recollect)
Where do you find—apart from, towering-o'er
The secondary temporary aims
Which satisfy the gross tastes you despise—
Where do you find his star?—his crazy trust
God knows through what or in what? it's alive
And shines and leads him and that's all we want.
Have we aught in our sober night shall point
Such ends as his were, and direct the means
Of working out our purpose straight as his,
Nor bring a moment's trouble on success
With after-care to justify the same?
—Be a Napoleon, and yet disbelieve!
Why, the man's mad, friend, take his light away.
What's the vague good of the world, for which you'd dare
With comfort to yourself blow millions up?
We neither of us see it! we do see

The blown-up millions—spatter of their brains
And writhing of their bowels and so forth,
In that bewildering entanglement
Of horrible eventualities
Past calculation to the end of time!
Can I mistake for some clear word of God
(Which were my ample warrant for it all)
His puff of hazy instincts, idle talk,
"The state, that's I," quack-nonsense about kings,
And (when one beats the man to his last hold)
A vague idea of setting things to rights,
Policing people efficaciously,
More to their profit, most of all to his own;
The whole to end that dismallest of ends
By an Austrian marriage, cant to us the church,
And resurrection of the old *régime*.
Would I, who hope to live a dozen years,
Fight Austerlitz for reasons such and such?
No: for, concede me but the merest chance
Doubt may be wrong—there's judgment, life to come!
With just that chance, I dare not. Doubt proves right?
This present life is all? you offer me
Its dozen noisy years, with not a chance
That wedding an Arch-Duchess, wearing lace,
And getting called by divers new-coined names,
Will drive off ugly thoughts and let me dine,
Sleep, read and chat in quiet as I like!
Therefore I will not.

Take another case;
Fit up the cabin yet another way.
What say you to the poets? shall we write
Hamlets, Othellos—make the world our own,
Without a risk to run of either sort?
I can't—to put the strongest reason first.
"But try," you urge, "the trying shall suffice:
The aim, if reached or not, makes great the life.
Try to be Shakspeare, leave the rest to fate!"
Spare my self-knowledge—there's no fooling me!
If I prefer remaining my poor self,

I say so not in self-dispraise but praise.
If I'm a Shakspeare, let the well alone—
Why should I try to be what now I am?
If I'm no Shakspeare, as too probable,—
His power and consciousness and self-delight
And all we want in common, shall I find—
Trying for ever? while on points of taste
Wherewith, to speak it humbly, he and I
Are dowered alike—I'll ask you, I or he,
Which in our two lives realises most?
Much, he imagined—somewhat, I possess.
He had the imagination; stick to that!
Let him say "In the face of my soul's works
Your world is worthless and I touch it not
Lest I should wrong them"—I'll withdraw my plea.
But does he say so? look upon his life!
Himself, who only can, gives judgment there.
He leaves his towers and gorgeous palaces
To build the trimmest house in Stratford town;
Saves money, spends it, owns the worth of things,
Giulio Romano's pictures, Dowland's lute;
Enjoys a show, respects the puppets, too,
And none more, had he seen its entry once,
Than "Pandulph, of fair Milan cardinal."
Why then should I who play that personage,
The very Pandulph Shakspeare's fancy made,
Be told that had the poet chanced to start
From where I stand now (some degree like mine
Being just the goal he ran his race to reach)
He would have run the whole race back, forsooth,
And left being Pandulph, to begin write plays?
Ah, the earth's best can be but the earth's best!
Did Shakspeare live, he could but sit at home
And get himself in dreams the Vatican,
Greek busts, Venetian paintings, Roman walls,
And English books, none equal to his own,
Which I read, bound in gold, (he never did).
—Terni and Naples' bay and Gothard's top—
Eh, friend? I could not fancy one of these—
But, as I pour this claret, there they are—

I've gained them—crossed St. Gothard last July
With ten mules to the carriage and a bed
Slung inside; is my hap the worse for that?
We want the same things, Shakspeare and myself,
And what I want, I have: he, gifted more,
Could fancy he too had them when he liked,
But not so thoroughly that if fate allowed
He would not have it also in my sense.
We play one game. I send the ball aloft
No less adroitly that of fifty strokes
Scarce five go o'er the wall so wide and high
Which sends them back to me: I wish and get
He struck balls higher and with better skill,
But at a poor fence level with his head,
And hit—his Stratford house, a coat of arms,
Successful dealings in his grain and wool,—
While I receive heaven's incense in my nose
And style myself the cousin of Queen Bess.
Ask him, if this life's all, who wins the game?

Believe—and our whole argument breaks up.
Enthusiasm's the best thing, I repeat;
Only, we can't command it; fire and life
Are all, dead matter's nothing, we agree:
And be it a mad dream or God's very breath,
The fact's the same,—belief's fire once in us,
Makes of all else mere stuff to show itself.
We penetrate our life with such a glow
As fire lends wood and iron—this turns steel,
That burns to ash—all's one, fire proves its power
For good or ill, since men call flare success.
But paint a fire, it will not therefore burn.
Light one in me, I'll find it food enough!
Why, to be Luther—that's a life to lead,
Incomparably better than my own.
He comes, reclaims God's earth for God, he says,
Sets up God's rule again by simple means,
Re-opens a shut book, and all is done.
He flared out in the flaring of mankind;
Such Luther's luck was—how shall such be mine?
If he succeeded, nothing's left to do:

And if he did not altogether—well,
Strauss is the next advance. All Strauss should be
I might be also. But to what result?
He looks upon no future: Luther did.
What can I gain on the denying side?
Ice makes no conflagration. State the facts,
Read the text right, emancipate the world—
The emancipated world enjoys itself
With scarce a thank-you—Blougram told it first
It could not owe a farthing,—not to him
More than St. Paul! 'twould press its pay, you think?
Then add there's still that plaguey hundredth chance
Strauss may be wrong. And so a risk is run—
For what gain? not for Luther's, who secured
A real heaven in his heart throughout his life,
Supposing death a little altered things!

"Ay, but since really I lack faith," you cry,
"I run the same risk really on all sides,
In cool indifference as bold unbelief.
As well be Strauss as swing 'twixt Paul and him.
It's not worth having, such imperfect faith,
No more available to do faith's work
Than unbelief like yours. Whole faith, or none!"

Softly, my friend! I must dispute that point.
Once own the use of faith, I'll find you faith.
We're back on Christian ground. You call for faith:
I show you doubt, to prove that faith exists.
The more of doubt, the stronger faith, I say,
If faith o'ercomes doubt. How I know it does?
By life and man's free will, God gave for that!
To mould life as we choose it, shows our choice:
That's our one act, the previous work's His own.
You criticise the soil? it reared this tree—
This broad life and whatever fruit it bears!
What matter though I doubt at every pore,
Head-doubts, heart-doubts, doubts at my fingers' ends,
Doubts in the trivial work of every day,
Doubts at the very bases of my soul

In the grand moments when she probes herself—
If finally I have a life to show,
The thing I did, brought out in evidence
Against the thing done to me underground
By Hell and all its brood, for aught I know?
I say, whence sprang this? shows it faith or doubt?
All's doubt in me; where's break of faith in this?
It is the idea, the feeling and the love,
God means mankind should strive for and show forth,
Whatever be the process to that end,—
And not historic knowledge, logic sound,
And metaphysical acumen, sure!
"What think ye of Christ," friend? when all's done and said,
Like you this Christianity or not?
It may be false, but will you wish it true?
Has it your vote to be so if it can?
Trust you an instinct silenced long ago
That will break silence and enjoin you love
What mortified philosophy is hoarse,
And all in vain, with bidding you despise?
If you desire faith—then you've faith enough.
What else seeks God—nay, what else seek ourselves?
You form a notion of me, we'll suppose,
On hearsay; it's a favourable one:
"But still," (you add), "there was no such good man,
Because of contradictions in the facts.
One proves, for instance, he was born in Rome,
This Blougram—yet throughout the tales of him
I see he figures as an Englishman."
Well, the two things are reconcileable.
But would I rather you discovered that,
Subjoining—"Still, what matter though they be?
Blougram concerns me nought, born here or there."

Pure faith indeed—you know not what you ask!
Naked belief in God the Omnipotent,
Omniscient, Omnipresent, sears too much
The sense of conscious creatures to be borne.
It were the seeing him, no flesh shall dare.
Some think, Creation's meant to show him forth:
I say, it's meant to hide him all it can,

And that's what all the blessed Evil's for.
Its use in time is to environ us,
Our breath, our drop of dew, with shield enough
Against that sight till we can bear its stress.
Under a vertical sun, the exposed brain
And lidless eye and disemprisoned heart
Less certainly would wither up at once
Than mind, confronted with the truth of Him.
But time and earth case-harden us to live;
The feeblest sense is trusted most; the child
Feels God a moment, ichors o'er the place,
Plays on and grows to be a man like us.
With me, faith means perpetual unbelief
Kept quiet like the snake 'neath Michael's foot
Who stands calm just because he feels it writhe.
Or, if that's too ambitious,—here's my box—
I need the excitation of a pinch
Threatening the torpor of the inside-nose
Nigh on the imminent sneeze that never comes.
"Leave it in peace" advise the simple folk—
Make it aware of peace by itching-fits,
Say I—let doubt occasion still more faith!

You'll say, once all believed, man, woman, child,
In that dear middle-age these noodles praise.
How you'd exult if I could put you back
Six hundred years, blot out cosmogony,
Geology, ethnology, what not
(Greek endings with the little passing-bell
That signifies some faith's about to die)
And set you square with Genesis again,—
When such a traveller told you his last news,
He saw the ark a-top of Ararat
But did not climb there since 'twas getting dusk
And robber-bands infest the mountain's foot!
How should you feel, I ask, in such an age,
How act? As other people felt and did;
With soul more blank than this decanter's knob,
Believe—and yet lie, kill, rob, fornicate
Full in belief's face, like the beast you'd be!

No, when the fight begins within himself
A man's worth something. God stoops o'er his head,
Satan looks up between his feet—both tug—
He's left, himself, in the middle: the soul wakes
And grows. Prolong that battle through his life!
Never leave growing till the life to come!
Here, we've got callous to the Virgin's winks
That used to puzzle people wholesomely—
Men have outgrown the shame of being fools.
What are the laws of Nature, not to bend
If the Church bid them, brother Newman asks.
Up with the Immaculate Conception, then—
On to the rack with faith—is my advice!
Will not that hurry us upon our knees
Knocking our breasts, "It can't be—yet it shall!
Who am I, the worm, to argue with my Pope?
Low things confound the high things!" and so forth.
That's better than acquitting God with grace
As some folk do. He's tried—no case is proved,
Philosophy is lenient—He may go!

You'll say—the old system's not so obsolete
But men believe still: ay, but who and where?
King Bomba's lazzaroni foster yet
The sacred flame, so Antonelli writes;
But even of these, what ragamuffin-saint
Believes God watches him continually,
As he believes in fire that it will burn,
Or rain that it will drench him? Break fire's law,
Sin against rain, although the penalty
Be just a singe or soaking? No, he smiles;
Those laws are laws that can enforce themselves.

The sum of all is—yes, my doubt is great,
My faith's the greater—then my faith's enough.
I have read much, thought much, experienced much,
Yet would die rather than avow my fear
The Naples' liquefaction may be false,
When set to happen by the palace-clock
According to the clouds or dinner-time.

I hear you recommend, I might at least
Eliminate, decrassify my faith
Since I adopt it; keeping what I must
And leaving what I can—such points as this!
I won't—that is, I can't throw one away.
Supposing there's no truth in what I said
About the need of trials to man's faith,
Still, when you bid me purify the same,
To such a process I discern no end,
Clearing off one excrescence to see two;
There's ever a next in size, now grown as big,
That meets the knife—I cut and cut again!
First cut the Liquefaction, what comes last
But Fichte's clever cut at God himself?
Experimentalize on sacred things?
I trust nor hand nor eye nor heart nor brain
To stop betimes: they all get drunk alike.
The first step, I am master not to take.

You'd find the cutting-process to your taste
As much as leaving growths of lies unpruned,
Nor see more danger in it, you retort.
Your taste's worth mine; but my taste proves more wise
When we consider that the steadfast hold
On the extreme end of the chain of faith
Gives all the advantage, makes the difference
With the rough purblind mass we seek to rule.
We are their lords, or they are free of us
Just as we tighten or relax our hold.
So, others matters equal, we'll revert
To the first problem—which if solved my way
And thrown into the balance turns the scale—
How we may lead a comfortable life,
How suit our luggage to the cabin's size.

Of course you are remarking all this time
How narrowly and grossly I view life,
Respect the creature-comforts, care to rule
The masses, and regard complacently

"The cabin," in our old phrase. Well, I do.
I act for, talk for, live for this world now,
As this world calls for action, life and talk—
No prejudice to what next world may prove,
Whose new laws and requirements, my best pledge
To observe then, is that I observe these now,
Doing hereafter what I do meanwhile.
Let us concede (gratuitously though)
Next life relieves the soul of body, yields
Pure spiritual enjoyments: well, my friend,
Why lose this life in the meantime, since its use
May be to make the next life more intense?

Do you know, I have often had a dream
(Work it up in your next month's article)
Of man's poor spirit in its progress still
Losing true life for ever and a day
Through ever trying to be and ever being
In the evolution of successive spheres,
Before its actual sphere and place of life,
Halfway into the next, which having reached,
It shoots with corresponding foolery
Halfway into the next still, on and off!
As when a traveller, bound from north to south,
Scouts fur in Russia—what's its use in France?
In France spurns flannel—where's its need in Spain?
In Spain drops cloth—too cumbrous for Algiers!
Linen goes next, and last the skin itself,
A superfluity at Timbuctoo.
When, through his journey, was the fool at ease?
I'm at ease now, friend—worldly in this world
I take and like its way of life; I think
My brothers who administer the means
Live better for my comfort—that's good too;
And God, if he pronounce upon it all,
Approves my service, which is better still.
If He keep silence,—why, for you or me
Or that brute-beast pulled-up in to-day's "Times,"
What odds is't, save to ourselves, what life we lead?

You meet me at this issue—you declare,
All special-pleading done with, truth is truth,
And justifies itself by undreamed ways.
You don't fear but it's better, if we doubt,
To say so, acting up to our truth perceived
However feebly. Do then,—act away!
'Tis there I'm on the watch for you! How one acts
Is, both of us agree, our chief concern:
And how you'll act is what I fain would see
If, like the candid person you appear,
You dare to make the most of your life's scheme
As I of mine, live up to its full law
Since there's no higher law that counterchecks.
Put natural religion to the test
You've just demolished the revealed with—quick,
Down to the root of all that checks your will,
All prohibition to lie, kill and thieve,
Or even to be an atheistic priest!
Suppose a pricking to incontinence—
Philosophers deduce you chastity
Or shame, from just the fact that at the first
Whoso embraced a woman in the plain,
Threw club down, and forewent his brains beside,
So stood a ready victim in the reach
Of any brother-savage club in hand—
Hence saw the use of going out of sight
In wood or cave to prosecute his loves—
I read this in a French book t'other day.
Does law so analyzed coerce you much?
Oh, men spin clouds of fuzz where matters end,
But you who reach where the first thread begins,
You'll soon cut that!—which means you can, but won't,
Through certain instincts, blind, unreasoned-out,
You dare not set aside, you can't tell why,
But there they are, and so you let them rule.
Then, friend, you seem as much a slave as I,
A liar, conscious coward and hypocrite,
Without the good the slave expects to get,
Suppose he has a master after all!
You own your instincts—why, what else do I,
Who want, am made for, and must have a God

Ere I can be aught, do aught?—no mere name
Want, but the true thing with what proves its truth,
To wit, a relation from that thing to me,
Touching from head to foot—which touch I feel,
And with it take the rest, this life of ours!
I live my life here; yours you dare not live.

Not as I state it, who (you please subjoin)
Disfigure such a life and call it names,
While, in your mind, remains another way
For simple men: knowledge and power have rights,
But ignorance and weakness have rights too.
There needs no crucial effort to find truth
If here or there or anywhere about—
We ought to turn each side, try hard and see,
And if we can't, be glad we've earned at least
The right, by one laborious proof the more,
To graze in peace earth's pleasant pasturage.
Men are not gods, but, properly, are brutes.
Something we may see, all we cannot see—
What need of lying? I say, I see all,
And swear to each detail the most minute
In what I think a man's face—you, mere cloud:
I swear I hear him speak and see him wink,
For fear, if once I drop the emphasis,
Mankind may doubt there's a cloud at all.
You take the simpler life—ready to see,
Willing to see—for no cloud's worth a face—
And leaving quiet what no strength can move,
And which, who bids you move? who has the right?
I bid you; but you are God's sheep, not mine—
"*Pastor est tui Dominus.*" You find
In these the pleasant pastures of this life
Much you may eat without the least offence,
Much you don't eat because your maw objects,
Much you would eat but that your fellow-flock
Open great eyes at you and even butt,
And thereupon you like your friends so much
You cannot please yourself, offending them—
Though when they seem exorbitantly sheep,

You weigh your pleasure with their butts and kicks
And strike the balance. Sometimes certain fears
Restrain you—real checks since you find them so—
Sometimes you please yourself and nothing checks;
And thus you graze through life with not one lie,
And like it best.

But do you, in truth's name?
If so, you beat—which means—you are not I—
Who needs must make earth mine and feed my fill
Not simply unbutted at, unbickered with,
But motioned to the velvet of the sward
By those obsequious wethers' very selves.
Look at me, sir; my age is double yours.
At yours, I knew beforehand, so enjoyed,
What now I should be—as, permit the word,
I pretty well imagine your whole range
And stretch of tether twenty years to come.
We both have minds and bodies much alike.
In truth's name, don't you want my bishopric,
My daily bread, my influence and my state?
You're young, I'm old, you must be old one day;
Will you find then, as I do hour by hour,
Women their lovers kneel to, that cut curls
From your fat lap-dog's ears to grace a brooch—
Dukes, that petition just to kiss your ring—
With much beside you know or may conceive?
Suppose we die to-night: well, here am I,
Such were my gains, life bore this fruit to me,
While writing all the same my articles
On music, poetry, the fictile vase
Found at Albano, or Anacreon's Greek.
But you—the highest honour in your life,
The thing you'll crown yourself with, all your days,
Is—dining here and drinking this last glass
I pour you out in sign of amity
Before we part for ever. Of your power
And social influence, worldly worth in short,
Judge what's my estimation by the fact—
I do not condescend to enjoin, beseech,
Hint secresy on one of all these words!

You're shrewd and know that should you publish it
The world would brand the lie—my enemies first,
Who'd sneer—"the bishop's an arch-hypocrite,
And knave perhaps, but not so frank a fool."
Whereas I should not dare for both my ears
Breathe one such syllable, smile one such smile,
Before my chaplain who reflects myself—
My shade's so much more potent than your flesh.
What's your reward, self-abnegating friend?
Stood you confessed of those exceptional
And privileged great natures that dwarf mine—
A zealot with a mad ideal in reach,
A poet just about to print his ode,
A statesman with a scheme to stop this war,
An artist whose religion is his art,
I should have nothing to object! such men
Carry the fire, all things grow warm to them,
Their drugget's worth my purple, they beat me.
But you,—you're just as little those as I—
You, Gigadibs, who, thirty years of age,
Write statedly for Blackwood's Magazine,
Believe you see two points in Hamlet's soul
Unseized by the Germans yet—which view you'll print—
Meantime the best you have to show being still
That lively lightsome article we took
Almost for the true Dickens,—what's the name?
"The Slum and Cellar—or Whitechapel life
Limned after dark!" it made me laugh, I know,
And pleased a month and brought you in ten pounds.
—Success I recognise and compliment,
And therefore give you, if you please, three words
(The card and pencil-scratch is quite enough)
Which whether here, in Dublin or New York,
Will get you, prompt as at my eyebrow's wink,
Such terms as never you aspired to get
In all our own reviews and some not ours.
Go write your lively sketches—be the first
"Blougram, or The Eccentric Confidence"—
Or better simply say, "The Outward-bound."
Why, men as soon would throw it in my teeth

As copy and quote the infamy chalked broad
About me on the church-door opposite.
You will not wait for that experience though,
I fancy, howsoever you decide,
To discontinue—not detesting, not
Defaming, but at least—despising me!

Over his wine so smiled and talked his hour
Sylvester Blougram, styled *in partibus*
Episcopus, nec non—(the deuce knows what
It's changed to by our novel hierarchy)
With Gigadibs the literary man,
Who played with spoons, explored his plate's design,
And ranged the olive-stones about its edge,
While the great bishop rolled him out his mind.

For Blougram, he believed, say, half he spoke.
The other portion, as he shaped it thus
For argumentatory purposes,
He felt his foe was foolish to dispute.
Some arbitrary accidental thoughts
That crossed his mind, amusing because new,
He chose to represent as fixtures there,
Invariable convictions (such they seemed
Beside his interlocutor's loose cards
Flung daily down, and not the same way twice)
While certain hell-deep instincts, man's weak tongue
Is never bold to utter in their truth
Because styled hell-deep ('tis an old mistake
To place hell at the bottom of the earth)
He ignored these,—not having in readiness
Their nomenclature and philosophy:
He said true things, but called them by wrong names.
"On the whole," he thought, "I justify myself
On every point where cavillers like this
Oppugn my life: he tries one kind of fence—
I close—he's worsted, that's enough for him;
He's on the ground! if the ground should break away
I take my stand on, there's a firmer yet

Beneath it, both of us may sink and reach.
His ground was over mine and broke the first.
So let him sit with me this many a year!"

He did not sit five minutes. Just a week
Sufficed his sudden healthy vehemence.
(Something had struck him in the "Outward-bound"
Another way than Blougram's purpose was)
And having bought, not cabin-furniture
But settler's-implements (enough for three)
And started for Australia—there, I hope,
By this time he has tested his first plough,
And studied his last chapter of St. John.

Memorabilia

1.

Ah, did you once see Shelley plain,
And did he stop and speak to you?
And did you speak to him again?
How strange it seems, and new!

2.

But you were living before that,
And also you are living after,
And the memory I started at—
My starting moves your laughter!

3.

I crossed a moor with a name of its own
And a certain use in the world no doubt,
Yet a hand's-breadth of it shines alone
'Mid the blank miles round about—

4.

For there I picked up on the heather
And there I put inside my breast
A moulted feather, an eagle-feather—
Well, I forget the rest.

FROM *MEN AND WOMEN*, VOL. II (1855)

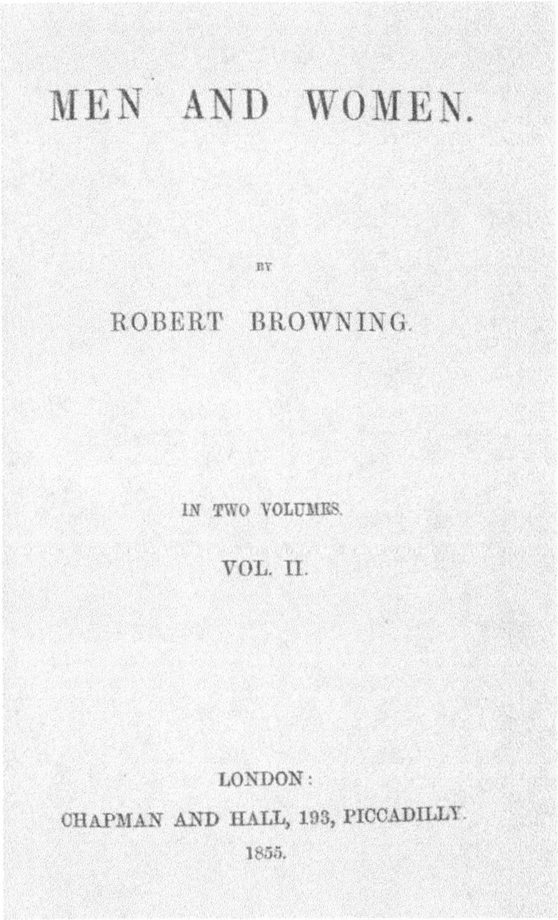

MEN AND WOMEN.

BY

ROBERT BROWNING.

IN TWO VOLUMES.

VOL. II.

LONDON:

CHAPMAN AND HALL, 193, PICCADILLY.

1855.

FIG. 6 Title-page of *Men and Women*, Vol. II (1855).

FIG. 7 *Doppio Ritrato* (Double Portrait), once thought to be a portrait by Andrea del Sarto of himself and his wife, Galleria Palatino, Palazzo Pitti, Florence.

Andrea del Sarto

(CALLED "THE FAULTLESS PAINTER")

But do not let us quarrel any more,
No, my Lucrezia; bear with me for once:
Sit down and all shall happen as you wish.
You turn your face, but does it bring your heart?
I'll work then for your friend's friend, never fear,
Treat his own subject after his own way,
Fix his own time, accept too his own price,
And shut the money into this small hand
When next it takes mine. Will it? tenderly?
Oh, I'll content him,—but to-morrow, Love!

I often am much wearier than you think,
This evening more than usual, and it seems
As if—forgive now—should you let me sit
Here by the window with your hand in mine
And look a half hour forth on Fiesole,
Both of one mind, as married people use,
Quietly, quietly, the evening through,
I might get up to-morrow to my work
Cheerful and fresh as ever. Let us try.
To-morrow how you shall be glad for this!
Your soft hand is a woman of itself,
And mine the man's bared breast she curls inside.
Don't count the time lost, either; you must serve
For each of the five pictures we require—
It saves a model. So! keep looking so—
My serpentining beauty, rounds on rounds!
—How could you ever prick those perfect ears,
Even to put the pearl there! oh, so sweet—
My face, my moon, my everybody's moon,
Which everybody looks on and calls his,
And, I suppose, is looked on by in turn,
While she looks—no one's: very dear, no less!
You smile? why, there's my picture ready made.
There's what we painters call our harmony!
A common greyness silvers everything,—
All in a twilight, you and I alike
—You, at the point of your first pride in me
(That's gone you know),—but I, at every point;
My youth, my hope, my art, being all toned down
To yonder sober pleasant Fiesole.
There's the bell clinking from the chapel-top;
That length of convent-wall across the way
Holds the trees safer, huddled more inside;
The last monk leaves the garden; days decrease
And autumn grows, autumn in everything.
Eh? the whole seems to fall into a shape
As if I saw alike my work and self
And all that I was born to be and do,
A twilight-piece. Love, we are in God's hand.
How strange now, looks the life he makes us lead!
So free we seem, so fettered fast we are:

I feel he laid the fetter: let it lie!
This chamber for example—turn your head—
All that's behind us! You don't understand
Nor care to understand about my art,
But you can hear at least when people speak;
And that cartoon, the second from the door
—It is the thing, Love! so such things should be—
Behold Madonna, I am bold to say.
I can do with my pencil what I know,
What I see, what at bottom of my heart
I wish for, if I ever wish so deep—
Do easily, too—when I say perfectly,
I do not boast, perhaps: yourself are judge,
Who listened to the Legate's talk last week,
And just as much they used to say in France.
At any rate 'tis easy, all of it,
No sketches first, no studies, that's long past—
I do what many dream of all their lives
—Dream? strive to do, and agonise to do,
And fail in doing. I could count twenty such
On twice your fingers, and not leave this town,
Who strive—you don't know how the others strive
To paint a little thing like that you smeared
Carelessly passing with your robes afloat,
Yet do much less, so much less, some one says,
(I know his name, no matter) so much less!
Well, less is more, Lucrezia! I am judged.
There burns a truer light of God in them,
In their vexed, beating, stuffed and stopped-up brain,
Heart, or whate'er else, than goes on to prompt
This low-pulsed forthright craftsman's hand of mine.
Their works drop groundward, but themselves, I know,
Reach many a time a heaven that's shut to me,
Enter and take their place there sure enough,
Though they come back and cannot tell the world.
My works are nearer heaven, but I sit here.
The sudden blood of these men! at a word—
Praise them, it boils, or blame them, it boils too.
I, painting from myself and to myself,
Know what I do, am unmoved by men's blame
Or their praise either. Somebody remarks

Morello's outline there is wrongly traced,
His hue mistaken—what of that? or else,
Rightly traced and well ordered—what of that?
Ah, but a man's reach should exceed his grasp,
Or what's a Heaven for? all is silver-grey
Placid and perfect with my art—the worse!
I know both what I want and what might gain—
And yet how profitless to know, to sigh
"Had I been two, another and myself,
Our head would have o'erlooked the world!" No doubt.
Yonder's a work, now, of that famous youth
The Urbinate who died five years ago.
('Tis copied, George Vasari sent it me).
Well, I can fancy how he did it all,
Pouring his soul, with kings and popes to see,
Reaching, that Heaven might so replenish him,
Above and through his art—for it gives way;
That arm is wrongly put—and there again—
A fault to pardon in the drawing's lines,
Its body, so to speak! its soul is right,
He means right—that, a child may understand.
Still, what an arm! and I could alter it.
But all the play, the insight and the stretch—
Out of me! out of me! And wherefore out?
Had you enjoined them on me, given me soul,
We might have risen to Rafael, I and you.
Nay, Love, you did give all I asked, I think—
More than I merit, yes, by many times.
But had you—oh, with the same perfect brow,
And perfect eyes, and more than perfect mouth,
And the low voice my soul hears, as a bird
The fowler's pipe, and follows to the snare—
Had you, with these the same, but brought a mind!
Some women do so. Had the mouth there urged
"God and the glory! never care for gain.
The present by the future, what is that?
Live for fame, side by side with Angelo—
Rafael is waiting. Up to God, all three!"
I might have done it for you. So it seems—
Perhaps not. All is as God over-rules.
Beside, incentives come from the soul's self;

The rest avail not. Why do I need you?
What wife had Rafael, or has Angelo?
In this world, who can do a thing, will not—
And who would do it, cannot, I perceive:
Yet the will's somewhat—somewhat, too, the power—
And thus we half-men struggle. At the end,
God, I conclude, compensates, punishes.
'Tis safer for me, if the award be strict,
That I am something underrated here,
Poor this long while, despised, to speak the truth.
I dared not, do you know, leave home all day,
For fear of chancing on the Paris lords.
The best is when they pass and look aside;
But they speak sometimes; I must bear it all.
Well may they speak! That Francis, that first time,
And that long festal year at Fontainebleau!
I surely then could sometimes leave the ground,
Put on the glory, Rafael's daily wear,
In that humane great monarch's golden look,—
One finger in his beard or twisted curl
Over his mouth's good mark that made the smile,
One arm about my shoulder, round my neck,
The jingle of his gold chain in my ear,
You painting proudly with his breath on me,
All his court round him, seeing with his eyes,
Such frank French eyes, and such a fire of souls
Profuse, my hand kept plying by those hearts,—
And, best of all, this, this, this face beyond,
This in the back-ground, waiting on my work,
To crown the issue with a last reward!
A good time, was it not, my kingly days?
And had you not grown restless—but I know—
'Tis done and past; 'twas right, my instinct said;
Too live the life grew, golden and not grey—
And I'm the weak-eyed bat no sun should tempt
Out of the grange whose four walls make his world.
How could it end in any other way?
You called me, and I came home to your heart.
The triumph was to have ended there—then if
I reached it ere the triumph, what is lost?
Let my hands frame your face in your hair's gold,

You beautiful Lucrezia that are mine!
"Rafael did this, Andrea painted that—
The Roman's is the better when you pray,
But still the other's Virgin was his wife—"
Men will excuse me. I am glad to judge
Both pictures in your presence; clearer grows
My better fortune, I resolve to think.
For, do you know, Lucrezia, as God lives,
Said one day Angelo, his very self,
To Rafael . . . I have known it all these years . . .
(When the young man was flaming out his thoughts
Upon a palace-wall for Rome to see,
Too lifted up in heart because of it)
"Friend, there's a certain sorry little scrub
Goes up and down our Florence, none cares how,
Who, were he set to plan and execute
As you are pricked on by your popes and kings,
Would bring the sweat into that brow of yours!"
To Rafael's!—And indeed the arm is wrong.
I hardly dare—yet, only you to see,
Give the chalk here—quick, thus the line should go!
Ay, but the soul! he's Rafael! rub it out!
Still, all I care for, if he spoke the truth,
(What he? why, who but Michael Angelo?
Do you forget already words like those?)
If really there was such a chance, so lost,
Is, whether you're—not grateful—but more pleased.
Well, let me think so. And you smile indeed!
This hour has been an hour! Another smile?
If you would sit thus by me every night
I should work better, do you comprehend?
I mean that I should earn more, give you more.
See, it is settled dusk now; there's a star;
Morello's gone, the watch-lights shew the wall,
The cue-owls speak the name we call them by,
Come from the window, Love,—come in, at last,
Inside the melancholy little house
We built to be so gay with. God is just.
King Francis may forgive me. Oft at nights
When I look up from painting, eyes tired out,
The walls become illumined, brick from brick

Distinct, instead of mortar fierce bright gold,
That gold of his I did cement them with!
Let us but love each other. Must you go?
That Cousin here again? he waits outside?
Must see you—you, and not with me? Those loans!
More gaming debts to pay? you smiled for that?
Well, let smiles buy me! have you more to spend?
While hand and eye and something of a heart
Are left me, work's my ware, and what's it worth?
I'll pay my fancy. Only let me sit
The grey remainder of the evening out,
Idle, you call it, and muse perfectly
How I could paint were I but back in France,
One picture, just one more—the Virgin's face,
Not your's this time! I want you at my side
To hear them—that is, Michael Angelo—
Judge all I do and tell you of its worth.
Will you? To-morrow, satisfy your friend.
I take the subjects for his corridor,
Finish the portrait out of hand—there, there,
And throw him in another thing or two
If he demurs; the whole should prove enough
To pay for this same Cousin's freak. Beside,
What's better and what's all I care about,
Get you the thirteen scudi for the ruff
Love, does that please you? Ah, but what does he,
The Cousin! what does he to please you more?

I am grown peaceful as old age to-night.
I regret little, I would change still less.
Since there my past life lies, why alter it?
The very wrong to Francis! it is true
I took his coin, was tempted and complied,
And built this house and sinned, and all is said.
My father and my mother died of want.
Well, had I riches of my own? you see
How one gets rich! Let each one bear his lot.
They were born poor, lived poor, and poor they died:
And I have laboured somewhat in my time
And not been paid profusely. Some good son
Paint my two hundred pictures—let him try!

No doubt, there's something strikes a balance. Yes,
You loved me quite enough, it seems to-night.
This must suffice me here. What would one have?
In heaven, perhaps, new chances, one more chance—
Four great walls in the New Jerusalem
Meted on each side by the angel's reed,
For Leonard, Rafael, Angelo and me
To cover—the three first without a wife,
While I have mine! So—still they overcome
Because there's still Lucrezia,—as I choose.

Again the Cousin's whistle! Go, my Love.

In a Year

1.

Never any more,
While I live,
Need I hope to see his face
As before.
Once his love grown chill,
Mine may strive—
Bitterly we re-embrace,
Single still.

2.

Was it something said,
Something done,
Vexed him? was it touch of hand,
Turn of head?
Strange! that very way
Love begun.
I as little understand
Love's decay.

3.

When I sewed or drew,
I recall
How he looked as if I sang,
—Sweetly too.

If I spoke a word,
First of all
Up his cheek the color sprang,
Then he heard.

4.

Sitting by my side,
At my feet,
So he breathed the air I breathed,
Satisfied!
I, too, at love's brim
Touched the sweet:
I would die if death bequeathed
Sweet to him.

5.

"Speak, I love thee best!"
He exclaimed.
"Let thy love my own foretell,—"
I confessed:
"Clasp my heart on thine
Now unblamed,
Since upon thy soul as well
Hangeth mine!"

6.

Was it wrong to own,
Being truth?
Why should all the giving prove
His alone?
I had wealth and ease,
Beauty, youth—
Since my lover gave me love,
I gave these.

7.

That was all I meant,
—To be just,
And the passion I had raised,
To content.

Since he chose to change
  Gold for dust,
If I gave him what he praised
  Was it strange?

8.

Would he loved me yet,
  On and on,
While I found some way undreamed
  —Paid my debt!
Gave more life and more,
  Till, all gone,
He should smile "She never seemed
  Mine before.

9.

"What—she felt the while,
  Must I think?
Love's so different with us men!"
  He should smile,
"Dying for my sake—
  White and pink!
Can't we touch these bubbles then
  But they break?"

10.

Dear, the pang is brief,
  Do thy part,
Have thy pleasure. How perplext
  Grows belief!
Well, this cold clay clod
  Was man's heart.
Crumble it—and what comes next?
  Is it God?

Old Pictures in Florence

1.

The morn when first it thunders in March,
  The eel in the pond gives a leap, they say.
As I leaned and looked over the aloed arch
  Of the villa-gate, this warm March day,
No flash snapt, no dumb thunder rolled
  In the valley beneath, where, white and wide,
And washed by the morning's water-gold,
  Florence lay out on the mountain-side.

2.

River and bridge and street and square
  Lay mine, as much at my beck and call,
Through the live translucent bath of air,
  As the sights in a magic crystal ball.
And of all I saw and of all I praised,
  The most to praise and the best to see,
Was the startling bell-tower Giotto raised:
  But why did it more than startle me?

3.

Giotto, how, with that soul of yours,
  Could you play me false who loved you so?
Some slights if a certain heart endures
  It feels, I would have your fellows know!
'Faith—I perceive not why I should care
  To break a silence that suits them best,
But the thing grows somewhat hard to bear
  When I find a Giotto join the rest.

4.

On the arch where olives overhead
  Print the blue sky with twig and leaf,
(That sharp-curled leaf which they never shed)
  'Twixt the aloes, I used to lean in chief,
And mark through the winter afternoons,
  By a gift God grants me now and then,
In the mild decline of those suns like moons,
  Who walked in Florence, besides her men.

5.

They might chirp and chaffer, come and go
  For pleasure or profit, her men alive—
My business was hardly with them, I trow,
  But with empty cells of the human hive;
—With the chapter-room, the cloister-porch,
  The church's apsis, aisle or nave,
Its crypt, one fingers along with a torch—
  Its face, set full for the sun to shave.

6.

Wherever a fresco peels and drops,
  Wherever an outline weakens and wanes
Till the latest life in the painting stops,
  Stands One whom each fainter pulse-tick pains!
One, wishful each scrap should clutch its brick,
  Each tinge not wholly escape the plaster,
—A lion who dies of an ass's kick,
  The wronged great soul of an ancient Master.

7.

For oh, this world and the wrong it does!
  They are safe in heaven with their backs to it,
The Michaels and Rafaels, you hum and buzz
  Round the works of, you of the little wit!
Do their eyes contract to the earth's old scope,
  Now that they see God face to face,
And have all attained to be poets, I hope?
  'Tis their holiday now, in any case.

8.

Much they reck of your praise and you!
  But the wronged great souls—can they be quit
Of a world where all their work is to do,
  Where you style them, you of the little wit,
Old Master this and Early the other,
  Not dreaming that Old and New are fellows,
A younger succeeds to an elder brother,
  Da Vincis derive in good time from Dellos.

9.

And here where your praise might yield returns
  And a handsome word or two give help,
Here, after your kind, the mastiff girns
  And the puppy pack of poodles yelp.
What, not a word for Stefano there
  —Of brow once prominent and starry,
Called Nature's ape and the world's despair
  For his peerless painting (see Vasari)?

10.

There he stands now. Study, my friends,
  What a man's work comes to! so he plans it,
Performs it, perfects it, makes amends
  For the toiling and moiling, and there's its transit!
Happier the thrifty blind-folk labour,
  With upturned eye while the hand is busy,
Not sidling a glance at the coin of their neighbour!
  'Tis looking downward that makes one dizzy.

11.

If you knew their work you would deal your dole.
  May I take upon me to instruct you?
When Greek Art ran and reached the goal,
  Thus much had the world to boast *in fructu*—
The truth of Man, as by God first spoken,
  Which the actual generations garble,
Was re-uttered,—and Soul (which Limbs betoken)
  And Limbs (Soul informs) made new in marble.

12.

So you saw yourself as you wished you were,
  As you might have been, as you cannot be;
And bringing your own shortcomings there,
  You grew content in your poor degree
With your little power, by those statues' godhead,
  And your little scope, by their eyes' full sway,
And your little grace, by their grace embodied,
  And your little date, by their forms that stay.

13.

You would fain be kinglier, say than I am?
  Even so, you will not sit like Theseus.
You would fain be a model? the Son of Priam
  Has yet the advantage in arms' and knees' use.
You're wroth—can you slay your snake like Apollo?
  You're grieved—still Niobe's the grander!
You live—there's the Racers' frieze to follow—
  You die—there's the dying Alexander.

14.

So, testing your weakness by their strength,
  Your meagre charms by their rounded beauty,
Measured by Art in your breadth and length,
  You learned—to submit is the worsted's duty.
—When I say "you" 'tis the common soul,
  The collective, I mean—the race of Man
That receives life in parts to live in a whole,
  And grow here according to God's own plan.

15.

Growth came when, looking your last on them all,
  You turned your eyes inwardly one fine day
And cried with a start—What if we so small
  Be greater, ay, greater the while than they!
Are they perfect of lineament, perfect of stature?
  In both, of such lower types are we
Precisely because of our wider nature;
  For time, theirs—ours, for eternity.

16.

To-day's brief passion limits their range,
  It seethes with the morrow for us and more.
They are perfect—how else? they shall never change:
  We are faulty—why not? we have time in store.
The Artificer's hand is not arrested
  With us—we are rough-hewn, no-wise polished:
They stand for our copy, and, once invested
  With all they can teach, we shall see them abolished.

17.

'Tis a life-long toil till our lump be leaven—
  The better! what's come to perfection perishes.
Things learned on earth, we shall practise in heaven:
  Works done least rapidly, Art most cherishes.
Thyself shalt afford the example, Giotto!
  Thy one work, not to decrease or diminish,
Done at a stroke, was just (was it not?) "O!"
  Thy great Campanile is still to finish.

18.

Is it true, we are now, and shall be hereafter,
  And what—is depending on life's one minute?
Hails heavenly cheer or infernal laughter
  Our first step out of the gulf or in it?
And Man, such step within his endeavour,
  His face, have no more play and action
Than joy which is crystallized for ever,
  Or grief, an eternal petrifaction!

19.

On which I conclude, that the early painters,
  To cries of "Greek Art and what more wish you?"—
Replied, "To become now self-acquainters,
  And paint man, man,—whatever the issue!
Make new hopes shine through the flesh they fray,
  New fears aggrandise the rags and tatters.
So bring the invisible full into play,
  Let the visible go to the dogs—what matters?"

20.

Give these, I say, full honour and glory
  For daring so much, before they well did it.
The first of the new, in our race's story,
  Beats the last of the old, 'tis no idle quiddit.
The worthies began a revolution
  Which if on the earth we intend to acknowledge
Honour them now—(ends my allocution)
  Nor confer your degree when the folk leave college.

21.

There's a fancy some lean to and others hate—
 That, when this life is ended, begins
New work for the soul in another state,
 Where it strives and gets weary, loses and wins—
Where the strong and the weak, this world's congeries,
 Repeat in large what they practised in small,
Through life after life in unlimited series;
 Only the scale's to be changed, that's all.

22.

Yet I hardly know. When a soul has seen
 By the means of Evil that Good is best,
And through earth and its noise, what is heaven's serene,—
 When our faith in the same has stood the test—
Why, the child grown man, you burn the rod,
 The uses of labour are surely done.
There remaineth a rest for the people of God,
 And I have had troubles enough for one.

23.

But at any rate I have loved the season
 Of Art's spring-birth so dim and dewy,
My sculptor is Nicolo the Pisan;
 My painter—who but Cimabue?
Nor ever was man of them all indeed,
 From these to Ghiberti and Ghirlandajo,
Could say that he missed my critic-meed.
 So, now to my special grievance—heigh ho!

24.

Their ghosts now stand, as I said before,
 Watching each fresco flaked and rasped,
Blocked up, knocked out, or whitewashed o'er
 —No getting again what the church has grasped
The works on the wall must take their chance,
 "Works never conceded to England's thick clime!"
(I hope they prefer their inheritance
 Of a bucketful of Italian quick-lime.)

25.

When they go at length, with such a shaking
  Of heads o'er the old delusions, sadly
Each master his way through the black streets taking,
  Where many a lost work breathes though badly—
Why don't they bethink them of who has merited?
  Why not reveal, while their pictures dree
Such doom, that a captive's to be out-ferreted?
  Why do they never remember me?

26.

Not that I expect the great Bigordi
  Nor Sandro to hear me, chivalric, bellicose;
Nor the wronged Lippino—and not a word I
  Say of a scrap of Fra Angelico's.
But are you too fine, Taddeo Gaddi,
  To grant me a taste of your intonaco—
Some Jerome that seeks the heaven with a sad eye?
  Not a churlish saint, Lorenzo Monaco?

27.

Could not the ghost with the close red cap,
  My Pollajolo, the twice a craftsman,
Save me a sample, give me the hap
  Of a muscular Christ that shows the draughtsman?
No Virgin by him, the somewhat petty,
  Of finical touch and tempera crumbly—
Could not Alesso Baldovinetti
  Contribute so much, I ask him humbly?

28.

Margheritone of Arezzo,
  With the grave-clothes garb and swaddling barret,
(Why purse up mouth and beak in a pet so,
  You bald, saturnine, poll-clawed parrot?)
Not a poor glimmering Crucifixion,
  Where in the foreground kneels the donor?
If such remain, as is my conviction,
  The hoarding it does you but little honour.

29.

They pass: for them the panels may thrill,
The tempera grow alive and tinglish—
Rot or are left to the mercies still
Of dealers and stealers, Jews and the English!
Seeing mere money's worth in their prize,
Who sell it to some one calm as Zeno
At naked Art, and in ecstacies
Before some clay-cold, vile Carlino!

30.

No matter for these! But Giotto, you,
Have you allowed, as the town-tongues babble it,
Never! it shall not be counted true—
That a certain precious little tablet
Which Buonarroti eyed like a lover,—
Buried so long in oblivion's womb,
Was left for another than I to discover,—
Turns up at last, and to whom?—to whom?

31.

I, that have haunted the dim San Spirito,
(Or was it rather the Ognissanti?)
Stood on the altar-steps, patient and weary too!
Nay, I shall have it yet, *detur amanti!*
My Koh-i-noor—or (if that's a platitude)
Jewel of Giamschid, the Persian Sofi's eye!
So, in anticipative gratitude,
What if I take up my hope and prophesy?

32.

When the hour grows ripe, and a certain dotard
Pitched, no parcel that needs invoicing,
To the worse side of the Mont St. Gothard,
Have, to begin by way of rejoicing,
None of that shooting the sky (blank cartridge),
Nor a civic guards, all plumes and lacquer,
Hunting Radetzky's soul like a partridge
Over Morello with squib and cracker.

33.

We'll shoot this time better game and bag 'em hot—
No display at the stone of Dante,
But a kind of Witan-agemot
("Casa Guidi," quod videas ante)
To ponder Freedom restored to Florence,
How Art may return that departed with her.
Go, hated house, go each trace of the Loraine's!
And bring us the days of Orgagna hither.

34.

How we shall prologuise, how we shall perorate,
Say fit things upon art and history—
Set truth at blood-heat and false at a zero rate,
Make of the want of the age no mystery!
Contrast the fructuous and sterile eras,
Show, monarchy its uncouth cub licks
Out of the bear's shape into chimæra's—
Pure Art's birth being still the republic's!

35.

Then one shall propose (in a speech, curt Tuscan,
Sober, expurgate, spare of an "*issimo*,")
Ending our half-told tale of Cambuscan,
Turning the Bell-tower's alt altissimo.
And fine as the beak of a young beccaccia
The Campanile, the Duomo's fit ally,
Soars up in gold full fifty braccia,
Completing Florence, as Florence, Italy.

36.

Shall I be alive that morning the scaffold
Is broken away, and the long-pent fire
Like the golden hope of the world unbaffled
Springs from its sleep, and up goes the spire—
As, "God and the People" plain for its motto,
Thence the new tricolor flaps at the sky?
Foreseeing the day that vindicates Giotto
And Florence together, the first am I!

In a Balcony

FIRST PART

CONSTANCE *and* NORBERT.

NORBERT.

Now.

CONSTANCE.

Not now.

NORBERT.

Give me them again, those hands—
Put them upon my forehead, how it throbs!
Press them before my eyes, the fire comes through.
You cruellest, you dearest in the world,
Let me! The Queen must grant whate'er I ask—
How can I gain you and not ask the Queen?
There she stays waiting for me, here stand you.
Some time or other this was to be asked,
Now is the one time—what I ask, I gain—
Let me ask now, Love!

CONSTANCE.

Do, and ruin us.

NORBERT.

Let it be now, Love! All my soul breaks forth.
How I do love you! give my love its way!
A man can have but one life and one death,
One heaven, one hell. Let me fulfil my fate—
Grant me my heaven now. Let me know you mine,
Prove you mine, write my name upon your brow,
Hold you and have you, and then die away
If God please, with completion in my soul.

CONSTANCE.

I am not yours then? how content this man?
I am not his, who change into himself,
Have passed into his heart and beat its beats,
Who give my hands to him, my eyes, my hair,
Give all that was of me away to him
So well, that now, my spirit turned his own,
Takes part with him against the woman here,
Bids him not stumble at so mere a straw
As caring that the world be cognisant
How he loves her and how she worships him.
You have this woman, not as yet that world.
Go on, I bid, nor stop to care for me
By saving what I cease to care about,
The courtly name and pride of circumstance—
The name you'll pick up and be cumbered with
Just for the poor parade's sake, nothing more;
Just that the world may slip from under you—
Just that the world may cry "So much for him—
The man predestined to the heap of crowns!
There goes his chance of winning one, at least."

NORBERT.

The world!

CONSTANCE.

You love it. Love me quite as well,
And see if I shall pray for this in vain!
Why must you ponder what it knows or thinks?

NORBERT.

You pray for—what, in vain?

CONSTANCE.

Oh my heart's heart,
How I do love you, Norbert!—that is right!
But listen, or I take my hands away.
You say, "let it be now"—you would go now

And tell the Queen, perhaps six steps from us,
You love me—so you do, thank God!

NORBERT.

Thank God!

CONSTANCE.

Yes, Norbert—but you fain would tell your love,
And, what succeeds the telling, ask of her
My hand. Now take this rose and look at it,
Listening to me. You are the minister,
The Queen's first favourite, nor without a cause.
To-night completes your wonderful year's-work
(This palace-feast is held to celebrate)
Made memorable by her life's success,
The junction of two crowns, on her sole head
Her house had only dreamed of anciently.
That this mere dream is grown a stable truth
To-night's feast makes authentic. Whose the praise?
Whose genius, patience, energy, achieved
What turned the many heads and broke the hearts?
You are the fate,—your minute's in the heaven.
Next comes the Queen's turn. Name your own reward!
With leave to clench the past, chain the to-come,
Put out an arm and touch and take the sun
And fix it ever full-faced on your earth,
Possess yourself supremely of her life,
You choose the single thing she will not grant—
The very declaration of which choice
Will turn the scale and neutralise your work.
At best she will forgive you, if she can.
You think I'll let you choose—her cousin's hand?

NORBERT.

Wait. First, do you retain your old belief
The Queen is generous,—nay, is just?

CONSTANCE.

There, there!
So men make women love them, while they know
No more of women's hearts than . . . look you here,
You that are just and generous beside,
Make it your own case. For example now,
I'll say—I let you kiss me and hold my hands—
Why? do you know why? I'll instruct you, then—
The kiss, because you have a name at court,
This hand and this, that you may shut in each
A jewel, if you please to pick up such.
That's horrible! Apply it to the Queen—
Suppose, I am the Queen to whom you speak.
"I was a nameless man: you needed me:
Why did I proffer you my aid? there stood
A certain pretty Cousin at your side.
Why did I make such common cause with you?
Access to her had not been easy else.
You give my labours here abundant praise:
'Faith, labour, which she overlooked, grew play.
How shall your gratitude discharge itself?
Give me her hand!"

NORBERT.

And still I urge the same.
Is the Queen just? just—generous or no!

CONSTANCE.

Yes, just. You love a rose—no harm in that—
But was it for the rose's sake or mine
You put it in your bosom? mine, you said—
Then mine you still must say or else be false.
You told the Queen you served her for herself:
If so, to serve her was to serve yourself
She thinks, for all your unbelieving face!
I know her. In the hall, six steps from us,
One sees the twenty pictures—there's a life
Better than life—and yet no life at all;
Conceive her born in such a magic dome,

Pictures all round her! why, she sees the world,
Can recognise its given things and facts,
The fight of giants or the feast of gods,
Sages in senate, beauties at the bath,
Chaces and battles, the whole earth's display,
Landscape and sea-piece, down to flowers and fruit—
And who shall question that she knows them all
In better semblance than the things outside?
Yet bring into the silent gallery
Some live thing to contrast in breath and blood,
Some lion, with the painted lion there—
You think she'll understand composedly?
—Say, "that's his fellow in the hunting-piece
Yonder, I've turned to praise a hundred times?"
Not so. Her knowledge of our actual earth,
Its hopes and fears, concerns and sympathies,
Must be too far, too mediate, too unreal.
The real exists for us outside, not her—
How should it, with that life in these four walls.
That father and that mother, first to last
No father and no mother—friends, a heap,
Lovers, no lack—a husband in due time,
And everyone of them alike a lie!
Things painted by a Rubens out of nought
Into what kindness, friendship, love should be;
All better, all more grandiose than life,
Only no life; mere cloth and surface-paint
You feel while you admire. How should she feel?
And now that she has stood thus fifty years
The sole spectator in that gallery,
You think to bring this warm real struggling love
In to her of a sudden, and suppose
She'll keep her state untroubled? Here's the truth—
She'll apprehend its value at a glance,
Prefer it to the pictured loyalty!
You only have to say, "so men are made,
For this they act, the thing has many names
But this the right one—and now, Queen, be just!"
Your life slips back—you lose her at the word—
You do not even for amends gain me.
He will not understand! oh, Norbert, Norbert,
Do you not understand?

NORBERT.

The Queen's the Queen,
I am myself—no picture, but alive
In every nerve and every muscle, here
At the palace-window or in the people's street,
As she in the gallery where the pictures glow.
The good of life is precious to us both.
She cannot love—what do I want with rule?
When first I saw your face a year ago
I knew my life's good—my soul heard one voice
"The woman yonder, there's no use of life
But just to obtain her! heap earth's woes in one
And bear them—make a pile of all earth's joys
And spurn them, as they help or help not here;
Only, obtain her!"—How was it to be?
I found you were the cousin of the Queen;
I must then serve the Queen to get to her—
No other way. Suppose there had been one,
And I by saying prayers to some white star
With promise of my body and my soul
Might gain you,—should I pray the star or no?
Instead, there was the Queen to serve! I served,
And did what other servants failed to do.
Neither she sought nor I declared my end.
Her good is hers, my recompense be mine,
And let me name you as that recompense.
She dreamed that such a thing could never be?
Let her wake now. She thinks there was some cause—
The love of power, of fame, pure loyalty?
—Perhaps she fancies men wear out their lives
Chasing such shades. Then I've a fancy too,
I worked because I want you with my soul—
I therefore ask your hand. Let it be now.

CONSTANCE.

Had I not loved you from the very first,
Were I not yours, could we not steal out thus
So wickedly, so wildly, and so well,

You might be thus impatient. What's conceived
Of us without here, by the folks within?
Where are you now? immersed in cares of state—
Where am I now?—intent on festal robes—
We two, embracing under death's spread hand!
What was this thought for, what this scruple of yours
Which broke the council up, to bring about
One minute's meeting in the corridor?
And then the sudden sleights, long secresies,
The plots inscrutable, deep telegraphs,
Long-planned chance-meetings, hazards of a look,
"Does she know? does she not know? saved or lost?"
A year of this compression's ecstasy
All goes for nothing? you would give this up
For the old way, the open way, the world's,
His way who beats, and his who sells his wife?
What tempts you? their notorious happiness,
That you're ashamed of ours? The best you'll get
Will be, the Queen grants all that you require,
Concedes the cousin, and gets rid of you
And her at once, and gives us ample leave
To live like our five hundred happy friends.
The world will show us with officious hand
Our chamber-entry and stand sentinel,
Where we so oft have stolen across her traps!
Get the world's warrant, ring the falcon's foot,
And make it duty to be bold and swift,
When long ago 'twas nature. Have it so!
He never hawked by rights till flung from fist?
Oh, the man's thought!—no woman's such a fool.

NORBERT.

Yes, the man's thought and my thought, which is more—
One made to love you, let the world take note.
Have I done worthy work? be love's the praise,
Though hampered by restrictions, barred against
By set forms, blinded by forced secresies.
Set free my love, and see what love will do
Shown in my life—what work will spring from that!

The world is used to have its business done
On other grounds, find great effects produced
For power's sake, fame's sake, motives you have named.
So, good. But let my low ground shame their high.
Truth is the strong thing. Let man's life be true!
And love's the truth of mine. Time prove the rest!
I choose to have you stamped all over me,
Your name upon my forehead and my breast,
You, from the sword's blade to the ribbon's edge,
That men may see, all over, you in me—
That pale loves may die out of their pretence
In face of mine, shames thrown on love fall off—
Permit this, Constance! Love has been so long
Subdued in me, eating me through and through,
That now it's all of me and must have way.
Think of my work, that chaos of intrigues,
Those hopes and fears, surprises and delays,
That long endeavour, earnest, patient, slow,
Trembling at last to its assured result—
Then think of this revulsion. I resume
Life, after death, (it is no less than life
After such long unlovely labouring days)
And liberate to beauty life's great need
Of the beautiful, which, while it prompted work,
Suppress itself erewhile. This eve's the time—
This eve intense with yon first trembling star
We seem to pant and reach; scarce aught between
The earth that rises and the heaven that bends—
All nature self-abandoned—every tree
Flung as it will, pursuing its own thoughts
And fixed so, every flower and every weed,
No pride, no shame, no victory, no defeat:
All under God, each measured by itself!
These statues round us, each abrupt, distinct,
The strong in strength, the weak in weakness fixed,
The Muse for ever wedded to her lyre,
Nymph to her fawn, and Silence to her rose,
And God's approval on his universe!
Let us do so—aspire to live as these
In harmony with truth, ourselves being true.
Take the first way, and let the second come.

My first is to possess myself of you;
The music sets the march-step—forward, then!
And there's the Queen, I go to claim you of,
The world to witness, wonder and applaud.
Our flower of life breaks open. No delay!

CONSTANCE.

And so shall we be ruined, both of us.
Norbert, I know her to the skin and bone—
You do not know her, were not born to it,
To feel what she can see or cannot see.
Love, she is generous,—ay, despite your smile,
Generous as you are. For, in that thin frame
Pain-twisted, punctured through and through with cares,
There lived a lavish soul until it starved
Debarred all healthy food. Look to the soul—
Pity that, stoop to that, ere you begin
(The true man's way) on justice and your rights,
Exactions and acquittance of the past.
Begin so—see what justice she will deal!
We women hate a debt as men a gift.
Suppose her some poor keeper of a school
Whose business is to sit thro' summer-months
And dole out children's leave to go and play,
Herself superior to such lightness—she
In the arm-chair's state and pædagogic pomp,
To the life, the laughter, sun and youth outside—
We wonder such an one looks black on us?
I do not bid you wake her tenderness,
—That were vain truly—none is left to wake—
But, let her think her justice is engaged
To take the shape of tenderness, and mark
If she'll not coldly do its warmest deed!
Does she love me, I ask you? not a whit:
Yet, thinking that her justice was engaged
To help a kinswoman, she took me up—
Did more on that bare ground than other loves
Would do on greater argument. For me,
I have no equivalent of that cold kind
To pay her with; my love alone to give

If I give anything. I give her love.
I feel I ought to help her, and I will.
So for her sake, as yours, I tell you twice
That women hate a debt as men a gift.
If I were you, I could obtain this grace—
Would lay the whole I did to love's account,
Nor yet be very false as courtiers go—
Declare that my success was recompense;
It would be so, in fact: what were it else?
And then, once loosed her generosity
As you will mark it—then,—were I but you
To turn it, let it seem to move itself,
And make it give the thing I really take,
Accepting so, in the poor cousin's hand,
All value as the next thing to the queen—
Since none loves her directly, none dares that!
And shadow if a thing, a name's mere echo
Suffices those who miss the name and thing;
You pick up just a ribbon she has worn
To keep in proof how near her breath you came.
Say I'm so near I seem a piece of her—
Ask for me that way—(oh, you understand)
And find the same gift yielded with a grace,
Which, if you make the least show to extort
—You'll see! and when you have ruined both of us,
Disertate on the Queen's ingratitude!

NORBERT.

Then, if I turn it that way, you consent?
'Tis not my way; I have more hope in truth.
Still, if you won't have truth—why, this indeed,
Is scarcely false, I'll so express the sense.
Will you remain here?

CONSTANCE.

O best heart of mine,
How I have loved you! then, you take my way?
Are mine as you have been her minister,
Work out my thought, give it effect for me,
Paint plain my poor conceit and make it serve?

I owe that withered woman everything—
Life, fortune, you, remember! Take my part—
Help me to pay her! Stand upon your rights?
You, with my rose, my hands, my heart on you?
Your rights are mine—you have no rights but mine.

NORBERT.

Remain here. How you know me!

CONSTANCE.

Ah, but still—
[He breaks from her: she remains. Dance-music from within.

SECOND PART

Enter the QUEEN.

QUEEN.

Constance?—She is here as he said. Speak! quick!
Is it so? Is it true or false? One word!

CONSTANCE.

True.

QUEEN.

Mercifullest Mother, thanks to thee!

CONSTANCE.

Madam!

QUEEN.

I love you, Constance, from my soul.
Now say once more, with any words you will,
'Tis true, all true, as true as that I speak.

CONSTANCE.

Why should you doubt it?

QUEEN.

Ah, why doubt? why doubt?
Dear, make me see it! Do you see it so?
None see themselves—another sees them best.
You say "why doubt it?"—you see him and me.
It is because the Mother has such grace
That if we had but faith—wherein we fail—
Whate'er we yearn for would be granted us;
Yet still we let our whims prescribe despair,
Our very fancies thwart and cramp our will,
And so accepting life, abjure ourselves!
Constance, I had abjured the hope of love
And being loved, as truly as yon palm
The hope of seeing Egypt from that turf.

CONSTANCE.

Heaven!

QUEEN.

But it was so, Constance, it was so.
Men say—or do men say it? fancies say—
"Stop here, your life is set, you are grown old.
Too late—no love for you, too late for love—
Leave love to girls. Be queen—let Constance love!"
One takes the hint—half meets it like a child,
Ashamed at any feelings that oppose.
"Oh love, true, never think of love again!
I am a queen—I rule, not love, indeed."
So it goes on; so a face grows like this,
Hair like this hair, poor arms as lean as these,
Till,—nay, it does not end so, I thank God!

CONSTANCE.

I cannot understand—

QUEEN.

The happier you!
Constance, I know not how it is with men.
For women, (I am a woman now like you)
There is no good of life but love—but love!
What else looks good, is some shade flung from love—
Love gilds it, gives it worth. Be warned by me,
Never you cheat yourself one instant. Love,
Give love, ask only love, and leave the rest!
O Constance, how I love you!

CONSTANCE.

I love you.

QUEEN.

I do believe that all is come through you.
I took you to my heart to keep it warm
When the last chance of love seemed dead in me;
I thought your fresh youth warmed my withered heart.
Oh, I am very old now, am I not?
Not so! it is true and it shall be true!

CONSTANCE.

Tell it me! let me judge if true or false.

QUEEN.

Ah, but I fear you—you will look at me
And say, "she's old, she's grown unlovely quite
Who ne'er was beauteous! men want beauty still."
Well, so I feared—the curse! so I felt sure.

CONSTANCE.

Be calm. And now you feel not sure, you say?

QUEEN.

Constance, he came, the coming was not strange—
Do not I stand and see men come and go?

I turned a half-look from my pedestal
Where I grow marble—"one young man the more!
He will love some one,—that is nought to me—
What would he with my marble stateliness?"
Yet this seemed somewhat worse than heretofore;
The man more gracious, youthful, like a god,
And I still older, with less flesh to change—
We two those dear extremes that long to touch.
It seemed still harder when he first began
Absorbed to labour at the state-affairs
The old way for the old end, interest.
Oh, to live with a thousand beating hearts
Around you, swift eyes, serviceable hands,
Professing they've no care but for your cause,
Thought but to help you, love but for yourself,
And you the marble statue all the time
They praise and point at as preferred to life,
Yet leave for the first breathing woman's cheek,
First dancer's, gipsy's or street baladine's!
Why, how I have ground my teeth to hear men's speech
Stifled for fear it should alarm my ear,
Their gait subdued lest step should startle me,
Their eyes declined, such queendom to respect,
Their hands alert, such treasure to preserve,
While not a man of them broke rank and spoke,
Or wrote me a vulgar letter all of love,
Or caught my hand and pressed it like a hand.
There have been moments, if the sentinel
Lowering his halbert to salute the queen,
Had flung it brutally and clasped my knees,
I would have stooped and kissed him with my soul.

CONSTANCE.

Who could have comprehended?

QUEEN.

Ay, who—who?
Why, no one, Constance, but this one who did.
Not they, not you, not I. Even now perhaps
It comes too late—would you but tell the truth.

CONSTANCE.

I wait to tell it.

QUEEN.

Well, you see, he came,
Outfaced the others, did a work this year
Exceeds in value all was ever done
You know—it is not I who say it—all
Say it. And so (a second pang and worse)
I grew aware not only of what he did,
But why so wondrously. Oh, never work
Like his was done for work's ignoble sake—
It must have finer aims to spur it on!
I felt, I saw he loved—loved somebody.
And Constance, my dear Constance, do you know,
I did believe this while 'twas you he loved.

CONSTANCE.

Me, madam?

QUEEN.

It did seem to me your face
Met him where'er he looked: and whom but you
Was such a man to love? it seemed to me
You saw he loved you, and approved his love,
And both of you were in intelligence.
You could not loiter in the garden, step
Into this balcony, but I straight was stung
And forced to understand. It seemed so true,
So right, so beautiful, so like you both
That all this work should have been done by him
Not for the vulgar hope of recompense,
But that at last—suppose, some night like this—
Borne on to claim his due reward of me
He might say, "Give her hand and pay me so."
And I (O Constance, you shall love me now)
I thought, surmounting all the bitterness,
—"And he shall have it. I will make her blest,
My flower of youth, my woman's self that was,

My happiest woman's self that might have been!
These two shall have their joy and leave me here."
Yes—yes!

CONSTANCE.

Thanks!

QUEEN.

And the word was on my lips
When he burst in upon me. I looked to hear
A mere calm statement of his just desire
For payment of his labour. When, O Heaven,
How can I tell you? cloud was on my eyes
And thunder in my ears at that first word
Which told 'twas love of me, of me, did all—
He loved me—from the first step to the last,
Loved me!

CONSTANCE.

You did not hear . . . you thought he spoke
Of love? what if you should mistake?

QUEEN.

No, no—
No mistake! Ha, there shall be no mistake!
He had not dared to hint the love he felt—
You were my reflex—how I understood!
He said you were the ribbon I had worn,
He kissed my hand, he looked into my eyes,
And love, love was the end of every phrase.
Love is begun—this much is come to pass,
The rest is easy. Constance, I am yours!—
I will learn, I will place my life on you,
But teach me but how to keep what I have won.
Am I so old? this hair was early grey;
But joy ere now has brought hair brown again,
And joy will bring the cheek's red back, I feel.
I could sing once too; that was in my youth.
Still, when men paint me, they declare me . . . yes,

Beautiful—for the last French painter did!
I know they flatter somewhat; you are frank—
I trust you. How I loved you from the first!
Some queens would hardly seek a cousin out
And set her by their side to take the eye:
I must have felt that good would come from you.
I am not generous—like him—like you!
But he is not your lover after all—
It was not you he looked at. Saw you him?
You have not been mistaking words or looks?
He said you were the reflex of myself—
And yet he is not such a paragon
To you, to younger women who may choose
Among a thousand Norberts. Speak the truth!
You know you never named his name to me—
You know, I cannot give him up—ah God,
Not up now, even to you!

CONSTANCE.

Then calm yourself.

QUEEN.

See, I am old—look here, you happy girl,
I will not play the fool, deceive myself;
'Tis all gone—put your cheek beside my cheek—
Ah, what a contrast does the moon behold!
But then I set my life upon one chance,
The last chance and the best—am *I* not left,
My soul, myself? All women love great men
If young or old—it is in all the tales—
Young beauties love old poets who can love—
Why should not he the poems in my soul,
The love, the passionate faith, the sacrifice,
The constancy? I throw them at his feet.
Who cares to see the fountain's very shape
Whether it be a Triton's or a Nymph's
That pours the foam, makes rainbows all around?
You could not praise indeed the empty conch;
But I'll pour floods of love and hide myself.
How I will love him! cannot men love love?

Who was a queen and loved a poet once
Humpbacked, a dwarf? ah, women can do that!
Well, but men too! at least, they tell you so.
They love so many women in their youth,
And even in age they all love whom they please;
And yet the best of them confide to friends
That 'tis not beauty makes the lasting love—
They spend a day with such and tire the next;
They like soul,—well then, they like phantasy,
Novelty even. Let us confess the truth
Horrible though it be—that prejudice,
Prescription . . . Curses! they will love a queen.
They will—they do. And will not, does not—he?

CONSTANCE.

How can he? You are wedded—'tis a name
We know, but still a bond. Your rank remains,
His rank remains. How can he, nobly souled
As you believe and I incline to think,
Aspire to be your favourite, shame and all?

QUEEN.

Hear her! There, there now—could she love like me?
What did I say of smooth-cheeked youth and grace?
See all it does or could do! so youth loves!
Oh, tell him, Constance, you could never do
What I will—you, it was not born in! I
Will drive these difficulties far and fast
As yonder mists curdling before the moon.
I'll use my light too, gloriously retrieve
My youth from its enforced calamity,
Dissolve that hateful marriage, and be his,
His own in the eyes alike of God and man.

CONSTANCE.

You will do—dare do—Pause on what you say!

QUEEN.

Hear her! I thank you, Sweet, for that surprise.

You have the fair face: for the soul, see mine!
I have the strong soul: let me teach you, here.
I think I have borne enough and long enough,
And patiently enough, the world remarks,
To have my own way now, unblamed by all.
It does so happen, I rejoice for it,
This most unhoped-for issue cuts the knot.
There's not a better way of settling claims
Than this; God sends the accident express;
And were it for my subjects' good, no more,
'Twere best thus ordered. I am thankful now,
Mute, passive, acquiescent. I receive,
And bless God simply, or should almost fear
To walk so smoothly to my ends at last.
Why, how I baffle obstacles, spurn fate!
How strong I am! could Norbert see me now!

CONSTANCE.

Let me consider. It is all too strange.

QUEEN.

You, Constance, learn of me; do you, like me
You are young, beautiful: my own, best girl,
You will have many lovers, and love one—
Light hair, not hair like Norbert's, to suit yours,
Taller than he is, for you are tall.
Love him like me! give all away to him;
Think never of yourself; throw by your pride,
Hope, fear,—your own good as you saw it once,
And love him simply for his very self.
Remember, I (and what am I to you?)
Would give up all for one, leave throne, lose life,
Do all but just unlove him! he loves me.

CONSTANCE.

He shall.

QUEEN.

You, step inside my inmost heart.
Give me your own heart—let us have one heart—
I'll come to you for counsel; "This he says,
This he does, what should this amount to, pray?
Beseech you, change it into current coin.
Is that worth kisses? shall I please him there?"
And then we'll speak in turn of you—what else?
Your love (according to your beauty's worth)
For you shall have some noble love, all gold—
Whom choose you? we will get him at your choice.
—Constance, I leave you. Just a minute since
I felt as I must die or be alone
Breathing my soul into an ear like yours.
Now, I would face the world with my new life,
Wear my new crown. I'll walk around the rooms,
And then come back and tell you how it feels.
How soon a smile of God can change the world!
How we are all made for happiness—how work
Grows play, adversity a winning fight!
True, I have lost so many years. What then?
Many remain—God has been very good.
You, stay here. 'Tis as different from dreams,—
From the mind's cold calm estimate of bliss,
As these stone statues from the flesh and blood.
The comfort thou hast caused mankind, God's moon!
[*She goes out. Dance-music from within.*

PART THIRD

NORBERT *enters.*

NORBERT.

Well? we have but one minute and one word—

CONSTANCE.

I am yours, Norbert!

NORBERT.

Yes, mine.

CONSTANCE.

Not till now!
You were mine. Now I give myself to you.

NORBERT.

Constance?

CONSTANCE.

Your own! I know the thriftier way
Of giving—haply, 'tis the wiser way.
Meaning to give a treasure, I might dole
Coin after coin out (each, as that were all,
With a new largess still at each despair)
And force you keep in sight the deed, reserve
Exhaustless till the end my part and yours,
My giving and your taking, both our joys
Dying together. Is it the wiser way?
I choose the simpler; I give all at once.
Know what you have to trust to, trade upon.
Use it, abuse it,—anything but say
Hereafter, "Had I known she loved me so,
And what my means, I might have thriven with it."
This is your means. I give you all myself.

NORBERT.

I take you and thank God.

CONSTANCE.

Look on through years!
We cannot kiss, a second day like this,
Else were this earth no earth.

NORBERT.

With this day's heat
We shall go on through years of cold.

CONSTANCE.

So, best.
I try to see those years—I think I see.
You walk quick and new warmth comes; you look back
And lay all to the first glow—not sit down
For ever brooding on a day like this
While seeing embers whiten and love die.
Yes, love lives best in its effect; and mine,
Full in its own life, yearns to live in yours.

NORBERT.

Just so. I take and know you all at once.
Your soul is disengaged so easily,
Your face is there, I know you; give me time,
Let me be proud and think you shall know me.
My soul is slower: in a life I roll
The minute out in which you condense yours—
The whole slow circle round you I must move,
To be just you. I look to a long life
To decompose this minute, prove its worth.
'Tis the sparks' long succession one by one
Shall show you in the end what fire was crammed
In that mere stone you struck: you could not know,
If it lay ever unproved in your sight,
As now my heart lies? your own warmth would hide
Its coldness, were it cold.

CONSTANCE.

But how prove, how?

NORBERT.

Prove in my life, you ask?

CONSTANCE.

Quick, Norbert—how?

NORBERT.

That's easy told. I count life just a stuff
To try the soul's strength on, educe the man.
Who keeps one end in view makes all things serve.
As with the body—he who hurls a lance
Or heaps up stone on stone, shows strength alike,
So must I seize and task all means to prove
And shew this soul of mine, you crown as yours,
And justify us both.

CONSTANCE.

Could you write books,
Paint pictures! one sits down in poverty
And writes or paints, with pity for the rich.

NORBERT.

And loves one's painting and one's writing too,
And not one's mistress! All is best, believe,
And we best as no other than we are.
We live, and they experiment on life
Those poets, painters, all who stand aloof
To overlook the farther. Let us be
The thing they look at! I might take your face
And write of it and paint it—to what end?
For whom? what pale dictatress in the air
Feeds, smiling sadly, her fine ghost-like form
With earth's real blood and breath, the beauteous life
She makes despised for ever? You are mine,
Made for me, not for others in the world,
Nor yet for that which I should call my art,
The cold calm power to see how fair you look.
I come to you—I leave you not, to write
Or paint. You are, I am: let Rubens there
Paint us.

CONSTANCE.

So, best!

NORBERT.

I understand your soul.
You live, and rightly sympathise with life,
With action, power, success: this way is straight.
And days were short beside, to let me change
The craft my childhood learnt; my craft shall serve.
Men set me here to subjugate, enclose,
Manure their barren lives and force the fruit
First for themselves, and afterward for me
In the due tithe; the task of some one man,
By ways of work appointed by themselves.
I am not bid create, they see no star
Transfiguring my brow to warrant that—
But bind in one and carry out their wills.
So I began: to-night sees how I end.
What if it see, too, my first outbreak here
Amid the warmth, surprise and sympathy,
The instincts of the heart that teach the head?
What if the people have discerned in me
The dawn of the next nature, the new man
Whose will they venture in the place of theirs,
And whom they trust to find them out new ways
To the new heights which yet he only sees?
I felt it when you kissed me. See this Queen,
This people—in our phrase, this mass of men—
See how the mass lies passive to my hand
Now that my hand is plastic, and you by
To make the muscles iron! Oh, an end
Shall crown this issue as this crowns the first.
My will be on this people! then, the strain,
The grappling of the potter with his clay,
The long uncertain struggle,—the success
In that uprising of the spirit-work,
The vase shaped to the curl of the god's lip,
While rounded fair for lower men to see
The Graces in a dance they recognise
With turbulent applause and laughs of heart!
So triumph ever shall renew itself;
Ever to end in efforts higher yet,
Ever begun——

CONSTANCE.

I ever helping?

NORBERT.

Thus!

[As he embraces her, enter the QUEEN.

CONSTANCE.

Hist, madam—so have I performed my part.
You see your gratitude's true decency,
Norbert? A little slow in seeing it!
Begun, to end the sooner. What's a kiss?

NORBERT.

Constance!

CONSTANCE.

Why, must I teach it you again?
You want a witness to your dulness, sir?
What was I saying these ten minutes long?
Then I repeat—when some young handsome man
Like you has acted out a part like yours,
Is pleased to fall in love with one beyond,
So very far beyond him, as he says—
So hopelessly in love that but to speak
Would prove him mad, he thinks judiciously,
And makes some insignificant good soul
Like me, his friend, adviser, confidant
And very stalking-horse to cover him
In following after what he dares not face—
When his end's gained—(sir, do you understand?)
When she, he dares not face, has loved him first,
—May I not say so, madam?—tops his hope,
And overpasses so his wildest dream,
With glad consent of all, and most of her
The confidant who brought the same about—
Why, in the moment when such joy explodes,

I do hold that the merest gentleman
Will not start rudely from the stalking-horse,
Dismiss it with a "There, enough of you!"
Forget it, show his back unmannerly;
But like a liberal heart will rather turn
And say, "A tingling time of hope was ours—
Betwixt the fears and faulterings—we two lived
A chanceful time in waiting for the prize.
The confidant, the Constance, served not ill;
And though I shall forget her in due time,
Her use being answered now, as reason bids,
Nay as herself bids from her heart of hearts,
Still, she has rights, the first thanks go to her,
The first good praise goes to the prosperous tool,
And the first—which is the last—thankful kiss."

NORBERT.

—Constance? it is a dream—ah see you smile!

CONSTANCE.

So, now his part being properly performed,
Madam, I turn to you and finish mine
As duly—I do justice in my turn.
Yes, madam, he has loved you—long and well—
He could not hope to tell you so—'twas I
Who served to prove your soul accessible,
I led his thoughts on, drew them to their place,
When oft they had wandered out into despair,
And kept love constant toward its natural aim.
Enough—my part is played; you stoop half-way
And meet us royally and spare our fears—
'Tis like yourself—he thanks you, so do I.
Take him—with my full heart! my work is praised
By what comes of it. Be you happy, both!
Yourself—the only one on earth who can—
Do all for him, much more than a mere heart
Which though warm is not useful in its warmth
As the silk vesture of a queen! fold that
Around him gently, tenderly. For him—
For him,—he knows his own part.

NORBERT.

Have you done?
I take the jest at last. Should I speak now?
Was yours the wager, Constance, foolish child,
Or did you but accept it? Well—at least
You lose by it.

CONSTANCE.

Now, madam, 'tis your turn.
Restrain him still from speech a little more
And make him happier as more confident!
Pity him, madam, he is timid yet.
Mark, Norbert! Do not shrink now! Here I yield
My whole right in you to the Queen, observe!
With her go put in practice the great schemes
You teem with, follow the career else closed—
Be all you cannot be except by her!
Behold her.—Madam, say for pity's sake
Anything—frankly say you love him. Else
He'll not believe it: there's more earnest in
His fear than you conceive—I know the man.

NORBERT.

I know the woman somewhat, and confess
I thought she had jested better—she begins
To overcharge her part. I gravely wait
Your pleasure, madam: where is my reward?

QUEEN.

Norbert, this wild girl (whom I recognise
Scarce more than you do, in her fancy-fit,
Eccentric speech and variable mirth,
Not very wise perhaps and somewhat bold
Yet suitable, the whole night's work being strange)
—May still be right: I may do well to speak
And make authentic what appears a dream
To even myself. For, what she says, is true—

Yes, Norbert—what you spoke but now of love,
Devotion, stirred no novel sense in me,
But justified a warmth felt long before.
Yes, from the first—I loved you, I shall say,—
Strange! but I do grow stronger, now 'tis said.
Your courage helps mine: you did well to speak
To-night, the night that crowns your twelvemonths' toil—
But still I had not waited to discern
Your heart so long, believe me! From the first
The source of so much zeal was almost plain,
In absence even of your own words just now
Which opened out the truth. 'Tis very strange,
But takes a happy ending—in your love
Which mine meets: be it so—as you choose me,
So I choose you.

NORBERT.

And worthily you choose!
I will not be unworthy your esteem,
No, madam. I do love you; I will meet
Your nature, now I know it; this was well.
I see,—you dare and you are justified:
But none had ventured such experiment,
Less versed than you in nobleness of heart,
Less confident of finding it in me.
I like that thus you test me ere you grant
The dearest richest beauteousest and best
Of women to my arms! 'tis like yourself!
So—back again into my part's set words—
Devotion to the uttermost is yours,
But no, you cannot, madam, even you,
Create in me the love our Constance does.
Or—something truer to the tragic phrase—
Not yon magnolia-bell superb with scent
Invites a certain insect—that's myself—
But the small eye-flower nearer to the ground:
I take this lady!

CONSTANCE.

Stay—not her's, the trap—
Stay, Norbert—that mistake were worst of all.

(He is too cunning, madam!) it was I.
I, Norbert, who...

NORBERT.

You, was it, Constance? Then,
But for the grace of this divinest hour
Which gives me you, I might not pardon here.
I am the Queen's: she only knows my brain—
She may experiment therefore on my heart
And I instruct her too by the result;
But you, sweet, you who know me, who so long
Have told my heart-beats over, held my life
In those white hands of yours,—it is not well!

CONSTANCE.

Tush! I have said it, did I not say it all?
The life, for her—the heart-beats, for her sake!

NORBERT.

Enough! my cheek grows red, I think. Your test!
There's not the meanest woman in the world,
Not she I least could love in all the world,
Whom, did she love me, did love prove itself,
I dared insult as you insult me now.
Constance, I could say, if it must be said,
"Take back the soul you offer—I keep mine"
But—"Take the soul still quivering on your hand,
The soul so offered, which I cannot use,
And, please you, give it to some friend of mine,
For—what's the trifle he requites me with?"
I, tempt a woman, to amuse a man,
That two may mock her heart if it succumb?
No! fearing God and standing 'neath his heaven,
I would not dare insult a woman so,
Were she the meanest woman in the world,
And he, I cared to please, ten emperors!

CONSTANCE.

Norbert!

NORBERT.

I love once as I live but once.
What case is this to think or talk about?
I love you. Would it mend the case at all
Should such a step as this kill love in me?
Your part were done: account to God for it.
But mine—could murdered love get up again,
And kneel to whom you pleased to designate
And make you mirth? It is too horrible.
You did not know this, Constance? now you know
That body and soul have each one life, but one:
And here's my love, here, living, at your feet.

CONSTANCE.

See the Queen. Norbert—this one more last word—
If thus you have taken jest for earnest—thus
Loved me in earnest...

NORBERT.

Ah, no jest holds here!
Where is the laughter in which jests break up?
And what this horror that grows palpable?
Madam—why grasp you thus the balcony?
Have I done ill? Have I not spoken the truth?
How could I other? Was it not your test,
To try me, and what my love for Constance meant?
Madam, your royal soul itself approves,
The first, that I should choose thus! so one takes
A beggar—asks him, what would buy his child,
And then approves the expected laugh of scorn
Returned as something noble from the rags.
Speak, Constance, I'm the beggar! Ha, what's this?
You two glare each at each like panthers now.
Constance—the world fades; only you stand there!
You did not, in to-night's wild whirl of things
Sell me—your soul of souls, for any price?
No—no—'tis easy to believe in you.
Was it your love's mad trial to o'ertop

Mine by this vain self-sacrifice? well, still—
Though I should curse, I love you. I am love.
And cannot change: love's self is at your feet!
[QUEEN *goes out.*

CONSTANCE.

Feel my heart; let it die against your own

NORBERT.

Against my own! explain not; let this be.
This is life's height.

CONSTANCE.

Yours! Yours! Yours!

NORBERT.

You and I—
Why care by what meanders we are here
In the centre of the labyrinth? men have died
Trying to find this place out, which we have found.

CONSTANCE.

Found, found!

NORBERT.

Sweet, never fear what she can do—
We are past harm now.

CONSTANCE.

On the breast of God.
I thought of men—as if you were a man.
Tempting him with a crown!

NORBERT.

This must end here—
It is too perfect!

CONSTANCE.

There's the music stopped.
What measured heavy tread? It is one blaze
About me and within me.

NORBERT.

Oh, some death
Will run its sudden finger round this spark
And sever us from the rest—

CONSTANCE.

And so do well.
Now the doors open—

NORBERT.

'Tis the guard comes.

CONSTANCE.

Kiss!

"De Gustibus——"

I.

Your ghost will walk, you lover of trees,
(If our loves remain)
In an English lane,
By a cornfield-side a-flutter with poppies.
Hark, those two in the hazel coppice—
A boy and a girl, if the good fates please,
Making love, say,—
The happier they!
Draw yourself up from the light of the moon,
And let them pass, as they will too soon,
With the beanflowers' boon,
And the blackbird's tune,
And May, and June!

2.

What I love best in all the world,
Is, a castle, precipice-encurled,
In a gash of the wind-grieved Apennine.
Or look for me, old fellow of mine,
(If I get my head from out the mouth
O' the grave, and loose my spirit's bands,
And come again to the land of lands)—
In a sea-side house to the farther south,
Where the baked cicalas die of drouth,
And one sharp tree ('tis a cypress) stands,
By the many hundred years red-rusted,
Rough iron-spiked, ripe fruit-o'ercrusted,
My sentinel to guard the sands
To the water's edge. For, what expands
Without the house, but the great opaque
Blue breadth of sea, and not a break?
While, in the house, for ever crumbles
Some fragment of the frescoed walls,
From blisters where a scorpion sprawls.
A girl bare-footed brings and tumbles
Down on the pavement, green-flesh melons,
And says there's news to-day—the king
Was shot at, touched in the liver-wing,
Goes with his Bourbon arm in a sling.
—She hopes they have not caught the felons.
  Italy, my Italy!
Queen Mary's saying serves for me—
  (When fortune's malice
  Lost her, Calais.)
Open my heart and you will see
Graved inside of it, "Italy."
Such lovers old are I and she;
So it always was, so it still shall be!

Cleon

"AS CERTAIN ALSO OF YOUR OWN POETS HAVE SAID"—

Cleon the poet, (from the sprinkled isles,
Lily on lily, that o'erlace the sea,
And laugh their pride when the light wave lisps "Greece")—
To Protos in his Tyranny: much health!

They give thy letter to me, even now:
I read and seem as if I heard thee speak.
The master of thy galley still unlades
Gift after gift; they block my court at last
And pile themselves along its portico
Royal with sunset, like a thought of thee:
And one white she-slave from the group dispersed
Of black and white slaves, (like the chequer-work
Pavement, at once my nation's work and gift,
Now covered with this settle-down of doves)
One lyric woman, in her crocus vest
Woven of sea-wools, with her two white hands
Commends to me the strainer and the cup
Thy lip hath bettered ere it blesses mine.

Well-counselled, king, in thy munificence!
For so shall men remark, in such an act
Of love for him whose song gives life its joy,
Thy recognition of the use of life;
Nor call thy spirit barely adequate
To help on life in straight ways, broad enough
For vulgar souls, by ruling and the rest.
Thou, in the daily building of thy tower,
Whether in fierce and sudden spasms of toil,
Or through dim lulls of unapparent growth,
Or when the general work 'mid good acclaim
Climbed with the eye to cheer the architect,
Didst ne'er engage in work for mere work's sake—
Hadst ever in thy heart the luring hope
Of some eventual rest a-top of it,
Whence, all the tumult of the building hushed,
Thou first of men mightst look out to the east.

The vulgar saw thy tower; thou sawest the sun.
For this, I promise on thy festival
To pour libation, looking o'er the sea,
Making this slave narrate thy fortunes, speak
Thy great words, and describe thy royal face—
Wishing thee wholly where Zeus lives the most
Within the eventual element of calm.

Thy letter's first requirement meets me here.
It is as thou hast heard: in one short life
I, Cleon, have effected all those things
Thou wonderingly dost enumerate.
That epos on thy hundred plates of gold
Is mine,—and also mine the little chaunt,
So sure to rise from every fishing-bark
When, lights at prow, the seamen haul their nets.
The image of the sun-god on the phare
Men turn from the sun's self to see, is mine;
The Pœcile, o'er-storied its whole length,
As thou didst hear, with painting, is mine too.
I know the true proportions of a man
And woman also, not observed before;
And I have written three books on the soul,
Proving absurd all written hitherto,
And putting us to ignorance again.
For music,—why, I have combined the moods,
Inventing one. In brief, all arts are mine;
Thus much the people know and recognise,
Throughout our seventeen islands. Marvel not.
We of these latter days, with greater mind
Than our forerunners, since more composite,
Look not so great (beside their simple way)
To a judge who only sees one way at once,
One mind-point, and no other at a time,—
Compares the small part of a man of us
With some whole man of the heroic age,
Great in his way,—not ours, nor meant for ours.
And ours is greater, had we skill to know.
Yet, what we call this life of men on earth,
This sequence of the soul's achievements here,
Being, as I find much reason to conceive,

Intended to be viewed eventually
As a great whole, not analysed to parts,
But each part having reference to all,—
How shall a certain part, pronounced complete,
Endure effacement by another part?
Was the thing done?—Then, what's to do again?
See, in the chequered pavement opposite,
Suppose the artist made a perfect rhomb,
And next a lozenge, then a trapezoid—
He did not overlay them, superimpose
The new upon the old and blot it out,
But laid them on a level in his work,
Making at last a picture; there it lies.
So, first the perfect separate forms were made,
The portions of mankind—and after, so,
Occurred the combination of the same.
Or where had been a progress, otherwise?
Mankind, made up of all the single men,—
In such a synthesis the labour ends.
Now, mark me—those divine men of old time
Have reached, thou sayest well, each at one point
The outside verge that rounds our faculty;
And where they reached, who can do more than reach?
It takes but little water just to touch
At some one point the inside of a sphere,
And, as we turn the sphere, touch all the rest
In due succession: but the finer air
Which not so palpably nor obviously,
Though no less universally, can touch
The whole circumference of that emptied sphere,
Fills it more fully than the water did;
Holds thrice the weight of water in itself
Resolved into a subtler element.
And yet the vulgar call the sphere first full
Up to the visible height—and after, void;
Not knowing air's more hidden properties.
And thus our soul, misknown, cries out to Zeus
To vindicate his purpose in its life—
Why stay we on the earth unless to grow?
Long since, I imaged, wrote the fiction out,
That he or other God, descended here

And, once for all, showed simultaneously
What, in its nature, never can be shown
Piecemeal or in succession;—showed, I say,
The worth both absolute and relative
Of all His children from the birth of time,
His instruments for all appointed work.
I now go on to image,—might we hear
The judgment which should give the due to each,
Shew where the labour lay and where the ease,
And prove Zeus' self, the latent, everywhere!
This is a dream. But no dream, let us hope,
That years and days, the summers and the springs
Follow each other with unwaning powers—
The grapes which dye thy wine, are richer far
Through culture, than the wild wealth of the rock;
The suave plum than the savage-tasted drupe;
The pastured honey-bee drops choicer sweet;
The flowers turn double, and the leaves turn flowers;
That young and tender crescent-moon, thy slave,
Sleeping upon her robe as if on clouds,
Refines upon the women of my youth.
What, and the soul alone deteriorates?
I have not chanted verse like Homer's, no—
Nor swept string like Terpander, no—nor carved
And painted men like Phidias and his friend:
I am not great as they are, point by point:
But I have entered into sympathy
With these four, running these into one soul,
Who, separate, ignored each other's arts.
Say, is it nothing that I know them all?
The wild flower was the larger—I have dashed
Rose-blood upon its petals, pricked its cup's
Honey with wine, and driven its seed to fruit,
And show a better flower if not so large.
I stand, myself. Refer this to the gods
Whose gift alone it is! which, shall I dare
(All pride apart) upon the absurd pretext
That such a gift by chance lay in my hand,
Discourse of lightly or depreciate?
It might have fallen to another's hand—what then?
I pass too surely—let at least truth stay!

And next, of what thou followest on to ask.
This being with me as I declare, O king,
My works, in all these varicoloured kinds,
So done by me, accepted so by men—
Thou askest if (my soul thus in men's hearts)
I must not be accounted to attain
The very crown and proper end of life.
Inquiring thence how, now life closeth up,
I face death with success in my right hand:
Whether I fear death less than dost thyself
The fortunate of men. "For" (writest thou)
"Thou leavest much behind, while I leave nought:
Thy life stays in the poems men shall sing,
The pictures men shall study; while my life,
Complete and whole now in its power and joy,
Dies altogether with my brain and arm,
Is lost indeed; since,—what survives myself?
The brazen statue that o'erlooks my grave,
Set on the promontory which I named.
And that—some supple courtier of my heir
Shall use its robed and sceptred arm, perhaps,
To fix the rope to, which best drags it down.
I go then: triumph thou, who dost not go!"

Nay, thou art worthy of hearing my whole mind.
Is this apparent, when thou turn'st to muse
Upon the scheme of earth and man in chief,
That admiration grows as knowledge grows?
That imperfection means perfection hid,
Reserved in part, to grace the after-time?
If, in the morning of philosophy,
Ere aught had been recorded, aught perceived,
Thou, with the light now in thee, couldst have looked
On all earth's tenantry, from worm to bird,
Ere man had yet appeared upon the stage—
Thou wouldst have seen them perfect, and deduced
The perfectness of others yet unseen.
Conceding which,—had Zeus then questioned thee
"Wilt thou go on a step, improve on this,
Do more for visible creatures than is done?"
Thou wouldst have answered, "Ay, by making each
Grow conscious in himself—by that alone.

All's perfect else: the shell sucks fast the rock,
The fish strikes through the sea, the snake both swims
And slides; the birds take flight, forth range the beasts,
Till life's mechanics can no further go—
And all this joy in natural life, is put,
Like fire from off Thy finger into each,
So exquisitely perfect is the same.
But 'tis pure fire—and they mere matter are;
It has them, not they it: and so I choose,
For man, Thy last premeditated work
(If I might add a glory to the scheme)
That a third thing should stand apart from both,
A quality arise within his soul,
Which, intro-active, made to supervise
And feel the force it has, may view itself,
And so be happy." Man might live at first
The animal life: but is there nothing more?
In due time, let him critically learn
How he lives; and, the more he gets to know
Of his own life's adaptabilities,
The more joy-giving will his life become.
Thus man who hath this quality, is best.

But thou, king, hadst more reasonably said:
"Let progress end at once,—man make no step
Beyond the natural man, the better beast,
Using his senses, not the sense of sense."
In man there's failure, only since he left
The lower and inconscious forms of life.
We called it an advance, the rendering plain
A spirit might grow conscious of that life,
And, by new lore so added to the old,
Take each step higher over the brute's head.
This grew the only life, the pleasure-house,
Watch-tower and treasure-fortress of the soul,
Which whole surrounding flats of natural life
Seemed only fit to yield subsistence to;
A tower that crowns a country. But alas!
The soul now climbs it just to perish there,
For thence we have discovered ('tis no dream—
We know this, which we had not else perceived)
That there's a world of capability
For joy, spread round about us, meant for us,

Inviting us; and still the soul craves all,
And still the flesh replies, "Take no jot more
Than ere you climbed the tower to look abroad!
Nay, so much less, as that fatigue has brought
Deduction to it." We struggle—fain to enlarge
Our bounded physical recipiency,
Increase our power, supply fresh oil to life,
Repair the waste of age and sickness. No,
It skills not: life's inadequate to joy,
As the soul sees joy, tempting life to take.
They praise a fountain in my garden here
Wherein a Naiad sends the water-spurt
Thin from her tube; she smiles to see it rise.
What if I told her, it is just a thread
From that great river which the hills shut up,
And mock her with my leave to take the same?
The artificer has given her one small tube
Past power to widen or exchange—what boots
To know she might spout oceans if she could?
She cannot lift beyond her first straight thread.
And so a man can use but a man's joy
While he sees God's. Is it, for Zeus to boast,
"Scc, man, how happy I live, and despair—
That I may be still happier—for thy use!"
If this were so, we could not thank our Lord,
As hearts beat on to doing: 'tis not so—
Malice it is not. Is it carelessness?
Still, no. If care—where is the sign? I ask—
And get no answer: and agree in sum,
O king, with thy profound discouragement,
Who seest the wider but to sigh the more,
Most progress is most failure! thou sayest well.

The last point now:—thou dost except a case—
Holding joy not impossible to one
With artist-gifts—to such a man as I—
Who leave behind me living works indeed;
For, such a poem, such a painting lives.
What? dost thou verily trip upon a word,
Confound the accurate view of what joy is
(Caught somewhat clearer by my eyes than thine)
With feeling joy? confound the knowing how
And showing how to live (my faculty)

With actually living?—Otherwise
Where is the artist's vantage o'er the king?
Because in my great epos I display
How divers men young, strong, fair, wise, can act—
Is this as though I acted? if I paint,
Carve the young Phoebus, am I therefore young?
Methinks I'm older that I bowed myself
The many years of pain that taught me art!
Indeed, to know is something, and to prove
How all this beauty might be enjoyed, is more:
But, knowing nought, to enjoy is something too.
Yon rower, with the moulded muscles there
Lowering the sail, is nearer it than I.
I can write love-odes—thy fair slave's an ode.
I get to sing of love, when grown too grey
For being beloved: she turns to that young man
The muscles all a-ripple on his back.
I know the joy of kingship: well—thou art king!

"But," sayest thou—(and I marvel, I repeat
To find thee tripping on a mere word) "what
Thou writest, paintest, stays: that does not die:
Sappho survives, because we sing her songs,
And Æschylus, because we read his plays!"
Why, if they live still, let them come and take
Thy slave in my despite—drink from thy cup—
Speak in my place. Thou diest while I survive?
Say rather that my fate is deadlier still—
In this, that every day my sense of joy
Grows more acute, my soul (intensified
By power and insight) more enlarged, more keen;
While every day my hairs fall more and more,
My hand shakes, and the heavy years increase—
The horror quickening still from year to year,
The consummation coming past escape
When I shall know most, and yet least enjoy—
When all my works wherein I prove my worth,
Being present still to mock me in men's mouths,
Alive still, in the phrase of such as thou,
I, I, the feeling, thinking, acting man,
The man who loved his life so over much,
Shall sleep in my urn. It is so horrible,

I dare at times imagine to my need
Some future state revealed to us by Zeus,
Unlimited in capability
For joy, as this is in desire for joy,
To seek which, the joy-hunger forces us.
That, stung by straitness of our life, made strait
On purpose to make sweet the life at large—
Freed by the throbbing impulse we call death,
We burst there as the worm into the fly,
Who, while a worm still, wants his wings. But no!
Zeus has not yet revealed it; and, alas!
He must have done so—were it possible!

Live long and happy, and in that thought die,
Glad for what was. Farewell. And for the rest,
I cannot tell thy messenger aright
Where to deliver what he bears of thine
To one called Paulus—we have heard his fame
Indeed, if Christus be not one with him—
I know not, nor am troubled much to know.
Thou canst not think a mere barbarian Jew,
As Paulus proves to be, one circumcised,
Hath access to a secret shut from us?
Thou wrongest our philosophy, O king,
In stooping to inquire of such an one,
As if his answer could impose at all.
He writeth, doth he? well, and he may write.
Oh, the Jew findeth scholars! certain slaves
Who touched on this same isle, preached him and Christ;
And (as I gathered from a bystander)
Their doctrine could be held by no sane man.

Two in the Campagna

I.

I wonder do you feel to-day
As I have felt, since, hand in hand,
We sat down on the grass, to stray
In spirit better through the land,
This morn of Rome and May?

2.

For me, I touched a thought, I know,
  Has tantalised me many times,
(Like turns of thread the spiders throw
  Mocking across our path) for rhymes
To catch at and let go.

3.

Help me to hold it: first it left
  The yellowing fennel, run to seed
There, branching from the brickwork's cleft,
  Some old tomb's ruin: yonder weed
Took up the floating weft,

4.

Where one small orange cup amassed
  Five beetles,—blind and green they grope
Among the honey-meal,— and last,
  Everywhere on the grassy slope
I traced it. Hold it fast!

5.

The champaign with its endless fleece
  Of feathery grasses everywhere!
Silence and passion, joy and peace,
  An everlasting wash of air—
Rome's ghost since her decease.

6.

Such life there, through such lengths of hours,
  Such miracles performed in play,
Such primal naked forms of flowers,
  Such letting Nature have her way
While Heaven looks from its towers!

7.

How say you? Let us, O my dove,
  Let us be unashamed of soul,

As earth lies bare to heaven above.
  How is it under our control
To love or not to love?

8.

I would that you were all to me,
  You that are just so much, no more—
Nor yours, nor mine,—nor slave nor free!
  Where does the fault lie? what the core
O' the wound, since wound must be?

9.

I would I could adopt your will,
  See with your eyes, and set my heart
Beating by yours, and drink my fill
  At your soul's springs,—your part, my part
In life, for good and ill.

10.

No. I yearn upward—touch you close,
  Then stand away. I kiss your cheek,
Catch your soul's warmth,—I pluck the rose
  And love it more than tongue can speak—
Then the good minute goes.

11.

Already how am I so far
  Out of that minute? Must I go
Still like the thistle-ball, no bar,
  Onward, whenever light winds blow
Fixed by no friendly star?

12.

Just when I seemed about to learn!
  Where is the thread now? Off again!
The old trick! Only I discern—
  Infinite passion, and the pain
Of finite hearts that yearn.

A Grammarian's Funeral

(*Time*—Shortly after the revival of learning in Europe.)

Let us begin and carry up this corpse,
  Singing together.
Leave we the common crofts, the vulgar thorpes
  Each in its tether
Sleeping safe on the bosom of the plain,
  Cared-for till cock-crow.
Look out if yonder's not the day again
  Rimming the rock-row!
That's the appropriate country—there, man's thought,
  Rarer, intenser,
Self-gathered for an outbreak, as it ought,
  Chafes in the censer!
Leave we the unlettered plain its herd and crop;
  Seek we sepulture
On a tall mountain, citied to the top,
  Crowded with culture!
All the peaks soar, but one the rest excels;
  Clouds overcome it;
No, yonder sparkle is the citadel's
  Circling its summit!
Thither our path lies—wind we up the heights—
  Wait ye the warning?
Our low life was the level's and the night's;
  He's for the morning!
Step to a tune, square chests, erect the head,
  'Ware the beholders!
This is our master, famous, calm, and dead,
  Borne on our shoulders.

Sleep, crop and herd! sleep, darkling thorpe and croft,
  Safe from the weather!
He, whom we convoy to his grave aloft,
  Singing together,
He was a man born with thy face and throat,
  Lyric Apollo!
Long he lived nameless: how should spring take note
  Winter would follow?
Till lo, the little touch, and youth was gone!
  Cramped and diminished,

Moaned he, "New measures, other feet anon!
  My dance is finished?"
No, that's the world's way! (keep the mountain-side,
  Make for the city.)
He knew the signal, and stepped on with pride
  Over men's pity;
Left play for work, and grappled with the world
  Bent on escaping:
"What's in the scroll," quoth he, "thou keepest furled?
  Shew me their shaping,
Theirs, who most studied man, the bard and sage,—
  Give!"—So he gowned him,
Straight got by heart that book to its last page:
  Learned, we found him!
Yea, but we found him bald too—eyes like lead,
  Accents uncertain:
"Time to taste life," another would have said,
  "Up with the curtain!"
This man said rather, "Actual life comes next?
  Patience a moment!
Grant I have mastered learning's crabbed text,
  Still, there's the comment.
Let me know all. Prate not of most or least,
  Painful or easy:
Even to the crumbs I'd fain eat up the feast,
  Ay, Nor feel queasy!"
Oh, such a life as he resolved to live,
  When he had learned it,
When he had gathered all books had to give;
  Sooner, he spurned it!
Image the whole, then execute the parts—
  Fancy the fabric
Quite, ere you build, ere steel strike fire from quartz,
  Ere mortar dab brick!

(Here's the town-gate reached: there's the market-place
  Gaping before us.)
Yea, this in him was the peculiar grace
  (Hearten our chorus)
That before living he'd learn how to live—
  No end to learning.
Earn the means first—God surely will contrive
  Use for our earning.

Others mistrust and say—"But time escapes,—
"Live now or never!"
He said, "What's time? Leave Now for dogs and apes!
Man has For ever."
Back to his book then: deeper drooped his head;
Calculus racked him:
Leaden before, his eyes grew dross of lead;
Tussis attacked him.
"Now, Master, take a little rest!"—not he!
(Caution redoubled!
Step two a-breast, the way winds narrowly.)
Not a whit troubled,
Back to his studies, fresher than at first,
Fierce as a dragon
He, (soul-hydroptic with a sacred thirst)
Sucked at the flagon.
Oh, if we draw a circle premature,
Heedless of far gain,
Greedy for quick returns of profit, sure
Bad is our bargain!
Was it not great? did not he throw on God,
(He loves the burthen)—
God's task to make the heavenly period
Perfect the earthen?
Did not he magnify the mind, shew clear
Just what it all meant?
He would not discount life, as fools do here,
Paid by instalment!
He ventured neck or nothing—heaven's success
Found, or earth's failure:
"Wilt thou trust death or not?" he answered "Yes.
"Hence with life's pale lure!"
That low man seeks a little thing to do,
Sees it and does it:
This high man, with a great thing to pursue,
Dies ere he knows it.
That low man goes on adding one to one,
His hundred's soon hit:
This high man, aiming at a million,
Misses an unit.
That, has the world here—should he need the next,
Let the world mind him!

This, throws himself on God, and unperplext
  Seeking shall find Him.
So, with the throttling hands of Death at strife,
  Ground he at grammar;
Still, thro' the rattle, parts of speech were rife.
  While he could stammer
He settled *Hoti's* business—let it be!—
  Properly based *Oun*—
Gave us the doctrine of the enclitic *De*,
  Dead from the waist down.
Well, here's the platform, here's the proper place.
  Hail to your purlieus,
All ye highfliers of the feathered race,
  Swallows and curlews!
Here's the top-peak! the multitude below
  Live, for they can there.
This man decided not to Live but Know—
  Bury this man there?
Here—here's his place, where meteors shoot, clouds form,
  Lightnings are loosened,
Stars come and go! let joy break with the storm—
  Peace let the dew send!
Lofty designs must close in like effects:
  Loftily lying,
Leave him—still loftier than the world suspects,
  Living and dying.

"*Transcendentalism*"

A POEM IN TWELVE BOOKS

Stop playing, poet! may a brother speak?
'Tis you speak, that's your error. Song's our art:
Whereas you please to speak these naked thoughts
Instead of draping them in sights and sounds.
—True thoughts, good thoughts, thoughts fit to treasure up!
But why such long prolusion and display,
Such turning and adjustment of the harp,
And taking it upon your breast, at length,
Only to speak dry words across its strings?
Stark-naked thought is in request enough—

Speak prose and holloa it till Europe hears!
The six-foot Swiss tube, braced about with bark,
Which helps the hunter's voice from Alp to Alp—
Exchange our harp for that,—who hinders you?

But here's your fault; grown men want thought, you think;
Thought's what they mean by verse, and seek in verse:
Boys seek for images and melody,
Men must have reason—so, you aim at men.
Quite otherwise! Objects throng our youth, 'tis true,
We see and hear and do not wonder much.
If you could tell us what they mean, indeed!
As Swedish Bœhme never cared for plants
Until it happed, a-walking in the fields,
He noticed all at once that plants could speak,
Nay, turned with loosened tongue to talk with him.
That day the daisy had an eye indeed—
Colloquised with the cowslip on such themes!
We find them extant yet in Jacob's prose.
But by the time youth slips a stage or two
While reading prose in that tough book he wrote,
(Collating, and emendating the same
And settling on the sense most to our mind)
We shut the clasps and find life's summer past.
Then, who helps more, pray, to repair our loss—
Another Bœhme with a tougher book
And subtler meanings of what roses say,—
Or some stout Mage like him of Halberstadt,
John, who made things Bœhme wrote thoughts about?
He with a "look you!" vents a brace of rhymes,
And in there breaks the sudden rose herself,
Over us, under, round us every side,
Nay, in and out the tables and the chairs
And musty volumes, Bœhme's book and all,—
Buries us with a glory, young once more,
Pouring heaven into this shut house of life.

So come, the harp back to your heart again!
You are a poem, though your poem's naught.
The best of all you showed before, believe,
Was your own boy-face o'er the finer chords
Bent, following the cherub at the top
That points to God with his paired half-moon wings.

One Word More

To E.B.B.

1.

There they are, my fifty men and women
Naming me the fifty poems finished!
Take them, Love, the book and me together:
Where the heart lies, let the brain lie also.

2.

Rafael made a century of sonnets,
Made and wrote them in a certain volume
Dinted with the silver-pointed pencil
Else he only used to draw Madonnas:
These, the world might view—but One, the volume.
Who that one, you ask? Your heart instructs you.
Did she live and love it all her life-time?
Did she drop, his lady of the sonnets,
Die, and let it drop beside her pillow
Where it lay in place of Rafael's glory,
Rafael's cheek so duteous and so loving—
Cheek, the world was wont to hail a painter's,
Rafael's cheek, her love had turned a poet's?

3.

You and I would rather read that volume,
(Taken to his beating bosom by it)
Lean and list the bosom-beats of Rafael,
Would we not? than wonder at Madonnas—
Her, San Sisto names, and Her, Foligno,
Her, that visits Florence in a vision,
Her, that's left with lilies in the Louvre—
Seen by us and all the world in circle.

4.

You and I will never read that volume.
Guido Reni, like his own eye's apple

Guarded long the treasure-book and loved it.
Guido Reni dying, all Bologna
Cried, and the world with it, "Ours—the treasure!"
Suddenly, as rare things will, it vanished.

5.

Dante once prepared to paint an angel:
Whom to please? You whisper "Beatrice."
While he mused and traced it and retraced it,
(Peradventure with a pen corroded
Still by drops of that hot ink he dipped for,
When, his left-hand i' the hair o' the wicked,
Back he held the brow and pricked its stigma,
Bit into the live man's flesh for parchment,
Loosed him, laughed to see the writing rankle,
Let the wretch go festering thro' Florence)—
Dante, who loved well because he hated,
Hated wickedness that hinders loving,
Dante standing, studying his angel,—
In there broke the folk of his Inferno.
Says he—"Certain people of importance"
(Such he gave his daily, dreadful line to)
Entered and would seize, forsooth, the poet.
Says the poet—"Then I stopped my painting."

6.

You and I would rather see that angel,
Painted by the tenderness of Dante,
Would we not?—than read a fresh Inferno.

7.

You and I will never see that picture.
While he mused on love and Beatrice,
While he softened o'er his outlined angel,
In they broke, those "people of importance:"
We and Bice bear the loss for ever.

8.

What of Rafael's sonnets, Dante's picture?

9.

This: no artist lives and loves that longs not
Once, and only once, and for One only,
(Ah, the prize!) to find his love a language
Fit and fair and simple and sufficient—
Using nature that's an art to others,
Not, this one time, art that's turned his nature.
Ay, of all the artists living, loving,
None but would forego his proper dowry,—
Does he paint? he fain would write a poem,—
Does he write? he fain would paint a picture,
Put to proof art alien to the artist's,
Once, and only once, and for One only,
So to be the man and leave the artist,
Gain the man's joy, miss the artist's sorrow.

10.

Wherefore? Heaven's gift takes earth's abatement!
He who smites the rock and spreads the water,
Bidding drink and live a crowd beneath him,
Even he, the minute makes immortal,
Proves, perchance, his mortal in the minute,
Desecrates, belike, the deed in doing.
While he smites, how can he but remember,
So he smote before, in such a peril,
When they stood and mocked—"Shall smiting help us?"
When they drank and sneered—"A stroke is easy!"
When they wiped their mouths and went their journey,
Throwing him for thanks—"But drought was pleasant."
Thus old memories mar the actual triumph;
Thus the doing savours of disrelish;
Thus achievement lacks a gracious somewhat;
O'er-importuned brows becloud the mandate,
Carelessness or consciousness, the gesture.
For he bears an ancient wrong about him,
Sees and knows again those phalanxed faces,
Hears, yet one time more, the 'customed prelude—
"How shouldst thou, of all men, smite, and save us?"
Guesses what is like to prove the sequel—
"Egypt's flesh-pots—nay, the drought was better."

11.

Oh, the crowd must have emphatic warrant!
Theirs, the Sinai-forehead's cloven brilliance,
Right-arm's rod-sweep, tongue's imperial fiat.
Never dares the man put off the prophet.

12.

Did he love one face from out the thousands,
(Were she Jethro's daughter, white and wifely,
Were she but the Æthiopian bondslave,)
He would envy yon dumb patient camel,
Keeping a reserve of scanty water
Meant to save his own life in the desert;
Ready in the desert to deliver
(Kneeling down to let his breast be opened)
Hoard and life together for his mistress.

13.

I shall never, in the years remaining,
Paint you pictures, no, nor carve you statues,
Make you music that should all-express me;
So it seems: I stand on my attainment.
This of verse alone, one life allows me;
Verse and nothing else have I to give you.
Other heights in other lives, God willing—
All the gifts from all the heights, your own, Love!

14.

Yet a semblance of resource avails us—
Shade so finely touched, love's sense must seize it.
Take these lines, look lovingly and nearly,
Lines I write the first time and the last time.
He who works in fresco, steals a hair-brush,
Curbs the liberal hand, subservient proudly,
Cramps his spirit, crowds its all in little,
Makes a strange art of an art familiar,
Fills his lady's missal-marge with flowerets.
He who blows thro' bronze, may breathe thro' silver,
Fitly serenade a slumbrous princess.
He who writes, may write for once, as I do.

15.

Love, you saw me gather men and women,
Live or dead or fashioned by my fancy,
Enter each and all, and use their service,
Speak from every mouth,—the speech, a poem.
Hardly shall I tell my joys and sorrows,
Hopes and fears, belief and disbelieving:
I am mine and yours—the rest be all men's,
Karshook, Cleon, Norbert and the fifty.
Let me speak this once in my true person,
Not as Lippo, Roland or Andrea,
Though the fruit of speech be just this sentence—
Pray you, look on these my men and women,
Take and keep my fifty poems finished;
Where my heart lies, let my brain lie also!
Poor the speech; be how I speak, for all things.

16.

Not but that you know me! Lo, the moon's self!
Here in London, yonder late in Florence,
Still we find her face, the thrice-transfigured.
Curving on a sky imbrued with colour,
Drifted over Fiesole by twilight,
Came she, our new crescent of a hair's-breadth.
Full she flared it, lamping Samminiato,
Rounder 'twixt the cypresses and rounder,
Perfect till the nightingales applauded.
Now, a piece of her old self, impoverished,
Hard to greet, she traverses the houseroofs,
Hurries with unhandsome thrift of silver,
Goes dispiritedly,—glad to finish.

17.

What, there's nothing in the moon note-worthy?
Nay—for if that moon could love a mortal,
Use, to charm him (so to fit a fancy)
All her magic ('tis the old sweet mythos)
She would turn a new side to her mortal,
Side unseen of herdsman, huntsman, steersman—
Blank to Zoroaster on his terrace,
Blind to Galileo on his turret,
Dumb to Homer, dumb to Keats—him, even!
Think, the wonder of the moonstruck mortal—

When she turns round, comes again in heaven,
Opens out anew for worse or better?
Proves she like some portent of an ice-berg
Swimming full upon the ship it founders,
Hungry with huge teeth of splintered chrystals?
Proves she as the paved work of a sapphire
Seen by Moses when he climbed the mountain?
Moses, Aaron, Nadab and Abihu
Climbed and saw the very God, the Highest,
Stand upon the paved-work of a sapphire.
Like the bodied heaven in his clearness
Shone the stone, the sapphire of that paved-work
When they ate and drank and saw God also!

18.

What were seen? None knows, none ever shall know.
Only this is sure—the sight were other,
Not the moon's same side, born late in Florence,
Dying now impoverished here in London.
God be thanked, the meanest of his creatures
Boasts two soul-sides, one to face the world with,
One to show a woman when he loves her.

19.

This I say of me, but think of you, Love!
This to you—yourself my moon of poets!
Ah, but that's the world's side—there's the wonder—
Thus they see you, praise you, think they know you,
There, in turn I stand with them and praise you,
Out of my own self, I dare to phrase it.
But the best is when I glide from out them,
Cross a step or two of dubious twilight,
Come out on the other side, the novel
Silent silver lights and darks undreamed of,
Where I hush and bless myself with silence.

20.

Oh, their Rafael of the dear Madonnas,
Oh, their Dante of the dread Inferno,
Wrote one song—and in my brain I sing it,
Drew one angel—borne, see, on my bosom.

THE END

Letter to John Ruskin,
10 *December* 1855

PARIS, Dec. 10th, '55

My dear Ruskin,—for so you let me begin, with the honest friendliness that befits,—You never were more in the wrong than when you professed to say "your unpleasant things" to me. This is pleasant and proper at all points, over-liberal of praise here and there, kindly and sympathetic everywhere, and with enough of yourself in even—what I fancy—the misjudging, to make the whole letter precious indeed. I wanted to thank you thus much at once,—that is, when the letter reached me; but the strife of lodging-hunting was too sore, and only now that I can sit down for a minute without self-reproach do I allow my thoughts to let go south-aspects, warm bedrooms, and the like, and begin as you see. For the deepnesses you think you discern,—may they be more than mere blacknesses! For the hopes you entertain of what may come of subsequent readings,—all success to them! For your bewilderment more especially noted—how shall I help *that*? We don't read poetry the same way, by the same law; it is too clear. I cannot begin writing poetry till my imaginary reader has conceded licences to me which you demur at altogether. I *know* that I don't make out my conception by my language; all poetry being a putting the infinite within the finite. You would have me paint it all plain out, which can't be; but by various artifices I try to make shift with touches and bits of outlines which *succeed* if they bear the conception from me to you. You ought, I think, to keep pace with the thought tripping from ledge to ledge of my "glaciers," as you call them; not stand poking your alpenstock into the holes, and demonstrating that no foot could have stood there;—suppose it sprang over there? In *prose* you may criticise so—because that is the absolute representation of portions of truth, what chronicling is to history—but in asking for more *ultimates* you must accept less *mediates*, nor expect that a Druid stone-circle will be traced for you with as few breaks to the eye as the North Crescent and South Crescent that go together so cleverly in many a suburb. Why, you look at my little song as if it were Hobbs' or Nobbs' lease of his house, or testament of his devisings, wherein, I grant you, not a "then and there," "to him and his heirs," "to have and to hold," and so on, would be superfluous; and so you begin:—"Stand still—why?" For the reason indicated in the verse, to be sure—*to let me draw him*—and because he is at present going his way, and fancying nobody notices him,—and moreover, "going on" (as we say) against the injustice of that,—and lastly, inasmuch as one night he'll fail us, as a star is apt to drop out of heaven, in authentic astronomic records, and I want to make the most of my time. So much may be in "stand still." And how much more was (for instance) in that "stay!" of Samuel's (I. xv. 16). So could I twit you through the whole series of your objurgations, but the declaring my own notion of the law on the subject will do. And why,—I prithee, friend and fellow and fellow-student,—why, having told the Poet what you read,—may I not turn to the bystanders, and tell them a bit of my own mind about their own stupid thanklessness and mistaking? Is the jump too much there? The whole is all but a simultaneous feeling with me.

The other hard measure you deal me I won't bear—about my requiring you to pronounce words short and long, exactly as I like. Nay, but exactly as the language likes, in this case. *Fold-skirts* not a trochee? A spondee possible in English? Two of the "longest monosyllables" continuing to be each of the old length when in junction? Sentence: let the delinquent be forced to supply the stone-cutter with a thousand companions to "Affliction sore—long time he bore", after the fashion of "He lost his life—by a pen-knife"—"He turned to clay—last Good Friday," "Departed hence—nor owed six-pence," and so on—so would pronounce a jury accustomed from the nipple to say lord and landlord, bridge and Cambridge, Gog and Magog, man and woman, house and workhouse, coal and charcoal, cloth and broadcloth, skirts and fold-skirts, more and once more,—in short! Once *more* I prayed!—is the confession of a self-searching professor! "I stand here for law!"

The last change I cannot answer, for you may be right in preferring it, however unwitting I am of the fact. I *may* put Robert Browning into Pippa and then other men and maids. If so, *peccavi*: but I don't see myself in them, at all events.

Do you think poetry was ever generally understood—or can be? Is the business of it to tell people what they know already, as they know it, and so precisely that they shall be able to cry out—"Here you should supply *this—that*, you evidently pass over, and I'll help you from my own stock"? It is all teaching, on the contrary, and the people hate to be taught. They say otherwise,—make foolish fables about Orpheus enchanting stocks and stones, poets standing up and being worshipped,—all nonsense and impossible dreaming. A poet's affair is with God, to whom he is accountable, and of whom is his reward: look elsewhere, and you find misery enough. Do you believe people understand *Hamlet*? The last time I saw it acted, the heartiest applause of the night went to a little by-play of the actor's own—who, to simulate madness in a hurry, plucked forth his handkerchief and flourished it hither and thither: certainly a third of the play, with no end of noble things, had been (as from time immemorial) suppressed, with the auditory's amplest acquiescence and benediction. Are these wasted, therefore? No—they act upon a very few, who react upon the rest: as Goldsmith says, "some lords, my acquaintance, that settle the nation, are pleased to be kind."

Don't let me lose *my* lord by any seeming self-sufficiency or petulance: I look on my own shortcomings too sorrowfully, try to remedy them too earnestly: but I shall never change my point of sight, or feel other than disconcerted and apprehensive when the public, critics and all, begin to understand and approve me. But what right have *you* to disconcert me in the other way? Why won't you ask the next perfumer for a packet of *orris*-root? Don't everybody know 'tis a corruption of *iris*-root—the Florentine lily, the *giaggolo*, of world-wide fame as a good savour? And because "iris" means so many objects already, and I use the old word, you blame me! But I write in the blind-dark and bitter cold, and past post-time as I fear. Take my truest thanks, and understand at least this rough writing, and, at all events, the real affection with which I venture to regard you. And "I" means my wife as well as

Yours ever faithfully,
Robert Browning

Letter To Euphrasia (Fanny) Haworth, 20 July 1861

Florence, July 20, '61

My dear friend, I well know you feel as you say, for her once and for me now. Isa Blagden, perfect in all kindness to me, will have told you something perhaps—and one day I shall see you and be able to tell you myself as much as I can. The main comfort is that she suffered very little pain, none beside that ordinarily attending the simple attacks of cold and cough she was subject to, had no presentiment of the result whatever, and was consequently spared the misery of knowing she was about to leave us: she was smilingly assuring me she was "better," "quite comfortable—if I would but come to bed—" to within a few minutes of the last. I think I foreboded evil even at Rome, certainly from the beginning of the week's illness—but when I reasoned about it, there was no justifying fear: she said on the last evening "It is merely the old attack, nor so severe a one as that of two years ago—there is no doubt I shall soon recover"—And we talked over plans for the summer and next year. I sent the servants away and her maid to bed—so little reason for disquietude did there seem. Thro' the night she slept heavily, and brokenly—that was the bad sign. But then she would sit up, take her medicine, say unrepeatable things to me and sleep again. At four o'clock there were symptoms that alarmed me,—I called the maid and sent for the Doctor,—She smiled as I proposed to bathe her feet "Well, you *are* making an exaggerated case of it!" Then came what my heart will keep till I see her and longer—the most perfect expression of her love to me within my whole knowledge of her—always smilingly, happily, and with a face like a girl's—and in a few minutes she died in my arms, her head on my cheek. These incidents so sustain me that I tell them to her beloved ones as their right: there was no lingering, nor acute pain, nor consciousness of separation, but God took her to himself as you would lift a sleeping child from a dark, uneasy bed into your arms and the light. Thank God. Annunziata thought by her earnest ways with me, happy and smiling as they were, that she must have been aware of our parting's approach—but she was quite conscious, had words at command, and yet did not even speak of Peni who was in the next room. Her last word was—when I asked "How do you feel?"—"*Beautiful.*"

You know I have her dearest interest to attend to *at once*—her child to care for, educate, establish properly,—and my own life to fulfil as properly,—all, just as she would require were she here. I shall leave Italy altogether for years—go to London for a few days talk with Arabel—than go to my father, and begin to try leisurely what will be the best for Peni—but no more "housekeeping" for me, even with my family. I shall grow, still, I hope—but my root is taken, remains.

I know you always loved her, and me too in my degree. Forgive my old peevish ways, which came from being too rich,—I shall trouble nobody with them now—but always be grateful to those who loved her—and that, I repeat, *you* did.

She was, is, lamented with extraordinary demonstrations if one consider it: the Italians seem to have understood her by an instinct. I have received strange kindness from everybody. Pen is very well, very dear and good, anxious to "comfort me" as he calls it. He can't know his loss yet. After years, his will be more than mine, he will want what he never had—that is, for the time when he could be helped by her wisdom, and genius and piety: I *have* had everything, and shall not forget.

God bless you, dear friend: I believe I set out in a week: Isa goes with me,— dear, true heart. You, too, would do what you could for us were you here and your assistance needful. A letter from you came a day or two before the end—she made me enquire about the "Frescobaldi Palace" for you,—Isa wrote to you in consequence. I shall be heard of at 151. Rue de Grenelle, Faubourg St Germ^{n}.

Faithfully and affectionately yours

Robert Browning

FROM *DRAMATIS PERSONÆ* (1864)

[*James Lee's Wife*] *James Lee*

I. At The Window.

1.

Ah, love, but a day,
 And the world has changed!
The sun's away,
 And the bird's estranged;
The wind has dropped,
 And the sky's deranged:
Summer has stopped.

2.

Look in my eyes!
 Wilt thou change too?
Should I fear surprise?
 Shall I find aught new
In the old and dear,
 In the good and true,
With the changing year?

3.

Thou art a man,
 But I am thy love!
For the lake, its swan;
 For the dell, its dove;
And for thee—(oh, haste!)
 Me, to bend above,
Me, to hold embraced!

II. By The Fireside.

1.

Is all our fire of shipwreck wood,
 Oak and pine?
Oh, for the ills half-understood,

The dim, dead woe
Long ago
Befallen this bitter coast of France!
Well, poor sailors took their chance;
I take mine.

2.

A ruddy shaft our fire must shoot
O'er the sea:
Do sailors eye the casement—mute,
Drenched and stark,
From their bark—
And envy, gnash their teeth for hate
O' the warm safe house and happy freight
—Thee and me?

3.

God help you, sailors, at your need!
Spare the curse!
For some ships, safe in port indeed,
Rot and rust,
Run to dust,
All through worms i' the wood, which crept,
Gnawed our hearts out while we slept:
That is worse!

4.

Who lived here before us two?
Old-world pairs!
Did a woman ever—would I knew!—
Watch the man
With whom began
Love's voyage full-sail,—(now, gnash your teeth!)
When planks start, open hell beneath
Unawares?

III. In The Doorway

1.

The swallow has set her six young on the rail,
  And looks sea-ward:
The water's in stripes like a snake, olive-pale
  To the leeward,—
On the weather-side, black, spotted white with the wind:
"Good fortune departs, and disaster's behind,"—
Hark, the wind with its wants and its infinite wail!

2.

Our fig-tree, that leaned for the saltness, has furled
  Her five fingers,
Each leaf like a hand opened wide to the world
  Where there lingers
No glint of the gold, Summer sent for her sake:
How the vines writhe in rows, each impaled on its stake!
My heart shrivels up and my spirit shrinks curled.

3.

Yet here are we two; we have love, house enough,
  With the field there,
This house of four rooms, that field red and rough,
  Though it yield there,
For the rabbit that robs, scarce a blade or a bent;
If a magpie alight now, it seems an event;
And they both will be gone at November's rebuff.

4.

But why must cold spread? but wherefore bring change
  To the spirit,
God meant should mate His with an infinite range,
  And inherit
His power to put life in the darkness and cold?
Oh, live and love worthily, bear and be bold!
Whom Summer made friends of, let Winter estrange!

IV. Along The Beach.

1.

I will be quiet and talk with you,
   And reason why you are wrong:
You wanted my love—is that much true?
   And so I did love, so I do:
What has come of it all along?

2.

I took you—how could I otherwise?
   For a world to me, and more;
For all, love greatens and glorifies
Till God's a-glow, to the loving eyes,
   In what was mere earth before.

3.

Yes, earth—yes, mere ignoble earth!
   Now do I mis-state, mistake?
Do I wrong your weakness and call it worth?
Expect all harvest, dread no dearth,
   Seal my sense up for your sake?

4.

Oh, love, love, no, love! not so, indeed!
   You were just weak earth, I knew:
With much in you waste, with many a weed,
And plenty of passions run to seed,
   But a little good grain too.

5.

And such as you were, I took you for mine:
   Did not you find me yours,
To watch the olive and wait the vine,
And wonder when rivers of oil and wine
   Would flow, as the Book assures?

6.

Well, and if none of these good things came,
  What did the failure prove?
The man was my whole world, all the same,
With his flowers to praise, or his weeds to blame,
  And, either or both, to love.

7.

Yet this turns now to a fault—there! there!
  That I do love, watch too long,
And wait too well, and weary and wear;
And 'tis all an old story, and my despair
  Fit subject for some new song:

8.

How the light, light love, he has wings to fly
  At suspicion of a bond:
My wisdom has bidden your pleasure good-bye,
Which will turn up next in a laughing eye,
  And why should you look beyond?

V. On The Cliff.

1.

I leaned on the turf,
I looked at a rock
Left dry by the surf;
For the turf, to call it grass were to mock:
Dead to the roots, so deep was done
The work of the summer sun.

2.

And the rock lay flat
As an anvil's face:
No iron like that!
Baked dry; of a weed, of a shell, no trace:
Sunshine outside, but ice at the core,
Death's altar by the lone shore.

3.

On the turf, sprang gay
With his films of blue,
No cricket, I'll say,
But a warhorse, barded and chanfroned too,
The gift of a quixote-mage to his knight,
Real fairy, with wings all right.

4.

On the rock, they scorch
Like a drop of fire
From a brandished torch,
Fall two red fans of a butterfly:
No turf, no rock, in their ugly stead,
See, wonderful blue and red!

5.

Is it not so
With the minds of men?
The level and low,
The burnt and bare, in themselves; but then
With such a blue and red grace, not theirs,
Love settling unawares!

VI. Under The Cliff.

1.

"Still ailing, Wind? Wilt be appeased or no?
Which needs the other's office, thou or I?
Dost want to be disburthened of a woe,
And can, in truth, my voice untie
Its links, and let it go?

2.

"Art thou a dumb, wronged thing that would be righted,
Entrusting thus thy cause to me? Forbear,
No tongue can mend such pleadings; faith, requited
With falsehood,—love, at last aware
Of scorn,—hopes, early blighted,—

3.

"We have them; but I know not any tone
So fit as thine to falter forth a sorrow:
Dost think men would go mad without a moan,
If they knew any way to borrow
A pathos like thy own?

4.

"Which sigh wouldst mock, of all the sighs? The one
So long escaping from lips starved and blue,
That lasts while on her pallet-bed the nun
Stretches her length; her foot comes through
The straw she shivers on;

5.

"You had not thought she was so tall: and spent,
Her shrunk lids open, her lean fingers shut
Close, close, their sharp and livid nails indent
The clammy palm; then all is mute:
That way, the spirit went.

6.

"Or wouldst thou rather that I understand
Thy will to help me?—like the dog I found
Once, pacing sad this solitary strand,
Who would not take my food, poor hound,
But whined and licked my hand."

7.

All this, and more, comes from some young man's pride
Of power to see,—in failure and mistake,
Relinquishment, disgrace, on every side,—
Merely examples for his sake,
Helps to his path untried:

8.

Instances he must—simply recognize?
Oh, more than so!—must, with a learner's zeal,

Make doubly prominent, twice emphasize,
By added touches that reveal
The god in babe's disguise.

9.

Oh, he knows what defeat means, and the rest!
Himself the undefeated that shall be:
Failure, disgrace, he flings them you to test,—
His triumph, in eternity
Too plainly manifest!

10.

Whence, judge if he learn forthwith what the wind
Means in its moaning—by the happy, prompt,
Instinctive way of youth, I mean; for kind
Calm years, exacting their accompt
Of pain, mature the mind:

11.

And some midsummer morning, at the lull
Just about daybreak, as he looks across
A sparkling foreign country, wonderful
To the sea's edge for gloom and gloss,
Next minute must annul,—

12.

Then, when the wind begins among the vines,
So low, so low, what shall it mean but this?
"Here is the change beginning, here the lines
Circumscribe beauty, set to bliss
The limit time assigns."

13.

Nothing can be as it has been before;
Better, so call it, only not the same.
To draw one beauty into our hearts' core,
And keep it changeless! such our claim;
So answered,—Never more!

14.

Simple? Why this is the old woe o' the world;
  Tune, to whose rise and fall we live and die.
Rise with it, then! Rejoice that man is hurled
  From change to change unceasingly,
His soul's wings never furled!

15.

That's a new question; still replies the fact,
  Nothing endures: the wind moans, saying so;
We moan in acquiescence: there's life's pact,
  Perhaps probation—do *I* know?
God does: endure His act!

16.

Only, for man, how bitter not to grave
  On his soul's hands' palms one fair, good, wise thing
Just as he grasped it! For himself, death's wave;
  While time first washes—ah, the sting!—
O'er all he'd sink to save.

VII. Among The Rocks.

1.

Oh, good gigantic smile o' the brown old earth,
  This autumn morning! How he sets his bones
To bask i' the sun, and thrusts out knees and feet
For the ripple to run over in its mirth;
  Listening the while, where on the heap of stones
The white breast of the sea-lark twitters sweet.

2.

That is the doctrine, simple, ancient, true;
  Such is life's trial, as old earth smiles and knows.
If you loved only what were worth your love,
Love were clear gain, and wholly well for you:
  Make the low nature better by your throes!
Give earth yourself, go up for gain above!

VIII. Beside The Drawing Board.

1.

"As like as a Hand to another Hand:"
  Whoever said that foolish thing,
Could not have studied to understand
  The counsels of God in fashioning,
Out of the infinite love of His heart,
This Hand, whose beauty I praise, apart
From the world of wonder left to praise,
If I tried to learn the other ways
Of love, in its skill, or love, in its power.
"As like as a Hand to another Hand:"
Who said that, never took his stand,
Found and followed, like me, an hour,
The beauty in this,—how free, how fine
To fear, almost,—of the limit-line!
As I looked at this, and learned and drew,
Drew and learned, and looked again,
While fast the happy minutes flew,
Its beauty mounted into my brain,
And a fancy seized me; I was fain
To efface my work, begin anew,
Kiss what before I only drew;
Ay, laying the red chalk 'twixt my lips,
With soul to help if the mere lips failed,
I kissed all right where the drawing ailed,
Kissed fast the grace that somehow slips
Still from one's soulless finger-tips.

2.

Go, little girl with the poor coarse hand!
I have my lesson, shall understand.

IX. On Deck.

1.

There is nothing to remember in me,
  Nothing I ever said with a grace,
Nothing I did that you care to see,
  Nothing I was that deserves a place
In your mind, now I leave you, set you free.

2.

Conceded! In turn, concede to me,
  Such things have been as a mutual flame.
Your soul's locked fast; but, love for a key,
  You might let it loose, till I grew the same
In your eyes, as in mine you stand: strange plea!

3.

For then, then, what would it matter to me
  That I was the harsh, ill-favoured one?
We both should be like as pea and pea;
  It was ever so since the world begun:
So, let me proceed with my reverie.

4.

How strange it were if you had all me,
  As I have all you in my heart and brain,
You, whose least word brought gloom or glee,
  Who never lifted the hand in vain
Will hold mine yet, from over the sea!

5.

Strange, if a face, when you thought of me,
  Rose like your own face present now,
With eyes as dear in their due degree,
  Much such a mouth, and as bright a brow,
Till you saw yourself, while you cried "'Tis She!"

6.

Well, you may, you must, set down to me
  Love that was life, life that was love;
A tenure of breath at your lips' decree,
  A passion to stand as your thoughts approve,
A rapture to fall where your foot might be.

7.

But did one touch of such love for me
  Come in a word or a look of yours,
Whose words and looks will, circling, flee
  Round me and round while life endures,—
Could I fancy "As I feel, thus feels He;"

8.

Why, fade you might to a thing like me,
  And your hair grow these coarse hanks of hair,
Your skin, this bark of a gnarled tree,—
  You might turn myself;—should I know or care,
When I should be dead of joy, James Lee?

Gold Hair: A Legend of Pornic

1.

Oh, the beautiful girl, too white,
  Who lived at Pornic, down by the sea,
Just where the sea and the Loire unite!
  And a boasted name in Brittany
She bore, which I will not write.

2.

Too white, for the flower of life is red;
  Her flesh was the soft seraphic screen
Of a soul that is meant (her parents said)
  To just see earth, and hardly be seen,
And blossom in Heaven instead.

3.

Yet earth saw one thing, one how fair!
  One grace that grew to its full on earth:
Smiles might be sparse on her cheek so spare,
  And her waist want half a girdle's girth,
But she had her great gold hair.

4.

Hair, such a wonder of flix and floss,
  Freshness and fragrance—floods of it, too!
Gold, did I say? Nay, gold's mere dross:
  Here, Life smiled, "Think what I meant to do!"
And Love sighed, "Fancy my loss!"

5.

So, when she died, it was scarce more strange
  Than that, when delicate evening dies,
And you follow its spent sun's pallid range,
  There's a shoot of colour startles the skies
With sudden, violent change,—

6.

That, while the breath was nearly to seek,
  As they put the little cross to her lips,
She changed; a spot came out on her cheek,
  A spark from her eye in mid-eclipse,
And she broke forth, "I must speak!"

7.

"Not my hair!" made the girl her moan—
  "All the rest is gone or to go;
But the last, last grace, my all, my own,
  Let it stay in the grave, that the ghosts may know!
Leave my poor gold hair alone!"

8.

The passion thus vented, dead lay she;
  Her parents sobbed their worst on that,
All friends joined in, nor observed degree:
  For indeed the hair was to wonder at,
As it spread—not flowing free,

9.

But curled around her brow, like a crown,
  And coiled beside her cheeks, like a cap,
And calmed about her neck—ay, down
  To her breast, pressed flat, without a gap
I' the gold, it reached her gown.

10.

All kissed that face, like a silver wedge
  Mid the yellow wealth, nor disturbed its hair;
E'en the priest allowed death's privilege,
  As he planted the crucifix with care
On her breast, 'twixt edge and edge.

11.

And thus was she buried, inviolate
  Of body and soul, in the very space
By the altar; keeping saintly state
  In Pornic church, for her pride of race,
Pure life, and piteous fate.

12.

And in after-time would your fresh tear fall,
  Though your mouth might twitch with a dubious smile,
As they told you of gold both robe and pall,
  How she prayed them leave it alone awhile,
So it never was touched at all.

13.

Years flew; this legend grew at last
  The life of the lady; all she had done,

All been, in the memories fading fast
  Of lover and friend, was summed in one
Sentence survivors passed:

14.

To wit, she was meant for Heaven, not earth;
  Had turned an angel before the time:
Yet, since she was mortal, in such dearth
  Of frailty, all you could count a crime
Was—she knew her gold hair's worth.

15.

At little pleasant Pornic church,
  It chanced, the pavement wanted repair,
Was taken to pieces: left in the lurch,
  A certain sacred space lay bare,
And the boys began research.

16.

'Twas the space where our sires would lay a saint,
  A benefactor,—a bishop, suppose;
A baron with armour-adornments quaint;
  Dame with chased ring and jewelled rose,
Things sanctity saves from taint:

17.

So we come to find them in after-days
  When the corpse is presumed to have done with gauds
Of use to the living, in many ways;
  For the boys get pelf, and the town applauds,
And the church deserves the praise.

18.

They grubbed with a will: and at length—*O cor*
  Humanum, pectora cæca, and the rest!—
They found—no gaud they were prying for,
  No ring, no rose, but—who would have guessed?—
A double Louis-d'or!

19.

Here was a case for the priest: he heard,
   Marked, inwardly digested, laid
Finger on nose, smiled, "A little bird
   Chirps in my ear": then, "Bring a spade,
Dig deeper!"—he gave the word.

20.

And lo! when they came to the coffin-lid,
   Or the rotten planks which composed it once,
Why, there lay the girl's skull wedged amid
   A mint of money, it served for the nonce
To hold in its hair-heaps hid.

21.

Louis-d'ors, some six times five;
   And duly double, every piece.
Now do you see? With the priest to shrive,
   With parents preventing her soul's release
By kisses that kept alive,—

22.

With Heaven's gold gates about to ope,
   With friends' praise, gold-like, lingering still,
What instinct had bidden the girl's hand grope
   For gold, the true sort—"Gold in heaven, I hope;
But I keep earth's, if God will!"

23.

Enough! The priest took the grave's grim yield:
   The parents, they eyed that price of sin
As if *thirty pieces* lay revealed
   On the place *to bury strangers in*,
The hideous Potter's Field.

24.

But the priest bethought him: "'Milk that's spilt'
   —You know the adage! Watch and pray!

Saints tumble to earth with so slight a tilt!
   It would build a new altar; that, we may!"
And the altar therewith was built.

25.

Why I deliver this horrible verse?
   As the text of a sermon, which now I preach:
Evil or good may be better or worse
   In the human heart, but the mixture of each
Is a marvel and a curse.

26.

The candid incline to surmise of late
   That the Christian faith proves false, I find;
For our Essays-and-Reviews' debate
   Begins to tell on the public mind,
And Colenso's words have weight:

27.

I still, to suppose it true, for my part,
   See reasons and reasons; this, to begin:
'Tis the faith that launched point-blank her dart
   At the head of a lie—taught Original Sin,
The Corruption of Man's Heart.

[Additional stanzas which became 21–3, written into George Eliot's copy of *DP* when she said the lady had insufficient motivation]

21.

Hid there? Why? Could the girl be wont
   (She the stainless soul) to treasure up
Money, earth's trash and heaven's affront?
   Had a spider found out the communion-cup,
Was a toad in the christening-font?

22.

Truth is truth: too true it was.
   Gold! She hoarded and hugged it first,
Longed for it, leaned o'er it, loved it—alas—

Till the humour grew to a head and burst,
And she cried, at the final pass,—

23.

"Talk not of God, my heart is stone!
"Nor lover nor friend—be gold for both!
"Gold I lack; and, my all, my own,
"It shall hide in my hair. I scarce die loth
"If they let my hair alone!"]

Dîs Aliter Visum; or, Le Byron de Nos Jours

1.

Stop, let me have the truth of that!
Is that all true? I say, the day
Ten years ago when both of us
Met on a morning, friends—as thus
We meet this evening, friends or what?—

2.

Did you—because I took your arm
And sillily smiled, "A mass of brass
That sea looks, blazing underneath!"
While up the cliff-road edged with heath,
We took the turns nor came to harm—

3.

Did you consider "Now makes twice
That I have seen her, walked and talked
With this poor pretty thoughtful thing,
Whose worth I weigh: she tries to sing;
Draws, hopes in time the eye grows nice;

4.

"Reads verse and thinks she understands;
Loves all, at any rate, that's great,
Good, beautiful; but much as we
Down at the Bath-house love the sea,
Who breathe its salt and bruise its sands:

5.

"While . . do but follow the fishing-gull
 That flaps and floats from wave to cave!
There's the sea-lover, fair my friend!
 What then? Be patient, mark and mend!
Had you the making of your scull?"

6.

And did you, when we faced the church
 With spire and sad slate roof, aloof
From human fellowship so far,
 Where a few graveyard crosses are,
And garlands for the swallows' perch,—

7.

Did you determine, as we stepped
 O'er the lone stone fence, "Let me get
Her for myself, and what's the earth
 With all its art, verse, music, worth—
Compared with love, found, gained, and kept?

8.

"Schumann's our music-maker now;
 Has his march-movement youth and mouth?
Ingres's the modern man that paints;
 Which will lean on me, of his saints?
Heine for songs; for kisses, how?"

9.

And did you, when we entered, reached
 The votive frigate, soft aloft
Riding on air this hundred years,
 Safe-smiling at old hopes and fears,—
Did you draw profit while she preached?

10.

Resolving, "Fools we wise men grow!
 Yes, I could easily blurt out curt

Some question that might find reply
  As prompt in her stopped lips, dropped eye,
And rush of red to cheek and brow:

11.

"Thus were a match made, sure and fast,
  'Mid the blue weed-flowers round the mound
Where, issuing, we shall stand and stay
  For one more look at Baths and bay,
Sands, sea-gulls, and the old church last—

12.

"A match 'twixt me, bent, wigged and lamed,
  Famous, however, for verse and worse,
Sure of the Fortieth spare Arm-chair
  When gout and glory seat me there,
So, one whose love-freaks pass unblamed,—

13.

"And this young beauty, round and sound
  As a mountain-apple, youth and truth
With loves and doves, at all events
  With money in the Three per Cents;
Whose choice of me would seem profound:—

14.

"She might take me as I take her.
  Perfect the hour would pass, alas!
Climb high, love high, what matter? Still,
  Feet, feelings, must descend the hill:
An hour's perfection can't recur.

15.

"Then follows Paris and full time
  For both to reason: 'Thus with us!'
She'll sigh, 'Thus girls give body and soul
  At first word, think they gain the goal,
When 'tis the starting-place they climb!

16.

"'My friend makes verse and gets renown;
Have they all fifty years, his peers?
He knows the world, firm, quiet and gay;
Boys will become as much one day:
They're fools; he cheats, with beard less brown.

17.

"'For boys say, *Love me or I die!*
He did not say, *The truth is, youth*
I want, who am old and know too much;
I'd catch youth: lend me sight and touch!
Drop heart's blood where life's wheels grate dry!

18.

"While I should make rejoinder"—(then
It was, no doubt, you ceased that least
Light pressure of my arm in yours)
"'I can conceive of cheaper cures
For a yawning-fit o'er books and men.

19.

"'What? All I am, was, and might be,
All, books taught, art brought, life's whole strife,
Painful results since precious, just
Were fitly exchanged in wise disgust
For two cheeks freshened by youth and sea?

20.

"'All for a nosegay!—what came first;
With fields on flower, untried each side;
I rally, need my books and men,
And find a nosegay: drop it, then,
No match yet made for best or worst!'"

21.

That ended me. You judged the porch
We left by, Norman; took our look

At sea and sky; wondered so few
  Find out the place for air and view;
Remarked the sun began to scorch;

22.

Descended, soon regained the Baths,
  And then, good bye! Years ten since then:
Ten years! We meet: you tell me, now,
  By a window-seat for that cliff-brow,
On carpet-stripes for those sand-paths.

23.

Now I may speak: you fool, for all
  Your lore! Who made things plain in vain?
What was the sea for? What, the grey
  Sad church, that solitary day,
Crosses and graves and swallows' call?

24.

Was there nought better than to enjoy?
  No feat which, done, would make time break,
And let us pent-up creatures through
  Into eternity, our due?
No forcing earth teach Heaven's employ?

25.

No wise beginning, here and now,
  What cannot grow complete (earth's feat)
And Heaven must finish, there and then?
  No tasting earth's true food for men,
Its sweet in sad, its sad in sweet?

26.

No grasping at love, gaining a share
  O' the sole spark from God's life at strife
With death, so, sure of range above
  The limits here? For us and love,
Failure; but, when God fails, despair.

27.

This you call wisdom? Thus you add
  Good unto good again, in vain?
You loved, with body worn and weak;
  I loved, with faculties to seek:
Were both loves worthless since ill-clad?

28.

Let the mere star-fish in his vault
  Crawl in a wash of weed, indeed,
Rose-jacynth to the finger-tips:
  He, whole in body and soul, outstrips
Man, found with either in default.

29.

But what's whole, can increase no more,
  Is dwarfed and dies, since here's its sphere.
The devil laughed at you in his sleeve!
  You knew not? That, I well believe;
Or you had saved two souls: nay, four.

30.

For Stephanie sprained last night her wrist,
  Ancle, or something. "Pooh," cry you?
At any rate she danced, all say,
  Vilely: her vogue has had its day.
Here comes my husband from his whist.

Abt Vogler

(After he has been extemporizing upon the musical instrument of his invention)

1.

Would that the structure brave, the manifold music I build,
  Bidding my organ obey, calling its keys to their work,
Claiming each slave of the sound, at a touch, as when Solomon willed
  Armies of angels that soar, legions of demons that lurk,

Man, brute, reptile, fly,—alien of end and of aim,
Adverse, each from the other heaven-high, hell-deep removed,—
Should rush into sight at once as he named the ineffable Name,
And pile him a palace straight, to pleasure the princess he loved!

2.

Would it might tarry like his, the beautiful building of mine,
This which my keys in a crowd pressed and importuned to raise!
Ah, one and all, how they helped, would dispart now and now combine,
Zealous to hasten the work, heighten their master his praise!
And one would bury his brow with a blind plunge down to hell,
Burrow awhile and build, broad on the roots of things,
Then up again swim into sight, having based me my palace well,
Founded it, fearless of flame, flat on the nether springs.

3.

And another would mount and march, like the excellent minion he was,
Ay, another and yet another, one crowd but with many a crest,
Raising my rampired walls of gold as transparent as glass,
Eager to do and die, yield each his place to the rest:
For higher still and higher (as a runner tips with fire,
When a great illumination surprises a festal night—
Outlining round and round Rome's dome from space to spire)
Up, the pinnacled glory reached, and the pride of my soul was in sight.

4.

In sight? Not half! for it seemed, it was certain, to match man's birth,
Nature in turn conceived, obeying an impulse as I;
And the emulous heaven yearned down, made effort to reach the earth,
As the earth had done her best, in my passion, to scale the sky:
Novel splendours burst forth, grew familiar and dwelt with mine,
Not a point nor peak but found and fixed its wandering star;
Meteor-moons, balls of blaze: and they did not pale nor pine,
For earth had attained to heaven, there was no more near nor far.

5.

Nay more; for there wanted not who walked in the glare and glow,
Presences plain in the place; or, fresh from the Protoplast,
Furnished for ages to come, when a kindlier wind should blow,
Lured now to begin and live, in a house to their liking at last;
Or else the wonderful Dead who have passed through the body and gone,
But were back once more to breathe in an old world worth their new:
What never had been, was now; what was, as it shall be anon;
And what is,—shall I say, matched both? for I was made perfect too.

6.

All through my keys that gave their sounds to a wish of my soul,
All through my soul that praised as its wish flowed visibly forth,
All through music and me! For think, had I painted the whole,
Why, there it had stood, to see, nor the process so wonder-worth:
Had I written the same, made verse—still, effect proceeds from cause,
Ye know why the forms are fair, ye hear how the tale is told;
It is all triumphant art, but art in obedience to laws,
Painter and poet are proud in the artist-list enrolled:—

7.

But here is the finger of God, a flash of the will that can,
Existent behind all laws, that made them and, lo, they are!
And I know not if, save in this, such gift be allowed to man,
That out of three sounds he frame, not a fourth sound, but a star.
Consider it well: each tone of our scale in itself is nought;
It is everywhere in the world—loud, soft, and all is said:
Give it to me to use! I mix it with two in my thought:
And, there! Ye have heard and seen: consider and bow the head!

8.

Well, it is gone at last, the palace of music I reared;
Gone! and the good tears start, the praises that come too slow;
For one is assured at first, one scarce can say that he feared,
That he even gave it a thought, the gone thing was to go.
Never to be again! But many more of the kind
As good, nay, better perchance: is this your comfort to me?
To me, who must be saved because I cling with my mind
To the same, same self, same love, same God: ay, what was, shall be.

9.

Therefore to whom turn I but to Thee, the ineffable Name?
  Builder and maker, Thou, of houses not made with hands!
What, have fear of change from Thee who art ever the same?
  Doubt that Thy power can fill the heart that Thy power expands?
There shall never be one lost good! What was, shall live as before;
  The evil is null, is nought, is silence implying sound;
What was good, shall be good, with, for evil, so much good more;
  On the earth the broken arcs; in the heaven, a perfect round.

10.

All we have willed or hoped or dreamed of good, shall exist;
  Not its semblance, but itself; no beauty, nor good, nor power
Whose voice has gone forth, but each survives for the melodist
  When eternity affirms the conception of an hour.
The high that proved too high, the heroic for earth too hard,
  The passion that left the ground to lose itself in the sky,
Are music sent up to God by the lover and the bard;
  Enough that He heard it once: we shall hear it by-and-by.

11.

And what is our failure here but a triumph's evidence
  For the fulness of the days? Have we withered or agonized?
Why else was the pause prolonged but that singing might issue thence?
  Why rushed the discords in but that harmony should be prized?
Sorrow is hard to bear, and doubt is slow to clear,
  Each sufferer says his say, his scheme of the weal and woe:
But God has a few of us whom He whispers in the ear;
  The rest may reason and welcome: 'tis we musicians know.

12.

Well, it is earth with me; silence resumes her reign:
  I will be patient and proud, and soberly acquiesce.
Give me the keys. I feel for the common chord again,
  Sliding by semitones, till I sink to the minor,—yes,
And I blunt it into a ninth, and I stand on alien ground,
  Surveying awhile the heights I rolled from into the deep;
Which, hark, I have dared and done, for my resting-place is found,
  The C Major of this life: so, now I will try to sleep.

Rabbi Ben Ezra

1.

Grow old along with me!
The best is yet to be,
The last of life, for which the first was made:
Our times are in His hand
Who saith "A whole I planned,
Youth shows but half; trust God: see all, nor be afraid!"

2.

Not that, amassing flowers,
Youth sighed "Which rose make ours,
Which lily leave and then as best recall?"
Not that, admiring stars,
It yearned "Nor Jove, nor Mars;
Mine be some figured flame which blends, transcends them all!"

3.

Not for such hopes and fears
Annulling youth's brief years,
Do I remonstrate: folly wide the mark!
Rather I prize the doubt
Low kinds exist without,
Finished and finite clods, untroubled by a spark.

4.

Poor vaunt of life indeed,
Were man but formed to feed
On joy, to solely seek and find and feast:
Such feasting ended, then
As sure an end to men;
Irks care the crop-full bird? Frets doubt the maw-crammed beast?

5.

Rejoice we are allied
To That which doth provide
And not partake, effect and not receive!
A spark disturbs our clod;
Nearer we hold of God
Who gives, than of His tribes that take, I must believe.

6.

Then, welcome each rebuff
That turns earth's smoothness rough,
Each sting that bids nor sit nor stand but go!
Be our joys three-parts pain!
Strive, and hold cheap the strain;
Learn, nor account the pang; dare, never grudge the throe!

7.

For thence,—a paradox
Which comforts while it mocks,—
Shall life succeed in that it seems to fail:
What I aspired to be,
And was not, comforts me:
A brute I might have been, but would not sink i' the scale.

8.

What is he but a brute
Whose flesh has soul to suit,
Whose spirit works lest arms and legs want play?
To man, propose this test—
Thy body at its best,
How far can that project thy soul on its lone way?

9.

Yet gifts should prove their use:
I own the Past profuse
Of power each side, perfection every turn:
Eyes, ears took in their dole,
Brain treasured up the whole;
Should not the heart beat once "How good to live and learn?"

10.

Not once beat "Praise be Thine!
I see the whole design,
I, who saw Power, see now Love perfect too:
Perfect I call Thy plan:
Thanks that I was a man!
Maker, remake, complete,—I trust what Thou shalt do!"

11.

For pleasant is this flesh;
Our soul, in its rose-mesh
Pulled ever to the earth, still yearns for rest:
Would we some prize might hold
To match those manifold
Possessions of the brute,—gain most, as we did best!

12.

Let us not always say
"Spite of this flesh to-day
I strove, made head, gained ground upon the whole!"
As the bird wings and sings,
Let us cry "All good things
Are ours, nor soul helps flesh more, now, than flesh helps soul!"

13.

Therefore I summon age
To grant youth's heritage,
Life's struggle having so far reached its term:
Thence shall I pass, approved
A man, for aye removed
From the developed brute; a God though in the germ.

14.

And I shall thereupon
Take rest, ere I be gone
Once more on my adventure brave and new:
Fearless and unperplexed,
When I wage battle next,
What weapons to select, what armour to indue.

15.

Youth ended, I shall try
My gain or loss thereby;
Be the fire ashes, what survives is gold:
And I shall weigh the same,
Give life its praise or blame:
Young, all lay in dispute; I shall know, being old.

16.

For note, when evening shuts,
A certain moment cuts
The deed off, calls the glory from the grey:
A whisper from the west
Shoots—"Add this to the rest,
Take it and try its worth: here dies another day."

17.

So, still within this life,
Though lifted o'er its strife,
Let me discern, compare, pronounce at last,
"This rage was right i' the main,
That acquiescence vain:
The Future I may face now I have proved the Past."

18.

For more is not reserved
To man, with soul just nerved
To act to-morrow what he learns to-day:
Here, work enough to watch
The Master work, and catch
Hints of the proper craft, tricks of the tool's true play.

19.

As it was better, youth
Should strive, through acts uncouth,
Toward making, than repose on aught found made:
So, better, age, exempt
From strife, should know, than tempt
Further. Thou waitedst age; wait death nor be afraid!

20.

Enough now, if the Right
And Good and Infinite
Be named here, as thou callest thy hand thine own,
With knowledge absolute,
Subject to no dispute
From fools that crowded youth, nor let thee feel alone.

21.

Be there, for once and all,
Severed great minds from small,
Announced to each his station in the Past!
Was I, the world arraigned,
Were they, my soul disdained,
Right? Let age speak the truth and give us peace at last!

22.

Now, who shall arbitrate?
Ten men love what I hate,
Shun what I follow, slight what I receive;
Ten, who in ears and eyes
Match me: we all surmise,
They, this thing, and I, that: whom shall my soul believe?

23.

Not on the vulgar mass
Called "work," must sentence pass,
Things done, that took the eye and had the price;
O'er which, from level stand,
The low world laid its hand,
Found straightway to its mind, could value in a trice:

24.

But all, the world's coarse thumb
And finger failed to plumb,
So passed in making up the main account;
All instincts immature,
All purposes unsure,
That weighed not as his work, yet swelled the man's amount:

25.

Thoughts hardly to be packed
Into a narrow act,
Fancies that broke through language and escaped;
All I could never be,
All, men ignored in me,
This, I was worth to God, whose wheel the pitcher shaped.

26.

Ay, note that Potter's wheel,
That metaphor! and feel
Why time spins fast, why passive lies our clay,—
Thou, to whom fools propound,
When the wine makes its round,
"Since life fleets, all is change; the Past gone, seize to-day!"

27.

Fool! All that is, at all,
Lasts ever, past recall;
Earth changes, but thy soul and God stand sure:
What entered into thee,
That was, is, and shall be:
Time's wheel runs back or stops; Potter and clay endure.

28.

He fixed thee mid this dance
Of plastic circumstance,
This Present, thou, forsooth, wouldst fain arrest:
Machinery just meant
To give thy soul its bent,
Try thee and turn thee forth, sufficiently impressed.

29.

What though the earlier grooves
Which ran the laughing loves
Around thy base, no longer pause and press?
What though, about thy rim,
Scull-things in order grim
Grow out, in graver mood, obey the sterner stress?

30.

Look not thou down but up!
To uses of a cup,
The festal board, lamp's flash and trumpet's peal,
The new wine's foaming flow,
The Master's lips a-glow!
Thou, heaven's consummate cup, what need'st thou with
earth's wheel?

31.

But I need, now as then,
Thee, God, who mouldest men;
And since, not even while the whirl was worst,
Did I,—to the wheel of life
With shapes and colours rife,
Bound dizzily,—mistake my end, to slake Thy thirst:

32.

So, take and use Thy work:
Amend what flaws may lurk,
What strain o' the stuff, what warpings past the aim!
My times be in Thy hand!
Perfect the cup as planned!
Let age approve of youth, and death complete the same!

A Death in the Desert

[Supposed of Pamphylax the Antiochene:
It is a parchment, of my rolls the fifth,
Hath three skins glued together, is all Greek,
And goeth from *Epsilon* down to *Mu*:
Lies second in the surnamed Chosen Chest,
Stained and conserved with juice of terebinth,
Covered with cloth of hair, and lettered *Xi*,
From Xanthus, my wife's uncle, now at peace:
Mu and *Epsilon* stand for my own name,
I may not write it, but I make a cross
To show I wait His coming, with the rest,
And leave off here: beginneth Pamphylax.]
I said, "If one should wet his lips with wine,
And slip the broadest plantain-leaf we find,
Or else the lappet of a linen robe,
Into the water-vessel, lay it right,
And cool his forehead just above the eyes,
The while a brother, kneeling either side,
Should chafe each hand and try to make it warm,—
He is not so far gone but he might speak."

This did not happen in the outer cave,
Nor in the secret chamber of the rock,
Where, sixty days since the decree was out,
We had him, bedded on a camel-skin,
And waited for his dying all the while;
But in the midmost grotto: since noon's light
Reached there a little, and we would not lose
The last of what might happen on his face.

I at the head, and Xanthus at the feet,
With Valens and the Boy, had lifted him,
And brought him from the chamber in the depths,
And laid him in the light where we might see:
For certain smiles began about his mouth,
And his lids moved, presageful of the end.

Beyond, and half way up the mouth o' the cave,
The Bactrian convert, having his desire,
Kept watch, and made pretence to graze a goat
That gave us milk, on rags of various herb,
Plantain and quitch, the rocks' shade keeps alive:
So that if any thief or soldier passed,
(Because the persecution was aware)
Yielding the goat up promptly with his life,
Such man might pass on, joyful at a prize,
Nor care to pry into the cool o' the cave.
Outside was all noon and the burning blue.

"Here is wine," answered Xanthus,—dropped a drop;
I stooped and placed the lap of cloth aright,
Then chafed his right hand, and the Boy his left:
But Valens had bethought him, and produced
And broke a ball of nard, and made perfume.
Only, he did—not so much wake, as—turn
And smile a little, as a sleeper does
If any dear one call him, touch his face—
And smiles and loves, but will not be disturbed.

Then Xanthus said a prayer, but still he slept:
It is the Xanthus that escaped to Rome,
Was burned, and could not write the chronicle.

Then the Boy sprang up from his knees, and ran,
Stung by the splendour of a sudden thought,
And fetched the seventh plate of graven lead
Out of the secret chamber, found a place,
Pressing with finger on the deeper dints,
And spoke, as 'twere his mouth proclaiming first,
"I am the Resurrection and the Life."

Whereat he opened his eyes wide at once,
And sat up of himself, and looked at us;
And thenceforth nobody pronounced a word:
Only, outside, the Bactrian cried his cry
Like the lone desert-bird that wears the ruff,
As signal we were safe, from time to time.

First he said, "If a friend declared to me,
This my son Valens, this my other son,
Were James and Peter,—nay, declared as well
This lad was very John,—I could believe!
—Could, for a moment, doubtlessly believe:
So is myself withdrawn into my depths,
The soul retreated from the perished brain
Whence it was wont to feel and use the world
Through these dull members, done with long ago.
Yet I myself remain; I feel myself:
And there is nothing lost. Let be, awhile!"

[This is the doctrine he was wont to teach,
How divers persons witness in each man,
Three souls which make up one soul: first, to wit,
A soul of each and all the bodily parts,
Seated therein, which works, and is what Does,
And has the use of earth, and ends the man
Downward: but, tending upward for advice,
Grows into, and again is grown into
By the next soul, which, seated in the brain,
Useth the first with its collected use,
And feeleth, thinketh, willeth,—is what Knows:
Which, duly tending upward in its turn,
Grows into, and again is grown into
By the last soul, that uses both the first,
Subsisting whether they assist or no,

And, constituting man's self, is what Is—
And leans upon the former, makes it play,
As that played off the first: and, tending up,
Holds, is upheld by, God, and ends the man
Upward in that dread point of intercourse,
Nor needs a place, for it returns to Him
What Does, what Knows, what Is; three souls, one man.
I give the glossa of Theotypas.]

And then, "A stick, once fire from end to end;
Now, ashes save the tip that holds a spark!
Yet, blow the spark, it runs back, spreads itself
A little where the fire was: thus I urge
The soul that served me, till it task once more
What ashes of my brain have kept their shape,
And these make effort on the last o' the flesh,
Trying to taste again the truth of things—"
(He smiled)—"their very superficial truth;
As that ye are my sons, that it is long
Since James and Peter had release by death,
And I am only he, your brother John,
Who saw and heard, and could remember all.
Remember all! It is not much to say.
What if the truth broke on me from above
As once and oft-times? Such might hap again:
Doubtlessly He might stand in presence here,
With head wool-white, eyes flame, and feet like brass,
The sword and the seven stars, as I have seen—
I who now shudder only and surmise
'How did your brother bear that sight and live?'

"If I live yet, it is for good, more love
Through me to men: be nought but ashes here
That keep awhile my semblance, who was John,—
Still, when they scatter, there is left on earth
No one alive who knew (consider this!)
—Saw with his eyes and handled with his hands
That which was from the first, the Word of Life.
How will it be when none more saith 'I saw'?

"Such ever was love's way: to rise, it stoops.
Since I, whom Christ's mouth taught, was bidden teach,

I went, for many years, about the world,
Saying 'It was so; so I heard and saw,'
Speaking as the case asked: and men believed.
Afterward came the message to myself
In Patmos isle; I was not bidden teach,
But simply listen, take a book and write,
Nor set down other than the given word,
With nothing left to my arbitrament
To choose or change: I wrote, and men believed.
Then, for my time grew brief, no message more,
No call to write again, I found a way,
And, reasoning from my knowledge, merely taught
Men should, for love's sake, in love's strength, believe;
Or I would pen a letter to a friend
And urge the same as friend, nor less nor more:
Friends said I reasoned rightly, and believed.
But at the last, why, I seemed left alive
Like a sea-jelly weak on Patmos strand,
To tell dry sea-beach gazers how I fared
When there was mid-sea, and the mighty things;
Left to repeat, 'I saw, I heard, I knew,'
And go all over the old ground again,
With Antichrist already in the world,
And many Antichrists, who answered prompt
'Am I not Jasper as thyself art John?
Nay, young, whereas through age thou mayest forget:
Wherefore, explain, or how shall we believe?'
I never thought to call down fire on such,
Or, as in wonderful and early days,
Pick up the scorpion, tread the serpent dumb;
But patient stated much of the Lord's life
Forgotten or misdelivered, and let it work:
Since much that at the first, in deed and word,
Lay simply and sufficiently exposed,
Had grown (or else my soul was grown to match,
Fed through such years, familiar with such light,
Guarded and guided still to see and speak)
Of new significance and fresh result;
What first were guessed as points, I now knew stars,
And named them in the Gospel I have writ.
For men said, 'It is getting long ago:'

'Where is the promise of His coming?'—asked
These young ones in their strength, as loth to wait,
Of me who, when their sires were born, was old.
I, for I loved them, answered, joyfully,
Since I was there, and helpful in my age;
And, in the main, I think such men believed.
Finally, thus endeavouring, I fell sick,
Ye brought me here, and I supposed the end,
And went to sleep with one thought that, at least,
Though the whole earth should lie in wickedness,
We had the truth, might leave the rest to God.
Yet now I wake in such decrepitude
As I had slidden down and fallen afar,
Past even the presence of my former self,
Grasping the while for stay at facts which snap,
Till I am found away from my own world,
Feeling for foot-hold through a blank profound,
Along with unborn people in strange lands,
Who say—I hear said or conceive they say—
'Was John at all, and did he say he saw?
Assure us, ere we ask what he might see!'

"And how shall I assure them? Can they share
—They, who have flesh, a veil of youth and strength
About each spirit, that needs must bide its time,
Living and learning still as years assist
Which wear the thickness thin, and let man see—
With me who hardly am withheld at all,
But shudderingly, scarce a shred between,
Lie bare to the universal prick of light?
Is it for nothing we grow old and weak,
We whom God loves? When pain ends, gain ends too.
To me, that story—ay, that Life and Death
Of which I wrote 'it was'—to me, it is;
—Is, here and now: I apprehend nought else.
Is not God now i' the world His power first made?
Is not His love at issue still with sin,
Closed with and cast and conquered, crucified
Visibly when a wrong is done on earth?
Love, wrong, and pain, what see I else around?
Yea, and the Resurrection and Uprise

To the right hand of the throne—what is it beside,
When such truth, breaking bounds, o'erfloods my soul,
And, as I saw the sin and death, even so
See I the need yet transiency of both,
The good and glory consummated thence?
I saw the Power; I see the Love, once weak,
Resume the Power: and in this word 'I see,'
Lo, there is recognized the Spirit of both
That, moving o'er the spirit of man, unblinds
His eye and bids him look. These are, I see;
But ye, the children, His beloved ones too,
Ye need,—as I should use an optic glass
I wondered at erewhile, somewhere i' the world,
It had been given a crafty smith to make;
A tube, he turned on objects brought too close,
Lying confusedly insubordinate
For the unassisted eye to master once:
Look through his tube, at distance now they lay,
Become succinct, distinct, so small, so clear!
Just thus, ye needs must apprehend what truth
I see, reduced to plain historic fact,
Diminished into clearness, proved a point
And far away: ye would withdraw your sense
From out eternity, strain it upon time,
Then stand before that fact, that Life and Death,
Stay there at gaze, till it dispart, dispread,
As though a star should open out, all sides,
And grow the world on you, as it is my world.

"For life, with all it yields of joy and woe,
And hope and fear,—believe the aged friend,—
Is just our chance o' the prize of learning love,
How love might be, hath been indeed, and is;
And that we hold thenceforth to the uttermost
Such prize despite the envy of the world,
And, having gained truth, keep truth: that is all.
But see the double way wherein we are led,
How the soul learns diversely from the flesh!
With flesh, that hath so little time to stay,
And yields mere basement for the soul's emprise,
Expect prompt teaching. Helpful was the light,

And warmth was cherishing and food was choice
To every man's flesh, thousand years ago,
As now to yours and mine; the body sprang
At once to the height, and stayed: but the soul,—no!
Since sages who, this noontide, meditate
In Rome or Athens, may descry some point
Of the eternal power, hid yestereve;
And as thereby the power's whole mass extends,
So much extends the æther floating o'er,
The love that tops the might, the Christ in God.
Then, as new lessons shall be learned in these
Till earth's work stop and useless time run out,
So duly, daily, needs provision be
For keeping the soul's prowess possible,
Building new barriers as the old decay,
Saving us from evasion of life's proof,
Putting the question ever, 'Does God love,
And will ye hold that truth against the world?'
Ye know there needs no second proof with good
Gained for our flesh from any earthly source:
We might go freezing, ages,—give us fire,
Thereafter we judge fire at its full worth,
And guard it safe through every chance, ye know!
That fable of Prometheus and his theft,
How mortals gained Jove's fiery flower, grows old
(I have been used to hear the pagans own)
And out of mind; but fire, howe'er its birth,
Here is it, precious to the sophist now
Who laughs the myth of Æschylus to scorn,
As precious to those satyrs of his play,
Who touched it in gay wonder at the thing.
While were it so with the soul,—this gift of truth
Once grasped, were this our soul's gain safe, and sure
To prosper as the body's gain is wont,—
Why, man's probation would conclude, his earth
Crumble; for he both reasons and decides,
Weighs first, then chooses: will he give up fire
For gold or purple once he knows its worth?
Could he give Christ up were His worth as plain?
Therefore, I say, to test man, shift the proofs,
Nor may he grasp that fact like other fact,

And straightway in his life acknowledge it,
As, say, the indubitable bliss of fire.
Sigh ye, 'It had been easier once than now'?
To give you answer I am left alive;
Look at me who was present from the first!
Ye know what things I saw; then came a test,
My first, befitting me who so had seen:
'Forsake the Christ thou sawest transfigured, Him
Who trod the sea and brought the dead to life?
What should wring this from thee?'—ye laugh and ask.
What wrung it? Even a torchlight and a noise,
The sudden Roman faces, violent hands,
And fear of what the Jews might do! Just that,
And, it is written, 'I forsook and fled':
There was my trial, and it ended thus.
Ay, but my soul had gained its truth, could grow:
Another year or two,—what little child,
What tender woman that had seen no least
Of all my sights, but barely heard them told,
Who did not clasp the cross with a light laugh,
Or wrap the burning robe round, thanking God?
Well, was truth safe for ever, then? Not so.
Already had begun the silent work
Whereby truth, deadened of its absolute blaze,
Might need love's eye to pierce the o'erstretched doubt:
Teachers were busy, whispering 'All is true
As the aged ones report; but youth can reach
Where age gropes dimly, weak with stir and strain,
And the full doctrine slumbers till to-day.'
Thus, what the Roman's lowered spear was found,
A bar to me who touched and handled truth,
Now proved the glozing of some new shrewd tongue,
This Ebion, this Cerinthus or their mates,
Till imminent was the outcry 'Save us Christ!'
Whereon I stated much of the Lord's life
Forgotten or misdelivered, and let it work.
Such work done, as it will be, what comes next?
What do I hear say, or conceive men say,
'Was John at all, and did he say he saw?
Assure us, ere we ask what he might see!'

"Is this indeed a burthen for late days,
And may I help to bear it with you all,
Using my weakness which becomes your strength?
For if a babe were born inside this grot,
Grew to a boy here, heard us praise the sun,
Yet had but yon sole glimmer in light's place,—
One loving him and wishful he should learn,
Would much rejoice himself was blinded first
Month by month here, so made to understand
How eyes, born darkling, apprehend amiss:
I think I could explain to such a child
There was more glow outside than gleams he caught,
Ay, nor need urge 'I saw it, so believe!'
It is a heavy burthen you shall bear
In latter days, new lands, or old grown strange,
Left without me, which must be very soon.
What is the doubt, my brothers? Quick with it!
I see you stand conversing, each new face,
Either in fields, of yellow summer eves,
On islets yet unnamed amid the sea;
Or pace for shelter 'neath a portico
Out of the crowd in some enormous town
Where now the larks sing in a solitude;
Or muse upon blank heaps of stone and sand
Idly conjectured to be Ephesus:
And no one asks his fellow any more
'Where is the promise of His coming?' but
'Was he revealed in any of His lives,
As Power, as Love, as Influencing Soul?'

"Quick, for time presses, tell the whole mind out,
And let us ask and answer and be saved!
My book speaks on, because it cannot pass;
One listens quietly, nor scoffs but pleads
'Here is a tale of things done ages since;
What truth was ever told the second day?
Wonders, that would prove doctrine, go for nought.
Remains the doctrine, love; well, we must love,
And what we love most, power and love in one,
Let us acknowledge on the record here,
Accepting these in Christ: must Christ then be?

Has He been? Did not we ourselves make Him?
Our mind receives but what it holds, no more.
First of the love, then; we acknowledge Christ—
A proof we comprehend His love, a proof
We had such love already in ourselves,
Knew first what else we should not recognize.
'Tis mere projection from man's inmost mind,
And, what he loves, thus falls reflected back,
Becomes accounted somewhat out of him;
He throws it up in air, it drops down earth's,
With shape, name, story added, man's old way.
How prove you Christ came otherwise at least?
Next try the power: He made and rules the world:
Certes there is a world once made, now ruled,
Unless things have been ever as we see.
Our sires declared a charioteer's yoked steeds
Brought the sun up the east and down the west,
Which only of itself now rises, sets,
As if a hand impelled it and a will,—
Thus they long thought, they who had will and hands:
But the new question's whisper is distinct,
'Wherefore must all force needs be like ourselves?
We have the hands, the will; what made and drives
The sun is force, is law, is named, not known,
While will and love we do know; marks of these,
Eye-witnesses attest, so books declare—
As that, to punish or reward our race,
The sun at undue times arose or set
Or else stood still: what do not men affirm?
But earth requires as urgently reward
Or punishment to-day as years ago,
And none expects the sun will interpose:
Therefore it was mere passion and mistake,
Or erring zeal for right, which changed the truth.
Go back, far, farther, to the birth of things;
Ever the will, the intelligence, the love,
Man's!—which he gives, supposing he but finds,
As late he gave head, body, hands and feet,
To help these in what forms he called his gods.
First, Jove's brow, Juno's eyes were swept away,
But Jove's wrath, Juno's pride continued long;

As last, will, power, and love discarded these,
So law in turn discards power, love, and will.
What proveth God is otherwise at least?
All else, projection from the mind of man!'

"Nay, do not give me wine, for I am strong,
But place my gospel where I put my hands.

"I say that man was made to grow, not stop;
That help, he needed once, and needs no more,
Having grown but an inch by, is withdrawn:
For he hath new needs, and new helps to these.
This imports solely, man should mount on each
New height in view; the help whereby he mounts,
The ladder-rung his foot has left, may fall,
Since all things suffer change save God the Truth.
Man apprehends Him newly at each stage
Whereat earth's ladder drops, its service done;
And nothing shall prove twice what once was proved.
You stick a garden-plot with ordered twigs
To show inside lie germs of herbs unborn,
And check the careless step would spoil their birth;
But when herbs wave, the guardian twigs may go,
Since should ye doubt of virtues, question kinds,
It is no longer for old twigs ye look,
Which proved once underneath lay store of seed,
But to the herb's self, by what light ye boast,
For what fruit's signs are. This book's fruit is plain,
Nor miracles need prove it any more.
Doth the fruit show? Then miracles bade 'ware
At first of root and stem, saved both till now
From trampling ox, rough boar and wanton goat.
What? Was man made a wheelwork to wind up,
And be discharged, and straight wound up anew?
No!—grown, his growth lasts; taught, he ne'er forgets:
May learn a thousand things, not twice the same.

"This might be pagan teaching: now hear mine.

"I say, that as the babe, you feed awhile,
Becomes a boy and fit to feed himself,
So, minds at first must be spoon-fed with truth:
When they can eat, babe's nurture is withdrawn.

I fed the babe whether it would or no:
I bid the boy or feed himself or starve.
I cried once, 'That ye may believe in Christ,
Behold this blind man shall receive his sight!'
I cry now, 'Urgest thou, *for I am shrewd*
And smile at stories how John's word could cure—
Repeat that miracle and take my faith?'
I say, that miracle was duly wrought
When, save for it, no faith was possible.
Whether a change were wrought i' the shows o' the world,
Whether the change came from our minds which see
Of shows o' the world so much as and no more
Than God wills for His purpose,—(what do I
See now, suppose you, there where you see rock
Round us?)—I know not; such was the effect,
So faith grew, making void more miracles
Because too much: they would compel, not help.
I say, the acknowledgment of God in Christ
Accepted by thy reason, solves for thee
All questions in the earth and out of it,
And has so far advanced thee to be wise.
Wouldst thou unprove this to re-prove the proved?
In life's mere minute, with power to use that proof,
Leave knowledge and revert to how it sprung?
Thou hast it; use it and forthwith, or die!

"For I say, this is death and the sole death,
When a man's loss comes to him from his gain,
Darkness from light, from knowledge ignorance,
And lack of love from love made manifest;
A lamp's death when, replete with oil, it chokes;
A stomach's when, surcharged with food, it starves.
With ignorance was surety of a cure.
When man, appalled at nature, questioned first
'What if there lurk a might behind this might?'
He needed satisfaction God could give,
And did give, as ye have the written word:
But when he finds might still redouble might,
Yet asks, 'Since all is might, what use of will?'
—Will, the one source of might,—he being man
With a man's will and a man's might, to teach

In little how the two combine in large,—
That man has turned round on himself and stands,
Which in the course of nature is, to die.

"And when man questioned, 'What if there be love
Behind the will and might, as real as they?'—
He needed satisfaction God could give,
And did give, as ye have the written word:
But when, beholding that love everywhere,
He reasons, 'Since such love is everywhere,
And since ourselves can love and would be loved,
We ourselves make the love, and Christ was not,'—
How shall ye help this man who knows himself,
That he must love and would be loved again,
Yet, owning his own love that proveth Christ,
Rejecteth Christ through very need of Him?
The lamp o'erswims with oil, the stomach flags
Loaded with nurture, and that man's soul dies.

"If he rejoin, 'But this was all the while
A trick; the fault was, first of all, in thee,
Thy story of the places, names and dates,
Where, when and how the ultimate truth had rise,
—Thy prior truth, at last discovered none,
Whence now the second suffers detriment.
What good of giving knowledge if, because
Of the manner of the gift, its profit fail?
And why refuse what modicum of help
Had stopped the after-doubt, impossible
I' the face of truth—truth absolute, uniform?
Why must I hit of this and miss of that,
Distinguish just as I be weak or strong,
And not ask of thee and have answer prompt,
Was this once, was it not once?—then and now
And evermore, plain truth from man to man.
Is John's procedure just the heathen bard's?
Put question of his famous play again
How for the ephemerals' sake Jove's fire was filched,
And carried in a cane and brought to earth:
The fact is in the fable, cry the wise,
Mortals obtained the boon, so much is fact,
Though fire be spirit and produced on earth.

As with the Titan's, so now with thy tale:
Why breed in us perplexity, mistake,
Nor tell the whole truth in the proper words?'

"I answer, Have ye yet to argue out
The very primal thesis, plainest law,
—Man is not God but hath God's end to serve,
A master to obey, a course to take,
Somewhat to cast off, somewhat to become?
Grant this, then man must pass from old to new,
From vain to real, from mistake to fact:
From what once seemed good, to what now proves best.
How could man have progression otherwise?
Before the point was mooted 'What is God?'
No savage man inquired 'What am myself?'
Much less replied, 'First, last, and best of things.'
Man takes that title now if he believes
Might can exist with neither will nor love,
In God's case—what he names now Nature's Law—
While in himself he recognizes love
No less than might and will: and rightly takes.
Since if man prove the sole existent thing
Where these combine, whatever their degree,
However weak the might or will or love,
So they be found there, put in evidence,—
He is as surely higher in the scale
Than any might with neither love nor will,
As life, apparent in the poorest midge,
When the faint dust-speck flits, ye guess its wing
Is marvellous beyond dead Atlas' self:
I give such to the midge for resting-place!
Thus, man proves best and highest—God, in fine,
And thus the victory leads but to defeat,
The gain to loss, best rise to the worst fall,
His life becomes impossible, which is death.

"But if, appealing thence, he cower, avouch
He is mere man, and in humility
Neither may know God nor mistake himself;
I point to the immediate consequence
And say, by such confession straight he falls
Into man's place, a thing nor God nor beast,

Made to know that he can know and not more:
Lower than God who knows all and can all,
Higher than beasts which know and can so far
As each beast's limit, perfect to an end,
Nor conscious that they know, nor craving more;
While man knows partly but conceives beside,
Creeps ever on from fancies to the fact,
And in this striving, this converting air
Into a solid he may grasp and use,
Finds progress, man's distinctive mark alone,
Not God's, and not the beasts': God is, they are,
Man partly is and wholly hopes to be.
Such progress could no more attend his soul
Were all it struggles after found at first
And guesses changed to knowledge absolute,
Than motion wait his body, were all else
Than it the solid earth on every side,
Where now through space he moves from rest to rest.
Man, therefore, thus conditioned, must expect
He could not, what he knows now, know at first;
What he considers that he knows to-day,
Come but to-morrow, he will find misknown;
Getting increase of knowledge, since he learns
Because he lives, which is to be a man,
Set to instruct himself by his past self:
First, like the brute, obliged by facts to learn,
Next, as man may, obliged by his own mind,
Bent, habit, nature, knowledge turned to law.
God's gift was that man should conceive of truth
And yearn to gain it, catching at mistake,
As midway help till he reach fact indeed.
The statuary ere he mould a shape
Boasts a like gift, the shape's idea, and next
The aspiration to produce the same;
So, taking clay, he calls his shape thereout,
Cries ever 'Now I have the thing I see':
Yet all the while goes changing what was wrought,
From falsehood like the truth, to truth itself.
How were it had he cried 'I see no face,
No breast, no feet i' the ineffectual clay?'
Rather commend him that he clapped his hands,

And laughed 'It is my shape and lives again!'
Enjoyed the falsehood, touched it on to truth,
Until yourselves applaud the flesh indeed
In what is still flesh-imitating clay.
Right in you, right in him, such way be man's!
God only makes the live shape at a jet.
Will ye renounce this pact of creatureship?
The pattern on the Mount subsists no more,
Seemed awhile, then returned to nothingness;
But copies, Moses strove to make thereby,
Serve still and are replaced as time requires:
By these, make newest vessels, reach the type!
If ye demur, this judgment on your head,
Never to reach the ultimate, angels' law,
Indulging every instinct of the soul
There where law, life, joy, impulse are one thing!

"Such is the burthen of the latest time.
I have survived to hear it with my ears,
Answer it with my lips: does this suffice?
For if there be a further woe than such,
Wherein my brothers struggling need a hand,
So long as any pulse is left in mine,
May I be absent even longer yet,
Plucking the blind ones back from the abyss,
Though I should tarry a new hundred years!"

But he was dead; 'twas about noon, the day
Somewhat declining: we five buried him
That eve, and then, dividing, went five ways,
And I, disguised, returned to Ephesus.

By this, the cave's mouth must be filled with sand.
Valens is lost, I know not of his trace;
The Bactrian was but a wild, childish man,
And could not write nor speak, but only loved:
So, lest the memory of this go quite,
Seeing that I to-morrow fight the beasts,
I tell the same to Phoebas, whom believe!
For many look again to find that face,
Beloved John's to whom I ministered,
Somewhere in life about the world; they err:

Either mistaking what was darkly spoke
At ending of his book, as he relates,
Or misconceiving somewhat of this speech
Scattered from mouth to mouth, as I suppose.
Believe ye will not see him any more
About the world with his divine regard!
For all was as I say, and now the man
Lies as he lay once, breast to breast with God.

[Cerinthus read and mused; one added this:

"If Christ, as thou affirmest, be of men
Mere man, the first and best but nothing more,—
Account Him, for reward of what He was,
Now and for ever, wretchedest of all.
For see; Himself conceived of life as love,
Conceived of love as what must enter in,
Fill up, make one with His each soul He loved:
Thus much for man's joy, all men's joy for Him.
Well, He is gone, thou sayest, to fit reward.
But by this time are many souls set free,
And very many still retained alive:
Nay, should His coming be delayed awhile,
Say, ten years longer (twelve years, some compute)
See if, for every finger of thy hands,
There be not found, that day the world shall end,
Hundreds of souls, each holding by Christ's word
That He will grow incorporate with all,
With me as Pamphylax, with him as John,
Groom for each bride! Can a mere man do this?
Yet Christ saith, this He lived and died to do.
Call Christ, then, the illimitable God,
Or lost!"

But 'twas Cerinthus that is lost.]

Caliban upon Setebos; or, Natural Theology in the Island

"Thou thoughtest that I was altogether such an one as thyself."

['Will sprawl, now that the heat of day is best,
Flat on his belly in the pit's much mire,
With elbows wide, fists clenched to prop his chin;
And, while he kicks both feet in the cool slush,
And feels about his spine small eft-things course,
Run in and out each arm, and make him laugh;
And while above his head a pompion-plant,
Coating the cave-top as a brow its eye,
Creeps down to touch and tickle hair and beard,
And now a flower drops with a bee inside,
And now a fruit to snap at, catch and crunch:
He looks out o'er yon sea which sunbeams cross
And recross till they weave a spider-web,
(Meshes of fire, some great fish breaks at times)
And talks to his own self, howe'er he please,
Touching that other, whom his dam called God.
Because to talk about Him, vexes—ha,
Could He but know! and time to vex is now,
When talk is safer than in winter-time.
Moreover Prosper and Miranda sleep
In confidence he drudges at their task,
And it is good to cheat the pair, and gibe,
Letting the rank tongue blossom into speech.]

Setebos, Setebos, and Setebos!
'Thinketh, He dwelleth i' the cold o' the moon.

'Thinketh He made it, with the sun to match,
But not the stars; the stars came otherwise;
Only made clouds, winds, meteors, such as that:
Also this isle, what lives and grows thereon,
And snaky sea which rounds and ends the same.

'Thinketh, it came of being ill at ease:
He hated that He cannot change His cold,
Nor cure its ache. 'Hath spied an icy fish
That longed to 'scape the rock-stream where she lived,

And thaw herself within the lukewarm brine
O' the lazy sea her stream thrusts far amid,
A crystal spike 'twixt two warm walls of wave;
Only she ever sickened, found repulse
At the other kind of water, not her life,
(Green-dense and dim-delicious, bred o' the sun)
Flounced back from bliss she was not born to breathe,
And in her old bounds buried her despair,
Hating and loving warmth alike: so He.

'Thinketh, He made thereat the sun, this isle,
Trees and the fowls here, beast and creeping thing.
Yon otter, sleek-wet, black, lithe as a leech;
Yon auk, one fire-eye in a ball of foam,
That floats and feeds; a certain badger brown
He hath watched hunt with that slant white-wedge eye
By moonlight; and the pie with the long tongue
That pricks deep into oakwarts for a worm,
And says a plain word when she finds her prize,
But will not eat the ants; the ants themselves
That build a wall of seeds and settled stalks
About their hole—He made all these and more,
Made all we see, and us, in spite: how else?
He could not, Himself, make a second self
To be His mate; as well have made Himself.
He would not make what He mislikes or slights,
An eyesore to Him, or not worth His pains:
But did, in envy, listlessness or sport,
Make what Himself would fain, in a manner, be—
Weaker in most points, stronger in a few,
Worthy, and yet mere playthings all the while,
Things He admires and mocks too,—that is it.
Because, so brave, so better though they be,
It nothing skills if He begin to plague.
Look now, I melt a gourd-fruit into mash,
Add honeycomb and pods, I have perceived,
Which bite like finches when they bill and kiss,—
Then, when froth rises bladdery, drink up all,
Quick, quick, till maggots scamper through my brain;
And throw me on my back i' the seeded thyme,
And wanton, wishing I were born a bird.

Put case, unable to be what I wish,
I yet could make a live bird out of clay:
Would not I take clay, pinch my Caliban
Able to fly?—for, there, see, he hath wings,
And great comb like the hoopoe's to admire,
And there, a sting to do his foes offence,
There, and I will that he begin to live,
Fly to yon rock-top, nip me off the horns
Of grigs high up that make the merry din,
Saucy through their veined wings, and mind me not.
In which feat, if his leg snapped, brittle clay,
And he lay stupid-like,—why, I should laugh;
And if he, spying me, should fall to weep,
Beseech me to be good, repair his wrong,
Bid his poor leg smart less or grow again,—
Well, as the chance were, this might take or else
Not take my fancy: I might hear his cry,
And give the manikin three legs for his one,
Or pluck the other off, leave him like an egg,
And lessoned he was mine and merely clay.
Were this no pleasure, lying in the thyme,
Drinking the mash, with brain become alive,
Making and marring clay at will? So He.

'Thinketh, such shows nor right nor wrong in Him,
Nor kind, nor cruel: He is strong and Lord.
'Am strong myself compared to yonder crabs
That march now from the mountain to the sea;
'Let twenty pass, and stone the twenty-first,
Loving not, hating not, just choosing so.
'Say, the first straggler that boasts purple spots
Shall join the file, one pincer twisted off;
'Say, this bruised fellow shall receive a worm,
And two worms he whose nippers end in red;
As it likes me each time, I do: so He.

Well then, 'supposeth He is good i' the main,
Placable if His mind and ways were guessed,
But rougher than His handiwork, be sure!
Oh, He hath made things worthier than Himself,
And envieth that, so helped, such things do more
Than He who made them! What consoles but this?

That they, unless through Him, do nought at all,
And must submit: what other use in things?
'Hath cut a pipe of pithless elder-joint
That, blown through, gives exact the scream o' the jay
When from her wing you twitch the feathers blue:
Sound this, and little birds that hate the jay
Flock within stone's throw, glad their foe is hurt:
Put case such pipe could prattle and boast forsooth
"I catch the birds, I am the crafty thing,
I make the cry my maker cannot make
With his great round mouth; he must blow through mine!"
Would not I smash it with my foot? So He.

But wherefore rough, why cold and ill at ease?
Aha, that is a question! Ask, for that,
What knows,—the something over Setebos
That made Him, or He, may be, found and fought,
Worsted, drove off and did to nothing, perchance.
There may be something quiet o'er His head,
Out of His reach, that feels nor joy nor grief,
Since both derive from weakness in some way.
I joy because the quails come; would not joy
Could I bring quails here when I have a mind:
This Quiet, all it hath a mind to, doth.
'Esteemeth stars the outposts of its couch,
But never spends much thought nor care that way.
It may look up, work up,—the worse for those
It works on! 'Careth but for Setebos
The many-handed as a cuttle-fish,
Who, making Himself feared through what He does,
Looks up, first, and perceives He cannot soar
To what is quiet and hath happy life;
Next looks down here, and out of very spite
Makes this a bauble-world to ape yon real,
These good things to match those as hips do grapes.
'Tis solace making baubles, ay, and sport.
Himself peeped late, eyed Prosper at his books
Careless and lofty, lord now of the isle:
Vexed, 'stitched a book of broad leaves, arrow-shaped,
Wrote thereon, he knows what, prodigious words;
Has peeled a wand and called it by a name;

Weareth at whiles for an enchanter's robe
The eyed skin of a supple oncelot;
And hath an ounce sleeker than youngling mole,
A four-legged serpent he makes cower and couch,
Now snarl, now hold its breath and mind his eye,
And saith she is Miranda and my wife:
'Keeps for his Ariel a tall pouch-bill crane
He bids go wade for fish and straight disgorge;
Also a sea-beast, lumpish, which he snared,
Blinded the eyes of, and brought somewhat tame,
And split its toe-webs, and now pens the drudge
In a hole o' the rock and calls him Caliban;
A bitter heart that bides its time and bites.
'Plays thus at being Prosper in a way,
Taketh his mirth with make-believes: so He.

His dam held that the Quiet made all things
Which Setebos vexed only: 'holds not so.
Who made them weak, meant weakness He might vex.
Had He meant other, while His hand was in,
Why not make horny eyes no thorn could prick,
Or plate my scalp with bone against the snow,
Or overscale my flesh 'neath joint and joint,
Like an orc's armour? Ay,—so spoil His sport!
He is the One now: only He doth all.

'Saith, He may like, perchance, what profits Him.
Ay, himself loves what does him good; but why?
'Gets good no otherwise. This blinded beast
Loves whoso places flesh-meat on his nose,
But, had he eyes, would want no help, but hate
Or love, just as it liked him: He hath eyes.
Also it pleaseth Setebos to work,
Use all His hands, and exercise much craft,
By no means for the love of what is worked.
'Tasteth, himself, no finer good i' the world
When all goes right, in this safe summer time,
And he wants little, hungers, aches not much,
Than trying what to do with wit and strength.
'Falls to make something: 'piled yon pile of turfs,
And squared and stuck there squares of soft white chalk,
And, with a fish-tooth, scratched a moon on each,

And set up endwise certain spikes of tree,
And crowned the whole with a sloth's skull a-top,
Found dead i' the woods, too hard for one to kill.
No use at all i' the work, for work's sole sake;
'Shall some day knock it down again: so He.

'Saith He is terrible: watch His feats in proof!
One hurricane will spoil six good months' hope.
He hath a spite against me, that I know,
Just as He favours Prosper, who knows why?
So it is, all the same, as well I find.
'Wove wattles half the winter, fenced them firm
With stone and stake to stop she-tortoises
Crawling to lay their eggs here: well, one wave,
Feeling the foot of Him upon its neck,
Gaped as a snake does, lolled out its large tongue,
And licked the whole labour flat: so much for spite.
'Saw a ball flame down late (yonder it lies)
Where, half an hour before, I slept i' the shade:
Often they scatter sparkles: there is force!
'Dug up a newt He may have envied once
And turned to stone, shut up inside a stone.
Please Him and hinder this?—What Prosper does?
Aha, if He would tell me how! Not He!
There is the sport: discover how or die!
All need not die, for of the things o' the isle
Some flee afar, some dive, some run up trees;
Those at His mercy,—why, they please Him most
When . . when . . well, never try the same way twice!
Repeat what act has pleased, He may grow wroth.
You must not know His ways, and play Him off,
Sure of the issue. 'Doth the like himself:
'Spareth a squirrel that it nothing fears
But steals the nut from underneath my thumb,
And when I threat, bites stoutly in defence:
'Spareth an urchin that contrariwise,
Curls up into a ball, pretending death
For fright at my approach: the two ways please.
But what would move my choler more than this,
That either creature counted on its life
To-morrow and next day and all days to come,

Saying forsooth in the inmost of its heart,
"Because he did so yesterday with me,
And otherwise with such another brute,
So must he do henceforth and always."—Ay?
'Would teach the reasoning couple what "must" means!
'Doth as he likes, or wherefore Lord? So He.

'Conceiveth all things will continue thus,
And we shall have to live in fear of Him
So long as He lives, keeps His strength: no change,
If He have done His best, make no new world
To please Him more, so leave off watching this,—
If He surprise not even the Quiet's self
Some strange day,—or, suppose, grow into it
As grubs grow butterflies: else, here are we,
And there is He, and nowhere help at all.

'Believeth with the life, the pain shall stop.
His dam held different, that after death
He both plagued enemies and feasted friends:
Idly! He doth His worst in this our life,
Giving just respite lest we die through pain,
Saving last pain for worst,—with which, an end.
Meanwhile, the best way to escape His ire
Is, not to seem too happy. Sees, himself,
Yonder two flies, with purple films and pink,
Bask on the pompion-bell above: kills both.
'Sees two black painful beetles roll their ball
On head and tail as if to save their lives:
Moves them the stick away they strive to clear.

Even so, 'would have Him misconceive, suppose
This Caliban strives hard and ails no less,
And always, above all else, envies Him.
Wherefore he mainly dances on dark nights,
Moans in the sun, gets under holes to laugh,
And never speaks his mind save housed as now:
Outside, 'groans, curses. If He caught me here,
O'erheard this speech, and asked "What chucklest at?"
'Would, to appease Him, cut a finger off,
Or of my three kid yearlings burn the best,
Or let the toothsome apples rot on tree,

Or push my tame beast for the orc to taste:
While myself lit a fire, and made a song
And sung it, "*What I hate, be consecrate*
To celebrate Thee and Thy state, no mate
For Thee; what see for envy in poor me?"
Hoping the while, since evils sometimes mend,
Warts rub away and sores are cured with slime,
That some strange day, will either the Quiet catch
And conquer Setebos, or likelier He
Decrepit may doze, doze, as good as die.

[What, what? A curtain o'er the world at once!
Crickets stop hissing; not a bird—or, yes,
There scuds His raven that hath told Him all!
It was fool's play, this prattling! Ha! The wind
Shoulders the pillared dust, death's house o' the move,
And fast invading fires begin! White blaze—
A tree's head snaps—and there, there, there, there, there,
His thunder follows! Fool to gibe at Him!
Lo! 'Lieth flat and loveth Setebos!
'Maketh his teeth meet through his upper lip,
Will let those quails fly, will not eat this month
One little mess of whelks, so he may 'scape!]

Confessions

1.

What is he buzzing in my ears?
"Now that I come to die,
Do I view the world as a vale of tears?"
Ah, reverend sir, not I!

2.

What I viewed there once, what I view again
Where the physic bottles stand
On the table's edge,—is a suburb lane,
With a wall to my bedside hand.

3.

That lane sloped, much as the bottles do,
  From a house you could descry
O'er the garden-wall: is the curtain blue
  Or green to a healthy eye?

4.

To mine, it serves for the old June weather
  Blue above lane and wall;
And that farthest bottle labelled "Ether"
  Is the house o'ertopping all.

5.

At a terrace, somewhere near the stopper,
  There watched for me, one June,
A girl: I know, sir, it's improper,
  My poor mind's out of tune.

6.

Only, there was a way . . you crept
  Close by the side, to dodge
Eyes in the house, two eyes except:
  They styled their house "The Lodge."

7.

What right had a lounger up their lane?
  But, by creeping very close,
With the good wall's help,—their eyes might strain
  And stretch themselves to Oes.

8.

Yet never catch her and me together,
  As she left the attic, there,
By the rim of the bottle labelled "Ether,"
  And stole from stair to stair,

9.

And stood by the rose-wreathed gate. Alas,
  We loved, sir—used to meet:
How sad and bad and mad it was—
  But then, how it was sweet!

Prospice

Fear death?—to feel the fog in my throat,
  The mist in my face,
When the snows begin, and the blasts denote
  I am nearing the place,
The power of the night, the press of the storm,
  The post of the foe;
Where he stands, the Arch Fear in a visible form,
  Yet the strong man must go:
For the journey is done and the summit attained,
  And the barriers fall,
Though a battle's to fight ere the guerdon be gained,
  The reward of it all.
I was ever a fighter, so—one fight more,
  The best and the last!
I would hate that death bandaged my eyes, and forbore,
  And bade me creep past.
No! let me taste the whole of it, fare like my peers
  The heroes of old,
Bear the brunt, in a minute pay glad life's arrears
  Of pain, darkness and cold.
For sudden the worst turns the best to the brave,
  The black minute's at end,
And the elements' rage, the fiend-voices that rave,
  Shall dwindle, shall blend,
Shall change, shall become first a peace, then a joy,
  Then a light, then thy breast,
O thou soul of my soul! I shall clasp thee again,
  And with God be the rest!

Youth and Art

1.

It once might have been, once only:
We lodged in a street together,
You, a sparrow on the housetop lonely,
I, a lone she-bird of his feather.

2.

Your trade was with sticks and clay,
You thumbed, thrust, patted and polished,
Then laughed "They will see some day
Smith made, and Gibson demolished."

3.

My business was song, song, song;
I chirped, cheeped, trilled and twittered,
"Kate Brown's on the boards ere long,
And Grisi's existence embittered!"

4.

I earned no more by a warble
Than you by a sketch in plaster;
You wanted a piece of marble,
I needed a music-master.

5.

We studied hard in our styles,
Chipped each at a crust like Hindoos,
For air, looked out on the tiles,
For fun, watched each other's windows.

6.

You lounged, like a boy of the South,
Cap and blouse—nay, a bit of beard too;
Or you got it, rubbing your mouth
With fingers the clay adhered to.

7.

And I—soon managed to find
  Weak points in the flower-fence facing,
Was forced to put up a blind
  And be safe in my corset-lacing.

8.

No harm! It was not my fault
  If you never turned your eyes' tail up
As I shook upon E *in alt.*,
  Or ran the chromatic scale up:

9.

For spring bade the sparrows pair,
  And the boys and girls gave guesses,
And stalls in our street looked rare
  With bulrush and watercresses.

10.

Why did not you pinch a flower
  In a pellet of clay and fling it?
Why did not I put a power
  Of thanks in a look, or sing it?

11.

I did look, sharp as a lynx,
  (And yet the memory rankles)
When models arrived, some minx
  Tripped up-stairs, she and her ankles.

12.

But I think I gave you as good!
  "That foreign fellow,—who can know
How she pays, in a playful mood,
  For his tuning her that piano?"

13.

Could you say so, and never say
  "Suppose we join hands and fortunes,
And I fetch her from over the way,
  Her, piano, and long tunes and short tunes?"

14.

No, no: you would not be rash,
  Nor I rasher and something over:
You've to settle yet Gibson's hash,
  And Grisi yet lives in clover.

15.

But you meet the Prince at the Board,
  I'm queen myself at *bals-paré* ,
I've married a rich old lord,
  And you're dubbed knight and an R.A.

16.

Each life unfulfilled, you see;
  It hangs still, patchy and scrappy:
We have not sighed deep, laughed free,
  Starved, feasted, despaired,—been happy.

17.

And nobody calls you a dunce,
  And people suppose me clever:
This could but have happened once,
  And we missed it, lost it for ever.

A Face

If one could have that little head of hers
Painted upon a background of pale gold,
Such as the Tuscan's early art prefers!
No shade encroaching on the matchless mould
Of those two lips, which should be opening soft

In the pure profile; not as when she laughs,
For that spoils all: but rather as if aloft
Yon hyacinth, she loves so, leaned its staff's
Burthen of honey-coloured buds to kiss
And capture 'twixt the lips apart for this.
Then her lithe neck, three fingers might surround,
How it should waver on the pale gold ground
Up to the fruit-shaped, perfect chin it lifts!
I know, Correggio loves to mass, in rifts
Of heaven, his angel faces, orb on orb
Breaking its outline, burning shades absorb:
But these are only massed there, I should think,
Waiting to see some wonder momently
Grow out, stand full, fade slow against the sky
(That's the pale ground you'd see this sweet face by),
All heaven, meanwhile, condensed into one eye
Which fears to lose the wonder, should it wink.

Mr. Sludge, "The Medium"

Now, don't, sir! Don't expose me! Just this once!
This was the first and only time, I'll swear,—
Look at me,—see, I kneel,—the only time,
I swear, I ever cheated,—yes, by the soul
Of Her who hears—(your sainted mother, sir!)
All, except this last accident, was truth—
This little kind of slip!—and even this,
It was your own wine, sir, the good champagne,
(I took it for Catawba,—you're so kind)
Which put the folly in my head!

"Get up?"
You still inflict on me that terrible face?
You show no mercy?—Not for Her dear sake,
The sainted spirit's, whose soft breath even now
Blows on my cheek—(don't you feel something, sir?)
You'll tell?

Go tell, then! Who the devil cares
What such a rowdy chooses to...

Aie—aie—aie!
Please, sir! your thumbs are through my windpipe, sir!
Ch—ch!

Well, sir, I hope you've done it now!
Oh Lord! I little thought, sir, yesterday,
When your departed mother spoke those words
Of peace through me, and moved you, sir, so much,
You gave me—(very kind it was of you)
These shirt-studs—(better take them back again,
Please, sir!)—yes, little did I think so soon
A trifle of trick, all through a glass too much
Of his own champagne, would change my best of friends
Into an angry gentleman!

Though, 'twas wrong.
I don't contest the point; your anger's just:
Whatever put such folly in my head,
I know 'twas wicked of me. There's a thick,
Dusk, undeveloped spirit (I've observed)
Owes me a grudge—a negro's, I should say,
Or else an Irish emigrant's; yourself
Explained the case so well last Sunday, sir,
When we had summoned Franklin to clear up
A point about those shares in the telegraph:
Ay, and he swore . . or might it be Tom Paine? . . .
Thumping the table close by where I crouched,
He'd do me soon a mischief: that's come true!

Why, now your face clears! I was sure it would!
Then, this one time . . don't take your hand away,
Through yours I surely kiss your mother's hand . .
You'll promise to forgive me?—or, at least,
Tell nobody of this? Consider, sir!
What harm can mercy do? Would but the shade
Of the venerable dead-one just vouchsafe
A rap or tip! What bit of paper's here?
Suppose we take a pencil, let her write,
Make the least sign, she urges on her child
Forgiveness? There now! Eh? Oh! 'Twas your foot,
And not a natural creak, sir?

Answer, then!
Once, twice, thrice . . . see, I'm waiting to say "thrice!"
All to no use? No sort of hope for me?
It's all to post to Greeley's newspaper?

What? If I told you all about the tricks?
Upon my soul!—the whole truth, and nought else,
And how there's been some falsehood—for your part,
Will you engage to pay my passage out,
And hold your tongue until I'm safe on board?
England's the place, not Boston—no offence!
I see what makes you hesitate: don't fear!
I mean to change my trade and cheat no more,
Yes, this time really it's upon my soul!
Be my salvation!—under Heaven, of course.
I'll tell some queer things. Sixty Vs must do.
A trifle, though, to start with! We'll refer
The question to this table?

How you're changed!
Then split the difference; thirty more, we'll say.
Ay, but you leave my presents! Else I'll swear
'Twas all through those: you wanted yours again,
So, picked a quarrel with me, to get them back!
Tread on a worm, it turns, sir! If I turn,
Your fault! 'Tis you'll have forced me! Who's obliged
To give up life yet try no self-defence?
At all events, I'll run the risk. Eh?

Done!
May I sit, sir? This dear old table, now!
Please, sir, a parting egg-nogg and cigar!
I've been so happy with you! Nice stuffed chairs,
And sympathetic sideboards; what an end
To all the instructive evenings! (It's alight.)
Well, nothing lasts, as Bacon came and said!
Here goes,—but keep your temper, or I'll scream!

Fol-lol-the-rido-liddle-iddle-ol!
You see, sir, it's your own fault more than mine;
It's all your fault, you curious gentlefolk!
You're prigs,—excuse me,—like to look so spry,
So clever, while you cling by half a claw

To the perch whereon you puff yourselves at roost,
Such piece of self-conceit as serves for perch
Because you chose it, so it must be safe.
Oh, otherwise you're sharp enough! You spy
Who slips, who slides, who holds by help of wing,
Wanting real foothold,—who can't keep upright
On the other perch, your neighbour chose, not you:
There's no outwitting you respecting him!
For instance, men love money—that, you know—
And what men do to gain it: well, suppose
A poor lad, say a help's son in your house,
Listening at keyholes, hears the company
Talk grand of dollars, V-notes, and so forth,
How hard they are to get, how good to hold,
How much they buy,—if, suddenly, in pops he—
"*I* 've got a V-note!"—what do you say to him?
What's your first word which follows your last kick?
"Where did you steal it, rascal?" That's because
He finds you, fain would fool you, off your perch,
Not on the special piece of nonsense, sir,
Elected your parade-ground: let him try
Lies to the end of the list,—"He picked it up,
His cousin died and left it him by will,
The President flung it to him, riding by,
An actress trucked it for a curl of his hair,
He dreamed of luck and found his shoe enriched,
He dug up clay, and out of clay made gold"—
How would you treat such possibilities?
Would not you, prompt, investigate the case
With cow-hide? "Lies, lies, lies," you'd shout: and why?
Which of the stories might not prove mere truth?
This last, perhaps, that clay was turned to coin!
Let's see, now, give him me to speak for him!
How many of your rare philosophers,
In plaguy books I've had to dip into,
Believed gold could be made thus, saw it made
And made it? Oh, with such philosophers
You're on your best behaviour! While the lad—
With him, in a trice, you settle likelihoods,
Nor doubt a moment how he got his prize:
In his case, you hear, judge and execute,
All in a breath: so would most men of sense.

But let the same lad hear you talk as grand
At the same keyhole, you and company,
Of signs and wonders, the invisible world;
How wisdom scouts our vulgar unbelief
More than our vulgarest incredulity;
How good men have desired to see a ghost,
What Johnson used to say, what Wesley did,
Mother Goose thought, and fiddle-diddle-dee:—
If he break in with, "Sir, *I* saw a ghost!"
Ah, the ways change! He finds you perched and prim;
It's a conceit of yours that ghosts may be:
There's no talk now of cow-hide. "Tell it out!
Don't fear us! Take your time and recollect!
Sit down first: try a glass of wine, my boy!
And, David, (is not that your Christian name?)
Of all things, should this happen twice—it may—
Be sure, while fresh in mind, you let us know!"
Does the boy blunder, blurt out this, blab that,
Break down in the other, as beginners will?
All's candour, all's considerateness—"No haste!
Pause and collect yourself! We understand!
That's the bad memory, or the natural shock,
Or the unexplained *phenomena*!"

Egad,
The boy takes heart of grace; finds, never fear,
The readiest way to ope your own heart wide,
Show—what I call your peacock-perch, pet post
To strut, and spread the tail, and squawk upon!
"Just as you thought, much as you might expect!
There be more things in heaven and earth, Horatio," . .
And so on. Shall not David take the hint,
Grow bolder, stroke you down at quickened rate?
If he ruffle a feather, it's "Gently, patiently!
Manifestations are so weak at first!
Doubting, moreover, kills them, cuts all short,
"Cures with a vengeance!"

There, sir, that's your style!
You and your boy—such pains bestowed on him,
Or any headpiece of the average worth,
To teach, say, Greek, would perfect him apace,

Make him a Person ("Porson?" thank you, sir!)
Much more, proficient in the art of lies.
You never leave the lesson! Fire alight,
Catch you permitting it to die! You've friends;
There's no withholding knowledge,—least from those
Apt to look elsewhere for their souls' supply:
Why should not you parade your lawful prize?
Who finds a picture, digs a medal up,
Hits on a first edition,—he henceforth
Gives it his name, grows notable: how much more,
Who ferrets out a "medium"? "David's yours,
You highly-favoured man? Then, pity souls
Less privileged! Allow us share your luck!"
So, David holds the circle, rules the roast,
Narrates the vision, peeps in the glass ball,
Sets to the spirit-writing, hears the raps,
As the case may be.

Now mark! To be precise—
Though I say, "lies" all these, at this first stage,
'Tis just for science' sake: I call such grubs
By the name of what they'll turn to, dragonflies.
Strictly, it's what good people style untruth;
But yet, so far, not quite the full-grown thing:
It's fancying, fable-making, nonsense-work—
What never meant to be so very bad—
The knack of story-telling, brightening up
Each dull old bit of fact that drops its shine.
One does see somewhat when one shuts one's eyes,
If only spots and streaks; tables do tip
In the oddest way of themselves: and pens, good Lord,
Who knows if you drive them or they drive you?
'Tis but a foot in the water and out again;
Not that duck-under which decides your dive.
Note this, for it's important: listen why.

I'll prove, you push on David till he dives
And ends the shivering. Here's your circle, now:
Two-thirds of them, with heads like you their host,
Turn up their eyes, and cry, as you expect,
"Lord, who'd have thought it!" But there's always one
Looks wise, compassionately smiles, submits

"Of your veracity no kind of doubt,
But—do you feel so certain of that boy's?
Really, I wonder! I confess myself
More chary of my faith!" That's galling, sir!
What, he the investigator, he the sage,
When all's done? Then, you just have shut your eyes,
Opened your mouth, and gulped down David whole,
You! Terrible were such catastrophe!
So, evidence is redoubled, doubled again,
And doubled besides; once more, "He heard, we heard,
You and they heard, your mother and your wife,
Your children and the stranger in your gates:
Did they or did they not?" So much for him,
The black sheep, guest without the wedding-garb,
The doubting Thomas! Now's your turn to crow:
"He's kind to think you such a fool: Sludge cheats?
Leave you alone to take precautions!"

Straight
The rest join chorus. Thomas stands abashed,
Sips silent some such beverage as this,
Considers if it be harder, shutting eyes
And gulping David in good fellowship,
Than going elsewhere, getting, in exchange,
With no egg-nogg to lubricate the food,
Some just as tough a morsel. Over the way,
Holds Captain Sparks his court: is it better there?
Have not you hunting-stories, scalping-scenes,
And Mexican War exploits to swallow plump
If you'd be free o' the stove-side, rocking-chair,
And trio of affable daughters?

Doubt succumbs!
Victory! All your circle's yours again!
Out of the clubbing of submissive wits,
David's performance rounds, each chink gets patched,
Every protrusion of a point's filed fine,
All's fit to set a-rolling round the world,
And then return to David finally,
Lies seven-feet thick about his first half-inch.
Here's a choice birth o' the supernatural,
Poor David's pledged to! You've employed no tool

That laws exclaim at, save the devil's own,
Yet screwed him into henceforth gulling you
To the top o' your bent,—all out of one half-lie!

You hold, if there's one half or a hundredth part
Of a lie, that's his fault,—his be the penalty!
I dare say! You'd prove firmer in his place?
You'd find the courage,—that first flurry over,
That mild bit of romancing-work at end,—
To interpose with "It gets serious, this;
Must stop here. Sir, I saw no ghost at all.
Inform your friends I made . . well, fools of them,
And found you ready made. I've lived in clover
These three weeks: take it out in kicks of me!"
I doubt it. Ask your conscience! Let me know,
Twelve months hence, with how few embellishments
You've told almighty Boston of this passage
Of arms between us, your first taste of the foil
From Sludge who could not fence, sir! Sludge, your boy!
I lied, sir,—there! I got up from my gorge
On offal in the gutter, and preferred
Your canvass-backs: I took their carver's size,
Measured his modicum of intelligence,
Tickled him on the cockles of his heart
With a raven feather, and next week found myself
Sweet and clean, dining daintily, dizened smart,
Set on a stool buttressed by ladies' knees,
Every soft smiler calling me her pet,
Encouraging my story to uncoil
And creep out from its hole, inch after inch,
"How last night, I no sooner snug in bed,
Tucked up, just as they left me,—than came raps!
While a light whisked" . . "Shaped somewhat like a star?"
"Well, like some sort of stars, ma'am."—"So we thought!
And any voice? Not yet? Try hard, next time,
If you can't hear a voice; we think you may:
At least, the Pennsylvanian 'mediums' did."
Oh, next time comes the voice! "Just as we hoped!"
Are not the hopers proud now, pleased, profuse
O' the natural acknowledgment?

Of course!
So, off we push, illy-oh-yo, trim the boat,
On we sweep with a cataract ahead,
We're midway to the Horse-shoe: stop, who can.
The dance of bubbles gay about our prow!
Experiences become worth waiting for,
Spirits now speak up, tell their inmost mind,
And compliment the "medium" properly,
Concern themselves about his Sunday coat,
See rings on his hand with pleasure. Ask yourself
How you'd receive a course of treats like these!
Why, take the quietest hack and stall him up,
Cram him with corn a month, then out with him
Among his mates on a bright April morn,
With the turf to tread; see if you find or no
A caper in him, if he bucks or bolts!
Much more a youth whose fancies sprout as rank
As toadstool-clump from melon-bed. 'Tis soon,
"Sirrah, you spirit, come, go, fetch and carry,
Read, write, rap, rub-a-dub, and hang yourself!"
I'm spared all further trouble; all's arranged;
Your circle does my business; I may rave
Like an epileptic dervish in the books,
Foam, fling myself flat, rend my clothes to shreds;
No matter: lovers, friends and countrymen
Will lay down spiritual laws, read wrong things right
By the rule of reverse. If Francis Verulam
Styles himself Bacon, spells the name beside
With a *y* and a *k* , says he drew breath in York,
Gave up the ghost in Wales when Cromwell reigned,
(As, sir, we somewhat fear he was apt to say,
Before I found the useful book that knows)
Why, what harm's done? The circle smiles apace,
"It was not Bacon, after all, do you see!
We understand; the trick's but natural:
Such spirits' individuality
Is hard to put in evidence: they incline
To gibe and jeer, these undeveloped sorts.
You see, their world's much like a jail broke loose,
While this of ours remains shut, bolted, barred,
With a single window to it. Sludge, our friend,

Serves as this window, whether thin or thick,
Or stained or stainless; he's the medium-pane
Through which, to see us and be seen, they peep:
They crowd each other, hustle for a chance,
Tread on their neighbour's kibes, play tricks enough!
Does Bacon, tired of waiting, swerve aside?
Up in his place jumps Barnum—'I'm your man,
I'll answer you for Bacon!' Try once more!"

Or else it's—"What's a 'medium'? He's a means,
Good, bad, indifferent, still the only means
Spirits can speak by; he may misconceive,
Stutter and stammer,—he's their Sludge and drudge,
Take him or leave him; they must hold their peace,
Or else, put up with having knowledge strained
To half-expression through his ignorance.
Suppose, the spirit Beethoven wants to shed
New music he's brimful of; why, he turns
The handle of this organ, grinds with Sludge,
And what he poured in at the mouth o' the mill
As a Thirty-third Sonata, (fancy now!)
Comes from the hopper as bran-new Sludge, nought else,
The Shakers' Hymn in G, with a natural F,
Or the 'Stars and Stripes' set to consecutive fourths."

Sir, where's the scrape you did not help me through,
You that are wise? And for the fools, the folk
Who came to see,—the guests, (observe that word!)
Pray do you find guests criticize your wine,
Your furniture, your grammar, or your nose?
Then, why your "medium"? What's the difference?
Prove your madeira red-ink and gamboge,—
Your Sludge, a cheat—then, somebody's a goose
For vaunting both as genuine. "Guests!" Don't fear!
They'll make a wry face, nor too much of that,
And leave you in your glory.

"No, sometimes
They doubt and say as much!" Ay, doubt they do!
And what's the consequence? "Of course they doubt"—
(You triumph) "that explains the hitch at once!
Doubt posed our 'medium,' puddled his pure mind;
He gave them back their rubbish: pitch chaff in,

Could flour come out o' the honest mill?" So, prompt
Applaud the faithful: cases flock in point,
"How, when a mocker willed a 'medium' once
Should name a spirit James whose name was George,
'James' cried the 'medium,'—'twas the test of truth!"
In short, a hit proves much, a miss proves more.
Does this convince? The better: does it fail?
Time for the double-shotted broadside, then—
The grand means, last resource. Look black and big!
"You style us idiots, therefore—why stop short?
Accomplices in rascality: this we hear
In our own house, from our invited guest
Found brave enough to outrage a poor boy
Exposed by our good faith! Have you been heard?
Now, then, hear us; one man's not quite worth twelve.
You see a cheat? Here's some twelve see an ass:
Excuse me if I calculate: good day!"
Out slinks the sceptic, all the laughs explode,
Sludge waves his hat in triumph!

Or—he don't.
There's something in real truth (explain who can!)
One casts a wistful eye at, like the horse
Who mopes beneath stuffed hay-racks and won't munch
Because he spies a corn-bag: hang that truth,
It spoils all dainties proffered in its place!
I've felt at times when, cockered, cossetted
And coddled by the aforesaid company,
Bidden enjoy their bullying,—never fear,
But o'er their shoulders spit at the flying man,—
I've felt a child; only, a fractious child
That, dandled soft by nurse, aunt, grandmother,
Who keep him from the kennel, sun and wind,
Good fun and wholesome mud,—enjoined be sweet,
And comely and superior,—eyes askance
The ragged sons o' the gutter at their game,
Fain would be down with them i' the thick o' the filth,
Making dirt-pies, laughing free, speaking plain,
And calling granny the grey old cat she is.
I've felt a spite, I say, at you, at them,
Huggings and humbug—gnashed my teeth to mark
A decent dog pass! It's too bad, I say,
Ruining a soul so!

But what's "so," what's fixed,
Where may one stop? Nowhere! The cheating's nursed
Out of the lying, softly and surely spun
To just your length, sir! I'd stop soon enough:
But you're for progress. "All old, nothing new?
Only the usual talking through the mouth,
Or writing by the hand? I own, I thought
This would develop, grow demonstrable,
Make doubt absurd, give figures we might see,
Flowers we might touch. There's no one doubts you, Sludge!
You dream the dreams, you see the spiritual sights,
The speeches come in your head, beyond dispute.
Still, for the sceptics' sake, to stop all mouths,
We want some outward manifestation!—well,
The Pennsylvanians gained such; why not Sludge?
He may improve with time!"

Ay, that he may!
He sees his lot: there's no avoiding fate.
'Tis a trifle at first. "Eh, David? Did you hear?
You jogged the table, your foot caused the squeak,
This time you're... joking, are you not, my boy?"
"N-n-no!"—and I'm done for, bought and sold henceforth.
The old good easy jog-trot way, the... eh?
The... not so very false, as falsehood goes,
The spinning out and drawing fine, you know,—
Really mere novel-writing of a sort,
Acting, or improvising, make-believe,
Surely not downright cheatery! Any how,
'Tis done with and my lot cast; Cheat's my name:
The fatal dash of brandy in your tea
Has settled what you'll have the souchong's smack:
The caddy gives way to the dram-bottle.

Then, it's so cruel easy! Oh, those tricks
That can't be tricks, those feats by sleight of hand,
Clearly no common conjuror's!—no indeed!
A conjuror? Choose me any craft in the world
A man puts hand to; and with six months' pains
I'll play you twenty tricks miraculous
To people untaught the trade: have you seen glass blown,
Pipes pierced? Why, just this biscuit that I chip,

Did you ever watch a baker toss one flat
To the oven? Try and do it! Take my word,
Practise but half as much, while limbs are lithe,
To turn, shove, tilt a table, crack your joints,
Manage your feet, dispose your hands aright,
Work wires that twitch the curtains, play the glove
At end of your slipper,—then put out the lights
And . . . there, there, all you want you'll get, I hope!
I found it slip, easy as an old shoe.

Now, lights on table again! I've done my part,
You take my place while I give thanks and rest.
"Well, Judge Humgruffin, what's your verdict, sir?
You, hardest head in the United States,—
Did you detect a cheat here? Wait! Let's see!
Just an experiment first, for candour's sake!
I'll try and cheat you, Judge! The table tilts:
Is it I that move it? Write! I'll press your hand:
Cry when I push, or guide your pencil, Judge!"
Sludge still triumphant! "That a rap, indeed?
That, the real writing? Very like a whale!
Then, if, sir you—a most distinguished man,
And, were the Judge not here, I'd say, . . no matter!
Well, sir, if you fail, you can't take us in,—
There's little fear that Sludge will!"

Won't he, ma'am?
But what if our distinguished host, like Sludge,
Bade God bear witness that he played no trick,
While you believed that what produced the raps
Was just a certain child who died, you know,
And whose last breath you thought your lips had felt?
Eh? That's a capital point, ma'am: Sludge begins
At your entreaty with your dearest dead,
The little voice set lisping once again,
The tiny hand made feel for yours once more,
The poor lost image brought back, plain as dreams,
Which image, if a word had chanced recall,
The customary cloud would cross your eyes,
Your heart return the old tick, pay its pang!
A right mood for investigation, this!
One's at one's ease with Saul and Jonathan,

Pompey and Cæsar: but one's own lost child . . .
I wonder, when you heard the first clod drop
From the spadeful at the grave-side, felt you free
To investigate who twitched your funeral scarf
Or brushed your flounces? Then, it came of course
You should be stunned and stupid; then, (how else?)
Your breath stopped with your blood, your brain struck work.
But now, such causes fail of such effects,
All's changed,—the little voice begins afresh,
Yet you, calm, consequent, can test and try
And touch the truth. "Tests? Didn't the creature tell
Its nurse's name, and say it lived six years,
And rode a rocking-horse? Enough of tests!
Sludge never could learn that!"

He could not, eh?
You compliment him. "Could not?" Speak for yourself!
I'd like to know the man I ever saw
Once,—never mind where, how, why, when,—once saw,
Of whom I do not keep some matter in mind
He'd swear I "could not" know, sagacious soul!
What? Do you live in this world's blow of blacks,
Palaver, gossipry, a single hour
Nor find one smut has settled on your nose,
Of a smut's worth, no more, no less?—one fact
Out of the drift of facts, whereby you learn
What some one was, somewhere, somewhen, somewhy?
You don't tell folk—"See what has stuck to me!
Judge Humgruffin, our most distinguished man,
Your uncle was a tailor, and your wife
Thought to have married Miggs, missed him, hit you!"—
Do you, sir, though you see him twice a-week?
"No," you reply, "what use retailing it?
Why should I?" But, you see, one day you *should*,
Because one day there's much use,—when this fact
Brings you the Judge upon both gouty knees
Before the supernatural; proves that Sludge
Knows, as you say, a thing he "could not" know:
Will not Sludge thenceforth keep an outstretched face,
The way the wind drives?

"Could not!" Look you now,
I'll tell you a story! There's a whiskered chap,
A foreigner, that teaches music here
And gets his bread,—knowing no better way:
He says, the fellow who informed of him
And made him fly his country and fall West,
Was a hunchback cobbler, sat, stitched soles and sang.
In some outlandish place, the city Rome,
In a cellar by their Broadway, all day long;
Never asked questions, stopped to listen or look,
Nor lifted nose from lapstone; let the world
Roll round his three-legged stool, and news run in
The ears he hardly seemed to keep pricked up.
Well, that man went on Sundays, touched his pay,
And took his praise from government, you see;
For something like two dollars every week,
He'd engage tell you some one little thing
Of some one man, which led to many more,
(Because one truth leads right to the world's end,)
And make you that man's master—when he dined
And on what dish, where walked to keep his health
And to what street. His trade was, throwing thus
His sense out, like an anteater's long tongue,
Soft, innocent, warm, moist, impassible,
And when 'twas crusted o'er with creatures—slick,
Their juice enriched his palate. "Could not Sludge!"

I'll go yet a step further, and maintain,
Once the imposture plunged its proper depth
In the rotten of your natures, all of you,—
(If one's not mad nor drunk, and hardly then)
It's impossible to cheat—that's, be found out!
Go tell your brotherhood this first slip of mine,
All to-day's tale, how you detected Sludge,
Behaved unpleasantly, till he was fain confess,
And so has come to grief! You'll find, I think,
Why Sludge still snaps his fingers in your face.
There now, you've told them! What's their prompt reply?
"Sir, did that youth confess he had cheated me,
I'd disbelieve him. He may cheat at times;
That's in the 'medium'-nature, thus they're made,

Vain and vindictive, cowards, prone to scratch.
And so all cats are; still, a cat's the beast
You coax the strange electric sparks from out,
By rubbing back its fur; not so a dog,
Nor lion, nor lamb: 'tis the cat's nature, sir!
Why not the dog's? Ask God, who made them beasts!
D'ye think the sound, the nicely-balanced man
(Like me"—aside)—"like you yourself,"—(aloud)
"—He's stuff to make a 'medium'? Bless your soul,
'Tis these hysteric, hybrid half-and-halfs,
Equivocal, worthless vermin yield the fire!
We take such as we find them, 'ware their tricks,
Wanting their service. Sir, Sludge took in you—
How, I can't say, not being there to watch:
He was tried, was tempted by your easiness,—
He did not take in me!"

Thank you for Sludge!
I'm to be grateful to such patrons, eh,
When what you hear's my best word? 'Tis a challenge
"Snap at all strangers, half-tamed prairie-dog,
So you cower duly at your keeper's nod!
Cat, show what claws were made for, muffling them
Only to me! Cheat others if you can,
Me, if you dare!" And, my wise sir, I dared—
Did cheat you first, made you cheat others next,
And had the help of your vaunted manliness
To bully the incredulous. You used me?
Have not I used you, taken full revenge,
Persuaded folk they knew not their own name,
And straight they'd own the error! Who was the fool
When, to an awe-struck, wide-eyed, open-mouthed
Circle of sages, Sludge would introduce
Milton composing baby-rhymes, and Locke
Reasoning in gibberish, Homer writing Greek
In noughts and crosses, Asaph setting psalms
To crotchet and quaver? I've made a spirit squeak
In sham voice for a minute, then outbroke
Bold in my own, defying the imbeciles—
Have copied some ghost's pothooks, half a page,
Then ended with my own scrawl undisguised.

"All right! The ghost was merely using Sludge,
Suiting itself from his imperfect stock!"
Don't talk of gratitude to me! For what?
For being treated as a showman's ape,
Encouraged to be wicked and make sport,
Fret or sulk, grin or whimper, any mood
So long as the ape be in it and no man—
Because a nut pays every mood alike.
Curse your superior, superintending sort,
Who, since you hate smoke, send up boys that climb
To cure your chimney, bid a "medium" lie
To sweep you truth down! Curse your women too.
Your insolent wives and daughters, that fire up
Or faint away if a male hand squeeze theirs,
Yet, to encourage Sludge, may play with Sludge
As only a "medium," only the kind of thing
They must humour, fondle . . oh, to misconceive
Were too preposterous! But I've paid them out!
They've had their wish—called for the naked truth,
And in she tripped, sat down and bade them stare:
They had to blush a little and forgive!
"The fact is, children talk so; in next world
All our conventions are reversed,—perhaps
Made light of: something like old prints, my dear!
The Judge has one, he brought from Italy,
A metropolis in the background,—o'er a bridge,
A team of trotting roadsters,—cheerful groups
Of wayside travellers, peasants at their work,
And, full in front, quite unconcerned, why not?
Three nymphs conversing with a cavalier,
And never a rag among them: 'fine,' folk cry—
And heavenly manners seem not much unlike!
Let Sludge go on; we'll fancy it's in print!"
If such as came for wool, sir, went home shorn,
Where is the wrong I did them? 'Twas their choice;
They tried the adventure, ran the risk, tossed up
And lost, as some one's sure to do in games;
They fancied I was made to lose,—smoked glass
Useful to spy the sun through, spare their eyes:
And had I proved a red-hot iron plate
They thought to pierce, and, for their pains, grew blind,

Whose were the fault but theirs? While, as things go,
Their loss amounts to gain, the more's the shame!
They've had their peep into the spirit-world,
And all this world may know it! They've fed fat
Their self-conceit which else had starved: what chance
Save this, of cackling o'er a golden egg
And compassing distinction from the flock,
Friends of a feather? Well, they paid for it,
And not prodigiously; the price o' the play,
Not counting certain pleasant interludes,
Was scarce a vulgar play's worth. When you buy
The actor's talent, do you dare propose
For his soul beside? Whereas, my soul you buy!
Sludge acts Macbeth, obliged to be Macbeth,
Or you will not hear his first word! Just go through
That slight formality, swear himself's the Thane,
And thenceforth he may strut and fret his hour,
Spout, spawl, or spin his target, no one cares!
Why hadn't I leave to play tricks, Sludge as Sludge?
Enough of it all! I've wiped out scores with you—
Vented your fustian, let myself be streaked
Like tom-fool with your ochre and carmine,
Worn patchwork your respectable fingers sewed
To metamorphose somebody,—yes, I've earned
My wages, swallowed down my bread of shame,
And shake the crumbs off—where but in your face?

As for religion—why, I served it, sir!
I'll stick to that! With my *phenomena*
I laid the atheist sprawling on his back,
And propped Saint Paul up, or, at least, Swedenborg!
In fact, it's just the proper way to baulk
These troublesome fellows—liars, one and all,
Are not these sceptics? Well, to baffle them,
No use in being squeamish: lie yourself!
Erect your buttress just as wide o' the line,
Your side, as they've built up the wall on theirs;
Where both meet, midway in a point, is truth,
High overhead: so, take your room, pile bricks,
Lie! Oh, there's titillation in all shame!
What snow may lose in white, it gains in rose:

Miss Stokes turns—Rahab,—nor a bad exchange!
Glory be on her, for the good she wrought,
Breeding belief anew 'neath ribs of death,
Brow-beating now the unabashed before,
Ridding us of their whole life's gathered straws
By a live coal from the altar! Why, of old,
Great men spent years and years in writing books
To prove we've souls, and hardly proved it then:
Miss Stokes with her live coal, for you and me!
Surely, to this good issue, all was fair—
Not only fondling Sludge, but, even suppose
He let escape some spice of knavery,—well,
In wisely being blind to it! Don't you praise
Nelson for setting spy-glass to blind eye
And saying . . what was it—that he could not see
The signal he was bothered? Ay, indeed!

I'll go beyond: there's a real love of a lie,
Liars find ready-made for lies they make,
As hand for glove, or tongue for sugar-plum.
At best, 'tis never pure and full belief;
Those furthest in the quagmire,—don't suppose
They strayed there with no warning, got no chance
Of a filth-speck in their face, which they clenched teeth,
Bent brow against! Be sure they had their doubts,
And fears, and fairest challenges to try
The floor o' the seeming solid sand! But no!
Their faith was pledged, acquaintance too apprised,
All but the last step ventured, kerchiefs waved,
And Sludge called "pet": 'twas easier marching on
To the promised land; join those who, Thursday next
Meant to meet Shakespeare; better follow Sludge—
Prudent, oh sure!—on the alert, how else?
But making for the mid-bog, all the same!
To hear your outcries, one would think I caught
Miss Stokes by the scuff o' the neck, and pitched her flat,
Foolish-face-foremost! Hear these simpletons,
That's all I beg, before my work's begun,
Before I've touched them with my finger-tip!
Thus they await me (do but listen, now!
It's reasoning, this is,—I can't imitate

The baby voice, though) "In so many tales
Must be some truth, truth though a pin-point big,
Yet, some: a single man's deceived, perhaps—
Hardly, a thousand: to suppose one cheat
Can gull all these, were more miraculous far
Than aught we should confess a miracle"—
And so on. Then the Judge sums up—(it's rare)—
Bids you respect the authorities that leap
To the judgment-seat at once,—why don't you note
The limpid nature, the unblemished life,
The spotless honour, indisputable sense
Of the first upstart with his story? What—
Outrage a boy on whom you ne'er till now
Set eyes, because he finds raps trouble him?

Fools, these are: ay, and how of their opposites
Who never did, at bottom of their hearts,
Believe for a moment?—Men emasculate,
Blank of belief, who played, as eunuchs use,
With superstition safely,—cold of blood,
Who saw what made for them in the mystery,
Took their occasion, and supported Sludge
—As proselytes? No, thank you, far too shrewd!
—But promisers of fair play, encouragers
Of the claimant; who in candour needs must hoist
Sludge up on Mars' Hill, get speech out of Sludge
To carry off, criticize, and cant about!
Didn't Athens treat Saint Paul so?—at any rate,
It's "a new thing," philosophy fumbles at.
Then there's the other picker out of pearl
From dung heaps,—ay, your literary man,
Who draws on his kid gloves to deal with Sludge
Daintily and discreetly,—shakes a dust
Of the doctrine, flavours thence, he well knows how,
The narrative or the novel,—half-believes,
All for the book's sake, and the public's stare,
And the cash that's God's sole solid in this world!
Look at him! Try to be too bold, too gross
For the master! Not you! He's the man for muck;
Shovel it forth, full-splash, he'll smooth your brown
Into artistic richness, never fear!

Find him the crude stuff; when you recognize
Your lie again, you'll doff your hat to it,
Dressed out for company! "For company,"
I say, since there's the relish of success:
Let all pay due respect, call the lie truth,
Save the soft silent smirking gentleman
Who ushered in the stranger: you must sigh
"How melancholy, he, the only one
Fails to perceive the bearing of the truth
Himself gave birth to!"—There's the triumph's smack!
That man would choose to see the whole world roll
I' the slime o' the slough, so he might touch the tip
Of his brush with what I call the best of browns—
Tint ghost-tales, spirit-stories, past the power
Of the outworn umber and bistre!

Yet I think
There's a more hateful form of foolery—
The social sage's, Solomon of saloons
And philosophic diner-out, the fribble
Who wants a doctrine for a chopping-block
To try the edge of his faculty upon,
Prove how much common sense he'll hack and hew
In the critical minute 'twixt the soup and fish!
These were my patrons: these, and the like of them
Who, rising in my soul now, sicken it,—
These I have injured! Gratitude to these?
The gratitude, forsooth, of a prostitute
To the greenhorn and the bully—friends of hers,
From the wag that wants the queer jokes for his club,
To the snuff-box-decorator, honest man,
Who just was at his wits' end where to find
So genial a Pasiphae! All and each
Pay, compliment, protect from the police,
And how she hates them for their pains, like me!
So much for my remorse at thanklessness
Toward a deserving public!

But, for God?
Ay, that's a question! Well, sir, since you press—
(How you do teaze the whole thing out of me!
I don't mean you, you know, when I say "them":

Hate you, indeed! But that Miss Stokes, that Judge!
Enough, enough—with sugar: thank you, sir!)
Now for it, then! Will you believe me, though?
You've heard what I confess; I don't unsay
A single word: I cheated when I could,
Rapped with my toe-joints, set sham hands at work,
Wrote down names weak in sympathetic ink,
Rubbed odic lights with ends of phosphor-match,
And all the rest; believe that: believe this,
By the same token, though it seem to set
The crooked straight again, unsay the said,
Stick up what I've knocked down; I can't help that
It's truth! I somehow vomit truth to-day.
This trade of mine—I don't know, can't be sure
But there was something in it, tricks and all!
Really, I want to light up my own mind.
They were tricks,—true, but what I mean to add
Is also true. First,—don't it strike you, sir?
Go back to the beginning,—the first fact
We're taught is, there's a world beside this world,
With spirits, not mankind, for tenantry;
That much within that world once sojourned here,
That all upon this world will visit there,
And therefore that we, bodily here below,
Must have exactly such an interest
In learning what may be the ways o' the world
Above us, as the disembodied folk
Have (by all analogic likelihood)
In watching how things go in the old world
With us, their sons, successors, and what not.
Oh, yes, with added powers probably,
Fit for the novel state,—old loves grown pure,
Old interests understood aright,—they watch!
Eyes to see, ears to hear, and hands to help,
Proportionate to advancement: they're ahead,
That's all—do what we do, but noblier done—
Use plate, whereas we eat our meals off delf,
(To use a figure).

Concede that, and I ask
Next what may be the mode of intercourse
Between us men here, and those once-men there?
First comes the Bible's speech; then, history
With the supernatural element,—you know—
All that we sucked in with our mothers' milk,
Grew up with, got inside of us at last,
Till it's found bone of bone and flesh of flesh.
See now, we start with the miraculous,
And know it used to be, at all events:
What's the first step we take, and can't but take,
In arguing from the known to the obscure?
Why this: "What was before, may be to-day.
Since Samuel's ghost appeared to Saul,—of course
My brother's spirit may appear to me."
Go tell your teacher that! What's his reply?
What brings a shade of doubt for the first time
O'er his brow late so luminous with faith?
"Such things have been," says he, "and there's no doubt
Such things may be: but I advise mistrust
Of eyes, ears, stomach, and, more than all, your brain,
Unless it be of your great-grandmother,
Whenever they propose a ghost to you!"
The end is, there's a composition struck;
'Tis settled, we've some way of intercourse
Just as in Saul's time; only, different:
How, when and where, precisely,—find it out!
I want to know, then, what's so natural
As that a person born into this world
And seized on by such teaching, should begin
With firm expectancy and a frank look-out
For his own allotment, his especial share
In the secret,—his particular ghost, in fine?
I mean, a person born to look that way,
Since natures differ: take the painter-sort,
One man lives fifty years in ignorance
Whether grass be green or red,—"No kind of eye
For colour," say you; while another picks
And puts away even pebbles, when a child,
Because of bluish spots and pinky veins—
"Give him forthwith a paint-box!" Just the same

Was I born . . . "medium," you won't let me say,—
Well, seer of the supernatural
Everywhen, everyhow and everywhere,—
Will that do?

I and all such boys of course
Started with the same stock of bible-truth;
Only,—what in the rest you style their sense,
Instinct, blind reasoning but imperative,
This, betimes, taught them the old world had one law
And ours another: "New world, new laws," cried they:
"None but old laws, seen everywhere at work,"
Cried I, and by their help explained my life
The Jews' way, still a working way to me.
Ghosts made the noises, fairies waved the lights,
Or Santaclaus slid down on New Year's Eve
And stuffed with cakes the stocking at my bed,
Changed the worn shoes, rubbed clean the fingered slate
Of the sum that came to grief the day before.

This could not last long: soon enough I found
Who had worked wonders thus, and to what end:
But did I find all easy, like my mates?
Henceforth no supernatural any more?
Not a whit: what projects the billiard-balls?
"A cue," you answer: "Yes, a cue," said I;
"But what hand, off the cushion, moved the cue?
What unseen agency, outside the world,
Prompted its puppets to do this and that,
Put cakes and shoes and slates into their mind,
These mothers and aunts, nay even schoolmasters?"
Thus high I sprang, and there have settled since.
Just so I reason, in sober earnest still,
About the greater godsends, what you call
The serious gains and losses of my life.
What do I know or care about your world
Which either is or seems to be? This snap
Of my fingers, sir! My care is for myself;
Myself am whole and sole reality
Inside a raree-show and a market-mob
Gathered about it: that's the use of things.
'Tis easy saying they serve vast purposes,

Advantage their grand selves: be it true or false,
Each thing may have two uses. What's a star?
A world, or a world's sun: doesn't it serve
As taper also, time-piece, weather-glass,
And almanac? Are stars not set for signs
When we should shear our sheep, sow corn, prune trees?
The Bible says so.

Well, I add one use
To all the acknowledged uses, and declare
If I spy Charles's Wain at twelve to-night,
It warns me, "Go, nor lose another day,
And have your hair cut, Sludge!" You laugh: and why?
Were such a sign too hard for God to give?
No: but Sludge seems too little for such grace:
Thank you, sir! So you think, so does not Sludge!
When you and good men gape at Providence,
Go into history and bid us mark
Not merely powder-plots prevented, crowns
Kept on kings' heads by miracle enough,
But private mercies—oh, you've told me, sir,
Of such interpositions! How yourself
Once, missing on a memorable day
Your handkerchief—just setting out, you know,—
You must return to fetch it, lost the train,
And saved your precious self from what befell
The thirty-three whom Providence forgot.
You tell, and ask me what I think of this?
Well, sir, I think then, since you needs must know,
What matter had you and Boston city to boot
Sailed skyward, like burnt onion-peelings? Much
To you, no doubt: for me—undoubtedly
The cutting of my hair concerns me more,
Because, however sad the truth may seem,
Sludge is of all-importance to himself.
You set apart that day in every year
For special thanksgiving, were a heathen else:
Well, I who cannot boast the like escape,
Suppose I said "I don't thank Providence
For my part, owing it no gratitude?"
"Nay, but you owe as much"—you'd tutor me,

"You, every man alive, for blessings gained
In every hour of the day, could you but know!
I saw my crowning mercy: all have such,
Could they but see!" Well, sir, why don't they see?
Because they won't look,—or perhaps, they can't."
Then, sir, suppose I can, and will, and do
Look, microscopically as is right,
Into each hour with its infinitude
Of influences at work to profit Sludge?
For that's the case: I've sharpened up my sight
To spy a providence in the fire's going out,
The kettle's boiling, the dime's sticking fast
Despite the hole i' the pocket. Call such facts
Fancies, too petty a work for Providence,
And those same thanks which you exact from me
Prove too prodigious payment: thanks for what,
If nothing guards and guides us little men?
No, no, sir! You must put away your pride,
Resolve to let Sludge into partnership!
I live by signs and omens: looked at the roof
Where the pigeons settle—"If the further bird,
The white, takes wing first, I'll confess when thrashed;
Not, if the blue does"—so I said to myself
Last week, lest you should take me by surprise:
Off flapped the white,—and I'm confessing, sir!
Perhaps 'tis Providence's whim and way
With only me, in the world: how can you tell?
"Because unlikely!" Was it likelier, now,
That this our one out of all worlds beside,
The what-d'you-call-'em millions, should be just
Precisely chosen to make Adam for,
And the rest o' the tale? Yet the tale's true, you know:
Such undeserving clod was graced so once;
Why not graced likewise undeserving Sludge?
Are we merit-mongers, flaunt we filthy rags?
All you can bring against my privilege
Is, that another way was taken with you,—
Which I don't question. It's pure grace, my luck:
I'm broken to the way of nods and winks,
And need no formal summoning. You've a help;
Holloa his name or whistle, clap your hands,

Stamp with your foot or pull the bell: all's one,
He understands you want him, here he comes.
Just so, I come at the knocking: you, sir, wait
The tongue of the bell, nor stir before you catch
Reason's clear tingle, nature's clapper brisk,
Or that traditional peal was wont to cheer
Your mother's face turned heavenward: short of these
There's no authentic intimation, eh?
Well, when you hear, you'll answer them, start up
And stride into the presence, top of toe,
And there find Sludge beforehand, Sludge that sprung
At noise o' the knuckle on the partition-wall!
I think myself the more religious man.
Religion's all or nothing; it's no mere smile
Of contentment, sigh of aspiration, sir—
No quality of the finelier-tempered clay
Like its whiteness or its lightness; rather, stuff
Of the very stuff, life of life, and self of self.
I tell you, men won't notice; when they do,
They'll understand. I notice nothing else,
I'm eyes, ears, mouth of me, one gaze and gape,
Nothing eludes me, everything's a hint,
Handle and help. It's all absurd, and yet
There's something in it all, I know: how much?
No answer! What does that prove? Man's still man,
Still meant for a poor blundering piece of work
When all's done; but, if somewhat's done, like this,
Or not done, is the case the same? Suppose
I blunder in my guess at the true sense
O' the knuckle-summons, nine times out of ten,—
What if the tenth guess happen to be right?
If the tenth shovel-load of powdered quartz
Yield me the nugget? I gather, crush, sift all,
Pass o'er the failure, pounce on the success.
To give you a notion, now—(let who wins, laugh!)
When first I see a man, what do I first?
Why, count the letters which make up his name,
And as their number chances, even or odd,
Arrive at my conclusion, trim my course:
Hiram H. Horsefall is your honoured name,
And haven't I found a patron, sir, in you?

"Shall I cheat this stranger?" I take apple-pips,
Stick one in either *canthus* of my eye,
And if the left drops first—(your left, sir, stuck)
I'm warned, I let the trick alone this time.
You, sir, who smile, superior to such trash,
You judge of character by other rules:
Don't your rules sometimes fail you? Pray, what rule
Have you judged Sludge by hitherto?

Oh, be sure,
You, everybody blunders, just as I,
In simpler things than these by far! For see:
I knew two farmers,—one, a wiseacre
Who studied seasons, rummaged almanacs,
Quoted the dew-point, registered the frost,
And then declared, for outcome of his pains,
Next summer must be dampish: 'twas a drought.
His neighbour prophesied such drought would fall,
Saved hay and corn, made cent. per cent. thereby,
And proved a sage indeed: how came his lore?
Because one brindled heifer, late in March,
Stiffened her tail of evenings, and somehow
He got into his head that drought was meant!
I don't expect all men can do as much:
Such kissing goes by favour. You must take
A certain turn of mind for this,—a twist
I' the flesh, as well. Be lazily alive,
Open-mouthed, like my friend the anteater,
Letting all nature's loosely-guarded motes
Settle and, slick, be swallowed! Think yourself
The one i' the world, the one for whom the world
Was made, expect it tickling at your mouth!
Then will the swarm of busy buzzing flies,
Clouds of coincidence, break egg-shell, thrive,
Breed, multiply, and bring you food enough.

I can't pretend to mind your smiling, sir!
Oh, what you mean is this! Such intimate way,
Close converse, frank exchange of offices,
Strict sympathy of the immeasurably great
With the infinitely small, betokened here
By a course of signs and omens, raps and sparks,—

How does it suit the dread traditional text
Of the "Great and Terrible Name"? Shall the Heaven of Heavens
Stoop to such child's play?

Please, sir, go with me
A moment, and I'll try to answer you.
The "*Magnum et terribile*" (is that right?)
Well, folk began with this in the early day;
And all the acts they recognized in proof
Were thunders, lightnings, earthquakes, whirlwinds, dealt
Indisputably on men whose death they caused.
There, and there only, folk saw Providence
At work,—and seeing it, 'twas right enough
All heads should tremble, hands wring hands amain,
And knees knock hard together at the breath
Of the Name's first letter; why, the Jews, I'm told,
Won't write it down, no, to this very hour,
Nor speak aloud: you know best if 't be so.
Each ague-fit of fear at end, they crept
(Because somehow people once born must live)
Out of the sound, sight, swing and sway of the Name,
Into a corner, the dark rest of the world,
And safe space where as yet no fear had reached;
'Twas there they looked about them, breathed again,
And felt indeed at home, as we might say.
The current of common things, the daily life,
This had their due contempt; no Name pursued
Man from the mountain-top where fires abide,
To his particular mouse-hole at its foot
Where he ate, drank, digested, lived in short:
Such was man's vulgar business, far too small
To be worth thunder: "small," folk kept on, "small,"
With much complacency in those great days!
A mote of sand, you know, a blade of grass—
What was so despicable as mere grass,
Except perhaps the life of the worm or fly
Which fed there? These were "small" and men were great.
Well, sir, the old way's altered somewhat since,
And the world wears another aspect now:
Somebody turns our spyglass round, or else
Puts a new lens in it: grass, worm, fly grow big:

We find great things are made of little things,
And little things go lessening till at last
Comes God behind them. Talk of mountains now?
We talk of mould that heaps the mountain, mites
That throng the mould, and God that makes the mites.
The Name comes close behind a stomach-cyst,
The simplest of creations, just a sac
That's mouth, heart, legs and belly at once, yet lives
And feels, and could do neither, we conclude,
If simplified still further one degree:
The small becomes the dreadful and immense!
Lightning, forsooth? No word more upon that!
A tin-foil bottle, a strip of greasy silk,
With a bit of wire and knob of brass, and there's
Your dollar's-worth of lightning! But the cyst—
The life of the least of the little things?

No, no!
Preachers and teachers try another tack,
Come near the truth this time: they put aside
Thunder and lightning: "That's mistake," they cry,
"Thunderbolts fall for neither fright nor sport,
But do appreciable good, like tides,
Changes of the wind, and other natural facts—
'Good' meaning good to man, his body or soul.
Mediate, immediate, all things minister
To man,—that's settled: be our future text
'We are His children!'" So, they now harangue
About the intention, the contrivance, all
That keeps up an incessant play of love,—
See the Bridgewater book.

Amen to it!
Well, sir, I put this question: I'm a child?
I lose no time, but take you at your word:
How shall I act a child's part properly?
Your sainted mother, sir,—used you to live
With such a thought as this a-worrying you?
"She has it in her power to throttle me,
Or stab or poison: she may turn me out,
Or lock me in,—nor stop at this, to-day,
But cut me off to-morrow from the estate

I look for"—(long may you enjoy it, sir!)
"In brief, she may unchild the child I am."
You never had such crotchets? Nor have I!
Who, frank confessing childship from the first,
Cannot both fear and take my ease at once,
So, don't fear,—know what might be, well enough,
But know too, child-like, that it will not be,
At least in my case, mine, the son and heir
Of the kingdom, as yourself proclaim my style.
But do you fancy I stop short at this?
Wonder if suit and service, sons and heirs
Needs must expect, I dare pretend to find?
If, looking for signs proper to such an one,
I straight perceive them irresistible?
Concede that homage is a son's plain right,
And, never mind the nods and raps and winks,
'Tis the pure obvious supernatural
Steps forward, does its duty: why, of course!
I have presentiments; my dreams come true:
I fancy a friend stands whistling all in white
Blithe as a boblink, and he's dead I learn.
I take dislike to a dog my favourite long,
And sell him; he goes mad next week and snaps.
I guess that stranger will turn up to-day
I have not seen these three years; there's his knock
I wager "sixty peaches on that tree!"—
That I pick up a dollar in my walk,
That your wife's brother's cousin's name was George—
And win on all points. Oh, you wince at this?
You'd fain distinguish between gift and gift,
Washington's oracle and Sludge's itch
O' the elbow when at whist he ought to trump?
With Sludge it's too absurd? *Fine, draw the line*
Somewhere, but, sir, your somewhere is not mine!

Bless us, I'm turning poet! It's time to end.
How you have drawn me out, sir! All I ask
Is—am I heir or not heir? If I'm he,
Then, sir, remember, that same personage
(To judge by what we read in the newspaper)
Requires, beside one nobleman in gold

To carry up and down his coronet,
Another servant, probably a duke,
To hold egg-nogg in readiness: why want
Attendance, sir, when helps in his father's house
Abound, I'd like to know?

Enough of talk!
My fault is that I tell too plain a truth.
Why, which of those who say they disbelieve,
Your clever people, but has dreamed his dream,
Caught his coincidence, stumbled on his fact
He can't explain, (he'll tell you smilingly)
Which he's too much of a philosopher
To count as supernatural, indeed,
So calls a puzzle and problem, proud of it:
Bidding you still be on your guard, you know,
Because one fact don't make a system stand,
Nor prove this an occasional escape
Of spirit beneath the matter: that's the way!
Just so wild Indians picked up, piece by piece,
The fact in California, the fine gold
That underlay the gravel—hoarded these,
But never made a system stand, nor dug!
So wise men hold out in each hollowed palm
A handful of experience, sparkling fact
They can't explain; and since their rest of life
Is all explainable, what proof in this?
Whereas I take the fact, the grain of gold,
And fling away the dirty rest of life,
And add this grain to the grain each fool has found
Of the million other such philosophers,—
Till I see gold, all gold and only gold,
Truth questionless though unexplainable,
And the miraculous proved the commonplace!
The other fools believed in mud, no doubt—
Failed to know gold they saw: was that so strange?
Are all men born to play Bach's fiddle-fugues,
"Time" with the foil in carte, jump their own height,
Cut the mutton with the broadsword, skate a five,
Make the red hazard with the cue, clip nails
While swimming, in five minutes row a mile,

Pull themselves three feet up with the left arm,
Do sums of fifty figures in their head,
And so on, by the scores of instances?
The Sludge with luck, who sees the spiritual facts,
His fellows strive and fail to see, may rank
With these, and share the advantage!

Ay, but share
The drawback! Think it over by yourself;
I have not heart, sir, and the fire's gone grey.
Defect somewhere compensates for success,
Everyone knows that! Oh, we're equals, sir!
The big-legged fellow has a little arm
And a less brain, though big legs win the race:
Do you suppose I 'scape the common lot?
Say, I was born with flesh so sensitive,
Soul so alert, that, practice helping both,
I guess what's going on outside the veil,
Just as a prisoned crane feels pairing-time
In the islands where his kind are, so must fall
To capering by himself some shiny night,
As if your back-yard were a plot of spice—
Thus am I 'ware o' the spirit-world: while you,
Blind as a beetle that way,—for amends,
Why, you can double fist and floor me, sir!
Ride that hot, hardmouthed, horrid horse of yours,
Laugh while it lightens, play with the great dog,
Speak your mind though it vex some friend to hear,
Never brag, never bluster, never blush,—
In short, you've pluck, when I'm a coward—there!
I know it, I can't help it,—folly or no,
I'm paralyzed, my hand's no more a hand,
Nor my head, a head, in danger: you can smile
And change the pipe in your cheek. Your gift's not mine.
Would you swap for mine? No! but you'd add my gift
To yours: I dare say! I too sigh at times,
Wish I were stouter, could tell truth nor flinch,
Kept cool when threatened, did not mind so much
Being dressed gaily, making strangers stare,
Eating nice things; when I'd amuse myself,
I shut my eyes and fancy in my brain

I'm—now the President, now Jenny Lind,
Now Emerson, now the Benicia Boy—
With all the civilized world a-wondering
And worshipping! I know it's folly and worse:
I feel such tricks sap, honeycomb the soul,
But I can't cure myself,—despond, despair,
And then, hey, presto, there's a turn of the wheel,
Under comes uppermost, fate makes full amends;
Sludge knows and sees and hears a hundred things
You all are blind to,—I've my taste of truth,
Likewise my touch of falsehood,—vice no doubt,
But you've your vices also: I'm content.

What, sir? You won't shake hands? "Because I cheat!
You've found me out in cheating!" That's enough
To make an apostle swear! Why, when I cheat,
Mean to cheat, do cheat, and am caught in the act,
Are you, or, rather, am I sure of the fact?
(There's verse again, but I'm inspired somehow.)
Well then, I'm not sure! I may be, perhaps,
Free as a babe from cheating: how it began,
My gift,—no matter; what 'tis got to be
In the end now, that's the question; answer that!
Had I seen, perhaps, what hand was holding mine,
Leading me whither, I had died of fright,
So, I was made believe I led myself.
If I should lay a six-inch plank from roof
To roof, you would not cross the street, one step,
Even at your mother's summons: but, being shrewd,
If I paste paper on each side the plank
And swear 'tis solid pavement, why, you'll cross
Humming a tune the while, in ignorance
Beacon Street stretches a hundred feet below:
I walked thus, took the paper-cheat for stone.
Some impulse made me set a thing on the move
Which, started once, ran really by itself;
Beer flows thus, suck the siphon; toss the kite,
It takes the wind and floats of its own force.
Don't let truth's lump rot stagnant for the lack
Of a timely helpful lie to leaven it!
Put a chalk-egg beneath the clucking hen,

She'll lay a real one, laudably deceived,
Daily for weeks to come. I've told my lie,
And seen truth follow, marvels none of mine;
All was not cheating, sir, I'm positive!
I don't know if I move your hand sometimes
When the spontaneous writing spreads so far,
If my knee lifts the table all that height,
Why the inkstand don't fall off the desk a-tilt,
Why the accordion plays a prettier waltz
Than I can pick out on the piano-forte,
Why I speak so much more than I first intend,
Describe so many things I never saw.
I tell you, sir, in one sense, I believe
Nothing at all,—that everybody can,
Will, and does cheat: but in another sense
I'm ready to believe my very self—
That every cheat's inspired, and every lie
Quick with a germ of truth.

You ask perhaps
Why I should condescend to trick at all
If I know a way without it? This is why!
There's a strange secret sweet self-sacrifice
In any desecration of one's soul
To a worthy end,—isn't it Herodotus
(I wish I could read Latin!) who describes
The single gift of the land's virginity,
Demanded in those old Egyptian rites,
(I've but a hazy notion—help me, sir!)
For one purpose in the world, one day in a life,
One hour in the day—thereafter, purity,
And a veil thrown o'er the past for evermore!
Well, now, they understood a many things
Down by Nile city, or wherever it was!
I've always vowed, after the minute's lie,
And the good end's gain,—truth should be mine
henceforth.
This goes to the root of the matter, sir,—this plain
Plump fact: accept it and unlock with it
The wards of many a puzzle!

Or, finally,
Why should I set so fine a gloss on things?
What need I care? I cheat in self-defence,
And there's my answer to a world of cheats!
Cheat? To be sure, sir! What's the world worth else?
Who takes it as he finds, and thanks his stars?
Don't it want trimming, turning, furbishing up
And polishing over? Your so-styled great men,
Do they accept one truth as truth is found,
Or try their skill at tinkering? What's your world?
Here are you born, who are, I'll say at once,
One of the luckiest whether in head and heart,
Body and soul, or all that helps the same.
Well, now, look back: what faculty of yours
Came to its full, had ample justice done
By growing when rain fell, biding its time,
Solidifying growth when earth was dead,
Spiring up, broadening wide, in seasons due?
Never! You shot up and frost nipped you off,
Settled to sleep when sunshine bade you sprout;
One faculty thwarted its fellow: at the end,
All you boast is, "I had proved a topping tree
In other climes"—yet this was the right clime
Had you foreknown the seasons. Young, you've force
Wasted like well-streams: old,—oh, then indeed,
Behold a labyrinth of hydraulic pipes
Through which you'd play off wondrous waterwork;
Only, no water left to feed their play!
Young,—you've a hope, an aim, a love; it's tossed
And crossed and lost: you struggle on, some spark
Shut in your heart against the puffs around,
Through cold and pain; these in due time subside,
Now then for age's triumph, the hoarded light
You mean to loose on the altered face of things,—
Up with it on the tripod! It's extinct.
Spend your life's remnant asking, which was best,
Light smothered up that never peeped forth once,
Or the cold cresset with full leave to shine?
Well, accept this too,—seek the fruit of it
Not in enjoyment, proved a dream on earth,
But knowledge, useful for a second chance,

Another life,—you've lost this world—you've gained
Its knowledge for the next.—What knowledge, sir,
Except that you know nothing? Nay, you doubt
Whether 'twere better have made you man or brute,
If aught be true, if good and evil clash.
No foul, no fair, no inside, no outside,
There's your world!

Give it me! I slap it brisk
With harlequin's pasteboard sceptre: what's it now?
Changed like a rock-flat, rough with rusty weed,
At first wash-over of the returning wave!
All the dry, dead, impracticable stuff
Starts into life and light again; this world
Pervaded by the influx from the next.
I cheat, and what's the happy consequence?
You find full justice straightway dealt you out,
Each want supplied, each ignorance set at ease,
Each folly fooled. No life-long labour now
As the price of worse than nothing! No mere film
Holding you chained in iron, as it seems,
Against the outstretch of your very arms
And legs in the sunshine moralists forbid!
What would you have? Just speak and, there, you see!
You're supplemented, made a whole at last,
Bacon advises, Shakespeare writes you songs,
And Mary Queen of Scots embraces you.
Thus it goes on, not quite like life perhaps,
But so near, that the very difference piques,
Shows that e'en better than this best will be—
This passing entertainment in a hut
Whose bare walls take your taste since, one stage more,
And you arrive at the palace: all half real,
And you, to suit it, less than real beside,
In a dream, lethargic kind of death in life,
That helps the interchange of natures, flesh
Transfused by souls, and such souls! Oh, 'tis choice!
And if at whiles the bubble, blown too thin,
Seem nigh on bursting,—if you nearly see
The real world through the false,—what *do* you see?
Is the old so ruined? You find you're in a flock

Of the youthful, earnest, passionate—genius, beauty,
Rank and wealth also, if you care for these,
And all depose their natural rights, hail you,
(That's me, sir) as their mate and yoke-fellow,
Participate in Sludgehood—nay, grow mine,
I veritably possess them—banish doubt,
And reticence and modesty alike!
Why, here's the Golden Age, old Paradise
Or new Eutopia! Here is life indeed,
And the world well won now, yours for the first time!

And all this might be, may be, and with good help
Of a little lying shall be: so, Sludge lies!
Why, he's at worst your poet who sings how Greeks
That never were, in Troy which never was,
Did this or the other impossible great thing!
He's Lowell—it's a world you smile and say,
Of his own invention—wondrous Longfellow,
Surprising Hawthorne! Sludge does more than they,
And acts the books they write: the more his praise!

But why do I mount to poets? Take plain prose—
Dealers in common sense, set these at work,
What can they do without their helpful lies?
Each states the law and fact and face of the thing
Just as he'd have them, finds what he thinks fit,
Is blind to what missuits him, just records
What makes his case out, quite ignores the rest.
It's a History of the World, the Lizard Age,
The Early Indians, the Old Country War,
Jerome Napoleon, whatsoever you please,
All as the author wants it. Such a scribe
You pay and praise for putting life in stones,
Fire into fog, making the past your world.
There's plenty of "How did you contrive to grasp
The thread which led you through this labyrinth?
How build such solid fabric out of air?
How on so slight foundation found this tale,
Biography, narrative?" or, in other words,
"How many lies did it require to make
The portly truth you here present us with?"
"Oh," quoth the penman, purring at your praise,

"'Tis fancy all; no particle of fact:
I was poor and threadbare when I wrote that book
'Bliss in the Golden City.' I, at Thebes?
We writers paint out of our heads, you see!"
"Ah, the more wonderful the gift in you,
The more creativeness and godlike craft!'
But I, do I present you with my piece,
It's "What, Sludge? When my sainted mother spoke
The verses Lady Jane Grey last composed
About the rosy bower in the seventh heaven
Where she and Queen Elizabeth keep house,—
You made the raps? 'Twas your invention that?
Cur, slave and devil!"—eight fingers and two thumbs
Stuck in my throat!

Well, if the marks seem gone,
'Tis because stiffish cock-tail, taken in time,
Is better for a bruise than arnica.

There, sir! I bear no malice: 'tisn't in me.
I know I acted wrongly: still, I've tried
What I could say in my excuse,—to show
The devil's not all devil . . . I don't pretend,
An angel, much less such a gentleman
As you, sir! And I've lost you, lost myself,
Lost all, l-l-l- . . . .

No—are you in earnest, sir?
O, yours, sir, is an angel's part! I know
What prejudice must be, what the common course
Men take to soothe their ruffled self-conceit:
Only you rise superior to it all!
No, sir, it don't hurt much; it's speaking long
That makes me choke a little: the marks will go!
What? Twenty V-notes more, and outfit too,
And not a word to Greeley? One—one kiss
Of the hand that saves me! You'll not let me speak,
I well know, and I've lost the right, too true!
But I must say, sir, if She hears (she does)
Your sainted . . . Well, sir,—be it so! That's, I think,
My bed-room candle. Good-night! Bl-l-less you, sir!

R-r-r, you brute-beast and blackguard! Cowardly scamp!
I only wish I dared burn down the house
And spoil your sniggering! Oh what, you're the man?
You're satisfied at last? You've found out Sludge?
We'll see that presently: my turn, sir, next!
I too can tell my story: brute,—do you hear?—
You throttled your sainted mother, that old hag,
In just such a fit of passion: no, it was...
To get this house of hers, and many a note
Like these... I'll pocket them, however... five,
Ten, fifteen... ay, you gave her throat the twist,
Or else you poisoned her! Confound the cuss!
Where was my head? I ought to have prophesied
He'll die in a year and join her: that's the way.

I don't know where my head is: what had I done?
How did it all go? I said he poisoned her,
And hoped he'd have grace given him to repent,
Whereon he picked this quarrel, bullied me
And called me cheat: I thrashed him,—who could help?
He howled for mercy, prayed me on his knees
To cut and run and save him from disgrace:
I do so, and once off, he slanders me.
An end of him! Begin elsewhere anew!
Boston's a hole, the herring-pond is wide,
V-notes are something, liberty still more.
Beside, is he the only fool in the world?

FROM *HELEN'S TOWER, CLANDEBOYE* (1870)

Helen's Tower

Ἑλένη ἐπὶ πύργῳ

Who hears of Helen's Tower, may dream perchance
How the Greek Beauty from the Scœan Gate
Gazed on old friends unanimous in hate,
Death-doom'd because of her fair countenance.

Hearts would leap otherwise, at thy advance,
Lady to whom this Tower is consecrate!
Like her's, thy face once made all eyes elate,
Yet, unlike her's, was blessed by every glance.

The Tower of Hate is outworn, far and strange:
A transitory shame of long ago,
It dies into the sand from which it sprang;
But thine, Love's rock-built Tower, shall fear no change;
God's Self laid stable earth's foundations so,
When all the morning-stars together sang.

April 26, 1870.

FROM *FIFINE AT THE FAIR* (1872)

Prologue

AMPHIBIAN

1.

The fancy I had to-day,
   Fancy which turned a fear!
I swam far out in the bay,
   Since waves laughed warm and clear.

2.

I lay and looked at the sun,
   The noon-sun looked at me:
Between us two, no one
   Live creature, that I could see.

3.

Yes! There came floating by
   Me, who lay floating too,
Such a strange butterfly!
   Creature as dear as new:

4.

Because the membraned wings
   So wonderful, so wide,
So sun-suffused, were things
   Like soul and nought beside.

5.

A handbreadth over head!
   All of the sea my own,
It owned the sky instead;
   Both of us were alone.

6.

I never shall join its flight,
   For, nought buoys flesh in air.
If it touch the sea—good night!
   Death sure and swift waits there.

7.

Can the insect feel the better
   For watching the uncouth play
Of limbs that slip the fetter,
   Pretend as they were not clay?

8.

Undoubtedly I rejoice
   That the air comports so well
With a creature which had the choice
   Of the land once. Who can tell?

9.

What if a certain soul
   Which early slipped its sheath,
And has for its home the whole
   Of heaven, thus look beneath,

10.

Thus watch one who, in the world,
   Both lives and likes life's way,
Nor wishes the wings unfurled
   That sleep in the worm, they say?

11.

But sometimes when the weather
   Is blue, and warm waves tempt
To free oneself of tether,
   And try a life exempt

12.

From worldly noise and dust,
   In the sphere which overbrims
With passion and thought,—why, just
   Unable to fly, one swims!

13.

By passion and thought upborne,
  One smiles to oneself—"They fare
Scarce better, they need not scorn
  Our sea, who live in the air!"

14.

Emancipate through passion
  And thought, with sea for sky,
We substitute, in a fashion,
  For heaven—poetry:

15.

Which sea, to all intent,
  Gives flesh such noon-disport
As a finer element
  Affords the spirit-sort.

16.

Whatever they are, we seem:
  Imagine the thing they know;
All deeds they do, we dream;
  Can heaven be else but so?

17.

And meantime, yonder streak
  Meets the horizon's verge;
That is the land, to seek
  If we tire or dread the surge:

18.

Land the solid and safe—
  To welcome again (confess!)
When, high and dry, we chafe
  The body, and don the dress.

19.

Does she look, pity, wonder
  At one who mimics flight,
Swims—heaven above, sea under,
  Yet always earth in sight?

Epilogue

THE HOUSEHOLDER

1.

Savage I was sitting in my house, late, lone:
  Dreary, weary with the long day's work:
Head of me, heart of me, stupid as a stone:
  Tongue-tied now, now blaspheming like a Turk;
When, in a moment, just a knock, call, cry,
  Half a pang and all a rapture, there again were we!—
"What, and is it really you again?" quoth I:
  "I again, what else did you expect?" quoth She.

2.

"Never mind, hie away from this old house—
  Every crumbling brick embrowned with sin and shame!
Quick, in its corners ere certain shapes arouse!
  Let them—every devil of the night—lay claim,
Make and mend, or rap and rend, for me! Good-bye!
  God be their guard from disturbance at their glee,
Till, crash, comes down the carcass in a heap!" quoth I:
  "Nay, but there's a decency required!" quoth She.

3.

"Ah, but if you knew how time has dragged, days, nights!
  All the neighbour-talk with man and maid—such men!
All the fuss and trouble of street-sounds, window-sights:
  All the worry of flapping door and echoing roof; and then,
All the fancies . . . Who were they had leave, dared try
  Darker arts that almost struck despair in me?
If you knew but how I dwelt down here!" quoth I:
  "And was I so better off up there?" quoth She.

4.

"Help and get it over! *Re-united to his wife*
  (How draw up the paper lets the parish-people know?)
Lies M. or N., departed from this life,
  Day the this or that, month and year the so and so.
What i' the way of final flourish? Prose, verse? Try!
  Affliction sore, long time he bore, or, what is it to be?
Till God did please to grant him ease. Do end!" quoth I:
  "I end with—Love is all and Death is nought!" quoth She.

THE INN ALBUM (1875)

The Inn Album

"That oblong book's the Album; hand it here!
Exactly! page on page of gratitude
For breakfast, dinner, supper, and the view!
I praise these poets: they leave margin-space;
Each stanza seems to gather skirts around,
And primly, trimly, keep the foot's confine,
Modest and maidlike; lubber prose o'ersprawls
And straddling stops the path from left to right.
Since I want space to do my cipher-work,
Which poem spares a corner? What comes first?
'Hail, calm acclivity, salubrious spot!'
(Open the window, we burn daylight, boy!)
Or see—succincter beauty, brief and bold—
'If a fellow can dine On rumpsteaks and port wine,
He needs not despair Of dining well here—'
'*Here!'* I myself could find a better rhyme!
That bard's a Browning; he neglects the form:
But ah, the sense, ye gods, the weighty sense!
Still, I prefer this classic. Ay, throw wide!
I'll quench the bits of candle yet unburnt.
A minute's fresh air, then to cipher-work!
Three little columns hold the whole account:
Ecarté, after which—Blind Hookey—then
Cutting-the-Pack, five hundred pounds the cut.
'Tis easy reckoning: I have lost, I think."

Two personages occupy this room
Shabby-genteel, that's parlour to the inn
Perched on a view-commanding eminence;
—Inn which may be a veritable house
Where somebody once lived and pleased good taste
Till tourists found his coigne of vantage out,
And fingered blunt the individual mark
And vulgarized things comfortably smooth.
On a sprig-pattern-papered wall there brays
Complaint to sky Sir Edwin's dripping stag;
His couchant coast-guard creature corresponds;
They face the Huguenot and Light o' the World.
Grim o'er the mirror on the mantelpiece,

Varnished and coffined, *Salmo ferox* glares
—Possibly at the List of Wines which, framed
And glazed, hangs somewhat prominent on peg.

So much describes the stuffy little room—
Vulgar flat smooth respectability:
Not so the burst of landscape surging in,
Sunrise and all, as he who of the pair
Is, plain enough, the younger personage
Draws sharp the shrieking curtain, sends aloft
The sash, spreads wide and fastens back to wall
Shutter and shutter, shows you England's best.
He leans into a living glory-bath
Of air and light where seems to float and move
The wooded watered country, hill and dale
And steel-bright thread of stream, a-smoke with mist,
A-sparkle with May morning, diamond drift
O' the sun-touched dew. Except the red-roofed patch
Of half a dozen dwellings that, crept close
For hill-side shelter, make the village-clump,
This inn is perched above to dominate—
Except such sign of human neighbourhood,
And this surmised rather than sensible,
There's nothing to disturb absolute peace,
The reign of English nature—which means art
And civilized existence. Wildness' self
Is just the cultured triumph. Presently
Deep solitude, be sure, reveals a Place
That knows the right way to defend itself:
Silence hems round a burning spot of life.
Now, where a Place burns, must a village brood,
And where a village broods, an inn should boast—
Close and convenient: here you have them both.
This inn, the Something-arms—the family's—
(Don't trouble Guillim: heralds leave out half!)
Is dear to lovers of the picturesque,
And epics have been planned here; but who plan
Take holy orders and find work to do.
Painters are more productive, stop a week,
Declare the prospect quite a Corot,—ay,
For tender sentiment,—themselves incline

Rather to handsweep large and liberal;
Then go, but not without success achieved
—Haply some pencil-drawing, oak or beech,
Ferns at the base and ivies up the bole,
On this a slug, on that a butterfly.
Nay, he who hooked the *salmo* pendent here,
Also exhibited, this same May-month,
'*Foxgloves: a study*'—so inspires the scene,
The air, which now the younger personage
Inflates him with till lungs o'erfraught are fain
Sigh forth a satisfaction might bestir
Even those tufts of tree-tops to the South
I' the distance where the green dies off to grey,
Which, easy of conjecture, front the Place;
He eyes them, elbows wide, each hand to cheek.

His fellow, the much older—either say
A youngish-old man or man oldish-young—
Sits at the table: wicks are noisome-deep
In wax, to detriment of plated ware;
Above—piled, strewn—is store of playing-cards,
Counters and all that's proper for a game.
He sets down, rubs out figures in the book,
Adds and subtracts, puts back here, carries there,
Until the summed-up satisfaction stands
Apparent, and he pauses o'er the work:
Soothes what of brain was busy under brow,
By passage of the hard palm, curing so
Wrinkle and crow-foot for a second's space;
Then lays down book and laughs out. No mistake,
Such the sum-total—ask Colenso else!

Roused by which laugh, the other turns, laughs too—
The youth, the good strong fellow, rough perhaps.

"Well, what's the damage—three, or four, or five?
How many figures in a row? Hand here!
Come now, there's one expense all yours not mine—
Scribbling the people's Album over, leaf
The first and foremost too! You think, perhaps,
They'll only charge you for a bran-new book
Nor estimate the literary loss?

Wait till the small account comes! '*To one night's . . .*
Lodging,'—for 'beds,' they can't say,—'*pound or so*;
Dinner, Apollinaris,—what they please,
Attendance not included;' last looms large
'*Defacement of our Album, late enriched*
With'—let's see what! Here, at the window, though!
Ay, breathe the morning and forgive your luck!
Fine enough country for a fool like me
To own, as next month, I suppose I shall!
Eh? True fool's-fortune! so console yourself.
Let's see, however—hand the book, I say!
Well, you've improved the classic by romance.
Queer reading! Verse with parenthetic prose—
'*Hail, calm acclivity, salubrious spot!*'
(Three-two fives) '*life how profitably spent*'
(Five-nought, five-nine fives) '*yonder humble cot*,'
(More and more noughts and fives) '*in mild content*;
And did my feelings find the natural vent
In friendship and in love, how blest my lot!'
Then follow the dread figures—five! '*Content!*'
That's apposite! Are you content as he—
Simpkin the sonneteer? *Ten thousand pounds*
Give point to his effusion—by so much
Leave me the richer and the poorer you
After our night's play; who's content the most,
I, you, or Simpkin?"
So the polished snob.
The elder man, refinement every inch
From brow to boot-end, quietly replies:

"Simpkin's no name I know. I had my whim."

"Ay, had you! And such things make friendship thick.
Intimates, I may boast we were; henceforth,
Friends—shall it not be?—who discard reserve,
Use plain words, put each dot upon each i,
Till death us twain do part? The bargain's struck!
Old fellow, if you fancy—(to begin—)
I failed to penetrate your scheme last week,
You wrong your poor disciple. Oh, no airs!
Because you happen to be twice my age

And twenty times my master, must perforce
No blink of daylight struggle through the web
There's no unwinding? You entoil my legs,
And welcome, for I like it: blind me,—no!
A very pretty piece of shuttle-work
Was that—your mere chance question at the club—
'Do you go anywhere this Whitsuntide?
I'm off for Paris, there's the Opera—there's
The Salon, there's a china-sale,—beside
Chantilly; and, for good companionship,
There's Such-and-such and So-and-so. Suppose
We start together?' 'No such holiday!'
I told you: *'Paris and the rest be hanged!*
Why plague me who am pledged to home-delights?
I'm the engaged now; through whose fault but yours?
On duty. As you well know. Don't I drowse
The week away down with the Aunt and Niece?
No help: it's leisure, loneliness and love.
'Wish I could take you; but fame travels fast,—
A man of much newspaper-paragraph,
You scare domestic circles; and beside
Would not you like your lot, that second taste
Of nature and approval of the grounds!
You might walk early or lie late, so shirk
Week-day devotions: but stay Sunday o'er,
And morning church is obligatory:
No mundane garb permissible, or dread
The butler's privileged monition! No!
Pack off to Paris, nor wipe tear away!'
Whereon how artlessly the happy flash
Followed, by inspiration! ''*Tell you what—*
Let's turn their flank, try things on t'other side!
Inns for my money! Liberty's the life!
We'll lie in hiding: there's the crow-nest nook,
The tourist's joy, the Inn they rave about,
Inn that's out—out of sight and out of mind
And out of mischief to all four of us—
Aunt and niece, you and me. At night arrive;
At morn, find time for just a Pisgah-view
Of my friend's Land of Promise; then depart.
And while I'm whizzing onward by first train,

Bound for our own place (since my Brother sulks
And says I shun him like the plague) yourself—
Why, you have stepped thence, start from platform, gay
Despite the sleepless journey,—love lends wings,—
Hug aunt and niece who, none the wiser, wait
The faithful advent! Eh?' '*With all my heart,*'
Said I to you; said I to mine own self:
'*Does he believe I fail to comprehend*
He wants just one more final friendly snack
At friend's exchequer ere friend runs to earth,
Marries, renounces yielding friends such sport?'
And did I spoil sport, pull face grim,—nay, grave?
Your pupil does you better credit! No!
I parleyed with my pass-book,—rubbed my pair
At the big balance in my banker's hands,—
Folded a cheque cigar-case-shape,—just wants
Filling and signing,—and took train, resolved
To execute myself with decency
And let you win—if not Ten thousand quite,
Something by way of wind-up, farewell burst
Of firework-nosegay! Where's your fortune fled?
Or is not fortune constant after all?
You lose ten thousand pounds: had I lost half
Or half that, I should bite my lips, I think.
You man of marble! Strut and stretch my best
On tiptoe, I shall never reach your height.
How does the loss feel? Just one lesson more!"

The more refined man smiles a frown away.

"The lesson shall be—only boys like you
Put such a question at the present stage.
I had a ball lodge in my shoulder once,
And, full five minutes, never guessed the fact;
Next day, I felt decidedly: and still,
At twelve years' distance, when I lift my arm
A twinge reminds me of the surgeon's probe.
Ask me, this day month, how I feel my luck!
And meantime please to stop impertinence,
For—don't I know its object? All this chaff
Covers the corn, this preface leads to speech,

This boy stands forth a hero. '*There, my lord!*
Our play was true play, fun not earnest! I
Empty your purse, inside out, while my poke
Bulges to bursting? You can badly spare
A doit, confess now, Duke though brother be!
While I'm gold-daubed so thickly, spangles drop
And show my father's warehouse-apron: pshaw!
Enough! We've had a palpitating night!
Good morning! Breakfast and forget our dreams!
My mouth's shut, mind! I tell nor man nor mouse.'
There, see! He don't deny it! Thanks, my boy!
Hero and welcome—only, not on me
Make trial of your 'prentice-hand! Enough!
We've played, I've lost and owe ten thousand pounds,
Whereof I muster, at the moment,—well,
What's for the bill here and the back to town.
Still, I've my little character to keep:
You may expect your money at month's end."

The young man at the window turns round quick—
A clumsy giant handsome creature; grasps
In his large red the little lean white hand
Of the other, looks him in the sallow face.

"I say now—is it right to so mistake
A fellow, force him in mere self-defence
To spout like Mister *Mild Acclivity*
In album-language? You know well enough
Whether I like you—*like*'s no album-word,
Anyhow: point me to one soul beside
In the wide world I care one straw about!
I first set eyes on you a year ago;
Since when you've done me good—I'll stick to it—
More than I got in the whole twenty-five
That make my life up, Oxford years and all—
Throw in the three I fooled away abroad,
Seeing myself and nobody more sage
Until I met you, and you made me man
Such as the sort is and the fates allow.
I do think, since we two kept company,
I've learnt to know a little—all through you!

It's nature if I like you. Taunt away!
As if I need you teaching me my place—
The snob I am, the Duke your brother is,
When just the good you did was—teaching me
My own trade, how a snob and millionnaire
May lead his life and let the Duke's alone,
Clap wings, free jackdaw, on his steeple-perch,
Burnish his black to gold in sun and air,
Nor pick up stray plumes, strive to match in strut
Regular peacocks who can't fly an inch
Over the court-yard-paling. Head and heart
(That's album-style) are older than you know,
For all your knowledge: boy, perhaps—ay, boy
Had his adventure, just as he were man—
His ball-experience in the shoulder-blade,
His bit of life-long ache to recognize,
Although he bears it cheerily about,
Because you came and clapped him on the back,
Advised him '*Walk and wear the aching off!*'
Why, I was minded to sit down for life
Just in Dalmatia, build a sea-side tower
High on a rock, and so expend my days
Pursuing chemistry or botany
Or, very like, astronomy because
I noticed stars shone when I passed the place:
Letting my cash accumulate the while
In England—to lay out in lump at last
As Ruskin should direct me! All or some
Of which should I have done or tried to do,
And preciously repented, one fine day,
Had you discovered Timon, climbed his rock
And scaled his tower, some ten years thence, suppose,
And coaxed his story from him! Don't I see
The pair conversing! It's a novel writ
Already, I'll be bound,—our dialogue!
'What?' cried the elder and yet youthful man—
So did the eye flash 'neath the lordly front,
And the imposing presence swell with scorn,
As the haught high-bred bearing and dispose
Contrasted with his interlocutor
The flabby low-born who, of bulk before,

Had steadily increased, one stone per week,
Since his abstention from horse-exercise:—
'What? you, as rich as Rothschild, left, you say,
London the very year you came of age,
Because your father manufactured goods—
Commission-agent hight of Manchester—
Partly, and partly through a baby case
Of disappointment I've pumped out at last—
And here you spend life's prime in gaining flesh
And giving science one more asteroid?'
Brief, my dear fellow, you instructed me,
At Alfred's and not Istria! proved a snob
May turn a million to account although
His brother be no Duke, and see good days
Without the girl he lost and some one gained.
The end is, after one year's tutelage,
Having, by your help, touched society,
Polo, Tent-pegging, Hurlingham, the Rink—
I leave all these delights, by your advice,
And marry my young pretty cousin here
Whose place, whose oaks ancestral you behold.
(Her father was in partnership with mine—
Does not his purchase look a pedigree?)
My million will be tail and tassels smart
To this plump-bodied kite, this house and land
Which, set a-soaring, pulls me, soft as sleep,
Along life's pleasant meadow,—arm left free
To lock a friend's in,—whose, but yours, old boy?
Arm in arm glide we over rough and smooth,
While hand, to pocket held, saves cash from cards.
Now, if you don't esteem ten thousand pounds
(—Which I shall probably discover snug
Hid somewhere in the column-corner capped
With '*Credit*,' based on '*Balance*,'—which, I swear,
By this time next month I shall quite forget
Whether I lost or won—ten thousand pounds,
Which at this instant I would give . . let's see,
For Galopin—nay, for that Gainsborough
Sir Richard won't sell, and, if bought by me,
Would get my glance and praise some twice a year,—)
Well, if you don't esteem that price dirt-cheap

For teaching me Dalmatia was mistake—
Why then, my last illusion-bubble breaks,
My one discovered phoenix proves a goose,
My cleverest of all companions—oh,
Was worth nor ten pence nor ten thousand pounds!
Come! Be yourself again! So endeth here
The morning's lesson! Never while life lasts
Do I touch card again. To breakfast now!
To bed—I can't say, since you needs must start
For station early—oh, the down-train still,
First plan and best plan—townward trip be hanged!
You're due at your big brother's—pay that debt,
Then owe me not a farthing! Order eggs—
And who knows but there's trout obtainable?"—

The fine man looks well-nigh malignant: then—

"Sir, please subdue your manner! Debts are debts:
I pay mine—debts of this sort—certainly.
What do I care how you regard your gains,
Want them or want them not? The thing *I* want
Is—not to have a story circulate
From club to club—how, bent on clearing out
Young So-and-so, young So-and-so cleaned me,
Then set the empty kennel flush again,
Ignored advantage and forgave his friend—
For why? There was no wringing blood from stone!
Oh, don't be savage! You would hold your tongue,
Bite it in two, as man may; but those small
Hours in the smoking-room, when instance apt
Rises to tongue's root, tingles on to tip,
And the thinned company consists of six
Capital well-known fellows one may trust!
Next week, it's in the 'World.' No, thank you much.
I owe ten thousand pounds: I'll pay them!"

"Now,—
This becomes funny. You've made friends with me:
I can't help knowing of the ways and means!
Or stay! they say your brother closets up
Correggio's long-lost Leda: if he means
To give you that, and if you give it me . . ."

"*I* polished snob off to aristocrat?
You compliment me! father's apron still
Sticks out from son's court-vesture; still silk purse
Roughs finger with some bristle sow-ear-born!
Well, neither I nor you mean harm at heart!
I owe you and shall pay you: which premised,
Why should what follows sound like flattery?
The fact is—you do compliment too much
Your humble master, as I own I am;
You owe me no such thanks as you protest.
The polisher needs precious stone no less
Than precious stone needs polisher: believe
I struck no tint from out you but I found
Snug lying first 'neath surface hair-breadth-deep!
Beside, I liked the exercise: with skill
Goes love to show skill for skill's sake. You see,
I'm old and understand things: too absurd
It were you pitched and tossed away your life,
As diamond were Scotch-pebble! all the more,
That I myself misused a stone of price.
Born and bred clever—people used to say
Clever as most men, if not something more—
Yet here I stand a failure, cut awry
Or left opaque,—no brilliant named and known.
Whate'er my inner stuff, my outside's blank;
I'm nobody—or rather, look that same—
I'm—who I am—and know it; but I hold
What in my hand out for the world to see?
What ministry, what mission, or what book
—I'll say, book even? Not a sign of these!
I began—laughing—'*All these when I like!*'
I end with—well, you've hit it!—'*This boy's cheque*
For just as many thousands as he'll spare!'
The first—I could, and would not; your spare cash
I would, and could not: have no scruple, pray,
But, as I hoped to pocket yours, pouch mine
—When you are able!"

"Which is—when to be?
I've heard, great characters require a fall
Of fortune to show greatness by uprise:

They touch the ground to jollily rebound,
Add to the Album! Let a fellow share
Your secret of superiority!
I know, my banker makes the money breed
Money; I eat and sleep, he simply takes
The dividends and cuts the coupons off,
Sells out, buys in, keeps doubling, tripling cash,
While I do nothing but receive and spend.
But you, spontaneous generator, hatch
A wind-egg; cluck, and forth struts Capital
As Interest to me from egg of gold.
I am grown curious: pay me by all means!
How will you make the money?"
"Mind your own—
Not my affair. Enough: or money, or
Money's worth, as the case may be, expect
Ere month's end,—keep but patient for a month!
Who's for a stroll to station? Ten's the time;
Your man, with my things, follow in the trap;
At stoppage of the down-train, play the arrived
On platform and you'll show the due fatigue
Of the night-journey,—not much sleep,—perhaps,
Your thoughts were on before you—yes, indeed,
You join them, being happily awake
With thought's sole object as she smiling sits
At breakfast-table. I shall dodge meantime
In and out station-precinct, wile away
The hour till up my engine pants and smokes.
No doubt, she goes to fetch you. Never fear!
She gets no glance at me, who shame such saints!"

II.

So, they ring bell, give orders, pay, depart
Amid profuse acknowledgment from host
Who well knows what may bring the younger back,
Light the cigar, descend in twenty steps
The '*calm acclivity*,' inhale—beyond
Tobacco's balm—the better smoke of turf
And wood fire,—cottages at cookery

I' the morning,—reach the main road straightening on
'Twixt wood and wood, two black walls full of night
Slow to disperse, though mists thin fast before
The advancing foot, and leave the flint-dust fine
Each speck with its fire-sparkle. Presently
The road's end with the sky's beginning mix
In one magnificence of glare, due East,
So high the sun rides,—May's the merry month.

They slacken pace: the younger stops abrupt,
Discards cigar, looks his friend full in face.

"All right; the station comes in view at end;
Five minutes from the beech-clump, there you are!
I say: let's halt, let's borrow yonder gate
Of its two magpies, sit and have a talk!
Do let a fellow speak a moment! More
I think about and less I like the thing—
No, you must let me! Now, be good for once!
Ten thousand pounds be done for, dead and damned!
We played for love, not hate: yes, hate! I hate
Thinking you beg or borrow or reduce
To strychnine some poor devil of a lord
Licked at Unlimited Loo. I had the cash
To lose—you knew that!—lose and none the less
Whistle to-morrow: it's not every chap
Affords to take his punishment so well!
Now, don't be angry with a friend whose fault
Is that he thinks—upon my soul, I do—
Your head the best head going. Oh, one sees
Names in the newspaper—great this, great that,
Gladstone, Carlyle, the Laureate:—much I care!
Others have their opinion, I keep mine:
Which means—by right you ought to have the things
I want a head for. Here's a pretty place,
My cousin's place, and presently my place,
Not yours! I'll tell you how it strikes a man.
My cousin's fond of music and of course
Plays the piano (it won't be for long!)
A bran-new bore she calls a '*semi-grand*'
Rose-wood and pearl, that blocks the drawing-room,

And cost no end of money. Twice a week
Down comes Herr Somebody and seats himself,
Sets to work teaching—with his teeth on edge—
I've watched the rascal. '*Does he play first-rate?*'
I ask: '*I rather think so*,' answers she—
'*He's What's-his-Name!*'—'*Why give you lessons then?*'—
'*I pay three guineas and the train beside.*'—
'*This instrument, has he one such at home?*'—
'*He? Has to practise on a table-top,*
When he can't hire the proper thing.'—'*I see!*
You've the piano, he the skill, and God
The distribution of such gifts.' So here:
After your teaching, I shall sit and strum
Polkas on this piano of a Place
You'd make resound with '*Rule Britannia*'!"
"Thanks!
I don't say but this pretty cousin's place,
Appendaged with your million, tempts my hand
As key-board I might touch with some effect."

"Then, why not have obtained the like? House, land,
Money, are things obtainable, you see,
By clever head-work: ask my father else!
You, who teach me, why not have learned, yourself?
Played like Herr Somebody with power to thump
And flourish and the rest, not bend demure
Pointing out blunders—'*Sharp, not natural!*
Permit me—on the black key use the thumb!'
There's some fatality, I'm sure! You say
'*Marry the cousin, that's your proper move!*'
And I do use the thumb and hit the sharp:
You should have listened to your own head's hint,
As I to you! The puzzle's past my power,
How you have managed—with such stuff, such means—
Not to be rich nor great nor happy man:
Of which three good things where's a sign at all?
Just look at Dizzy! Come,—what tripped your heels?
Instruct a goose that boasts wings and can't fly!
I wager I have guessed it!—never found
The old solution of the riddle fail!
'*Who was the woman*?' I don't ask, but—*Where*

I' the path of life stood she who tripped you?'"
"Goose
You truly are! I own to fifty years.
Why don't I interpose and cut out—you?
Compete with five-and-twenty? Age, my boy!"

"Old man, no nonsense!—even to a boy
That's ripe at least for rationality
Rapped into him, as may be mine was, once!
I've had my small adventure lesson me
Over the knuckles!—likely, I forget
The sort of figure youth cuts now and then,
Competing with old shoulders but young head
Despite the fifty grizzling years!"

"Aha?
Then that means—just the bullet in the blade
Which brought Dalmatia on the brain,—that, too,
Came of a fatal creature? Can't pretend
Now for the first time to surmise as much!
Make a clean breast! Recount! a secret's safe
'Twixt you, me and the gate-post!"

"—Can't pretend,
Neither, to never have surmised your wish!
It's no use,—case of unextracted ball—
Winces at finger-touching. Let things be!"

"Ah, if you love your love still! I hate mine."

"I can't hate."

"I won't teach you; and won't tell
You, therefore, what you please to ask of me
As if I, also, may not have my ache!"

"My sort of ache? No, no! and yet—perhaps!
All comes of thinking you superior still.
But live and learn! I say! Time's up! Good jump!
You old, indeed! I fancy there's a cut
Across the wood, a grass path: shall we try?
It's venturesome, however!"

"Stop, my boy!

Don't think I'm stingy of experience! Life
—It's like this wood we leave. Should you and I
Go wandering about there, though the gaps
We went in and came out by were opposed
As the two poles, still, somehow, all the same,
By nightfall we should probably have chanced
On much the same main points of interest—
Both of us measured girth of mossy trunk,
Stript ivy from its strangled prey, clapped hands
At squirrel, sent a fir-cone after crow,
And so forth,—never mind what time betwixt.
So in our lives; allow I entered mine
Another way than you: 'tis possible
I ended just by knocking head against
That plaguy low-hung branch yourself began
By getting bump from; as at last you too
May stumble o'er that stump which first of all
Bade me walk circumspectly. Head and feet
Are vulnerable both, and I, foot-sure,
Forgot that ducking down saves brow from bruise.
I, early old, played young man four years since
And failed confoundedly: so, hate alike
Failure and who caused failure,—curse her cant!"

"Oh, I see! You, though somewhat past the prime,
Were taken with a rosebud beauty! Ah—
But how should chits distinguish? She admired
Your marvel of a mind, I'll undertake!
But as to body . . nay, I mean . . that is,
When years have told on face and figure . . ."

"Thanks,
Mister *Sufficiently-Instructed!* Such
No doubt was bound to be the consequence
To suit your self-complacency: she liked
My head enough, but loved some heart beneath
Some head with plenty of brown hair a-top
After my young friend's fashion! What becomes
Of that fine speech you made a minute since
About the man of middle age you found
A formidable peer at twenty-one?

So much for your mock-modesty! and yet
I back your first against this second sprout
Of observation, insight, what you please.
My middle age, Sir, had too much success!
It's odd: my case occurred four years ago—
I finished just while you commenced that turn
I' the wood of life that takes us to the wealth
Of honeysuckle, heaped for who can reach.
Now, I don't boast: it's bad style, and beside,
The feat proves easier than it looks: I plucked
Full many a flower unnamed in that bouquet
(Mostly of peonies and poppies, though!)
Good nature sticks into my button-hole.
Therefore it was with nose in want of snuff
Rather than Ess or Psidium, that I chanced
On what—so far from '*rosebud beauty*' . . Well—
She's dead: at least you never heard her name;
She was no courtly creature, had nor birth
Nor breeding—mere fine-lady-breeding; but
Oh, such a wonder of a woman! Grand
As a Greek statue! Stick fine clothes on that,
Style that a Duchess or a Queen,—you know,
Artists would make an outcry: all the more,
That she had just a statue's sleepy grace
Which broods o'er its own beauty. Nay, her fault
(Don't laugh!) was just perfection: for suppose
Only the little flaw, and I had peeped
Inside it, learned what soul inside was like.
At Rome some tourist raised the grit beneath
A Venus' forehead with his whittling-knife—
I wish,—now,—I had played that brute, brought blood
To surface from the depths I fancied chalk!
As it was, her mere face surprised so much
That I stopped short there, struck on heap, as stares
The cockney stranger at a certain bust
With drooped eyes,—she's the thing I have in mind,—
Down at my Brother's. All sufficient prize—
Such outside! Now,—confound me for a prig!—
Who cares? I'll make a clean breast once for all!
Beside, you've heard the gossip. My life long
I've been a woman-liker,—liking means

Loving and so on. There's a lengthy list
By this time I shall have to answer for—
So say the good folk: and they don't guess half—
For the worst is, let once collecting-itch
Possess you, and, with perspicacity
Keeps growing such a greediness that theft
Follows at no long distance,—there's the fact!
I knew that on my Leporello-list
Might figure this, that and the other name
Of feminine desirability,
But if I happened to desire inscribe,
Along with these, the only Beautiful—
Here was the unique specimen to snatch
Or now or never. 'Beautiful' I said—
'Beautiful' say in cold blood,—boiling then
To tune of '*Haste, secure whate'er the cost*
This rarity, die in the act, be damned,
So you complete collection, crown your list!'
It seemed as though the whole world, once aroused
By the first notice of such wonder's birth,
Would break bounds to contest my prize with me
The first discoverer, should she but emerge
From that safe den of darkness where she dozed
Till I stole in, that country-parsonage
Where, country-parson's daughter, motherless,
Brotherless, sisterless, for eighteen years
She had been vegetating lily-like.
Her father was my brother's tutor, got
The living that way: him I chanced to see—
Her I saw—her the world would grow one eye
To see, I felt no sort of doubt at all!
'*Secure her!*' cried the devil: '*afterward*
Arrange for the disposal of the prize!'
The devil's doing! yet I seem to think—
Now, when all's done,—think with '*a head reposed*'
In French phrase—hope I think I meant to do
All requisite for such a rarity
When I should be at leisure, have due time
To learn requirement. But in evil day—
Bless me, at week's end, long as any year,
The father must begin '*Young Somebody*,

Much recommended—for I break a rule—
Comes here to read, next Long Vacation.' 'Young!'
That did it. Had the epithet been '*rich* ,'
'*Noble,*' '*a genius,*' even '*handsome,*'—but
—'*Young*'*!*"

"I say—just a word! I want to know—
You are not married?"

"I?"

"Nor ever were?"

"Never! Why?"

"Oh, then—never mind! Go on!
I had a reason for the question."

"Come,—
You could not be the young man?"
"No, indeed!
Certainly—if you never married her!"

"That I did not: and there's the curse, you'll see!
Nay, all of it's one curse, my life's mistake
Which, nourished with manure that's warranted
To make the plant bear wisdom, blew out full
In folly beyond field-flower-foolishness!
The lies I used to tell my womankind,
Knowing they disbelieved me all the time
Though they required my lies, their decent due,
This woman—not so much believed, I'll say,
As just anticipated from my mouth:
Since being true, devoted, constant—she
Found constancy, devotion, truth, the plain
And easy commonplace of character.
No mock-heroics but seemed natural
To her who underneath the face, I knew
Was fairness' self, possessed a heart, I judged
Must correspond in folly just as far
Beyond the common,—and a mind to match,—
Not made to puzzle conjurers like me
Who, therein, proved the fool who fronts you, Sir,
And begs leave to cut short the ugly rest!

'*Trust me!*' I said: she trusted. '*Marry me!*'
Or rather, '*We are married: when, the rite?*'
That brought on the collector's next day qualm
At counting acquisition's cost. There lay
My marvel, there my purse more light by much
Because of its late lie-expenditure:
Ill-judged such moment to make fresh demand—
Bid cage as well as catch my rarity!
So, I began explaining. At first word
Outbroke the horror. '*Then, my truths were lies!*'
I tell you, such an outbreak, such new strange
All-unsuspected revelation—soul
As supernaturally grand as face
Was fair beyond example—that at once
Either I lost—or, if it please you, found
My senses,—stammered somehow—'*Jest! and now,*
Earnest! Forget all else but—heart has loved,
Does love, shall love you ever! take the hand!'
Not she! no marriage for superb disdain,
Contempt incarnate!"

"Yes, it's different,—
It's only like in being four years since.
I see now!"

"Well, what did disdain do next,
Think you?"

"That's past me: did not marry you!—
That's the main thing I care for, I suppose.
Turned nun, or what?"

"Why, married in a month
Some parson, some smug crop-haired smooth-chinned sort
Of curate-creature, I suspect,—dived down,
Down, deeper still, and came up somewhere else—
I don't know where—I've not tried much to know,—
In short she's happy: what the clodpoles call
'Countrified' with a vengeance! leads the life
Respectable and all that drives you mad:
Still—where, I don't know, and that's best for both."

"Well, that she did not like you, I conceive.
But why should you hate her, I want to know?"

"My good young friend,—because or her or else
Malicious Providence I have to hate.
For, what I tell you proved the turning-point
Of my whole life and fortune toward success
Or failure. If I drown, I lay the fault
Much on myself who caught at reed not rope,
But more on reed which, with a packthread's pith,
Had buoyed me till the minute's cramp could thaw
And I strike out afresh and so be saved.
It's easy saying—I had sunk before,
Disqualified myself by idle days
And busy nights, long since, from holding hard
On cable, even, had fate cast me such!
You boys don't know how many times men fail
Perforce o' the little to succeed i' the large,
Husband their strength, let slip the petty prey,
Collect the whole power for the final pounce.
My fault was the mistaking man's main prize
For intermediate boy's diversion; clap
Of boyish hands here frightened game away
Which, once gone, goes for ever. Oh, at first
I took the anger easily, nor much
Minded the anguish—having learned that storms
Subside, and teapot-tempests are akin.
Time would arrange things, mend whate'er might be
Somewhat amiss; precipitation, eh?
Reason and rhyme prompt—reparation! Tiffs
End properly in marriage and a dance!
I said 'We'll marry, make the past a blank'—
And never was such damnable mistake!
That interview, that laying bare my soul,
As it was first, so was it last chance—one
And only. Did I write? Back letter came
Unopened as it went. Inexorable
She fled, I don't know where, consoled herself
With the smug curate-creature: chop and change!
Sure am I, when she told her shaveling all
His Magdalen's adventure, tears were shed,

Forgiveness evangelically shewn,
'Loose hair and lifted eye,'—as someone says.
And now, he's worshipped for his pains, the sneak!"

"Well, but your turning-point of life,—what's here
To hinder you contesting Finsbury
With Orton, next election? I don't see . . ."

"Not you! But *I* see. Slowly, surely, creeps
Day by day o'er me the conviction—here
Was life's prize grasped at, gained, and then let go!
—That with her—may be, for her—I had felt
Ice in me melt, grow steam, drive to effect
Any or all the fancies sluggish here
I' the head that needs the hand she would not take
And I shall never lift now. Lo, your wood—
Its turnings which I likened life to! Well,—
There she stands, ending every avenue,
Her visionary presence on each goal
I might have gained had we kept side by side!
Still string nerve and strike foot? Her frown forbids:
The steam congeals once more: I'm old again!
Therefore I hate myself—but how much worse
Do not I hate who would not understand,
Let me repair things—no, but sent a-slide
My folly faulteringly, stumblingly
Down, down and deeper down until I drop
Upon—the need of your ten thousand pounds
And consequently loss of mine! I lose
Character, cash, nay, common-sense itself
Recounting such a lengthy cock-and-bull
Adventure—lose my temper in the act . . ."

"And lose beside,—if I may supplement
The list of losses,—train and ten-o'clock!
Hark, pant and puff, there travels the swart sign!
So much the better! You're my captive now!
I'm glad you trust a fellow: friends grow thick
This way—that's twice said; we were thickish, though,
Even last night, and, ere night comes again,
I prophesy good luck to both of us!
For see now!—back to '*balmy eminence*'

Or '*calm acclivity*' or what's the word,
Bestow you there an hour, concoct at ease
A sonnet for the Album, while I put
Bold face on, best foot forward, make for house,
March in to aunt and niece, and tell the truth—
(Even white-lying goes against my taste
After your little story.) Oh, the niece
Is rationality itself! The aunt—
If she's amenable to reason too—
Why, you stopped short to pay her due respect,
And let the Duke wait (I'll work well the Duke).
If she grows gracious, I return for you;
If thunder's in the air, why—bear your doom,
Dine on rump-steaks and port, and shake the dust
Of aunty from your shoes as off you go
By evening-train, nor give the thing a thought
How you shall pay me—that's as sure as fate,
Old fellow! Off with you, face left about!
Yonder's the path I have to pad. You see,
I'm in good spirits, God knows why! Perhaps
Because the woman did not marry you
—Who look so hard at me,—and have the right,
One must be fair and own!"

The two stand still
Under an oak.

"Look here!" resumes the youth.
"I never quite knew how I came to like
You—so much—whom I ought not court at all:
Nor how you had a leaning just to me
Who am assuredly not worth your pains
For there must needs be plenty such as you
Somewhere about,—although I can't say where,—
Able and willing to teach all you know;
While—how can you have missed a score like me
With money and no wit, precisely each
A pupil for your purpose, were it—ease
Fool's poke of tutor's *honorarium*-fee?
And yet, howe'er it came about, I felt

At once my master: you as prompt descried
Your man, I warrant, so was bargain struck.
Now, these same lines of liking, loving, run
Sometimes so close together they converge—
Life's great adventures—you know what I mean—
In people. Do you know, as you advanced,
It got to be uncommonly like fact
We two had fallen in with—liked and loved
Just the same woman in our different ways?
I began life—poor groundling as I prove—
Winged and ambitious to fly high: why not?
There's something in 'Don Quixote' to the point,
My shrewd old father used to quote and praise—
'*Am I born man?*' asks Sancho: '*being man,*
By possibility I may be Pope!'
So, Pope I meant to make myself, by step
And step, whereof the first should be to find
A perfect woman; and I tell you this—
If what I fixed on, in the order due
Of undertakings, as next step, had first
Of all disposed itself to suit my tread,
And I had been, the day I came of age,
Returned at head of poll for Westminster
—Nay, and moreover summoned by the Queen
At week's end, when my maiden-speech bore fruit,
To form and head a Tory ministry—
It would not have seemed stranger, no, nor been
More strange to me, as now I estimate,
Than what did happen—sober truth, no dream.
I saw my wonder of a woman,—laugh,
I'm past that!—in Commemoration-week.
A plenty have I seen since, fair and foul,—
With eyes, too, helped by your sagacious wink;
But one to match that marvel—no least trace,
Least touch of kinship and community!
The end was—I did somehow state the fact,
Did, with no matter what imperfect words,
One way or other give to understand
That woman, soul and body were her slave
Would she but take, but try them—any test
Of will, and some poor test of power beside:

So did the strings within my brain grow tense
And capable of . . . hang similitudes!
She answered kindly but beyond appeal.
'*No sort of hope for me, who came too late.*
She was another's. Love went—mine to her,
Hers just as loyally to someone else.'
Of course! I might expect it! Nature's law—
Given the peerless woman, certainly
Somewhere shall be the peerless man to match!
I acquiesced at once, submitted me
In something of a stupor, went my way.
I fancy there had been some talk before
Of somebody—her father or the like—
To coach me in the holidays,—that's how
I came to get the sight and speech of her,—
But I had sense enough to break off sharp,
Save both of us the pain."

"Quite right there!"

"Eh?
Quite wrong, it happens! Now comes worst of all!
Yes, I did sulk aloof and let alone
Thc lovers *I* disturb the angel-mates?"

"Seraph paired off with cherub!"

"Thank you! While
I never plucked up courage to inquire
Who he was, even,—certain-sure of this,
That nobody I knew of had blue wings
And wore a star-crown as he needs must do,—
Some little lady,—plainish, pock-marked girl,—
Finds out my secret in my woeful face,
Comes up to me at the Apollo Ball,
And pityingly pours her wine and oil
This way into the wound: '*Dear f-f-friend,*
Why waste affection thus on—must I say,
A somewhat worthless object? Who's her choice—
Irrevocable as deliberate—
Out of the wide world? I shall name no names—
But there's a person in society,

Who, blessed with rank and talent, has grown grey
In idleness and sin of every sort
Except hypocrisy: he's thrice her age,
A byeword for 'successes with the sex'
As the French say—and, as we ought to say,
Consummately a liar and a rogue,
Since—show me where's the woman won without
The help of this one lie which she believes—
That—never mind how things have come to pass,
And let who loves have loved a thousand times—
All the same he now loves her only, loves
Her ever! if by 'won' you just mean 'sold,'
That's quite another compact. Well, this scamp,
Continuing descent from bad to worse,
Must leave his fine and fashionable prey
(Who—fathered, brothered, husbanded,—are hedged
About with thorny danger) and apply
His arts to this poor country ignorance
Who sees forthwith in the first rag of man
Her model hero! Why continue waste
On such a woman treasures of a heart
Would yet find solace,—yes, my f-f-friend—
In some congenial —fiddle-diddle-dee?'"

"Pray, is the pleasant gentleman described
Exact the portrait which my '*f-f-friends*'
Recognize as so like? 'Tis evident
You half surmised the sweet original
Could be no other than myself, just now!
Your stop and start were flattering!"

"Of course
Caricature's allowed for in a sketch!
The longish nose becomes a foot in length,
The swarthy cheek gets copper-coloured,—still,
Prominent beak and dark-hued skin are facts:
And '*parson's daughter*'—'*young man coachable*'—
'*Elderly party*'—'*four years since*'—were facts
To fasten on, a moment! Marriage, though—
That made the difference, I hope."

"All right!

I never married; wish I had—and then
Unwish it: people kill their wives, sometimes!
I hate my mistress, but I'm murder-free.
In your case, where's the grievance? You came last,
The earlier bird picked up the worm. Suppose
You, in the glory of your twenty-one,
Had happened to precede myself! 'tis odds
But this gigantic juvenility,
This offering of a big arm's bony hand—
I'd rather shake than feel shake me, I know—
Had moved *my* dainty mistress to admire
An altogether new Ideal—deem
Idolatry less due to life's decline
Productive of experience, powers mature
By dint of usage, the made man—no boy
That's all to make! I was the earlier bird—
And what I found, I let fall; what you missed,
Who is the fool that blames you for?"

"Myself—
For nothing, everything! For finding out
She, whom I worshipped, was a worshipper
In turn of . . . but why stir up settled mud?
She married him—the fifty-years-old rake—
How you have teazed the talk from me! At last
My secret's told you. I inquired no more,
Nay, stopped ears when informants unshut mouth;
Enough that she and he live, deuce take where,
Married and happy, or else miserable—
It's 'Cut-the-pack;' she turned up ace or knave,
And I left Oxford, England, dug my hole
Out in Dalmatia, till you drew me thence
Badger-like,—'*Back to London*' was the word—
'*Do things, a many, there, you fancy hard,*
I'll undertake are easy!'—the advice.
I took it, had my twelvemonth's fling with you—
(Little hand holding large hand pretty tight
For all its delicacy—eh, my lord?)
Until when, t'other day, I got a turn
Somehow and gave up tired: and '*Rest!*' bade you,
'*Marry your cousin, double your estate,*

And take your ease by all means!' So, I loll
On this the springy sofa, mine next month—
Or should loll, but that you must needs beat rough
The very down you spread me out so smooth.
I wish this confidence were still to make!
Ten thousand pounds? You owe me twice the sum
For stirring up the black depths! There's repose
Or, at least, silence when misfortune seems
All that one has to bear; but folly—yes,
Folly, it all was! Fool to be so meek,
So humble,—such a coward rather say!
Fool, to adore the adorer of a fool!
Not to have faced him, tried (a useful hint)
My big and bony, here, against the bunch
Of lily-coloured five with signet-ring,
Most like, for little-finger's sole defence—
Much as you flaunt the blazon there! I grind
My teeth, that bite my very heart, to think—
To know I might have made that woman mine
But for the folly of the coward—know—
Or what's the good of my apprenticeship
This twelvemonth to a master in the art?
Mine—had she been mine—just one moment mine
For honour, for dishonour—anyhow,
So that my life, instead of stagnant . . . Well,
You've poked and proved stagnation is not sleep—
Hang you!"

"Hang *you* for an ungrateful goose!
All this means—I who since I knew you first
Have helped you to conceit yourself this cock
O' the dunghill with all hens to pick and choose—
Ought to have helped you when shell first was chipped
By chick that wanted prompting '*Use the spur!*'
While I was elsewhere putting mine to use.
As well might I blame you who kept aloof,
Seeing you could not guess I was alive,
Never advised me '*Do as I have done—*
Reverence such a jewel as your luck
Has scratched up to enrich unworthiness!'
As your behaviour was, should mine have been,

—Faults which we both, too late, are sorry for—
Opposite ages, each with its mistake:
'*If youth but would—if age but could,*' you know!
Don't let us quarrel! Come, we're—young and old—
Neither so badly off! Go you your way,
Cut to the Cousin! I'll to Inn, await
The issue of diplomacy with Aunt,
And wait my hour on '*calm acclivity*'
In rumination manifold—perhaps
About ten thousand pounds I have to pay!"

III.

Now, as the elder lights the fresh cigar
Conducive to resource, and saunteringly
Betakes him to the left-hand backward path,—
While, much sedate, the younger strides away
To right and makes for—islanded in lawn
And edged with shrubbery—the brilliant bit
Of Barry's building that's the Place,—a pair
Of women, at this nick of time, one young,
One very young, are ushered with due pomp
Into the same Inn-parlour—'*disengaged*
Entirely now!' the obsequious landlord smiles,
'*Since the late occupants—whereof but one*
Was quite a stranger'—(smile enforced by bow)
'*Left, a full two hours since, to catch the train,*
Probably for the stranger's sake!' (Bow, smile,
And backing out from door soft-closed behind.)

Woman and girl, the two, alone inside,
Begin their talk: the girl, with sparkling eyes—

"Oh, I forewent him purposely! but you,
Who joined at—journeyed from the Junction here
I wonder how he failed your notice! Few
Stop at our station: fellow-passengers
Assuredly you were—I saw indeed
His servant, therefore he arrived all right.
I wanted, you know why, to have you safe
Inside here first of all, so dodged about
The dark end of the platform; that's his way—

To swing from station straight to avenue
And stride the half a mile for exercise.
I fancied you might notice the huge boy.
He soon gets o'er the distance; at the house
He'll hear I went to meet him and have missed;
He'll wait. No minute of the hour's too much
Meantime for our preliminary talk:
First word of which must be—O good beyond
Expression of all goodness—you to come!"

The elder, the superb one, answers slow.

"There was no helping that. You called for me,
Cried, rather: and my old heart answered you.
Still, thank me! since the effort breaks a vow—
At least, a promise to myself."

"I know!
How selfish get you happy folk to be!
If I should love my husband, must I needs
Sacrifice straightway all the world to him,
As you do? Must I never dare leave house
On this dread Arctic expedition, out
And in again, six mortal hours, though you—
You even, my own friend for evermore,
Adjure me—fast your friend till rude love pushed
Poor friendship from her vantage—just to grant
The quarter of a whole day's company
And counsel? This makes counsel so much more
Need and necessity. For here's my block
Of stumbling: in the face of happiness
So absolute, fear chills me. If such change
In heart be but love's easy consequence,
Do I love? If to marry mean—let go
All I now live for, should my marriage be?"

The other never once has ceased to gaze
On the great elm-tree in the open, posed
Placidly full in front, smooth bole, broad branch,
And leafage, one green plenitude of May.
The gathered thought runs into speech at last.

"O you exceeding beauty, bosomful
Of lights and shades, murmurs and silences,
Sun-warmth, dew-coolness,—squirrel, bee and bird,
High, higher, highest, till the blue proclaims
'*Leave earth, there's nothing better till next step
Heavenward!*'—so, off flies what has wings to help!"

And henceforth they alternate. Says the girl—

"That's saved then: marriage spares the early taste."

"Four years now, since my eye took note of tree!"

"If I had seen no other tree but this
My life long, while yourself came straight, you said,
From tree which overstretched you and was just
One fairy tent with pitcher-leaves that held
Wine, and a flowery wealth of suns and moons,
And magic fruits whereon the angels feed—
I looking out of window on a tree
Like yonder—otherwise well-known, much-liked,
Yet just an English ordinary elm—
What marvel if you cured me of conceit
My elm's bird bee and squirrel tenantry
Was quite the proud possession I supposed?
And there is evidence you tell me true.
The fairy marriage-tree reports itself
Good guardian of the perfect face and form,
Fruits of four years' protection! Married friend,
You are more beautiful than ever!"

"Yes—
I think that likely. I could well dispense
With all thought fair in feature, mine or no,
Leave but enough of face to know me by—
With all found fresh in youth except such strength
As lets a life-long labour earn repose
Death sells at just that price, they say; and so,
Possibly, what I care not for, I keep."

"How you must know he loves you! Chill, before,
Fear sinks to freezing. Could I sacrifice—
Assured my lover simply loves my soul—

One nose-breadth of fair feature? No, indeed!
Your own love . . .”

"The preliminary hour—
Don’t waste it!”

"But I can’t begin at once!
The angel’s self that comes to hear me speak
Drives away all the care about the speech.
What an angelic mystery you are—
Now—that is certain! when I knew you first,
No break of halo and no bud of wing!
I thought I knew you, saw you, round and through,
Like a glass ball; suddenly, four years since,
You vanished, how and whither? Mystery!
Wherefore? No mystery at all: you loved,
Were loved again, and left the world of course,—
Who would not? Lapped four years in fairyland,
Out comes, by no less wonderful a chance,
The changeling, touched athwart her trellised bliss
Of blush-rose bower by just the old friend’s voice
That’s now struck dumb at her own potency.
I talk of my small fortunes? Tell me yours—
Rather! The fool I ever was—I am,
You see that: the true friend you ever had,
You have, you also recognize. Perhaps,
Giving you all the love of all my heart,
Nature, that’s niggard in me, has denied
The after-birth of love there’s someone claims,
—This huge boy, swinging up the avenue;
And I want counsel—is defect in me,
Or him who has no right to raise the love?
My cousin asks my hand: he’s young enough,
Handsome,—my maid thinks,—manly’s more the word:
He asked my leave to ‘*drop*’ the elm-tree there,
Some morning before breakfast. Gentleness
Goes with the strength, of course. He’s honest too,
Limpidly truthful. For ability—
All’s in the rough yet. His first taste of life
Seems to have somehow gone against the tongue:
He travelled, tried things—came back, tried still more—
He says he’s sick of all. He’s fond of me

After a certain careless-earnest way
I like: the iron's crude,—no polished steel
Somebody forged before me. I am rich—
That's not the reason, he's far richer: no,
Nor is it that he thinks me pretty,—frank
Undoubtedly on that point! He saw once
The pink of face-perfection—oh, not you—
Content yourself, my beauty!—for she proved
So thoroughly a cheat, his charmer . . . nay,
He runs into extremes, I'll say at once,
Lest you say! Well, I understand he wants
Someone to serve, something to do: and both
Requisites so abound in me and mine
That here's the obstacle which stops consent—
The smoothness is too smooth, and I mistrust
The unseen cat beneath the counterpane.
Therefore I thought—'*Would she but judge for me,*
Who, judging for herself succeeded so?'
Do I love him, does he love me, do both
Mistake for knowledge—easy ignorance?
Appeal to the proficient in each art!
I got rough-smooth through a piano-piece,
Rattled away last week till tutor came,
Heard me to end, then grunted '*Ach, mein Gott!*
Sagen Sie 'easy'? Every note is wrong!
All thumped mit wrist—we'll trouble fingers now!
The Fräulein will please roll up Raff again
And exercise at Czerny for one month!'
Am I to roll up cousin, exercise
At Trollope's novels for one month? Pronounce!"

"Now, place each in the right position first,
Adviser and advised one! I perhaps
Am three—nay, four years older; am, beside,
A wife: advantages—to balance which,
You have a full fresh joyous sense of life
That finds you out life's fit food everywhere,
Detects enjoyment where I, slow and dull,
Fumble at fault. Already, these four years,
Your merest glimpses at the world without
Have shown you more than ever met my gaze;

And now, by joyance you inspire joy,—learn
While you profess to teach, and teach, although
Avowedly a learner. I am dazed
Like any owl by sunshine which just sets
The sparrow preening plumage! Here's to spy
—Your cousin! You have scanned him all your life,
Little or much; I never saw his face.
You have determined on a marriage—used
Deliberation therefore—I'll believe
No otherwise, with opportunity
For judgment so abounding! Here stand I—
Summoned to give my sentence, for a whim,
(Well, at first cloud-fleck thrown athwart your blue)
On what is strangeness' self to me,—say '*Wed!*'
Or '*Wed not!*' whom you promise I shall judge
Presently, at propitious lunch-time, just
While he carves chicken! Sends he leg for wing?
That revelation into character
And conduct must suffice me! Quite as well
Consult with yonder solitary crow
That eyes us from your elm-top!"

"Still the same
Do you remember, at the library
We saw together somewhere, those two books
Somebody said were notice-worthy? One
Lay wide on table, sprawled its painted leaves
For all the world's inspection; shut on shelf
Reclined the other volume, closed, clasped, locked—
Clear to be let alone. Which page had we
Preferred the turning over of? You were,
Are, ever will be the locked lady, hold
Inside you secrets written,—soul absorbed,
My ink upon your blotting-paper. *I*—
What trace of you have I to show in turn?
Delicate secrets! No one juvenile
Ever essayed at croquet and performed
Superiorly but I confided you
The sort of hat he wore and hair it held.
While you? One day a calm note comes by post—
'*I am just married, you may like to hear.*'

Most men would hate you, or they ought; we love
What we fear,—*I* do! '*Cold*' I shall expect
My cousin calls you. I—dislike not him,
But (if I comprehend what loving means)
Love you immeasurably more—more—more
Than even he who, loving you his wife,
Would turn up nose at me impertinent,
Frivolous, forward—*love* that excellence
Of all the earth he bows in worship to!
And who's this paragon of privilege?
Simply a country parson: his the charm
That worked the miracle! Oh, too absurd—
But that you stand before me as you stand!
Such beauty does prove something, everything!
Beauty's the prize-flower which dispenses eye
From peering into what has nourished root—
Dew or manure: the plant best knows its place.
Enough, from teaching youth and tending age
And hearing sermons,—haply writing tracts,—
From such strange love-besprinkled compost, lo,
Out blows this triumph! Therefore love's the soil
Plants find or fail of. You, with wit to find,
Exercise wit on the old friend's behalf,
Keep me from failure! Scan and scrutinize
This cousin! Surely he's as worth your pains
To study as my elm-tree, crow and all,
You still keep staring at. I read your thoughts."

"At last?"

"At first! '*Would, tree, a-top of thee*
I winged were, like crow perched moveless there,
And so could straightway soar, escape this bore,
Back to my nest where broods whom I love best—
The parson o'er his parish—garish—rarish—'
Oh I could bring the rhyme in if I tried:
The Album here inspires me! Quite apart
From lyrical expression, have I read
The stare aright, and sings not soul just so?"

"Or rather *so?* '*Cool comfortable elm*
That men make coffins out of,—none for me

At thy expense, so thou permit I glide
Under thy ferny feet, and there sleep, sleep,
Nor dread awaking though in heaven itself!"

The younger looks with face struck sudden white.
The elder answers its inquiry.

"Dear,
You are a guesser, not a '*clairvoyante*.'
I'll so far open you the locked and shelved
Volume, my soul, that you desire to see,
As let you profit by the title-page—"

"*Paradise Lost?*"
"*Inferno!*—All which comes
Of tempting me to break my vow. Stop here!
Friend, whom I love the best in the whole world,
Come at your call, be sure that I will do
At your requirement—see and say my mind.
It may be that by sad apprenticeship
I have a keener sense: I'll task the same.
Only indulge me—here let sight and speech
Happen—this Inn is neutral ground, you know!
I cannot visit the old house and home,
Encounter the old sociality
Abjured for ever. Peril quite enough
In even this first—last, I pray it prove—
Renunciation of my solitude!
Back, you, to house and cousin! Leave me here,
Who want no entertainment, carry still
My occupation with me. While I watch
The shadow inching round those ferny feet,
Tell him '*A school-friend wants a word with me*
Up at the inn: time, tide and train won't wait:
I must go see her—on and off again—
You'll keep me company?' Ten minutes' talk,
With you in presence, ten more afterward
With who, alone, convoys me station-bound,
And I see clearly—to say honestly
To-morrow: pen shall play tongue's part, you know!
Go—quick! for I have made our hand-in-hand
Return impossible. So scared you look,—

If cousin does not greet you with '*What ghost*
Has crossed your path?' I set him down obtuse."

And after one more look, with face still white,
The younger does go, while the elder stands
Occupied by the elm at window there.

IV.

Occupied by the elm; and, as its shade
Has crept clock-hand-wise till it ticks at fern
Five inches further to the South,—the door
Opens abruptly, someone enters sharp,
The elder man returned to wait the youth—
Never observes the room's new occupant,
Throws hat on table, stoops quick, elbow-propped
Over the Album wide there, bends down brow
A cogitative minute, whistles shrill,
Then,—with a cheery-hopeless laugh-and-lose
Air of defiance to fate visibly
Casting the toils about him,—mouths once more
'*Hail, calm acclivity, salubrious spot!*'
Then clasps-to cover, sends book spinning off
T'other side table, looks up, starts erect
Full-face with her who,—roused from that abstruse
Question, '*Will next tick tip the fern or no?*'—
Fronts him as fully.

All her languor breaks,
Away withers at once the weariness
From the black-blooded brow, anger and hate
Convulse. Speech follows slowlier, but at last—

"You here! I felt, I knew it would befall!
Knew, by some subtle undivinable
Trick of the trickster, I should, silly-sooth,
Late or soon, somehow be allured to leave
Safe hiding and come take of him arrears,
My torment due on four years' respite! Time
To pluck the bird's healed breast of down o'er wound!
Have your success! Be satisfied this sole
Seeing you has undone all heaven could do
These four years, puts me back to you and hell!

What will next trick be, next success? No doubt
When I shall think to glide into the grave,
There will you wait disguised as beckoning Death,
And catch and capture me for evermore!
But, God, though I am nothing, be thou all!
Contest him for me! Strive, for he is strong!"

Already his surprise dies palely out
In laugh of acquiescing impotence.
He neither gasps nor hisses: calm and plain—

"I also felt and knew—but otherwise!
You out of hand and sight and care of me
These four years, whom I felt, knew, all the while . . .
Oh, it's no superstition! It's a gift
O' the gamester that he snuffs the unseen powers
Which help or harm him! Well I knew what lurked,
Lay perdue paralysing me,—drugged, drowsed
And damnified my soul and body both!
Down and down, see where you have dragged me to,
You and your malice! I was, four years since,
—Well, a poor creature! I become a knave.
I squandered my own pence: I plump my purse
With other people's pounds. I practised play
Because I liked it: play turns labour now
Because there's profit also in the sport.
I gamed with men of equal age and craft:
I steal here with a boy as green as grass
Whom I have tightened hold on slow and sure
This long while, just to bring about to-day
When the boy beats me hollow, buries me
In ruin who was sure to beggar him.
O time indeed I should look up and laugh
'*Surely she closes on me!*' Here you stand!"

And stand she does: while volubility,
With him, keeps on the increase, for his tongue
After long locking-up is loosed for once.

"Certain the taunt is happy!" he resumes:
"So, I it was allured you—only I
—I, and none other—to this spectacle—

Your triumph, my despair—you woman-fiend
That front me! Well, I have my wish, then! See
The low wide brow oppressed by sweeps of hair
Darker and darker as they coil and swathe
The crowned corpse-wanness whence the eyes burn black
Not asleep now! not pin-points dwarfed beneath
Either great bridging eyebrow—poor blank beads—
Babies, I've pleased to pity in my time:
How they protrude and glow immense with hate!
The long triumphant nose attains—retains
Just the perfection; and there's scarlet-skein
My ancient enemy, her lip and lip,
Sense-free, sense-frighting lips clenched cold and bold
Because of chin, that based resolve beneath!
Then the columnar neck completes the whole
Greek-sculpture-baffling body! Do I see?
Can I observe? You wait next word to come?
Well, wait and want! since no one blight I bid
Consume one least perfection. Each and all,
As they are rightly shocking now to me,
So may they still continue! Value them?
Ay, as the vendor knows the money-worth
Of his Greek statue, fools aspire to buy,
And he to see the back of! Let us laugh!
You have absolved me from my sin at least!
You stand stout, strong, in the rude health of hate,
No touch of the tame timid nullity
My cowardice, forsooth, has practised on!
Ay, while you seemed to hint some fine fifth act
Of tragedy should freeze blood, end the farce,
I never doubted all was joke. I kept,
May be, an eye alert on paragraphs,
Newspaper-notice,—let no inquest slip,
Accident, disappearance: sound and safe
Were you, my victim, not of mind to die!
So, my worst fancy that could spoil the smooth
Of pillow, and arrest descent of sleep
Was '*Into what dim hole can she have dived* ,
She and her wrongs, her woe that's wearing flesh
And blood away?' Whereas, see, sorrow swells!
Or, fattened, fulsome, have you fed on me,

Sucked out my substance? How much gloss, I pray,
O'erbloomed those hair-swathes when there crept from you
To me that craze, else unaccountable,
Which urged me to contest our county-seat
With whom but my own brother's nominee?
Did that mouth's pulp glow ruby from carmine
While I misused my moment, pushed,—one word,—
One hair's breadth more of gesture,—idiot-like
Past passion, floundered on to the grotesque,
And lost the heiress in a grin? At least,
You made no such mistake! You tickled fish,
Landed your prize the true artistic way!
How did the smug young curate rise to tune
Of '*Friend, a fatal fact divides us! Love*
Suits me no longer! I have suffered shame,
Betrayal: past is past; the future—yours—
Shall never be contaminate by mine!
I might have spared me this confession, not
—O, never by some hideousest of lies,
Easy, impenetrable! No! but say,
By just the quiet answer—'I am cold.'
Falsehood avaunt, each shadow of thee, hence!
Had happier fortune willed . . but dreams are vain!
Now, leave me—yes, for pity's sake!' Aha,
Who fails to see the curate as his face
Reddened and whitened, wanted handkerchief
At wrinkling brow and twinkling eye, until
Out burst the proper '*Angel, whom the fiend*
Has thought to smirch,—thy whiteness, at one wipe
Of holy cambric, shall disgrace the swan!
Mine be the task' . . and so forth! Fool? not he!
Cunning in flavors, rather! What but sour
Suspected makes the sweetness doubly sweet?
And what stings love from faint to flamboyant
But the fear-sprinkle? Even horror helps—
'*Love's flame in me by such recited wrong*
Drenched, quenched, indeed? It burns the fiercelier thence!'
Why, I have known men never love their wives
Till somebody—myself, suppose—had '*drenched*
And quenched love,' so the blockheads whined: as if
The fluid fire that lifts the torpid limb

Were a wrong done to palsy. But I thrilled
No palsied person: half my age, or less
The curate was, I'll wager: o'er young blood
Your beauty triumphed! Eh, but—was it *he?*
Then, it *was* he, I heard of! None beside!
How frank you were about the audacious boy
Who fell upon you like a thunderbolt—
Passion and protestation! He it was
Reserved *in petto!* Ay, and '*rich*' beside—
'*Rich*'—how supremely did disdain curl nose!
All that I heard was—'*wedded to a priest;*'
Informants sunk youth, riches and the rest.
And so my lawless love disparted loves,
That loves might come together with a rush!
Surely this last achievement sucked me dry:
Indeed, that way my wits went! Mistress-queen,
Be merciful and let your subject slink
Into dark safety! He's a beggar, see—
Do not turn back his ship, Australia-bound,
And bid her land him right amid some crowd
Of creditors, assembled by your curse!
Don't cause the very rope to crack (you can!)
Whereon he spends his last (friend's) sixpence, just
The moment when he hoped to hang himself!
Be satisfied you beat him!"

She replies—

"Beat him! I do. To all that you confess
Of abject failure, I extend belief.
Your very face confirms it: God is just!
Let my face—fix your eyes!—in turn confirm
What I shall say. All-abject's but half truth;
Add to all-abject knave as perfect fool!
So is it you probed human nature, *so*
Prognosticated of me? Lay these words
To heart then, or where God meant heart should lurk!
That moment when you first revealed yourself,
My simple impulse prompted—end forthwith
The ruin of a life uprooted thus
To surely perish! How should such a tree
Henceforward baulk the wind of its worst sport,

Fail to go falling deeper, falling down
From sin to sin until some depth were reached
Doomed to the weakest by the wickedest
Of weak and wicked human kind? But when,
That self-display made absolute,—behold
A new revealment!—round you pleased to veer,
Propose me what should prompt annul the past,
Make me '*amends by marriage*'—in your phrase,
Incorporate me henceforth, body and soul,
With soul and body which mere brushing past
Brought leprosy upon me—'*marry*' these!
Why, then despair broke, re-assurance dawned,
Clear-sighted was I that who hurled contempt
As I—thank God!—at the contemptible,
Was scarce an utter weakling. Rent away
By treason from my rightful pride of place,
I was not destined to the shame below.
A cleft had caught me: I might perish there,
But thence to be dislodged and whirled at last
Where the black torrent sweeps the sewage—no!
'*Bare breast be on hard rock*,' laughed out my soul
In gratitude, '*howe'er rock's grip may grind!*
The plain, rough, wretched holdfast shall suffice
This wreck of me!' The wind,—I broke in bloom
At passage of,—which stripped me bole and branch,
Twisted me up and tossed me here,—turns back
And, playful ever, would replant the spoil?
Be satisfied, not one least leaf that's mine
Shall henceforth help wind's sport to exercise!
Rather I give such remnant to the rock
Which never dreamed a straw would settle there.
Rock may not thank me, may not feel my breast,
Even: enough that *I* feel, hard and cold,
Its safety my salvation. Safe and saved,
I lived, live. When the tempter shall persuade
His prey to slip down, slide off, trust the wind,—
Now that I know if God or Satan be
Prince of the Power of the Air,—then, then, indeed,
Let my life end and degradation too!"

"Good!" he smiles, "true Lord Byron! '*Tree and rock:*'
'*Rock*'—there's advancement! He's at first a youth,
Rich, worthless therefore; next he grows a priest:
Youth, riches prove a notable resource,
When to leave me for their possessor gluts
Malice abundantly; and now, last change,
The young rich parson represents a rock
—Bloodstone, no doubt. He's Evangelical?
Your Ritualists prefer the Church for spouse!"

She speaks. "I have a story to relate.
There was a parish-priest, my father knew,
Elderly, poor: I used to pity him
Before I learned what woes are pity-worth.
Elderly was grown old now, scanty means
Were straitening fast to poverty, beside
The ailments which await in such a case.
Limited every way, a perfect man
Within the bounds built up and up since birth
Breast-high about him till the outside world
Was blank save o'erhead one blue bit of sky—
Faith: he had faith in dogma, small or great,
As in the fact that if he clave his scull
He'd find a brain there: such a fact who proves
No falsehood by experiment at price
Of soul and body? The one rule of life
Delivered him in childhood was '*Obey!*
Labour!' He had obeyed and laboured—tame,
True to the mill-track blinked on from above.
Some scholarship he may have gained in youth:
Gone—dropt or flung behind. Some blossom-flake,
Spring's boon, descends on every vernal head,
I used to think; but January joins
December, as his year had known no May
Trouble its snow-deposit,—cold and old!
I heard it was his will to take a wife,
A helpmate. Duty bade him tend and teach—
How? with experience null, nor sympathy
Abundant,—while himself worked dogma dead,
Who would play ministrant to sickness, age,
Womankind, childhood? These demand a wife.
Supply the want, then! theirs the wife; for him—

No coarsest sample of the proper sex
But would have served his purpose equally
With God's own angel,—let but knowledge match
Her coarseness: zeal does only half the work.
I saw this—knew the purblind honest drudge
Was wearing out his simple blameless life,
And wanted help beneath a burthen—borne
To treasure-house or dust-heap, what cared I?
Partner he needed: I proposed myself,
Nor much surprised him—duty was so clear!
Gratitude? What for? Gain of Paradise—
Escape, perhaps, from the dire penalty
Of who hides talent in a napkin! No,
His scruple was—should I be strong enough
—In body? since of weakness in the mind,
Weariness in the heart—what fear of these?
He took me as these Arctic voyagers
Take an aspirant to their toil and pain:
Can he endure them?—that's the point, and not
—Will he? Who would not, rather! Whereupon,
I pleaded far more earnestly for leave
To give myself away, than you to gain
What you called priceless till you gained the heart
And soul and body! which, as beggars serve
Extorted alms, you straightway spat upon.
Not so my husband,—for I gained my suit,
And had my value put at once to proof.
Ask him! These four years I have died away
In village-life. The village? Ugliness
At best and filthiness at worst—inside.
Outside, sterility—earth sown with salt
Or what keeps even grass from growing fresh.
The life? I teach the poor and learn, myself,
That commonplace to such stupidity
Is all-recondite. Being brutalized
Their true need is brute-language, cheery grunts
And kindly cluckings, no articulate
Nonsense that's elsewhere knowledge. Tend the sick,
Sickened myself at pig-perversity,
Cat-craft, dog-snarling,—may be, snapping . . ."

"Brief—
You eat that root of bitterness called Man
—Raw: I prefer it cooked, with social sauce!
So, he was not the rich youth after all!
Well, I mistook. But somewhere needs must be
The compensation. If not young nor rich . . ."

"You interrupt!"

"Because you've daubed enough
Bistre for background. Play the artist now,
Produce your figure well-relieved in front!
The contrast—do not I anticipate?
Though neither rich nor young—what then? 'Tis all
Forgotten, all this ignobility,
In the dear home, the darling word, the smile,
The something sweeter . . ."

"Yes, you interrupt.
I have my purpose and proceed. Who lives
With beasts assumes beast-nature, look and voice,
And, much more, thought,—for beasts think. Selfishness
In us met selfishness in them, deserved
Such answer as it gained. My husband, bent
On saving his own soul by saving theirs,—
They, bent on being saved if saving soul
Included body's getting bread and cheese
Somehow in life and somehow after death,—
Both parties were alike in the same boat,
One danger, therefore one equality.
Safety induces culture: culture seeks
To institute, extend and multiply
The difference between safe man and man,
Able to live alone now; progress means
What but abandonment of fellowship?
We were in common danger, still stuck close.
No new books,—were the old ones mastered yet?
No pictures and no music: these divert
—What from? the staving danger off! You paint
The waterspout above, you set to words
The roaring of the tempest round you? Thanks!
Amusement? Talk at end of the tired day

Of the more tiresome morrow! I transcribed
The page on page of sermon-scrawlings—stopped
My intellectual eye and ear to sense and sound—
Vainly: the sound and sense would penetrate
To brain and plague there in despite of me
Maddened to know more moral good were done
Had we two simply sallied forth and preached
I' the '*Green*' they call their grimy,—I with twang
Of long-disused guitar,—with cut and slash
Of much misvalued horsewhip he,—to bid
The peaceable come dance, the peace-breaker
Pay in his person! Whereas—Heaven and Hell,
Excite with that, restrain with this!—so dealt
His drugs my husband; as he dosed himself,
He drenched his cattle: and, for all my part
Was just to dub the mortar, never fear
But drugs, hand pestled at, have poisoned nose!
Heaven he let pass, left wisely undescribed:
As applicable therefore to the sleep
I want, that knows no waking—as to what's
Conceived of as the proper prize to tempt
Souls less world-weary: there, no fault to find!
But Hell he made explicit. After death,
Life: man created new, ingeniously
Perfect for a vindictive purpose now
That man, first fashioned in beneficence,
Was proved a failure; intellect at length
Replacing old obtuseness, memory
Made mindful of delinquent's bygone deeds
Now that remorse was vain, which life-long lay
Dormant when lesson might be laid to heart;
New gift of observation up and down
And round man's self, new power to apprehend
Each necessary consequence of act
In man for well or ill—things obsolete—
Just granted to supplant the idiotcy
Man's only guide while act was yet to choose,
With ill or well momentously its fruit;
A faculty of immense suffering
Conferred on mind and body,—mind, erewhile
Unvisited by one compunctious dream

During sin's drunken slumber, startled up,
Stung through and through by sin's significance
Now that the holy was abolished—just
As body which, alive, broke down beneath
Knowledge, lay helpless in the path to good,
Failed to accomplish aught legitimate,
Achieve aught worthy,—which grew old in youth,
And at its longest fell a cut-down flower,—
Dying, this too revived by miracle
To bear no end of burthen now that back
Supported torture to no use at all,
And live imperishably potent—since
Life's potency was impotent to ward
One plague off which made earth a hell before.
This doctrine, which one healthy view of things,
One sane sight of the general ordinance—
Nature,—and its particular object,—man,—
Which one mere eye-cast at the character
Of Who made these and gave man sense to boot,
Had dissipated once and evermore,—
This doctrine I have dosed our flock withal.
Why? Because none believed it. *They* desire
Such Heaven and dread such Hell, whom everyday
The alehouse tempts from one, a dog-fight bids
Defy the other? All the harm is done
Ourselves—done my poor husband who in youth
Perhaps read Dickens, done myself who still
Could play both Bach and Brahms. Such life I lead—
Thanks to you, knave! You learn its quality—
Thanks to me, fool!"

He eyes her earnestly,
But she continues.

"—Life which, thanks once more
To you, arch-knave as exquisitest fool,
I acquiescingly—I gratefully
Take back again to heart! and hence this speech
Which yesterday had spared you. Four years long
Life—I began to find intolerable,
Only this moment. Ere your entry just,

The leap of heart which answered, spite of me,
A friend's first summons, first provocative
Authoritative, nay, compulsive call
To quit—though for a single day—my house
Of bondage—made return seem horrible.
I heard again a human lucid laugh
All trust, no fear; again saw earth pursue
Its narrow busy way amid small cares,
Smaller contentments, much weeds, some few flowers,—
Never suspicious of a thunderbolt
Avenging presently each daisy's death.
I recognized the beech-tree, knew the thrush
Repeated his old music-phrase,—all right,
How wrong was I, then! But your entry broke
Illusion, bade me back to bounds at once.
I honestly submit my soul: which sprang
At love, and losing love lies signed and sealed
'*Failure*.' No love more? then, no beauty more
Which tends to breed love! Purify my powers,
Effortless till some other world procure
Some other chance of prize! or, if none be,—
Nor second world nor chance,—undesecrate
Die then this aftergrowth of heart, surmised
Where May's precipitation left June blank!
Better have failed in the high aim, as I,
Than vulgarly in the low aim succeed
As, God be thanked, I do not! Ugliness
Had I called beauty, falsehood—truth, and you
My lover! No—this earth's unchanged for me,
By his enchantment whom God made the Prince
O' the Power o' the Air, into a Heaven: there is
Heaven, since there is Heaven's simulation—earth;
I sit possessed in patience; prison-roof
Shall break one day and Heaven beam overhead."

His smile is done with; he speaks bitterly.

"Take my congratulations, and permit
I wish myself had proved as teachable!
—Or, no! until you taught me, could I learn
A lesson from experience ne'er till now

Conceded? Please you listen while I show
How thoroughly you estimate my worth
And yours—the immeasurably superior! I
Believed at least in one thing, first to last,—
Your love to me: I was the vile and you
The precious; I abused you, I betrayed,
But doubted—never! Why else go my way
Judas-like plodding to this Potter's Field
Where fate now finds me? What has dinned my ear
And dogged my step? The spectre with the shriek
'*Such she was, such were you, whose punishment*
Is just!' And such she was not, all the while!
She never owned a love to outrage, faith
To pay with falsehood! For, myself know this—
Love once and you love always. Why, it's down
Here in the Album: every lover knows
Love may use hate but—turn to hate, itself—
Turn even to indifference—no, indeed!
Well, I have been spell-bound, deluded like
The witless negro by the Obeah-man
Who bids him wither: so, his eye grows dim,
His arm slack, arrow misses aim and spear
Goes wandering wide,—and all the woe because
He proved untrue to Fetish, who, he finds,
Was just a feather-phantom! I wronged love,
Am ruined,—and there was no love to wrong!"

"No love? Ah, dead love! I invoke thy ghost
To show the murderer where thy heart poured life
At summons of the stroke he doubts was dealt
On pasteboard and pretence! Not love, my love?
I changed for you the very laws of life:
Made you the standard of all right, all fair.
No genius but you could have been, no sage,
No sufferer—which is grandest—for the truth!
My hero—where the heroic only hid
To burst from hiding, brighten earth one day!
Age and decline were man's maturity;
Face, form were nature's type: more grace, more strength,
What had they been but just superfluous gauds,
Lawless divergence? I have danced through day

On tiptoe at the music of a word,
Have wondered where was darkness gone as night
Burst out in stars at brilliance of a smile!
Lonely, I placed the chair to help me seat
Your fancied presence; in companionship,
I kept my finger constant to your glove
Glued to my breast; then—where was all the world?
I schemed—not dreamed—how I might die some death
Should save your finger aching! Who creates
Destroys, he only: I had laughed to scorn
Whatever angel tried to shake my faith
And make you seem unworthy: you yourself
Only could do that! With a touch 'twas done.
'*Give me all, trust me wholly!*' At the word,
I did give, I did trust—and thereupon
The touch did follow. Ah, the quiet smile,
The masterfully folded arm in arm,
As trick obtained its triumph one time more!
In turn, my soul too triumphs in defeat:
Treason like faith moves mountains: love is gone!"

He paces to and fro, stops, stands quite close
And calls her by her name. Then—

"God forgives:
Forgive you, delegate of God, brought near
As never priests could bring him to this soul
That prays you both—forgive me! I abase—
Know myself mad and monstrous utterly
In all I did that moment; but as God
Gives me this knowledge—heart to feel and tongue
To testify—so be you gracious too!
Judge no man by the solitary work
Of—well, they do say and I can believe—
The devil in him: his, the moment,—mine
The life—your life!"

He names her name again.

"You were just—merciful as just, you were
In giving me no respite: punishment

Followed offending. Sane and sound once more,
The patient thanks decision, promptitude,
Which flung him prone and fastened him from hurt,
Haply to others, surely to himself.
I wake and would not you had spared one pang.
All's well that ends well!"

Yet again her name.

"Had *you* no fault? Why must you change, forsooth,
Parts, why reverse positions, spoil the play?
Why did your nobleness look up to me,
Not down on the ignoble thing confessed?
Was it your part to stoop, or lift the low?
Wherefore did God exalt you? Who would teach
The brute man's tameness and intelligence
Must never drop the dominating eye:
Wink—and what wonder if the mad fit break,
Followed by stripes and fasting? Sound and sane,
My life, chastised now, couches at your foot.
Accept, redeem me! Do your eyes ask '*How?*'
I stand here penniless, a beggar; talk
What idle trash I may, this final blow
Of fortune fells me. *I* disburse, indeed,
This boy his winnings? when each bubble-scheme
That danced athwart my brain, a minute since,
The worse the better,—of repairing straight
My misadventure by fresh enterprise,
Capture of other boys in foolishness
His fellows,—when these fancies fade away
At first sight of the lost so long, the found
So late, the lady of my life, before
Whose presence I, the lost, am also found
Incapable of one least touch of mean
Expedient, I who teemed with plot and wile—
That family of snakes your eye bids flee!
Listen! Our troublesomest dreams die off
In daylight: I awake and dream is—where?
I rouse up from the past: one touch dispels
England and all here. I secured long since
A certain refuge, solitary home

To hide in, should the head strike work one day,
The hand forget its cunning, or perhaps
Society grow savage,—there to end
My life's remainder, which, say what fools will,
Is or should be the best of life,—its fruit,
All tends to, root and stem and leaf and flower.
Come with me, love, loved once, loved only, come,
Blend loves there! Let this parenthetic doubt
Of love, in me, have been the trial test
Appointed to all flesh at some one stage
Of soul's achievement,—when the strong man doubts
His strength, the good man whether goodness be,
The artist in the dark seeks, fails to find
Vocation, and the saint forswears his shrine.
What if the lover may elude, no more
Than these, probative dark, must search the sky
Vainly for love, his soul's star? But the orb
Breaks from eclipse: I breathe again: I love!
Tempted, I fell; but fallen—fallen lie
Here at your feet, see! Leave this poor pretence
Of union with a nature and its needs
Repugnant to your needs and nature! Nay,
False, beyond falsity you reprehend
In me, is such mock marriage with such mere
Man-mask as—whom you witless wrong, beside,
By that expenditure of heart and brain
He recks no more of than would yonder tree
If watered with your life-blood: rains and dews
Answer its ends sufficiently, while me
One drop saves—sends to flower and fruit at last
The laggard virtue in the soul which else
Cumbers the ground! Quicken me! Call me yours—
Yours and the world's—yours and the world's and God's!
Yes, for you can, you only! Think! Confirm
Your instinct! Say, a minute since, I seemed
The castaway you count me,—all the more
Apparent shall the angelic potency
Lift me from out perdition's deep of deeps
To light and life and love!—that's love for you—
Love that already dares match might with yours.
You loved one worthy,—in your estimate,—

When time was; you descried the unworthy taint,
And where was love then? No such test could e'er
Try my love: but you hate me and revile;
Hatred, revilement—had you these to bear
Would you, as I do, nor revile, nor hate,
But simply love on, love the more, perchance?
Abide by your own proof! '*Your love was love* :
Its ghost knows no forgetting!' Heart of mine,
Would that I dared remember! Too unwise
Were he who lost a treasure, did himself
Enlarge upon the sparkling catalogue
Of gems to her his queen who trusted late
The keeper of her caskets! Can it be
That I, custodian of such relic still
As your contempt permits me to retain,
All I dare hug to breast is—'*How your glove*
Burst and displayed the long thin lily-streak!'
What may have followed—that is forfeit now!
I hope the proud man has grown humble! True—
One grace of humbleness absents itself—
Silence! yet love lies deeper than all words,
And not the spoken but the speechless love
Waits answer ere I rise and go my way."

Whereupon, yet one other time the name.

To end she looks the large deliberate look,
Even prolongs it somewhat; then the soul
Bursts forth in a clear laugh that lengthens on,
On, till—thinned, softened, silvered, one might say
The bitter runnel hides itself in sand,
Moistens the hard grey grimly comic speech.

"Ay—give the baffled angler even yet
His supreme triumph as he hales to shore
A second time the fish once 'scaped from hook—
So artfully has new bait hidden old
Blood-imbrued iron! Ay, no barb's beneath
The gilded minnow here! You bid break trust,
This time, with who trusts me,—not simply bid
Me trust you, me who ruined but myself,
In trusting but myself! Since, thanks to you,

I know the feel of sin and shame,—be sure,
I shall obey you and impose them both
On one who happens to be ignorant
Although my husband—for the lure is love,
Your love! Try other tackle, fisher-friend!
Repentance, expiation, hopes and fears,
What you had been, may yet be, would I but
Prove helpmate to my hero—one and all
These silks and worsteds round the hook, seduce
Hardly the late torn throat and mangled tongue.
Pack up, I pray, the whole assortment prompt!
Who wonders at variety of wile
In the Arch-cheat? You are the Adversary!
Your fate is of your choosing: have your choice!
Wander the world,—God has some end to serve,
Ere he suppress you! He waits: I endure,
But interpose no finger-tip, forsooth,
To stop your passage to the pit. Enough
That I am stable, uninvolved by you
In the rush downwards: free I gaze and fixed;
Your smiles, your tears, prayers, curses move alike
My crowned contempt. You kneel? Prostrate yourself!
To earth, and would the whole world saw you there!"

Whereupon—"All right!" carelessly begins
Somebody from outside, who mounts the stair,
And sends his voice for herald of approach:
Half in half out the doorway as the door
Gives way to push.

"Old fellow, all's no good!
The train's your portion! Lay the blame on me!
I'm no diplomatist, and Bismarck's self
Had hardly braved the awful Aunt at broach
Of proposition—so has world-repute
Preceded the illustrious stranger! Ah!—"

Quick the voice changes to astonishment,
Then horror, as the youth stops, sees, and knows.

The man who knelt starts up from kneeling, stands
Moving no muscle, and confronts the stare.

The lady's proud pale queenliness of scorn
Buries with one red outbreak throat and brow—
Then her great eyes that turned so quick, become
Intenser: quail at gaze, not they indeed!

V.

It is the young man shatters silence first.

"Well, my lord—for indeed my lord you are,
I little guessed how rightly—this last proof
Of lordship-paramount confounds too much
My simple head-piece! Let's see how we stand
Each to the other! how we stood i' the game
Of life an hour ago,—the magpies, stile
And oak-tree witnessed. Truth exchanged for truth—
My lord confessed his four-years-old affair—
How he seduced and then forsook the girl
Who married somebody and left him sad.
My pitiful experience was—I loved
A girl whose gown's hem had I dared to touch
My finger would have failed me, palsy-fixed;
She left me, sad enough, to marry—whom?
A better man,—then possibly not you!
How does the game stand? Who is who and what
Is what, o' the board now, since an hour went by?
My lord's '*seduced, forsaken, sacrificed*'—
Starts up, my lord's familiar instrument,
Associate and accomplice, mistress-slave—
Shares his adventure, follows on the sly,
—Ay, and since 'bag and baggage' is a phrase—
Baggage lay hid in carpet-bag belike,
Was but unpadlocked when occasion came
For holding council, since my back was turned,
On how invent ten thousand pounds which, paid,
Would lure the winner to lose twenty more,
Beside refunding these! Why else allow
The fool to gain them? So displays herself
The lady whom my heart believed—oh, laugh!

Noble and pure: whom my heart loved at once,
And who at once did speak truth when she said
'*I am not mine now but another's*'—thus
Being that other's! Devil's-marriage, eh?
'*My lie weds thine till lucre us do part?*'
But pity me the snobbish simpleton,
You two aristocratic tip-top swells
At swindling! Quits, I cry! Decamp content
With skin I'm peeled of: do not strip bones bare—
As that you could, I have no doubt at all!
O you two rare ones! Male and female, Sir!
The male there smirked, this morning, '*Come, my boy—*
Out with it! You've been crossed in love, I think:
I recognize the lover's hangdog look;
Make a clean breast and match my confidence,
For, I'll be frank, I too have had my fling,
Am punished for my fault, and smart enough!
Where now the victim hides her head, God knows!'
Here loomed her head, life-large, the devil knew!
Look out, Salvini! Here's your man, your match!
He and I sat applauding, stall by stall,
Last Monday—'*Here's Othello*' was our word,
'*But where's Iago?*' Where? Why, there! And now
The fellow-artist, female specimen—
Oh, lady, you must needs describe yourself!
He's great in art, but you—how greater still
—(If I can rightly, out of all I learned,
Apply one bit of Latin that assures
'*Art means just art's concealment*'—tower yourself!
For he stands plainly visible henceforth—
Liar and scamp: while you, in artistry
Prove so consummate—or I prove perhaps
So absolute an ass—that—either way—
You still do seem to me who worshipped you
And see you take the homage of this man,
Your master, who played slave and knelt, no doubt,
Before a mistress in his very craft . . .
Well, take the fact, I nor believe my eyes,
Nor trust my understanding! Still you seem
Noble and pure as when we had the talk
Under the tower, beneath the trees, that day.

And there's the key explains the secret: down
He knelt to ask your leave to rise a grade
I' the mystery of humbug: well he may!
For how you beat him! Half an hour ago,
I held your master for my best of friends;
And now I hate him! Four years since, you seemed
My heart's one love: well, and you so remain!
What's he to you in craft?"

She looks him through.

"My friend, 'tis just that friendship have its turn—
Interrogate thus me whom one, of foes
The worst, has questioned and is answered by.
Take you as frank an answer! answers both
Begin alike so far, divergent soon
World-wide—I own superiority
Over you, over him. As him I searched,
So do you stand seen through and through by me
Who, this time, proud, report your crystal shrines
A dewdrop, plain as amber prisons round
A spider in the hollow heart his house!
Nowise are you that thing my fancy feared
When out you stepped on me, a minute since,
—This man's confederate! no, you step not thus
Obsequiously at beck and call to help
At need some second scheme, and supplement
Guile by force, use my shame to pinion me
From struggle and escape! I fancied that!
Forgive me! Only by strange chance,—most strange
In even this strange world,—you enter now,
Obtain your knowledge. Me you have not wronged
Who never wronged you—least of all, my friend,
That day beneath the College tower and trees,
When I refused to say,—'*not friend but, love!*'
Had I been found as free as air when first
We met, I scarcely could have loved you. No—
For where was that in you which claimed return
Of love? My eyes were all too weak to probe
This other's seeming, but that seeming loved
The soul in me, and lied—I know too late!

While your truth was truth: and I knew at once
My power was just my beauty—bear the word—
As I must bear, of all my qualities,
To name the poorest one that serves my soul
And simulates myself! So much in me
You loved, I know: the something that's beneath
Heard not your call,—uncalled, no answer comes!
For, since in every love, or soon or late
Soul must awake and seek out soul for soul,
Yours, overlooking mine then, would, some day,
Take flight to find some other; so it proved—
Missing me, you were ready for this man.
I apprehend the whole relation: his—
The soul wherein you saw your type of worth
At once, true object of your tribute. Well
Might I refuse such half-heart's homage! Love
Divining, had assured you I no more
Stand his participant in infamy
Than you—I need no love to recognize
As simply dupe and nowise fellow-cheat!
Therefore accept one last friend's-word,—your friend's,
All men's friend, save a felon's. Ravel out
The bad embroilment howsoe'er you may,
Distribute as it please you praise or blame
To me—so you but fling this mockery far—
Renounce this rag-and-feather hero-sham,
This poodle clipt to pattern, lion-like!
Throw him his thousands back, and lay to heart
The lesson I was sent,—if man discerned
Ever God's message,—just to teach. I judge—
Far to another issue than could dream
Your cousin,—younger, fairer, as befits—
Who summoned me to judgment's exercise.
I find you, save in folly, innocent.
And in my verdict lies your fate; at choice
Of mine your cousin takes or leaves you. '*Take!*'
I bid her—for you tremble back to truth!
She turns the scale,—one touch of the pure hand
Shall so press down, emprison past relapse
Farther vibration twixt veracity—
That's honest solid earth—and falsehood, theft

And air, that's one illusive emptiness!
That reptile capture you? I conquered him:
You saw him cower before me! Have no fear
He shall offend you farther! Spare to spurn—
Safe let him slink hence till some subtler Eve
Than I, anticipate the snake—bruise head
Ere he bruise heel—or, warier than the first,
Some Adam purge earth's garden of its pest
Before the slaver spoil the Tree of Life!

"You! Leave this youth, as he leaves you, as I
Leave each! There's caution surely extant yet
Though conscience in you were too vain a claim.
Hence quickly! Keep the cash but leave unsoiled
The heart I rescue and would lay to heal
Beside another's! Never let her know
How near came taint of your companionship!"

"Ah"—draws a long breath with a new strange look
The man she interpellates—soul a-stir
Under its covert, as, beneath the dust,
A coppery sparkle all at once denotes
The hid snake has conceived a purpose.

"Ah—
Innocence should be crowned with ignorance?
Desirable indeed, but difficult!
As if yourself, now, had not glorified
Your helpmate by imparting him a hint
Of how a monster made the victim bleed
Ere crook and courage saved her—hint, I say,—
Not the whole horror,—that were needless risk,—
But just such inkling, fancy of the fact,
As should suffice to qualify henceforth
The shepherd, when another lamb would stray,
For warning '*Ware the wolf!*' No doubt at all,
Silence is generosity,—keeps wolf
Unhunted by flock's warder! Excellent,
Did—generous to me, mean—just to him!
But, screening the deceiver, lamb were found
Outraging the deceitless! So,—he knows!
And yet, unharmed I breathe—perchance, repent—
Thanks to the mercifully-politic!"

"Ignorance is not innocence but sin—
Witness your own ignoring after-pangs
Pursue the plague-infected. Merciful
Am I? Perhaps! the more contempt, the less
Hatred; and who so worthy of contempt
As you that rest assured I cooled the spot
I could not cure, by poisoning, forsooth,
Whose hand I pressed there? Understand for once
That, sick, of all the pains corroding me
This burnt the last and nowise least—the need
Of simulating soundness. I resolved—
No matter how the struggle tasked weak flesh—
To hide the truth away as in a grave
From—most of all—my husband: he nor knows
Nor ever shall be made to know your part,
My part, the devil's part,—I trust, God's part
In the foul matter. Saved, I yearn to save
And not destroy: and what destruction like
The abolishing of faith in him, that's faith
In me as pure and true? Acquaint some child
Who takes yon tree into his confidence,
That, where he sleeps now, was a murder done,
And that the grass which grows so thick, he thinks,
Only to pillow him is product just
Of what lies festering beneath! 'Tis God
Must bear such secrets and disclose them. Man?
The miserable thing I have become
By dread acquaintance with my secret—*you*—
That thing had he become by learning *me*—
The miserable, whom his ignorance
Would wrongly call the wicked: ignorance
Being, I hold, sin ever, small or great.
No, he knows nothing!"

"He and I alike
Are bound to you for such discreetness, then.
What if our talk should terminate awhile?
Here is a gentleman to satisfy,
Settle accounts with, pay ten thousand pounds
Before we part—as, by his face, I fear,
Results from your appearance on the scene.

Grant me a minute's parley with my friend
Which scarce admits of a third personage!
The room from which you made your entry first
So opportunely—still untenanted—
What if you please return there? Just a word
To my young friend first—then, a word to you,
And you depart to fan away each fly
From who, grass-pillowed, sleeps so sound at home!"

"So the old truth comes back! A wholesome change,—
At last the altered eye, the rightful tone!
But even to the truth that drops disguise
And stands forth grinning malice which but now
Whined so contritely—I refuse assent
Just as to malice. I, once gone, come back?
No, my lord! I enjoy the privilege
Of being absolutely loosed from you
Too much—the knowledge that your power is null
Which was omnipotence. A word of mouth,
A wink of eye would have detained me once,
Body and soul your slave; and now, thank God,
Your fawningest of prayers, your frightfulest
Of curses—neither would avail to turn
My footstep for a moment!"

"Prayer, then, tries
No such adventure. Let us cast about
For something novel in expedient: take
Command,—what say you? I profess myself
One fertile in resource. Commanding, then,
I bid—not only wait there, but return
Here, where I want you! Disobey and—good!
On your own head the peril!"

"Come!" breaks in
The boy with his good glowing face. "Shut up!
None of this sort of thing while I stand here
—Not to stand that! No bullying, I beg!
I also am to leave you presently
And never more set eyes upon your face—
You won't mind that much; but—I tell you frank—
I do mind having to remember this

For your last word and deed—my friend who were!
Bully a woman you have ruined, eh?
Do you know,—I give credit all at once
To all those stories everybody told
And nobody but I would disbelieve:
They all seem likely now,—nay, certain, sure!
I dare say you did cheat at cards that night
The row was at the Club: '*sauter la coupe*'—
That was your 'cut,' for which your friends 'cut' you
While I, the booby, 'cut'—acquaintanceship
With who so much as laughed when I said '*luck!*'
I daresay you had bets against the horse
They doctored at the Derby; little doubt,
That fellow with the sister found you shirk
His challenge and did kick you like a ball,
Just as the story went about! Enough:
It only serves to show how well advised,
Madam, you were in bidding such a fool
As I, go hang. You see how the mere sight
And sound of you suffice to tumble down
Conviction topsy-turvy: no,—that's false,—
There's no unknowing what one knows; and yet
Such is my folly that, in gratitude
For . . . well, I'm stupid; but you seemed to wish
I should know gently what I know, should slip
Softly from old to new, not break my neck
Between beliefs of what you were and are.
Well then, for just the sake of such a wish
To cut no worse a figure than needs must
In even eyes like mine, I'd sacrifice
Body and soul! But don't think danger—pray!—
Menaces either! He do harm to us?
Let me say "us" this one time! You'd allow
I lent perhaps my hand to rid your ear
Of some cur's yelping—hand that's fortified,
Into the bargain, with a horsewhip? Oh,
One crack and you shall see how curs decamp!
My lord, you know your losses and my gains.
Pay me my money at the proper time!
If cash be not forthcoming,—well, yourself
Have taught me, and tried often, I'll engage,

The proper course: I post you at the Club,
Pillory the defaulter. Crack, to-day,
Shall, slash, to-morrow, slice through flesh and bone!
There, Madam, you need mind no cur, I think!"

"Ah, what a gain to have an apt no less
Than grateful scholar! Nay, he brings to mind
My knowledge till he puts me to the blush,
So long has it lain rusty! Post my name!
That were indeed a wheal from whipcord! Whew!
I wonder now if I could rummage out
—Just to match weapons—some old scorpion-scourge!
Madam, you hear my pupil, may applaud
His triumph o'er the master. I—no more
Bully, since I'm forbidden: but entreat—
Wait and return—for my sake, no! but just
To save your own defender, should he chance
Get thwacked thro' awkward flourish of his thong.
And what if—since all waiting's weary work—
I help the time pass 'twixt your exit now
And entry then? for—pastime proper—here's
The very thing, the Album, verse and prose
To make the laughing minutes launch away!
Each of us must contribute. I'll begin—
'*Hail, calm acclivity, salubrious spot!*'
I'm confident I beat the bard,—for why?
My young friend owns me an Iago—him
Confessed, among the other qualities,
A ready rhymer. Oh, he rhymed! Here goes!
—Something to end with '*horsewhip!*' No, that rhyme
Beats me; there's '*cowslip*,' '*boltsprit*,' nothing else!
So, Tennyson take my benison,—verse for bard,
Prose suits the gambler's book best! Dared and done!'

Wherewith he dips pen, writes a line or two,
Closes and clasps the cover, gives the book,
Bowing the while, to her who hesitates,
Turns half away, turns round again, at last
Takes it as you touch carrion, then retires.
The door shuts fast the couple.

VI.

With a change
Of his whole manner, opens out at once
The Adversary.

"Now, my friend, for you!
You who, protected late, aggressive grown,
Brandish, it seems, a weapon I must 'ware!
Plain speech in me becomes respectable
Therefore, because courageous; plainly, then—
(Have lash well loose, hold handle tight and light!)
Throughout my life's experience, you indulged
Yourself and friend by passing in review
So courteously but now, I vainly search
To find one record of a specimen
So perfect of the pure and simple fool
As this you furnish me. Ingratitude
I lump with folly,—all's one lot,—so—fool!
Did I seek you or you seek me? Seek? sneak
For service to, and service you would style—
And did style—godlike, scarce an hour ago!
Fool, there again, yet not precisely there
First-rate in folly: since the hand you kissed
Did pick you from the kennel, did plant firm
Your footstep on the pathway, did persuade
Your awkward shamble to true gait and pace,
Fit for the world you walk in. Once a-strut
On that firm pavement which your cowardice
Was for renouncing as a pitfall, next
Came need to clear your brains of their conceit
They cleverly could distinguish who was who,
Whatever folk might tramp the thoroughfare.
Men, now—familiarly you read them off,
Each phyz at first sight! O you had an eye!
Who couched it? made you disappoint each fox
Eager to strip my gosling of his fluff
So golden as he cackled 'Goose trusts lamb?'
'*Ay, but I saved you—wolf defeated fox—
Wanting to pick your bones myself?*' then, wolf
Has got the worst of it with goose for once.
I, penniless, pay you ten thousand pounds

(—No gesture, pray! I pay ere I depart!)
And how you turn advantage to account
Here's the example! Have I proved so wrong
In my peremptory '*debt must be discharged?*'
O you laughed lovelily, were loth to leave
The old friend out at elbows—pooh, a thing
Not to be thought of! I must keep my cash,
And you forget your generosity!
Ha ha, I took your measure when I laughed
My laugh to that! First quarrel—nay, first faint
Pretence at taking umbrage—'*Down with debt,*
Both interest and principal!—The Club,
Exposure and expulsion!—stamp me out!'
That's the magnanimous magnificent
Renunciation of advantage! Well,
But whence and why did you take umbrage, Sir?
Because your master, having made you know
Somewhat of men, was minded to advance,
Expound you women, still a mystery!
My pupil pottered with a cloud on brow,
A clod in breast: had loved, and vainly loved:
Whence blight and blackness, just for all the world
As Byron used to teach us boys. Thought I—
'*Quick rid him of that rubbish! Clear the cloud,*
And set the heart a-pulsing!'—heart, this time:
'Twas nothing but the head I doctored late
For ignorance of Man; now heart's to dose,
Palsied by over-palpitation due
To Woman-worship—so, to work at once
On first avowal of the patient's ache!
This morning you described your malady,—
How you dared love a piece of virtue—lost
To reason, as the upshot showed: for scorn
Fitly repaid your stupid arrogance;
And, parting, you went two ways, she resumed
Her path—perfection, while forlorn you paced
The world that's made for beasts like you and me.
My remedy was—tell the fool the truth!
Your paragon of purity had plumped
Into these arms at their first outspread—'*fallen*
My victim,' she prefers to turn the phrase—

And, in exchange for that frank confidence,
Asked for my whole life present and to come—
Marriage: a thing uncovenanted for!
Never so much as put in question! Life—
Implied by marriage—throw that trifle in
And round the bargain off, no otherwise
Than if, when we played cards, because you won
My money you should also want my head!
That, I demurred to: we but played '*for love*'—
She won my love; had she proposed for stakes
'*Marriage*,'—why, that's for whist, a wiser game.
Whereat she raved at me, as losers will,
And went her way. So far the story's known,
The remedy's applied, no farther—which
Here's the sick man's first *honorarium* for—
Posting his medicine-monger at the Club!
That being, Sir, the whole you mean my fee—
In gratitude for such munificence
I'm bound in common honesty to spare
No droplet of the draught: so,—pinch your nose,
Pull no wry faces!—drain it to the dregs!
I say '*She went off*'—'*went off*,' you subjoin,
'*Since not to wedded bliss, as I supposed,*
Sure to some convent: solitude and peace
Help her to hide the shame from mortal view,
With prayer and fasting.' No, my sapient Sir!
Far wiselier, straightway she betook herself
To a prize-portent from the donkey-show
Of leathern long-ears that compete for palm
In clerical absurdity: since he,
Good ass, nor practises the shaving-trick,
The candle-crotchet, nonsense which repays
When you've young ladies congregant,—but schools
The poor,—toils, moils and grinds the mill nor means
To stop and munch one thistle in this life
Till next life smother him with roses: just
The parson for her purpose! Him she stroked
Over the muzzle; into mouth with bit,
And on to back with saddle,—there he stood,
The serviceable beast who heard, believed
And meekly bowed him to the burden,—borne

Off in a canter to seclusion—ay,
The lady's lost! But had a friend of mine
—While friend he was—imparted his sad case
To sympathizing counsellor, full soon
One cloud at least had vanished from his brow.
'*Don't fear!*' had followed reassuringly—
'*The lost will in due time turn up again,*
Probably just when, weary of the world,
You think of nothing less than settling-down
To country life and golden days, beside
A dearest best and brightest virtuousest
Wife: who needs no more hope to hold her own
Against the naughty-and-repentant—no,
Than water-gruel against Roman punch!'
And as I prophesied, it proves! My youth,—
Just at the happy moment when, subdued
To spooniness, he finds that youth fleets fast,
That town-life tires, that men should drop boy's-play,
That property, position have, no doubt,
Their exigency with their privilege,
And if the wealthy wed with wealth, how dire
The double duty!—in, behold, there beams
Our long-lost lady, form and face complete!
And where's my moralizing pupil now,
Had not his master missed a train by chance?
But, by your side instead of whirled away,
How have I spoiled scene, stopped catastrophe,
Struck flat the stage-effect I know by heart!
Sudden and strange the meeting—improvised?
Bless you, the last event she hoped or dreamed!
But rude sharp stroke will crush out fire from flint—
Assuredly from flesh. '*'Tis you?*' '*Myself.*'
'*Changed?*' '*Changeless!*' '*Then, what's earth to me?*' '*To me*
What's heaven?' '*So,—thine!*' '*And thine!*' '*And likewise mine!*'
Had laughed '*Amen*' the devil, but for me
Whose intermeddling hinders this hot haste,
And bids you, ere concluding contract, pause—
Ponder one lesson more, then sign and seal
At leisure and at pleasure,—lesson's price
Being, if you have skill to estimate,
—How say you?—I'm discharged my debt in full!

Since paid you stand, to farthing uttermost,
Unless I fare like that black majesty
A friend of mine had visit from last Spring.
Coasting along the Cape-side, he's becalmed
Off an uncharted bay, a novel town
Untouched at by the trader: here's a chance!
Out paddles straight the king in his canoe,
Comes over bulwark, says he means to buy
Ship's cargo—being rich and having brought
A treasure ample for the purpose. See!
Four dragons, stalwart blackies, guard the same
Wrapped round and round: its hulls, a multitude,—
Palm-leaf and cocoa-mat and goat's-hair cloth
All duly braced about with bark and board,—
Suggest how brave, 'neath coat, must kernel be!
At length the peeling is accomplished, plain
The casket opens out its core, and lo
—A bran-new British silver sixpence—bid
That's ample for the Bank,—thinks majesty!
You are the Captain; call my sixpence cracked
Or copper; '*what I've said is calumny;*
The lady's spotless!' Then, I'll prove my words,
Or make you prove them true as truth—yourself,
Here, on the instant! I'll not mince my speech,
Things at this issue. When she enters, then,
Make love to her! No talk of marriage now—
The point-blank bare proposal! Pick no phrase—
Prevent all misconception! Soon you'll see
How different the tactics when she deals
With an instructed man, no longer boy
Who blushes like a booby. Woman's wit!
Because you have instruction, blush no more!
Such your five minutes' profit by my pains,
'Tis simply now—demand and be possessed!
Which means—you may possess—may strip the tree
Of fruit desirable to make one wise!
More I nor wish nor want: your act's your act,
My teaching is but—there's the fruit to pluck
Or let alone at pleasure. Next advance
In knowledge were beyond you! Don't expect
I bid a novice—pluck, suck, send sky-high

Such fruit, once taught that neither crab nor sloe
Falls readier prey to who but robs a hedge,
Than this gold apple to my Hercules.
Were you no novice but proficient—then,
Then, truly, I might prompt you—Touch and taste,
Try flavour and be tired as soon as I!
Toss on the prize to greedy mouths agape,
Betake yours, sobered as the satiate grow,
To wise man's solid meal of house and land,
Consols and cousin! but my boy, my boy,
Such lore's above you! Here's the lady back!
So, Madam, you have conned the Album-page
And come to thank its last contributor?
How kind and condescending! I retire
A moment, lest I spoil the interview,
And mar my own endeavour to make friends—
You with him, him with you, and both with me!
If I succeed—permit me to inquire
Five minutes hence! Friends bid good-bye, you know."
And out he goes.

VII.

She, face, form, bearing, one
Superb composure—

"He has told you all?
Yes, he has told you all, your silence says—
What gives him, as he thinks the mastery
Over my body and my soul!—has told
That instance, even, of their servitude
He now exacts of me? A silent blush!
That's well, though better would white ignorance
Beseem your brow, undesecrate before—
Ay, when I left you! I too learn at last
—Hideously learned as I seemed so late—
What sin may swell to. Yes,—I needed learn
That, when my prophet's rod became the snake
I fled from, it would, one day, swallow up
—Incorporate whatever serpentine
Falsehood and treason and unmanliness
Beslime earth's pavement: such the power of Hell,

And so beginning, ends no otherwise
The Adversary! I was ignorant,
Blameworthy—if you will; but blame I take
Nowise upon me as I ask myself
—*You*—how can you, whose soul I seemed to read
The limpid eyes through, have declined so deep
Even with him for consort? I revolve
Much memory, pry into the looks and words
Of that day's walk beneath the College wall,
And nowhere can distinguish, in what gleams
Only pure marble through my dusky past,
A dubious cranny where such poison-seed
Might harbour, nourish what should yield to-day
This dread ingredient for the cup I drink.
Do not I recognize and honour truth
In seeming?—take your truth and for return,
Give you my truth, a no less precious gift?
You loved me: I believed you. I replied
—How could I other? '*I was not my own*,'
—No longer had the eyes to see, the ears
To hear, the mind to judge, since heart and soul
Now were another's. My own right in me,
For well or ill, consigned away—my face
Fronted the honest path, deflection whence
Had shamed me in the furtive backward look
At the late bargain—fit such chapman's phrase!—
As though—less hasty and more provident—
Waiting had brought advantage. Not for me,
The chapman's chance! Yet while thus much was true,
I spared you—as I knew you then—one more
Concluding word which, truth no less, seemed best
Buried away for ever. Take it now
Its power to pain is past! Four years—that day—
Those limes that make the College avenue!
I would that—friend and foe—by miracle,
I had, that moment, seen into the heart
Of either, as I now am taught to see!
I do believe I should have straight assumed
My proper function, and sustained a soul,
—Not aimed at being just sustained myself
By some man's soul—the weaker woman's-want!

So had I missed the momentary thrill
Of finding me in presence of a god,
But gained the god's own feeling when he gives
Such thrill to what turns life from death before.
'*Gods many and Lords many*,' says the Book:
You would have yielded up your soul to me
—Not to the false god who has burned its clay
In his own image. I had shed my love
Like Spring dew on the clod all flowery thence,
Not sent up a wild vapour to the sun
That drinks and then disperses. Both of us
Blameworthy,—I first meet my punishment—
And not so hard to bear. I breathe again!
Forth from those arms' enwinding leprosy
At last I struggle—uncontaminate:
Why must I leave *you* pressing to the breast
That's all one plague-spot? Did you love me once?
Then take love's last and best return! I think,
Womanliness means only motherhood;
All love begins and ends there,—roams enough,
But, having run the circle, rests at home.
Why is your expiation yet to make?
Pull shame with your own hands from your own head
Now,—never wait the slow envelopment
Submitted to by unelastic age!
One fierce throe frees the sapling: flake on flake
Lull till they leave the oak snow-stupified.
Your heart retains its vital warmth—or why
That blushing reassurance? Blush, young blood!
Break from beneath this icy premature
Captivity of wickedness—I warn
Back, in God's name! No fresh encroachment here!
This May breaks all to bud—no winter now!
Friend, we are both forgiven! Sin no more!
I am past sin now, so shall you become!
Meanwhile I testify that, lying once,
My foe lied ever, most lied last of all.
He, waking, whispered to your sense asleep
The wicked counsel,—and assent might seem;
But, roused, your healthy indignation breaks
The idle dream-pact. You would die—not dare

Confirm your dream-resolve,—nay, find the word
That fits the deed to bear the light of day!
Say I have justly judged you! then farewell
To blushing—nay, it ends in smiles, not tears!
Why tears now? I have justly judged, thank God!"

He does blush boy-like, but the man speaks out,
—Makes the due effort to surmount himself.

"I don't know what he wrote—how should I? Nor
How he could read my purpose which, it seems,
He chose to somehow write—mistakenly
Or else for mischief's sake. I scarce believe
My purpose put before you fair and plain
Would need annoy so much; but there's my luck—
From first to last I blunder. Still, one more
Turn at the target, try to speak my thought!
Since he could guess my purpose, won't you read
Right what he set down wrong? He said—let's think!
Ay, so!—he did begin by telling heaps
Of tales about you. Now, you see—suppose
Anyone told me—my own mother died
Before I knew her—told me—to his cost!—
Such tales about my own dead mother: why,
You would not wonder surely if I knew,
By nothing but my own heart's help, he lied,
Would you? No reason's wanted in the case.
So with you! In they burnt on me, his tales,
Much as when madhouse-inmates crowd around,
Make captive any visitor and scream
All sorts of stories of their keeper—he's
Both dwarf and giant, vulture, wolf, dog, cat,
Serpent and scorpion, yet man all the same;
Sane people soon see through the gibberish!
I just made out, you somehow lived somewhere
A life of shame—I can't distinguish more—
Married or single—how, don't matter much:
Shame which himself had caused—that point was clear,
That fact confessed—that thing to hold and keep.
Oh, and he added some absurdity
—That you were here to make me—ha, ha, ha!—

Still love you, still of mind to die for you,
Ha, ha—as if that needed mighty pains!
Now, foolish as . . . but never mind myself
—What I am, what I am not, in the eye
Of the world, is what I never cared for much.
Fool then or no fool, not one single word
In the whole string of lies did I believe,
But this—this only—if I choke, who minds?—
I believe somehow in your purity
Perfect as ever! Else what use is God?
He is God, and work miracles He can!
Then, what shall I do? Quite as clear, my course!
They've got a thing they call their Labyrinth
I' the garden yonder: and my cousin played
A pretty trick once, led and lost me deep
Inside the briery maze of hedge round hedge;
And there might I be staying now, stock-still,
But that I laughing bade eyes follow nose
And so straight pushed my path through let and stop
And soon was out in the open, face all scratched,
But well behind my back the prison-bars
In sorry plight enough, I promise you!
So here: I won my way to truth through lies—
Said, as I saw light,—if her shame be shame
I'll rescue and redeem her,—shame's no shame?
Then, I'll avenge, protect—redeem myself
The stupidest of sinners! Here I stand!
Dear,—let me once dare call you so,—you said
Thus ought you to have done, four years ago,
Such things and such! Ay, dear, and what ought I?
You were revealed to me: where's gratitude,
Where's memory even, where the gain of you
Discernible in my low after-life
Of fancied consolation? why, no horse
Once fed on corn, will, missing corn, go munch
Mere thistles like a donkey! I missed you,
And in your place found—him, made him my love,
Ay, did I,—by this token, that he taught
So much beast-nature that I meant . . . God knows
Whether I bow me to the dust enough! . . .
To marry—yes, my cousin here! I hope

That was a master-stroke! Take heart of hers,
And give her hand of mine with no more heart
Than now you see upon this brow I strike!
What atom of a heart do I retain
Not all yours? Dear, you know it! Easily
May she accord me pardon when I place
My brow beneath her foot, if foot so deign,
Since uttermost indignity is spared—
Mere marriage and no love! And all this time
Not one word to the purpose! Are you free?
Only wait! only let me serve—deserve
Where you appoint and how you see the good!
I have the will—perhaps the power—at least
Means that have power against the world. For time—
Take my whole life for your experiment!
If you are bound—in marriage, say—why, still,
Still, sure, there's something for a friend to do,
Outside? A mere well-wisher, understand!
I'll sit, my life long, at your gate, you know,
Swing it wide open to let you and him
Pass freely,—and you need not look, much less
Fling me a '*Thank you—are you there, old friend?*'
Don't say that even: I should drop like shot!
So I feel now at least: some day, who knows?
After no end of weeks and months and years
You might smile '*I believe you did your best!*'
And that shall make my heart leap—leap such leap
As lands the feet in Heaven to wait you there!
Ah, there's just one thing more! How pale you look!
Why? Are you angry? If there's, after all,
Worst come to worst—if still there somehow be
The shame—I said was no shame,—none, I swear!—
In that case, if my hand and what it holds,—
My name,—might be your safeguard now—at once—
Why, here's the hand—you have the heart! Of course—
No cheat, no binding you, because I'm bound,
To let me off probation by one day,
Week, month, year, lifetime! Prove as you propose!
Here's the hand with the name to take or leave!
That's all—and no great piece of news, I hope!"

"Give me the hand, then!" she cries hastily.
"Quick, now! I hear his footstep!"

Hand in hand
The couple face him as he enters, stops
Short, stands surprised a moment, laughs away
Surprise, resumes the much-experienced man.

"So, you accept him?"

"Till us death do part!"

"No longer? Come, that's right and rational!
I fancied there was power in common sense,
But did not know it worked thus promptly. Well—
At last each understands the other, then?
Each drops disguise, then? So, at supper-time
These masquerading people doff their gear,
Grand Turk his pompous turban, Quakeress
Her stiff-starched bib and tucker,—make-believe
That only bothers when, ball-business done,
Nature demands champagne and *mayonnaise*.
Just so has each of us sage three abjured
His and her moral pet particular
Pretension to superiority,
And, cheek by jowl, we henceforth munch and joke!
Go, happy pair, paternally dismissed
To live and die together—for a month,
Discretion can award no more! Depart
From whatsoe'er the calm sweet solitude
Selected—Paris not improbably—
At month's end, when the honeycomb's left wax,
—You, daughter, with a pocketful of gold
Enough to find your village boys and girls
In duffel cloaks and hobnailed shoes from May
To—what's the phrase?—Christmas-come-never-mas!
You, son and heir of mine, shall re-appear
Ere Spring-time, that's the ring-time, lose one leaf,
And—not without regretful smack of lip
The while you wipe it free of honey-smear—
Marry the cousin, play the magistrate,
Stand for the county, prove perfection's pink—

Master of hounds, gay-coated dine—nor die
Sooner than needs of gout, obesity,
And sons at Christ Church! As for me,—ah me,
I abdicate—retire on my success,
Four years well occupied in teaching youth
—My son and daughter the exemplary!
Time for me to retire now, having placed
Proud on their pedestal the pair: in turn,
Let them do homage to their master! You,—
Well, your flushed cheek and flashing eye proclaim
Sufficiently your gratitude: you paid
The *honorarium*, the ten thousand pounds
To purpose, did you not? I told you so!
And you,—but, bless me, why so pale—so faint
At influx of good fortune? Certainly,
No matter how or why or whose the fault,
I save your life—save it, nor less nor more!
You blindly were resolved to welcome death
In that black boor-and-bumpkin-haunted hole
Of his, the prig with all the preachments! *You*
Installed as nurse and matron to the crones
And wenches, while there lay a world outside
Like Paris (which again I recommend)
In company and guidance of—first, this,
Then—all in good time—some new friend as fit—
What if I were to say, some fresh myself,
As I once figured? Each dog has his day,
And mine's at sunset: what should old dog do
But eye young litters' frisky puppyhood?
O I shall watch this beauty and this youth
Frisk it in brilliance! But don't fear! Discreet,
I shall pretend to no more recognize
My quondam pupils than the doctor nods
When certain old acquaintances may cross
His path in Park, or sit down prim beside
His plate at dinner-table: tip nor wink
Scares patients he has put, for reason good,
Under restriction,—maybe, talked sometimes
Of douche or horsewhip to,—for why? because
The gentleman would crazily declare
His best friend was—Iago! Ay, and worse—

The lady, all at once grown lunatic,
In suicidal monomania vowed,
To save her soul, she needs must starve herself!
They're cured now, both, and I tell nobody.
Why don't you speak? Nay, speechless, each of you
Can spare,—without unclasping plighted troth,—
At least one hand to shake! Left-hands will do—
Yours first, my daughter! Ah, it guards—it gripes
The precious Album fast—and prudently!
As well obliterate the record there
On page the last: allow me tear the leaf!
Pray, now! And afterward, to make amends,
What if all three of us contribute each
A line to that prelusive fragment,—help
The embarrassed bard who broke out to break down
Dumbfoundered at such unforseen success?
'*Hail, calm acclivity, salubrious spot*'
You begin—*place aux dames!* I'll prompt you then!
'*Here do I take the good the gods allot!*'
Next you, Sir! What, still sulky? Sing, O Muse!
'*Here does my lord in full discharge his shot!*'
Now for the crowning flourish! mine shall be . . ."

"Nothing to match your first effusion, mar
What was, is, shall remain your masterpiece!
Authorship has the alteration-itch!
No, I protest against erasure. Read,
My friend!" (she gasps out.) "Read and quickly read
'*Before us death do part*,' what made you mine
And made me yours—the marriage-licence here!
Decide if he is like to mend the same!"

And so the lady, white to ghastliness,
Manages somehow to display the page
With left-hand only, while the right retains
The other hand, the young man's,—dreaming-drunk
He, with this drench of stupifying stuff,
Eyes wide, mouth open,—half the idiot's stare
And half the prophet's insight,—holding tight,
All the same, by his one fact in the world—
The lady's right-hand: he but seems to read—

Does not, for certain; yet, how understand
Unless he reads?

So, understand he does,
For certain. Slowly, word by word, *she* reads
Aloud that licence—or that warrant, say.

'*One against two—and two that urge their odds*
To uttermost—I needs must try resource!
Madam, I laid me prostrate, bade you spurn
Body and soul: you spurned and safely spurned
So you had spared me the superfluous taunt
'*Prostration means no power to stand erect,*
Stand, trampling on who trampled—prostrate now!'
So, with my other fool-foe: I was fain
Let the boy touch me with the buttoned foil,
And him the infection gains, he too must needs
Catch up the butcher's cleaver. Be it so!
Since play turns earnest, here's my serious fence.
He loves you; he demands your love: both know
What love means in my language. Love him then!
Pursuant to a pact, love pays my debt:
Therefore, deliver me from him, thereby
Likewise delivering from me yourself!
For, hesitate—much more, refuse consent—
I tell the whole truth to your husband. Flat
Cards lie on table, in our gamester-phrase!
Consent—you stop my mouth, the only way.'

"I did well, trusting instinct: knew your hand
Had never joined with his in fellowship
Over this pact of infamy. You known—
As he was known through every nerve of me.
Therefore I '*stopped his mouth the only way*'
But *my* way! none was left for you, my friend—
The loyal—near, the loved one! No—no—no!
Threaten? Chastise? The coward would but quail.
Conquer who can, the cunning of the snake!
Stamp out his slimy strength from tail to head,
And still you leave vibration of the tongue.
His malice had redoubled—not on me

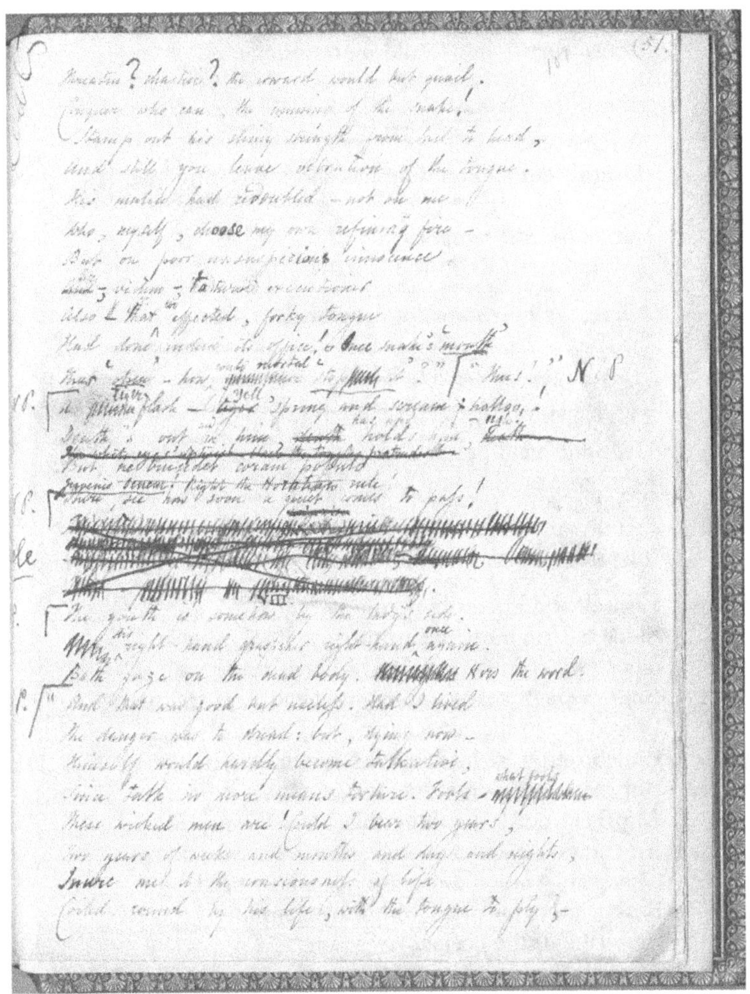

FIG. 8 MS in Browning's hand of *The Inn Album* (1875), VII, ll. 368–83 and VIII, ll. 1–11, Balliol College Library.

Who, myself, choose my own refining fire—
But on poor unsuspicious innocence;
And,—victim,—to turn executioner
Also—that feat effected, forky tongue

Had done indeed its office! Once snake's '*mouth*'
Thus '*open*'—how could mortal '*stop it*'?"

"So!"

A tiger-flash—yell, spring, and scream: halloo!
Death's out and on him, has and holds him—ugh!

But *ne trucidet coram populo*
Juvenis senem! Right the Horatian rule!

There, see how soon a quiet comes to pass!

VIII.

The youth is somehow by the lady's side.
His right-hand grasps her right-hand once again.
Both gaze on the dead body. Hers the word.

"And that was good but useless. Had I lived
The danger was to dread: but, dying now—

Himself would hardly become talkative,
Since talk no more means torture. Fools—what fools
These wicked men are! Had I borne four years,
Four years of weeks and months and days and nights,
Inured me to the consciousness of life
Coiled round by his life, with the tongue to ply,—
But that I bore about me, for prompt use
At urgent need, the thing that '*stops the mouth*'
And stays the venom? Since such need was now
Or never,—how should use not follow need?
Bear witness for me, I withdraw from life
By virtue of the licence—warrant, say,
That blackens yet this Album—white again,
Thanks still to my one friend who tears the page!
Now, let me write the line of supplement,
As counselled by my foe there: '*each a line!*'

And she does falteringly write to end.

'*I die now through the villain who lies dead,*
Righteously slain. He would have outraged me,
So, my defender slew him. God protect
The right! Where wrong lay, I bear witness now.

Let man believe me, whose last breath is spent
In blessing my defender from my soul!'

And so ends the Inn Album.

As she dies,
Begins outside a voice that sounds like song,
And is indeed half song though meant for speech
Muttered in time to motion—stir of heart
That unsubduably must bubble forth
To match the fawn-step as it mounts the stair.

"All's ended and all's over! Verdict found
'*Not guilty*'—prisoner forthwith set free,
Mid cheers the Court pretends to disregard!
Now Portia, now for Daniel, late severe,
At last appeased, benignant! '*This young man—*
Hem—has the young man's foibles but no fault.
He's virgin soil—a friend must cultivate.
I think no plant called 'love' grows wild—a friend

May introduce, and name the bloom, the fruit!'
Here somebody dares wave a handkerchief—
She'll want to hide her face with presently!
Good-bye then! '*Cigno fedel, cigno fedel,*
Addio!' Now, was ever such mistake—
Ever such foolish ugly omen? Pshaw!
Wagner, beside! '*Amo te solo, te*
Solo amai!' That's worth fifty such!
But, mum, the grave face at the opened door!"

And so the good gay girl, with eyes and cheeks
Diamond and damask,—cheeks so white erewhile
Because of a vague fancy, idle fear
Chased on reflection!—pausing, taps discreet;
And then, to give herself a countenance,
Before she comes upon the pair inside,
Loud—the oft-quoted, long-laughed-over line—
"'*Hail, calm acclivity, salubrious spot!*'
Open the door!"

No: let the curtain fall!

FROM *PACCHIAROTTO AND HOW HE WORKED IN DISTEMPER: WITH OTHER POEMS* (1876)

House

1.

Shall I sonnet-sing you about myself?
  Do I live in a house you would like to see?
Is it scant of gear, has it store of pelf?
  "Unlock my heart with a sonnet-key?"

2.

Invite the world, as my betters have done?
  "Take notice: this building remains on view,
Its suites of reception every one,
  Its private apartment and bedroom too;

3.

"For a ticket, apply to the Publisher."
  No: thanking the public, I must decline.
A peep through my window, if folks prefer;
  But, please you, no foot over threshold of mine!

4.

I have mixed with a crowd and heard free talk
  In a foreign land where an earthquake chanced
And a house stood gaping, nought to baulk
  Man's eye wherever he gazed or glanced.

5.

The whole of the frontage shaven sheer,
  The inside gaped: exposed to day,
Right and wrong and common and queer,
  Bare, as the palm of your hand, it lay.

6.

The owner? Oh, he had been crushed, no doubt!
  "Odd tables and chairs for a man of wealth!
What a parcel of musty old books about!
  He smoked,—no wonder he lost his health!

7.

"I doubt if he bathed before he dressed.
A brasier?—the pagan, he burned perfumes!
You see it is proved, what the neighbours guessed:
His wife and himself had separate rooms."

8.

Friends, the goodman of the house at least
Kept house to himself till an earthquake came:
'Tis the fall of its frontage permits you feast
On the inside arrangement you praise or blame.

9.

Outside should suffice for evidence:
And whoso desires to penetrate
Deeper, must dive by the spirit-sense—
No optics like yours, at any rate!

10.

"Hoity toity! A street to explore,
Your house the exception! '*With this same key*
Shakespeare unlocked his heart,' once more!"
Did Shakespeare? If so, the less Shakespeare he!

Bifurcation

We were two lovers; let me lie by her,
My tomb beside her tomb. On hers inscribe—
"I loved him; but my reason bade prefer
Duty to love, reject the tempter's bribe
Of rose and lily when each path diverged,
And either I must pace to life's far end
As love should lead me, or, as duty urged,
Plod the worn causeway arm in arm with friend.
So, truth turned falsehood: '*How I loathe a flower,*
How prize the pavement!' still caressed his ear—
The deafish friend's—through life's day, hour by hour,
As he laughed (coughing) '*Ay, it would appear!*'

But deep within my heart of hearts there hid
Ever the confidence, amends for all,
That heaven repairs what wrong earth's journey did,
When love from life-long exile comes at call.
Duty and love, one broadway, were the best—
Who doubts? But one or other was to choose.
I chose the darkling half, and wait the rest
In that new world where light and darkness fuse."

Inscribe on mine—"I loved her: love's track lay
O'er sand and pebble, as all travellers know.
Duty led through a smiling country, gay
With greensward where the rose and lily blow.
'Our roads are diverse: farewell, love!' said she:
''Tis duty I abide by: homely sward
And not the rock-rough picturesque for me!
Above, where both roads join, I wait reward.
Be you as constant to the path whereon
I leave you planted!' But man needs must move,
Keep moving—whither, when the star is gone
Whereby he steps secure nor strays from love?
No stone but I was tripped by, stumbling-block
But brought me to confusion. Where I fell,
There I lay flat, if moss disguised the rock,
Thence, if flint pierced, I rose and cried '*All's well!*
Duty be mine to tread in that high sphere
Where love from duty ne'er disparts, I trust,
And two halves make that whole, whereof—since here
One must suffice a man—why, this one must!' "

Inscribe each tomb thus: then, some sage acquaint
The simple—which holds sinner, which holds saint!

Numpholeptos

Still you stand, still you listen, still you smile!
Still melts your moonbeam through me, white awhile,
Softening, sweetening, till sweet and soft
Increase so round this heart of mine, that oft
I could believe your moonbeam-smile has past
The pallid limit and, transformed at last,

Lies, sunlight and salvation—warms the soul
It sweetens, softens! Would you pass that goal,
Gain love's birth at the limit's happier verge,
And, where an iridescence lurks, but urge
The hesitating pallor on to prime
Of dawn!—true blood-streaked, sun-warmth, action-time,
By heart-pulse ripened to a ruddy glow
Of gold above my clay—I scarce should know
From gold's self, thus suffused! For gold means love.
What means the sad slow silver smile above
My clay but pity, pardon?—at the best,
But acquiescence that I take my rest,
Contented to be clay, while in your heaven
The sun reserves love for the Spirit-Seven
Companioning God's throne they lamp before,
—Leaves earth a mute waste only wandered o'er
By that pale soft sweet disempassioned moon
Which smiles me slow forgiveness! Such, the boon
I beg? Nay, dear, submit to this—just this
Supreme endeavour! As my lips now kiss
Your feet, my arms convulse your shrouding robe,
My eyes, acquainted with the dust, dare probe
Your eyes above for—what, if born, would blind
Mine with redundant bliss, as flash may find
The inert nerve, sting awake the palsied limb,
Bid with life's ecstasy sense overbrim
And suck back death in the resurging joy—
Love, the love whole and sole without alloy!

Vainly! The promise withers! I employ
Lips, arms, eyes, pray the prayer which finds the word,
Make the appeal which must be felt, not heard,
And none the more is changed your calm regard:
Rather, its sweet and soft grow harsh and hard—
Forbearance, then repulsion, then disdain.
Avert the rest! I rise, see!—make, again
Once more, the old departure for some track
Untried yet through a world which brings me back
Ever thus fruitlessly to find your feet,
To fix your eyes, to pray the soft and sweet
Which smile there—take from his new pilgrimage

Your outcast, once your inmate, and assuage
With love—not placid pardon now—his thirst
For a mere drop from out the ocean erst
He drank at! Well, the quest shall be renewed.
Fear nothing! Though I linger, unembued
With any drop, my lips thus close. I go!
So did I leave you, I have found you so,
And doubtlessly, if fated to return,
So shall my pleading persevere and earn
Pardon—not love in that same smile, I learn,
And lose the meaning of, to learn once more,
Vainly!

What fairy track do I explore?
What magic hall return to, like the gem
Centuply-angled o'er a diadem?
You dwell there, hearted; from your midmost home
Rays forth—through that fantastic world I roam
Ever—from centre to circumference,
Shaft upon coloured shaft: this crimsons thence,
That purples out its precinct through the waste.
Surely I had your sanction when I faced,
Fared forth upon that untried yellow ray
Whence I retrack my steps? They end to-day
Where they began, before your feet, beneath
Your eyes, your smile: the blade is shut in sheath,
Fire quenched in flint; irradiation, late
Triumphant through the distance, finds its fate,
Merged in your blank pure soul, alike the source
And tomb of that prismatic glow: divorce
Absolute, all-conclusive! Forth I fared,
Treading the lambent flamelet: little cared
If now its flickering took the topaz tint,
If now my dull-caked path gave sulphury hint
Of subterranean rage—no stay nor stint
To yellow, since you sanctioned that I bathe,
Burnish me, soul and body, swim and swathe
In yellow licence. Here I reek suffused
With crocus, saffron, orange, as I used
With scarlet, purple, every dye o' the bow
Born of the storm-cloud. As before, you show

Scarce recognition, no approval, some
Mistrust, more wonder at a man become
Monstrous in garb, nay—flesh disguised as well,
Through his adventure. Whatsoe'er befell,
I followed, whereso'er it wound, that vein
You authorised should leave your whiteness, stain
Earth's sombre stretch beyond your midmost place
Of vantage,—trode that tinct whereof the trace
On garb and flesh repel you! Yes, I plead
Your own permission—your command, indeed,
That who would worthily retain the love
Must share the knowledge shrined those eyes above,
Go boldly on adventure, break through bounds
O' the quintessential whiteness that surrounds
Your feet, obtain experience of each tinge
That bickers forth to broaden out, impinge
Plainer his foot its pathway all distinct
From every other. Ah, the wonder, linked
With fear, as exploration manifests
What agency it was first tipped the crests
Of unnamed wildflower, soon protruding grew
Portentous mid the sands, as when his hue
Betrays him and the burrowing snake gleams through;
Till, last... but why parade more shame and pain?
Are not the proofs upon me? Here again
I pass into your presence, I receive
Your smile of pity, pardon, and I leave...
No, not this last of times I leave you, mute,
Submitted to my penance, so my foot
May yet again adventure, tread, from source
To issue, one more ray of rays which course
Each other, at your bidding, from the sphere
Silver and sweet, their birthplace, down that drear
Dark of the world,—you promise shall return
Your pilgrim jewelled as with drops o' the urn
The rainbow paints from, and no smatch at all
Of ghastliness at edge of some cloud-pall
Heaven cowers before, as earth awaits the fall
O' the bolt and flash of doom. Who trusts your word
Tries the adventure: and returns—absurd

As frightful—in that sulphur-steeped disguise
Mocking the priestly cloth-of-gold, sole prize
The arch-heretic was wont to bear away
Until he reached the burning. No, I say:
No fresh adventure! No more seeking love
At end of toil, and finding, calm above
My passion, the old statuesque regard,
The sad petrific smile!

O you—less hard
And hateful than mistaken and obtuse
Unreason of a she-intelligence!
You very woman with the pert pretence
To match the male achievement! Like enough!
Ay, you were easy victors, did the rough
Straightway efface itself to smooth, the gruff
Grind down and grow a whisper,—did man's truth
Subdue, for sake of chivalry and ruth,
Its rapier-edge to suit the bulrush-spear
Womanly falsehood fights with! O that ear
All fact pricks rudely, that thrice-superfine
Feminity of sense, with right divine
To waive all process, take result stain-free
From out the very muck wherein...

Ah me!
The true slave's querulous outbreak! All the rest
Be resignation! Forth at your behest
I fare. Who knows but this—the crimson-quest—
May deepen to a sunrise, not decay
To that cold sad sweet smile?—which I obey.

A Forgiveness

I am indeed the personage you know.
As for my wife,—what happened long ago—
You have a right to question me, as I
Am bound to answer.

"Son, a fit reply!"
The monk half spoke, half ground through his clenched teeth,
At the confession-grate I knelt beneath.

Thus then all happened, Father! Power and place
I had as still I have. I ran life's race,
With the whole world to see, as only strains
His strength some athlete whose prodigious gains
Of good appal him: happy to excess,—
Work freely done should balance happiness
Fully enjoyed; and, since beneath my roof
Housed she who made home heaven, in heaven's behoof
I went forth every day, and all day long
Worked for the world. Look, how the labourer's song
Cheers him! Thus sang my soul, at each sharp throe
Of labouring flesh and blood—"She loves me so!"

One day, perhaps such song so knit the nerve
That work grew play and vanished. "I deserve
Haply my heaven an hour before the time!"
I laughed, as silverly the clockhouse-chime
Surprised me passing through the postern-gate
—Not the main entry where the menials wait
And wonder why the world's affairs allow
The master sudden leisure. That was how
I took the private garden-way for once.

Forth from the alcove, I saw start, ensconce
Himself behind the porphyry vase, a man.

My fancies in the natural order ran:
"A spy,—perhaps a foe in ambuscade,—
A thief,—more like, a sweetheart of some maid
Who pitched on the alcove for tryst perhaps."

"Stand there!" I bid.

Whereat my man but wraps
His face the closelier with uplifted arm
Whereon the cloak lies, strikes in blind alarm
This and that pedestal as,—stretch and stoop,—
Now in, now out of sight, he thrids the group
Of statues, marble god and goddess ranged
Each side the pathway, till the gate's exchanged
For safety: one step thence, the street, you know!

Thus far I followed with my gaze. Then, slow,
Near on admiringly, I breathed again,

And—back to that last fancy of the train—
"A danger risked for hope of just a word
With—which of all my nest may be the bird
This poacher covets for her plumage, pray?
Carmen? Juana? Carmen seems too gay
For such adventure, while Juana's grave
—Would scorn the folly. I applaud the knave!
He had the eye, could single from my brood
His proper fledgeling!"

As I turned, there stood
In face of me, my wife stone-still stone-white.
Whether one bound had brought her,—at first sight
Of what she judged the encounter, sure to be
Next moment, of the venturous man and me,—
Brought her to clutch and keep me from my prey
Whether impelled because her death no day
Could come so absolutely opportune
As now at joy's height, like a year in June
Stayed at the fall of its first ripened rose;
Or whether hungry for my hate—who knows?—
Eager to end an irksome lie, and taste
Our tingling true relation, hate embraced
By hate one naked moment:—anyhow
There stone-still stone-white stood my wife, but now
The woman who made heaven within my house.
Ay, she who faced me was my very spouse
As well as love—you are to recollect!

"Stay!" she said. "Keep at least one soul unspecked
With crime, that's spotless hitherto—your own!
Kill me who court the blessing, who alone
Was, am and shall be guilty, first to last!
The man lay helpless in the toils I cast
About him, helpless as the statue there
Against that strangling bell-flower's bondage: tear
Away and tread to dust the parasite,
But do the passive marble no despite!
I love him as I hate you. Kill me! Strike
At one blow both infinitudes alike
Out of existence—hate and love! Whence love?

That's safe inside my heart, nor will remove
For any searching of your steel, I think.
Whence hate? The secret lay on lip, at brink
Of speech, in one fierce tremble to escape,
At every form wherein your love took shape,
At each new provocation of your kiss.
Kill me!
We went in.

Next day after this,
I felt as if the speech might come. I spoke—
Easily, after all.

"The lifted cloak
Was screen sufficient: I concern myself
Hardly with laying hands on who for pelf—
Whate'er the ignoble kind—may prowl and brave
Cuffing and kicking proper to a knave
Detected by my household's vigilance.
Enough of such! As for my love-romance—
I, like our good Hidalgo, rub my eyes
And wake and wonder how the film could rise
Which changed for me a barber's bason straight
Into—Mambrino's helm? I hesitate
Nowise to say—God's sacramental cup!
Why should I blame the brass which, burnished up,
Will blaze, to all but me, as good as gold?
To me—a warning I was overbold
In judging metals. The Hidalgo waked
Only to die, if I remember,—staked
His life upon the bason's worth, and lost:
While I confess torpidity at most
In here and there a limb; but, lame and halt,
Still should I work on, still repair my fault
Ere I took rest in death,—no fear at all!
Now, work—no word before the curtain fall!"

The "curtain"? That of death on life, I meant:
My "word" permissible in death's event,
Would be—truth, soul to soul; for, otherwise,
Day by day, three years long, there had to rise
And, night by night, to fall upon our stage—

Ours, doomed to public play by heritage—
Another curtain, when the world, perforce
Our critical assembly, in due course
Came and went, witnessing, gave praise or blame
To art-mimetic. It had spoiled the game
If, suffered to set foot behind our scene,
The world had witnessed how stage-king and queen,
Gallant and lady, but a minute since
Enarming each the other, would evince
No sign of recognition as they took
His way and her way to whatever nook
Waited them in the darkness either side
Of that bright stage where lately groom and bride
Had fired the audience to a frenzy-fit
Of sympathetic rapture—every whit
Earned as the curtain fell on her and me,
—Actors. Three whole years, nothing was to see
But calm and concord: where a speech was due
There came the speech; when smiles were wanted too
Smiles were as ready. In a place like mine,
Where foreign and domestic cares combine,
There's audience every day and all day long;
But finally the last of the whole throng
Who linger lets one see his back. For her—
Why, liberty and liking: I aver,
Liking and liberty! For me—I breathed,
Let my face rest from every wrinkle wreathed
Smile-like about the mouth, unlearned my task
Of personation till next day bade mask,
And quietly betook me from that world
To the real world, not pageant: there unfurled
In work, its wings, my soul, the fretted power.
Three years I worked, each minute of each hour
Not claimed by acting:—work I may dispense
With talk about, since work in evidence,
Perhaps in history; who knows or cares?

After three years, this way, all unawares,
Our acting ended. She and I, at close
Of a loud night-feast, led, between two rows
Of bending male and female loyalty,

Our lord the king down staircase, while, held high
At arm's length did the twisted tapers' flare
Herald his passage from our palace where
Such visiting left glory evermore.
Again the ascent in public, till at door
As we two stood by the saloon—now blank
And disencumbered of its guests—there sank
A whisper in my ear, so low and yet
So unmistakable!

"I half forget
The chamber you repair to, and I want
Occasion for one short word—if you grant
That grace—within a certain room you called
Our '*Study*,' for you wrote there while I scrawled
Some paper full of faces for my sport.
That room I can remember. Just one short
Word with you there, for the remembrance' sake!"

"Follow me thither!" I replied.

We break
The gloom a little, as with guiding lamp
I lead the way, leave warmth and cheer, by damp
Blind disused serpentining ways afar
From where the habitable chambers are,—
Ascend, descend stairs tunnelled through the stone,—
Always in silence,—till I reach the lone
Chamber sepulchred for my very own
Out of the palace-quarry. When a boy,
Here was my fortress, stronghold from annoy,
Proof-positive of ownership; in youth
I garnered up my gleanings here—uncouth
But precious relics of vain hopes, vain fears;
Finally, this became in after years
My closet of entrenchment to withstand
Invasion of the foe on every hand—
The multifarious herd in bower and hall,
State-room,—rooms whatsoe'er the style, which call
On masters to be mindful that, before
Men, they must look like men and something more.
Here,—when our lord the king's bestowment ceased

To deck me on the day that, golden-fleeced,
I touched ambition's height,—'twas here, released
From glory (always symboled by a chain!)
No sooner was I privileged to gain
My secret domicile than glad I flung
That last toy on the table—gazed where hung
On hook my father's gift, the arquebuss—
And asked myself "Shall I envisage thus
The new prize and the old prize, when I reach
Another year's experience?—own that each
Equalled advantage—sportsman's—statesman's tool?
That brought me down an eagle, this—a fool!"

Into which room on entry, I set down
The lamp, and turning saw whose rustled gown
Had told me my wife followed, pace for pace.
Each of us looked the other in the face,
She spoke. "Since I could die now . . . "

(To explain
Why that first struck me, know—not once again
Since the adventure at the porphyry's edge
Three years before, which sundered like a wedge
Her soul from mine, though daily, smile to smile,
We stood before the public,—all the while
Not once had I distinguished, in that face
I paid observance to, the faintest trace
Of feature more than requisite for eyes
To do their duty by and recognize:
So did I force mine to obey my will
And pry no further. There exists such skill,—
Those know who need it. What physician shrinks
From needful contact with a corpse? He drinks
No plague so long as thirst for knowledge,—not
An idler impulse,—prompts inquiry. What,
And will you disbelieve in power to bid
Our spirit back to bounds, as though we chid
A child from scrutiny that's just and right
In manhood? Sense, not soul, accomplished sight,
Reported daily she it was—not how
Nor why a change had come to cheek and brow.)

"Since I could die now of the truth concealed,
Yet dare not, must not die,—so seems revealed
The Virgin's mind to me,—for death means peace,
Wherein no lawful part have I, whose lease
Of life and punishment the truth avowed
May haply lengthen,—let me push the shroud
Away, that steals to muffle ere is just
My penance-fire in snow! I dare—I must
Live, by avowal of the truth—this truth—
I loved you! Thanks for the fresh serpent's tooth
That, by a prompt new pang more exquisite
Than all preceding torture, proves me right!
I loved you yet I lost you! May I go
Burn to the ashes, now my shame you know?"

I think there never was such—how express?—
Horror coquetting with voluptuousness,
As in those arms of Eastern workmanship—
Yataghan, kandjar, things that rend and rip,
Gash rough, slash smooth, help hate so many ways,
Yet ever keep a beauty that betrays
Love still at work with the artificer
Throughout his quaint devising. Why prefer,
Except for love's sake, that a blade should writhe
And bicker like a flame?—now play the scythe
As if some broad neck tempted,—now contract
And needle off into a fineness lacked
For just that puncture which the heart demands?
Then, such adornment! Wherefore need our hands
Enclose not ivory alone, nor gold
Roughened for use, but jewels? Nay, behold!
Fancy my favourite—which I seem to grasp
While I describe the luxury. No asp
Is diapered more delicate round throat
Than this below the handle! These denote
—These mazy lines meandering, to end
Only in flesh they open—what intend
They else but water-purlings—pale contrast
With the life-crimson where they blend at last?
And mark the handle's dim pellucid green,
Carved, the hard jadestone, as you pinch a bean,

Into a sort of parrot-bird! He pecks
A grape-bunch; his two eyes are ruby-specks
Pure from the mine: seen this way,—glassy blank,
But turn them,—lo the inmost fire, that shrank
From sparkling, sends a red dart right to aim!
Why did I choose such toys? Perhaps the game
Of peaceful men is warlike, just as men
War-wearied get amusement from that pen
And paper we grow sick of—statesfolk tired
Of merely (when such measures are required)
Dealing out doom to people by three words,
A signature and seal: we play with swords
Suggestive of quick process. That is how
I came to like the toys described you now,
Store of which glittered on the walls and strewed
The table, even, while my wife pursued
Her purpose to its ending. "Now you know
This shame, my three years' torture, let me go,
Burn to the very ashes! You—I lost,
Yet you—I loved!"

The thing I pity most
In men is—action prompted by surprise
Of anger: men? nay, bulls—whose onset lies
At instance of the firework and the goad!
Once the foe prostrate,—trampling once bestowed,—
Prompt follows placability, regret,
Atonement. Trust me, blood-warmth never yet
Betokened strong will! As no leap of pulse
Pricked me, that first time, so did none convulse
My veins at this occasion for resolve.
Had that devolved which did not then devolve
Upon me, I had done—what now to do
Was quietly apparent.

"Tell me who
The man was, crouching by the porphyry vase!"

"No, never! All was folly in his case,
All guilt in mine. I tempted, he complied."

"And yet you loved me?"

"Loved you. Double-dyed
In folly and in guilt, I thought you gave
Your heart and soul away from me to slave
At statecraft. Since my right in you seemed lost,
I stung myself to teach you, to your cost,
What you rejected could be prized beyond
Life, heaven, by the first fool I threw a fond
Look on, a fatal word to."

"And you still
Love me? Do I conjecture well or ill?"

"Conjecture—well or ill! I had three years
To spend in learning you."

"We both are peers
In knowledge, therefore: since three years are spent
Ere thus much of yourself *I* learn—who went
Back to the house, that day, and brought my mind
To bear upon your action, uncombined
Motive from motive, till the dross, deprived
Of every purer particle, survived
At last in native simple hideousness,
Utter contemptibility, nor less
Nor more. Contemptibility—exempt
How could I, from its proper due—contempt?
I have too much despised you to divert
My life from its set course by help or hurt
Of your all-despicable life—perturb
The calm, I work in, by—men's mouths to curb,
Which at such news were clamorous enough—
Men's eyes to shut before my broidered stuff
With the huge hole there, my emblazoned wall
Blank where a scutcheon hung,—by, worse than all,
Each day's procession, my paraded life
Robbed and impoverished through the wanting wife
—Now that my life (which means—my work) was grown
Riches indeed! Once, just this worth alone
Seemed work to have, that profit gained thereby
Of good and praise would—how rewardingly!—
Fall at your feet,—a crown I hoped to cast

Before your love, my love should crown at last.
No love remaining to cast crown before,
My love stopped work now: but contempt the more
Impelled me task as ever head and hand,
Because the very fiends weave ropes of sand
Rather than taste pure hell in idleness.
Therefore I kept my memory down by stress
Of daily work I had no mind to stay
For the world's wonder at the wife away.
Oh, it was easy all of it, believe,
For I despised you! But your words retrieve
Importantly the past. No hate assumed
The mask of love at any time! There gloomed
A moment when love took hate's semblance, urged
By causes you declare; but love's self purged
Away a fancied wrong I did both loves
—Yours and my own: by no hate's help, it proves,
Purgation was attempted. Then, you rise
High by how many a grade! I did despise—
I do but hate you. Let hate's punishment
Replace contempt's! First step to which ascent—
Write down your own words I re-utter you!
'I loved my husband and I hated—who
He was, I took up as my first chance, mere
Mud-ball to fling and make love foul with!' Here
Lies paper!"

"Would my blood for ink suffice!"

"It may: this minion from a land of spice,
Silk, feather—every bird of jewelled breast—
This poignard's beauty, ne'er so lightly prest
Above your heart there . . . "

"Thus?"

"It flows, I see.
Dip there the point and write!"

"Dictate to me!
Nay, I remember."

And she wrote the words.
I read them. Then—"Since love, in you, affords
Licence for hate, in me, to quench (I say)
Contempt—why, hate itself has passed away
In vengeance—foreign to contempt. Depart
Peacefully to that death which Eastern art
Imbued this weapon with, if tales be true!
Love will succeed to hate. I pardon you—
Dead in our chamber!"

True as truth the tale.
She died ere morning; then, I saw how pale
Her cheek was ere it wore day's paint-disguise,
And what a hollow darkened 'neath her eyes,
Now that I used my own. She sleeps, as erst
Beloved, in this your church: ay, yours!

Immersed
In thought so deeply, Father? Sad, perhaps?
For whose sake, hers or mine or his who wraps
—Still plain I seem to see!—about his head
The idle cloak,—about his heart (instead
Of cuirass) some fond hope he may elude
My vengeance in the cloister's solitude?
Hardly, I think! As little helped his brow
The cloak then, Father—as your grate helps now!

FROM *LA SAISIAZ AND THE TWO POETS OF CROISIC* (1878)

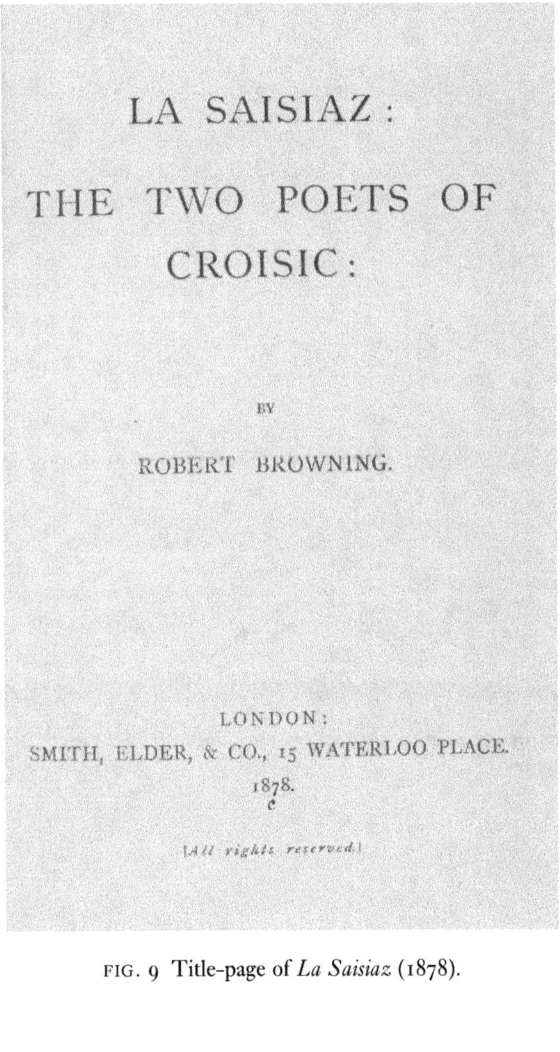

LA SAISIAZ:

THE TWO POETS OF CROISIC:

BY

ROBERT BROWNING.

LONDON:
SMITH, ELDER, & CO., 15 WATERLOO PLACE.
1878.

FIG. 9 Title-page of *La Saisiaz* (1878).

FIG. 10 MS in Browning's hand of opening lines of *La Saisiaz* (1878), Balliol College Library.

La Saisiaz

1.

Good, to forgive;
  Best, to forget!
  Living, we fret;
Dying, we live.
Fretless and free,
  Soul, clap thy pinion!
  Earth have dominion,
Body, o'er thee!

2.

Wander at will,
  Day after day,—
  Wander away,
Wandering still—
Soul that canst soar!
  Body may slumber:
  Body shall cumber
Soul-flight no more.

3.

Waft of soul's wing!
  What lies above?
  Sunshine and Love,
Skyblue and Spring!
Body hides—where?
  Ferns of all feather,
  Mosses and heather,
Yours be the care!

La Saisiaz

A.E.S. September 14, 1877.

Dared and done: at last I stand upon the summit, Dear and True!
Singly dared and done; the climbing both of us were bound to do.
Petty feat and yet prodigious: every side my glance was bent
O'er the grandeur and the beauty lavished through the whole ascent.
Ledge by ledge, out broke new marvels, now minute and now immense:
Earth's most exquisite disclosure, heaven's own God in evidence!
And no berry in its hiding, no blue space in its outspread,
Pleaded to escape my footstep, challenged my emerging head,
(As I climbed or paused from climbing, now o'erbranched by shrub and tree,
Now built round by rock and boulder, now at just a turn set free,
Stationed face to face with—Nature? rather with Infinitude)
—No revealment of them all, as singly I my path pursued,
But a bitter touched its sweetness, for the thought stung "Even so
Both of us had loved and wondered just the same, five days ago!"
Five short days, sufficient hardly to entice, from out its den
Splintered in the slab, this pink perfection of the cyclamen;
Scarce enough to heal and coat with amber gum the sloe-tree's gash,
Bronze the clustered wilding apple, redden ripe the mountain-ash:
Yet of might to place between us—Oh the barrier! Yon Profound
Shrinks beside it, proves a pin-point: barrier this, without a bound!
Boundless though it be, I reach you: somehow seem to have you here
—Who are there. Yes, there you dwell now, plain the four low walls appear;
Those are vineyards they enclose from; and the little spire which points
—That's Collonge, henceforth your dwelling! All the same, howe'er disjoints
Past from present, no less certain you are here, not there: have dared,
Done the feat of mountain-climbing,—five days since, we both prepared
Daring, doing, arm in arm, if other help should haply fail.
For you asked, as forth we sallied to see sunset from the vale,
"Why not try for once the mountain,—take a foretaste, snatch by stealth

Sight and sound, some unconsidered fragment of the hoarded wealth?
Six weeks at its base, yet never once have we together won
Sight or sound by honest climbing: let us two have dared and done
Just so much of twilight journey as may prove tomorrow's jaunt
Not the only mode of wayfare—wheeled to reach the eagle's haunt!"
So, we turned from the low grass-path you were pleased to call "your own,"
Set our faces to the rose-bloom o'er the summit's front of stone
Where Salève obtains, from Jura and the sunken sun she hides,
Due return of blushing "Good Night," rosy as a borne-off bride's,
For his masculine "Good Morrow" when, with sunrise still in hold,
Gay he hails her, and, magnific, thrilled her black length burns to gold.
Up and up we went, how careless—nay, how joyous! All was new,
All was strange. "Call progress toilsome? that were just insulting you!
How the trees must temper noontide! Ah, the thicket's sudden break!
What will be the morning glory, when at dusk thus gleams the lake?
Light by light puts forth Geneva: what a land—and, of the land,
Can there be a lovelier station than this spot where now we stand?
Is it late, and wrong to linger? True, to-morrow makes amends.
Toilsome progress? child's play, call it—specially when one descends!
There, the dread descent is over—hardly our adventure, though!
Take the vale where late we left it, pace the grass-path, 'mine,' you know!
Proud completion of achievement!" And we paced it, praising still
That soft tread on velvet verdure as it wound through hill and hill;
And at very end there met us, coming from Collonge, the pair
—All our people of the Chalet—two, enough and none to spare.
So, we made for home together, and we reached it as the stars
One by one came lamping—chiefly that prepotency of Mars—
And your last word was "I owe you this enjoyment!"—met with "Nay:
With yourself it rests to have a month of morrows like to-day!"
Then the meal, with talk and laughter, and the news of that rare nook
Yet untroubled by the tourist, touched on by no travel-book,
All the same—though latent—patent, hybrid birth of land and sea,
And (our travelled friend assured you)—if such miracle might be—
Comparable for completeness of both blessings—all around
Nature, and, inside her circle, safety from world's sight and sound—
Comparable to our Saisiaz. "Hold it fast and guard it well!
Go and see and vouch for certain, then come back and never tell

Living soul but us; and haply, prove our sky from cloud as clear,
There may we four meet, praise fortune just as now, another year!"

Thus you charged him on departure: not without the final charge
"Mind to-morrow's early meeting! We must leave our journey marge
Ample for the wayside wonders: there's the stoppage at the inn
Three-parts up the mountain, where the hardships of the track begin;
There's the convent worth a visit; but, the triumph crowning all—
There's Salève's own platform facing glory which strikes greatness small,
—Blanc, supreme above his earth-brood, needles red and white and green,
Horns of silver, fangs of crystal set on edge in his demesne.
So, some three weeks since, we saw them: so, to-morrow we intend
You shall see them likewise; therefore Good Night till to-morrow, friend!"
Last, the nothings that extinguish embers of a vivid day:
"What might be the Marshal's next move, what Gambetta's counter-play"
Till the landing on the staircase saw escape the latest spark:
"Sleep you well!" "Sleep but as well, you!"—lazy love quenched, all was dark.

Nothing dark next day at sundawn! Up I rose and forth I fared:
Took my plunge within the bath-pool, pacified the watch-dog scared,
Saw proceed the transmutation—Jura's black to one gold glow,
Trod your level path that let me drink the morning deep and slow,
Reached the little quarry—ravage recompensed by shrub and fern—
Till the overflowing ardours told me time was for return.
So, return I did, and gaily. But, for once, from no far mound
Waved salute a tall white figure. "Has her sleep been so profound?
Foresight, rather, prudent saving strength for day's expenditure!
Ay, the chamber-window's open: out and on the terrace, sure!"

No, the terrace showed no figure, tall, white, leaning through the wreaths,
Tangle-twine of leaf and bloom that intercept the air one breathes,
Interpose between one's love and Nature's loving, hill and dale
Down to where the blue lake's wrinkle marks the river's inrush pale
—Mazy Arve: whereon no vessel but goes sliding white and plain,
Not a steamboat pants from harbour but one hears pulsate amain,

Past the city's congregated peace of homes and pomp of spires
—Man's mild protest that there's something more than Nature, man requires,
And that, useful as is Nature to attract the tourist's foot,
Quiet slow sure money-making proves the matter's very root,—
Need for body,—while the spirit also needs a comfort reached
By no help of lake or mountain, but the texts whence Calvin preached.
"Here's the veil withdrawn from landscape: up to Jura and beyond,
All awaits us ranged and ready; yet she violates the bond,
Neither leans nor looks nor listens: why is this?" A turn of eye
Took the whole sole answer, gave the undisputed reason "why!"

This dread way you had your summons! No premonitory touch,
As you talked and laughed ('tis told me) scarce a minute ere the clutch
Captured you in cold forever. Cold? nay, warm you were as life
When I raised you, while the others used, in passionate poor strife,
All the means that seemed to promise any aid, and all in vain.
Gone you were, and I shall never see that earnest face again
Grow transparent, grow transfigured with the sudden light that leapt,
At the first word's provocation, from the heart-deeps where it slept.

Therefore, paying piteous duty, what seemed you have we consigned
Peacefully to—what I think were, of all earth-beds, to your mind
Most the choice for quiet, yonder: low walls stop the vines' approach,
Lovingly Salève protects you; village-sports will ne'er encroach
On the stranger lady's silence, whom friends bore so kind and well
Thither "just for love's sake,"—such their own word was: and who can tell?
You supposed that few or none had known and loved you in the world:
May be! flower that's full-blown tempts the butterfly, not flower that's furled.
But more learned sense unlocked you, loosed the sheath and let expand
Bud to bell and outspread flower-shape at the least warm touch of hand
—May be, throb of heart, beneath which,—quickening farther than it knew,—
Treasure oft was disembosomed, scent all strange and unguessed hue.
Disembosomed, re-embosomed,—must one memory suffice,
Prove I knew an Alpine-rose which all beside named Edelweiss?

Rare thing, red or white, you rest now: two days slumbered through; and since
One day more will see me rid of this same scene whereat I wince,
Tetchy at all sights and sounds and pettish at each idle charm

Proffered me who pace now singly where we two went arm in arm,—
I have turned upon my weakness: asked "And what, forsooth, prevents
That, this latest day allowed me, I fulfil of her intents
One she had the most at heart—that we should thus again survey
From Salève Mont Blanc together?" Therefore,—dared and
done to-day
Climbing,—here I stand: but you—where?

If a spirit of the place
Broke the silence, bade me question, promised answer,—what
disgrace
Did I stipulate "Provided answer suit my hopes, not fears!"
Would I shrink to learn my life-time's limit—days, weeks, months
or years?
Would I shirk assurance on each point whereat I can but guess—
"Does the soul survive the body? Is there God's self, no or yes?"
If I know my mood, 'twere constant—come in whatso'er uncouth
Shape it should, nay, formidable—so the answer were but truth.

Well, and wherefore shall it daunt me, when 'tis I myself am tasked,
When, by weakness weakness questioned, weakly answers—weakly
asked?
Weakness never needs be falseness: truth is truth in each degree
—Thunderpealed by God to Nature, whispered by my soul
to me.
Nay, the weakness turns to strength and triumphs in a truth beyond:
"Mine is but man's truest answer—how were it did God respond?"
I shall no more dare to mimic such response in futile speech,
Pass off human lisp as echo of the sphere-song out of reach,
Than,—because it well may happen yonder, where the far
snows blanch
Mute Mont Blanc, that who stands near them sees and hears
an avalanche,—
I shall pick a clod and throw,—cry "Such the sight and such the
sound!
What though I nor see nor hear them? Others do, the proofs abound!"
Can I make my eye an eagle's, sharpen ear to recognize
Sound o'er league and league of silence? Can I know, who but
surmise?
If I dared no self-deception when, a week since, I and you
Walked and talked along the grass-path, passing lightly in review
What seemed hits and what seemed misses in a certain
fence-play,—strife

Sundry minds of mark engaged in "On the Soul and Future Life,"—
If I ventured estimating what was come of parried thrust,
Subtle stroke, and, rightly, wrongly, estimating could be just
—Just, though life so seemed abundant in the form which moved
by mine,
I might well have played at feigning, fooling,—laughed "What need opine
Pleasure must succeed to pleasure else past pleasure turns to pain,
And this first life claims a second, else I count its good
no gain?"—
Much less have I heart to palter when the matter to decide
Now becomes "Was ending ending once and always, when you died?"
Did the face, the form I lifted as it lay, reveal the loss
Not alone of life but soul? A tribute to yon flowers and moss,
What of you remains beside? A memory! Easy to attest
"Certainly from out the world that one believes who knew her best
Such was good in her, such fair, which fair and good were great perchance
Had but fortune favored, bidden each shy faculty advance;
After all—who knows another? Only as I know, I speak."
So much of you lives within me while I live my year or week.
Then my fellow takes the tale up, not unwilling to aver
Duly in his turn "I knew him best of all, as he knew her:
Such he was, and such he was not, and such other might have been
But that somehow every actor, somewhere in this earthly scene,
Fails." And so both memories dwindle, yours and mine together linked,
Till there is but left for comfort, when the last spark proves extinct,
This—that somewhere new existence led by men and women new
Possibly attains perfection coveted by me and you;
While ourselves, the only witness to what work our life evolved,
Only to ourselves proposing problems proper to be solved
By ourselves alone,—who working ne'er shall know if work bear fruit
Others reap and garner, heedless how produced by stalk and root,—
We who, darkling, timed the day's birth,—struggling, testified to peace,—
Earned, by dint of failure, triumph,—we, creative thought, must cease
In created word, thought's echo, due to impulse long since sped!
Why repine? There's ever someone lives although ourselves be dead!

Well, what signifies repugnance? Truth is truth howe'er it strike.
Fair or foul the lot apportioned life on earth, we bear alike.
Stalwart body idly yoked to stunted spirit, powers, that fain
Else would soar, condemned to grovel, groundlings through the
fleshly chain,—

Help that hinders, hindrance proved but help disguised when all too late,—
Hindrance is the fact acknowledged, howsoe'er explained as Fate,
Fortune, Providence: we bear, own life a burthen more or less.
Life thus owned unhappy, is there supplemental happiness
Possible and probable in life to come? or must we count
Life a curse and not a blessing, summed-up in its whole amount,
Help and hindrance, joy and sorrow?
Why should I want courage here?
I will ask and have an answer,—with no favour, with no fear,—
From myself. How much, how little, do I inwardly believe
True that controverted doctrine? Is it fact to which I cleave,
Is it fancy I but cherish, when I take upon my lips
Phrase the solemn Tuscan fashioned, and declare the soul's eclipse
Not the soul's extinction? take his "I believe and I declare—
Certain am I—from this life I pass into a better, there
Where that lady lives of whom enamoured was my soul"—where this
Other lady, my companion dear and true, she also is?

I have questioned and am answered. Question, answer presuppose
Two points: that the thing itself which questions, answers,—is, it knows;
As it also knows the thing perceived outside itself,—a force
Actual ere its own beginning, operative through its course,
Unaffected by its end,—that this thing likewise needs must be;
Call this—God, then, call that—soul, and both—the only facts for me.
Prove them facts? that they o'erpass my power of proving, proves them such:
Fact it is I know I know not something which is fact as much.
What before caused all the causes, what effect of all effects
Haply follows,—these are fancy. Ask the rush if it suspects
Whence and how the stream which floats it had a rise, and where and how
Falls or flows on still! What answer makes the rush except that now
Certainly it floats and is, and, no less certain than itself,
Is the everyway external stream that now through shoal and shelf
Floats it onward, leaves it—may be—wrecked at last, or lands on shore
There to root again and grow and flourish stable evermore.
—May be! mere surmise not knowledge: much conjecture styled belief,
What the rush conceives the stream means through the voyage blind and brief.

Why, because I doubtless am, shall I as doubtless be? "Because
God seems good and wise." Yet under this our life's apparent laws
Reigns a wrong which, righted once, would give quite other laws to life.
"He seems potent." Potent here, then: why are right and wrong at strife?
Has in life the wrong the better? Happily life ends so soon!
Right predominates in life? Then why two lives and double boon?
"Anyhow, we want it: wherefore want?" Because, without the want,
Life, now human, would be brutish: just that hope, however scant,
Makes the actual life worth leading; take the hope therein away,
All we have to do is surely not endure another day.
This life has its hopes for this life, hopes that promise joy: life done—
Out of all the hopes, how many had complete fulfilment? none.
"But the soul is not the body:" and the breath is not the flute;
Both together make the music: either marred and all is mute.
Truce to such old sad contention whence, according as we shape
Most of hope or most of fear, we issue in a half-escape:
"We believe" is sighed. I take the cup of comfort proffered thus,
Taste and try each soft ingredient, sweet infusion, and discuss
What their blending may accomplish for the cure of doubt, till—slow,
Sorrowful, but how decided! needs must I o'erturn it—so!
Cause before, effect behind me—blanks! The midway point I am,
Caused, itself—itself efficient: in that narrow space must cram
All experience—out of which there crowds conjecture manifold,
But, as knowledge, this comes only—things may be as I behold,
Or may not be, but, without me and above me, things there are;
I myself am what I know not—ignorance which proves no bar
To the knowledge that I am, and, since I am, can recognize
What to me is pain and pleasure: this is sure, the rest—surmise.
If my fellows are or are not, what may please them and what pain,—
Mere surmise: my own experience—that is knowledge, once again!

I have lived, then, done and suffered, loved and hated, learnt and taught
This—there is no reconciling wisdom with a world distraught,
Goodness with triumphant evil, power with failure in the aim,
If—(to my own sense, remember! though none other feel the same!)—
If you bar me from assuming earth to be a pupil's place,
And life, time,—with all their chances, changes,—just probation-space,
Mine, for me. But those apparent other mortals—theirs, for them?
Knowledge stands on my experience: all outside its narrow hem,

Free surmise may sport and welcome! Pleasures, pains affect mankind
Just as they affect myself? Why, here's my neighbour colour-blind,
Eyes like mine to all appearance: "green as grass" do I affirm?
"Red as grass" he contradicts me: which employs the proper term?
Were we two the earth's sole tenants, with no third for referee,
How should I distinguish? Just so, God must judge 'twixt man and me.
To each mortal peradventure earth becomes a new machine,
Pain and pleasure no more tally in our sense than red and green;
Still, without what seems such mortal's pleasure, pain, my life were lost
—Life, my whole sole chance to prove—although at man's apparent cost—
What is beauteous and what ugly, right to strive for, right to shun,
Fit to help and fit to hinder,—prove my forces everyone,
Good and evil,—learn life's lesson, hate of evil, love of good,
As 'tis set me, understand so much as may be understood—
Solve the problem: "From thine apprehended scheme of things, deduce
Praise or blame of its contriver, shown a niggard or profuse
In each good or evil issue! nor miscalculate alike
Counting one the other in the final balance, which to strike,
Soul was born and life allotted: ay, the show of things unfurled
For thy summing-up and judgment,—thine, no other mortal's world!"
What though fancy scarce may grapple with the complex and immense
—"His own world for every mortal?" Postulate omnipotence!
Limit power, and simple grows the complex: shrunk to atom size,
That which loomed immense to fancy low before my reason lies,—
I survey it and pronounce it work like other work: success
Here and there, the workman's glory,—here and there, his shame no less,
Failure as conspicuous. Taunt not "Human work ape work divine?"
As the power, expect performance! God's be God's as mine is mine!
God whose power made man and made man's wants, and made, to meet those wants,
Heaven and earth which, through the body, prove the spirit's ministrants,
Excellently all,—did he lack power or was the will in fault
When he let blue heaven be shrouded o'er by vapours of the vault,
Gay earth drop her garlands shrivelled at the first infecting breath
Of the serpent pains which herald, swarming in, the dragon death?
What, no way but this that man may learn and lay to heart how rife
Life were with delights would only death allow their taste to life?
Must the rose sigh "Pluck—I perish!" must the eve weep "Gaze—I fade!"

—Every sweet warn "'Ware my bitter!" every shine bid "Wait my shade?"
Can we love but on condition, that the thing we love must die?
Needs there groan a world in anguish just to teach us sympathy—
Multitudinously wretched that we, wretched too, may guess
What a preferable state were universal happiness?
Hardly do I so conceive the outcome of that power which went
To the making of the worm there in yon clod its tenement,
Any more than I distinguish aught of that which, wise and good,
Framed the leaf, its plain of pasture, dropped the dew, its fineless food.
Nay, were fancy fact, were earth and all it holds illusion mere,
Only a machine for teaching love and hate and hope and fear
To myself, the sole existence, single truth mid falsehood,—well!
If the harsh throes of the prelude die not off into the swell
Of that perfect piece they sting me to become a-strain for,—if
Roughness of the long rock-clamber lead not to the last of cliff,
First of level country where is sward my pilgrim-foot can prize,—
Plainlier! if this life's conception new life fail to realize,—
Though earth burst and proved a bubble glassing hues of hell, one huge
Reflex of the devil's doings—God's work by no subterfuge—
(So death's kindly touch informed me as it broke the glamour, gave
Soul and body both release from life's long nightmare in the grave)
Still,—with no more Nature, no more Man as riddle to be read,
Only my own joys and sorrows now to reckon real instead,—
I must say—or choke in silence—"Howsoever came my fate,
Sorrow did and joy did nowise,—life well weighed,—preponderate."
By necessity ordained thus? I shall bear as best I can;
By a cause all-good, all-wise, all-potent? No, as I am man!
Such were God: and was it goodness that the good within my range
Or had evil in admixture or grew evil's self by change?
Wisdom—that becoming wise meant making slow and sure advance
From a knowledge proved in error to acknowledged ignorance?
Power? 'tis just the main assumption reason most revolts at! power
Unavailing for bestowment on its creature of an hour,
Man, of so much proper action rightly aimed and reaching aim,
So much passion,—no defect there, no excess, but still the same,—
As what constitutes existence, pure perfection bright as brief
For yon worm, man's fellow-creature, on yon happier world—its leaf!
No, as I am man, I mourn the poverty I must impute:
Goodness, wisdom, power, all bounded, each a human attribute!

But, O world outspread beneath me! only for myself I speak,
Nowise dare to play the spokesman for my brothers strong and weak,
Full and empty, wise and foolish, good and bad, in every age,
Every clime, I turn my eyes from, as in one or other stage
Of a torture writhe they, Job-like couched on dung and crazed with blains
—Wherefore? whereto? ask the whirlwind what the dread voice thence explains!
I shall "vindicate no way of God's to man," nor stand apart,
"Laugh, be candid." while I watch it traversing the human heart!
Traversed heart must tell its story uncommented on: no less
Mine results in "Only grant a second life, I acquiesce
In this present life as failure, count misfortune's worst assaults
Triumph, not defeat, assured that loss so much the more exalts
Gain about to be. For at what moment did I so advance
Near to knowledge as when frustrate of escape from ignorance?
Did not beauty prove most precious when its opposite obtained
Rule, and truth seem more than ever potent because falsehood reigned?
While for love—Oh how but, losing love, does whoso loves succeed
By the death-pang to the birth-throe—learning what is love indeed?
Only grant my soul may carry high through death her cup unspilled,
Brimming though it be with knowledge, life's loss drop by drop distilled,
I shall boast it mine—the balsam, bless each kindly wrench that wrung
From life's tree its inmost virtue, tapped the root whence pleasure sprung,
Barked the bole, and broke the bough, and bruised the berry, left all grace
Ashes in death's stern alembic, loosed elixir in its place!

Witness, Dear and True, how little I was 'ware of—not your worth
—That I knew, my heart assures me—but of what a shade on earth
Would the passage from my presence of the tall white figure throw
O'er the ways we walked together! Somewhat narrow, somewhat slow
Used to seem the ways, the walking: narrow ways are well to tread
When there's moss beneath the footstep, honeysuckle overhead:
Walking slow to beating bosom surest solace soonest gives,
Liberates the brain o'erloaded—best of all restoratives.
Nay, do I forget the open vast where soon or late converged

Ways though winding?—world-wide heaven-high sea where music
  slept or surged
As the angel had ascendant, and Beethoven's Titan mace
Smote the immense to storm, Mozart would by a finger's lifting chase?
Yes, I knew—but not with knowledge such as thrills me while I view
Yonder precinct which henceforward holds and hides the Dear
  and True.
Grant me (once again) assurance we shall each meet each some day,
Walk—but with how bold a footstep! on a way—but what a way!
—Worst were best, defeat were triumph, utter loss were utmost gain.
Can it be, and must, and will it?
                    Silence! Out of fact's domain,
Just surmise prepared to mutter hope, and also fear—dispute
Fact's inexorable ruling "Outside fact, surmise be mute!"
Well!
    Ay, well and best, if fact's self I may force the answer from!
'Tis surmise I stop the mouth of! Not above in yonder dome
All a rapture with its rose-glow,—not around, where pile and peak
Strainingly await the sun's fall,—not beneath, where crickets creak,
Birds assemble for their bed-time, soft the tree-top swell subsides,—
No, nor yet within my deepest sentient self the knowledge hides!
Aspiration, reminiscence, plausibilities of trust
Now the ready "Man were wronged else," now the rash "and
  God unjust"—
None of these I need! Take thou, my soul, thy solitary stand,
Umpire to the champions Fancy, Reason, as on either hand
Amicable war they wage and play the foe in thy behoof!
Fancy thrust and Reason parry! Thine the prize who stand aloof!

FANCY.

I concede the thing refused: henceforth no certainty more plain
Than this mere surmise that after body dies soul lives again.
Two, the only facts acknowledged late, are now increased to three—
God is, and the soul is, and, as certain, after death shall be.
Put this third to use in life, the time for using fact!

REASON.

                    I do:
Find it promises advantage, coupled with the other two.
Life to come will be improvement on the life that's now; destroy

Body's thwartings, there's no longer screen betwixt soul and soul's joy.
Why should we expect new hindrance, novel tether? In this first
Life, I see the good of evil, why our world began at worst:
Since time means amelioration, tardily enough displayed,
Yet a mainly onward moving, never wholly retrograde.
We know more though we know little, we grow stronger though still weak,
Partly see though all too purblind, stammer though we cannot speak.
There is no such grudge in God as scared the ancient Greek, no fresh
Substitute of trap for dragnet, once a breakage in the mesh.
Dragons were, and serpents are, and blindworms will be: ne'er emerged
Any new-created Python for man's plague since earth was purged.
Failing proof, then, of invented trouble to replace the old,
O'er this life the next presents advantage much and manifold:
Which advantage—in the absence of a fourth and farther fact
Now conceivably surmised, of harm to follow from the act—
I pronounce for man's obtaining at this moment. Why delay?
Is he happy? happiness will change: anticipate the day!
Is he sad? there's ready refuge: of all sadness death's prompt cure!
Is he both, in mingled measure? cease a burthen to endure!
Pains with sorry compensations, pleasures stinted in the dole,
Power that sinks and pettiness that soars, all halved and nothing whole,
Idle hopes that lure man onward, forced back by as idle fears—
What a load he stumbles under through his glad sad seventy years,
When a touch sets right the turmoil, lifts his spirit where, flesh-freed,
Knowledge shall be rightly named so, all that seems be truth indeed!
Grant his forces no accession, nay, no faculty's increase,
Only let what now exists continue, let him prove in peace
Power whereof the interrupted unperfected play enticed
Man through darkness, which to lighten any spark of hope sufficed,—
What shall then deter his dying out of darkness into light?
Death itself perchance, brief pain that's pang, condensed and infinite?
But at worst, he needs must brave it one day, while, at best, he laughs—
Drops a drop within his chalice, sleep not death his science quaffs!
Any moment claims more courage when, by crossing cold and gloom,
Manfully man quits discomfort, makes for the provided room
Where the old friends want their fellow, where the new acquaintance wait,
Probably for talk assembled, possibly to sup in state!

I affirm and re-affirm it therefore: only make as plain
As that man now lives, that after dying man will live again,—
Make as plain the absence, also, of a law to contravene
Voluntary passage from this life to that by change of scene,—
And I bid him—at suspicion of first cloud athwart his sky,
Flower's departure, frost's arrival—never hesitate, but die!

FANCY.

Then I double my concession: grant, along with new life sure,
This same law found lacking now: ordain that, whether rich or poor
Present life is judged in aught man counts advantage—be it hope,
Be it fear that brightens, blackens most or least his horoscope,—
He, by absolute compulsion such as made him live at all,
Go on living to the fated end of life whate'er befall.
What though, as on earth he darkling grovels, man descry the sphere,
Next life's—call it, heaven of freedom, close above and crystal-clear?
He shall find—say, hell to punish who in aught curtails the term,
Fain would act the butterfly before he has played out the worm!
God, soul, earth, heaven, hell,—five facts now: what is to desiderate?

REASON.

Nothing! Henceforth man's existence bows to the monition "Wait!
Take the joys and bear the sorrows—neither with extreme concern!
Living here means nescience simply: 'tis next life that helps to learn.
Shut those eyes, next life will open,—stop those ears, next life will teach
Hearing's office,—close those lips, next life will give the power of speech!
Or, if action more amuse thee than the passive attitude,
Bravely bustle through thy being, busy thee for ill or good,
Reap this life's success or failure! Soon shall things be unperplexed
And the right and wrong, now tangled, lie unravelled in the next."

FANCY.

Not so fast! Still more concession! not alone do I declare
Life must needs be borne,—I also will that man become aware
Life has worth incalculable, every moment that he spends
So much gain or loss for that next life which on this life depends.
Good, done here, be there rewarded,—evil, worked here, there amerced!
Six facts now, and all established, plain to man the last as first.

REASON.

There was good and evil, then, defined to man by this decree?
Was—for at its promulgation both alike have ceased to be.
Prior to this last announcement "Certainly as God exists,
As he made man's soul, as soul is quenchless by the deathly mists,
Yet is, all the same, forbidden premature escape from time
To eternity's provided purer air and brighter clime,—
Just so certainly depends it on the use to which man turns
Earth, the good or evil done there, whether after death he earns
Life eternal,—heaven, the phrase be, or eternal death,—say, hell.
As his deeds, so proves his portion, doing ill or doing well!"
—Prior to this last announcement, earth was man's probation-place:
Liberty of doing evil gave his doing good a grace;
Once lay down the law, with Nature's simple "Such effects succeed
Causes such, and heaven or hell depends upon man's earthly deed
Just as surely as depends the straight or else the crooked line
On his making point meet point or with or else without incline,"—
Thenceforth neither good nor evil does man, doing what he must.
Lay but down that law as stringent "Wouldst thou live again, be just!"
As this other "Wouldst thou live now, regularly draw thy breath!
For, suspend the operation, straight law's breach results in death—"
And (provided always, man, addressed this mode, be sound and sane)
Prompt and absolute obedience, never doubt, will law obtain!
Tell not me "Look round us! nothing each side but acknowledged law,
Now styled God's—now, Nature's edict!" Where's obedience without flaw
Paid to either? What's the adage rife in man's mouth? Why, "The best
I both see and praise, the worst I follow"—which, despite professed
Seeing, praising, all the same he follows, since he disbelieves
In the heart of him that edict which for truth his head receives.
There's evading and persuading and much making law amends
Somehow, there's the nice distinction 'twixt fast foes and faulty friends,
—Any consequence except inevitable death when "Die,
Whoso breaks our law!" they publish, God and Nature equally.
Law that's kept or broken—subject to man's will and pleasure! Whence?
How comes law to bear eluding? Not because of impotence:
Certain laws exist already which to hear means to obey;

Therefore not without a purpose these man must, while those man may
Keep and, for the keeping, haply gain approval and reward.
Break through this last superstructure, all is empty air—no sward
Firm like my first fact to stand on "God there is, and soul there is,"
And soul's earthly life-allotment: wherein, by hypothesis,
Soul is bound to pass probation, prove its powers, and exercise
Sense and thought on fact, and then, from fact educing fit surmise,
Ask itself, and of itself have solely answer, "Does the scope
Earth affords of fact to judge by warrant future fear or hope?"

Thus have we come back full circle: fancy's footsteps one by one
Go their round conducting reason to the point where they begun,
Left where we were left so lately, Dear and True! When, half a week
Since, we walked and talked and thus I told you, how suffused a cheek
You had turned me had I sudden brought the blush into the smile
By some word like "Idly argued! you know better all the while!"
Now, from me—Oh not a blush but, how much more, a joyous glow,
Laugh triumphant, would it strike did your "Yes, better I do know"
Break, my warrant for assurance! which assurance may not be
If, supplanting hope, assurance needs must change this life to me.
So, I hope—no more than hope, but hope—no less than hope, because
I can fathom, by no plumb-line sunk in life's apparent laws,
How I may in any instance fix where change should meetly fall
Nor involve, by one revisal, abrogation of them all
—Which again involves as utter change in life thus law-released,
Whence the good of goodness vanished when the ill of evil
ceased.
Whereas, life and laws apparent re-instated,—all we know,
All we know not,—o'er our heaven again cloud closes, until, lo—
Hope the arrowy, just as constant, comes to pierce its gloom, compelled
By a power and by a purpose which, if no one else beheld,
I behold in life, so—hope!

Sad summing-up of all to say!
Athanasius contra mundum, why should he hope more than they?
So are men made notwithstanding, such magnetic virtue darts
From each head their fancy haloes to their unresisting hearts!

Here I stand, methinks a stone's throw from yon village I this morn
Traversed for the sake of looking one last look at its forlorn
Tenement's ignoble fortune: through a crevice, plain its floor
Piled with provender for cattle, while a dung-heap blocked the door.

In that squalid Bossex, under that obscene red roof, arose,
Like a fiery flying serpent from its egg, a soul—Rousseau's.
Turn thence! Is it Diodati joins the glimmer of the lake?
There I plucked a leaf, one week since,—ivy, plucked for Byron's sake.
Famed unfortunates! And yet, because of that phosphoric fame
Swathing blackness' self with brightness till putridity looked flame,
All the world was witched: and wherefore? what could lie beneath, allure
Heart of man to let corruption serve man's head as cynosure?
Was the magic in the dictum "All that's good is gone and past;
Bad and worse still grows the present, and the worst of all comes last:
Which believe—for I believe it?" So preached one his gospel-news;
While melodious moaned the other "Dying day with dolphin-hues!
Storm, for loveliness and darkness like a woman's eye! Ye mounts
Where I climb to 'scape my fellow, and thou sea wherein he counts
Not one inch of vile dominion! What were your especial worth
Failed ye to enforce the maxim 'Of all objects found on earth
Man is meanest, much too honored when compared with—what by odds
Beats him—any dog: so, let him go a-howling to his gods!'
Which believe—for I believe it!" such the comfort man received
Sadly since perforce he must: for why? the famous bard believed!

Fame! Then, give me fame, a moment! As I gather at a glance
Human glory after glory vivifying yon expanse,
Let me grasp them all together, hold on high and brandish well
Beacon-like above the rapt world ready, whether heaven or hell
Send the dazzling summons downward, to submit itself the same,
Take on trust the hope or else despair flashed full on face by—Fame!
Thanks, thou pine-tree of Makistos, wide thy giant torch I wave!
Know ye whence I plucked the pillar, late with sky for architrave?
This the trunk, the central solid Knowledge, kindled core, began
Tugging earth-deeps, trying heaven-heights, rooted yonder at Lausanne.
This which flits and spits, the aspic,—sparkles in and out the boughs
Now, and now condensed, the python, coiling round and round allows
Scarce the bole its due effulgence, dulled by flake on flake of Wit—
Laughter so bejewels Learning,—what but Ferney nourished it?
Nay, nor fear—since every resin feeds the flame—that I dispense
With yon Bossex terebinth-tree's all-explosive Eloquence:
No, be sure! nor, any more than thy resplendency, Jean-Jacques,
Dare I want thine, Diodati! What though monkeys and macaques
Gibber "Byron"? Byron's ivy rears a branch beyond the crew,

Green for ever, no deciduous trash macaques and monkeys chew!
As Rousseau, then, eloquent, as Byron prime in poet's power,—
Detonations, fulgurations, smiles—the rainbow, tears—the shower,—
Lo, I lift the corruscating marvel—Fame! and, famed, declare
—Learned for the nonce as Gibbon, witty as wit's self Voltaire...
O the sorriest of conclusions to whatever man of sense
Mid the millions stands the unit, takes no flare for evidence!
Yet the millions have their portion, live their calm or troublous day,
Find significance in fireworks: so, by help of mine, they may
Confidently lay to heart and lock in head their life long—this:
"He there with the brand flamboyant, broad o'er night's forlorn abyss,
Crowned by prose and verse; and wielding, with Wit's bauble, Learning's rod...
Well? Why, he at least believed in Soul, was very sure of God.

So the poor smile played, that evening: pallid smile long since extinct
Here in London's mid-November! Not so loosely thoughts were linked,
Six weeks since as I, descending in the sunset from Salève,
Found the chain, I seemed to forge there, flawless till it reached your grave,—
Not so filmy was the texture, but I bore it in my breast
Safe thus far. And since I found a something in me would not rest
Till I, link by link, unravelled any tangle of the chain,
—Here it lies, for much or little! I have lived all o'er again
That last pregnant hour: I saved it, just as I could save a root
Disinterred for re-interment when the time best helps to shoot.
Life is stocked with germs of torpid life; but may I never wake
Those of mine whose resurrection could not be without earthquake!
Rest all such, unraised forever! Be this, sad yet sweet, the sole
Memory evoked from slumber! Least part this: then what the whole?

November 9, 1877.

FROM *DRAMATIC IDYLS*: *SECOND SERIES* (1880)

Pan and Luna

Si credere dignum est.—*Georgic.* III. 390.

O worthy of belief I hold it was,
Virgil, your legend in those strange three lines!
No question, that adventure came to pass
One black night in Arcadia: yes, the pines,
Mountains and vallies mingling made one mass
Of black with void black heaven: the earth's confines,
The sky's embrace,—below, above, around,
All hardened into black without a bound.

Fill up a swart stone chalice to the brim
With fresh-squeezed yet fast-thickening poppy-juice:
See how the sluggish jelly, late a-swim,
Turns marble to the touch of who would loose
The solid smooth, grown jet from rim to rim,
By turning round the bowl! So night can fuse
Earth with her all-comprising sky. No less,
Light, the least spark, shows air and emptiness.

And thus it proved when—diving into space,
Stript of all vapour, from each web of mist
Utterly film-free—entered on her race
The naked Moon, full-orbed antagonist
Of night and dark, night's dowry: peak to base,
Upstarted mountains, and each valley, kissed
To sudden life, lay silver-bright: in air
Flew she revealed, Maid-Moon with limbs all bare.

Still as she fled, each depth—where refuge seemed—
Opening a lone pale chamber, left distinct
Those limbs: mid still-retreating blue, she teemed
Herself with whiteness,—virginal, uncinct
By any halo save what finely gleamed
To outline not disguise her: heaven was linked
In one accord with earth to quaff the joy,
Drain beauty to the dregs without alloy.

Whereof she grew aware. What help? When, lo,
A succourable cloud with sleep lay dense:
Some pine-tree-top had caught it sailing slow,

And tethered for a prize: in evidence
Captive lay fleece on fleece of piled-up snow
Drowsily patient: flake-heaped how or whence,
The structure of that succourable cloud,
What matter? Shamed she plunged into its shroud.

Orbed—so the woman-figure poets call
Because of rounds on rounds—that apple-shaped
Head which its hair binds close into a ball
Each side the curving ears—that pure undraped
Pout of the sister paps—that . . . Once for all,
Say—her consummate circle thus escaped
With its innumerous circlets, sank absorbed,
Safe in the cloud—O naked Moon full-orbed!

But what means this? The downy swathes combine,
Conglobe, the smothery coy-caressing stuff
Curdles about her! Vain each twist and twine
Those lithe limbs try, encroached on by a fluff
Fitting as close as fits the dented spine
Its flexile ivory outside-flesh: enough!
The plumy drifts contract, condense, constringe,
Till she is swallowed by the feathery springe.

As when a pearl slips lost in the thin foam
Churned on a sea-shore, and, o'er-frothed, conceits
Herself safe-housed in Amphitrite's dome,—
If, through the bladdery wave-worked yeast, she meets
What most she loathes and leaps from,—elf from gnome
No gladlier,—finds that safest of retreats
Bubble about a treacherous hand wide ope
To grasp her—(divers who pick pearls so grope)—

So lay this Maid-Moon clasped around and caught
By rough red Pan, the god of all that tract:
He it was schemed the snare thus subtly wrought
With simulated earth-breath,—wool-tufts packed
Into a billowy wrappage. Sheep far-sought
For spotless shearings yield such: take the fact
As learned Virgil gives it,—how the breed
Whitens itself for ever: yes, indeed!

If one fore-father ram, though pure as chalk
From tinge on fleece, should still display a tongue
Black 'neath the beast's moist palate, prompt men baulk
The propagating plague: he gets no young:
They rather slay him,—sell his hide to caulk
Ships with, first steeped in pitch,—nor hands are wrung
In sorrow for his fate: protected thus,
The purity we love is gained for us.

So did Girl-Moon, by just her attribute
Of unmatched modesty betrayed, lie trapped,
Bruised to the breast of Pan, half god half brute,
Raked by his bristly boar-sward while he lapped
—Never say, kissed her! that were to pollute
Love's language—which moreover proves unapt
To tell how she recoiled—as who finds thorns
Where she sought flowers—when, feeling, she touched—horns!

Then—does the legend say?—first moon-eclipse
Happened, first swooning-fit which puzzled sore
The early sages? Is that why she dips
Into the dark, a minute and no more,
Only so long as serves her while she rips
The cloud's womb through and, faultless as before,
Pursues her way? No lesson for a maid
Left she, a maid herself thus trapped, betrayed?

Ha, Virgil? Tell the rest, you! "To the deep
Of his domain the wildwood, Pan forthwith
Called her, and so she followed"—in her sleep,
Surely?—"by no means spurning him." The myth
Explain who may! Let all else go, I keep
—As of a ruin just a monolith—
Thus much, one verse of five words, each a boon:
Arcadia, night, a cloud, Pan, and the moon.

FROM *JOCOSERIA* (1883)

Never the Time and the Place

Never the time and the place
  And the loved one all together!
This path—how soft to pace!
  This May—what magic weather!
Where is the loved one's face?—
In a dream that loved one's face meets mine,
  But the house is narrow, the place is bleak
Where, outside, rain and wind combine
  With a furtive ear, if I strive to speak,
  With a hostile eye at my flushing cheek,
With a malice that marks each word, each sign!
O enemy sly and serpentine,
  Uncoil thee from the waking man!
    Do I hold the Past
    Thus firm and fast
  Yet doubt if the Future hold I can?
This path so soft to pace shall lead
Thro' the magic of May to herself indeed!
Or narrow if needs the house must be,
Outside are the storms and strangers: we—
Oh, close, safe, warm sleep I and she,
—I and she!

FROM *FERISHTAH'S FANCIES* (1884)

Epilogue

Oh, Love—no, Love! All the noise below, Love,
  Groanings all and moanings—none of Life I lose!
All of Life's a cry just of weariness and woe, Love—
  "Hear at least, thou happy one!" How can I, Love, but choose?

Only, when I do hear, sudden circle round me
  —Much as when the moon's might frees a space from cloud—
Iridescent splendours: gloom—would else confound me—
  Barriered off and banished far—bright-edged the blackest shroud!

Thronging through the cloud-rift, whose are they, the faces
  Faint revealed yet sure divined, the famous ones of old?
"What"—they smile—"our names, our deeds so soon erases
  Time upon his tablet where Life's glory lies enrolled?

"Was it for mere fool's-play, make-believe and mumming,
  So we battled it like men, not boylike sulked or whined?
Each of us heard clang God's 'Come!' and each was coming:
  Soldiers all, to forward-face, not sneaks to lag behind!

"How of the field's fortune? That concerned our Leader!
  Led, we struck our stroke nor cared for doings left and right:
Each as on his sole head, failer or succeeder,
  Lay the blame or lit the praise: no care for cowards: fight!"

Then the cloud-rift broadens, spanning earth that's under,
  Wide our world displays its worth, man's strife and strife's
    success:
All the good and beauty, wonder crowning wonder,
  Till my heart and soul applaud perfection, nothing less.

Only, at heart's utmost joy and triumph, terror
  Sudden turns the blood to ice: a chill wind disencharms
All the late enchantment! What if all be error—
  If the halo irised round my head were, Love, thine arms?

Palazzo Giustinian-Recanati, Venice: December 1, 1883.

FROM ANDREW REID, ED., *WHY I AM A LIBERAL* (1885)

Why I am a Liberal

"Why?" Because all I haply can and do,
  All that I am now, all I hope to be,—
  Whence comes it save from fortune setting free
Body and soul the purpose to pursue,
God traced for both? If fetters, not a few,
  Of prejudice, convention, fall from me,
  These shall I bid men—each in his degree
Also God-guided—bear, and gaily too?

But little do or can the best of us:
  THAT LITTLE IS ACHIEVED THROUGH LIBERTY.
Who, then, dares hold—emancipated thus—
  His fellow shall continue bound? Not I,
Who live, love, labour freely, nor discuss
  A brother's right to freedom. That is "Why."
ROBERT BROWNING.

FROM *PARLEYINGS WITH CERTAIN PEOPLE OF IMPORTANCE IN THEIR DAY* (1887)

PARLEYINGS WITH CERTAIN PEOPLE

OF IMPORTANCE IN THEIR DAY:

TO WIT: BERNARD DE MANDEVILLE,
DANIEL BARTOLI,
CHRISTOPHER SMART,
GEORGE BUBB DODINGTON,
FRANCIS FURINI,
GERARD DE LAIRESSE,
AND CHARLES AVISON.

INTRODUCED BY

A DIALOGUE BETWEEN APOLLO AND THE FATES;

CONCLUDED BY

ANOTHER BETWEEN JOHN FUST AND HIS FRIENDS.

BY ROBERT BROWNING.

LONDON:
SMITH, ELDER, & CO., 15 WATERLOO PLACE.
1887.

[*All rights reserved.*]

FIG. 11 Title page of *Parleyings with Certain People of Importance in Their Day* (1887).

VI. *With Gerard de Lairesse*

I.

Ah, but—because you were struck blind, could bless
Your sense no longer with the actual view
Of man and woman, those fair forms you drew
In happier days so duteously and true,—
Must I account my Gerard de Lairesse
All sorrow-smitten? He was hindered too
—Was this no hardship?—from producing, plain
To us who still have eyes, the pageantry
Which passed and passed before his busy brain
And, captured on his canvas, showed our sky
Traversed by flying shapes, earth stocked with brood
Of monsters,—centaurs bestial, satyrs lewd,—
Not without much Olympian glory, shapes
Of god and goddess in their gay escapes
From the severe serene: or haply paced
The antique ways, god-counselled, nymph-embraced,
Some early human kingly personage.
Such wonders of the teeming poet's-age
Were still to be: nay, these indeed began—
Are not the pictures extant?—till the ban
Of blindness struck both palate from his thumb
And pencil from his finger.

II.

Blind—not dumb,
Else, Gerard, were my inmost bowels stirred
With pity beyond pity: no, the word
Was left upon your unmolested lips:
Your mouth unsealed, despite of eyes' eclipse,
Talked all brain's yearning into birth. I lack
Somehow the heart to wish your practice back
Which boasted hand's achievement in a score
Of veritable pictures, less or more,
Still to be seen: myself have seen them,—moved
To pay due homage to the man I loved
Because of that prodigious book he wrote
On Artistry's Ideal, by taking note,

Making acquaintance with his artist-work.
So my youth's piety obtained success
Of all-too dubious sort: for, though it irk
To tell the issue, few or none would guess
From extant lines and colours, De Lairesse,
Your faculty, although each deftly-grouped
And aptly-ordered figure-piece was judged
Worthy a prince's purchase in its day.
Bearded experience bears not to be duped
Like boyish fancy: 'twas a boy that budged
No foot's breadth from your visioned steps away
The while that memorable "Walk" he trudged
In your companionship,—the Book must say
Where, when and whither,—"Walk," come what
  come may,
No measurer of steps on this our globe
Shall ever match for marvels. Faustus' robe,
And Fortunatus' cap were gifts of price:
But—oh, your piece of sober sound advice
That artists should descry abundant worth
In trivial commonplace, nor groan at dearth
If fortune bade the painter's craft be plied
In vulgar town and country! Why despond
Because hemmed round by Dutch canals? Beyond
The ugly actual, lo, on every side
Imagination's limitless domain
Displayed a wealth of wondrous sounds and sights
Ripe to be realized by poet's brain
Acting on painter's brush! "Ye doubt? Poor wights,
What if I set example, go before,
While you come after, and we both explore
Holland turned Dreamland, taking care to note
Objects whereto my pupils may devote
Attention with advantage?"

III.

So commenced
That "Walk" amid true wonders—none to you,
But huge to us ignobly common-sensed,
Purblind, while plain could proper optics view

In that old sepulchre by lightning split,
Whereof the lid bore carven,—any dolt
Imagines why,—Jove's very thunderbolt:
You who could straight perceive, by glance at it,
This tomb must needs be Phaeton's! In a trice,
Confirming that conjecture, close on hand,
Behold, half out, half in the ploughed-up sand,
A chariot-wheel explained its bolt-device:
What other than the Chariot of the Sun
Ever let drop the like? Consult the tome—*
I bid inglorious tarriers-at-home—
For greater still surprise the while that "Walk"
Went on and on, to end as it begun,
Chokefull of chances, changes, every one
No whit less wondrous. What was there to baulk
Us, who had eyes, from seeing? You with none
Missed not a marvel: wherefore? Let us talk.

IV.

Say am I right? Your sealed sense moved your mind,
Free from obstruction, to compassionate
Art's power left powerless, and supply the blind
With fancies worth all facts denied by fate.
Mind could invent things, and to—take away,
At pleasure, leave out trifles mean and base
Which vex the sight that cannot say them nay
But, where mind plays the master, have no place.
And bent on banishing was mind, be sure,
All except beauty from its mustered tribe
Of objects apparitional which lure
Painter to show and poet to describe—
That imagery of the antique song
Truer than truth's self. Fancy's rainbow-birth
Conceived mid clouds in Greece, could glance along
Your passage o'er Dutch veritable earth,
As with ourselves, who see, familiar throng
About our pacings men and women worth
Nowise a glance—so poets apprehend—

* *The Art of Painting, etc.*, by Gerard de Lairesse; translated by J. F. Fritsch. 1778.

Since nought avails portraying them in verse:
While painters turn upon the heel, intend
To spare their work the critic's ready curse
Due to the daily and undignified.

V.

I who myself contentedly abide
Awake, nor want the wings of dream,—who tramp
Earth's common surface, rough, smooth, dry or damp,
—I understand alternatives, no less
Conceive your soul's leap, Gerard de Lairesse
How were it could I mingle false with true,
Boast, with the sights I see, your vision too?
Advantage would it prove or detriment
If I saw double? Could I gaze intent
On Dryope plucking the blossoms red,
As you, whereat her lote-tree writhed and bled,
Yet lose no gain, no hard fast wide-awake
Having and holding nature for the sake
Of nature only—nymph and lote-tree thus
Gained by the loss of fruit not fabulous,
Apple of English homesteads, where I see
Nor seek more than crisp buds a struggling bee
Uncrumples, caught by sweet he clambers through?
Truly, a moot point: make it plain to me,
Who, bee-like, sate sense with the simply true,
Nor seek to heighten that sufficiency
By help of feignings proper to the page—
Earth's surface-blank whereon the elder age
Put colour, poetizing—poured rich life
On what were else a dead ground—nothingness—
Until the solitary world grew rife
With Joves and Junos, nymphs and satyrs. Yes,
The reason was, fancy composed the strife
'Twixt sense and soul: for sense, my De Lairesse,
Cannot content itself with outward things,
Mere beauty: soul must needs know whence there springs—
How, when and why—what sense but loves, nor lists
To know at all.

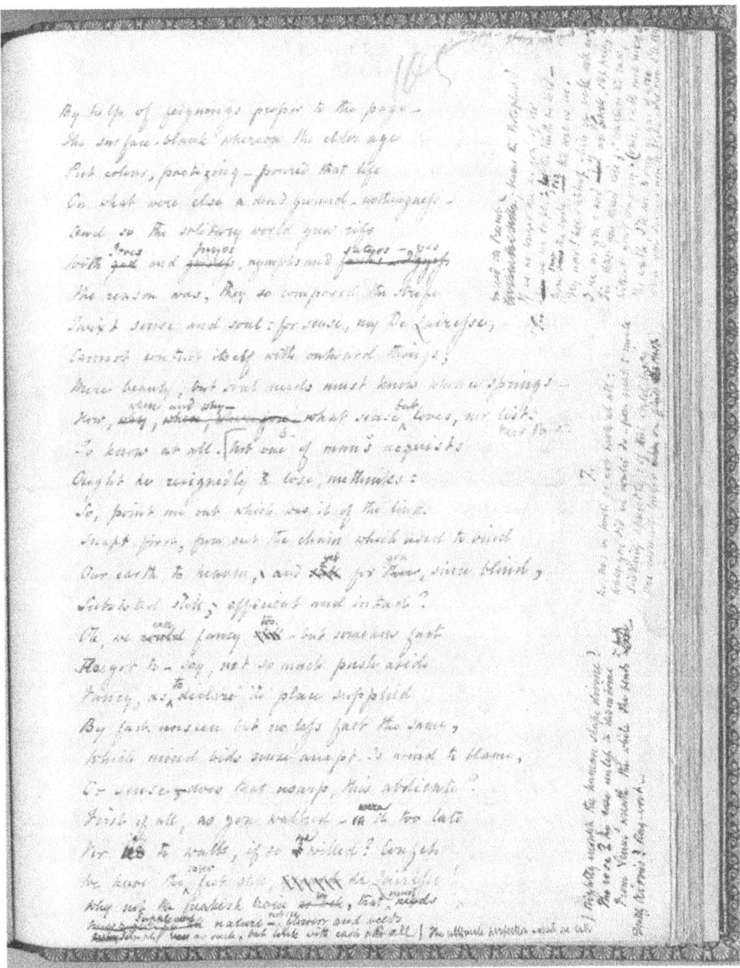

FIG. 12 MS in Browning's hand of *Gérard de Lairesse*, ll. 132–80, Balliol College Library.

VI.

Not one of man's acquists
Ought he resignedly to lose, methinks:
So, point me out which was it of the links
Snapt first, from out the chain which used to bind

Our earth to heaven, and yet for you, since blind,
Subsisted still efficient and intact?
Oh, we can fancy too! but somehow fact
Has got to—say, not so much push aside
Fancy, as to declare its place supplied
By fact unseen but no less fact the same,
Which mind bids sense accept. Is mind to blame,
Or sense,—does that usurp, this abdicate?
First of all, as you "walked"—were it too late
For us to walk, if so we willed? Confess
We have the sober feet still, De Lairesse!
Why not the freakish brain too, that must needs
Supplement nature—not see flowers and weeds
Simply as such, but link with each and all
The ultimate perfection—what we call
Rightly enough the human shape divine?
The rose? No rose unless it disentwine
From Venus' wreath the while she bends to kiss
Her deathly love?

VII.

Plain retrogression, this!
No, no: we poets go not back at all:
What you did we could do—from great to small
Sinking assuredly: if this world last
One moment longer when Man finds its Past
Exceed its Present—blame the Protoplast!
If we no longer see as you of old,
'Tis we see deeper. Progress for the bold!
You saw the body, 'tis the soul we see.
Try now! Bear witness while you walk with me,
I see as you: if we loose arms, stop pace,
'Tis that you stand still, I conclude the race
Without your company. Come, walk once more
The "Walk": if I to-day as you of yore
See just like you the blind—then sight shall cry
—The whole long day quite gone through—victory!

VIII.

Thunders on thunders, doubling and redoubling
Doom o'er the mountain, while a sharp white fire
Now shone, now sheared its rusty herbage, troubling
Hardly the fir-boles, now discharged its ire
Full where some pine-tree's solitary spire
Crashed down, defiant to the last: till—lo,
The motive of the malice!—all a-glow,
Circled with flame there yawned a sudden rift
I' the rock-face, and I saw a form erect
Front and defy the outrage, while—as checked,
Chidden, beside him dauntless in the drift—
Cowered a heaped creature, wing and wing outspread
In deprecation o'er the crouching head
Still hungry for the feast foregone awhile.
O thou, of scorn's unconquerable smile,
Was it when this—Jove's feathered fury—slipped
Gore-glutted from the heart's core whence he ripped—
This eagle-hound—neither reproach nor prayer—
Baffled, in one more fierce attempt to tear
Fate's secret from thy safeguard,—was it then
That all these thunders rent earth, ruined air
To reach thee, pay thy patronage of men?
He thundered,—to withdraw, as beast to lair,
Before the triumph on thy pallid brow.
Gather the night again about thee now,
Hate on, love ever! Morn is breaking there—
The granite ridge pricks through the mist, turns gold
As wrong turns right. O laughters manifold
Of ocean's ripple at dull earth's despair!

IX.

But morning's laugh sets all the crags alight
Above the baffled tempest: tree and tree
Stir themselves from the stupor of the night
And every strangled branch resumes its right
To breathe, shakes loose dark's clinging dregs, waves free
In dripping glory. Prone the runnels plunge,
While earth, distent with moisture like a spunge,
Smokes up, and leaves each plant its gem to see,

Each grass-blade's glory-glitter. Had I known
The torrent now turned river?—masterful
Making its rush o'er tumbled ravage—stone
And stub which barred the froths and foams: no bull
Ever broke bounds in formidable sport
More overwhelmingly, till lo, the spasm
Sets him to dare that last mad leap: report
Who may—his fortunes in the deathly chasm
That swallows him in silence! Rather turn
Whither, upon the upland, pedestalled
Into the broad day-splendour, whom discern
These eyes but thee, supreme one, rightly called
Moon-maid in heaven above and, here below,
Earth's huntress-queen? I note the garb succinct
Saving from smirch that purity of snow
From breast to knee—snow's self with just the tinct
Of the apple-blossom's heart-blush. Ah, the bow
Slack-strung her fingers grasp, where, ivory-linked
Horn curving blends with horn, a moonlike pair
Which mimic the brow's crescent sparkling so—
As if a star's live restless fragment winked
Proud yet repugnant, captive in such hair!
What hope along the hillside, what far bliss
Lets the crisp hair-plaits fall so low they kiss
Those lucid shoulders? Must a morn so blithe,
Needs have its sorrow when the twang and hiss
Tell that from out thy sheaf one shaft makes writhe
Its victim, thou unerring Artemis?
Why did the chamois stand so fair a mark
Arrested by the novel shape he dreamed
Was bred of liquid marble in the dark
Depths of the mountain's womb which ever teemed
With novel births of wonder? Not one spark
Of pity in that steel-grey glance which gleamed
At the poor hoof's protesting as it stamped
Idly the granite? Let me glide unseen
From thy proud presence: well may'st thou be queen
Of all those strange and sudden deaths which damped
So oft Love's torch and Hymen's taper lit
For happy marriage till the maidens paled
And perished on the temple-step, assailed

By—what except to envy must man's wit
Impute that sure implacable release
Of life from warmth and joy? But death means peace.

X.

Noon is the conqueror,—not a spray, nor leaf,
Nor herb, nor blossom but has rendered up
Its morning dew: the valley seemed one cup
Of cloud-smoke, but the vapour's reign was brief,
Sun-smitten, see, it hangs—the filmy haze—
Grey-garmenting the herbless mountain-side,
To soothe the day's sharp glare: while far and wide
Above unclouded burns the sky, one blaze
With fierce immitigable blue, no bird
Ventures to spot by passage. E'en of peaks
Which still presume there, plain each pale point speaks
In wan transparency of waste incurred
By over-daring: far from me be such!
Deep in the hollow, rather, where combine
Tree, shrub and briar to roof with shade and cool
The remnant of some lily-strangled pool,
Edged round with mossy fringing soft and fine.
Smooth lie the bottom slabs, and overhead
Watch elder, bramble, rose, and service-tree
And one beneficent rich barberry
Jewelled all over with fruit-pendents red.
What have I seen! O Satyr, well I know
How sad thy case, and what a world of woe
Was hid by the brown visage furry-framed
Only for mirth: who otherwise could think—
Marking thy mouth gape still on laughter's brink,
Thine eyes a-swim with merriment unnamed
But haply guessed at by their furtive wink?
And all the while a heart was panting sick
Behind that shaggy bulwark of thy breast—
Passion it was that made those breath-bursts thick
I took for mirth subsiding into rest.
So, it was Lyda—she of all the train
Of forest-thridding nymphs,—'twas only she
Turned from thy rustic homage in disdain,

Saw but that poor uncouth outside of thee,
And, from her circling sisters, mocked a pain
Echo had pitied—whom Pan loved in vain—
For she was wishful to partake thy glee,
Mimic thy mirth—who loved her not again,
Savage for Lyda's sake. She crouches there—
Thy cruel beauty, slumberously laid
Supine on heaped-up beast-skins, unaware
Thy steps have traced her to the briery glade,
Thy greedy hands disclose the cradling lair,
Thy hot eyes reach and revel on the maid!

XI.

Now, what should this be for? The sun's decline
Seems as he lingered lest he lose some act
Dread and decisive, some prodigious fact
Like thunder from the safe sky's sapphirine
About to alter earth's conditions, packed
With fate for nature's self that waits, aware
What mischief unsuspected in the air
Menaces momently a cataract.
Therefore it is that yonder space extends
Untrenched upon by any vagrant tree,
Shrub, weed well nigh; they keep their bounds, leave free
The platform for what actors? Foes or friends,
Here come they trooping silent: heaven suspends
Purpose the while they range themselves. I see!
Bent on a battle, two vast powers agree
This present and no after-contest ends
One or the other's grasp at rule in reach
Over the race of man—host fronting host,
As statue statue fronts—wrath-molten each,
Solidified by hate,—earth halved almost,
To close once more in chaos. Yet two shapes
Show prominent, each from the universe
Of minions round about him, that disperse
Like cloud-obstruction when a bolt escapes.
Who flames first? Macedonian is it thou?
Ay, and who fronts thee, King Darius, drapes
His form with purple, fillet-folds his brow.

XII.

What, then the long day dies at last? Abrupt
The sun that seemed, in stooping, sure to melt
Our mountain ridge, is mastered: black the belt
Of westward crags, his gold could not corrupt,
Barriers again the valley, lets the flow
Of lavish glory waste itself away
—Whither? For new climes, fresh eyes breaks the day!
Night was not to be baffled. If the glow
Were all that's gone from us! Did clouds, afloat
So filmily but now, discard no rose,
Sombre throughout the fleeciness that grows
A sullen uniformity. I note
Rather displeasure,—in the overspread
Change from the swim of gold to one pale lead
Oppressive to malevolence,—than late
Those amorous yearnings when the aggregate
Of cloudlets pressed that each and all might sate
Its passion and partake in relics red
Of day's bequeathment: now, a frown instead
Estranges, and affrights who needs must fare
On and on till his journey ends: but where?
Caucasus? Lost now in the night. Away
And far enough lies that Arcadia.
The human heroes tread the world's dark way
No longer. Yet I dimly see almost—
Yes, for my last adventure! 'Tis a ghost.
So drops away the beauty! There he stands
Voiceless, scarce strives with deprecating hands

XIII.

Enough! Stop further fooling, De Lairesse!
My fault, not yours! Some fitter way express
Heart's satisfaction that the Past indeed
Is past, gives way before Life's best and last,
The all-including Future! What were life
Did soul stand still therein, forego her strife
Through the ambiguous Present to the goal
Of some all-reconciling Future? Soul,
Nothing has been which shall not bettered be

Hereafter,—leave the root, by law's decree
Whence springs the ultimate and perfect tree!
Busy thee with unearthing root? Nay, climb—
Quit trunk, branch, leaf and flower—reach, rest sublime
Where fruitage ripens in the blaze of day!
O'erlook, despise, forget, throw flower away,
Intent on progress? No whit more than stop
Ascent therewith to dally, screen the top
Sufficiency of yield by interposed
Twistwork bold foot gets free from. Wherefore glozed
The poets—"Dream afresh old godlike shapes,
Recapture ancient fable that escapes,
Push back reality, repeople earth
With vanished falseness, recognize no worth
In fact new-born unless 'tis rendered back
Pallid by fancy, as the western rack
Of fading cloud bequeaths the lake some gleam
Of its gone glory!"

XIV.

Let things be—not seem,
I counsel rather,—do, and nowise dream!
Earth's young significance is all to learn:
The dead Greek lore lies buried in the urn
Where who seeks fire finds ashes. Ghost, forsooth!
What was the best Greece babbled of as truth?
"A shade, a wretched nothing,—sad, thin, drear,
Cold, dark, it holds on to the lost loves here,
If hand have haply sprinkled o'er the dead
Three charitable dust-heaps, made mouth red
One moment by the sip of sacrifice:
Just so much comfort thaws the stubborn ice
Slow-thickening upward till it choke at length
The last faint flutter craving—not for strength,
Not beauty, not the riches and the rule
O'er men that made life life indeed." Sad school
Was Hades! Gladly,—might the dead but slink
To life, back,—to the dregs once more would drink
Each interloper, drain the humblest cup
Fate mixes for humanity.

XV.

Cheer up,—
Be death with me, as with Achilles erst,
Of Man's calamities the last and worst:
Take it so! By proved potency that still
Makes perfect, be assured, come what come will,
What once lives never dies—what here attains
To a beginning, has no end, still gains
And never loses aught: when, where, and how—
Lies in Law's lap. What's death then? Even now
With so much knowledge is it hard to bear
Brief interposing ignorance? Is care
For a creation found at fault just there—
There where the heart breaks bond and outruns time,
To reach, not follow what shall be?

XVI.

Here's rhyme
Such as one makes now,—say, when Spring repeats
That miracle the Greek Bard sadly greets:
"Spring for the tree and herb—no Spring for us!"
Let Spring come: why, a man salutes her thus:

Dance, yellows and whites and reds,—
Lead your gay orgy, leaves, stalks, heads
Astir with the wind in the tulip-beds!

There's sunshine; scarcely a wind at all
Disturbs starved grass and daisies small
On a certain mound by a churchyard wall.

Daisies and grass be my heart's bedfellows
On the mound wind spares and sunshine mellows:
Dance you, reds and whites and yellows!

FROM *THE ATHENAEUM*, NO. 3220, JULY 13, 1889, 64

To Edward FitzGerald

I chanced upon a new book yesterday:
I opened it, and, where my finger lay
  'Twixt page and uncut page, these words I read
—Some six or seven at most—and learned thereby
That you, Fitzgerald, whom by ear and eye
  She never knew, "thanked God my wife was dead."

Aye, dead! and were yourself alive, good Fitz,
How to return you thanks would task my wits:
  Kicking you seems the common lot of curs—
While more appropriate greeting lends you grace:
Surely to spit there glorifies your face—
  Spitting—from lips once sanctified by Hers.

July 8, 1889 ROBERT BROWNING

FROM *ASOLANDO: FANCIES AND FACTS* (1889)

Development

My Father was a scholar and knew Greek.
When I was five years old, I asked him once
"What do you read about?"
"The siege of Troy."
"What is a siege and what is Troy?"
Whereat
He piled up chairs and tables for a town,
Set me a-top for Priam, called our cat
—Helen, enticed away from home (he said)
By wicked Paris, who couched somewhere close
Under the footstool, being cowardly,
But whom—since she was worth the pains, poor puss—
Towzer and Tray,—our dogs, the Atreidai,—sought
By taking Troy to get possession of
—Always when great Achilles ceased to sulk,
(My pony in the stable)—forth would prance
And put to flight Hector—our page-boy's self.
This taught me who was who and what was what:
So far I rightly understood the case
At five years old: a huge delight it proved
And still proves—thanks to that instructor sage
My Father, who knew better than turn straight
Learning's full flare on weak-eyed ignorance,
Or, worse yet, leave weak eyes to grow sand-blind,
Content with darkness and vacuity.

It happened, two or three years afterward,
That—I and playmates playing at Troy's Siege—
My Father came upon our make-believe.
"How would you like to read yourself the tale
Properly told, of which I gave you first
Merely such notion as a boy could bear?
Pope, now, would give you the precise account
Of what, some day, by dint of scholarship,
You'll hear—who knows?—from Homer's very mouth.
Learn Greek by all means, read the 'Blind Old Man,
Sweetest of Singers'—*tuphlos* which means 'blind,'
Hedistos which means 'sweetest.' Time enough!
Try, anyhow, to master him some day;

Until when, take what serves for substitute,
Read Pope, by all means!"
So I ran through Pope,
Enjoyed the tale—what history so true?
Also attacked my Primer, duly drudged,
Grew fitter thus for what was promised next—
The very thing itself, the actual words,
When I could turn—say, Buttmann to account.

Time passed, I ripened somewhat: one fine day,
"Quite ready for the Iliad, nothing less?
There's Heine, where the big books block the shelf:
Don't skip a word, thumb well the Lexicon!"

I thumbed well and skipped nowise till I learned
Who was who, what was what, from Homer's tongue,
And there an end of learning. Had you asked
The all-accomplished scholar, twelve years old,
"Who was it wrote the Iliad?"—what a laugh!
"Why, Homer, all the world knows: of his life
Doubtless some facts exist: it's everywhere:
We have not settled, though, his place of birth:
He begged, for certain, and was blind beside:
Seven cities claimed him—Scio, with best right,
Thinks Byron. What he wrote? Those Hymns we have.
Then there's the 'Battle of the Frogs and Mice,'
That's all—unless they dig 'Margites' up
(I'd like that) nothing more remains to know."

Thus did youth spend a comfortable time;
Until—"What's this the Germans say is fact
That Wolf found out first? It's unpleasant work
Their chop and change, unsettling one's belief:
All the same, while we live, we learn, that's sure."
So, I bent brow o'er *Prolegomena*.

And, after Wolf, a dozen of his like
Proved there was never any Troy at all,
Neither Besiegers nor Besieged,—nay, worse,—
No actual Homer, no authentic text,
No warrant for the fiction I, as fact,
Had treasured in my heart and soul so long—
Ay, mark you! and as fact held still, still hold,

Spite of new knowledge, in my heart of hearts
And soul of souls, fact's essence freed and fixed
From accidental fancy's guardian sheath.
Assuredly thenceforward—thank my stars!—
However it got there, deprive who could—
Wring from the shrine my precious tenantry,
Helen, Ulysses, Hector and his Spouse,
Achilles and his Friend?—though Wolf—ah, Wolf!
Why must he needs come doubting, spoil a dream?

But then "No dream's worth waking"—Browning says:
And here's the reason why I tell thus much.
I, now mature man, you anticipate,
May blame my Father justifiably
For letting me dream out my nonage thus,
And only by such slow and sure degrees
Permitting me to sift the grain from chaff,
Get truth and falsehood known and named as such.
Why did he ever let me dream at all,
Not bid me taste the story in its strength?
Suppose my childhood was scarce qualified
To rightly understand mythology,
Silence at least was in his power to keep:
I might have—somehow—correspondingly—
Well, who knows by what method, gained my gains,
Been taught, by forthrights not meanderings,
My aim should be to loathe, like Peleus' son,
A lie as Hell's Gate, love my wedded wife,
Like Hector, and so on with all the rest.
Could not I have excogitated this
Without believing such men really were?
That is—he might have put into my hand
The "Ethics"? In translation, if you please,
Exact, no pretty lying that improves,
To suit the modern taste: no more, no less—
The "Ethics": 'tis a treatise I find hard
To read aright now that my hair is grey,
And I can manage the original.
At five years old—how ill had fared its leaves!
Now, growing double o'er the Stagirite,
At least I soil no page with bread and milk,
Nor crumple, dogsear and deface—boys' way.

Epilogue

At the midnight in the silence of the sleep-time,
  When you set your fancies free,
Will they pass to where—by death, fools think, imprisoned—
Low he lies who once so loved you, whom you loved so,
    —Pity me?

Oh to love so, be so loved, yet so mistaken!
  What had I on earth to do
With the slothful, with the mawkish, the unmanly?
Like the aimless, helpless, hopeless, did I drivel
    —Being—who?

One who never turned his back but marched breast forward,
  Never doubted clouds would break,
Never dreamed, though right were worsted, wrong would triumph,
Held we fall to rise, are baffled to fight better,
    Sleep to wake.

No, at noonday in the bustle of man's work-time
  Greet the unseen with a cheer!
Bid him forward, breast and back as either should be,
"Strive and thrive!" cry "Speed,—fight on, fare ever
    There as here!"

NOTES

PAULINE: A FRAGMENT OF A CONFESSION (1833)

Pauline was published anonymously in March 1833. RB's first publication attracted several reviews, the fullest and warmest by his friend W. J. Fox, in the *Monthly Repository*, but towards the end of his life RB could not recall that a single copy of the poem was ever sold. Its fate might have been different had John Stuart Mill succeeded in placing the review of the poem that he had planned to write. His annotated copy of the poem (now in the National Art Library, Victoria and Albert Museum), which was later returned to RB who took the opportunity to respond to some of Mill's objections, constitutes the most searching and intelligent criticism that any poem of RB's attracted during the lifetime of the poet. The poem is daringly experimental. It is far more radically fragmentary than any of the poems of RB's Romantic predecessors who had established the fashion for the poetical fragment. It more closely recalls the fragmentation common in novels of sensibility such as Henry Mackenzie's *Man of Feeling* or P. B. Shelley's Gothic novel *St Irvyne*. Perhaps the most pertinent formal models were the fragmentary poems by Shelley such as *Prince Athanase* that Mary Shelley excavated from her husband's notebooks and published posthumously. *Pauline* is presented rather similarly as if it had been edited for the press by the Swiss woman to whom the poem is addressed (Pauline even appends a long note in French). The poem includes several tributes to Shelley, the poet that the young RB most admired, and is much his most Shelleyan poem. The poem that leaves the clearest mark on it is *Alastor*, Shelley's study of a youthful poet unable to escape from his 'self-centred seclusion', and the poem also recalls *Epipsychidion*, and other Romantic studies of troubled young men, most obviously Byron's *Childe Harold's Pilgrimage*. But it is also a poem of its time. In the early 1830s Tennyson and many of his Cambridge friends wrote confessional poems that explored a spiritual crisis, the best known of which is Tennyson's *Supposed Confessions of a Second-Rate Sensitive Mind Not in Unity with Itself* (1830). A poem such as 'A Spirit's Return' (also 1830) by Felicia Hemans shares similar preoccupations. These poems, like RB's, are dramatic lyrics. They share a character that RB seeks to define by his references to Edward Kean who in the last months of his life invited his audiences not so much to witness his performance in the Shakespearian tragic roles that had made him famous as to witness his performance of his own demise. In *Pauline*, RB attempts to bring to his performance of himself the same demonic energy that Kean brought to the stage.

RB added the following note by way of a preface in Mill's copy of the poem:

The following Poem was written in pursuance of a foolish plan which occupied me mightily for a time, and which had for its object the enabling me to assume & realize I know not how many different characters;—meanwhile the world was never to guess that "Brown, Smith, Jones, & Robinson" (as the spelling-books have it), the respective authors of this poem, the other novel, such an opera, such a speech &c &c were no other than one and the same individual. The present abortion was the first work of the *Poet* of the batch, who would have been more legitimately *myself* than most of the others; but I surrounded him with all manner of (to my then notion) poetical accessories and had planned quite a delightful life for him: Only this crab remains of the shapely tree of life in this fools paradise of mine.

Plus ne suis . . . jamais être. Clément Marot (1496–1544), 'De Soy mesme', 1–2, *Epigrammes diverses*, ccix. 'I am no longer what I have been, and I do not know how I may ever again be it.' The poem continues:

Mon beau printemps & mon esté
Ont faict le sault par la fenestre,
Amour, tu as esté mon maistre
Ie t'ay servy sur toutes les Dieux;
O si je pouvois deux fois naistre,
Comme ie te serviroys mieux

'My fine spring and my summer have jumped out of the window. Love, you have been my master; I have served you above all other gods. Oh, if I could be born twice, how much better I would serve you.'

Non Dubito . . . opus compsui. The Latin epigraph is taken from the preface to Heinrich Cornelius Agrippa, *De Occulta Philosophia*, 1531. Maynard notes that the work was included in an anthology which RB's father had in his library; John Maynard, *Browning's Youth*, 1977, 210. RB's version shortens and adapts the preface. The following translation is that of F. A. Pottle in his *Shelley and Browning: A Myth and Some Facts*, 1923, 40–1:

I have no doubt that the title of our book may by its unusual character entice very many to read it, and that among them some of biased opinions, with weak minds—many even hostile and churlish—will attack our genius, who in the rashness of their ignorance will cry out, almost before they have read the title, that we are teaching forbidden things, are scattering the seeds of heresies, that we are an annoyance to righteous ears, to enlightened minds an object of offense; so taking care for their consciences that neither Apollo, nor all the Muses, nor an angel from heaven could save me from their execration. To these I now give counsel not to read our book, neither to understand it nor remember it; for it is harmful, poisonous; the gate of Hell is in this book; it speaks of stones—let them beware lest by them, it beat out their brains. But if you who come to its perusal with unprejudiced minds will exercise as much discernment and prudence as bees gathering honey, then read with safety. For I think you will receive not a little of instruction and a great deal of enjoyment. On the other hand, if you find things which do not please you, pass over them and make no use of them. FOR I DO NOT RECOMMEND THESE THINGS TO YOU: I MERELY TELL YOU OF THEM. Yet do not on that account reject the rest. Therefore if anything has been said rather freely, forgive my youth; I wrote this work when I was less than a youth.

V.A. XX. RB explained to Wise that the phrase means '*Vixi annos*—"I was twenty years old"—that is, the imaginary subject of the poem was of that age' (*Wise*, 256).

l. 11. *Whoso sucks a poisoned wound.* Possibly alluding to the legend that Eleanor of Castile saved the life of her husband Edward I when he was stabbed at Acre by sucking the poison from the wound.

l. 18. *Nature would point at one.* 'not I think an appropriate image and it throws considerable obscurity over the meaning of the passage' (Mill's note); *quivering lip.* Compare *Alastor*: 'A gloomy smile | Of desperate hope wrinkled his quivering lips' (290–1).

l. 27. *as I shall be no more.* Mill comments 'same remark' (as on line 18).

l. 36. Mill comments, 'not even *poetically* grammatical.'

l. 45. *and veil without a fear.* Mill underlines, and notes 'qu. meaning?'

ll. 69–70. Mill comments 'not *distinct* enough'.

l. 83. *faithful found.* Compare Milton's 'Abdiel faithful found, | Among the faithless', *Paradise Lost*, V. 896–7. The quotation suggests that lines 78–9 in which the speaker sings as one who is acclaimed recall the 'shout' with which the 'universal host' of fallen angels respond when Azazel unfurls the 'imperial ensign', *Paradise Lost*, I. 533–43.

l. 89. *I am ruined.* Compare Satan, who did not appear 'Less than archangel ruined', *Paradise Lost*, I. 593.

l. 91. *wide dominion.* Compare 'wide dominions', *Prometheus Unbound*, I. 763.

l. 97. *I seemed the fate from which I fled.* Compare Shelley, *Adonais*: 'And his own thoughts, along that rugged way, | Pursued, like raging hounds, their father and their prey' (278–9).

l. 102. *A white swan.* Compare the swan that the speaker of Shelley's *Alastor* blesses as it flies away to be reunited with its mate, 275–84.

l. 119. *his perishing.* The story of the god seduced by a witch has a very general resemblance to Keats's account of Glaucus seduced by the witch Circe in Book III of *Endymion.*

l. 122. After this line, which ends a page, Mill comments, 'a curious idealization of self-worship. very fine, though'.

l. 140. Compare Wordsworth, 'Tintern Abbey', 52–3: 'The fretful stir | Unprofitable, and the fever of the world.'

l. 142. Mill asked 'What does this mean?' and adds, 'only at the fourth reading of the poem I found out what this means'. RB added an explanatory note, 'The award of fame to Him. The late acknowledgement of Shelley's genius.'

l. 150. Compare *Adonais*, 249–51, in which Byron appears as Apollo: 'from his golden bow | The Pythian of the age one arrow sped | And smiled.'

ll. 163–7. Mill marked the passage 'beautiful'.

ll. 171–80. Mill marked the passage 'most beautiful'.

ll. 179–90. Of the many Romantic evocations of great rivers, the closest in tone is perhaps Leigh Hunt's sonnet 'The Nile', written in competition with Keats. Notice Shelley's preface to *The Revolt of Islam* in which he offers as one of his qualifications as a poet, 'I have sailed down mighty rivers'.

l. 199. *when all the world was in his praise*. When the lover's praise meant the whole world to the girl. Mill found the line 'obscurely expressed'.

l. 205. *as thou art*. i.e. 'alive', 'as thou art' rather than 'as thou wert', because, as the following lines reveal, the speaker believes that Shelley still lives.

l. 207. *set this final seal*. Compare John 3: 33: 'He that hath received this testimony hath set to his seal that God is true.'

ll. 207, 209, 219. *Remember me*. Compare the Ghost in *Hamlet*, I. v. 91, 'Adieu, adieu, adieu, remember me.'

l. 212. *shapes*. Compare *Alastor*, 696–8: 'Thou canst no longer know or love the shapes | Of this phantasmal scene, who have to thee | Been purest ministers.'

l. 213. *foul forms*. Compare Shelley's 'lovely forms | After some foul disguise had fallen', *Prometheus Unbound*, III. iv. 69–70.

ll. 213–18, Mill comments, 'The obscurity of this is the greater fault as the meaning if I can guess it right is really poetical.'

l. 221. *imaginings*. A word Shelley uses four times, most famously in 'Mont Blanc', 143, 'the human mind's imaginings'.

ll. 222–9. Mill comments 'beautiful'.

ll. 227–8. Compare Keats, 'On First Looking into Chapman's Homer', 9–10: 'Then felt I like some watcher of the skies | When a new planet swims into his ken.'

ll. 233–4. *but full of sober thoughts | Of fading years*. Mill comments 'might be improved'.

l. 252. *day dies soft*. Compare Keats, 'To Autumn', 25, 'the soft-dying day.'

l. 267. *my present state, and what it is*. Mill comments, 'this only says you shall see what you shall see & is more prose than poetry'.

l. 268. *intensest*. A word Shelley uses four times, as in 'Ode to Heaven', 18, 'Atoms of intensest light'.

l. 284. *imagination*. Mill commented 'not imagination but Imagination. The absence of that capital letter obscures the meaning.' RB inked in the alteration.

ll. 293–4. *wasted | Or progressed*. Changed in 1888 to 'halted | Or hastened' which makes the sense clearer.

ll. 310–12. Mill comments, 'explain better what this means'.

l. 311. Sensuality acts as a substitute for the love that the speaker cannot feel.

l. 321. I lived my own life through the tales that I read.

ll. 321–2. The giant may be Atlas, who, after his defeat in the war against the Olympians, was punished by being exiled to the furthest western edge of the world where he supported the sky on his shoulders: the hunter may be Orion who, after his death, ascended to the heavens as a constellation.

l. 324. *a high-crested chief.* One of the Greek chieftains in the war against Troy, Tenedos being, according to Virgil, the island where the Greeks hid their fleet when they wished the Trojans to believe that they had abandoned the siege.

l. 334. *the naked Swift-footed.* Possibly Atalanta, the swift-footed huntress who had taken a vow of chastity.

l. 335. *Proserpine's hair.* The lock of hair kept unshorn through life, which Proserpine cuts after death in order to release the soul from the body.

l. 342. *those shadowy times.* Mill asks, 'what times? your own imaginative times?'

l. 361. *lampless.* A word used by Shelley nine times.

l. 367. *is as a voice.* Mill asks, 'do you mean to *you* as a voice &c?'

l. 370. *she.* Mill asks, 'who? Fancy or Music?'

l. 392. *so much was light.* Mill objected that 'The writer seems to use "so" according to the colloquial vulgarism, in the sense of therefore or accordingly, from which occasionally comes great obscurity & ambiguity as here.' RB seems to have been stung by the charge and responds with a number of quotations adducing Milton as an authority for the usage.

l. 403. *the white way.* The Milky Way.

l. 404. Probably a second address to Shelley.

l. 425. Mary Shelley observes in her note to *Prometheus Unbound*, 'The prominent feature of Shelley's theory of the destiny of the human species was that evil is not inherent in the system of the creation, but an accident that might be expelled.'

ll. 430–1. Mill notes, 'fine'.

l. 433. Reverses the traditional romance plot in which the 'loathly lady' is transformed into a beautiful damsel when accepted by the knight as his bride.

ll. 433–5. The speaker contrasts himself with Wordsworth who, in his youth, 'bounded o'er the mountains' 'like a roe' ('Tintern Abbey', 67–8), and compares himself with Coleridge whose schooldays were spent 'In the great city, pent 'mid cloisters dim' ('Frost at Midnight', 52).

l. 437. Compare *Prometheus Unbound*, II. iii. 40–1, 'As thought by thought is piled, till some great truth | Is loosened, and the nations echo round'.

ll. 447–88. Mill notes that the passage is 'finely painted & evidently from experience'.

ll. 447–8. Mimics Shelleyan awakenings, as when the hero of *Alastor* awakes to the 'cold white light of morning' after dreaming of the 'veilèd maid' (193), but the dream that RB's speaker awakens from is a dream of Shelley.

l. 458. In his preface to *Prometheus Unbound*, Shelley confessed to 'a passion for reforming the world'.

l. 460. *motives' ends.* In 1888 the line reads 'motives, ends'.

l. 472. *dark spirit.* Compare the address to the 'Dark Spirit!' in Byron's 'Ode to Napoleon Bonaparte'. Byron here and elsewhere identified Napoleon as an alter ego, and RB may be referring to a period when Byron usurped Shelley as the god of his allegiance.

l. 479. *Arab birds.* Possibly a reference to huma birds which, in Persian legend, never alight on the ground.

ll. 518–21. Compare Shelley, 'A Defence of Poetry': 'the mind in creation is as a fading coal, which some invisible influence, like an inconstant wind, awakens to transitory brightness.'

l. 527. *One branch.* The golden bough that in Virgil's *Aeneid* allows Aeneas safe passage through the Underworld.

l. 540. *my soul's idol.* Presumably Shelley.

l. 553. *decaying wits.* The reference may be to Wordsworth.

ll. 567–71. RB explained to Wise, 'The "King" is Agamemnon, in the Tragedy of that name by Æschylos, whose treading the purple carpets spread before him by his wife, preparatory to his murder, is a notable passage' (*Wise*, 256). In Mill's copy he explains the allusion by a quotation from the play.

ll. 572–3. RB identified this figure as Ajax in his madness by quoting in the margin from Sophocles' *Ajax*.

ll. 573–5. RB explained to Wise, '"The boy" is Orestes, as described at the end of the *Choephoroi* by the same author' (*Wise*, 256). In Mill's copy he adds a quotation from the play.

l. 588. RB was an admirer of John Donne, who wrote 'Of the Progresse of the Soule'.

ll. 621–3. The argument is that a commanding will can only be demonstrated by showing itself able to repress the craving after knowledge.

l. 622. *that power.* Mill notes, 'you should make clear *what* power.'

l. 624. *harpy.* A legendary monster with the body of a bird and the face of an old woman that acts as the minister of divine vengeance.

ll. 627, 629. *wild eyes.* As in Wordsworth, 'Tintern Abbey', 119 and 148.

ll. 636–7. If each was in its element my capacity to love would outstrip my capacity to reason. It is not so in this world where love can only find inadequate objects.

ll. 638–43. Mill comments, 'self-flattery'.

l. 646–7. The paradox is that the kind of love he describes does not release him from himself but makes that self still more obtrusive.

ll. 648–9. Mill comments, 'inconsistent with what precedes'.

l. 656. *Andromeda*. The princess rescued by Perseus as she was about to be sacrificed to a sea-monster. RB owned a print of Polidoro da Caravaggio's *Perseus and Andromeda*. Both the legend and the painting had a special significance for him.

ll. 669–75. RB in a note in Mill's copy identified these lines as a reference to Edmund Kean's performance in *Richard III* that he had witnessed at Richmond on 22 October 1830, the place and date he appends to the poem. Kean died after collapsing on stage less than six months later.

l. 670. Mill marked the line as obscure. The point is that his errors bring his wondrous soul within range of human sympathy.

ll. 679–80. Mill comments, 'deeply true'.

l. 681. *juggle*. Trick.

l. 690. *prejudice*. Compare Edmund Burke's warning in his *Reflections on the Revolution in France*, 1790, against those prepared 'to cast away the coat of prejudice and to leave nothing but the naked reason'.

l. 703. *all conjuncture*. All imaginable circumstances.

l. 712. *slight flower*. *The Ring and the Book*, XI. 1103–4, suggests that RB has in mind the dog-rose, but this is not a winter flower.

ll. 736–7. Either a reference to the giants by whom the daughters of men bore children, Genesis 6: 4, or to the slain Gigantes from whose blood a race of men was born, Ovid, *Metamorphoses*, 1. 151.

l. 746. *foam-sheet*. Compare 'a slumberous sheet of foam', Tennyson, *The Lotos-Eaters*, 1832, 13.

l. 761. Compare 'a shelving bank of turf', Shelley, 'The Question', l. 5.

ll. 768–77. Mill comments, 'good descriptive writing'.

l. 773. Compare Spenser's Serena, watched as she slept by the cannibalistic wildmen, *The Faerie Queene*, 6. VIII. xxxix.

l. 776. *flag-knots*. Clumps of reeds or rushes.

l. 811. We translate the French note: 'I am much afraid that my poor friend may not be wholly comprehensible in what remains to be read of this strange fragment—but he is less fitted than anyone to throw light on what of its nature can only be dream and confusion. Moreover I hardly know if in seeking better to make sense of certain parts one does not run the risk of damaging the sole merit a production so singular can lay claim to—that of giving a reasonably accurate notion of the kind of work that it has merely sketched out.—This unpretentious beginning, this stirring of the passions, which at first swells and then gradually subsides, these impulses of the soul, this sudden return upon itself.—And above all, my friend's very special cast of mind issues in almost impossible shifts in feeling. Besides the reasons he advances, and others even more powerful, have made me sympathetic towards this piece of writing which I would otherwise have thrown in the fire—I have even less confidence in the grand principle of the whole composition—this principle derived from Shakespeare, Raphael, Beethoven, from which it follows that the intensity of the ideas owes more to their conception than their execution . . . I have every reason for supposing that the former of these qualities is still foreign to my friend—and I very much doubt that even twice as much effort would enable him to achieve the latter. The best thing would be to burn the thing; but what is one to do?

I'm afraid that in what follows he alludes to a kind of examination that he once made of the soul or rather of his soul, in order to find out a sequence of goals that it would be possible for him to attempt, each of which once achieved might form a kind of plateau from which it might be possible for him to perceive other goals, other projects, other satisfactions, which in their turn might be achieved. This may well all end in sleep and oblivion. The whole notion which I do not perfectly grasp is perhaps as unintelligible to him as it is to me.' The spelling 'Shakspeare' used in the poem was quite common up to the middle of the nineteenth century.

ll. 831–6. Mill asks, 'Why should this follow the description of scenery.'

l. 831. *this hell-dress.* Compare 'Curst Pride, the dress of hell,' Isaac Watts, 'An Elegiac Thought on Mrs. Anne Warner', 73.

ll. 850–4. Unlike the disciples who fell asleep when asked by Jesus to watch with him in the garden of Gethsemane near the Mount of Olives (see Mark 14: 34–8), they did not share his crucifixion and did not witness his resurrection. His ambition is to be the 'one of his disciples, whom Jesus loved' (traditionally identified as John), who is represented 'leaning on Jesus' bosom' (see John 13: 23).

l. 859. Mill comments, 'strange transition.'

l. 870. Compare 'I vowed that I would dedicate my powers | To thee', Shelley, 'Hymn to Intellectual Beauty', 61–2.

l. 904. *All these words are wild and weak.* Compare Alaric Watts, 'A Farewell' (1828), 17, 'But worlds are wild and weak.'

ll. 920–1. A reference to the lotos-eaters, probably brought to mind by Tennyson's 'The Lotos-Eaters' (1832).

l. 931. *a clue.* A ball of thread like that given by Ariadne to Theseus that enables him to escape from the labyrinth after killing the minotaur.

l. 932. Mill commented, 'poor.'

l. 946. Possibly a reference to the transformation of Geraldine in Coleridge's *Christabel.*

ll. 955–6. *a race | Most stunted and deformed.* Travellers commonly noted the deformity of the peasants living in the Swiss valleys as opposed to the stalwart mountaineers. Charles Tennant, for example, notices 'the race of idiots, in many of the fertile valleys of Switzerland, bearing round their necks the badge and curse of indolence and filthiness, the hideous goitre' (*Tour in the Year 1821–2*, 2 vols., 1824, 2. 350).

l. 964. *The fair pale sister.* In Mill's copy RB appends a quotation from Sophocles' *Antigone* to identify the reference to Antigone, buried alive by Cleon for performing the burial rites for her brother.

ll. 974–5. *I shall be | Prepared.* Mill comments, 'he is always talking of being *prepared*—what for?' RB responds, 'Why, "that's telling," as schoolboys say.'

l. 1016. *beauteous shapes.* As in *Prometheus Unbound*, I. 202.

RICHMOND October 22, 1832.

Mill comments, 'this transition from speaking to Pauline to writing a letter to the public with *place* & *date*, is quite horrible.' RB added an explanation, 'Kean was acting there: I saw him in Richard III that night, and conceived the childish scheme already mentioned: there is an allusion to Kean, page 47 [ll. 669–75]. I don't know whether I had not made up my mind to *act*, as well as to make verses, music, and God knows what—que de châteaux en Espagne!'

On the endleaf of his copy Mill wrote:

With considerable poetic power, this writer seems to me possessed with a more intense and morbid self-consciousness than I ever knew in any sane human being—I should think it a sincere confession though of a most unloveable state, if the 'Pauline' were not evidently a mere phantom. All about *her* is full of inconsistency—he neither loves her nor fancies he loves her, yet insists upon *talking* love to her—then he *pays her off* towards the end by a piece of flummery, amounting to the modest request that she will love him, *without* his loving *her*, *moyennant quoi* he will think her and call her everything that is handsome and he promises her that she shall find it mighty pleasant. Then he leaves off by saying he knows he shall have changed his mind by tomorrow & despise 'these intents which seem so fair' but that having been thus visited once no doubt he will again—& is therefore in perfect joy bad luck to him! as the Irish say.

A canto of most beautiful passages might be made from this poem & the psychological history of himself is powerful and truthful, *truth-like* certainly all but the last stage. That he evidently has not yet got into. The self-seeking and self-worshipping state is well described & beyond that I should think the writer had made, as yet, only the next step; viz. into despising his own state. I even question whether part even of that self-disdain is not *assumed*. He is evidently *dissatisfied* and feels part of the badness of his state, but he does not write as if it were purged out of him—if he once could muster a hearty hatred of his selfishness, it would *go*—as it is he feels only the *lack* of *good*, not the positive *evil*. He feels not remorse, but only disappointment. A mind in that state can only be regenerated by some new passion, and I know not what to wish for him but that he may meet with a real Pauline.

Meanwhile he should not attempt to shew how a person may be *recovered* from this morbid state—for *he* is hardly convalescent and 'what shall we speak of but that which we know?'

FROM *THE MONTHLY REPOSITORY*, VOL. 10, NS 1836, 43–6

[*Porphyria's Lover*] *Porphyria*

First published as *Porphyria* in the *Monthly Repository*, NS 10 (January 1836), 43–4, signed 'Z'. Two sources have been suggested, John Wilson's 'Extracts from Gosschen's Diary no I', *Blackwood's Edinburgh Magazine*, 3 (1818), 596–8, and a passage from Barry Cornwall's *Marcian Colonna* (1820), Part III, 507–30. See Michael Mason, 'Browning and the Dramatic Monologue', in Isobel Armstrong (ed.), *Writers and their Background: Robert Browning* (London: Bell and Hyman, 1978), 255–7. But neither seems very close. It seems more pertinent to note how RB feels his way into the murderer's state of mind by drawing on his own darker proclivities. In a letter to EBB, for example, he seems to draw, rather unnervingly, on his own poem: 'if you chose to come out of a whirl of balls and parties and excursions and visitings—to my side, I should love you as you sate still by me' (15 August 1846). Lines from *Pauline* are also significant:

> How the blood lies upon her cheek, all spread
> As thinned by kisses; only in her lips
> It wells and pulses like a living thing,
> And her neck looks, like marble misted o'er
> With love-breath,—a dear thing to kiss and love,
> Standing beneath me—looking out to me,
> As I might kill her and be loved for it. (896–902)

RB may also draw upon *Othello*. RB's lover projects onto his mistress the sentiment that Othello directs towards himself: 'If it were now to die, | 'Twere now to be most happy; for, I fear, | My soul hath her content so absolute | That not another comfort like to this | Succeeds in unknown fate' (II. i. 189–93). RB's decision to obscure the five-line stanza in which the poem is written by using a continuous lineation contributes to the sinister effect.

Porphyria. The name which derives from the Latin for purple may suggest her aristocratic birth, and may also recall Porphyro in Keats's *The Eve of St Agnes*, though Porphyro is divided from Madeline not by difference in rank but because their families are at feud.

l. 8. *cheerless grate*. As in Crabbe, *The Parish*, III. 237.

l. 24. *pride and vainer ties*. Suggesting that Porphyria is prevented from making her love public because of a difference in rank.

l. 33. *Porphyria worshipped me*. Compare the 'troops of shadows' who kneel to the speaker and cry 'let us worship thee!', *Pauline*, 476.

l. 48. *blushed bright*. The face is presumably discoloured after strangulation.

[Johannes Agricola in Meditation] Johannes Agricola

First published as *Johannes Agricola* in the *Monthly Repository*, NS 10 (January 1836), 45–6, signed 'Z'. Johannes Agricola (originally Schneider or Schnitter), 1494–1566, enjoyed the patronage of Martin Luther after the two had met at Wittenberg. He at first fell out with Melanchthon, who had been given a Chair at the university in preference to Agricola, attacking as papist Melanchthon's insistence on the duty to obey the commandments of the law. After seeming to recant his views, he fell out with Luther himself. Agricola's heresy was to maintain that Christians, unlike non-Christians, were freed from the duty of obedience to the Mosaic law, being bound only by the teachings of the Gospels. It was Luther who first ascribed to Agricola the belief that those who followed Christ were freed from the moral law, and categorized the heresy as antinomianism. RB also attributes to Agricola the doctrines of absolute predestination, that is, the notion that God, even before the Creation, had elected who was to be saved, and that his choice had no reference to the individual's merits, and the perseverance of the saints, that is, the notion that once elected by God the election cannot for forfeited by any action of the elected individual.

ll. 4–5. Longman compares *Hermetica*, ed. W. Scott (Oxford, 1924), I. 221, 'Bid it [your soul] fly up to heaven, and it will have no need of wings; nothing can bar its way, neither the fiery heat of the sun, nor the swirl of the planet-spheres; cleaving its way through all, it will fly up till it reaches the outermost of all corporeal things.' Johannes cares as little for God's works as he does for man's.

l. 5. *aloof.* To windward (prompting the nautical metaphor explicit in 'shoals', 9), figuratively at a distance, with the further implication that he holds the stars in contempt.

l. 14. *thundergirt.* Compare *Pauline*, 666–7, 'some god | To save will come in thunder from the stars'.

ll. 31–2. The contrast between the two trees, one of them poisonous, may echo the difference between the Tree of Life and the Tree of Death, sometimes identified as the upas tree, in the Garden of Eden. There may also be a reference to the gourd that sheltered Job until God prepared a worm to wither it (Job 4: 6–8).

ll. 33–7. Mithridates VI is reputed to have secured his immunity from poison by ingesting small quantities of poison over a long period. Johannes claims that his immunity from the poison of sin is directly granted by God. Mithridates' prophylactic measures did not benefit him. When captured by the Romans, he attempted to poison himself, failed, and had to ask a follower to run him through with a sword.

ll. 43–5. The spectacle of the agony of the damned is often represented by early Christians as contributing to the joy of the saved. In *De Spectaculis* chapter 30 Tertullian represents the sight as superior to the 'circus, and both theatres, and every race-course'. Johannes' distinction is that he enjoys the agonies of those he believes will be damned because they trusted their good works might save them.

l. 47. *Altar-smoke.* Compare *Pippa Passes*, III, 216.

ll. 51–4. The damned are distinctively Roman Catholic.

ll. 54–5. The doctrine of predestination, most closely associated with Calvin but characteristic of all Pauline Christianity, as in Romans 8: 30, 'Moreover, whom he did predestinate, them he also called: and whom he called, them he also justified: and whom he justified, them he also glorified.'

ll. 56–8. It is orthodox to hold with Augustine that 'God's judgements' are 'inscrutable, and His ways past finding out', but Augustine insists on the obligation to 'seek those things that belong only to good men, and especially to shun those evils which belong only to bad men'. *The City of God*, Book 20, chapter 2.

ll. 59–60. Johannes can only understand virtuous action as an attempt to buy salvation.

l. 60. *at his right hand.* That is in the place usually assigned to Christ. See Hebrews 1: 3; or Romans 8: 34.

BELLS AND POMEGRANATES, NO. I, PIPPA PASSES (1841)

Pippa Passes

Pippa Passes was published in April 1841 as the first number of the series *Bells and Pomegranates.* The play is set in 'delicious Asolo' (IV. 68), first visited by RB in 1838. He visited the town again in 1878, and for the last time in 1889, when he wrote much of the volume *Asolando* to which the town gives a title. Mrs Sutherland Orr reports that, at some point after that first visit, 'RB was walking alone, in a wood near Dulwich, when the image flashed upon him of someone walking thus alone through life; one apparently too obscure to leave a trace of his or her passage, yet exercising a lasting though unconscious influence at every step of it, and the image shaped itself into the little silk-winder of Asolo, Felippa or Pippa' (Orr, *Handbook*, 55). The form of the drama, four scenes linked by the decisive effect in the action of each of Pippa's song, overheard as she passes, seems to have been invented by RB. No close parallels have been adduced. The drama is built around a contrast between the sunny optimism of Pippa and a degraded and degrading cynicism best exemplified by Bluphocks, the 'English vagabond' who speaks at the end of scene II. RB explained the name as a coded reference to the buff and blue wrapper of the *Edinburgh Review*, which may suggest that the contrast between the two characters parallels at least in burlesque mode the troubled relationship between poets and their critics (the *Edinburgh Review* had published a wounding notice of RB's *Strafford* (*Edinburgh Review*, 65 (July 1837), 132–51), in which the broken dramatic speech given to Strafford himself puts the reviewer in mind of Mr Jingle in *Pickwick Papers* (144), and RB is identified as a member of 'the "Cockney school" of dramatic authorship' (147)). Bluphocks's cynicism, best revealed in an obscure speech (II. 254–270) in which he degrades a temple into a thieves' den and a rabbi into a receiver of stolen goods (RB was probably at work on *Pippa Passes* in 1838 when *Oliver Twist* was published), seems irredeemable, but Pippa's idealism is itself revealed as unacceptably naive, as in the speech (introduction, 80–147), in which she places on a simple ascending scale Sebald's adulterous love for Ottima, Jules's love for his bride, Phene, the love that his mother feels for Luigi, the patriotic assassin, and the worldly Bishop's love of God. The same simplicity is revealed in her firm persuasion that 'God's in his heaven— | All's right with the world!', a view that has often, though absurdly, been ascribed to RB himself. The decisions that her songs inspire in those who overhear them are matters of life and death (even for Jules, the sculptor, who represses his first impulse, to challenge his tormentors to a duel), but it does not follow that the reader is invited to approve them. Most often they induce mixed responses. Sebald's revulsion from the woman whose husband he has murdered does not seem manifestly superior to Ottima's anguished plea that God be merciful not to her but her lover, Luigi's mother offers a characterization of the revolutionary idealist too shrewd to dismiss out of hand—'he loves himself—and then, the world'—and there is a fine moral balance between the brutish Intendant, willing to purchase immunity by murdering Pippa, and the silkily ruthless Monsignor. *Pippa Passes* was the first of RB's plays that he chose to publish without offering it for production. RB wrote to Elizabeth Barrett, 26 February 1845, 'I like "Pippa" better than anything else I have done yet', *Correspondence*, x. 99.

New Year's Day. RB seems undecided whether the day is 1 January or the old new year's day, 25 March, new year's day in England until 1752. 25 March is suggested in I. 214 'The year's at the spring', III. 137–9 'Sure he's arrived— | The Tell-tale cuckoo—spring's his confidant, | And he lets out his April purposes!', but 1 January at the beginning of scene IV when Monsignor notes that the mildness is 'very unlike winter-weather', and that it is fourteen years and a month 'all but three days' since the death of his brother on 3 December.

l. 14. *my twelve-hours' treasure*. As Ottima notes in II. 225–6, 'we give | Them but one holiday the whole year round.'

l. 22. *happy tribes*. As in Milton, *Paradise Lost*, III. 532.

ll. 49–66. Longman compares Virgil, *Aeneid*, VIII. 22–5, and notes that the passage is quoted in Montaigne's essay 'Of Idleness' to figure how the idle mind may 'run into a thousand extravagances'.

l. 64. Probably the scarlet martagon (*lilium chalcedonicum*), the flowers of which are bright red and turban-shaped.

l. 66. *Turk bird*. Turkey.

l. 76. The weevil and chafer are beetles.

l. 78. *Gibe*. Mock, because the bee cannot reach the flower's pollen through the pane.

l. 90. *shrub-house*. Greenhouse or conservatory.

l. 100. The temple that Canova built at Possagno, his birthplace, in imitation of the Pantheon.

l. 142. *the dome*. The duomo or cathedral.

ll. 157–9. The point is that God is as fully present in events thought of as small as he is in events thought of as great.

l. 177. *cicale*. The cicada.

1. —Morning

l. 16. *Herds*. Herdsmen.

ll. 25–8. St Mark's and its belfry, the cathedral of Venice and its campanile, are some 30 miles from Asolo, Vicenza and Padua a little less. Asolo, the city of a thousand horizons, is celebrated for the views it affords. The glimpse of the campanile of St Mark's is disconcerting because it houses the Maleficio bell, rung to signal an execution.

l. 50. *wittol*. A complaisant cuckold.

l. 49. *passion's fruit*. As in Shelley, *Queen Mab*, VIII. 129.

l. 53. *Black?* Dark red wine is called 'vino nero', literally 'black wine'.

l. 56. *Benet the Capuchin*. A Franciscan friar, who is named after St Benet, a saint who had cured himself of fleshly desires by rolling in thorns and nettles, and who resolutely imposed stern discipline on all the abbeys he governed. The friars were called Capuchins after the pointed hood or 'capuche' which formed part of their habit.

l. 73. *proof-mark*. RB may mean the plate mark, the indentation left by the outline of the copper plate that proves an engraving genuine. Alternatively he may mean the mark, usually the artist's initials, with which the artist indicated that a print is approved.

l. 80. *officious coil*. Eagerness to please, fuss.

l. 124. *sputter*. Splutter.

l. 164. *campanula*. Bell-flower.

l. 188. *God's messenger*. Messenger translates angel. The angel most closely associated with the punishment of evil-doers and a sword is the Archangel Michael.

l. 201. Compare *Othello*, II. i. 186–7: 'If it were now to die, | 'Twere now to be most happy', and Keats 'Ode to a Nightingale', 55, 'Now more than ever seems it rich to die.'

l. 210. Compare Virgil, Eclogue VIII. 74–5, in which the lover binds three threads around the beloved. These constitute 'vincula Veneris', 78, the chains of Venus.

l. 229. *double heartsease*. A cultivated pansy, W. R. Campbell notes that 'the heartsease (viola tricolor) represents both thought (pensée) and willingness to love', 'A Note on Flowers in *Pippa Passes*', *Victorian Poetry*, 14.1 (Spring 1976), 62.

l. 249. *morbid.* Derived from the Italian 'morbidezza', used of paintings to signify a lifelike delicacy in flesh tints, though the ordinary English sense, diseased, lurks behind it.

[Stage direction]: *Talk* . . . *Statuary.* The conversation takes place as Pippa walks from the hillside to the valley of Orcana.

Statuary. Sculptor.

l. 280. *who's a defaulter?* Who has failed to turn up?

l. 283. *moonstrike.* Let him be moonstruck, that is distracted or deranged.

l. 285. *Trieste.* A port city north-east of Venice; *immortal poem* . . . *cramp couplets.* An arch allusion to RB's 'mammoth' poem *Sordello* and its hostile critical reception seems probable. The 'butterflies' are presumably the frivolous readers or critics who have responded unappreciatively to it.

l. 287. Bluphocks, identified by Furnivall as a play on the *Edinburgh Review*, the cover of which was buff, or fox, and blue.

l. 291. *Æsculapius* . . . *Cures.* A ponderous joke in which the absent poet is invited to write an epic poem entitled Aesculapius after the god of medicine, a poem in which a catalogue of drugs substitutes for the *Iliad*'s catalogue of ships. Hebe is the goddess of youth and cupbearer to the gods, and her 'plaister' is presumably a kiss. Phoebus Apollo is god of the sun, medicine, and poetry, and his 'emulsion', a medicine in which the active agent is held in suspension, is presumably wine. Mercury is the messenger of the gods, but also a drug commonly used to treat venereal disease. A bolus is a large pill. The reader is invited to supply the ellipsis with the words 'your pox'.

l. 297. *Delia* . . . *boy.* A strained allusion to Virgil, Eclogue III. 66–7, in which Menalcas boasts that his boy lover comes to him unasked so often that Delia or the moon (from Artemis' birth at Delos) is not better known to his dogs. The point seems to be that if the poet, Giovacchino, had written the poem suggested by the second student, he would have become as well known to the dogs or critics as Delia is to Amyntas' dogs.

l. 300. *in a tale.* In agreement.

l. 302. *stone-squarer.* The expression comically degrades the sculptor to a stonemason.

l. 304. *Possagno.* A small town less than 4 miles from Asolo, the birthplace of Canova.

l. 305. *He take up his portion.* He recognize himself as one of.

l. 308. *coxcomb as much as you choose.* However much of a coxcomb he may be.

ll. 317–320. Canova responded to the surprise of a gentleman who found the model for his Venus 'almost ugly rather than beautiful' that ideal beauty is perceived by the mind rather than by the 'material eyes' that see women in the flesh.

l. 335. *fribble.* Trifler.

l. 336. *The Model-Gallery*. The Canova Museum, the gypsoteca, built in 1836, that displays an almost complete collection of plaster casts of Canova's statues.

l. 338. *Psiche-fanciulla*. Psyche as a young girl. Psyche holds a butterfly, her name in Greek, to signify that she represents the soul. Jules recognizes it as a plaster cast of a statue the original of which he knows from Munich.

l. 341. *the unfinished Pietá*. Left at Canova's death as a clay model. The statue contrasts the Virgin with Mary Magdalen, both women grieving over the body of Christ.

l. 348. *predestinated*. The suggestion is that Jules believes that his artistic genius is divinely predestined.

l. 355. *Malamocco* is to the south of the Venetian Lido, separated from it by a canal. *Ohio* notes that much of the population was of Greek descent.

l. 356. *hair like sea-moss*. Compare Glaucippe's description of Ephebus, 'His hair curls more delightfully than sea-moss', in the first English translation of *Alciphron's Epistles* (1791), 146.

l. 359. *Tydeus*. One of the princes in Aeschylus' *Seven against Thebes*, who was exiled from his native Calydon after committing a murder.

l. 361. *Paolina* has copied the letter written by 1 Student in a feminine hand.

l. 364. *monitress*. Female mentor.

l. 366. *relations were in the way*. The bride's family would obstruct the match.

l. 368. *St—St!* Exclamations calling for silence.

l. 374. *Hannibal Scratchy*. That is Annibale Caracci, a nickname for 5 Student. Fielding had given the same comical misrendering of Caracci's name in *Joseph Andrews* 3, chapter 6.

II. —Noon.

l. 1. *Phene*. The name is chosen to suggest an appearance (as opposed to a reality).

l. 14. He has made a clay model of Tydeus but has still to carve the figure in marble.

l. 17. *block-work*. Probably roughly hewn, unfinished sculptures.

ll. 31–2. *minion of Coluthus*. Coluthus' poem on the rape of Helen, described, because of the poem's subject matter, as the poet's minion or mistress. The poem had been discovered by Cardinal Bessarion, the foremost Greek scholar of the earlier 15th century; *Bistre*. A brown pigment.

l. 33. Jules determines that the first Greek he hears Phene pronounce should be a line from Homer.

ll. 36–7. *Odyssey*, XXII. 8.

l. 39. *Almaign Kaiser*. German emperor.

ll. 43–4. Hippolyta was Queen of the Amazons. The horse she sits on reflects the fame of the Numidian cavalry.

l. 49. Harmodius is celebrated as a champion of democracy because of his killing of Hipparchus, brother of the Athenian tyrant. The sculpture that Phene has instructed Jules to carve illustrates the famous hymn, ascribed to Callistratus, in praise of Harmodius and his fellow assassin Aristogeiton. A paper in *Blackwood's Edinburgh Magazine*, 34 (1833), 265 complains that the magazine has been sent eight versions of the hymn, which is 'sufficient in all taste and in all conscience'. The singer or 'Praiser' is depicted wearing a bay wreath, which offers protection against thunder and lightning, his eyes blind to the outside world as he focuses his inward gaze on Harmodius. The singer's face is depicted at the centre of a tangle of arms and hands all reaching for the myrtle branch in which Harmodius concealed his sword.

l. 65. *fantastic*. Fanciful, the fancy being that Phene, rapt in the contemplation of Jules's statue, has become herself as fixed and silent as a statue.

ll. 68–78. The passage conflates two thoughts; that nature supplies the materials from which the artist produces a better nature, that is, art, and that all beauty has its ideal type in the beauty of the human body, as Jules demonstrates when he produces from the curves of a peach the body of a dryad or wood nymph.

ll. 80–98. Jules describes how he releases the potentialities of the materials with which he works; first the chalk with which he sketches his subjects, then the steel with which an engraving is produced, and finally the marble in which the potentialities of chalk and steel are combined.

l. 121. *Lutwyche*. The 1st Student.

ll. 195–210. Pippa sings a love song sung by a humble page to 'Kate', that is, Catherine Cornaro, who had been Queen of Cyprus until deposed by the Venetian Republic, after which she established her court at Asolo.

l. 202. *messes*. Meals.

ll. 218–19. Jules has summoned a soul in Phene, and is responsible for the new soul that he has brought into being.

l. 222. *Ancona*. The principal Italian port for Greece.

l. 234. *meet Lutwyche, in a duel*. In the courtship correspondence duelling elicited the most serious disagreement between RB and EBB. He persisted in defending the practice despite her objections to it.

l. 236. Jules's dream may owe something to Shelley's *Epipsychidion*, the speaker of which, the Preface indicates, died 'as he was preparing for a voyage to one of the wildest of the Sporades' with Emilia 'where it was his hope to have realised a scheme of life, suited perhaps to that happier and better world of which he is now an inhabitant'.

l. 244. *grig*. Cricket.

l. 245. *christmas faggot*. Bundle of twigs, usually ash, burnt ceremonially at Christmas.

l. 246. *the Armenian*. The Armenian Apostolic Orthodox Church or Gregorian Church is the most ancient of all Christian national churches.

l. 247. *Prussia Improper.* A play on 'Prussia Proper'. Compare *Don Juan*, X. 80. 1–2, 'From Poland they came on through Prussia Proper, | And Königsberg, the capital.'

l. 249. *Chaldee.* Aramaic, the language of the Bible. 'Translation of an Ancient Chaldee Manuscript', a celebrated satiric hoax produced by James Hogg and others, appeared in *Blackwood's Edinburgh Magazine* (October 1817).

l. 254. *Syriac.* A dialect of Aramaic.

l. 255. A scrap of a mnemonic poem devised by William of Sherwood to help students remember the valid forms of syllogism.

ll. 257–61. Jocular references to biblical stories; the plagues on Egypt called down by Moses, Jonah's escape to Tarshish, and Balaam's ass.

l. 263. William Beveridge, 1637–1708, Bishop of St Asaph's, was an expert on oriental languages, but Bluphocks is punning on beverage, and the use of the word bishop to refer to mulled, spiced port.

l. 264. *Greek dog-sage.* The Greek Cynics were thought to be named for their 'dog-like' qualities. The best known Cynic sage was Diogenes.

ll. 264–70. Charon is the ferryman who, on payment of a coin such as an obolus, transported dead souls over the Styx, one of the rivers of Hell, the gates of which were guarded by the three-headed dog Cerberus. Lupin seeds were commonly chewed in Italy. Hecate is the three-headed goddess of the underworld. A coble is a boat, Charon's ferry. An Intendant is an Austrian officer, either civil or military. Zwanzigers are Austrian coins.

l. 274. *Prince Metternich.* The Austrian foreign minister and chief architect of the post-Napoleonic settlement of Europe at the Congress of Vienna under which Lombardy-Venetia passed to Austria.

l. 280. Panurge consults Hertrippa, an astrologer who predicts that Panurge will be cuckolded, robbed, and beaten by his wife in Rabelais's *Gargantua and Pantagruel*, III. 25. In Acts 26: 27, St Paul asks, 'King Agrippa, believest thou the prophets?'

ll. 288–92. Marks in the Austrian passport prepared for Luigi constitute a code that 2 Policeman interprets.

l. 298. *the Carbonari.* Members of a revolutionary secret society that opposed Austrian rule in Italy.

l. 299. *Spielberg.* Spielberg or Spilberk Castle in Brno was the most secure prison in the Austro-Hungarian empire.

III

Turret. The turret of the castle of Rocca in Asolo.

ll. 6–7. Luigi chooses to call out the names of two republican heroes; Aristogeiton who assassinated Hipparchus, and Lucius Junius Brutus, who expelled Lucius Tarquinius Superbus, the last king of Rome. Katharine Bronson records that in 1889 RB recalled the echo that he had discovered on his first visit to Asolo fifty years earlier. 'Browning in Asolo', *Century Magazine*, 59 (April 1900), 928.

l. 18. *Pellicos.* Silvio Pellico was a dramatist and journalist, an associate of the Carbonari and determined opponent of Austrian rule, who was imprisoned in Spielberg from 1822 until 1830. He is best known for his account of his prison experiences *Le mie prigioni* (*My Prisons*), 1832.

ll. 23–4. The reference is probably to Francis I, who ruled as Emperor of Austria 1804–35. He was an implacable opponent of reform but was also distinguished by his domestic virtues and personal affability.

l. 50. *cicales.* Cicadas.

l. 67. The metaphor is of a wine-press.

ll. 121–2. The names seem to be imaginary.

ll. 134–7. Austria acquired the provinces of Milan, Lombardy, and Venetia at the Congress of Vienna, 1814–15.

ll. 145–6. Astrologically, Jupiter is a bringer of good fortune.

ll. 147–9. Revelation 22: 16, 'I am the root and the off-spring of David, and the bright and morning star', and Revelation 2: 28, 'I will give him the morning star', he being responsible for the nations being 'broken to shivers'.

l. 150. Chiara is Luigi's betrothed.

ll. 161–2. The 'Malchiostro Annunciation' in the cathedral of Treviso: the subject would have an obvious significance for a couple planning to marry.

ll. 163ff. Pippa's song was first published in Fox's *Monthly Repository*, immediately after an article 'On Organic [that is, root and branch] Reforms', in which Fox protests against a speech in which Lord John Russell repudiates such reforms, distinguishes between the 'Whig' and the 'Radical' reformers on the grounds that the Whig reformers espouse a principle of expediency that make them always willing to compromise, and ends by setting itself against hereditary privilege, which is located principally in the unreformed House of Lords, but Fox hints that he might even be prepared to extend his objection to the monarchy.

l. 230. *fig-peckers.* That is, beccaficos, small songbirds eaten as a delicacy in Italy.

l. 231. *lampreys.* Eel-like fish commonly cooked in wine, compare John Gay, 'To a Young Lady, with some Lampreys': 'Why then send lampreys? Fye, for shame! | 'Twill set a virgin's blood on flame', 19–20; the area around Breganze is famous for wine.

l. 244. A 'deuzan' is an apple, so called because it is supposed to keep two years, a 'junketing' (jenneting) an early apple named after St John, and a 'leather coat' a russet apple named for the roughness of its skin.

l. 275. Those sunshiny beetles, probably the golden fly beetle, *cetonia aurata*.

l. 279. *Cecco.* Abbreviation of Francesco.

l. 286. *ortolans.* Small birds much prized by epicures.

l. 290. The young women have been suborned by Bluphocks to approach Pippa.

ll. 305–6. All that remains of me will be the one violet growing from a grave.

IV

l. 1. *Monsignor*, the form of address used for a bishop.

l. 3. *Benedicto benedicatur*. A standard but significantly terse grace said at the end of a meal, which the Bishop has presumably just finished.

l. 7. *Assumption Day*. Commonly 15 August.

ll. 14–15. Ascoli Piceno, Fermo, and Fossombrone are cathedral cities in the Italian Marche which was at that time under papal rule.

l. 42. *Antonio da Correggio* (1490–1534). Vasari identifies Correggio as 'the first who began to work in the modern manner in Lombardy', and stresses that he worked independently, without being influenced by 'the ancient or the best of the modern', although Vasari views this as a deficiency.

l. 59. *liberty*. A specially granted privilege or immunity.

ll. 66–8. Forli and Cesena are towns in Emilio-Romagna. Both had been occupied by Napoleon, and both, in consequence were in some turmoil in the 1820s. The Carbonari were strong in the area.

l. 67. *interdict*. A sentence by which an individual is debarred from taking the sacraments.

l. 84. *soldo*. A coin of little value (a twentieth of a lira); *Millet-cake*. Millet is a cheap alternative to wheat.

l. 89. *off-scouring*. 1 Corinthians 4: 13, 'we are made as the filth of the world, and are the offscouring of all things unto this day'.

l. 91. *unaccountably*. That is, abominations for which he has not been held to account.

l. 100. *forgive us our trespasses*. From the Lord's Prayer as given in the Anglican Book of Common Prayer. Trespasses are sins.

ll. 101. *a very worm*. Compare Job 25: 6: 'man, that is a worm, and the son of man, which is a worm.'

l. 122. *complot*. Conspiracy.

l. 127. *seven times*. A biblical intensifier, as when Peter asks if he should forgive his brother 'seven times' and Jesus replies that he should rather forgive him 'seventy times seven', Matthew 18: 21–2.

l. 138. *English knave*. i.e. Bluphocks.

l. 155. *the Seven and One*. 'Seek him that maketh the seven stars . . . The Lord is his name' (Amos 5: 8).

l. 164. *Miserere mei, Domine*. 'Have mercy on me, O God', the opening of Psalm 51, one of the Seven Penitential Psalms.

l. 166. *dray*. Nest.

l. 167. *tomb*. That is, its chrysalis.

l. 169. *hedge-shrew*. *OED* guesses this to be the shrew-mouse, but this is the only citation; *lob-worm*. More commonly the lug-worm.

l. 199. *Psalms* 8: 5, in answer to the question, 'What is man?': 'For thou hast made him a little lower than the angels'.

l. 201. *that regard to spare*. That expression to forgive, Monsignor's sanctimonious expression. 'Regard' in later editions became 'proud look'.

ll. 215–22. Compare Pippa's distaste for the cultivated pansy with Perdita's distaste for cultivated flowers such as carnations and 'streak'd gillyvors', *The Winter's Tale*, IV. iv. 81–5.

l. 229. Pippa arrests herself before remarking on Zanze's breasts.

l. 234. The markings on the pansy's petals resemble eyes.

l. 244. *mavis, merle and throstle*. The song thrush, the blackbird, and thrush.

l. 247. *Howlet*. Owl.

l. 248. *chantry*. A chapel in which masses are sung for the souls of the dead.

l. 249. *sisterhoods*. Communities of nuns.

l. 250. *complines*. The last service of the day in Catholic ritual.

l. 251. *twats*. RB explained to Furnivall that he was misled into believing that the word denoted some part of a nun's attire by his creditably innocent interpretation of a ribald 17th-century couplet, ''Tis said they will give him a Cardinal's hat: | They sooner will give him an old nun's twat!' (Furnivall, 135).

FROM *BELLS AND POMEGRANATES*, NO. III, *DRAMATIC LYRICS* (1842)

[*My Last Duchess*] *Italy and France. I. Italy*

Published in *Dramatic Lyrics* as *Italy*, entitled *My Last Duchess* from 1849. Louis S. Friedland, 'Ferrara and "My Last Duchess"', *Studies in Philology*, 33.4 (1936), 656–84, argues that RB's Duke is based on Alfonso II (1533–98), fifth Duke of Ferrara, who in 1558 took as his first wife Lucrezia, the 14-year-old daughter of Cosimo de' Medici. When she died, just turned 17, there were suspicions that she had been poisoned. His second wife, Barbara, the daughter of Ferdinand I Emperor of Austria, was first introduced to Alfonso at Innsbruck. After her death Alfonso married for a third time. Alfonso was a patron of the arts, and of the poets Tasso and Guarini. The details are suggestive, but RB's Duke seems more generic than Friedland is prepared to admit.

l. 1. *Painted on the wall*. The expression may suggest a fresco, but intimate portraits of this kind were more commonly in the 16th century painted in oil on board, and the attempt to capture a 'faint | Half-flush' (18–19) seems to accord better with oil.

l. 3. *Fra Pandolf*. An imaginary painter monk, though Pilkington's *Dictionary of Artists* (1805), known to RB, lists as flourishing in 1640 a Pesaro painter named Gian (Giovanni) Giacomo Pandolfi.

l. 25. Either a love token given her by the Duke, or a family crest.

l. 27. *bough of cherries*. In the traditional 'Cherry-Tree Carol' the cherries, at the behest of the unborn Jesus, attest the pregnant Mary's innocence by bowing down to her after she has been accused of infidelity by Joseph. The carol ends when the unborn baby sings, 'O eat your cherries, Mary, | O eat your cherries now; | O eat your cherries, Mary, | That grow upon the bough.'

l. 28. *white mule*. The Queen rides a 'cream-white mule' in Tennyson's 'Sir Launcelot and Queen Guinevere', 31, published in May 1842. 'My Last Duchess' appeared in November.

l. 30. *forward*. Prompt or eager, though shaded by the pejorative sense, immodest.

l. 33. *nine hundred years old name*. The Este family could date its claim to Ferrara only to 1146, though the House of Este traced itself back to the time of Charlemagne (742–814).

l. 35. *trifling*. Frivolous behaviour.

l. 38. *disgusts*. Weaker than the modern sense, signifying that the behaviour is not to his taste.

ll. 45–6. Hiram Corson records that when he asked RB in the 1880s about the fate of the Duchess RB replied, '"Yes, I meant that the commands were that she be put to death." And then, after a pause, he added, with a characteristic dash of expression, and as if the thought had just started up in his mind, "Or he might have had her shut up in a convent"', *An Introduction to the Study of Robert Browning's Poetry*, 3rd edn., 1903, p. viii.

l. 49. *Count*. In Italian titles of nobility count ranks below marquis, which itself ranks below duke.

l. 54. *Neptune*. God of the sea, but also, as Neptunus Equester, god of horses; *Claus of Innsbruck*. An imaginary sculptor, but Innsbruck, that RB had visited in 1838, was famous for its bronzes, particularly the 28 historical bronzes in the Hofkirche or Court Church.

[*Soliloquy of the Spanish Cloister*] *Camp and Cloister. II. Cloister (Spanish)*

On its first publication in 1842, the poem was paired with *Incident of the French Camp* under the title *Camp and Cloister*, suggesting that both poems are studies of enclosed male communities. As in *My Last Duchess* the object of the speaker's vituperation, although entirely silent, somehow achieves a strongly marked character. Brother Lawrence seems as innocent as the Duchess, though far more Miss Bates-like in the harmless inconsequentiality of his conversation. The sins that the speaker imputes to Brother Lawrence, especially lust, clearly indicate the sins that he is most anxious to deny in himself.

l. 3. *Brother Lawrence*. The name may recall the kindly Friar Lawrence in *Romeo and Juliet*; *God's blood*. The context exacerbates the blasphemy of the oath.

l. 10. *Salve tibi*. Greetings to you, presumably Brother Lawrence's friendly acknowledgement of the speaker.

l. 13. The crop from cork trees is vulnerable to drought.

l. 14. *oak-galls*. Growths produced on oaks after gall wasps have laid their eggs in the bark. The galls were used to produce a fine ink for use on vellum or parchment.

l. 15. The Latin name for parsley is 'apium', although Brother Lawrence's enquiry seems inconsequential.

l. 16. Swine's Snout, latin *Rostrum porcinum*, a name for the dandelion. The insult has biblical authority: 'As a jewel of gold in a swine's snout, so is a fair woman which is without discretion' (Proverbs 11: 22).

l. 24. *his lily snaps*. Presumably indicating that the speaker has destroyed one of Brother Lawrence's flowers (see l. 48).

l. 25. *Dolores*. The name, meaning sorrows, refers to the Seven Sorrows of the Virgin.

l. 27. *Sanchicha*. The Spanish name means 'holy'.

l. 31. Barbary corsairs or pirates were notorious for taking captive Christian women.

l. 33. *refection*. The communal meal taken by monks.

ll. 33–6. The speaker, unlike Brother Lawrence, after he has finished eating lays his knife and fork across his plate in the shape of a cross, a custom that Charles Panati claims had its origin in 17th-century Italy, where it marked 'a pious act of thanksgiving' for the meal, *Extraordinary Origin of Everyday Things*, 1987, 81.

ll. 37–40. Augustine illustrates the doctrine of the Trinity by arguing that a spring, a river, and drinking water are all 'members in the trinity called water' (*Augustine in his Own Words*, ed. William Harmless, 2010, 283). The speaker exemplifies the doctrine more literally by drinking his orange juice in three sips. Arianism is the heresy of those who deny that Jesus Christ is of the same substance as God.

ll. 47–8. Melon plants will not fruit unless the melon flowers are pollinated.

ll. 49–52. RB admitted in a letter of April 1888 that he was 'not careful to be correct' (*Studies in Browning and his Circle*, 2 (1974), 62). His reference may be to Galatians 5: 19–22 which lists a catalogue of some eighteen sins of the flesh: 'Adultery, fornication, uncleanness, lasciviousness, idolatry, witchcraft, hatred, variance, emulations, wrath, strife, seditions, heresies, envying, murders, drunkenness, revellings, and such like.' The speaker is evidently guilty of a good number of these. A text from Galatians that has clearly failed to catch the speaker's attention is, 'For all the law is fulfilled in one word, even in this; thou shalt love thy neighbour as thyself' (5: 14).

ll. 53–6. Compare *Hamlet*, III. iii. 91–6 in which Hamlet proposes to kill Claudius when he is 'about some act | That has no relish of salvation in't, | Then trip him that his heels may kick at heaven, | And that his soul may be as damned and black | As hell whereto it goes.'

l. 56. *Manichee*. Literally a follower of the prophet Mani, who conceived of the world as the scene of a contest between independent principles of light and darkness or good and evil. The speaker seems to use the word in a more general sense, implying simply that Brother Lawrence is a heretic. The irony is that Galatians, the book of the Bible that the speaker most values, makes so emphatic a distinction between 'the flesh' and 'the Spirit' (4: 29) that it was frequently cited by Manichaeans. A further irony is that in Galatians Paul emphasizes that salvation comes not from 'the works of the law' but from 'the faith of Jesus Christ' (2: 16), which serves only to expose the speaker's belief in the efficacy of formal ritual. See Miriam K. Starkman, 'The Manichee in the Cloister: A Reading of Browning's "Soliloquy of the Spanish Cloister"', *Modern Language Notes*, 75.5 (1960), 399–405.

l. 57. *scrofulous*. In a general metaphorical sense, to suggest that the novel is corrupt and corrupting. The reference suggests that the monologue is contemporary rather than historical.

l. 58. The cheap production suggests that the novel is pornographic rather than racy, a novel such as *Gamiani ou deux nuits d'excès*, cheaply published in 1833 and commonly ascribed to Alfred de Musset. Like many pornographic novels it was illustrated by lithographs that have been attributed to Achille Deveria.

l. 60. *Belial*. 'than whom a Spirit more lewd | Fell not from heaven' (*Paradise Lost*, I. 490–1).

l. 64. *sieve*. A gardener's basket.

ll. 65–8. Folk tales are common of wily peasants who outwit the devil by leaving a loophole in their indenture or contract with him.

l. 69. *rose acacia*. An impressive flowering shrub which produces pendent rose-pink blooms.

l. 70. *Hy, Zy, Hine*. The reference is obscure. James F. Loucks offers as a source the *Heptameron* or *Elementa Magica* ascribed to Pietro of Abano, whose life and work RB knew, in which the words occur, though not consecutively and 'Zy' only approximately, in a section on spells used to conjure demons. '"Hy, Zy, Hine" and Peter of Abano', *Victorian Poetry*, 12.2 (1974), 165–9.

l. 71. *Vespers*. The speaker hears the bell summoning him to Vespers, in Catholic ritual the sixth of the seven canonical hours.

l. 71–2. The 'Hail, Mary' prayer begins, 'Ave Maria, gratia plena'. The point is, presumably, that the prayer to the Virgin immediately follows the spell to raise a demon, revealing the Manichaean character of the speaker.

In a Gondola

RB wrote the first seven lines of the poem extempore as a catalogue entry for Daniel Maclise's *The Serenade* before it was exhibited at the British Institute in 1842. RB had not yet seen the painting, having only John Forster's description to work from, and when he did thought it 'somewhat too jolly' for the lines that he had composed (Furnivall, 24). *The Art-Union*, 4 (April 1842), 76, agreed, quoting RB's lines 'as an example of exceedingly rich and graceful versification from the pen of a poet, kindred to Maclise in imagination and mind', but describing Maclise's cavalier as 'a sonneteering galliard, who will sing the same vows to many other maidens before he sleeps'. RB had visited Venice in 1838. The date at which the poem is set is uncertain, but, given the reference to a painting by Giordano, cannot be earlier than the mid-17th century. RB's poem is operatic in its form, and in its heady blending of the erotic and the violent, but also suggests the influence of Shakespeare's *Romeo and Juliet*, and possibly *The Merchant of Venice*. The elopement of Lorenzo and Jessica may have prompted the uncomfortable references to Jews in 64–9, and 113.

I. Later editions add the direction 'He sings'.

l. 3. *bears part.* Accompanies, as in music.

II. later editions add the direction, 'She speaks'.

l. 22. *the Three.* Presumably family members, possibly the husband and his brothers, from whom the relationship must be hidden. The term is chosen as evocatively Venetian. Compare the Venetian councils commonly referred to as 'the Ten' and 'the Forty', both terms that RB knew from Byron's *Marino Faliero* and *The Two Foscari*.

l. 26. The rich fabrics curtaining the partition wall may suggest a disparity in wealth between the mistress and her lover, a difference that the mistress may be repudiating in ll. 122–3 when she throws away the 'foolish jewel' that she had been wearing in her hair.

ll. 31–6. The alchemist's art was introduced into medieval Europe by Arab practitioners. Alchemists sought to rid substances, amongst them precious stones, of their impurities, by dissolving them to produce a spirit or elixir of the substance.

l. 33. *cruce.* crucible.

l. 34 *mage.* A possessor of esoteric wisdom.

l. 35 *use.* May have a specifically sexual sense.

IV. Later editions add the direction 'He sings'.

l. 44. The Palazzo Pucci is in Florence, not Venice.

l. 47. *wried.* Twisted.

V. Later editions add the direction 'She sings'.

l. 49. Moth's kiss, a term coined through analogy with a butterfly kiss, often understood as a kiss with the eyelashes. Longman compares Shelley, *The Sensitive-Plant*, 50–1: 'soft moths that kiss | The sweet lips of the flowers.'

VI. Later editions add the direction 'He sings'

ll. 63–78. Vampiric or Eucharistic fantasies in which the lover imagines the blood of his mistress being consumed. Blood libels against the Jews of the kind indicated in the first of the two stanzas were widely disseminated. In the second stanza the speaker seems to imagine himself a spirit whose wings will only achieve their full power through an infusion of the mistress's blood.

l. 69. The word omitted is presumably 'blood'.

VII. Later editions add the direction 'He muses'.

VIII. Later editions add the direction 'He speaks, musing'.

l. 104. *He and the Couple*. The Three.

l. 107. *Himself*. Presumably the husband.

l. 111. *sains*. Blesses (by making the sign of the cross).

l. 113. There is a Jewish cemetery at San Nicolo on the Lido.

X. Later editions add the direction 'She replies, musing'.

l. 117. Compare Shelley, *Queen Mab*, 1–2: 'How wonderful is Death, | Death and his brother Sleep!'

XI. Later editions add the direction 'He speaks'.

l. 127. The Giudecca, the canal that separates the island of Giudecca from the central islands of Venice to its north.

l. 141. *loory*. Commonly 'lory', a bird rather like a parakeet.

l. 148. Smyrna, modern-day Izmir in Turkey. The area is still famous for its peaches.

ll. 151–4. An unlikely tale, prompted perhaps by goddesses such as Hygeia, the goddess of health, often represented holding a snake, or by the popularity of the snake in Roman jewellery.

l. 172. *chords*. Strings.

ll. 174–6. Babylon is associated with pillars because the Temple of Solomon was plundered by the Babylonians, and its pillars carried back to Babylon (2 Kings 25: 13).

l. 179. *lymph*. Water.

ll. 182–3. Longman compares Hazlitt, 'Of Persons One Would Wish to Have Seen'. In a 'room that was hung round with several portraits of eminent painters [amongst them paintings by Titian and Giorgione] . . . it seemed that all at once they glided from their frames, and seated themselves at some little distance from us'; *Schidone*. Bartolomeo Schedoni (1578–1615). The eager Duke is presumably his patron, the Duke of Parma.

l. 187. *Haste-thee-luke*. Luca Giordano (1634–1705), Italian painter nicknamed 'Luca Fa-presto' (Luke Work-quickly) in tribute to the speed with which he completed paintings, or, in a popular story, because his mercenary father used these words to encourage him to work more quickly.

l. 189. *Castelfranco*. Giorgione, formally Giorgio Barbarelli da Castelfranco (in or before 1477– 1510). There is no Magdalen amongst Giorgione's authenticated works, but a great number of paintings have at some time been attributed to him.

l. 191. *Ser*. An Italian honorific, roughly equivalent to the English 'Sir'.

l. 192. *the Tizian*. That is, a portrait by Titian (1485/90–1576) of a Venetian politician. As Vasari notes, 'There has been scarce a single lord of great name, or prince, or great lady, who has not been portrayed by Tiziano.' The speaker fancifully imagines the portrait's subject gazing at a desk, littered now with feminine gewgaws, on which he had once put his signature to a document, an act for which he was later murdered.

XIII. Later editions add the direction 'She speaks'.

ll. 205–6. Zorzi is presumably the name of the lover's manservant, Zanze (a name that RB also uses in *Sordello* and *Pippa Passes*) of the mistress's maidservant.

l. 214. The epithet, 'vigilant', is transferred from Zanze to her taper or candle.

l. 221. Siora, a contraction of Signora, and the strongest indication in the poem that the mistress is a married woman.

XV. Later editions add the direction 'He is surprised, and stabbed'.

l. 230. Longman compares *Romeo and Juliet*, V. iii. 120: 'Thus with a kiss I die.'

Artemis Prologuizes

RB reported in a letter to Julia Wedgwood that on 10 April 1841 while lying ill in bed he had begun to compose in his head a play of which he could remember on his recovery only the prologue (*Wedgwood*, 102). The anecdote recalls the story that Coleridge prefaced to 'Kubla Khan' in which he presents the poem as the fragment that he managed to transcribe of a much longer poem that he had composed in his sleep. The play RB imagined was a sequel to Euripides' *Hippolytus*, which ends when Hippolytus is killed at the instigation of Aphrodite because Hippolytus pays his devotions not to her, but to Artemis, goddess of chastity. Hippolytus refuses the love offered him by his stepmother Phaedra, who responds by hanging herself, leaving a letter accusing Hippolytus of rape. Her husband Theseus curses his son, who is killed when he falls from his chariot and is dragged to death by the horses, a death contrived by Poseidon, Theseus' father, who terrifies the horses when he emerges from the sea in the form of a monstrous bull. Artemis explains to Theseus his mistake, and Hippolytus lives long enough to forgive his father. In the sequel Artemis was to have restored Hippolytus to life with the help of Asclepios only to be disappointed when Hippolytus fell in love not with her but with Aricia, one of her nymphs, who gave her name to Arricia, the town near Rome founded by Hippolytus (DeVane, *Handbook*, 19–20). The poem was praised by Matthew Arnold as 'one of the very best antique fragments I know' (*Letters of Matthew Arnold*, ed. Cecily Y. Lang, 1996, 383). In the poem Browning uses the spelling 'Hippolutos' which we retain in the poem but we use the more common 'Hippolytus' in the notes.

Prologuizes. Speaks the prologue

l. 1. *ambrosial*. Celestial, ambrosia being the food of the Olympic gods. Here or Hera, wife of Zeus. Her emblem was the peacock, hence her association with pride.

l. 4. *lucid*. Bright

l. 6. Artemis cares for animals as the goddess of hunting.

l. 7. *fox-bitch*. A vixen is more commonly termed a 'bitch fox'.

ll. 10–12. The temple of Artemis Agrotera (Artemis the huntress) is one of the most important classical sites in central Athens. It is Demeter rather than Artemis who is usually associated with the poppy.

l. 13. *Of such this youth*. Hippolytus, who is one of the chaste; *Asclepios*. God of medicine.

l. 14. *buskined*. Booted: a buskin is not only a hunting boot but the boot worn by Greek tragic actors.

l. 15. *wild-wood leafy ways*. Compare Thomas Dermody, 'An Heroic Epistle to M. G. Lewis Esq. M.P.', 'Oft in youth's idle summer have I stray'd | Delighted through the wild wood's leafy shade' (99–100). Oxford compares 'wild wood-leaves', *Cymbeline*, IV. ii. 393.

l. 17. *ounce*. Usually the lynx.

l. 21. *gadbee*. Gadfly.

l. 27. Hippolytus was Theseus' son by the Amazon, Hippolyta.

l. 30. *swerving*. Deviating from right conduct, as in 'Firm we subsist, but possible to swerve' (*Paradise Lost*, IX. 359).

l. 39. *ai ai!* Alas!

l. 40. RB follows *Hippolytus*, 1189, in which Euripides explains that the charioteer fitted his feet into a foot-rest.

l. 42. Henetian or Enetian horses were much esteemed. RB takes the detail from Euripides.

l. 46. *obscene*. Loathsome, but probably punning with the (false) etymological sense of the word to denote something that can only take place offstage.

l. 51. *trammelled*. Fettered.

l. 52. *circling rein*. Euripides explains that Hippolytus had fastened the reins around his body.

l. 54. *trace*. The strap harnessing the horse to the chariot.

l. 60. *mooned fronts*. The horses have a white star on the forehead.

l. 67. *in a flood of glory visible*. Artemis as Luna wears as a crown the crescent moon.

l. 73. *Athenai*. Athens.

l. 75. *cross-way*. Artemis was sometimes known as Artemis of the Cross-roads, because of her identification with Hecate.

l. 75–6. Honey-cake is a traditional offering to the gods. Dogs and dog sacrifice were especially associated with Artemis and Hecate.

l. 79. *favours*. The sense seems to be that the crowns, once devotional objects, have become merely decorative.

l. 87. Cutting the hair was a conventional sign of grief in ancient Greece.

ll. 101–2. Asclepios is the son of Phoebus (Phoibos) Apollo, who was Artemis' twin brother.

l. 106. *lavers*. Cleansing waters as in *Samson Agonistes*, 1726–8, 'and from the stream | With lavers pure, and cleansing herbs wash off | The clotted gore'.

l. 106. Compare the transferred epithet in 'murdered cheeks' with Keats's proleptic description of Lorenzo riding in the company of Isabella's two brothers as 'their murder'd man', *Isabella: or, the Pot of Basil*, 209.

l. 114–16. The asklepian, the serpent-entwined staff that Asklepios is commonly represented as carrying.

l. 117. *pharmacies.* Treatments with medicinal drugs.

l. 118. *sister nymphs.* Presumably the seven nymphs who were attendants on Artemis, and were saved from Orion, who had fallen in love with one of them, by being transformed into seven stars, the Pleiades.

l. 120. *the Twain.* Artemis and Hippolytus. Artemis imagines that she will lie on the grass with Hippolytus until he awakes rather as Cupid and Psyche lie together 'on the bedded grass' in the first stanza of Keats's 'Ode to Psyche'.

Waring

The poem has always been associated with the precipitate emigration to New Zealand of RB's friend Alfred Domett in April 1842. The association was first made by RB whose letter to Domett of 15 May 1843, as Longman notes, clearly paraphrases lines 192–6 of the poem: 'What shall I tell you?—that we are dead asleep in literary things and in great want of a "rousing word" (as the old puritans phrase it) from New Zealand or any place *out* of this snoring dormitory' (*Correspondence*, vii. 124). But the likeness is approximate. Waring paces London with 'no work done, but great works undone'. Domett had already published *Poems* in 1833, and an ambitious long poem *Venice* in 1839. 'Waring' seems as much a fanciful self-portrait as a portrait of Domett, embodying not only RB's recurrent dream of escape into a simpler, freer mode of life, but the sense of great but unfulfilled talents that suffuses *Pauline*, *Paracelsus*, and *Sordello*.

l. 4. The boots and chest are associated with sailors; the staff and scrip (or satchel) with pilgrims who travel by land.

l. 16. *prose-poet.* Still in 1842 a rare designation, but sometimes applied to Carlyle, by, for example, J. A. Heraud in his review of *The French Revolution* in *Fraser's Magazine*, 16 (July 1837), 100.

l. 20. At dawn ghosts must return to their resting place. The ghost in *Hamlet* fades 'on the crowing of the cock' (I. i. 157).

l. 22. Matthew Arnold's brother Tom, who met Domett in New Zealand in 1848, described him as 'of a passionate fiery nature; full of suppressed energy; as proud as Lucifer' (Jane Stafford and Mark Williams, *Maoriland: New Zealand Literature 1872–1914* (Wellington: University of Victoria Press, 2006), 29.

l. 27. Compare 'contrast | The petty Done the Undone vast', 'The Last Ride Together', 52–3.

l. 33. *blurs.* Ink-stains.

l. 38. *chance-blades.* Ears of corn growing where the seed fell by chance.

l. 54. Playing on Virgil's description of Polyphemus, 'Monstrum horrendum, informe, ingens', a horrid, shapeless, huge monster, *Aeneid*, III. 658. Lines 54–5 may be at once a description and a parody of the prose style already recognized as Carlylese. Domett was in fact an admirer of Carlyle, describing himself to C. A. Dillon in 1850 as 'all for inspiration, old prophets, and Carlyle' (*An Encyclopedia of New Zealand*, 1966, entry on Domett).

l. 56. *graphic*. Vivid description.

l. 59. *swimmingly*. Through tears.

ll. 65–73. The young men, priggishly believing themselves obliged to be strictly truthful, brutally insisted on sharing with the woman their opinion of her.

ll. 77–8. The point seems to be that, though an object of contempt, the woman has risen to a height that the young men cannot reach.

l. 78. *the flowers*. Of the grave.

l. 84. Compare *Hamlet*, III. ii. 374, 'They fool me to the top of my bent.'

ll. 92–3. Longman notes the allusion to Perrault's 'Little Thumb', in which an ogre and his wife have seven daughters each of whom wears a golden crown and has 'very long sharp teeth' with which they bite little children 'in order to suck their blood'.

ll. 99–100. Echoing 1 Samuel 4: 21: 'And she named the child Ichabod, saying, The glory is departed from Israel.'

l. 103. *upstarted*. Who has suddenly appeared.

l. 108. *Vishnu-land*. India where Vishnu is a principal god. *Avatar*. The incarnation of a God, as Krishna was an incarnation of Vishnu.

l. 109. RB had travelled to Russia in 1834, not to Moscow but St Petersburg, where he met a Russian diplomat named Waring (Maynard, *Browning's Youth*, 128).

l. 112. Serpentine and siennite (more commonly syenite or sienite) are ornamental rocks; serpentine is dull green with snake-like markings, sienite is a crystalline rock akin to granite.

ll. 115–19. Silk is an effective protection against sword cuts.

ll. 122–5. Aeschylus records in the *Agamemnon* that Agamemnon and Menelaus throw down their sceptres in grief when they realize that they can only appease Artemis, who has denied the Greek fleet wind, by sacrificing Agamemnon's daughter Iphigenia. Euripides in *Iphigenia at Aulis* represents Iphigenia as refusing the protection of Achilles and willingly sacrificing herself for her country. In *Iphigenia in Tauris* Artemis intervenes at the last moment and transports Iphigenia to Tauris (modern-day Crimea) where she becomes a priestess in Artemis' temple.

ll. 130–1. *myrrhy lands*. Arabia; Scythia included the modern Ukraine, Georgia, and southern Russia.

l. 131. *whirlblast*. Hurricane, a word introduced to poetry by Wordsworth, but here perhaps suggested by Shelley's description of the 'austral lake' in *The Witch of Atlas* as 'like a meadow which no scythe has shaven, | Which rain could never bend, or whirl-blast shake' (425–6), RB's Scythia recalling Shelley's scythe.

ll. 146–51. RB would have known of Benjamin Haydon and his ambition to revive fresco painting in Britain through his acquaintance and Haydon's follower, George Lance (Maynard, *Browning's Youth*, 102).

l. 152. *Polidoro da Caravaggio*. RB kept an engraving of his fresco of Andromeda above his desk.

l. 155–6. Cherries are picked in July, hops in September.

ll. 156–7. *prime | Of March*. Mid-March.

ll. 178–82. Waring is compared to monarchs who hold at their coronation an orb signifying their rule over the world.

ll. 185–6. *Garrick*. David Garrick (1717–79), foremost actor-manager of the 18th century. One of his most famous roles was Hamlet, who says to Guildenstern, 'you would pluck out the heart of my mystery' (III. ii. 368).

l. 188. *Junius*. The pseudonym of the author of a series of letters published between 1769 and 1772 attacking governmental corruption; *tuck*. Roll up.

ll. 190–1. Thomas Chatterton (1752–70), the precocious poet who had, before committing suicide when he was 17, written a series of pseudo-medieval poems that he claimed to have transcribed from the manuscripts of a 15th-century Bristol monk, Thomas Rowley. In his essay on Chatterton RB defended the escapade as an extravagant expression of the imitativeness essential to poets of genius in their earliest work.

l. 208. On his second trip to Italy in 1838 RB docked at Trieste.

l. 216. *lateen sail*. The triangular sail common on Mediterranean boats such as the felucca.

l. 223. *Lascar*. A sailor from the East Indies.

l. 231. *long-shore*. A commonly pejorative term for those employed along the shore.

l. 236. *grass hat*. Straw hat.

l. 249. *sea-calf*. Seal.

ll. 254–5. The point is that whenever a star sinks below the horizon it rises above the horizon at some other point on the globe.

l. 256. *Look East*. Reversing Walter Scott's contention that the European living in the east (Batavia is modern-day Indonesia) dreams only of home: 'Look east, and ask the Belgian why, | Beneath Batavia's sultry sky, | He seeks not eager to inhale | The freshness of the mountain gale.' Introduction to *Marmion*, Canto Third, 129–32.

The Pied Piper of Hamelin; A Child's Story

RB recalled that he wrote the poem in spring 1842, for Willie Macready, the 8-year-old son of the actor-manager William Macready, to illustrate when he was ill in bed. It has remained a favourite with children. RB first encountered the story in Nathaniel Wanley's *Wonders of the Little World, or A General and*

Complete History of Man (1678), a favourite book that had been presented to him by his father when he was 13. It was a favourite story of his father, who abandoned his own attempt to render it in verse after he had seen his son's effort, but later completed his poem which survives in two versions. Arthur Dickson has convincingly argued that some of the details are taken from the story as related by Richard Vestegan's *Restitution of Decayed Intelligence in Antiquities* (1605). See 'Browning's Source for "The Pied Piper of Hamelin"', *Studies in Philology*, 23.3 (1926), 327–36.

l. 1. Hamelin is not in Brunswick but Hanover. The mistake derives from Verstegan.

l. 4. The river washes the old town on its western rather than southern side.

l. 7. Wanley dates the story 1284, but Verstegan sets it in 1376.

l. l13. *vats.* The moulds in which the curds are pressed.

l. 23. *noddy.* Fool.

l. 24. *Corporation.* The Town Council, which is headed by the Mayor.

l. 25. The official robe of an alderman is a gown, often furred. The state gown of the Lord Mayor of London is of ermine.

l. 35. *guilder.* A German gold coin introduced in the 14th century. Its approximate value was half a guinea.

l. 76. *cheque.* Usually check.

l. 83. *Cham.* The leader or emperor, a form of Khan.

l. 85. *Nizam.* The ruler of Hyderabad, though the word may be used here generically.

l. 99. *candle flame.* In fact household salt burns with a yellow flame.

ll. 117–20. Plutarch relates how Caesar saved himself from the Egyptians at the Battle of Pharos by jumping into the sea and swimming ashore holding above his head a manuscript, popularly reputed as in Lemprière (1820) to be 'his commentaries on the Gallic wars', which he saved by swimming 'with his arms in one hand and his commentaries in the other', 144.

l. 127. *train-oil.* Oil obtained by boiling whale blubber.

l. 130. *psaltery.* A stringed instrument like a dulcimer.

l. 132. *drysaltery.* A shop selling sauces, pickles, preserved meats.

l. 133. *nuncheon.* Snack.

l. 135. *puncheon.* A large barrel.

l. 147. *peirked.* Started up

l. 154. *Rhenish.* Rhine wine.

l. 171. *Bagdat.* Baghdad.

l. 173. *Caliph.* A Muslim ruler, literally a successor to Muhammad.

l. 176. *bate a stiver.* Reduce my fee by as much as a small coin, a twentieth of a guilder.

l. 192. *pitch-and-hustle.* A children's game in which coins or other objects are thrown at a mark, pitch-and-toss.

ll. 251–3. 'And again I say unto you, it is easier for a camel to go through the eye of a needle, than for a rich man to enter into the kingdom of God' (Matthew 19: 24).

ll. 262–8. Verstegan records that it was 'established, that from that tyme forward in all publyke writings that should bee made in that town, after the date therein set down of the yeare of our Lord, the date of the yeare of the going forth of their children should bee added'. RB follows Verstegan as to the year. Wanley dates the event in 1284.

ll. 278–9. Wanley reports that the children's abduction is 'painted in their Windows, and in their Churches'.

ll. 282–92. The legend is reported, though doubted, by Verstegan.

l. 289. *trepanned.* Lured.

FROM *HOOD'S MAGAZINE*, vol. 1, June 1844; vol. 2, July 1844; vol. 3, March 1845; vol. 3, April 1845

The Laboratory

The poem was first published in *Hood's Magazine*, 1 (June 1844), 513–14, after Hood's friends were encouraged to submit contributions during Hood's illness. The poem was altered, and weakened, for its publication in *Bells and Pomegranates* VII, *Dramatic Romances and Lyrics*, in response to EBB's complaints about its 'uncertainty of rhythm'. RB clearly associated his speaker with the Marchioness de Brinvilliers (1632–76), who was executed for her complicity in the poisoning of her father and brothers. She had been taught the art by her lover, Saint Croix, who had himself learned it from an Italian with whom he had been imprisoned. Saint Croix died when the glass mask with which he protected himself from the poisons he was preparing slipped. The mask, so striking an appurtenance that Walter Scott borrowed it in *Kenilworth*, reappears in RB's poem. RB's speaker's relationship with her silent auditor may have been suggested by Brinvilliers's relationship with Saint Croix, although Saint Croix was not an old man. RB's speaker, like Brinvilliers, seems to be associated with the court of Louis XIV, and both women are diminutive. But in other respects the two women differ. Brinvilliers murdered to secure inheritances from her family and her husband: RB's speaker murders out of jealousy. RB would have known of Brinvilliers's career from the *Biographie universelle*. Her history was often recalled in 19th-century periodicals, for example in George Hogarth's 'The Poisoners of the Seventeenth Century', *Bentley's Miscellany*, 2 (July 1837), 229–39, and was rehearsed by Alexandre Dumas in *Crimes célèbres* (1839–40). Longman notes that a poem by RB's father entitled 'Brinvilliers' is in the Library of Northwestern University.

l. 3. *devil's smithy.* In chapter 6 of *Sartor Resartus* Carlyle speaks of 'this Devil's-smithy (*Teufels-schmiede*) of a world'.

l. 14. *oozings*. Compare Keats, 'To Autumn': 'Thou watchest the last oozings hours by hours.'

l. 15. *soft*. Possibly translating the French 'doux', hence also suggesting sweet.

l. 19. *a earring*. For 'an' earring; *a casket*. The Marchioness of Brinvilliers was finally exposed when, after Saint Croix's death, she attempted to recover a casket in his possession containing poison.

l. 20. *fan-mount*. The frame on which a fan is mounted, often elaborately painted. In a story recently published in *Hood's Magazine* a pretty young Frenchwoman is exposed as a spy, her secret messages secreted in various decorative items. The detective observes that 'comfit-box wrappers, aye, even fan-mounts play an important part in these plots'. 'Phoebe's Window', *Hood's Magazine and Comic Miscellany*, 1 (February 1844), 204; *filagree-basket*. A basket made from woven threads of silver or gold.

l. 23. *pastille*. A pellet of aromatic paste burned as a perfume.

l. 24. Longman compares a passage paying tribute to the beauty of the Marchioness de Ganges quoted by a reviewer of Dumas's *Crimes célèbres* immediately before an account of the Marchioness de Brinvilliers: 'her figure corresponded to the beauty of her face; indeed, her arms, her hands, her carriage, and her deportment, left nothing to desire', *Foreign Quarterly Review*, 30 (1842), 26–60.

l. 29. *minion*. Used here like the French 'mignon' to mean petite or delicate.

Garden Fancies, *1* and *2*

Unusually the two poems continued to be paired under the collective title 'Garden Fancies' after their first publication in *Hood's Magazine*, July 1844, possibly because RB understood them as an indirect tribute to his parents. His mother, like the Spanish lady in 'The Flower's Name', was a devoted gardener, and her love of animals extended to the kind that inhabit the hollow in the plum tree in 'Sibrandus Schafnaburgensis', but the second poem more particularly recalls RB's father, an indefatigable collector of antiquarian books. The lady in 'The Flower's Name' recalls, as has been noted, the Lady of Part Second of Shelley's *The Sensitive-Plant*. RB's interest in poetry that, because it is articulated in a language that the auditor cannot understand, inheres in the music rather than the meaning, recalls Wordsworth's 'The Solitary Reaper', in which the incomprehensible language is Gaelic rather than Spanish. 'Sibrandus Schafnaburgensis' engages with another of RB's central concerns, the pathos in the discrepancy between the dead letter and the living world that it seeks to describe, a discrepancy comically overcome by the worm, slug, water-beetle, and newt, and more cunningly threatened by a diction in which any word is likely to be enlisted into active service as a verb, 'suppling' the books covers, or leaving it to 'dry-rot at ease'.

1. *The Flower's Name*

ll. 7–8. Compare the Lady in Shelley's *The Sensitive-Plant*, who spares even 'killing insects and gnawing worms' because their 'intent | Although they did ill, was innocent', Part Second, 41 and 47–8.

l. 10. *the box*. The shrub, a dwarf form of which is often used to edge flower beds.

l. 12. Compare Shelley, *The Sensitive-Plant*, 'and soft moths that kiss, | The sweet lips of the flowers, and harm not, did she | Make her attendant angels be,' Part Second, 50–2.

l. 20. EBB commented on 'that beautiful & musical use of the word "meandering," which I never remember having seen used in relation to *sound* before' (*Correspondence*, x. 315).

l. 23. In December 1834, RB reported, 'I have learned Spanish enough [to] be able to read "the majestic tongue which Calderon along the desert flung!"' and added, 'I will not learn German . . . & can't help learning Spanish!' (*Correspondence*, iii. 111). But he did not persevere. The quotation, *Letter to Maria Gisborne*, 180–1, suggests that it was Shelley who had prompted the attempt.

l. 24. *slow, sweet*. Tennyson has 'slow sweet hours' paired with 'slow sad hours', 'Love and Duty' (1842), 56–7.

2. 31–2. Compare *The Sensitive-Plant*, Part Second, 39–40: 'If the flowers had been her own infants she | Could never have nursed them more tenderly.'

l. 36. Reversing the cliché of the rosebud mouth.

l. 47. *flout*. Scoff.

2. *Sibrandus Schafnaburgensis*. An invented pedant. DeVane follows Griffin and Minchin in claiming that RB found the name in a favourite childhood book, *Wanley's Wonders of the Little World*, but neither gives a reference and I cannot locate it. Schafnaburgensis means from Aschaffenburg, a town in Bavaria. There is a minor 16th-century scholar who takes his name from the town, Lambertus Schafnaburgensis. Sibrandus Lubbertus is a better-known Dutch theologian who engaged in a controversy with Grotius in the early 17th century.

l. 7. *matin-prime*. Literally the time, usually 6 a.m., of the first canonical prayer in the morning.

l. 10. The arbutus and laurustinus are evergreen shrubs, the former sometimes known as the strawberry tree.

l. 15. *the mortal amount*. Presumably seventy. The 'three-score years and ten' of mortal existence, Psalm 90: 10.

l. 19. *pont-levis*. Drawbridge.

l. 32. *Rabelais*. Author of the 16th-century comic masterpiece *Gargantua and Pantagruel*, selected presumably as a contemporary of Sibrandus but his antithesis.

l. 34. *limbo*. Prison or confinement, as in Carlyle's *Past and Present*, in which monks are enjoined to silence 'under penalty of foot-gyves, limbo, and bread and water'.

ll. 38–9. *de profundis, accentibus laetis, Cantate*. From the depths, sing in joy, parodying the opening of Psalm 130, the psalm used in prayers for the dead. RB revises the psalm to mark his resurrection of the book.

l. 50. *toused*. Worried.

l. 51. *eft*. Newt.

l. 52. *right of trover*. An action of trover makes a claim to ownership of a found object.

l. 61. *John Knox*. The leader of the Scottish Reformation, often cited as a type of the pleasure-hating, and hence theatre-despising, Calvinist.

l. 64. *trowsers*. In the 19th century male ballet dancers wore tight black trousers.

l. 67. *sufficit*. It's enough.

[*The Bishop Orders his Tomb at Saint Praxed's Church*]
The Tomb at Saint Praxed's (Rome, 15—)

Published in *Hood's Magazine* as *The Tomb at St Praxed's*. EBB identified it as 'the finest & most powerful' of 'the Hood poems' (*Correspondence*, x. 315), and Ruskin wrote in *Modern Painters* IV: 'I know of no other piece of modern English, prose or poetry, in which there is so much told, as in these lines, of the Renaissance spirit,—its worldliness, inconsistency, pride, hypocrisy, ignorance of itself, love of art, of luxury, and of good Latin.' But it is a poem as concerned with RB's own time as with 16th-century Italy. When he offered the poem for inclusion in *Hood's Magazine*, RB described it as 'a pet of mine, and just the thing for the time—what with the Oxford business, and Camden society and other embroilments' (x. 83). The poem speaks to a nation whose distrust of Catholicism had been greatly intensified by the Tractarian Movement ('the Oxford business'). K. I. D. Maslen has suggested ('Browning and Macaulay', *Notes and Queries*, NS 27 (1980), 525–7) that the poem recalls a review of Ranke's *History of the Popes* by Macaulay that surveys papal deficiencies with a gleeful Protestant disdain: 'They regarded those Christian mysteries of which they were stewards, just as the Augur Cicero and the Pontifex Maximus Caesar regarded the Sibylline books and the pecking of the sacred chickens. Among themselves they spoke, of the Incarnation, the Eucharist, and the Trinity, in the same tone in which Cotta and Velleius talked of the oracle of Delphi, or of the voice of Faunus in the mountains. Their years glided by in a soft dream of intellectual voluptuousness' (*Edinburgh Review*, 72 (October 1840), 242). But as R. A. Greenberg has shown ('Ruskin, Pugin, and the Contemporary Context of "The Bishop Orders his Tomb"', *PMLA* 84 (1969), 1588–94), Pugin, the Tractarians, and the members of the Camden Society who were their Cambridge counterparts were just as likely as Macaulay to condemn the manner in which the Renaissance Church allowed pagan sensuousness to contaminate Christian principle both in the decoration of their churches and in their behaviour. Santa Prassede was a saint of the early Church, and the contrast between the purity of the early Church and its later corruption was as important to Pugin and Newman as it was to their Protestant antagonists. It seems unlikely that either side would have allowed the pathos with which RB renders his dying Bishop who, even as his mind starts to wander, remains so incorrigibly himself that he may even inspire a measure of rough affection. There have been various attempts to identify the original of RB's Bishop, but the portrait seems to be generic. Attempts to identify the original of the tomb that the Bishop plans are still less persuasive since the clear implication of the poem is that the tomb will not be built.

l. 1. Compare Ecclesiastes 1: 2: 'Vanity of vanities, saith the Preacher, vanity of vanities; all is vanity.'

l. 2. *Anselm*. The English form of the Italian Anselmo. St Anselm the 11th-century Archbishop of Canterbury was born in Aosta.

l. 3. *Nephews*. A euphemism for the sons of those in divine orders. Compare the Prior's 'niece' in *Fra Lippo Lippi*.

l. 6. *What's done is done*. Proverbial, but also *Macbeth*, III. ii. 12.

l. 7. *I am bishop since*. That is, she died before I was raised to a bishopric.

l. 9. *the world's a dream*. Proverbial but compare Calderon's play *La vida es sueño* (Life is a Dream), and Prospero, 'We are such stuff | As dreams are made on' (*The Tempest*, IV. i. 156–7).

l. 17. *came me in*. *OED* explains this as a fencing expression, meaning 'got within my guard', quoting from plays by Shakespeare and Fletcher. The expression puzzled EBB, and in later editions became 'cozened me'.

l. 21. *the epistle-side*. The south side, the right-hand side of the church as the congregation looks at it, from which laymen would read from the lectern. The pulpit is on the north side, the left side as the congregation looks at it.

l. 22. *choir*. The part of the church east of the nave often, though not in Santa Prassede, separated from the rest of the church by a screen.

ll. 23–4. In fact Santa Prassede has an apse or half-dome with mosaics depicting Christ surrounded by saints.

l. 25. The Bishop imagines the recumbent statue of himself on its basalt slab.

l. 26. *tabernacle*. The stone canopy of the tomb.

l. 31. *onion-stone*. As RB explained to Ruskin, the expression is a translation of cippolino, the variety of marble named after the small, flat Italian onions called cippolini, 'good for pillars and the like, bad for finer work, thro' its being laid coat upon coat, onion-wise'.

l. 34. The implication is that the Bishop has had one of his churches burned down in order to conceal that he has plundered its treasures.

l. 37. Presumably a press for the extraction of olive oil.

l. 41. *olive-frail.* Rush basket used for storing olives.

l. 42. *lapis lazuli.* Literally stone of heaven, a blue-coloured rock that, because it is hard, and can be smoothed and polished, was frequently carved.

l. 43. Possibly a reference to the severed head of John the Baptist, which, resting on a dish held by Salome, was a common subject in Italian painting in the 16th and 17th centuries. There are celebrated examples by Titian, Caravaggio, Guido Reni, and Artemisia Gentileschi.

l. 44. Again suggesting the Bishop's connoisseurship as well as his sensuality. In Italian painting Madonnas are often represented suckling the infant.

l. 46. *Frascati.* A town 12 miles south-east of Rome. Ancient Romans had villas there, and the practice was revived by the Roman aristocracy in the 16th century.

ll. 47–8. The lapis lazuli sphere, representing the globe, on which the Trinity stand above the altar in the chapel of the Chiesa del Gesu in which St Ignatius is entombed is reputed to be the largest in the world. The reference is anachronistic: the chapel was not built until the end of the 17th century.

l. 51. Proverbial as in Edward Young, *Night Thoughts*, IV. 809: 'How swift the shuttle flies that weaves thy shroud!'

l. 54. *antique-black.* Translating 'nero antico', a rare and expensive black marble.

ll. 55–6. Unlike the bronze reliefs on Loyola's altar which depict episodes in the life of the saint.

l. 58. *tripod*; *thyrsus.* The tripod, a three-legged vessel, is associated with Apollo, and the thyrsus, a staff topped with a pine cone, vines wound around it, with Dionysus.

l. 60. *a glory.* The circle of light or aureole around the head of a saint.

l. 64. *Child of my bowels.* Compare 2 Samuel 16: 11: 'Behold, my son, which came forth of my bowels', and Bunyan, *Pilgrim's Progress*: '"O my dear wife," said he, "and you the children of my bowels."'

l. 65. *revel down.* Squander by revelling.

l. 66. *mouldy travertine.* See 'Pictor Ignotus', l. 67 and note.

l. 68. *jasper*, a precious stone, the most precious variety of which was green. The wall of the New Jerusalem is 'of jasper' (Revelation 21: 18).

l. 70. Melchiori suggests that RB is recalling the Emperor Constantine's green jasper bath preserved in the Baptistery of the Church of San Giovanni in Laterano in Rome, *Browning's Poetry of Reticence*, 1968, 27.

l. 77. *Tully's.* Cicero's. Cicero was the preferred model for prose in Renaissance Italy. Pietro Bembo was reputed to have vowed never to use a word that had not been used by Cicero. Contrast St Jerome, who gave up reading pagan authors after a dream in which Christ accused him of being a Ciceronian rather than a Christian.

l. 78. Polonius advises Laertes that his dress should be 'rich, not gaudy', *Hamlet*, I. iii. 67.

l. 79. *Ulpian*. Domitius Ulpianus, Roman jurist and prolific writer, whose Latin is despised because decadent (Ulpian died in 228).

l. 87. *crook*. The Bishop's crozier.

l. 89. *mortcloth*. Funeral pall.

l. 95. RB explained, 'the blunder about the sermon is the result of the dying man's haziness; he would not reveal himself as he does but for that.' *Select Poems*, ed. Rolfe and Hersey, 1886, 195. The Bishop also mistakes the gender of the saint.

l. 97. *agate*. A precious stone commonly marked by bands of colour.

l. 99. ELUCESCEBAT, shone, a word selected for ridicule from Gandolf's epitaph because it is used instead of the classical form 'elucebat'. The point is that it is the form despised as un-Ciceronian, 'elucesco', that is used in the Vulgate, for example in 2 Peter 1: 19.

ll. 105–6. Between these lines in *Bells and Pomegranates, No. VII*, 'Dramatic Romances and Lyrics' and after RB added the lines: 'Or ye would heighten my impoverished frieze, | Piece out it starved design, and fill my vase | With grapes, and add a vizor, and a term.'

ll. 106–7. Melchiori in *Browning's Poetry of Reticence*, 1968, 29–36, has suggested a reference to 'Sweet Repose disturbed by Lewdness. An Emblem' in Gerard de Lairesse's *The Art of Painting in all its Branches*, 1778, 249–51, the favourite book of RB's childhood. The resemblances are slight, although they became more substantial when RB expanded the passage in 1845. She understands the Bishop as fearing that his sons will introduce some emblem that will reflect satirically upon his life, but it seems more natural to understand the Bishop as devising an emblem that will enrich the tomb. Possibly the Bishop envisages an emblem in which Dionysus, associated with the thyrsus, is toppled leaving the tripod, associated with Apollonian calm, supreme.

l. 108. *entablature*. The reference seems to be to the basalt slab on which the Bishop's sculptured effigy will lie.

l. 113. *gritstone*. Sandstone.

l. 118. *altar-ministrants*. Altar servers.

The Flight of the Duchess [*I–IX*]

The poem was first published in *Hood's Magazine*, 3 (April 1845), 313–18, headed 'Part the First'. RB explained to EBB that it was 'only the beginning of a story written some time ago, and given to poor Hood in his emergency at a day's notice—the true stuff and story is all to come, the "*Flight*," and what you allude to is mere introduction'. He would put the rest of the poem in 'some "Bell" or other' (*Correspondence*, x. 201). EBB assumed, as have RB's editors, that most of the poem was written before its first part was published, and twice in May and again in June she asked to be shown the rest of the poem, but RB did not give her the next instalment until the beginning of July, and did not show her the conclusion of the poem until 16 July (*Correspondence*, x. 306). There is some reason to believe that, when he first published the poem in *Hood's*, it was, like 'Saul', a fragment. In 1883 RB wrote to Furnivall, 'There was an odd circumstance that either mended or marred the poem in the writing—I fancied the latter at the time. As I finished the line—which ends what was printed in Hood's Magazine as the First Part—"and the old one—you shall hear!" I saw from the window where I sat a friend opening the gate to our house—one Captain Lloyd—whom I jumped up to meet, judging from the time of day that something especially interesting had brought him—as proved to be the case, for he was in a strange difficulty. This took a deal of discussing,—next day, other interruptions occurred, and the end was I lost altogether the thing as it was in my head at the beginning' (*Wise*, 217). The consonance with Coleridge's account of how 'Kubla Khan' remained a fragment, Captain Lloyd standing in for the 'person on business from Porlock', seems more than coincidental. It is true that RB went on to suggest that a chance remark overheard during a visit to Wales in 1842 had prompted him to continue the poem, but even if his memory was accurate, his decision to publish in *Hood's* only its first part suggests that he retained an interest in it as a fragment. The poem's satire on medievalism, the Duke recalling Peacock's Mr Chainmail in *Crotchet Castle* (1831), had been given more point by Disraeli's formation of his 'Young England' group. The publication of *Historical Fancies* (1844) by one of Disraeli's associates, George Smythe, may have spurred RB on. The poem seems comically to rehearse the Young England penchant for superimposing on 19th-century England a visionary medieval England, as in the opening description that divides Moldavia between two landscapes separated by a range of mountains, one of them devoted to agriculture and the chase, the other busily industrial (the landscape is similarly divided in George Darley's pastoral drama *Sylvia; or, The May Queen*, 1825). The poem has strong biographical interest. Discussion of it (it was more frequently discussed in the letters between RB and EBB than any other poem), as Daniel Karlin has shown, played a significant role in their courtship. See *The Courtship of Robert Browning and Elizabeth Barrett*, 1985, 89–93.

Our text is taken from the poem's first publication in *Hood's Magazine* in order to focus attention in RB's youthful interest in the fragment as a poetic form. In the poem's continuation that recalls, by coincidence RB insisted, the traditional ballad 'Johnny Faa' or 'The Gypsy Laddie', the castle is visited by a group of gypsies, amongst them an old woman, who recognizes the Duchess as one of their own. Alone with the Duchess she abandons her disguise, reveals herself as a gypsy queen, and persuades the Duchess to ride away with her in a speech that reflects the metre that RB had devised for his poem, a 'wondrous chime' (557) contrived by a swift alternation between 'prose and rhyme' (558), a chant that pours into the Duchess all the vitality of which her married life has drained her.

l. 12. *open-chase*. Unenclosed land kept for hunting.

ll. 14–18. Compare James Grahame, *British Georgics* (1812), 'October', 140–1: '*woods* of pine, or sable belts, | Like funeral processions, long drawn out.'

l. 21. *red drear burnt-up plain*. Compare EBB, 'A Thought for a Lonely Death-Bed' (1844), 7–8, 'the red | Drear wine-press'.

l. 23. *dealt*. Traded.

l. 30. *salt sand*. Compare Keats 'Ode on Melancholy', 16: 'the salt sand wave'; *hoar*. White.

l. 33. Compare Coleridge. 'Youth and Age', 20–2: 'O! the joys, that came down shower-like, | Of Friendship, Love, and Liberty, | Ere I was old!'

l. 36. *the Kennel*. The gutter.

l. 46. *salt-pit*. A reservoir in which sea-water is evaporated for the manufacture of salt.

l. 51. *bantling*. Brat.

l. 53. *Kaiser's courier*. Prince's messenger.

l. 76. *tannage*. Tanning.

l. 78. *rough-foot*. With feathered legs; *merlin*. A small falcon.

l. 80. *lanner*. A falcon like a peregrine but smaller.

l. 83. *white beer*. Translating the German 'weissbier'. Weissbier is a wheat beer.

ll. 85–6. Cotnari is the most famous wine-producing region in Moldavia. It produces a sweet wine like sauternes or tokay.

l. 88. *ropy*. Sticky and stringy. In the continuation of the poem (838), the wine is described as 'streaky syrup'.

l. 101. *Struck at himself*. Struck with admiration for himself.

l. 104. *Land of Lays*. Suggesting a non-classical heritage preserved in 'wild nooks'. In a review in the *Monthly Magazine*, 46 (October 1842), of Cyrus Redding's book on Cornwall the county is referred to as 'the land of lays and legends' (p. 355).

l. 106. *Mid-Age*. The Middle Ages, the only use of the expression in this sense recorded in *OED*.

l. 107. *wild nooks*. Compare 'this wild nook', Wordsworth, 'It was an April morning: fresh and clear', 38.

l. 117. *fumed-forth*. Dispersed in vapour.

l. 119. *lathy*. Thin.

l. 120. *blood for bone*. Breeding as a substitute for substance.

l. 130. *urox*. More commonly urochs, the Lithuanian bison; *buffle*. Buffalo.

l. 164. *sullies*. By bringing cloud.

l. 201. *wheel-work image*. Automaton.

LETTER TO ELIZABETH BARRETT, JANUARY 10, 1845

RB's first letter to EBB, postmarked 10 January 1845, in which RB introduced himself to EBB as one poet to another. It is a remarkably self-conscious performance in which he seems anxious to exhibit himself as free from the bourgeois constraints that inhibit conventional correspondents: 'I do, as I say, love these Books with all my heart—and I love you too.' The correspondence ended a week after the two married on 12 September 1856, when they eloped, because they were never again separated. Our text is from *The Letters of Robert Browning and Elizabeth Barrett, 1845–46*, 2 vols., ed. Elvan Kinter (Cambridge, Mass.: Belknap Press, 1969).

l. 5. *your poems*. EBB's *Poems* in two volumes of 1844.

l. 16. *a "Flora"*. A descriptive catalogue of flowers.

l. 24. *Kenyon*. RB had met John Kenyon, EBB's cousin and a schoolfriend of his father's, in 1839. He was the couple's most important benefactor and, on his death in December 1856, left legacies that secured their financial independence.

l. 32. *was never to be!* Possibly a reference to Lancelot's finding the door of the chapel where the Holy Grail was kept but being prevented from entering.

FROM *BELLS AND POMEGRANATES, NO. VII, DRAMATIC ROMANCES AND LYRICS* (1845)

"*How They Brought the Good News from Ghent to Aix*"

RB wrote the poem in August 1844 on board the ship taking him from Sicily to Naples 'after I had been at sea long enough to appreciate even the fancy of a gallop on a certain good horse "York," then in my stable at home' (*The Leisure Hour* (July 1833), 403). It was perhaps the name of the horse that brought to mind the principal source for the poem, Dick Turpin's celebrated ride from London to York on Black Bess as recorded by Harrison Ainsworth in *Rookwood* (Book IV, chapters iv–xii), a connection first made, as Longman notes, by EBB. RB also borrowed his metre from Ainsworth. In Book IV, chapter ii, Turpin 'chanted' some rhymes entitled 'Black Bess' in the anapaestic tetrameters that RB uses in his poem. Turpin's auditors 'beat time to the melody'. RB's narrative bears the mark too of another boys' favourite, the tale of Pheidippides, who ran from Marathon to Athens to bring news of the Greek victory over the Persians, collapsing and dying on his arrival. The historical circumstances that the poem alludes to are imaginary, though presumably set at some point in the Eighty Years War (1568–1648) in which Flanders Protestants fought for their independence from Spain. The elderly RB responded to enquiries by suggesting that Aix was under siege, and that the good news the riders brought was to expect a relief force from Ghent. The distance from Ghent to Aix is a little over 100 miles (170 kilometres) in an east-south-east direction. Lokeren, Boom, Düffeld (now Duffel), Mecheln, Aerschot (Aarschot), Hasselt, Looz (now Borgloon), Tongres, and Dalhem are towns more or less en route. An early contributor to *Notes and Queries* deduced from RB's haphazard use of Flemish, French, and German forms of the names of towns, and his wrongly accenting Lokeren on its second syllable, that he 'had never personally explored the route' (James Platt, 'Browningiana', *Notes and Queries*, 12 (October 1897), 345), but in fact RB had travelled through Flanders in 1844 as he had in 1834 and 1838.

l. 5. *the postern.* A gate other than the main gate.

l. 10. *pique.* Longman quotes a letter of 1884 in which RB explains, 'I certainly had and have the impression that the old-fashioned projection in front of the military saddle on the Continent was called the pique.'

l. 11. *cheek strap.* A single strap that loops through the bit and the ring to a buckle on the cheek.

l. 17. Mecheln or Mechelen and the countryside around are dominated by the tower of St Rumbold's Cathedral, famous for its carillon of 49 bells.

l. 19. *up leaped of a sudden the sun.* Compare Coleridge, 'The Rime of the Ancient Mariner', 98: 'The glorious sun uprist'.

l. 22. *stout.* An epithet used of a horse that has staying power.

l. 24. *bluff.* Rising steeply.

l. 25. *crest.* The line of a horse's neck.

l. 29. *spume-flakes.* Foam.

l. 32. *Roos.* Flemish for rose, a common girl's name.

l. 41. Aachen (or Aix) Cathedral, otherwise the Imperial Cathedral or the Royal Church of St Mary at Aachen, has a cupola and a spire.

l. 44. *croup*, or crop, the horse's rump.

l. 49. *buffcoat.* A leather coat of a kind commonly worn by soldiers in the 17th century.

l. 50. *jack-boot.* A leather boot rising above the knee worn by cavalry soldiers in the 17th century.

ll. 58–9. Perhaps remembering how Dick Turpin 'poured the contents of the bottle down the throat of his mare' (*Rookwood*, Book IV, chapter xii), EBB praised 'that touch of natural feeling at the end, to prove that it was not in brutal carelessness that the poor horse was driven through all that suffering' (*Correspondence*, xi. 167).

l. 59. *burgesses.* Magistrates or town councillors.

Pictor Ignotus

Scholarly attention has focused on an attempt to identify the unknown painter. In an important article (*Review of English Studies*, 23 (1972), 313–19) J. B. Bullen suggests that he is modelled on Fra Bartolommeo (*c.*1472–1517). Like RB's painter, Fra Bartolommeo retreated to a convent (though he later left it to resume his artistic career), and his association with

Raphael points to the identity of the 'youth' mentioned by RB's painter. Two details are particularly striking. RB's reference in line 41 to the dramatic effect on his painter of 'a voice' is obscure, but Bartolommeo, as recorded by Vasari, was so moved by Savonarola's preaching that he publicly burned the paintings that Savonarola had denounced as pagan and lascivious nudes. Second, the thought with which the poem opens, that the speaker might have rivalled Raphael, echoes Anna Jameson's observation that 'Fra Bartolommeo seems to have been *the* Raphael had not fortune been determined in favour of the other' (Jameson, i. 225). J. B. Bullen is less persuasive in his attempt to repel the charge that there is an inherent absurdity in representing a well-known painter as a model for a painter whose defining characteristic is that his name has been lost to posterity. In a later article (*Nineteenth-Century Contexts*, 26.3 (2004), 273–88) Bullen argues that RB's poem offers a sideglance on a contemporary debate. The art-catholic historian Alexis-François Rio sought in his *De la poésie chrétienne* to revive in the 19th century the notion that he attributed to early Italian painters that art should subordinate itself to the expression of religious principle. He celebrated the German Nazarenes, who lived together in a convent and cultivated monk-like habits both in behaviour and dress, as painters that shared his convictions. Bullen's suggestion that RB's poem is an intervention in the debate that Rio precipitated is valuable. His additional suggestion that Johann Friedrich Overbeck should be recognized as the contemporary model for RB's painter just as Fra Bartolommeo is his Renaissance model is open to a similar criticism. Overbeck by the 1840s had achieved a European celebrity.

Pictor Ignotus [title]. The conventional designation used in galleries for an unidentified painter.

l. 1. *that youth's*. Most probably a reference to Raphael, who seems to have been active in Florence from 1504 when he was 21.

l. 4. *star by star*. Compare the stage direction after line 2004 in EBB's *A Drama of Exile* (1844): 'the earth-zodiac pales as the stars, star by star, shine out in the sky.'

l. 12. Compare the account in RB's *Easter-Day* of how the 'world of spirit' might be 'Made visible in verse, despite | The veiling weakness' (922–3).

l. 23. *hath it spilt, my cup*. The Psalmist rejoices because his 'cup runneth over' (Psalm 23: 5); Pictor Ignotus because not a drop from his cup has been spilled.

l. 24. Alluding to the man given one talent, who, fearing to lose it, saved it by burying it in the ground (Matthew 25: 24–5).

ll. 26–32. He dreams of a success like Cimabue's in a celebrated anecdote recounted by Vasari in which his Madonna is 'borne in solemn procession with trumpets and great rejoicing' to its installation in the Church of Santa Maria Novella in Florence.

l. 28. *Kaiser*. Emperor. Compare the reference in *Sordello*, 4. 380 to 'spokesmen for the Kaiser and the Pope'.

ll. 34–5. Longman compares Wordsworth's 'Ode: Intimations of Immortality', stanza 5, in which the 'youth' is attended by 'Life's Star' which the man sees 'fade into the light of common day'.

l. 41. For the possibility that the voice is Savonarola's see headnote.

l. 43. *House of Idols*. In 1 Samuel 31: 9, the expression denotes the temple of the Philistines.

l. 48. The speaker's comparison of himself to a nun enforces the contrast with Raphael who, according to Vasari, died of sexual excess.

l. 51. *garniture*, a merely decorative object, as in *Sordello*, 5. 712, in which a 'bauble' is described as 'a cumbrous garniture'.

l. 67. *travertine*. A kind of limestone. In his life of Michelangelo, Vasari explains that travertine does not dry quickly, and can encourage mould.

l. 71. Fame conventionally blows a golden trumpet, as in Marlowe, *Tamburlaine the Great Part Two*, III. iv: 'Fame hovereth, sounding of her golden trump.'

[*The Italian in England*] *Italy in England*

Many Italian political exiles took refuge in England after the failed revolts of 1820, amongst them RB's Italian tutor, Angelo Cerutti, and Giuseppe Mazzini, who came to England in 1837. Mazzini wrote to thank RB, who had presented him with a copy of *Dramatic Romances and Lyrics*, singling out this poem: 'I have read, re-read, and have read to my friends "Italy in England"' (*Correspondence*, xi. 169–70). He reciprocated RB's gift by sending him his pamphlet on the brothers Emilio and Attilio Bandiera, who had been inspired by Mazzini to lead a landing on the Calabrian coast in a disastrous attempt to overthrow Spanish rule. They were betrayed and executed with their followers in July 1844, prompting some commentators to suggest that they are the models for RB's revolutionary. But, given the very different circumstances of the men, the most that can be claimed is that the execution of the brothers may have played a part in prompting the poem by reawakening interest in their cause. Mazzini seems unaware that the poem is at least as concerned to reveal the cost of allowing political commitment precedence over human attachment as to inspire sympathy for the Italian cause.

l. 3. *Austria*. The Kingdom of Lombardy-Venetia was created by Metternich (see note to l. 19) in 1815 at the Congress of Vienna and ceded to Austria. Until 1835 it was ruled by Francis I, who was succeeded by Ferdinand I.

l. 5. *instant*. Close at hand.

l. 19. *Metternich our friend*. Metternich (1773–1859), Austrian statesman, principal architect of the Congress of Vienna, and instigator of Austrian rule in northern Italy.

l. 41. *crypt*. Hiding place.

l. 54. That is, he planned to tell her that hiding himself was only a youthful prank.

ll. 57–62. She resembles the woman who symbolized Italian national identity, 'Italia Turrita' or 'Stella d'Italia', figures often conflated and given new prominence by Italian nationalists.

l. 75. *Duomo*. Cathedral.

l. 76. *Tenebrae*. The morning service in the final three days of Easter week, the days in which Christ was entombed.

ll. 83–4. That is, put the letter through the grille or screen through which confession is spoken.

ll. 86–7. The emphasis on the youth of both the man and the woman, like the extreme youth of Luigi in *Pippa Passes*, may bring to mind 'La Giovine Italia', 'Young Italy', the nationalist movement founded by Mazzini in 1831.

ll. 95–6. Perhaps indicating disappointment that her lover is politically inactive.

l. 122. *distil*. Trickle.

l. 127. *new employers*. Presumably the Austrians.

[*The Englishman in Italy*] *England in Italy*

As Daniel Karlin notes in an important study of the poem, 'The Sources of "The Englishman in Italy"' (*Browning Society Notes*, 14.3 (1984), 23–4), it had its origin in EBB's recommendation that RB read Hans Christian Andersen's *The Improvisatore*, Mary Howitt's translation of which had been published in 1845. The vividly descriptive extracts of the novel that RB had read in reviews confirmed him in 'an old belief—that Italy is stuff for the use of the North, and no more', that even Dante's 'great wide black eyes' could 'stare nothing out of the earth that lies before them', and that Alfieri's plays are quite devoid of 'local colouring, touches of the soil they are said to spring from' (*Correspondence*, x. 184). He challenges EBB in his next letter to 'take up handfuls of sonnetti, rime, poemetti' and try to make out from them 'what flowers they tread on, or trees they walk under'. He remembers that the previous year, when he had visited the piano or plain of Sorrento, the landscape was familiar to him not from his reading of Italian poetry but from his reading of Shelley (see note to line 140). 'England in Italy' reasserts RB's claim, and yet complicates it. RB invites the Italian child to whom he speaks the poem to share the enraptured vitality of his vision of Italy, and the child responds by falling asleep, confirming, it may be, that RB's vision of the landscape, like his vision of the contents of the fish basket with its 'strange lumps, 'eyes open' and 'all manner | Of horns and of humps' (58–60), is a consequence rather than a contradiction of his estrangement. The poem ends with a dry reference to the parliamentary debates on the Corn Laws that works to further undermine any complacent sense of British superiority.

l. 1. *Fortù*. a diminutive of Fortunato (boy) or Fortunata (girl). The gender of the child is not specified.

l. 5. *Scirocco*. More commonly sirocco, a hot southerly wind often terminated by a storm.

l. 10. *beads*. Rosary beads.

l. 11. I weave into a garland all the memories I gathered like flowers on the piano or plain of Sorrento.

l. 13. *'Twas time*. Later editions explain 'Time for rain!'

l. 23. *chapping*. Bursting.

l. 35. *quail-nets*. 'nets spread to catch quails as they fly to or from the other side of the Mediterranean. They are slung by rings on to poles, and stand sufficiently high for the quails to fly into them' (Orr, *Handbook*, 287 n. 1).

l. 47. *frails*. Large rush baskets.

l. 51. *blind-rock*, a rock hidden under the surface of the water.

l. 53. *Amalfi*. A coastal town 11 miles west of Salerno.

l. 57. *sea-fruit*. Translating the Italian 'frutti di mare'.

l. 72. The grape harvest usually begins early in September.

l. 73. Possibly recalling Psalm 128: 3: 'Thy wife shall be as a fruitful vine by the sides of thine house.'

l. 74. *spins*. Gushes or spurts.

l. 87. *love-apple*. Tomato.

l. 92. *regales*. Feasts.

l. 99. *gourds*. 'Purple' suggests aubergines.

l. 103. *bloom*. The powdery deposit on the freshly picked grape.

l. 107. *cheese-ball*. Mozzarella, a cheese made from buffalo milk, formed into balls and kept in whey; it originated in the Naples region.

ll. 113–15. Longman compares a passage in Hans Christian Andersen's *Improvisatore*, a novel discussed by RB and EBB. The passage is quoted in two reviews that RB is likely to have seen: 'I thought in particular about the delicious green water-melons which lay on one another, divided in halves, and showed the purple-red flesh with black seeds.'

l. 131. *pasture*. feed

l. 140. *gold orbs*. RB quotes Shelley's 'Marenghi', 'those globes of deep red gold—which in the woods the strawberry-tree doth bear, suspended in their emerald atmosphere', in a letter to EBB describing his visit to the plain of Sorrento (*Correspondence*, x. 200).

l. 157. *fume-weed*. Fumitory or fumewort

l. 159. *ever a-dying*. Because of rosemary's association with funerals. Henry Kirk White addresses it as the 'funeral flower, who lovest to dwell | With the pale corse in lonely tomb', 'To the Herb Rosemary', 11–12; *lentisks*. Mastic trees.

l. 171. *Calvano*. RB refers to 'Monte Calvano' in his letter to EBB. (*Correspondence*, x. 200), but later admitted to Furnivall that he was 'far from sure that this is the right name' (*Browning Society Papers*, 1 (1881), 170). Penguin, Oxford, and Longman convincingly suggest that he is referring to Monte Vico Alvano.

l. 172. *profound.* The sky, as in the Virgilian expression 'caelumque profundum', 'and the depth of the sky', *Eclogues*, IV. 51, and *Aeneid*, I. 58.

l. 177. *terrible crystal.* Ezekiel 1: 22 describes the firmament as having 'the colour of the terrible crystal'.

ll. 199–208. The islands off the Sorrento peninsula called in Italian, because of their association with the Sirens, 'Le Sirenuse', or alternatively 'I Galli' (the Cockerels). In addition to the three main islands, there is a fourth island, Isca, referred to by RB as 'their sister', and between the group of three and the fourth island a rocky outcrop, Vetara, which RB calls 'the small one', that barely rises above the waves. In a letter to EBB of 12 May 1846 he notes, 'there are *three* siren's isles, you know' (*Correspondence*, xii. 320). According to Strabo, when Ulysses successfully resisted the lure of the Sirens' song they cast themselves into the sea and were metamorphosed into these islands (*Geography*, Book 5, chapter 4).

ll. 219–20. The Angevin tower on the largest of 'I Galli', 'il Gallo Lungo'.

l. 221. *loop.* Loop-hole.

ll. 222–3. In his letter of 15–16 April RB included a quick sketch of the islands: 'Three scratches with a pen, even with this pen,—and you have the green little Syrenusae where I have sate and heard the quails sing' (10. 166).

l. 225. Oxford notes a reference to Sir Thomas Browne's *Urn Burial*, chapter 5, 'What song the *Syrens* sang, or what name *Achilles* assumed when he hid himself among women, though puzzling Questions, are not beyond all conjecture.'

l. 230. *strikes.* Hauls down (like a flag).

l. 244. That is, the pig's cheek is as swollen as an abbot's.

ll. 249–50. The Feast of Our Lady of the Rosary, held on 7 October, originally commemorated the Christian victory over the Turks at the Battle of Lepanto in 1571.

l. 253. *off-hand.* Impromptu.

l. 255. The feast was instituted by Pius V, a Dominican. St Dominic was often identified as the creator of the rosary.

l. 258. *red and blue.* Red for the rosary (garland or garden of roses) and blue as Mary's colour.

l. 265. Vincenzo Bellini (1801–35), Italian composer, who visited London in 1833, and Daniel Auber (1782–1871), French composer.

l. 289. Corn Laws, a protective measure passed in 1815 prohibiting the import of grain until the price in Britain reached a certain level. The repeal of the measure was debated in Parliament every year from 1837 until the laws were at last repealed in 1846. RB's point is that the repeal is as obviously beneficial as the storm that will bring an end to the sirocco and as natural.

The Lost Leader

RB repeatedly acknowledged that the 'lost leader' that he had in mind was Wordsworth, although, as he grew older, he began to intimate that the figure should be understood as generic rather than simply individual. In excoriating Wordsworth's political apostasy RB repeated a charge already levelled by writers such as Leigh Hunt, William Hazlitt, Byron, and Shelley. Compare in particular Shelley's regret in 'To Wordsworth': 'thou leavest me to grieve, | Thus having been, that thou shouldst cease to be' (13–14), and the charge brought by Shelley in *Peter Bell the Third* that Wordsworth's apostasy had mercenary motives. He was determined to 'make a better thing by metre | Than e'er was made by living creature | Up to this blessed day' (631–3).

l. 1–2. Wordsworth became the recipient of a government salary when he was appointed Distributor of Stamps for Westmoreland in 1813, and on surrendering his distributorships and the salary of £400 attached to them in 1842 was awarded a Civil List pension of £300 p.a. for life. In describing this income as 'pieces of silver' RB suggests a comparison with Judas Iscariot who betrayed Jesus for thirty pieces of silver (Matthew 26: 15). The 'riband' refers to Wordsworth's acceptance in 1843 of the laureateship in succession to Robert Southey. The use of the word to signify a degrading decoration is in accord with its use by Byron in *The Irish Avatar* to refer to the honours bestowed on an Irish peer and court sycophant: 'Will thy yard of blue riband, poor Fingal, recall | The fetters from millions of Catholic limbs?' (69–70).

l. 3. *the one gift*. Riches, poets being proverbially poor.

l. 4. *devote*. Longman compares Leviticus 27: 28: 'Notwithstanding no devoted thing, that a man shall devote unto the LORD of all that he hath . . . shall be sold or redeemed: every devoted thing is most holy unto the LORD.'

l. 7. *copper*. Implying coinage of the lowest value (after gold and silver), and hence in the gift of the people rather than the court.

l. 8. *Rags*. Rags of money are coins of no value; RB exploits the pun on rags as clothes to accuse him of contempt for the people's offering and venal desire for purple, the royal colour.

ll. 13–14. In a letter to Ruskin on 1 February 1856, RB wrote: 'Shakespeare was *of* us—not *for* us, like Him of the Defensio [Shelley's *Defence of Poetry*], nor abreast with our political sympathies like the other two: I wish he had been more than *of* us' (published as Baylor Browning Interests, No. 17, Waco, Tex., 1958).

l. 17. *presence*, suggesting the divine presence to which the Bible attributes great power.

l. 25. *Life's night begins*. Implying that Wordsworth is approaching death. He was 75 when the poem was published.

l. 28. *glad confident morning*. Possibly remembering, 'Bliss was it in that dawn to be alive, | But to be young was very Heaven!' (*Prelude* (1850), XI. 108–9, but from a passage published in *Poems*, 1815).

l. 32. *the first by the throne!* The reference may compare Wordsworth to Jesus who is at God's right hand, or, more modestly, to one of the archangels who stand 'nearest to his throne', Milton, *Paradise Lost*, III. 649. In this passage Milton identifies the 'first' of these as Uriel.

Home-Thoughts, from Abroad, I and III

The poems are clearly a product of a trip to Italy, but whether of the 1838 trip or the trip in 1844 is disputed, though the latter seems on stylistic grounds more likely. Both are, like 'England in Italy' and 'Italy in England', expressions of RB's interest in the relationship between patriotic sentiment and foreign travel. The title was supplied in obedience to EBB's advice that if RB would only 'stoop to the vulgarism of prefixing some word of introduction, as other people do, you know . . . a title . . . a name?', he would save readers responding by saying 'to themselves . . . "Why who is this? . . . who's out of England?"' (*Correspondence*, xi. 109–10).

I.

l. 5. *brush-wood sheaf.* The delicate new-grown twigs sprouting directly from the bole or trunk of the tree.

l. 10. Whitethroats and swallows, unlike the chaffinch and the thrush, are migrant birds that winter in Africa, swallows returning to Britain to nest in March and whitethroats in mid-April.

l. 14. The description indicates the song thrush.

l. 19. *dower.* Because the golden buttercups constitute the only wealth that children accrue.

l. 20. The flower of the cantaloupe melon commonly grown in Italy is larger but of a paler yellow than the buttercup.

III.

l. 1. *Cape Saint Vincent.* Scene of a naval battle of 14 February 1797 in the Anglo-Spanish war in which the British defeated a larger Spanish fleet.

l. 2. *reeking.* Burning or smouldering; *Cadiz Bay.* On 29 April 1587, Francis Drake sailed into Cadiz harbour, destroying many Spanish vessels and plundering and torching the town, a raid that Drake famously described as singeing the King of Spain's beard.

l. 3. *Trafalgar.* Scene of the most famous of all British naval victories on 21 October 1805, when the British fleet under Nelson decisively defeated the combined fleets of France and Spain, the battle in which Nelson died.

l. 4. Gibraltar was seized by Britain in 1704. Because of its successful resistance to repeated Spanish attempts to reclaim it, it became known as 'the Rock', a symbol of British naval power.

l. 8. *Jove's planet.* Jupiter; *silent over Africa.* The line may recall the final line of Keats's sonnet 'On First Looking into Chapman's Homer', 'Silent, upon a peak in Darien'.

Saul, sections 1–9

The note at the end of the poem ('End of Part the First') was added only in proof, in obedience, it seems, to EBB, who had suggested that RB ought to end the poem with asterisks to mark it as unfinished (*Correspondence*, xi. 145). But the final monosyllabic line of the poem, 'Saul', a line that is at once defective (not being a dimeter), and finely conclusive, inviting the reader to supply silently the missing foot, seems to establish the poem as a fragment rather than incomplete. When RB extended the poem in *Men and Women*, he printed as long, anapaestic pentameters what in 1845 had been alternating trimeter and dimeter lines. The effect is to muffle the poem's rhythmic vitality, what John Kenyon called its 'lyrical whirl & life' (*Correspondence*, xi. 234). In 1845 the poem lacks the 'turn to religious philosophy' that, as Longman notes, distinguishes the poem as it appears in *Men and Women*. The later poem is a repudiation rather than a continuation of the poem that RB published in 1845. In *Men and Women* David praises Saul in ploddingly flat verse for 'rejecting mere comforts that spring | From the mere mortal life held in common by man and by brute' (148–9), but in 1845 those comforts are all David has to offer. RB seems to have been anxious about how EBB would respond to the poem's lack of doctrinal content. In a letter of 27 August 1845 she reassures him that the poem is 'unobjectionable', but it is unobjectionable, it seems, only because it is incomplete, or, as she puts it still more emphatically, the lines are 'broken as you have left them' (*Correspondence*, xi. 48). She advised him to include in *Dramatic Romances and Lyrics* only 'such poems as are fairly finished & require no retouching. "Saul" for instance, you might leave' (*Correspondence*, xi. 66). But RB ignored the advice, and included a poem in which David responds to Saul's retreat into self-enclosed depression with a paean to all those things that join human beings to the world they live in, and to each other. The tunes David plays seem to follow a simple generic progression, moving from the animal kingdom, through work-song, elegy, and epithalamium, to the 'chorus intoned' by the priests as they approach the altar (116–18), but the energies of the verse seem unconstrained by hierarchy, and the 'quick jerboa' (87), 'Half bird and half mouse' (90) (compare the address to EBB at the end of *The Ring and the Book*: 'O lyric Love, half angel and half bird'), seems at least as worthy of attention as the chorus of priests. In 1845 RB's David responds to Saul's gloom not with doctrine but with a hymn of praise, the most important model for which is a poem that RB greatly loved, Christopher Smart's *Song to David*.

l. 1. *Abner.* In 1 Samuel 14: 50 Abner is described as 'the captain of [Saul's] host' and his cousin.

l. 6. *thy countenance*. Compare the description of David, 1 Samuel 16: 12, 'Now he was ruddy, and withal of a beautiful countenance, and goodly to look to.'

l. 11. In 1 Samuel 14: 27 and 43, Saul's son Jonathan angers his father by eating honey when Saul has commanded his people to fast.

l. 13. *mid-tent*. Inner tent.

l. 14. Prefiguring the three days in which Jesus was entombed.

ll. 17–18. See 1 Samuel 16: 14: 'But the Spirit of the Lord departed from Saul, and an evil spirit from the Lord troubled him.'

l. 20. *his dew*. The dew suggests David's youthful innocence and may also recall the chrism with which Samuel anointed him, 1 Samuel 16: 13: 'Then Samuel took the horn of oil and anointed him in the midst of his brethren: and the Spirit of the Lord came upon David from that day forward.'

l. 22. *blue*. See RB to EBB, 16 March 1846: 'lilies are of all colours in Palestine—one sort is particularized as *white* with a dark blue spot and streak—the water lily, lotos, which I think I meant, is *blue* altogether' (*Correspondence*, xii. 154). Oxford plausibly suggests that RB is thinking of Thomas Moore's reference to 'Blue water-lilies' (*Lalla Rookh*, 2. 323), which Moore glosses as the 'blue lotus'.

l. 25. David explains, 67–9, that the lilies prevent the harp strings from becoming so dry that they snap. There may be an allegorical suggestion that the salutary effects of David's music are preserved by his lily-like innocence. The availability of water-lilies is miraculous given the 'wild heat' of the desert, as is David's innocence.

l. 27. *God of my fathers*. Compare Daniel 2: 23: 'I thank thee, and praise thee, O thou God of my fathers.'

l. 29. Ran because the sand was so hot.

l. 30. *unlooped*. Unfastened, not tied up.

l. 37. The inner tent would be carpeted.

l. 39. *foldskirts*. The flaps through which the tent is entered; the word seems to be RB's coinage.

ll. 44–52. The delay before David is able to distinguish Saul from the main prop of the tent suggests that he is the main prop of the nation. Saul is as vast and upright as the prop: 'from his shoulders and upward he was higher than any of the people', 1 Samuel 9: 2.

ll. 53–6. Prefiguring the Crucifixion.

ll. 57–63. Saul is imagined as a snake changing its skin. As Oxford points out the serpent may be a type of Christ crucified: 'And as Moses lifted up the serpent in the wilderness, even so must the Son of man be lifted up', John 3: 14, so that the casting of the old skin may figure resurrection. The serpent king is the basilisk (etymologically little king) or cockatrice. Isaiah 14: 29 warns the Philistines that 'out of the serpent's root shall come forth a cockatrice, and his fruit shall be a fiery flying serpent', a prophecy that might appropriately be retrospectively applied to Saul.

l. 75. *stifle*. Impede.

ll. 87–90. The jerboa is a mouse-like desert rodent that hops on long legs, which may suggest a bird.

l. 104. *balm-seeds*. The seeds of what will heal and soothe.

ll. 112–15. The Gothic cathedral (identified by the reference to the flying buttress) exemplifies endeavours only made possible by cooperation. The choice of example may owe something to Ruskin.

l. 117. *Levites*. Members of the priestly caste.

l. 124. Smart refers to gems' 'darts of lustre', *A Song to David*, 153.

l. 128. *Courageous*. Probably in an archaic sense, meaning lively.

l. 134. *waste*. Unused.

ll. 143–4. Because in the mid-day heat, lions rest rather than hunt.

l. 147. See Leviticus 11: 22: 'Even these of them ye may eat; the locust after his kind, and the bald locust after his kind.'

l. 157. *thy father*. Kish. See 1 Samuel 9: 1.

l. 158. When his father became old, his sword was passed to Saul.

l. 163. The song sung to the dying.

l. 172. *working*. Fermentation.

ll. 184–6. Rage is described as an earthquake that is creative rather than destructive: it functions as a midwife, assisting the earth to give birth to the gold that the earthquake uncovers.

FROM *LETTERS OF PERCY BYSSHE SHELLEY* (1852)

Introductory Essay

RB wrote the essay in response to Edward Moxon's invitation to introduce a volume of newly discovered letters by Shelley. Soon after its publication the volume was withdrawn when the letters were exposed as forgeries (Palgrave recognized one of the letters as drawing on an article he had published in the *Quarterly Review*). Shortly afterwards the forger was exposed as 'Major Byron'. Despite these unfortunate circumstances RB remained proud of the essay, his most substantial venture into literary criticism. He had acknowledged to Carlyle that the essay was indebted to him, and Carlyle welcomed it as 'a solid, well-wrought massive manful bit of discourse', even if it were 'a *little* too elaborate here and there' (*Collected Letters of Thomas and Jane Welsh Carlyle*, vol. xxvii, 1999, 65). RB's admiration for Shelley was long-standing and frankly acknowledged in *Pauline*, his first published poem. Like Carlyle in his essay on Burns published in the *Edinburgh Review* in 1828 RB is anxious to defend the poet from small-minded attacks on his moral character, and he shares, if less emphatically, the sense of the value of biography that led Carlyle to represent Burns's poems as 'little rhymed fragments scattered here and there in the grand unrhymed Romance of his earthly existence' (*Edinburgh Review*, 48 (1828), 290). RB rather similarly views Shelley's poetry as 'a sublime fragmentary essay towards the presentment of the correspondency of the universe to Deity' rather than dwelling on the perfection of individual poems. But RB, unlike Carlyle, distinguishes between a class of poet whose works are only comprehensible in relation to their lives, and a class of poet the value of whose work is independent of any such knowledge. The distinction was common enough. Keats had distinguished between 'the Wordsworthian or egotistical Sublime' and the poetical character that he assigned to himself, which 'has no self—It is everything and nothing—It has no character' (to Richard Woodhouse, 27 October 1818). But the terms that RB uses to distinguish the two classes of poet, the subjective and the objective, align him with Coleridge. Carlyle records his meetings with Coleridge at Highgate in his life of John Sterling: 'I still remember his "object" and "subject," terms of continual recurrence in the Kantean province; and how he sang and snuffled them into "om-m-mject" and "sum-m-ject," with a kind of solemn shake or quaver, as he rolled along.' Still more to the point is EBB's characterization of RB in her second letter to him: 'You have in your vision two worlds—or to use the language of the schools of the day, you are both subjective & objective in the habits of your mind' (*Correspondence*, x. 26). For RB the type of the objective poet is, predictably, Shakespeare, 'the inventor of "Othello"'. Shelley is his type of the subjective poet, except that RB ends his essay by pointing out 'successful instances of objectivity in Shelley: there is the unrivalled "Cenci;" there is the "Julian and Maddalo" too; there is the magnificent "Ode to Naples"'. RB insists that there is no reason 'why these two modes of poetic faculty may not issue hereafter from the same poet in successive perfect works', and suggests that, but for his early death, Shelley might have achieved the feat. As it is, he bequeathed it to his successors, amongst whom, RB implies, he numbers himself. Our text is from the withdrawn edition (London: Moxon, 1852) in the British Library.

Moxon, *Essays, Letters from Abroad, Translations and Fragments*, ed. Mary Shelley (London: Moxon, 1840).

l. 11. *Scenic universe.* Landscape, the natural world.

l. 15. *The poet's double faculty.* Compare EBB, *Aurora Leigh*, 5. 183–4: 'But poets should | Exert a double vision', and compare EBB to RB, 'You have in your vision two worlds' (*Correspondence*, x. 26).

l. 16. *seeing external objects more clearly, widely, and deeply, than is possible to the average mind.* Compare Wordsworth in the Preface to *Lyrical Ballads* claiming for the poet 'a greater knowledge of human nature, and a more comprehensive soul, than are supposed to be common among mankind'.

l. 20. *Auditory.* Audience.

l. 23. *abstract.* Ideal representation.

l. 28. *ποιητης.* Poet, but literally maker.

l. 29. *Substantive.* Independent (of the poet).

l. 29. *We are ignorant.* Compare Keats on 'the poetical Character': 'it is not itself—it has no self—it is everything and nothing—It has no character—it enjoys light and shade; it lives in gusto –It has as much delight in conceiving an Iago as an Imogen' (to Woodhouse, 27 October 1818).

l. 49. Compare 'the speculum or watch-tower of Teufelsdröckh; wherefrom, sitting at ease, he might see the whole life-circulation of that considerable City; the streets and lanes of which, with all their doing and driving (*Thun und Treiben*), were for the most part visible there' (Carlyle, *Sartor Resartus*, chapter 3).

l. 53. *some sunken and darkened chamber of imagery*. Possibly recalling Plato's allegory of the cave in Book VII of *The Republic*.

l. 65. *Anatomy*. Anatomical structure.

l. 77. *Seeds of creation lying burningly on the Divine Hand*. Compare Aurora Leigh on her own creative talent: 'And yet I felt it in me where it burnt, | Like those hot fire-seeds of creation held | In Jove's clenched palm before the worlds were sown' (*Aurora Leigh*, 3. 251–3).

l. 81. *The nearest reflex of that absolute Mind*. Compare Shelley's 'Essay on Life': 'The words *I*, *you*, *they*, are not signs of any actual difference subsisting between the assemblage of thoughts thus indicated, but are merely marks employed to denote the different modifications of the one mind. Let it not be supposed that this doctrine conducts to the monstrous presumption that I, the person who now write and think, am that one mind. I am but a portion of it.'

l. 89. *an effluence*. Compare Shelley's 'Defence of Poetry' in which poetry is the source 'whence as from a magnet the invisible effluence is sent forth, which at once connects, animates, and sustains the life of all'.

l. 117. *originative painters . . . that succeeding race of landscape-painters*. The contrast is between painters such as Giotto and later painters such as Turner.

l. 134. *the same poet in successive perfect works*. Compare Aristotle's claim in the *Poetics*, on several later occasions echoed by RB, that the best tragic writer should also be the best writer of comedy, that 'Tragic and Comic Poet prove one power' (*Aristophanes' Apology*, 1302).

l. 140. *The perfect shield with the gold and the silver side*. Apparently an allusion to 'The Party-coloured Shield' in which two knights who approach the shield from different directions fight to resolve a dispute as to whether the shield is gold or silver. A druid who cures their wounds explains that they are both right. See Joseph Spence, *Moralities by Sir Harry Beaumont* (1753), 99–101. Newman refers to the fable in the first of his 'Lectures on the Present Position of Catholics in England' delivered on 30 June 1851.

l. 152. *Homerides*. The successors of Homer.

l. 218. *The masses*. The first instance of the word used to denote the common people recorded in *OED* is 1837.

l. 228. *The "Remains"—produced within a period of ten years*. RB presumably included amongst Shelley's 'Remains' the writing from the publication of *Queen Mab* in 1813 until Shelley's death in 1822, when he was 29.

l. 232. *adaptitude*. The word seems to combine the senses, aptitude, and adaptation.

l. 239. *The shortcomings of his predecessors in art.* Compare Shelley's 'Defence of Poetry', 'every great poet must inevitably innovate upon the example of his predecessors'.

l. 249. *This ideal of a future man.* Compare the conclusion of Shelley's 'Defence of Poetry' in which poets are represented as 'the mirrors of the gigantic shadows which futurity casts upon the present'.

l. 264. *the spheric poetical faculty of Shelley.* The figure may recall the 'sphere, which is as many thousand spheres' from which emanate 'beams like spokes of some invisible wheel', *Prometheus Unbound*, IV. 236–318.

l. 280. *"E pur si muove".* 'And yet it does move', the comment Galileo is said to have made when forced to retract his belief that the earth circles the sun.

l. 312 *Full life of Shelley.* The fullest available to RB was Thomas Medwin's *Life of Percy Bysshe Shelley* (1847).

l. 329. *Titan of genius.* The phrase invites a comparison between Shelley and his own Prometheus.

l. 345. *basement.* Foundation.

l. 358. *the ostensible conch and dominant Triton of the fountain.* RB may specifically have in mind Bernini's Triton fountain in the Piazza Barberini in Rome.

l. 390. *The very first letter.* The first letter, dated 22 February 1811 and addressed to the Editor of the *New Statesman*, in which Shelley deprecates attacks on the liberty of the press and threats to the liberty of individuals.

l. 397–405. *"One whose heart . . . this earth". Julian and Maddalo*, 442–50. The lines are not authorial but given to a character, the Maniac, whose unhappy fate Julian and Maddalo discuss. RB obscures the dramatic character of the lines by replacing 'me' in the first and penultimate line of the quotation with 'One'. *Julian and Maddalo* was written in 1818–19, not 'at the close' of Shelley's life, although it was published only in the posthumous volume of 1824.

l. 437. *Red cloak . . . fireball.* The metaphor derives from bullfighting in which the bull might be enraged by fireballs attached to the horns.

l. 439. *"the sale of love".* A note is appended to the phrase, 'Even love is sold', *Queen Mab*, V. 189, arguing that 'prostitution is the legitimate offspring of marriage'.

l. 452. *Hate of hate.* Tennyson, 'The Poet', 1830, 3.

l. 458. *"a worship . . . Coleridge says".* Loosely paraphrasing a passage from a letter to Maria Gisborne: 'Hope, as Coleridge says, is a solemn duty, which we owe alike to ourselves & to the world—a worship to the spirit of good within, which requires, before it sends that inspiration forth, which impresses its likeness upon all that it creates, devoted and disinterested homage,' *Essays, Letters from Abroad, Translations and Fragments*, 1840, 234.

l. 461. *Paul.* The reference may be to Paul's distinction between those who are 'in the flesh' and those who are 'in the spirit' (Romans 8: 9).

l. 465. *"The stars . . . things that be"*. 'The Boat on the Serchio', first published in the *Posthumous Poems* of 1824, 7–17, with lines 9–10 and lines 15–16 omitted.

l. 473. *choragus-like*. Like the leader of the Chorus in an ancient Greek drama.

l. 475. *"All rose . . . can be known"*. Shelley, 'The Boat on the Serchio', 30–3.

l. 479. *David's pregnant conclusion*. The reference may be specifically to the conclusion of Psalm 90: 17: 'And let the beauty of the Lord our God be upon us: and establish thou the work of our hands upon us; yea, the work of our hands establish thou it.' RB seems oddly inattentive to Shelley's blasphemous description of Christian teaching as 'What none yet ever knew or can be known.'

l. 484. *Every audacious negative*. In *Queen Mab*, 7. 13, the claim 'There is no God' is supplemented by a long note in which Shelley claims that the assertion leaves unshaken the 'hypothesis of a pervading Spirit co-eternal with the universe'.

l. 489. *the politics of Junius*. Junius was the pseudonym adopted by the author (now commonly identified as Sir Philip Francis) of a series of attacks on the corruptions of the Duke of Grafton's administration collected in 1772 as the *Letters of Junius*. Rowley was the name under which Thomas Chatterton published his counterfeit medieval poems. RB extenuated the offence and insisted that Chatterton had determined before his death not to repeat it in his only other critical essay, ostensibly a review of a book on Tasso, published anonymously in the *Foreign Quarterly Review* for July 1842 but convincingly ascribed to RB.

l. 491. *"really, truly, nobody at all"*. In *The Vision of Judgment*, 639–40, Byron advances the witty hypothesis that 'what Junius we are wont to call, | Was *really—truly*—nobody at all.'

l. 495. *Stronger admiration for Guido (and Carlo Dolce!) than for Michelangelo*. Shelley much admired Guido Reni, and owned, as he records in the preface to *The Cenci*, a copy of the portrait by him that he believed to be of Beatrice Cenci, and disapproved of Michaelangelo's Bacchus, as he records in his remarks on the statues in Florence. The notion that Shelley admired Carlo Dolci may derive from Medwin's sketch of Professor Pacchiani, a Pisan acquaintance of the Shelleys, who always knew a '*Marchese* or *Marchesa*, ready to part with a Carlo Dolce or Andrea del Sarto' (*Life of Percy Bysshe Shelley*, ii. 59).

l. 497. *"a word . . . to a man"*. In Luke 12: 10, Jesus instructs the disciples, 'whosoever shall speak a word against the Son of man, it shall be forgiven him; but unto him that blasphemeth against the Holy Ghost it shall not be forgiven'.

l. 501. *Gold-region*. References to 'the gold region of California' became common after the gold rush of 1848.

l. 508. *Zastrozzi*. The Gothic novel that Shelley published in 1810 when he was 17.

l. 517. *Laudanum*. Opium dissolved in alcohol, taken by Shelley, as Medwin records, to ease the pain of his nephritis.

l. 522. *Creations of the imagination*. In a note to *Hellas*, 814–15, Shelley refers to 'that state of mind in which ideas may be supposed to assume the force of sensations through the confusion of thought with the objects of thought, and the excess of passion animating the creations of the imagination'.

ll. 526–8. The anecdotes that RB recalls are all gathered from Medwin's *Life*. Medwin tells the story of the attempt on Shelley's life 'that occurred, or which Shelley supposed to occur, in North Wales', and reports the general view that the incident was 'a horrid dream—the effect of an overheated imagination' (i. 178–81). He reports a story of a 'lady' who fell in love with Shelley, followed him to Naples, and died there (i. 324–9), and the story that, after hearing Shelley ask for his mail at the post office at Pisa, a soldier asked him, 'What, are you that damned atheist Shelley', and knocked him down (ii. 9).

l. 530–6. *Half-created shadow*. A fragment first published by Mary Shelley in the *Poetical Works* (1839).

l. 541. *"old rags"*. Medwin records of *The Cenci*, 'Whilst writing it he heard in the street the oft-repeated cry, "Cenci, Cenci," which he at first thought the echo of his own soul, but soon learnt was one of the cries of Rome—Cenci meaning old rags' (i. 133).

l. 541. *Somnambulism*. Medwin reports that Shelley took up again 'his old habit of sleep-walking' in the final months at Lerici (ii. 50).

l. 556. *The Koh-i-noor*. A topical reference to the 'mountain of light', then the largest known diamond in the world. In 1849 Sir Charles Napier dispatched it to Britain to be presented to Queen Victoria, after it had been seized from Duleep Singh.

l. 564. *The spirit . . . with God*. *Epipsychidion*, 128–9: Shelley's worm is 'beneath' the sod.

l. 576. *as perfect even as those*. The metaphor derives from Aphrodite (etymologically the 'foam-born') who was born of the sea.

l. 579. "Shelley", compare RB to EBB, 'I never have begun, even, what I hope I was born to begin and end,—"R.B. a poem"' (*Correspondence*, x. 69).

Note to p. 171. RB is mocking Shelley's description of a bas-relief that RB believes to be by Verrocchio as 'Probably the sides of a Sarcophagus' in his 'Remarks on some of the Statues in the Gallery of Florence'; his mistake in 'Ugolino', first published in 1847 in Thomas Medwin's *Life of Shelley*, as to which Pisan tower it was in which Ugolino and his sons starved to death; and his mistaking in *Julian and Maddalo* the Venetian island on which the madhouse stood, a mistake resulting in him describing it as a 'windowless, deformed and dreary pile' (101).

FROM *MEN AND WOMEN*, VOL. I (1855)

Love Among the Ruins

The poem may well have been prompted by the excursions to the Campagna that RB enjoyed in the spring of 1854, while resident in Rome. Much criticism of the poem has been concerned to identify ruins further afield that RB might have had in mind. Suggestions have ranged from the biblical Babylon and Nineveh (although Nineveh, recently excavated by Layard, had a topical interest), to Syracuse and Agrigentum in Sicily (in an early manuscript preserved in Harvard's Houghton Library the poem is entitled 'A Sicilian Pastoral'), but Ann Farkas seems right to conclude that the city RB describes conforms to the 'stereotype of an ancient city' that would have been familiar to any 'classically educated and well-read person like RB' from the writings of poets, travellers, and archaeologists over many centuries (see 'Digging Among the Ruins', *Victorian Poetry*, 29.1 (1991), 36). Nevertheless R. K. Thornton's suggestion that RB is indebted to Spenser's *Complaints*, *Notes and Queries*, 123 (May 1968), 178–9, seems unusually pertinent, not least because Thornton finds in Spenser's *Ruines of Rome* a passage that might have played in RB's ear when he devised his poem's metre: 'Ne ought save Tyber hastning to his fall | Remaines of all' (40–1). RB wrote his own meditation among the ruins in full consciousness that he was only the latest of a long line of poets prompted to meditation by evidence of the transience of even the most impressive human monuments. It was a complex tradition. Ruins might prompt a soothing melancholy, an indignantly prophetic insistence that the ruination of the city was the necessary consequence of the depravity of its inhabitants, or, closer to RB's own time, the republican satisfaction in the levelling of monarchic ambitions evident in the manner in which writers such as Volney or Shelley contemplate ruins. RB's poem seems to glance between all three manners, settling on none, rather in the same way that he devises a metre to which the reader's ear never becomes quite attuned. Ten-syllable lines, most often trimeters, most often anapaestic, alternate with lines that consist of a single foot, an English version of the cretic, in which two stressed are separated by an unstressed syllable. The short line sounds like an echo of the line it follows, but the echo may seem mocking or it may seem plangent. In 1855 the poem is divided into six-line stanzas, the stanzas alternating between past and present. In later editions the poem is in twelve-line stanzas, each stanza completing its own contrast between past and present. In the Harvard manuscript the poem is divided into sections of twelve lines but each section includes a break after the sixth line. RB clearly found it difficult to decide whether he should 'intersect' the poem after a group of six lines or let two such stanzas 'run | Into one' (17–18), and his hesitation seems appropriate to the poem. It is a poem full of doublets but RB cannot decide whether to disjoin or to conjoin them: 'Miles and miles', 'stray or stop', 'great and gay', 'Peace or war', 'plenty and perfection', 'Stock or stone', 'Bought and sold', 'South and north'. In the same way, the speaker seems uncertain whether to mourn or mock his monarch's attempt to make of 'the hundred-gated circuit' of the city walls, and the 'burning ring' that the chariots traced around it magic circles within which he could, like Coleridge's Kubla Khan with his 'walls and towers girdled round', dream that he was safe from the depredations of time. But he seems still more uncertain whether lingeringly to contemplate the ruins all around him as a natural emblem of mortality, or whether to focus his attention on the 'girl with eager eyes and yellow hair' who is awaiting him. RB's most distinctive innovation is to cross the meditation among ruins with a very different version of pastoral with which he would have been familiar from his favourite, John Donne, in which the poem celebrates erotic love as a refuge from the corrupt court life of power, gold, and glory, but remains recalcitrantly fascinated by the world that it repudiates.

l. 7. *great and gay*. Compare Spenser, *The Ruines of Time*, 55: 'all that in this world is great or gaie'.

l. 19. *shot its spires*. Compare Spenser, *Ruines of Rome by Bellay*, 16: 'And sharped steeples high shot up in Air.'

l. 21. *hundred-gated*. The Egyptian Thebes is commonly distinguished by its hundred gates from the Grecian city which had seven, but other great cities such as Babylon are credited with a similar number of gates.

l. 30. *Stock or stone*. The phrase usually refers to idols, graven images, as in Jeremiah 2: 27, but the phrase here seems simply to suggest the deadness of the ruins, as in Catherine Gore's *Mrs Armytage* (1836) in which a mother who has been persuaded to renounce her daughter has to endure that daughter growing up in her presence 'as in the presence of a stock or stone' (volume iii, chapter 19).

l. 35–6. Compare Shelley, *Prometheus Unbound*, I. 530–1: 'Kingly concaves, stern and cold, | Where blood with gold is bought and sold.'

l. 39. *caper*. A spiny shrub common in Mediterranean countries, the berries of which are pickled and eaten. John Armstrong refers to the plant's 'wandering roots', *The Oeconomy of Love*, 225. The gourd is a trailing plant.

l. 40. *Overscored*. Crossed out, as with a pen.

l. 41. *houseleek*. Sempervivum or live forever, a succulent so-called because of its ability to withstand dry and stony conditions.

l. 47. *minions*. Favourites.

l. 51. Venus, the evening star, is also known as the folding star; *many-tinkling*. Because the sheep are wearing bells; *fleece*. As a collective noun for sheep the usage is rare but not unique.

l. 59. *breathless*. Compare Wordsworth, 'It is a beauteous evening, calm and free', 3, 'Breathless with adoration'.

l. 64. *Colonnades*. Trees arranged in orderly rows, like Cowper's poplars which emit 'the whispering sound of the cool colonnade', 'The Poplar Field', 2.

l. 65. *causeys*. Embankments.

l. 75. *brazen pillar*. Compare 'brasen Pillours', Spenser, *The Ruines of Time*, 410.

Pillars are associated with architectural ambition through the 'pillars of brass' which Solomon erected in his temple (1 Kings 7: 15), and its frustration when the Babylonians take Jerusalem, break up the pillars and transport the brass to Babylon (2 Kings 25: 13). The pillar of the temple may be conflated with the Tower of Babel, the vainglorious attempt to erect a building 'whose top may reach unto heaven' (Genesis 11: 4).

l. 80. *returns*. As in the returns on an investment.

A Lovers' Quarrel

Given that the poem cites two issues on which RB and EBB differed, spiritualism and the character of Napoleon III, RB being in both cases antipathetic, it is inevitable that it has invited biographical understanding, but the interest of the poem is not exclusively, nor even primarily, personal.

l. 5. *the South*. The south wind.

l. 8. *Runnels, which rillets swell*. Streams which are swelled by little rills.

l. 11. The stone forming the bed of the stream is compared to beryl because of its colour, but the colour of beryl stones varies widely. RB is probably thinking of a yellow or orange variety.

l. 13. Possibly a memory of *As You Like It*, II. i. 16–17: 'books in the running brooks | Sermons in stones.'

ll. 17–19. The cutting edge of the wind is compared to the maul and wedge used to split wood.

l. 20. *ingle*. Hearth.

l. 28. Jackdaws nest in church steeples. Cowper describes the bird as 'A great frequenter of the church' ('The Jackdaw', 4). Jackdaws are commonly said to 'chatter'.

ll. 29–35. The marriage of Napoleon III and the Empress Eugenie was celebrated on 30 January 1853. An editorial in *The Times* for 31 January 1853, 4, notes that there are 'few instances upon record of a Royal marriage celebrated with so much pomp and publicity', and adds: 'Among the more stable sovereignties of Europe there is a greater sobriety of display, a more cautious use of the public money, and less disposition to catch the eye of a few thousand spectators by a species of exhibition which may be thought puerile or theatrical.' RB disliked and distrusted Napoleon III because, after being elected President, he elevated himself to the monarchy in 1851 by means of a coup d'état. RB always acknowledged that his 1871 monologue *Prince Hohenstiel-Schwangau, Saviour of Society* was a portrait of Napoleon III.

l. 35. *The Times* reported that at the religious ceremony in Notre Dame the Empress Eugenie wore 'a diadem of brilliants on her head', Tuesday, 1 February, 5.

ll. 36–42. RB's friend Alfred Domett has a vigorous description of the Pampas in his *Venice* (1839): 'Ye pampas wild—a thistly sea | Of rolling rank fertility' (87–8), as does his American friend William Wetmore Story in 'The Gaucho' (1848) in which the Pampas is an 'inland sea of grass' over which the gaucho rides on his 'sinewy horse' (2). RB's sunflowers may owe something to Tennyson's dandelion, a 'flower all gold' that propagates itself so successfully that 'the world | Like one great garden showed', 'The Poet' (1830), 24, 33–4.

ll. 43–9. In 1853 EBB held séances in which tables moved, but RB remained 'in a glorious minority' 'trying hard to keep his ground as a denier' (*EBB to Arabella*, i. 572).

ll. 46–7. Probably a reference to 'that od-force of German Reichenbach' (*Aurora Leigh*, 7. 566), an all-pervading force posited by Carl von Reichenbach which, as Margaret Reynolds explains, 'was especially visible to the sensitive as a light streaming from the fingertips' (*Aurora Leigh*, note to p. 231).

l. 55. *ocean-space*. Reversing the commonplace, 'the vast ocean of unbounded space', Edward Young, *Night Thoughts*, VI. 177.

l. 58. *vest*. A loose outer garment.

l. 61. *the lappet*. The lapel.

l. 64. *flirt a fan*. Snap a fan open and shut.

ll. 66–8. Applying a false moustache.

l. 72. *mesmeriser*. Franz Anton Mesmer (1754–1815) claimed to cure patients by passing 'animal magnetism' from his body to theirs, a process that involved making 'passes' with his hands. For RB's interest in this kind of therapy see 'Mesmerism'.

l. 82. The devil shoots arrows of temptation, but the figure is best understood as antithetical to Cupid with his bow.

ll. 90–1. 'Death and life are in the power of the tongue', Proverbs 18: 21.

l. 105. 'why beholdest thou the mote that is in thy brother's eye, but considerest not the beam that is in thine own eye', Matthew 7: 3.

l. 112. *brain's coat of curd*. The cerebral cortex.

l. 121. The almond is one of the first trees to blossom.

l. 123. *minor third*. The interval between the two notes of the cuckoo's call.

l. 125. *guelder-rose*. The viburnum or snowball tree.

ll. 131–3. Tom Thumb was commonly represented as heroic despite his diminutive stature and was once swallowed by a giant after being deposited in his castle. Giants traditionally exclaim 'fee-faw-fum' or some variant of the phrase.

ll. 134–47. The thought is that in summertime people can live separately, but in winter they need to cling to each other for warmth.

l. 138. *unnipped*. That is by frost.

l. 145. The metaphor is of a fire stirred once again to life.

l. 148. *the score*. The reckoning, the tally of how much is owed.

Evelyn Hope

A love poem distinguished by the oddity that the love it proclaims, for a 16-year-old girl by a man approaching 50, can be acknowledged only, as the speaker admits, because the girl is dead. He can claim her 'sweet cold hand' only in Heaven, where, according to some, everyone will be 33, the perfect age because the age at which Christ died, and almost precisely the mean of the ages of Evelyn and her admirer.

l. 15. Compare *Christmas-Eve*, 151–3: 'Whene'er 'twas the thought first struck him, | How death, at unawares, might duck him | Deeper than the grave.'

l. 19. Compare Dryden's Anne Killigrew Ode, 41–2: 'For sure the milder planets did combine | On thy auspicious horoscope to shine.'

l. 20. *spirit, fire and dew*. She is made up of three of the elements, air, fire, and water, but the fourth, earth, is absent.

l. 28. If love has the power to inspire love in return, then he can claim Evelyn on the strength of his love for her rather than of hers for him.

l. 35. *long still*. Long dead and gone, as in *Parleying with Certain People*, 1887, 'With Charles Avison', 43, 'the relic of a brain long still'.

l. 38. In 'Flower' Part Two, 5 (1833), RB's friend Alfred Domett notes of a young woman, 'Her lip's geranium-red'.

l. 44. *spoiled the climes*. Plundered the regions of the earth.

l. 53. *leaf*. Presumably a sheet of paper on which he has written his declaration of love, perhaps the poem itself.

Up at a Villa—Down in the City (As Distinguished by an Italian Person of Quality)

The subtitle suggests that, like 'England in Italy', the poem is designed to mock Italian insensitivity to the beauty of the Italian countryside, but its speaker occasionally displays, or is lent by RB, the sensitivity that he disclaims, as when he notes the flower of the wild tulip, 'a thin clear bubble of blood'. The poem is perhaps better understood as a study of national difference, persons of quality in England being much more likely to regret that their limited wealth does not allow them to retreat to their country seats when the London season ends with the end of June. The Cockney pleasure that the Italian takes in urban sights and sounds might render him absurd, but is perhaps just as likely to endear him to English readers, especially those who shared RB's own suburban upbringing.

l. 4. *by Bacchus*. A comical oath, used, for example, by 'Parsnippides' in the 1833 translation from Aristophanes' *The Clouds* by RB's friend Alfred Domett.

l. 9. *shag*. Seems to combine the use of the word to refer to a shrub with its derogatory use for a low or rascally person.

l. 12. *white as a curd*. The expression may be proverbial. Keats's fellow Cockney Cornelius Webbe describes eggs as 'white as a curd', 'The Miller's Treat' (1832), 63.

l. 13. *in four straight lines*. Along each side of the square.

l. 20. *over-smoked*. *OED* cites the line, and suggests that the expression means covered over as if by smoke. It refers to the effect of the olive trees dulling the hue of the hills.

ll. 26–30. The fountain seems to be imaginary, though hippocamps ('horses with curling fish-tails') are common, as in the Trevi fountain in Rome. Venus is also sometimes so represented, for example, in the fountain that was replaced by the Fonte Gaia in Siena.

l. 27. *foam-bows*. Rainbows formed when the sun shines on the foam of the fountain. The expression is used, and explained in a note, by Tennyson, 'Oenone' (1842), 60.

l. 29. *fifty gazers*. Compare the reference in *Sordello* to a woman giving birth on a 'chance heap of wet filth, reconciled | To fifty gazers' (5. 279–80).

l. 35. *the stunning cicala*. Compare *Aurora Leigh*, 7. 700–1: 'perfectly be stunned | By those insufferable cicale'.

l. 38. *blessed*. Used either to mean holy or as a euphemism for 'damned', or perhaps both.

l. 39. *diligence*. Public stage coach, by this date used only for the stage coaches of continental Europe.

l. 42. *Pulcinello*. More commonly Pulcinella, the Italian Punch. The trumpet announces the puppet show, which attracts those who had been shopping in the market.

l. 43. *scene-picture*. Compare *Fifine at the Fair*, 2014–15: 'unrolled, the strange scene-picture grew | Before me', where the expression seems to denote a panorama. The new play is advertised on a playbill.

l. 44. *three liberal thieves*. That is nationalists who have been shot as thieves.

l. 45. Several archbishops, including the Archbishop of Florence, were identified as reactionary supporters of Austrian rule. In *Casa Guidi Windows*, for example, EBB records how, in the course of their ineffective revolution, the Florentine republicans 'chased the Archbishop from the Duomo door' (Part II, 152).

l. 46. *The Duke's*. Leopold II, Grand Duke of Tuscany, was a frequent butt of both RB and EBB.

l. 47. *flowery marge*. The margin of the paper on which the sonnet is written, but also a hackneyed phrase commonly used for a riverbank, and hence a phrase that might appear in the sonnet itself.

l. 48. The literary figures are chosen for their incongruity one with another.

l. 50. *Lent-lectures*. A special series of sermons given for Lent, the most famous of which are the twelve sermons given in 1622 by St Francis de Sales: *unctuous*/ Because they provided spiritual unction, although RB would have been aware that the word was often derogatory, suggesting greasiness.

ll. 51–2. The procession probably celebrates the Feast of the Seven Sorrows of the Blessed Virgin Mary, held on the third Sunday of September. The feast was extended to Tuscany in 1807, and is most closely associated with the Servite order which was founded in Florence.

l. 54. Compare *Christmas-Eve*, 250–5, where the 'thump-thump and shriek-shriek' of the train 'from Manchester' makes 'my neighbour's haunches stir'.

l. 56. In Tuscany the Grand-Duke had a right to tax salt, a tax so resented that it is often invoked to explain the absence of salt from Tuscan bread.

ll. 60–1. Such processions are most common in Italy on good Friday.

A Woman's Last Word

It is proverbial that a woman always has the last word, but the echo of the proverb in the poem's title seems ironic, because, although only the woman speaks, she speaks to voice her surrender to a man who claims possession of her body and soul. It is not enough for him that she speaks his speech, unreasonable though the demand is: he makes the further and intolerable demand, or so she believes, that she think his thought. The tears with which the poem ends seem far from foolish. The poem should be contrasted rather than compared with 'A Lover's Quarrel'. It describes a relationship quite different from the kind of relationship that the RBs claimed for themselves. Longman appropriately quotes EBB's letter to her sister of 24 February 1847, in which she records RB's observation: 'When I . . . say unreasonable & improper things, which my own reason would recoil at another time, you do not give up to me, & attempt to soothe me by agreeing with me or letting it pass, as so many good-tempered women do to the eternal injury of foolish men.' EBB replies, 'The reason is, that I have too much *respect* for you not to tell you the truth, when I apprehend the truth myself' (*Correspondence*, xiv. 132).

ll. 7–8. A memory of the debate on Valentine's day in which birds choose their mates in Chaucer's *Parliament of Foules* may lie behind the thought, but RB's point is that the birds are so intent on their debate that they do not notice the imminent threat from the hawk that is stalking them.

l. 12. Compare 'By the Fireside', 161–2: 'Hither we walked then, side by side, | Arm in arm and cheek to cheek.'

ll. 13–14. The point is that to maintain in opposition to the beloved a position believed to be true is to be false to the beloved.

l. 15. The serpent's tooth is a type of ingratitude, from *King Lear*, I. iv. 288–9: 'How sharper than a serpent's tooth it is | To have a thankless child.'

ll. 17–20. The reference to the fruit of the knowledge of good and evil seems prompted by the reference to the serpent in the previous stanza. The word 'pry' may recall Satan's resolve to 'pry | In every bush and brake, where hap may find | The serpent sleeping', *Paradise Lost*, IX. 159–61.

Fra Lippo Lippi

RB follows Vasari closely in his understanding of Lippo Lippi's life, especially Vasari's claim that Lippo Lippi was 'much addicted to the pleasures of sense' (76), but for his understanding of his place in the history of art, he relies on Anna Jameson, who represents Fra Lippo Lippi and Fra Angelico as 'the very antipodes of each other'. The two painters initiated 'the great schism in modern art'. Fra Angelico began a school of painters 'to whom the cultivation of art was a sacred vocation—the representation of beauty a means, not an end; by whom Nature in her various aspects was studied and deeply studied, but only for the purpose of embodying whatever we can conceive or reverence as highest, holiest, purest in heaven and earth'. Lippo Lippi by contrast initiated a school 'profoundly versed in the knowledge of the human form, and intent on studying and imitating the various effects of nature in colour and in light and shade, without any other aspiration than the representation of beauty for its own sake, and the pleasure and the triumph of difficulties overcome' (Jameson, 67–8). But the poem engages issues that continued to divide in the 19th century as even an arch-realist such as George Eliot reveals when she defends Goethe's depiction in *Wilhelm Meister* of 'irregular relations in all the charms they really have for human nature' (*Leader*, 21 July 1855), and yet concedes that Balzac has 'overstepped' the necessary limits of art. The poem may suggest a nostalgia shared by a novelist such as Thackeray for the easy acceptance possible to an 18th-century writer like Fielding that irregular relations might be a more or less regrettable symptom of generous animal spirits. The poem also explores whether and how a knowledge of an artist's private life might inform an understanding of the work, an issue that RB had confronted in 1851 when writing his Introductory Essay to the volume of letters that drew attention to the irregular private life of Shelley, the poet he had once most admired.

l. 3. *Zooks.* A mildly blasphemous exclamation, usually explained as a shortening of God's hooks, the nails used to crucify Christ. A stock item in dramatic diction from the 17th century, but antiquated by the 19th.

l. 6. *sportive ladies.* That is, prostitutes.

l. 7. *Carmine.* The Carmelite convent: its church is Santa Maria del Carmine.

ll. 7–11. The watchmen who have apprehended him as he leaves the brothel are compared to terriers ratting, before the rat is diminished to a less threatening white mouse.

l. 9. *wrong hole.* Probably with a smutty double entendre.

l. 17. *Cosimo of the Medici.* Cosimo de' Medici (1389–1464). Although he refused all public office Cosimo was described by the Pope as the king of Florence in all but name. His great wealth derived from the family banking business.

l. 18. *the house.* The Medici Palace that caps or crowns the street corner on which it stands.

ll. 23–4. The watch do not discriminate between people of different status. The figure may recall the Clown in *Twelfth Night*, III. i. 32–3: 'fools are as like husbands as pilchards are to herrings; the husband's the bigger'.

l. 28. *quarter-florin*. A florin is a gold coin first issued in Florence and sometimes known as a Florence.

l. 31. *all's come square*. Neither party owes the other anything.

ll. 32–6. Lippo Lippi painted the beheading of John the Baptist in the series of frescoes representing the life of the saint he completed for Prato Cathedral between 1452 and 1466.

l. 38. *A wood-coal*. A piece of charcoal.

l. 44. *hip to haunch*. Side by side, with a suggestion of man to man.

ll. 45–6. The reference seems to be not to the carnival before Lent but to a second carnival peculiar to Florence that marks the beginning of spring on 1 May, and continues until the feast day of John the Baptist on 24 June. This was the carnival associated with carnival songs, many of them involving risqué double entendres.

l. 47. *mew*. Place of confinement.

ll. 48–9. C. F. Thomas suspects a reference to a specific picture, Fra Lippo Lippi's *Seven Saints*, painted for the Medici Palace and now in the National Gallery (*Art and Architecture in the Poetry of Robert Browning*, 1991, 425–6).

l. 52. *whifts*. Snatches.

ll. 53–4. The first of seven complete or partial examples of the 'stornello' included in the poem. The 'stornello' is an Italian verse form of two or three lines in which a short line is followed by one or two longer lines. Because the first linc usually invokes a flower the verse form is also termed a 'fiore'.

ll. 61–6. '[H]aving endured this confinement for two days, he then made ropes with the sheet of his bed, which he cut to pieces for that purpose, and so having let himself down from a window, escaped' (Vasari, 77).

l. 63. *bed furniture*. Bed linen.

l. 67. *St. Laurence*. San Lorenzo in the market district of Florence, the parish church of the Medici. The building by Brunelleschi was commissioned by Cosimo's father.

ll. 73–4. Vasari mentions as particularly fine 'a figure of St. Jerome doing penance' as 'now in the *guardaroba* of Duke Cosimo' (Vasari, 2. 83).

l. 80. *what am I a beast for?* Why do you think me bestial?

l. 86. *empty as your hat*. The officer is presumably carrying rather than wearing his hat.

88. 'Old Aunt Lapaccia', 'The child was for some time under the care of a certain Mona Lapaccia, his aunt' after the death of his parents (Vasari, 74); *trussed*. Clutched.

l. 89. *stinger*. In the habit of delivering stinging blows.

l. 94. *refection*. Commonly denotes a monastic meal; *Will you renounce*. Carmelites take vows of poverty and chastity. In particular they renounce personal property, agreeing to hold all property in common.

l. 104. *serge*. The rough woollen cloth from which the monk's habit is made.

l. 109. *waste*. Wasted labour.

ll. 117–20. Lippo Lippi alludes to the Processions of the Holy Sacrament or Eucharistic Processions most closely associated with the Feast of Corpus Christi. Some of those carrying candles would allow the boy to collect the melted wax to sell.

l. 121. *the Eight*. The Magistracy of the Eight responsible for maintaining law and order in Florence, an institution established by Machiavelli.

ll. 129–42. '[I]n place of studying, he never did anything but daub his own books, and those of the other boys, with caricatures, whereupon the prior determined to give him all means and every opportunity for learning to draw' (Vasari, 2. 74).

l. 130. *antiphonary*. Hymn book.

l. 131. *long music-notes*. Probably semibreves, a hollow oval note without a stem.

l. 137. *Lose a crow and catch a lark*. A seemingly invented proverb, meaning lose a shilling and find a pound, possibly suggested by *The Merchant of Venice*, V. i. 102–3: 'The crow doth sing as sweetly as the lark | When neither is attended.'

ll. 139–40. The Camaldolese had Lorenzo Monaco, active 1399, died 1423 or 1424, who entered the Camaldolese monastery of Santa Maria degli Angeli in Florence in 1391; the Preaching Friars or Dominicans had Fra Angelico, active 1417, died 1455, who became Prior of the Friary of San Domenici in Fiesole.

l. 141. The façade of Santa Maria del Carmine remained unfinished.

l. 145. *the black and white*. The Dominicans and Carmelites.

l. 148. *cribs of barrel-droppings*. Insignificant thefts.

ll. 149–50. The fellow has fled to the church to claim sanctuary.

l. 164. *laid the ladder flat*. So that the ladder on which he had been standing to paint did not obscure the painting.

l. 170. *Prior's niece*. A comical euphemism denoting the Prior's mistress. Compare the Bishop's 'nephews' in 'The Tomb at St Praxed's'.

l. 172. *triumph's straw-fire*. Fires of straw are proverbially quickly ignited but short-lived, as in Edward Fairfax, *Godfrey of Bulloigne*, 1. 504: 'Like fire of straw soone kindled, soone burnt out'; *funked*. Smoked (after the flames are extinguished).

l. 185. In medieval art the soul leaving the body of the dying is often represented as an infant.

l. 189. Giotto (1267/76–1337) was identified by Vasari as the first modern master. The reference may be specific to the cycle of frescoes in Assisi on the life of St Francis in which Giotto represents the soul ascending from the body of the dying saint.

ll. 196–7. The Prior ignorantly conflates Salome who asked for the head of John the Baptist as her reward after dancing before her stepfather, King

Herod, with Herodias, her mother, who instigated her choice. Vasari records that Fra Lippo painted a fresco in Prato Cathedral depicting 'the Feast of Herod, and the Decapitation of the Saint' (82).

ll. 200–1. *must go further | And can't fare worse!* Inverting the proverb, 'you may go further and fare worse'.

ll. 210–11. *if it means hope, fear, | Sorrow or joy?* Vasari praises Lippo Lippi's skill in rendering 'variety of expression' (2. 82).

l. 214. *threefold.* RB is referring to the distinctions between body, mind or life, and soul.

ll. 227–9. Cosimo in the Medici Palace, the gates to which have large metal rings to which Lippo Lippi imagines himself clinging.

ll. 235–6. See note to 139–40.

l. 250. *the cup runs o'er.* The Psalmist's 'cup runneth over' with the oil with which God has anointed him (Psalm 23: 5), but Lippo's cup overflows with his own vitality.

l. 251. Lippo denies two clichés, the association of the world and the flesh with the devil, and the thought that life is a dream.

l. 254. *mill-horse.* The horse harnessed to the mill-wheel that it turns, but often a figure for a person bound to humdrum tasks.

l. 257. Combines two thoughts: that 'all flesh is as grass' (1 Peter 1: 24), and that God will separate the wheat from the chaff and 'burn up the chaff with unquenchable fire' (Matthew 3: 12). The implication is that the flesh is irredeemable.

ll. 266–7. Masolino's fresco of the beautiful unfallen Adam and Eve is in the Brancacci Chapel of Santa Maria del Carmine, alongside Masaccio's frescoes.

l. 277. *They call him hulking Tom.* '[F]rom his abstracted air, his utter indifference to the usual sports and pursuits of boyhood, his negligent dress and manners, his companions called him *Masaccio*, which might be translated *ugly* or *slovenly Tom*' (Jameson, 80).

l. 278. *He picks my practice up.* RB believed and continued to maintain that Masaccio was a follower of Lippo Lippi rather than vice versa, misled by a note in the Le Monnier edition of Vasari's *Vite* that he owned. See Johnstone Parr, 'Browning's Fra Lippo Lippi, Baldinucci, and the Milanesi Edition of Vasari', *English Language Notes*, 3 (1966), 197–201. Anna Jameson would have entrenched RB in his mistake by placing her chapter on Masaccio after her chapter on Lippo Lippi and pairing him with Lippo's son Filippino Lippi.

ll. 286–90. Landscapes sometimes occupy the backgrounds of Lippo Lippi's paintings, as in his *Madonna with Child and Two Angels*.

l. 306. The painting allows all who look at it to borrow the manner in which the mind of the painter apprehended his subject.

l. 307. *cullion.* A contemptuous term for a low person; *hanging.* Gloomy-looking.

ll. 310–11. A Ruskinian view of the painter's function.

l. 318. In the Catholic Church, unlike the Church of England, matins is the night office.

l. 319. Friday for Catholics is the day of abstinence.

ll. 323–31. An imaginary painting of the martyrdom of St Lawrence who was roasted to death on a gridiron.

l. 330. *their own*. That is, their own hearts.

l. 337. *God wot*. God knows.

l. 339. *Chianti*. The typical wine of Tuscany.

ll. 344–74. Lippi plans the *The Coronation of the Virgin* that he painted for Sant'Ambrogio's in Florence.

l. 347. *cast of my office*. Specimen of my profession.

l. 351. *orris-root*. The root of the iris used as a scent.

l. 354. John the Baptist is patron saint of Florence.

l. 355. St Ambrose (339–97), who was Bishop of Milan, is on the left of the painting, identified by his mitre. RB imagines him recording the names of the patrons of the convent depicted in the painting.

l. 356. *A long day*. A legal term signifying a distant date at which accounts must be settled. Here it indicates that Ambrose will intercede to secure a long life for the donors.

l. 357. Job is the bearded figure in the left foreground, wearing a sash on which his name is written, looking, like St Ambrose, at the donors.

l. 358. *The man of Uz*. 'There was a man in the land of Uz, whose name was Job', Job 1: 1. Job is the Man of Patience.

l. 374. *Saint John*. John the Baptist, represented at the far right of the painting.

l. 375. *camel-hair*. 'John had his raiment of camel's hair', Matthew 3: 4.

ll. 375–6. RB imagined that the bald figure on the far right holding a scroll, on which is written, 'This man completed the work,' is Lippo's self-portrait, whereas it is certainly a portrait of Francesco Maringhi who had left money to pay for the painting. The figure popularly supposed to be Lippo's self-portrait is the tonsured monk kneeling in front of St Ambrose.

l. 380. *kirtles*. Skirts or outer petticoats.

l. 381. *hot cockles*. A party game in which one player must tap another, whose head in buried in someone's lap, without being identified, but the expression is often used lubriciously as in Aphra Behn, *The Lucky Chance*, III. iii, 'his gentlewoman has been at Hot-Cockles without her husband'.

l. 387. Lippo mimics the Prior in line 196; *Saint Lucy*. An early Christian martyr who was, like the Prior's niece, beautiful, but unlike her was sworn to preserve her virginity.

l. 392. *the grey beginning*. The darkness is thinning.

A Toccata of Galuppi's

RB's boyhood ambition was to be a musician. He took lessons in composition from his Camberwell neighbour John Relfe, as well as learning to play piano, cello, violin, and the organ. A toccata is a keyboard piece designed to show the touch of the performer. RB wrote to an enquirer: 'As for Galuppi, I had once in my possession two huge manuscript volumes almost exclusively made up of his "Toccata-pieces"—apparently a slighter form of the Sonata to be "touched" lightly off.' (Quoted in Herbert E. Greene, 'Browning's Knowledge of Music', *PMLA* 62 (1947), 1095–9.) Byron's speaker opens just such a volume, but, unlike RB, he 'was never out of England'. As his eye scans the score he hears inwardly, or perhaps he plays by sight, music that he has never heard performed, just as he tries to imagine Venice, a city he has never visited except in the pages of Shakespeare and Byron. The metre of the opening lines seems only to mark the discrepancy between Venice and the earnest, stiffly disapproving, and perhaps rather cockney speaker, but as the poem proceeds the metre, like the speaker, reveals unexpected capacities. He shows himself thrillingly alert, for example, to such things as 'a breast's superb abundance'. Oxford compares the poem to a Keats ode (see note to lines 19–21). The toccata makes its listeners aware of their own mortality as does Keats's Grecian urn, but, unlike the urn, it is a mortality that Galuppi's piece, no longer fashionable, taken from the shelf on a whim by a young Englishman who seems unfamiliar even with the composer's name, seems to share. The Englishman imagines Venetian lovers listening to Galuppi play and praising his music as 'good alike at grave and gay', which is surely a virtue that RB is quietly claiming for his own poem, which begins in broad comedy and ends in desolation: 'I feel chilly and grown old.'

l. 1. *Galuppi*. Baldassare Gallupi (1706–85), best known for his association with his fellow-Venetian Carlo Goldoni, that led to his nomination as the father of the comic opera, spent most of his life in Venice, although he stayed for some months in London, and for three years in St Petersburg. He was a prolific composer of music both sacred and secular.

l. 5. *where the merchants were the kings*. Venice's government, like its wealth, was built on its merchants, for which reason it was often compared with the City of London.

l. 6. *St Mark's*. The cathedral of Venice; in 1177 Pope Alexander III presented the Doge with a ring celebrating the marriage of Venice to the sea, a ceremony commemorated each year on Ascension Day in the Feast of Sensa, in which the current Doge throws a ring into the sea. Byron laments that the ceremony has fallen into disuse after the French occupation in *Childe Harold*, 14, stanza XI.

l. 8. *Shylock's bridge*. The Rialto bridge with its double row of shops and close to the mint was a commercial centre. In *The Merchant of Venice* Shylock tells Bassanio, who has come to borrow money on Antonio's surety, that he has heard about the state of Antonio's affairs on the Rialto.

l. 11. The Venetian carnival was famous for its masked balls. See Byron, *Beppo*, stanzas 2–7.

l. 14. *buoyant*. Floating; *bell-flower*. Campanula.

l. 18. *clavichord*. An early keyboard instrument still popular in the 18th century. It is only suitable for intimate performances, not being loud enough for large concerts.

ll. 19–21. *lesser thirds*. Lesser or, as would be said now, minor thirds, diminished sixths, suspensions, solutions, and sevenths, like dominant and octave in 24–5, are technical musical terms that might advertise RB's musical knowledge, or map the conflict in the speaker between analytic detachment and sensuous immersion. The reference to diminished sixths has been viewed especially suspiciously by RB's musically knowledgeable readers.

ll. 22–3 and 25–6. Imagined exchanges between the lovers listening to the music.

l. 33. *cold music*. The music, though gay, is now seen as cold because it takes no heed of human mortality. Compare Keats's address to the urn in the last stanza of the poem as 'Cold Pastoral!' ('Ode on a Grecian Urn', 45).

l. 34. *The Cricket on the Hearth* was consolidated as an emblem of domestic contentment by the publication of Dickens's Christmas story in 1845, but the cricket's creak takes on a new significance if the house has been burnt down. It may even suggest a miniaturized Nero fiddling while Rome burns.

ll. 35–43. What the speaker now imagines the music saying to him.

l. 39. *Butterflies*. Gaudily trivial people, as in Lear's invitation to Cordelia to laugh at 'guilded butterflies' (*King Lear*, V. iii. 13), but the speaker seems ignorant that the butterfly, in Greek the psyche, is also an emblem of the immortal soul.

l. 41. *fruitage*. Crop of fruit, possible recalling Matthew 7: 16: 'Ye shall know them by their fruits.'

l. 45. *I feel chilly and grown old*. Compare Thomas Hood, 'Ballad', 16–18: 'Youth may be silly, | Wisdom is chilly,— | What can an old man do but die?'

By the Fire-side

RB wrote of the poem, 'the portraiture only is intended to be like—the circumstances are a mere imaginary framework' (David George, 'Four New Browning Letters . . .', *Studies in Browning and his Circle*, 2.1 (1974), 62), confirming what all the poem's readers had surmised that the poem memorializes the love that he shared with EBB. Indeed, the repeated description of the woman with the 'great brow | And the spirit-small hand propping it' (113–14 and 258–9) has always been recognized as one of RB's most thrilling sketches of his wife. The reference to Pella identifies the poem's landscape as the Piedmontese Alps, an area that the RBs never visited, although in 1847 they had planned to, and they did own Murray's *Handbook for Travellers in Switzerland, and the Alps of Savoy and Piedmont*, from which RB may have taken some clues for his description of the region (see Jean Stirling Lindsay, 'The Central Episode of Browning's "By the Fireside"', *Studies in Philology*, 39.3 (1942), 571–9). Other details may have been drawn from the RBs' visit to Bagni di Lucca in the summer of 1853, the chapel in the poem recalling the Refubbri Chapel, both being reached by a way of a 'one-arched bridge' (68). The poem tests the power of the love the man and woman share to unify all of their lived experience. The poem's first and last lines echo each other, completing what Coleridge called with reference to 'Frost at Midnight' the poem's 'rondo': the poem shows, by allowing its present moment to anticipate the lovers' old age and recall their youth, how their love has redeemed them from linear time. But all this is revealed in an epiphanic moment that takes place in the midst of a gloriously multitudinous landscape, in which such things as the 'sudden coral nipple' of a wild mushroom seem reluctant to yield their own vitality to that of the lovers.

l. 3. Chatterton describes 'Conscience' as 'the soul-chameleon's varying hue', 'Happiness', 25.

l. 11. *the young ones*. Imagined grandchildren.

l. 18. *branch-work*. Possibly recalling Keats, 'Ode to Psyche', 52, 'branched thoughts'.

l. 23. In EBB's *A Vision of Poets* (1844) the Muse promises the poet, 'You may see | The trees grow rarer presently' (115–16). The rarer trees are presumably Italian in contrast to the English hazels that form the outer frame. It may be that RB is thinking of a 'cypress alley' like that down which EBB's Aurora Leigh walks (*Aurora Leigh*, 7. 1161).

ll. 28–30. A common figure as in Germaine de Staël's *Corinne, ou l'Italie*, 1807, in which the poet Corinne who as its laureate embodies Italy is wooed but not wed by the English aristocrat Oswald, Lord Nelvil.

l. 43. Pella is a village in Piedmont on the western shore of Lago di Orta.

l. 44. The pointed summits of the mountains seem as sharp as spear-heads.

l. 52. *the thorny balls*. The cupules of the sweet chestnut each contain at least three nuts. The cupules usually split open and fall in October.

l. 58. *from rim to boss*. From circumference to centre (of a shield).

ll. 59–60. Compare Felicia Hemans, 'The Streams', 45–6, 'the brightest cups on the emerald moss | Whose Fairy goblets the turf emboss'; the mat of moss looks as if it had been embroidered by elves.

l. 64. *freaked*. Streaked or variegated.

l. 73. *dyke*. Ditch, in which the hemp is soaked to release its fibres.

l. 75. *strike*. Score with lines.

l. 77. *festa-day*. Day of festival.

l. 81. RB wrote to George Barrett from Bagni di Lucca, 16–18 July 1853, 'there's nothing civilised beyond us on *this* side, but a few charcoal-burners' huts' (*George Barrett*, 195).

l. 84. *wattled cote*. A hut or fence made of woven twigs.

l. 89. *John in the Desert*. John the Baptist preaching in the wilderness.

l. 92. *pent-house*. A projecting roof.

l. 95. The date 1569, taken together with the primitive fresco still exemplifying 'art's early wont', testifies to the chapel's remoteness.

l. 98. *aware*. On its guard.

l. 101. *Leonor*. Possibly named to point the contrast with Leonora, sister of the Duke of Ferrara. Tasso's love for her was popularly represented as leading to his imprisonment and madness.

l. 103. As Orpheus looks back for Eurydice but without the fatal consequences.

l. 106. Compare the 'sheer edge' from which one drops into old age and death with the gentle 'slope' (24) down which the speaker imagines himself walking from his present age to his remembered youth.

l. 108. *contemn*. Scorn the fact of age.

l. 110. *life's safe hem*. Presumably on an analogy with the hem of Christ's robe to which the speaker clings in *Christmas-Eve*.

ll. 116–20. The couple respond to each other's unspoken thoughts.

ll. 126–31. A thought characteristic of John Donne, as in 'The Extasie', 35–6: 'Love, these mixt soules doth mixe again, | And makes both one, each this and that.'

ll. 128–30. After suggesting that the two souls mix like 'mists' the metaphor changes to suggest that they mix like two rivers at their confluence, the river that results having a more powerful current than either of the rivers singly.

l. 132. God says, 'Behold, I make all things new', Revelation 21: 5. God is 'the Word' after John 1: 1, 'In the beginning was the Word,' and is often referred to as 'the great Word', as in Milton, *Samson Agonistes*, 84.

l. 135. 2 Corinthians 5: 1: 'we have a building of God, an house not made with hands, eternal in the heavens.'

l. 145. *miss*. Fail to obtain.

ll. 149–50. Compare 'England in Italy', 7–10, in which memories are also compared to rosary beads.

l. 154. *Strained to a bell.* Presumably held tautly concave, to achieve maximum support from the air.

ll. 159–60. Compare 98 in which the 'place is silent and aware'. Here the silence makes it seem that the place is repressing an urge to confess.

l. 171. *settle*. Bench, which is presumably under the window grate that they look through.

l. 175. As if thieves are unafraid that they will be struck by thunder in punishment for their sacrilege.

l. 181. Compare 'the good minute', 'Two in the Campagna', 50, but RB often records such epiphanic moments.

l. 182. *stock and stone*. Very general, suggesting only organic and inorganic matter, as in Scott's *Lord of the Isles*, 4. 33–4: 'And see, brave Ronald, see him dart | O'er stock and stone like hunted hart.'

l. 185. *chrysolite*. The seventh foundation of the new Jerusalem is chrysolite. See Revelation 21: 20. Compare the conclusion of *Aurora Leigh*, which also names various stones of which the city's foundations are made: 'I saw his soul,—"Jasper first," I said; | "And second, sapphire; third, chalcedony; | The rest in order:—last an amethyst"' (9. 962–4).

l. 186. Compare Romney to Aurora in *Aurora Leigh*, 8. 257–8, 'I with you, | And no third troubling.'

ll. 191–2. Oxford points out that 'the little more' and 'the little less' translate Italian terms, 'il poco piu' and 'il poco meno', commonly used in art criticism to signify how an effect might be destroyed by tiny variance.

ll. 196–200. The thought is that Leonor might have insisted on a barrier between the pair allowing friendship but preventing them from becoming lovers.

ll. 201–15. The thought is that he had met Leonor when his youth was past, and he was no longer as ready to take emotional risks as he once had been. The metaphor may owe something to Shakespeare's sonnets in which the course of a human life is often compared to the annual cycle of a tree, youth marked by 'lusty leaves' (5. 7), and age represented as 'lofty trees . . . barren of leaves' (12. 5). Sonnet 73 seems especially pertinent: 'That time of year thou mayst in me behold, | When yellow leaves, or none, or few, do hang | Upon those boughs which shake against the cold' (1–3).

l. 202. Wanting to hibernate.

l. 205. Like earlier editors we have failed to locate a source.

ll. 211–15. The hope is that a breeze might by chance strip the last leaf from the tree, an action that Leonora would have feared to anticipate by stripping the leaf off herself.

l. 218. *agonise*. Struggle.

ll. 221–5. She might, like a lady in a romance, have demanded that her lover complete some task to prove his worthiness of her love.

ll. 228–30. If the joining of two lives leaves a scar that separates those lives, then, however thin the scar, the lovers remain 'too far' from one another.

l. 245. 'Ye shall know them by their fruits' (Matthew 7: 16).

ll. 246–50. The thought is that each individual's achievement contributes to the achievement of humanity.

Any Wife to Any Husband

The poem forms a pair with 'By the Fireside' which precedes it in RB's arrangement of *Men and Women*, the first poem spoken by the husband, the second by the wife, the first speaker serene, the second agonizingly attempting to extort a promise of behaviour after her death that she knows as well as the Bishop of St Praxed that she is unable to enforce. Like all RB's poems about marriage, this poem has been understood as autobiographical, but EBB wrote of her husband to her sister: 'I've stopped him twenty times in such vows as never to take another wife, & the like . . . I've held his lips together with both hands . . . I wouldn't have it!' (*EBB to Arabella*, ii. 70); her protestations may, however, strike some readers as too emphatic to be entirely convincing. The poem seems interested in the folly of allowing one's peace of mind to depend upon a guarantee that could never be strong enough to satisfy.

l. 9. The line may recall Henry King, 'The Exequy', 111–12: 'But heark! My Pulse like a soft Drum | Beats my approch, tells *Thee* I come.'

l. 12. Karshish notices that Lazarus' 'soul sometimes 'springs into his face' (191), and thinks it may be when he remembers his meeting with Christ.

l. 17. *soul makes all things new*. Compare Revelation 21: 5: 'Behold, I make all things new.'

l. 22. *fire of fires*. In George Chapman's dedication of his translation of Homer to Robert, Earl of Somerset, he speaks of 'Heavens great fire of fires | To whom, the Sunne it selfe is but a Beame' (65–6).

l. 26. *demesne*. Here probably the park or estate surrounding the house.

l. 28. *three-parts*. Of four, that is 'three-quarters'.

l. 30. The sense seems to be that the husband has only to live the rest of his life as he has lived it so far to achieve a place in Heaven. 'Stroke' may be used to signify a feat or achievement.

l. 35. *relic-flower*. The flower that acts as a memento of the festival at which it was worn.

l. 37. The glove is dropped flirtatiously, but the husband declines such invitations.

l. 45. The thought is probably that, unlike the other chairs, the chair the wife sat on is not pushed under the table, but still in the position in which she sat on it.

l. 47. Longman quotes Carlyle on Burns: 'No poet of any age or nation is more graphic than Burns: the characteristic features disclose themselves to him at a glance; three lines from his hand, and we have a likeness' (*Edinburgh Review*, 48 (1828), 280).

ll. 49–50. Compare the 'moment, one and infinite' in which the souls of the lovers in 'By the Fireside', 182, become one.

l. 52. *Who*. The capital letter indicates God.

l. 54. Possibly punning on the sense 'unpair'.

ll. 55–60. The comparison of the wife to the sun, and of the lesser light of the woman who might console him after her death to a firefly, might recall Shelley's comparisons of the women in his life to the sun, moon, and a comet, in *Epipsychidion*, conflated with one of Shelley's favourite thoughts, that the sun's light renders the stars invisible.

l. 58. *Glimpses*. Glimmers.

l. 66. The husband is represented as a sentry on duty.

l. 69. Presumably the hair is golden.

ll. 71–2. Compare Letitia Landon, 'April' (1835), 13–14: 'The wild-briar rose, a fragrant cup | To hold the morning's tear.'

l. 77. If RB has in mind a particular painting it is probably Titian's *Venus of Urbino* in the Uffizi Gallery in Florence.

ll. 79–81. The wife, watching from Heaven, will witness the husband claiming his wife's authority for his infidelities.

ll. 89–90. When the priests try to trap Jesus by asking whether it is lawful to give tribute to Rome, he takes a coin and asks, 'Whose image and superscription hath it? They answered and said Caesar's', Luke 20: 24. Also see Matthew 22: 20.

l. 91. *Re-coin.* The figure may derive from Charles Smith's translation of Kotzebue, *The Wild Youth* (1800), in which a servant describes a kiss that she is given by a young aristocrat as 'stolen money; it belongs to your bride', and is answered, 'I recoin this piece of money every minute' (III. v).

ll. 94–5. *sealing up the sum | Or lavish of my treasure*. Hoarding or spending, echoing Ezekiel 28: 12, 'Thou sealest up the sum, full of wisdom and perfect in beauty.'

ll. 105–6. In the 15th century a perpetual lamp supposedly still alight was found in the tomb of Cicero's much-loved daughter Tullia, after which a lighted lamp became a common figure for a love that extends beyond the tomb, as in John Donne, *Epithalamion*, 111–14 : 'Now, as in Tullias tombe, one lampe burnt cleare, | Unchang'd for fifteene hundred yeare, | May these love-lamps we here enshrine, | In warmth, light, lasting, equall the divine.'

ll. 107–8. She would remember the dead husband better because the walls of her soul would remain blank, with no likenesses of other men affixed to them.

l. 113. *'Neath the low door-way's lintel.* On the threshold of the tomb.

ll. 121–2. The thought is that the wife does not have to rely on the husband's pride to keep him faithful to her memory when the expression in his eyes already allows her to predict the life he will lead after her death.

ll. 125–6. *sleep*. The sleep, that will seem only a minute, between the time of her death and the Last Judgment.

An Epistle ... Karshish, the Arab Physician

In a letter to Abib, his senior colleague, the Arab physician Karshish writes of his meeting with Lazarus, and of his belief that he has been raised from the dead. His attention was perhaps drawn to the miracle, which is only recorded in RB's favourite Gospel John 11: 1–45, by Tennyson's reference in *In Memoriam* XXXI to the absence from the Bible of any account by Lazarus of the experience he had undergone: 'Behold a man raised up by Christ! | The rest remaineth unrevealed; | He told it not; or something sealed | The lips of that Evangelist' (13–16). Karshish's letter begins with a studiedly orientalized address that distances its writer. But the poem also keeps its eye on its own place and time. Karshish is an Arab travelling in Judea in the seventh decade of the Christian era, but he reflects as in a mirror the experience of many

Victorian intellectuals. The failure of his scientific cast of mind to repress its wonder at the notion of an incarnated God mirrors in reverse the failure of the childhood religious faith of some Victorians to survive their scientific education. Karshish's horrified fascination with Lazarus' belief that Jesus was 'God forgive me—who but God himself' (268) may anachronistically derive from the Islamic understanding of Incarnation as blasphemous, but it also anticipates the manner in which the likes of Matthew Arnold flinch from 'that favourite doctrine of our theologians, "the blessed truth that the God of the universe is a Person"' (*Literature and Dogma*, 1873, chapter 7). The Incarnation was not only central to RB's religious faith, but it also raised in its most intense form the moral implications of the relationship between the human and the divine. John Wesley in the hymn 'Glory be to God on high' comfortably addresses a 'Lord of Power and God of Love', but RB had been taught by Shelley amongst others that power and love were divine attributes not so easily reconciled. The Incarnation was also an idea central to RB's aesthetics that so often focus on the difficulty of reconciling the spirit or conception of a poem with its material embodiment.

l. 1. *Karshish*. The name means 'one who gathers' in Arabic.

l. 4. The line compares God in his role as creator of humankind first to a glass-blower and then to a baker.

ll. 5–6. The function of the body is to restrain the soul's natural disposition to fly from earth to God, from whom it derives.

l. 12. *term*. Due date.

l. 17. *snake-stone*. A stone supposed to offer protection against snake venom.

l. 20. The number of letters is recorded so that Abib can determine whether any has gone astray.

l. 28. Vespasian was deputed in 66 CE to suppress the Great Jewish Revolt. He commanded two legions, his eldest son, Titus, commanded a third. He took Jericho in 68 CE and Jerusalem in 70 CE.

ll. 34–7. Jericho is 17 miles from Jerusalem; Bethany, where Lazarus lived, less than 2 miles away, 'about fifteen furlongs' (John 11: 18).

l. 37. A man with buboes in their third and final stage.

l. 40. To empty the contents of my travel bag.

l. 42. *viscid choler*. Sticky or glutinous bile.

l. 43. *tertians*. A fever that produces a fit every other day.

l. 44. *falling-sickness*. Epilepsy.

l. 49. *run-a-gate*. The term may simply denote a vagabond, but may more specifically refer to a renegade or apostate, as for example a Syrian who had converted to Christianity.

l. 50. *payeth me a sublimate*. Pays me for a powder.

l. 55. *gum-tragacanth*. A medicinal gum, extracted from spiny shrubs, for which Judea was celebrated; it was commonly believed to be the substance translated in the King James Bible as 'spices'.

l. 57. *porphyry*. The stone from which the mortar is made.

ll. 58–9. He cannot readily distinguish between leprosy and a scalp disease such as psoriasis or alopecia.

l. 60. *Zoar*. The city neighbouring Sodom and Gomorrah spared the destruction that they suffered (known only from the references to it in the Bible).

l. 63. *my price*. What he will charge me.

l. 79. *mania*. Described in 1853 by W. B. Carpenter in *Principles of Human Physiology* as 'characterized by the combination of complete derangement of the intellectual powers, with passionate excitement about every point which in the least degree affects the feelings'; *subinduced by*. Brought about as a result of.

l. 82. *exhibition*. Application.

l. 88. Compare Luke 11: 24–5: 'When the unclean spirit is gone out of a man, he walketh through dry places, seeking rest; and finding none, he saith, I will return into my house whence I came out. And when he cometh, he findeth it swept and garnished.'

l. 93. *fancy-scrawls*. Scribbling of the fancy or imagination.

l. 103. *figment*. That is of the imagination; *fume*. Insubstantial belief.

l. 106. *saffron*. The spice produced from the stigmas of the saffron crocus also functions as a vivid orange-yellow dye.

l. 109. *Sanguine*, *proportioned*. Cheerful, equable.

l. 112. *As he . . . show*. As if he were an exhibition piece.

l. 116. *balm*. Medicinal ointment. The context suggests that RB is thinking of a spiritual equivalent of euphrasia or eyebright.

l. 128. *straightened*. More commonly 'straitened', narrowed.

l. 137. *golden mean*. The Aristotelian notion that virtue consists in choosing a position midway between opposing extremes.

l. 143. *witless*. Heedless.

l. 151. *stupor*. Wonder or amazement (archaic).

l. 161. *pretermission . . . craft*. Interruption of his daily business.

l. 167. *our lord*. The master of both Karshish and Abib.

ll. 172–3. The lines seem to describe the explosion of an old star to form a nebula.

l. 177. *Greek fire*. A combustible material that not even water will extinguish; its exact composition is unknown. It was so-called because it was believed to have been invented by the Greeks of Constantinople.

ll. 178–90. Lazarus is apt to live his finite, earthly life in obedience to values that are only applicable to the infinite life of the spirit.

l. 208. Body and soul are already separated because the soul has, as a consequence of Jesus's miracle, reached its full growth, at which point it is independent of the body.

l. 226. *apathetic*. Karshish imagines that Abib will diagnose Lazarus' failure to display conventional emotional responses as a clinical condition.

l. 228. *affects*. Has affection for.

l. 229. In this he is like Christ who in the sermon on the mount bids 'Behold the fowls of the air' and 'Consider the lilies of the field' (Matthew 6: 26 and 28).

l. 240. *sublimed.* Elevated.

l. 247. *leech.* Physician.

l. 249. *wizardry.* Witchcraft.

l. 252. As Jesus died, 'the earth did quake' (Matthew 27: 51).

ll. 257–9. Karshish connects the earthquake to Christ's death by postulating that Jesus was killed because the 'mad people' believed that he might have, had he wished, prevented it.

ll. 281–2. *Borage.* A herb that once had medical uses. Its flowers are most commonly blue. Aleppo is in Syria, from where borage is thought to derive; *Nitrous.* Salty.

l. 283. *case.* Record of an individual's medical condition.

ll. 291–2. Compare 'piles of loose stones | Like the loose broken teeth | Of some monster', *England in Italy*, 153–5.

l. 306. God's voice is frequently described as in Revelation 14: 2 'as the voice of a great thunder'.

Mesmerism

Franz Anton Mesmer developed in the 1770s a therapeutic method that he named animal magnetism (animal from the Latin *animus*, meaning the mind or soul), and was subsequently known as mesmerism. It depended on the notion that magnetism, an energy that pervaded the universe, might be passed from therapist to patient with beneficial results. Mesmer achieved this at first by the application of magnets, then by touching or by passes of the hands. It was subsequently believed that once a rapport had been established between a therapist and his patient the effect might operate at a distance, even a great distance. It was a follower of Mesmer who discovered the phenomenon that he termed magnetic sleep that would now be described as a hypnotic trance. EBB was persuaded of the efficacy of animal magnetism by Harriet Martineau who believed that it had cured her cancer. EBB's interest was re-galvanized in 1853 when mesmerism was associated by her and her acquaintances in Italy with phenomena such as spiritualism, table-rapping, etc. RB remained sceptical, even though the admired Shelley had given the technique his approval (see 'The Magnetic Lady to her Patient'). The Gothic opening stanzas seem designed to introduce a supernatural tale. Oxford and Longman compare the episode in Hawthorne's *The House of the Seven Gables* in which Matthew Maule has gained such power over Alice Pyncheon that he is able to summon her from a distance. But RB seems at least as concerned to explore questions about the nature of poetry, more particularly poetry of the kind that he wrote himself. The speaker seems to acknowledge at the last that the desire to exercise control over the body and soul of another is sinful, even allied to the several cases of demonic possession recorded in the Bible. The poem is remarkable for the intimacy with which RB occupies his speaker's mind. Lines 6–105 might even be construed as a single sentence, a remarkable syntactic enactment of the unremitting concentration with which the mesmerist exercises his tyrannical control over the woman who is his subject. The poem seems weighted with RB's suspicion that his own dramatic imagination, exercised in this poem on the mesmerist, is worryingly like the power that the mesmerist exerts over his subject. The moment at which the real woman and the woman that the mesmerist has so vividly conjured converge seems to figure at once the utmost triumph of the poet's art, and the point at which its moral recklessness is finally exposed.

l. 8. *death-watch.* The death watch beetle, of which wood-worms are the larvae. The ticking sound, designed to attract a mate, was understood as signalling an impending death.

l. 9. *flag of smut.* The sooty film that flutters on the grate and is supposed to presage the arrival of a stranger. See Cowper, *The Task*, 4. 292–5, and Coleridge, 'Frost at Midnight', 13–16.

l. 10. To drown a cat brings ill luck as is intimated in the nursery rhyme 'Ding, dong, bell': the cat may return to haunt its killer, the perpetrator may in turn be drowned, or the perpetrator may be taken by the devil.

l. 11. The socket holds the candle, which, the wax all melted, is emitting its final flare.

l. 15. *unawares.* Without explanation.

l. 30. The foot is caught inside a fold of the muslin dress the woman is wearing.

ll. 44–5. The calotype is an early kind of photograph, introduced by Fox Talbot in 1838, in which the image is imprinted upon sensitive paper by the sun's light.

ll. 51–5. The mesmerist commands the soul to reoccupy the body: that is, he brings the woman he has summoned to consciousness.

ll. 56–60. The transfer of magnetic fluid from the mesmerist to his patient often, although not always, involved passes with the hands.

l. 65. *flame.* The magnetic effluence that some patients claimed to see streaming from the hands of the mesmerist.

ll. 69–70. A toil is a net laid to catch game. Here, he captures her soul in a net from which there is no escape.

ll. 74. *Essence and earth-attire.* Soul and body.

l. 75. *tractile fire.* A flame capable of indefinite extension, of being drawn out like a thread.

ll. 76–80. The house seems at once to denote the woman's body from which the soul craves escape, and the house in which the mesmerist sits, a house of which she has taken possession, but feels compelled to escape in a somnambulist trance. Compare the house in 'The Householder'.

ll. 82–3. Compare George Crabbe, *The Ancient Mansion*, in which, after asking 'what being likes a bound?' (131), the speaker wishes that 'in the wild-wood maze I as of old might stray' (134).

l. 85. *blind with sight*. Unseeing though with open eyes.

l. 88. *stubs*. Stumps.

l. 94. Compare 'Pictor Ignotus', 7–8, 'my soul, with eyes uplift | And wide to heaven.'

l. 95. *drift*. Wind-driven shower.

l. 99. *gesture*. The mesmerist's pass with the hands.

l. 106. Was the hair the first feature set a-glow?

l. 107. *unfilleted*. Released from its fillet or head-band, let down.

ll. 111–15. The woman's two arms are compared to the richly jewelled doors of a reliquary which open to reveal the prized relic, which in this case as in many reliquaries in Italian churches is a heart.

ll. 116–25. The flesh and blood woman, summoned by the call of the mesmerist, arrives, and merges with the phantom woman that the mesmerist has conjured in his room. Compare the manner in which the real and the dream Porphyro come together in Keats's *The Eve of St Agnes*: 'Into her dream he melted' (320).

A Serenade at the Villa

The poem seems prompted by the heavy, stifling atmosphere of an Italian night not as yet refreshed by a storm of rain. It may owe something to Tennyson's Song 'A spirit haunts the year's last hours', when similar weather prompts similar thoughts of a deathbed: 'The air is damp and hushed and close | As a sick man's room when he taketh repose | An hour before death' (13–15). The dry comedy of the serenader who, because the mistress's window remains tight shut, cannot be certain whether his song was appreciated or, as he rather suspects, loathed, may echo RB's own frustration at the lack of response to the several volumes of poetry that he had already published.

ll. 6–7. *fly . . . worm*. Firefly and glow-worm.

l. 12. *suspired for proof*. Sighed in demonstration (of her lovelorn condition).

l. 15. *Bloodlike*. Suggesting the rain's warmth.

l. 22. The white flowers of the hemlock are small but grow in clusters. RB may have vaguely in mind Tennyson, 'A spirit haunts the year's last hours' (1830), 21, 'Heavily hangs the broad sunflower'.

l. 25. *past away*. Seems deliberately to play between his departure and his imagined death.

l. 33. *count*. Esteem or regard.

l. 36. *as something bodes*. As something makes me anticipate.

l. 39. *task-master*. The word used in Exodus to describe the Egyptian overseers of the enslaved Israelites.

l. 51. *some plague*. Referring either to the singer or the song, both of which, the suggestion is, should be avoided like the plague.

My Star

Mrs Orr remarks that the poem 'may be taken as a tribute to the personal element in love: the bright peculiar light in which the sympathetic soul reveals itself to the object of its sympathy' (*Handbook*, 293). Her phrasing reveals that she has heard in the poem an echo of Helena's acknowledgement of the hopelessness of her love for Bertram: ''twere all one | That I should love a bright particular star | And think to wed it, he is so above me' (*All's Well that Ends Well*, I. i. 79–81). RB often, like Helena, insists that the woman he loves is far above him. The suspicion that the poem has a strong personal significance for him is strengthened by his decision to place it first in his *Selections* of 1865, and by the echo in the poem of one of his letters to EBB: 'I believed in your glorious genius and knew it for a true star from the moment I saw it,—long before I had the blessing of knowing it was MY star, with my fortune and futurity in it' (*Correspondence*, xi. 159). The poem seems to map the moment referred to in the letter when 'a certain star' quite suddenly reveals itself as 'My Star'.

l. 4. *angled spar*. A crystal cut into a prismatic shape.

l. 9. *dartle*. RB's coinage, by analogy with 'sparkle'.

l. 11. Saturn may be chosen because its rings would for most viewers make it a more spectacular sight than the star that the speaker describes. If RB has in mind the opening of Keats's *Hyperion: A Fragment*, 'Far from the fiery noon, and eve's one star | Sat gray-hair'd Saturn, quiet as a stone,' the star might be associated with Venus.

"Childe Roland to the Dark Tower Came"

RB recollected that in January 1853 he decided to write a poem every day, and 'Childe Roland to the Dark Tower Came' was the second product of what turned out to be a short-lived resolution. The poem, he recalled, 'came upon me as a kind of dream. I had to write it, then and there, and I finished it the same day, I believe. But it was simply that I had to do it. I did not know then what I meant beyond that, and I'm sure I don't know now. But I am very fond of it' (Lilian Whiting, *The Brownings: Their Life and Art*, 1911, 261). The title comes from the snatch of song with which Edgar, disguised as the madman Poor Tom, ends Act III, scene iv of *King Lear*: '*Child Rowland to the dark tower came*, | His word was still: *Fie, foh, and fum,* | *I smell the blood of a British man*' (186–8). As RB acknowledged, the poem reads like a romance refracted in a dream. The landscape changes suddenly, unexpectedly, and the language itself is marked by odd, dream-like incongruities, as in the phrase, 'coloured gay and grim' (151). The poem clearly has its origins in knightly romance, and much commentary has been concerned to identify the romances it most resembles. A print of Perseus and Andromache hung over RB's desk, and the poems make frequent references to romance, as when in *Pauline* the speaker recalls how he dreamed of living 'like the knight | Of old tales' (527–8). In fact, only a single reference to a spear (123) suggests that the speaker of 'Childe Roland' has any of the accoutrements of the conventional knight. He travels by foot rather than on horse. He seems as close kin to Byron's Childe Harold as he is to Charlemagne's knight, Roland, blowing the trumpet with which he signals his glorious defeat. Orr describes the poem as a fantastic collage, the elements of which had their origin in RB's own experience, 'a tower which Mr RB once saw in the Carrara mountains, a painting which caught his eye years later in Paris; and the figure of a horse in the tapestry in his own drawing-room' (*Handbook*, 273). The anonymous speaker's perceptions (although he is repeatedly referred to as Childe Roland, his name is no more than an inference from the poem's final line) have a hallucinatory vividness that may suggest that RB, like Edgar in *King Lear*, is assuming the character of a madman. His most lurid encounters are not with items in the landscape but with items supplied by his own imaginings; the 'baby's shriek' (126), the 'toads in a poisoned tank', and the 'wild cats in a red-hot iron cage' (131–2). Even less sensational Gothic trappings such as the howlet and the bat (106) are anticipated rather than seen. The harrow and brake represented in stanza 24 as infernal instruments of torture might be quite ordinary agricultural implements as seen by a deranged spectator. The speaker seems to regard the world through which he wanders as threatening to infect him by contagion with its own disease: even a scanty growth of grass puts him in mind of leprosy (73–4). One may even suspect that the moral as well as the aesthetic lens through which he views the world is alarmingly distorted, as when he comments on a horse, 'his every bone a-stare' (76): 'I never saw a brute I hated so— | He must be wicked to deserve such pain' (83–4). But to read the poem as a study of neurosis need not preclude a recognition of its speaker's dauntless heroism.

l. 10. *skull-like laugh*. Skulls are often said to laugh or grin because of the set of a skeleton's mouth. Compare RB's Guido who, when confronted with 'death's gigantic skull', asks why he should 'Grin back his grin' (*The Ring and the Book*, XI. 1036–7).

ll. 16–18. Compare Matthew Arnold, 'Self-Deception' (1852), in which after noting that 'on earth we wander' (21), Arnold acknowledges that 'Ends we seek we never shall attain' (26), and concludes by asking, '*Some* end is there, we indeed may gain?' (28).

l. 19. *world-wide wandering*. Compare Shelley's description of Mercury in *Prometheus Unbound*, I. 325, as 'Jove's world-wandering Herald'.

ll. 25–30. Compare Donne, 'A Valediction: forbidding mourning', 1–4: 'As virtuous men pass mildly away, | And whisper to their soules, to goe, | Whilst some of their sad friends doe say, | The breath goes now, and some say, no.'

l. 34. *scarves*. Possibly the black scarves worn by mourners over the shoulder, but possibly sashes, which might accord better with the banners and the staves or poles from which they fly.

l. 44. *his highway*. Conventionally it is the King's highway. The phrase perhaps suggests that the 'hateful cripple' reigns over the poem's bleak landscape.

l. 48. *estray*. The word was popularized by Longfellow who entitled the selection of favourite poems that he published in 1846 *The Estray*, explaining in an epigraph, 'Estray in our Common Law signifieth any beast not wilde, found within any Lordship, and not owned by any man.'

l. 52. *safe road*. Possibly a reference to the highway, but possibly a metaphorical reference to the safe anchorage that the speaker has abandoned by turning into the plain, which seems like a featureless, threatening sea.

l. 57. *cedar-grove*. A conventional item in luxuriant landscapes, as in Samuel Rogers, *The Campagna of Florence*, in which he describes 'radiance' streaming through 'the cedar-grove' (233–4).

l. 58. *cockle, spurge*. Both are weeds. Compare Job 31: 40: 'Let thistles grow instead of wheat, and cockle instead of barley.' Spurge was used as a purgative, but *OED* quotes Benjamin Stillingfleet, 'The spurge, that is noxious to man.'

l. 60. The point is that a burr, both as the prickly flower-head of the burdock, and when used metaphorically to refer to a clinging person, is something that one usually tries to shake off.

l. 65. 'God is a consuming fire' (Hebrews 12: 29), and will consume the world at the Last Judgment.

l. 66. *calcine*. Reduce to powder.

l. 68. *bents*. Coarse grass.

ll. 73–4. Hair loss is an effect of leprosy.

l. 76. *a-stare*. Protruding. The horse is said by Mrs Orr to have been modelled on a horse in a tapestry, owned by the Brownings, of Hermes driving off the cattle of Apollo. See Philip Kelley and Betty A. Coley, *The Browning Collections* (Winfield: Wedgstone Press, 1984), H667 and plate 27.

l. 80. *colloped*. A collop is ordinarily a gobbet of flesh, but in this context the word seems more likely to refer to protruding sinews.

l. 89. *Think first*. One might expect 'Drink first', but the wine called for is the wine of memory.

ll. 91–102. Cuthbert and Giles are fellow knights.

l. 92. *garniture*. A decorative trimming, here the hair.

l. 95. *one night's disgrace*. A sexual misdemeanour is implied.

l. 99. Compare *Macbeth*, I. vii. 46–7: 'I dare do all that may become a man; | Who dares do more is none.'

l. 101. *a parchment*. Presumably naming the crime for which he is hanged, an ignoble means of execution.

l. 113. The devil is supposed to have the hooves of a goat rather than feet.

l. 114. *bespate*. *OED* records this as an instance of an archaic verb form meaning spat upon, but it seems more probably a coinage suggesting how the surface of a river in spate becomes agitated by flecks and froth.

l. 118. The association between willows and suicide was fixed by the reference in *Hamlet* to Ophelia's suicide by drowning at a place where 'There is a willow grows aslant a brook' (IV. vii. 166). But the willow is traditionally associated with mourning and with unrequited love.

l. 133. *fell cirque*. A savage or cruel amphitheatre such as the Colosseum designed for the staging of gladiatorial contests or fights between man and beast.

l. 135. *mews*. Usually stables, though used here in an antiquated sense to refer to a place of confinement.

l. 136. *brewage*. Fermentation.

ll. 137–8. A sadistic fantasy in which Turks are represented as staging gladiatorial contests between Christians and Jews chosen from the captives who have been condemned to row their galleys.

l. 141. *brake*. Here probably the toothed machine used for separating the fibre from the woody rind of flax or hemp; the harrow is the iron-toothed machine driven over ploughed lands to break up clods. The speaker understands ordinary agricultural machines as if they were instruments of torture.

l. 143. Tophet, originally the site near Jerusalem of human sacrifice (see Jeremiah 19: 5–6), but Tophet later became, as Milton puts it in *Paradise Lost*, I. 405, 'the Type of Hell'.

l. 145. *stubbed ground*. Ground from which the stumps of trees have been grubbed up.

l. 149. *rood*. A unit of length, 16.5 feet.

l. 150. *dearth*. Scarcity but punning with the word earth to suggest utterly infertile soil.

ll. 154–6. RB may have in mind the Yardley oak, a famous, hollowed-out oak tree described by Cowper in 'Yardley Oak'.

l. 160. In *Pilgrim's Progress* Apollyon is the monster with scales like a fish, wings like a dragon, and feet like a bear, who breathes fire and smoke, encountered by Christian in the Valley of Humiliation, who attempts to persuade Christian to abandon his pilgrimage to the Celestial City.

l. 161. *dragon-penned*. Winged like a dragon.

l. 179. *at the very nonce*. At the very moment. *OED* quotes this usage as unique.

l. 182. *blind*. Windowless, like the tower inhabited by the madman in Shelley's *Julian and Maddalo*, a 'windowless, deformed and dreary pile' (101); 'blind as the fool's heart', compare William Sotheby's invocation of Napoleon: *A Song of Triumph*, 'Fool! blind of heart', 51.

ll. 184–6. Possibly a distorted allusion to Ariel in *The Tempest*, who lures Alonso's ship to Prospero's island where those sailing in the fleet's other ships believe it to be wrecked. See *The Tempest*, I. ii. 193–236.

l. 192. *heft*. Alternative spelling of haft: hilt.

l. 203. *slug-horn*. RB follows Chatterton in using the word to signify an instrument like a trumpet, whereas the word is in fact an early spelling of the word slogan, signifying a war-cry. Turner compares the great horn in Book 7 of Malory's *Morte d'Arthur* that the Knight of the Red Laundes hangs on a sycamore: 'that if there came any errant-knight, he must blow that horn, and then he will make him ready and come to him to do battle.'

Respectability

The poem is a product of the Brownings' stay in Paris from September 1851 until July 1852, and in particular, perhaps, of their meetings at this time with the novelist George Sand, who, since separating from her husband, had lived the kind of free, passionate life that would have been impossible in London. Her lovers in that time included Mérimée, de Musset, and Chopin. EBB hero-worshipped her, believing her 'sanctified from blame' by her 'pure genius' ('To George Sand', 12). RB was less convinced, and recalled that 'his studied courtesy towards her was felt by her as a rebuke to the latitude which she granted to other men' (Orr, *Life*, 171). In other words, he received her rather as, in the poem, he records Guizot receiving Montalembert. It is entirely characteristic of RB that he should interrogate so aggressively in this poem a code of respectability to which he was himself so strongly attached.

l. 3. *Have . . . troth*. Have accepted that you are legally married. In the Church of England service of marriage the bride and groom, after repeating their vows, say 'and thereto I plight thee my troth'. The implication is that the man is not married to the woman to whom he speaks.

l. 4. *sponsor*. Guarantor, but the word is also used for a godparent.

l. 15. *Boulevart*. A spelling peculiar but not unique to RB.

ll. 21–2. The reference is to the ceremonial reception of Charles Forbes René de Montalembert into the Académie Française on 5 February 1852, at which the official speech of welcome was delivered by François Guizot (the Académie was a part of the Institut de France). RB, who disliked both men, thought the ceremony hypocritical because Montalembert and Guizot were political opponents, a difference exacerbated by religious differences. Montalembert was a devout Catholic, Guizot a Protestant. RB seems to have associated such shabbily polite compromises with Napoleon III, who had seized power by a coup d'état in 1851. Napoleon III, like George Sand, was much admired by EBB.

A Light Woman

The speaker of the poem, possibly a celebrated writer, looks forward to the worldly, plausible, corrupt men who came increasingly to interest RB in the latter half of his career. This speaker's chilling emotional detachment (his friend was 'already' (5) too good to lose and seemed in the process of becoming still more worth cultivating) extends even to himself when he presents his own behaviour as an interesting moral conundrum. In the poem's startling conclusion the poem's silent auditor ('You look away and your lip is curled?' 23) is revealed as 'Robert Browning', the 'writer of plays' (55), a discovery that serves only to start the question of how far RB as a dramatic poet imagines himself implicated in the cast of mind he so forcefully exposes in the speaker.

l. 7. Compare Pompilia to Margherita, officially her maid but thought to be acting in the service of Pompilia's husband, when she suspects Margherita of trying to compromise her with the priest Caponsacchi: 'The others hunt me, and you throw a noose!' *The Ring and the Book*, VII. 1132.

l. 9. *toils*. Nets.

ll. 15–16. The contrast is proverbial, as in Peter Pindar's address to Sir Joshua Reynolds: 'Compar'd, alas! to other men, | Thou art an eagle to a wren!' (*Lyric Odes to the Royal Academicians*, 1. 46–7).

l. 17. *take*. As a fish takes a fly.

l. 21. Eagles are conventionally associated with fame, as in Shelley, *Hellas*, 873: 'Fame, the eagle'.

l. 22. *maiden face*. Compare Julia's maid in Byron's *Don Juan*, who could understand her mistress breaking her marriage vows for a 'stout cavalier' but not for the 16-year-old Juan's 'half-girlish face' (1. 1368–9).

l. 26. *basilisk*. A fabulous serpent that can kill with a glance.

l. 28. Conveys two ideas: he has blackened the woman in his friend's eyes, and has interposed between her and his friend.

l. 34. *basking*. Sun-bathing.

l. 39. *blue flies*. Blue-bottles.

l. 55. RB who can so vociferously insist that his poems avoid personal expression is unusual amongst 19th-century poets in incorporating his own name into his verse. Compare, for example, *The Inn Album*, 17: 'That bard's a Browning; he neglects the form.' In this Shelley is a significant precursor ('Less oft is peace in Shelley's mind | Than calm in waters seen', 'To Jane: The Recollection', 87–8), as are John Donne and Ben Jonson.

The Statue and the Bust

Ferdinand de' Medici, Grand Duke of Tuscany, emerges in this poem as an odd counterpart to his predecessor, the Duke of Ferrara in 'My Last Duchess', who seems so much more content with his wife when she survives only as a painting. Ferdinand aspires, as does the woman he loves, to become a work of art himself. The pair prefer to live out their love for one another by proxy, in bronze and in terracotta, not so much too timid as too idle to live it for themselves, in the flesh. The Duke, the product of the fag-end of Florence's Renaissance, is endowed with a piquantly modern sensibility, an Italian aristocrat crossed with a character such as Dickens's Eugene Wrayburn (one of his fictional descendants, the Prince in Christina Rossetti's 'The Prince's

Progress', has a similar character). RB invites the reader to savour the contrast between Ferdinand and precursors such as Scott's 'The Young Lochinvar', but he also offers the poem, as its epilogue makes clear, as a challenge to his reader (*De te, fabula*, 250). The 19th century developed a moral rhetoric that identified heroism with self-restraint, and with the ability to exert disciplined control over insubordinate passions. The poem explores the alternative possibility that the regulation of the passions might just as commonly be a symptom of idleness and of cowardice, and that accidie, rather than virtue, might be the glue that binds husband and wife together. There is no direct reference to RB's elopement with EBB, both of whom were unmarried, but an indirect reference seems inescapable, and invited by the reference to the lady's 'pale brow spirit-pure' (50).

ll. 1–3. In the Piazza della SS. Annunziata in Florence Giambologna's equestrian statue of Ferdinand de' Medici (1549–1609) shows Ferdinand, who became Grand Duke of Tuscany in 1587, looking to his right at the building then known as the Palazzo Grifoni (now Budini Gattai). The central window on the first floor is flanked by two alcoves in either of which a bust might be placed. To Ferdinand's left is the Ospedale degli Innocente, the foundling hospital, designed by Brunelleschi with a nine-bay loggia facing the square. The columns of the loggia are surmounted by blue and white ceramic tondi by Andrea della Robbia. These tondi may have given RB the idea for the bust of the lady; in an irony which is not likely to have escaped RB, they depict babies, absent, of course, from the life of the pair of lovers.

l. 18. The Riccardi are a leading Florence family. The name may have been suggested to RB because the Riccardi purchased the Medici Palace in Florence in 1659, after which it was known as the Medici Riccardi Palace.

ll. 19–24. A portrait that seems to be playfully modelled on EBB. Compare 'By the Fireside', 113–14: 'that great brow | And the spirit-small hand propping it.'

l. 21. *coal-black tree.* Ebony.

l. 22. *Crisped.* Curled; *encolure.* Mane, RB's borrowing from the French where it signifies more specifically a horse's neck.

l. 25. *emprise.* A chivalric enterprise.

l. 33. The Medici Palace, which was on the Via Larga (now the Via Cavour).

ll. 34–9. 'The partial darkening of the Via Larga by the overhanging mass of the Riccardi (formerly Medici) Palace is figuratively connected in the poem with the "crime" of two of its inmates: the "murder" by Cosimo de' Medici and his grandson Lorenzo, of the liberties of the Florentine Republic', Orr, *Handbook*, 206.

l. 54. *blink.* Glimmer.

l. 57. *catafalk.* The movable platform on which the coffin is removed. The point is that the young bride is condemned to an entombment in her lifetime from which she will only be released by death.

l. 60. It was conventional in convents and monasteries for one of the order to act as the chronicler of the times, recording events in the secular world outside the walls.

l. 68. *loop.* Loop-hole.

l. 72. The *ave-bell* signals the end of the day, bedtime.

l. 74. Compare Constance de Beverley who escapes from her convent to follow Marmion, 'A horse-boy in his train to ride', Scott, *Marmion*, Canto Second, xxvii. 11.

l. 77. *state.* Married status.

ll. 89–90. Riccardi is a lord-in-waiting or lord of the bedchamber to Ferdinand.

l. 90. *alcove.* The recess in which the Duke's bed of state is placed.

ll. 94–6. The Duke suggests leaving Florence, referred to in a courtly circumlocution as Arno bowers from the river that runs through it, for the Villa Petraia outside the city, the gardens of which had been designed by Niccolo Tribolo who first defined the character of the Italian garden.

l. 100. *leaves the south.* That is, before arriving in Florence she lived in southern Italy, and was accustomed to its heat.

l. 111. Compare *King Lear*, in which the King asks, 'Dost thou call me fool, boy?' and the Fool answers, 'All thy other titles thou hast given away; that thou wast born with' (I. iv. 147–9).

ll. 113–14. Riccardi is still of use to Ferdinand in his negotiations with France. Ferdinand cultivated Henri IV as part of his policy to free Tuscany from Spanish domination.

l. 129. Compare Philip van Artevelde in Henry Taylor's play of that name: 'I too would live—I have a love for life— | But rather than to live to charge my soul | With one hour's lengthening out of ills like these, | I'd leap this parapet with as free a bound | As e'er was schoolboy's o'er a garden wall' (IV. i. 144–8).

l. 137. Rosehips have culinary uses, but the reference to fruits may be more general.

l. 150. That is tearing the picture out of the book.

ll. 151–3. Compare Wordsworth, 'Ode: Intimations of Immortality', 56–7: 'Whither is fled the visionary gleam? | Where is it now, the glory and the dream?'

l. 159. *The serpent's tooth.* The phrase derives from *King Lear* where Lear exclaims of Goneril, 'How sharper than a serpent's tooth it is | To have a thankless child! (I. iv. 288–9), after bidding Nature 'stamp wrinkles in her brow of youth' (284), but RB seems to have associated it with unsatisfactory loving relationships, as in 'One Word More', 15–16: 'Where the serpent's tooth is | Shun the tree'.

l. 160. *peaked.* Sharply pointed.

l. 166 *a hand to aid.* Whose hand can give me the assistance I require.

l. 169. An anachronism because the last distinguished member of the della Robbia family, Girolamo, left Florence for France in 1517, but until then the family, the first and most famous of whom was Luca della Robbia (*c.*1399–1482), were famous for the production of glazed terracotta sculptures, both sacred and secular, characteristically coloured blue and white.

l. 171 *rivet*. As one would repair a cracked vase.

ll. 172–4. The bust placed in the window is an invention of RB's, but Thomas Hardy recalled that when he questioned a Florentine waiter about it, the waiter 'remembered seeing it in its place, after which he gave further interesting details about it', Florence Hardy, *The Early Life of Thomas Hardy*, 1928, 262.

ll. 187–8. The bust of the lady is imagined within a decorative cornice or frame, probably arched, of flowers and fruits, like many della Robbia sculptures of the Madonna and child.

l. 202. Giovanni of Bologna or Giambologna (1529–1608), who was born in Douai.

l. 222. Pompilia refers to Caponsacchi, the priest who, at the risk of his own reputation, rescues her from her husband, as her 'soldier-saint'. *The Ring and the Book*, VII. 1786.

l. 225. Each soldier-saint had attained Heaven by single-mindedly pursuing what he had identified as the end of life.

l. 229. Possibly glancing ironically at the Aristotelian notion that virtue consists in moderation, following the golden mean.

ll. 232–46. The thought is that the character of a game is established by the passion with which it is played rather than the stakes that it is played for. To play for a button or for a coin, for an authentic coin or for a counterfeit, is all one.

l. 233. *epigram*. Pointed joke.

l. 234. The coin for which Florence is famous, the florin, was first minted in 1252 to mark the triumph of the Guelphs, the party of the merchants, over the aristocratic party, the Ghibellines.

l. 236. *counter*. A token, rather than a legal coin.

l. 237. When the crown of your hat serves for a card table, and the prize for winning is a shot of spirit.

l. 247. The parable of the foolish virgins who failed to gain entry to the wedding because they did not have the oil to light their lamps immediately precedes the parable in which the Lord excoriates as 'wicked and slothful' the servant who buried rather than used his single talent. Matthew 25: 1–30; the ungirt loin. Compare Job 38: 3: 'Gird up now thy loins like a man; for I will demand of thee, and answer thou me.'

l. 250. *De te, fabula*! Horace, *Satires*, I. i. 69–70: 'mutato nomine de te | fabula narratur', 'if names are changed, this is a story about you.'

Love in a Life

Sutherland Orr suggests that the two poems might be 'the utterance of the same person', 'Life in a Love' produced 'when he has grasped the fact that the loved one is determined to elude him. She may baffle his pursuit, but he will never desist from it, though it absorb his whole life' (Orr, *Handbook*, 228–9). But it seems more pertinent to note that in neither poem is the quest for the woman satisfied: the difference is rather that the speaker of the second poem suffers his frustration, whereas the speaker of the first experiences it as a condition of endlessly prolonged erotic anticipation. The house in 'Love in a Life' seems, like the houses in 'By the Fireside' and 'The Householder', to occupy at once a physical and a mental space. The poem is anticipated in RB's courtship letters to EBB: 'I fancy myself meeting you on "the stairs"—stairs and passages generally, and galleries, (ah, those indeed!)—all, with their picturesque *accidents*, of landing-places, and spiral heights & depths, and sudden turns, and visions of half-open doors into what Quarles calls "mollitious chambers"—and above all, *landing-places*—they are my heart's delight—I would come upon you unaware on a landing-place in my next dream:' 'In this House of Life,—where I go, you go,—where I ascend, you run before,—where I descend, it is after you' (*Correspondence*, xii. 6 and 215).

l. 5. *trouble.* The disturbance that the woman is imagined to produce in her passage through the house.

l. 7. *cornice-wreath.* An ornamental plaster moulding, probably at the top of the wainscoting. The plaster flowers are imagined to blossom when touched by the woman's skirt.

l. 9. *wears.* Wastes away. Compare Matthew Arnold, *Empedocles on Etna*, 464: 'But the day wears.'

l. 15. *suites.* RB seems to use the word suite to mean a single room, as in 'House', 7, where he speaks of 'suites of reception every one'.

l. 16. *importune.* Solicit, carrying, like the word solicit, erotic implications.

Life in a Love

l. 8. *a fault.* A failure, but it may be with the added sense that his life has missed its purpose, like a faulty serve in tennis.

l. 15. *chace.* Hunt. In the 19th century this spelling sometimes signified that the reference was to the field sport.

l. 20. *I shape me.* I fashion for myself.

How It Strikes a Contemporary

John Coates argues that the poem is set in Valladolid at the beginning of the 17th century ('How It Strikes a Contemporary and the Spain of Cervantes', *Studies in Browning and his Circle*, 11 (1983), 41–6), a date that accords well with the references to ruffs and the Inquisition, but not to cribbage or coffee or 'bold-print posters' or the Jews' quarter. Cribbage, for example, is a quintessentially English card game, reputed to have been invented in the early 17th century by the poet Sir John Suckling. The poem, as has often been noted, explores, through its shabbily genteel protagonist, Shelley's notion that poets are 'the unacknowledged legislators of the world'. It also explores, through the poet's service to the ambiguously titled 'our Lord the King', RB's sense of the poet's dual obligations. He repeatedly insisted that the poet had to answer not to man but to God for his use of his talent, and yet maintained at least as often the poet's obligation to the secular world, an obligation that he chose himself to satisfy by refusing to swerve from the liberal politics of his youth. At first it seems that both obligations might be met by the poet who acts as the quietly insistent moral conscience of his community: 'If any beat a horse, you felt he saw; | If any cursed a woman, he took note' (31–2). But the Spanish setting allows him to go on to interrogate his premises far more fiercely. He sets his poem in a society in which service to God might take the form of acting as an unacknowledged Grand Inquisitor and service to the secular state of acting as spy and informant to an autocratic monarch. 'Our Lord the King' seems less concerned with upholding the law, secular or divine, than with satisfying a salacious 'itch' to pry into the secrets of his subjects. Unacknowledged power is power without recognition, but, as the poem reveals, it may also be power without responsibility. The poem seems suffused also by a sense of the poet's separation from the community within which he lives, his separation even from himself. Its title, as G. W. Cooke long ago noted (*A Guide-Book to the Poetic and Dramatic Works of Robert Browning*, 1894, 444–5), recalls the title of a short fable by Jane Taylor, 'How It Strikes A Stranger', that was included in a volume that RB owned. Poem and story have little in common, except for the isolation of the protagonist. Taylor's central character is a Venusian trapped in a world that seems to him unimaginably strange.

l. 6. *conscientious still.* Longman paraphrases, 'still doing its duty'.

l. 15. *at the wrong time.* That is, not at the time when the main promenade would be crowded with citizens taking their early evening stroll, 'el paseo'.

l. 19. The Moors were expelled from Spain in 1609 but traces of Moorish architecture remained and remain still.

l. 20. *ferrel.* Ferrule, the metal tip that protects a walking stick.

l. 28. *fly-leaf ballads.* Ballads printed on a fly-sheet, that is, a single sheet of paper.

l. 39. *recording chief-inquisitor.* A phrase that seems to conflate the roles of the recording angel, traditionally Gabriel, whose function it is to keep a written record of the actions of every individual, and the chief-inquisitor, or grand inquisitor, that is, the head of the Holy Office of the Inquisition, the arm of the Church charged with the suppression of heresy. The first and most celebrated grand inquisitor in Spain, Torquemada, was appointed to that role in 1483.

l. 44. *our Lord the King*. The phrase refers ambiguously to the secular and divine authority.

l. 45. *He knows why*. Echoing the expression 'God knows why'.

l. 60. *shifts his ministry*. Shuffles his cabinet of ministers.

l. 69. *set the watch*. Appoint the watchmen.

ll. 72–7. Compare RB's letter to EBB, 9 July 1845: 'there's no denying the deep delight of playing the Eastern Jew's part here in this London—they go about, you know by travel-books, with the tokens of extreme destitution & misery, and steal by blind ways & bye-paths to some blank dreary house, one obscure door in it—which being well shut behind them, they grope on thro' a dark corridor or so, and then, a blaze follows the lifting a curtain or the like, for they are in a palace-hall with fountains and lights and marble and gold,—of which the envious are never to dream!' (*Correspondence*, x. 296).

l. 74. *Jewry*. Jews' quarter, the reference to cleanliness is ironic.

l. 83. *a decent cribbage*. A respectable card game (cribbage is not a game designed to be played for anything other than small stakes).

l. 85. *starved winter-pears*. Wrinkled pears. Pears were commonly said to be sweeter when preserved until the winter.

l. 86. Radishes, unlike pears, are best harvested early and eaten immediately.

l. 90. *Corregidor*. The chief administrative official of a town, roughly equivalent to an English magistrate, but directly appointed by the crown.

l. 95. *gave each church its turn*. Attended a different church in the town each week.

l. 96. He committed to memory whichever miracle was the current fashionable topic of conversation.

l. 97. He was the object of the boys' deference and respect.

l. 102. *truckle-bed*. A simple, small bed.

l. 103. *relieving guard*. That is, guardsmen come to relieve those currently on duty.

l. 106. *dim day*. Keble writes of being 'Wearied with the world's dim day', 'Lighting of Lamps' (1836), 9.

ll. 109–10. 'He that overcometh, the same shall be clothed in white raiment' (Revelation 3: 5).

l. 112. The Bible warns against respecting 'him that weareth gay clothing' more highly than 'a poor man in vile raiment' (James 2: 2–4).

l. 115. *Prado*. In the 1780s Charles III instructed the development of what became the Paseo del Prado ('prado' means meadow) as a wide avenue with a garden area to act as a promenade for the upper classes of Madrid. Here it signifies a similarly fashionable promenade.

The Last Ride Together

In this, as in many of RB's poems, the voice fails quite to coincide with the sentiments it expresses. The poem accommodates an unusual number of RB's favourite topics—the selflessness of true love, the saving failure of execution to match conception, the insistence that the value of life is in the striving rather than the achievement, the refusal to accept that artistic achievement might compensate for a failure to have lived one's life to the full, the power of the 'good minute' to redeem long years of dissatisfaction—but it accommodates them within a stanza and a metre that drains them of their customary energy. This is a speaker that seems, as J. K. Stephen insinuates in his parody, written from the woman's point of view, to revel in rather than suffer a rebuff that frees him restfully to contemplate might-have-beens. He shares with the woman who has rejected him 'one more last ride' (11), a revealingly paradoxical expression that suggests that he aspires to feel only the kind of joy that Keats identifies as a close companion of melancholy, 'Joy, whose hand is ever at his lips | Bidding adieu'.

l. 11. *one more last ride*. Compare 'one more last word', 'In a Balcony', 880.

l. 15. *a breathing-while*. Compare Shakespeare, *Venus and Adonis*, 1142.

l. 22. Oxford compares 'What if this present were the worlds last night', Donne, *Holy Sonnets*, XIII.

l. 24. *billowy-bosomed*. Compare *Don Juan*, VI. 108. 6: emotion 'Stirred up and down [Gulbeyaz's] bosom like a billow'.

l. 35. *scroll*. Pennant, as in Scott, *Marmion*, IV. xxviii. 6.

l. 57. Compare the final line of Smart's *A Song to David*, in which he celebrates his poem as 'DETERMINED, DARED, and DONE'.

l. 62. *Ten lines*. A standard length for an obituary.

l. 65. *the Abbey-stones*. Westminster Abbey, where a wide selection of national heroes are buried, including, in 1890, RB himself.

l. 90. *sublimate*. Dematerialize.

l. 91. *had I signed the bond*. The Faustian contract, as in Marlowe's play, according to which the prospect of heaven is surrendered in favour of happiness in this world.

l. 100. Uncomfortably echoing the final line of 'Porphyria's Lover', 'And yet God has not said a word!'

l. 108. *The instant mad eternity*. M. Kowal compares 'Der Augenblick ist Ewigkeit' in Goethe's 'Vermächtnis', 'An Allusion to Goethe in Browning', *Notes and Queries*, 235 (1990), 32–4.

The Patriot: An Old Story

RB, and, still more emphatically, EBB associated the word patriot with the liberal nationalist movements throughout Europe (see, for example, EBB's early poem on an executed Spanish patriot 'On a Picture of Riego's Widow' (1826)), and with Italian nationalism in particular. The reference to Brescia is significant because it was a town strongly associated with Italian nationalism after the 'Ten Days of Brescia', the brief period from 23 March to 1 April 1849, in which the townspeople rose successfully against the Austrians garrisoning the town. Thereafter the revolt was viciously suppressed. The leader of the rebellion, Tito Speri, was eventually captured and hanged by the Austrians in 1853. According to DeVane (*Handbook*, 239) RB denied that he had in mind the fate of Arnold of Brescia, the intellectual leader of the Commune of Rome, which, in the mid-12th century, successfully challenged the Pope's authority in the city. Arnold was hanged in 1155. A link between Arnold of Brescia and Tito Speri would at least serve amply to demonstrate RB's contention in his subtitle that his is an 'old story'.

ll. 1–2. Roses and myrtle are traditionally strewn by celebrating crowds, as in Henry Taylor, *Philip van Artevelde*, III. ii. 337.

l. 9. Possibly referring to Phaeton who demanded to ride the chariot of the sun as a proof that he was in fact the son of the sun god, Helios. When he failed to control the chariot, he was killed by Zeus. In 'In a Balcony', Constance invites Norbert to 'Name [his] own reward': 'Put out an arm and touch and take the sun' (63, 65).

l. 11. Compare the address in *Pauline* to the 'sun-treader' (almost certainly a reference to Shelley), and *Aurora Leigh*, 6. 305–6: 'My soul's in haste to leap into the sun | And scorch and seethe itself to a finer mood.'

l. 14. He offers his own case as a bitter exception to the biblical promise 'whatsoever a man soweth, that shall he also reap' (Galatians 6: 7).

l. 19. A shambles is a slaughterhouse, but here the word refers by extension to a place of execution. The Gate may derive from London's place of execution, Tyburn Gate.

ll. 26–30. The sense is that, had he died a year earlier in his moment of triumph, he would have been fully repaid in this world for his efforts. Dying the death he is about to suffer, his reward will come from God.

l. 30. 'I will repay, saith the Lord', Romans 12: 19.

Master Hugues of Saxe-Gotha

RB insisted that his fictional composer, oddly compounded from a French or Flemish name, and a German Duchy well known because of its association with Queen Victoria's consort, was not modelled on J. S. Bach but one of his 'dry-as-dust imitators' (letter to Henry G. Spaulding quoted in Herbert E. Greene, 'Browning's Knowledge of Music', *PMLA* 62.4 (1947), 1095–9). To Churton Collins he described the poem as 'little more than an actual description of what I saw with my own eyes'. In a church in Antwerp 'I made my way, I remember, to the organ-loft, where, though the service was over and the lights were being put out, the organ was still playing, and I looked down into the fast-emptying and fast-darkening church. I was struck with the picturesqueness of the scene and thought I would describe it in a poem'

(J. Churton Collins, 'Poetry and Symbolism: A Study of "The Tempest"', *Contemporary Review*, 93 (1908), 66). RB had been taught counterpoint by his music teacher, John Relfe, and claimed to have composed fugues. In the poem the fugue functions as an antiquated kind that focuses RB's interest on the manner in which cultural forms may not survive their historical moment. The organist's exasperation with the piece he is playing may also give comic expression to RB's recognition that many of his own readers were equally bemused. The organist's ingenious but unpersuasive effort to locate a sketch of the composer's own face in the score from which he plays may reflect ironically on the inability of RB's readers to conceive that poetry might serve any purpose other than self-expression, unless it were the transmission of edifying moral messages of the kind that the organist tries unpersuasively to identify in the fugue (106–10). But there is also perhaps a suggestion that the division between the organist and the composer acts as a clue to the divided character of RB's own work. The organist inhabits a cluttered, multitudinous world full of things, whereas the composer is interested in pure form, and in the cultivation of formal complexity for its own sake. RB might seem himself to have more in common with the organist, but it should be remembered that he is also a poet remarkable for his formal inventiveness. He was, for example, of all 19th-century poets, with the possible exception of Thomas Hardy, the most extreme and daring in his metrical experiments.

l. 13. *sacristan*. Sexton, the lay-person responsible for the material upkeep of the church.

l. 14. *crank*. Faulty.

l. 15. Prevents one from sustaining the bass note.

ll. 16–18. The hundreds of sounds generated by the organ are imagined as being summoned back to the organ after being released to wander through the church.

l. 16. *our huge house of the sounds*. The organ.

l. 20. The saints to which the church is dedicated, Aloys, Jurien, and Just, are imagined as watchmen patrolling the church.

l. 23. The saints walk east along the nave to the chancel, where the priest officiates, and then walks north and south along the transepts.

l. 26. Most likely St Aloysius Gonzaga and St Justus of Beauvais, but there are other possibilities. Jurien is a Low German variant of George.

l. 29. *sacrament-lace*. The lace of the altar cloth.

l. 30. *desk-velvet*. Probably the velvet covering the lectern.

l. 31. Younger people leave your book of fugues on the shelf.

l. 35. *helve*. Handle. The axe head is the music, the performance its handle, both being necessary if the music is to 'strike' the listener.

l. 37. *Every bar's rest*. Whenever the character appeared indicating a silent bar.

l. 39. *claviers*. Keyboards.

l. 40. The organist imagines the composer peeping at him from the pipes of the organ.

ll. 41–5. Developing the thought in the previous stanza, the portrait of Hugues is described as constructed from the score, the five lines of the stave the wrinkles on his brow, the breves his eyes, and the bar lines his nose.

l. 48. Hugues is imagined as having been, after auditioning, elected to his post, like Bach at Leipzig, by the Corporation or town council.

l. 49. *sciolists shent.* Those whose knowledge and skill are only superficial shamed.

l. 55. *a clinch.* A clinching proof.

ll. 56–60. The first voice states the subject of the fugue which is then restated by a second voice in a different key. The restatement is known as the answer.

ll. 61–5. A third, fourth, and fifth voice repeat the subject all in different keys; the resulting noise is compared to the baying of a pack of hounds in hot pursuit of their quarry which they maintain until the quarry is caught. The comparison is given point because packs of hounds were chosen in part for the harmony that their united voices produced. In *A Midsummer Night's Dream* Theseus claims that his hounds are 'match'd in mouth like bells' (IV. i. 120).

l. 66. *disertates.* Usually 'dissertates', makes a statement.

l. 67. *Two must discept,—has distinguished!* The second voice establishes its distinctness by entering into debate with the first.

l. 70. The subject is batted from one voice to another until it is returned to the first voice.

l. 72. The first section of a fugue is termed the exposition.

l. 80. Forty-nine of the fifty daughters of Danaus at their father's command murdered their husbands, and were subsequently punished in Tartarus by being compelled to undertake an endless task, filling with water a vessel that leaked like a sieve.

ll. 81–2. The music alternates between the super-robust and the super-delicate.

ll. 83–4. Antonio Escobar y Mendoza, a 17th-century Jesuit theologian, whose name was often invoked as an exemplary casuist, that is, as one who devised specious justifications for immoral behaviour. His arguments are as fine and flimsy as the linen thread used to make bonelace, that is, the lace manufactured with bobbins made of bone.

l. 85. *Two-bars.* The double bar line that indicates that a section of the music has ended.

l. 86. *Est fuga, volvitur rota!* It is a fugue, the wheel is turned. Oxford suggests that this should be understood as a direction given in the score.

l. 92. *risposting.* Responding. As Turner points out, the second voice's response to the first in a fugue is termed the 'risposta'; *subjoining.* Supplementing.

l. 94. *groining.* The edge where two vaults meet.

l. 98. Where the devil is the music?

ll. 99–100. The sense is that the gold or beauty of the music is obscured by the pointless elaborations.

l. 100. *tickens*. Ticking, coarse material of the kind used for mattresses.

l. 105. The bellows in 17th- and 18th-century pipe organs were operated manually by an assistant.

ll. 107–10. In RB's version of the traditional metaphor, the web of life is not woven by the Fates: each individual makes his own fate. Death, however, still functions as Atropos, cutting the thread.

l. 113. *a new legislature*. That is a new law-making body, the acts of which are given priority over the laws deriving from 'Truth and Nature'.

l. 114. *that*. Truth and Nature.

l. 117. *trophy*. Used in a general sense to describe the ornamentation in the church that supplements the cherubs and garlands.

l. 120. *glozes*. Glosses, marginal notes. The formal complexity of the fugue, after being compared with a cobweb, is compared to a commentary that obscures rather than illuminates a text.

l. 122. *make up a visage*. Assume an expression, no doubt of dutiful piety.

l. 127. In the Aesop fable the mountain labours to give birth to a mouse.

l. 129. The pipe and the tabor (small drum) probably represent simple, popular music, as in 'The Pied Piper of Hamelin', 279, wholly unlike Hugues's fugue.

l. 130. The key signature for F minor has four flats.

l. 136. *meâ pœnâ*. A truncated version of the well-known motto, 'nemo mea poena effugit', none shall escape my vengeance.

l. 137. Counterpoint is the technical musical term for the relationship one to another of the various voices in a fugue. The implication is that it is a musical technique that, like the Gorgon, turns the listener to stone. The organist, about to abandon the fugue, compares himself with Perseus killing the Gorgon.

l. 139. *unstop the Full-Organ*. Draw the stops to unleash the full power of the organ.

l. 140. *mode Palestrina*, RB explained that this was 'the name given to a certain simple and severe style like that of the Master [Palestrina]' (letter to Spaulding cited in the headnote): an abrupt contrast, then, to the fugue.

l. 144. The candle flares and is extinguished as quickly as a firework.

l. 149. If he carried the moon in his pocket he would need no candle, but to do so is famously impossible. As Cloten says to Cymbeline: 'If Caesar can hide the sun from us with a blanket, or put the moon in his pocket, we will pay him tribute for light' (*Cymbeline*, III. i. 41–3).

Bishop Blougram's Apology

RB acknowledged that Blougram was modelled on Nicholas Wiseman (1802–65) (Sir Charles Gavan Duffy, *My Life in Two Hemispheres*, 1898, ii. 261). The immediate occasion of RB's poem is clearly the re-establishment of the Catholic hierarchy in England, the so-called papal aggression, that produced Wiseman's appointment as cardinal-archbishop of Westminster. Julia Markus locates the poem in the context of the widespread attacks on Wiseman that accompanied his appointment, especially those in *Punch* and *The Globe*, in her fine article 'Bishop Blougram and the Literary Men', *Victorian Studies*, 21.2 (1978), 171–95. She also argues that Gigadibs is based on the lapsed Jesuit journalist Francis Sylvester Mahoney, who wrote under the name 'Father Prout'. This is less persuasive, though it is interesting that Blougram shares a forename, Sylvester, with Mahoney. The links between Blougram and Wiseman (note for example that both are born abroad, Blougram in Rome, Wiseman in Seville, and both had been, before being appointed as cardinals, bishops in partibus) were strong enough to prompt objections from one reviewer who thought it 'scandalous' of RB 'to show so plainly *whom* he means, when he describes an English Catholic bishop' (see the review of *Men and Women* in *The Rambler*, NS 5 (1856), 61). Wiseman had a reputation as a *bon vivant* borne out by his corpulence, but the resemblance between the two men is otherwise slight. RB's characterization seems to derive at least as much from the coincidence that he shared a name with Bunyan's Mr Worldly Wiseman as from traits peculiar to the cardinal. But it does seem significant that Wiseman occupied a high station in the Church while retaining his place, as co-founder and frequent contributor to the *Dublin Review*, as essayist and as novelist (*Fabiola, or the Church of the Catacombs* was published in 1854), in the literary world that Gigadibs inhabits. The poem is best thought of as an extended commentary on Matthew 6: 24: 'No man can serve two masters: for either he will hate the one, and love the other; or else he will hold to the one, and despise the other. Ye cannot serve God and Mammon.' Blougram's suavely argued attempt to refute Christ's injunction leaves chinks through which the Christian truths that Blougram fails to acknowledge are glimpsed, in particular the truth of the Passion, which so forcefully gives the lie to Blougram's claim that the Christian life might be compatible with a life of ease and comfort in this world. So, when Blougram complains of Gigadibs, 'No dogmas nail your faith' (154), when he claims 'There needs no crucial effort to find truth' (858), and whenever he takes a glass of wine or pushes the bottle to his companion, the nails, the Cross, and Christ's blood offer their own silent commentary on his argument. As his monologue ends Blougram's mask of affability slips as he reveals the depth of his contempt for the journalist, but, the reader by this time realizes, the contempt is so deep because it is a projection of the contempt that he feels for himself. 'Bishop Blougram's Apology' is one of the many poems in which RB investigates the relationship between the material and the spiritual worlds. Blougram is a contemporary, but in a direct line of descent from the Bishop of 'The Tomb at St Praxed's'. He also has an odd kinship with some of RB's most attractive characters, with Fra Lippo Lippi, for example, who is equally convinced that body and soul complement rather than contradict each other. The Bishop ends by making a convert of the man he despises. Gigadibs is not converted to Catholicism, but to a life of action rather than a life wasted in words. Like RB's boyhood friend Alfred Domett, he emigrates to New Zealand, determined to take Jesus's advice quite literally and 'put his hand to the plough' (Luke 9: 62).

l. 3. *Westminster Abbey*. The church where Britain's monarchs are crowned. The monastery to which it served as church was dissolved by Henry VIII in 1540. Mary Tudor briefly restored the monastery, but Elizabeth I removed the abbot and monks once again in 1559, since when it has remained a principal cathedral of the Church of England.

l. 4. *basilicas*. Blougram chooses the word to invite a comparison between Westminster Abbey and the four papal basilicas of Rome, chief amongst them, St Peter's.

l. 6. *this of brother Pugin's*. In 1850, when the English hierarchy was restored, St George's Southwark became the first British Catholic church in London to be raised to the status of a cathedral since the Reformation, but the building, designed by the leading architect of the Gothic Revival, Augustus Pugin, had only been completed in 1848, in which year it was formally inaugurated by Wiseman.

ll. 7–8. The use of stucco, and the profusion of meaningless decorative detail, suggests the Regency architecture that Pugin was reacting against rather than his own work.

l. 9. *lime-kiln*. A furnace used to produce quicklime from limestone, a proverbially dusty place as in *David Copperfield* (1850), chapter 12, 'From head to foot I was powdered almost as white with chalk and dust as if I had come out of a lime-kiln.'

ll. 11–12. The reward for officiating at the ceremonies more than repays what the ceremonies cost him in discomfort.

l. 16. *watch a dinner out*. The phrase characteristically conflates religious devotion, keeping vigil, with material self-indulgence, having dinner.

l. 19. *body gets its sop*. The body must be pacified, like Cerberus who must be given a sop before he allows dead souls to enter Hades.

l. 26. *entourage*. Surroundings, the italics suggest that the Bishop is using the word in its French sense.

ll. 28–9. To be up to the eyes in pride means simply to be deeply filled with pride. The eyes are 'protesting' because Gigadibs pretends to despise what he secretly admires, and also perhaps to allude to his Protestant upbringing.

l. 34. *Corpus Christi Day*. Celebrated on the first Thursday after Trinity Sunday, the feast of Corpus Christi celebrates Christ's inauguration of the Eucharist at the Last Supper.

l. 42. *the thing's his trade*. That is, he has entered the Church only to make a living.

l. 45. *che ch'é*. Corrected in later editions to 'che che', literally 'what? what?' The English expression 'Whatever' captures the impatient dismissal that Blougram wishes to express.

l. 48. The figure is from card playing. The Bishop leads and in doing so determines the suit that Gigadibs must play.

ll. 52–4. Blougram claims that Gigadibs would rather aspire to be a great man of letters such as Goethe, a military leader such as Napoleon, or even a dandy such as the Comte d'Orsay (1801–52). The thought is Carlylean in its implication that the modern hero cannot be a churchman such as Carlyle's own Abbot Samson (*Past and Present*, 1843), because he was a hero of the 12th century, faithful to religious forms that have become in the modern world no more than outworn clothing.

l. 62. After 1523 there was no non-Italian Pope until 1978.

l. 70. *tire-room*. The dressing room in a theatre.

l. 71. *shift himself*. Change out of his stage clothes.

l. 77. *imperial*. Probably echoing a Shelleyan ideal: 'man who man would be, | Must rule the empire of himself' ('Sonnet: To the Republic of Benevento', 10–11).

l. 84. Compare the speaker of *Pauline* who recognizes in himself a 'principle of restlessness | Which would be all, have, see, know, taste, feel, all' (277–8).

l. 109. An edition of Balzac's works in fifty-five volumes began to appear in 1856, but Blougram may be comically exaggerating the size of the twenty-volume edition of *La Comédie humaine* announced in 1853. In 1848 EBB wrote to Mary Mitford, 'When Robert and I are ambitious, we talk of buying Balzac in full some day, to put him up in our bookcase from the convent' (*Correspondence*, xv. 99).

ll. 110–11. The Tauchnitz editions of classic Greek authors set in stereotype, some of which the Brownings owned.

ll. 113–14. Antonio da Correggio's *Madonna of St Jerome* which has been exhibited since 1815 in the National Gallery of Parma. The painting is 81 by 56 inches.

l. 117. Modena is near Correggio, the village in which the painter was born.

ll. 119–20. Blougram is unsure of the name of the official responsible for regulating the amount of luggage passengers bring on board.

l. 122. *Six feet square*. The size of the cabin in which all belongings will have to be stowed.

l. 125. *overhauls*. Rejects after inspection.

l. 129. *half-seas o'er*. The mid-point of the voyage.

l. 133. *don't jog the ice*. The ice, if jogged, would dilute as well as cool the wine.

l. 154. *dogmas*. Used in the special theological sense of doctrines that the Church requires the faithful to accept.

l. 160. That he refuses to acknowledge doubts that would damage his career.

l. 168. (*To you, and over the wine*). I am prepared to acknowledge as much to a person such as yourself over a glass of wine.

l. 168. *dogmas*. Blougram uses the word to indicate that Gigadibs's secular opinions are no more demonstrable than the dogmas of the Church.

ll. 177–8. Oxford compares Donne's Holy Sonnet XIX, 12–13: 'So my devout fits come and go away | Like a fantastic ague.'

ll. 182–4. Penguin compares a passage from the Tractarian Isaac Williams, *The Gospel Narrative of Our Lord's Passion* (1841): 'The sound of distant music or a plaintive note, a passing word, or the momentary scent of a flower, or the sound of a bell, or the retiring of the day, or the falling leaf of autumn . . . all these will touch a chord' (434).

l. 187. 'Behold, I stand at the door, and knock: if any man hear my voice, and open the door, I will come in to him' (Revelation 3: 20). But Blougram's expression suggests that the susceptibility he describes may be of a kind with that which prompts belief in table-rapping.

l. 189. *the ancient idol*. A blasphemous reference to God, though Blougram would defend the expression as expressing Gigadibs's point of view. Compare Wiseman's objection to a Church of England document indicting the Catholic Church as idolatrous: 'from "idolatrous" to "not idolatrous," there is a monstrous leap: the whole gulf between heathenism and Christianity must be crossed by it'. *Dublin Review* (December 1850), 520.

l. 190. *The grand Perhaps*. The dying Rabelais was reported to have said, 'Je m'en vais chercher le grand peut-être.' The phrase became proverbial.

l. 197. 'Jesus saith unto him, I am the way, the truth, and the life' (John 14: 6).

ll. 198–203. Mountain paths may be difficult to make out for those travelling on them, but clearly visible to those viewing them from a distance.

l. 212. Julia Markus, '"Bishop Blougram's Apology" and the Literary Men', *Victorian Studies*, 21 (1977–8), 171–95, notes that Wiseman himself uses this metaphor in an article on the reintroduction of the Catholic hierarchy to characterize the unscrupulous behaviour of *The Times*: '*The Times* is a speculation, and a speculation has no conscience. Who that has followed its chequered career, seeing it now on the white, now on the black upon the board, sometimes shifted by the easy glide of queen or rook, now jerked equivocally by a knightly move, has not long known, that in every case it is playing a game, and is only intent on winning?', *Dublin Review*, 29 (December 1850), 528.

l. 311. *latter days*. The last days of the world, as in Job 19: 25: 'For I know that my redeemer liveth, and that he shall stand at the latter day upon the earth.'

l. 315. Compare Satan tempting Christ, Matthew 4: 3–4: 'And when the tempter came to him, he said, If thou be the Son of God, command that these stones be made bread. But he answered . . . Man shall not live by bread alone.'

l. 316. Popes traditionally trace their authority to St Peter. Blougram substitutes Hildebrand, who as Gregory VII served as Pope 1073–85, because it was Gregory who first established the secular power of the papacy.

l. 335. Blougram admits for form's sake that the reverence is offered not to himself but to the Church as embodied in his person.

l. 349. Compare 'Fra Lippo Lippi', 270: 'You understand me: I'm a beast, I know.'

l. 353. To cut their tails to a stump and cover up their hindquarters (though apes are in fact without tails).

l. 357. *steerage-hole*. Steerage was a term used to denote the cheapest cabins on board, in which the poorest passengers would travel.

l. 358. Live sheep and pigs would be carried on long voyages.

l. 360. *upholstery*. All the inessential, luxurious aspects of furniture.

l. 375. *dozen men of sense*. The number on a jury.

l. 377. In 1850 members of the congregation of Santa Chiara in Rimini saw the eyes of the Virgin in a painting move and the painting was taken in procession to St Augustine's, a larger church in the city. In 1851 a commission confirmed 'the truth of the prodigious movement of the eyes' that might now be 'regarded as a well-established historical fact' (Charles Raymond Dillon, *Miracles*, 2000, 79–80).

ll. 381–6. Oxford suggests that the opera is *Macbeth*, the only opera given its first performance in Florence in 1847, but it is a title Blougram is unlikely to have forgotten. In June 1851 the RBs attended performances of *Attila* and *Ernani* in Venice, EBB enjoying them more. The reference is possibly to *Attila*, which was wildly popular with contemporary audiences who understood it as approving liberal reform. RB met Rossini, whom he admired, in 1849. As RB implies, Verdi was an admirer of Rossini, whose approval he therefore values above popular plaudits.

l. 384. The primitive instruments are imagined because of the dissonance of the music.

l. 389. *catch a thing within a thing*. Are alert to the complexity of reality.

l. 393. Probably a factory rather than a domestic chimney.

l. 397. *demireps*. Women of doubtful reputation.

l. 406. *carats*. The measures of a little more than three grains in which diamonds are weighed.

l. 407. *your picked Twelve*. An imagined jury.

l. 411. *that's Schelling's way*. RB denied ever having read any Schelling, but he may still have been aware of Schelling's *naturphilosophie* as attempting to negotiate rather than choose between a subjective and an objective account of reality (Furnivall, 51).

l. 412. *the tail of time*. The latter days.

l. 413. *Nicking the minute*. Alert to the precise historical moment.

l. 425. *All Peter's chains about his waist*. Longman notes that both Father Prout and George Borrow ridicule pious Catholic noblemen who asked that the chains of Peter preserved as a relic in San Pietro in Vincoli in Rome be hung about their person.

l. 426. In Swift's *Tale of a Tub*, section VI, Catholicism is distinguished from Lutheranism and Calvinism by its representative Lord Peter's preference for a coat in which he had obscured the original material by covering it with 'an infinite quantity of lace and ribbons, and fringe, and embroidery, and points'. Noodledom is a collective term for noodles or fools.

l. 445. *his star.* The principle by which he guides his conduct like a ship that uses a star to steer by, or perhaps like the star that guides the Magi.

ll. 451–2. Nor compromise the moment of triumph by feeling a need to justify the means by which the triumph was obtained.

l. 454. If Napoleon were not understood to be following his star, he would properly be judged insane.

l. 466. Blougram seems to conflate the saying 'L'état, c'est moi' commonly ascribed to Louis XIV with the saying, 'Je suis la Révolution' commonly ascribed to Napoleon.

l. 467. The metaphor is from wrestling.

l. 472. In 1809 Napoleon divorced his first wife Josephine in order to marry the Archduchess Marie-Louise, daughter of the Emperor of Austria. He re-established relations with Pope Pius VII and the Church in 1801, but was later excommunicated.

l. 473. Napoleon crowned himself Emperor of France in 1804. The Pope was present at the ceremony.

l. 475. *Austerlitz.* The battle of 1805 in which Napoleon decisively defeated the Russian and Austrian armies.

ll. 476–85. Blougram loosely paraphrases Pascal's wager, the argument that, since to believe promises infinite rewards, and incurs, if belief is mistaken, only finite losses, disbelief is irrational.

l. 489. The poet, since he lives in his imagination, is spared the choice of living either for this world or the next.

l. 492. Compare 'Andrea del Sarto', 97–8, 'Ah, but a man's reach should exceed his grasp, | Or what's a heaven for?'

l. 493 *Shakspeare.* See note to *Pauline*, l. 811. The old spelling is used throught *Bishop Blougram's Apology*.

l. 513. Compare 'The Cloud-capp'd Tow'rs, the gorgeous Palaces' (*The Tempest*, IV. i. 152) that constitute for Prospero an imaginative vision that, for all its splendour, leaves 'not a rack behind'.

l. 516. Shakespeare pays his tribute to Giulio Romano in *The Winter's Tale*, V. ii. 94–6, and to Dowland's lute in *The Passionate Pilgrim*, VII. 5–6, published as Shakespeare's in 1599. The reference appears in a poem now ascribed to Richard Barnfield.

l. 519. *King John*, III. i. 136–46. In the play Pandulph demonstrates his power by excommunicating the king.

l. 523. *degree.* Rank.

l. 533. European beauty spots that the RBs like Blougram had visited, whereas Shakespeare had visited Italy only in his imagination. Terni is an ancient city north of Rome. Travellers take the St Gothard pass when crossing the Alps from Switzerland to Italy.

ll. 544–9. An imaginary racket game a little like rackets or real tennis. The point is that Blougram, though an inferior player, plays for higher rewards.

l. 553. Because as a cardinal he is a prince of the Church Blougram may call himself the cousin of the monarch to whom Shakespeare was no more than a servant.

ll. 556–65. Fire or spiritual energy gives life its value, whether the fire be illusory or god-given, and whether it be used constructively or destructively.

l. 563. Steel is made by fusing iron with other elements in a furnace.

l. 568. Blougram's tribute to Luther, the leader of the Protestant Reformation, is deliberately provocative.

l. 572. *Re-opens a shut book*. The reference may be specifically to Luther's translation of the Bible into German.

l. 577. David Friedrich Strauss (1808–74), the leading exponent of the 'Higher Criticism', the German theological movement that regarded the Bible as a historical document rather than as the Word of God.

ll. 579–81. Strauss, a scholarly critic, will not, like Luther, determine the future course of events. His scepticism brings no profit. He is ice against Luther's fire.

l. 591. Even if his belief in the reality of heaven were mistaken.

l. 597. *available*. Effectual.

ll. 602–4. Compare Tennyson, *In Memoriam*, XCVI. 11–12: 'There lives more faith in honest doubt, | Believe me, than in half the creeds.'

l. 611. *doubts at my fingers' ends*. Compare Thomas whose doubts are overcome when Jesus says, 'Reach hither thy finger', and he feels Jesus's wound (John 20: 27).

ll. 616–17. Blougram suggests that when he is tried, his devout actions will weigh more heavily than his sceptical thoughts that may be prompted by the devil.

l. 626. *"What think ye of Christ"*. Jesus's question to the Pharisees. See Matthew 22: 42.

ll. 638–43. Blougram investigates the grounds for believing in his own historical existence in parody of the manner in which Strauss investigates the Gospel accounts of Christ in his *Das Leben Jesu*, translated by George Eliot in 1846 as *The Life of Jesus*.

l. 640. *born in Rome*. Wiseman was born in Spain, in Seville, of Irish parents.

ll. 648–51. Compare Exodus 33: 20: 'And he said, Thou canst not see my face: for there shall no man see me, and live.'

l. 652. *Some think*. Such as William Paley in his *A View of the Evidences of Christianity* (1794), but in the mid-19th century the argument from design seemed less persuasive. See, for example, Tennyson, *In Memoriam*,

CXXIV. 4–5: 'I found Him not in world or sun | Or eagle's wing, or insect's eye.'

ll. 655–61. Blougram disconcertingly conflates two orthodox Christian notions; the notion that what we think of as evil is in fact providential, a part of God's plan, and the doctrine of accommodation or condescension, which maintains that God must accommodate his infinity to the finite capacities of human beings.

l. 662. *case-harden*. The process by which iron is strengthened by converting its surface to steel.

l. 664. *ichors o'er the place*. Ichors seems to refer to the manner in which the body releases white corpuscles to repair a wound. Ichor ordinarily refers to the blood of the gods.

l. 667. Michael is commonly represented as trampling on a dragon, after Revelation 12: 7–9.

l. 677. Probably a specific reference to Disraeli and his Young England movement.

ll. 679–80. *cosmogony | Geology, ethnology*. Representative modern sciences all of which threaten traditional Christian belief; cosmogony by offering alternatives to the biblical account of creation, geology by expanding time beyond the parameters that the Bible seemed to establish, and ethnology by exposing disconcerting parallels between Christian myth and myths current in other cultures. In 1836 Wiseman had published a series of lectures, *On the Connection between Science and Revealed Religion*.

ll. 681–2. RB plays between the sound of the Greek suffix 'ology', a tuneful dactyl, and its sense. The suffix marks the scientific disciplines that threaten religious faith.

l. 685. The ark is recorded as coming to rest on Mount Ararat in Genesis 8: 4.

l. 690. The stopper of the decanter is topped, presumably, by a plain globe of glass.

ll. 702–3. C. R. Tracy ('Bishop Blougram', *MLR* 34 (1939), 423) notes an exchange of letters between Newman and the Bishop of Norwich in *The Times*, 22 October 1851, in which Newman defends himself for having written, 'I think it impossible to withstand the evidence which is brought for the liquefaction of the blood of St Januarius, and for the motion of the eyes of the pictures of the Madonna in the Roman states' (compare note to l. 377), by arguing that biblical miracles have established 'the idea of a violation of nature' and hence have made subsequent miracles more probable.

l. 704. The doctrine of the Immaculate Conception, that is, that the Virgin Mary was born free from original sin, was promulgated by Pope Pius IX on 8 December 1854, but the new doctrine had been widely anticipated.

l. 708. Job 25: 6: 'man, that is a worm'.

l. 709. Contrast Corinthians 1: 27: 'But God hath chosen the foolish things of the world to confound the wise; and God hath chosen the weak things of the world to confound the things which are mighty.'

ll. 715–16. King Bomba was Ferdinand II of Naples; the lazzaroni, named after the beggar Lazarus in Luke 16: 20, are the poorest of the city's poor. Cardinal Giacomo Antonelli was secretary of state to Pope Pius IX and a vigorous opponent of Italian nationalism in general and Garibaldi in particular. Blougram insinuates that unthinking faith is now only possible amongst the very lowest, although their faith may be exploited by the more sophisticated for their own ends.

l. 728. See note to ll. 702–3.

ll. 729–30. Blougram alludes sardonically to the promptness with which the blood liquefies on each of the eighteen occasions on which it is required to do so each year.

l. 732. *eliminate*. Purge. *decrassify*. Divest of what is crass: a RB coinage.

l. 744. J. G. Fichte (1762–1814) held that consciousness was not grounded in anything other than itself. It follows that god is the creation of man rather than vice versa. Fichte defined God as the moral order of the universe. RB was urged to read Fichte, 'especially on Religion & Christianity', by his friend Joseph Arnould in 1847 (*Correspondence*, xiv. 349).

l. 748. *I am master not to take*. I am free not to take. As Oxford points out, a Gallicism.

ll. 769–74. Blougram offers his willingness to conform to the laws of this world as a guarantee of his readiness to conform to the requirements of the world hereafter. The Bible more often opposes 'the wisdom of this world' with true wisdom. See 1 Corinthians 2: 6.

l. 791. *scouts*. Scornfully rejects.

ll. 819–20. Natural religion appeals to the authority of experience, revealed religion to the authority of scripture.

l. 833. *a French book*. R. E. Neil Dodge, *TLS*, 21 March 1935, 176, suggests Balzac's *Physiologie du mariage*: 'Certain poets discern in modesty, in the alleged mysteries of love, some reason why the married couple should share the same bed; but the fact must be recognized that if primitive men sought the shade of caverns, the mossy couch of deep ravines, the flinty roof of grottoes to protect his pleasure, it was because the delight of love left him without defence against his enemies.'

l. 858. *crucial*. Critical, but the word is no doubt chosen to suggest Christ's Cross.

l. 868. The thought seems to conflate the frequent biblical references to God appearing in a cloud, as in Lamentations 3: 44: 'Thou hast covered thyself with a cloud', and the human facility for seeing determinate shapes in a cloud, as in *Hamlet*, III. ii. 366–72, in which Hamlet and Polonius discuss whether a particular cloud is like a camel, a weasel, or a whale.

ll. 877–8. *Pastor est tui Dominus*. Your Lord is a Shepherd, revising the opening of Psalm 23, which continues, 'He maketh me to lie down in green pastures.'

l. 892. *beat*. overcome with 'me' omitted.

l. 896. A wether is a castrated ram.

ll. 898–901. I could predict what I would become when I was your age, and can predict what you will be when you are mine.

ll. 907–8. The women cut curls from his dog's ears as mementoes of the bishop.

l. 914. *fictile*. Moulded into form by art.

l. 915. Roman artefacts were commonly uncovered at Albano, a city near Rome. Anacreon was a lyric poet best known for his drinking and love songs.

l. 942. Drugget is coarse woollen clothing; purple is the colour that signifies nobility, but may also, as an alternative to red, be the colour of a cardinal's robes.

l. 945. *statedly*. Regularly; *Blackwood's Magazine* by the mid-19th century was a respectable, Tory magazine, conservative in its tastes and only occasionally intellectual in its content. Gigadibs would have written for it out of economic necessity, not because it reflected his own views.

l. 947. For example, the discussion of *Hamlet* in A. W. Schlegel's *Lectures on Dramatic Art and Literature* (1809).

ll. 949–52. Dickens contributed several such sketches of London slum life to *Household Words*. See, for example, 'The Devil's Acre', 1 (June 1850), 297–301.

l. 960. *our own reviews*. Roman Catholic reviews.

l. 963. *Outward-bound*. Taking up Blougram's analogy of life as a sea voyage.

l. 972. Before the Catholic hierarchy was restored in Britain British bishops were given titles relating to foreign dioceses no longer in practical existence. Such titles were marked by the addition of the phrase *in partibus infidelium*, in the lands of unbelievers. Before he became Archbishop of Westminster Wiseman was Bishop of Melipotamus *in partibus infidelium*, Melipotamus being a see in Crete. The comment may suggest that in Britain Blougram thinks himself still in a land of unbelievers.

l. 987. *loose cards*. In whist a term for cards of no value.

l. 1003. That is, Gigadibs took the higher ground in their argument.

l. 1010. He plans, presumably, to marry and start a family, like Philip Hewson, who emigrates to New Zealand with his new wife at the end of Clough's *The Bothie of Toper-na-Fuosich* (a title later changed to *The Bothie of Tober-na-Vuolich*), 1848, a poem that RB much enjoyed.

l. 1013. Gigadibs has taken literally the instruction that the resurrected Jesus gives three times to Peter in the last chapter of John: 'Feed my lambs'; 'Feed my sheep', 'Feed my sheep' (21: 15–17). Jesus also instructs Peter to leave Judas's punishment to Jesus: 'If I will that he tarry till I come, what is that to thee?' (21; 23). The implication is that Gigadibs should not busy himself to expose Blougram.

Memorabilia

RB explained, 'I was once in the shop of Hodgson, the bookseller, when a stranger, who was in conversation with Hodgson, spoke of something which Shelley had once told him. Suddenly the stranger turned towards me, bursting into a loud laugh as he saw my blanched face—for I was strangely moved' (W. G. Kingland, 'Browning: Some Personal Reminiscences', *Baylor Bulletin*, 34 (July 1931), 28–40, 32. The word memorabilia seems to signify mementoes, objects that have an uncanny power to revive the past, a sense that *OED* records only from 1855, rather than its then more common meaning, memorable thoughts. The poem registers the power certain events have to shock an individual out of a conventional acceptance of the linearity of time, as RB is shocked by meeting someone who had met the poet of the past he most admired, and as the memory of finding an eagle feather on an otherwise forgotten day retains its potency. It is a power that, as 'To a Skylark' intimates, Shelley and others have often attributed to poetry.

ll. 5–6. Compare 'To a Skylark', 86–7: 'We look before and after | And pine for what is not.' Shelley is echoing Hamlet, *Hamlet*, IV. iv. 37.

l. 15. Oxford compares Edward Young, *Night Thoughts*, 'Night the Second', 602–4: 'Had he dropt | That eagle Genius! O had he let fall | One feather as he flew.'

FROM *MEN AND WOMEN*, VOL. II (1855)

Andrea del Sarto

The poem seems to have been prompted when in 1853 John Kenyon, the Brownings' closest friend, asked Robert to commission a copy of a double portrait in the Pitti Palace then identified as by Andrea of himself and his wife (the portrait is now attributed to Tommaso di Stefano Lunetti). The biographical details that RB incorporates are taken from Vasari, who had been apprenticed to Andrea, which helps to explain why the life of Andrea is one of his longest and most elaborate. The notion that Andrea is a 'faultless' painter derives, though, from Anna Jameson: 'he attained so much excellence that he was called in his own time "Andrea senza errori," that is, Andrea *the Faultless*' (Jameson, 212). Vasari ascribes Andrea's misfortunes largely to the malign influence of his wife Lucrezia, and claims that Andrea was jealous of her, but it was RB who furnished the wife with a lover. Julia Markus has suggested the impact on the poem of the marital troubles of the American painter William Page, whose much younger wife left him in 1854 for a still younger Italian. The young couple had pursued their affair so openly that it had become a notorious scandal in the expatriate community. See Julia Markus, 'Andrea del Sarto (Called "The Faultless Painter") and William Page (Called "The American Titian")', *Browning Institute Studies*, 2.2 (1974), 1–24. RB clearly intended the poem as a companion to 'Fra Lippo Lippi', Lippo's reckless love of life contrasting with Andrea's timidity, a difference most feelingly enacted in the handling of the blank verse in the two poems. The contrast between Andrea's perfect but limited talent, and the imperfect genius of the three great contemporaries in competition with whom Andrea imagines painting frescoes in Heaven, is also RB's own. Through it, he adumbrates a thought central to his own aesthetic, and significant too in the aesthetic thought of his contemporaries, in which it often elicited a contrast between the fixed perfection of classical architecture and the vital straining towards the infinite found in Gothic or Christian architecture. RB holds that the finite medium with which any artist has to work (whether the medium be paint or language) can only register the infinite by admitting rather than seeking to eradicate imperfection. Andrea's faultlessness on this reckoning is itself a fault, and a decisive one. RB misrepresents the character of Andrea's work the more strongly to associate it with the mediocrity of perfection. Its 'twilight' character, the 'common greyness' that 'silvers everything' (35–6), belies the deserved reputation as a colourist that both Vasari and Jameson grant Andrea (though it should be borne in mind that the colour of the paintings RB saw in Florence would have been dulled by time and varnish). It is at once curious and characteristic that RB, the most famously married poet in literature, should have adopted the voice of a painter eager to ascribe his failure to match Leonardo, Raphael, and Michaelangelo to his married status: 'the three first without a wife, | While I have mine! So—still they overcome' (263–4).

l. 7. *Fix his own time*. The commissioned painting is presumably a portrait. Andrea promises that he will allow the 'friend's friend' to decide when to sit.

l. 15. *Fiesole*. A hill-town 5 miles outside Florence.

l. 16. *use*. Are supposed to be.

ll. 23–4. A point insisted on both by Vasari and Jameson. 'His only model for all his females was his wife; and even when he did not paint from her, she so possessed his thoughts that unconsciously he repeated the same features in every face he drew, whether Virgin, or saint, or goddess' (Jameson, 214–15). Compare Vasari, 3. 203.

l. 26. *serpentining*. The 'figura serpentinata', the figure with its body twisted in a manner that reveals its musculature, was commonly deployed by Michelangelo, and, following him, by the other major Florentine artists. In this context the word also suggests Lucrezia's serpentine duplicity; *rounds on rounds*. Compare the use of the phrase in 'Pan and Luna', 42.

ll. 29–30. For woman as the moon, see 'One Word More', 157–68, and 'Pan and Luna'.

l. 34. *harmony*. A word often used to indicate a painterly refinement lost on the common viewer. Hazlitt in 'On the Pleasure of Painting' claims that it is a quality 'lost upon the common observer'. Those blind, for example, to the 'exquisite gradations in a sky of Claude's' will not feel the painting's 'harmony'. Vasari claims that it is a quality for which Andrea is remarkable (3. 192, 236).

l. 49. *twilight-piece*. As Oxford suggests, the phrase is analogous to 'night-piece', a painting representing a night-time scene.

l. 54. Andrea indicates the paintings displayed on the wall.

l. 57. *cartoon*. A full-size preparatory design on paper for an art-work in another medium

l. 65. *Legate*. Probably the Papal Legate, the representative of the Pope, but the word may be used of a representative more generally, for an ambassador, for example.

l. 68. '[W]hen he drew the different objects from nature which he proposed to use in his works, it was his custom for the most part to sketch them but very slightly, since these few memoranda sufficed him, although, when the object in question was executed in the paintings, he completed it to the utmost perfection' (Vasari, 3. 233).

l. 86. Compare Tennyson on Lazarus: 'Behold a man raised up by Christ! | The rest remaineth unreveal'd; | He told it not, or something seal'd | The lips of that Evangelist', *In Memoriam*, XXXI. 12–15.

l. 93. *Morello's outline*. Monte Morello, north-west of Florence, is the highest mountain in the Florentine valley.

ll. 103–16. Vasari, by contrast, reports that when the Duke of Mantua demanded that Raphael's portrait of Pope Leo be given to him, Andrea painted a copy so perfect that the Duke was deceived and even Giulio Romano believed it to be the work of Raphael (3. 216–18).

l. 104. *The Urbinate*. That is, Raphael, born in Urbino, 1483, who died in 1520.

l. 105. Vasari was one of Andrea's pupils.

l. 116. *Out of me!* Beyond me!

ll. 123–4. The voice is contrasted with the still small voice of God. In Psalm 91: 3, it is promised that God 'shall deliver thee from the snare of the fowler'.

l. 128. *by the future*. In comparison with the future.

ll. 129–30. Michelangelo is still alive, but Raphael, as Andrea reports in 104, has been dead five years.

l. 132. *over-rules*. Ultimately determines.

l. 139. *half-men*. Compare Carlyle, *Sartor Resartus*, Book 2, chapter 9: 'Unhappy if we are but Half-men, in whom that divine handwriting has never blazed forth, all-subduing, in true sun-splendour.'

l. 145. *the Paris lords*. Vasari and Jameson both report that Andrea was entrusted with a large sum of money by the King of France, Francis I, for the purchase of works of art, a sum that Andrea subsequently 'embezzled' (Jameson, 213).

ll. 148–9. In 1518, at the King's invitation, Andrea entered into the service of Francis I. The royal hunting lodge at Fontainebleau, some 35 miles outside Paris, became, through his patronage, the most important conduit through which the Renaissance was introduced to France. Francis was patron not only to Andrea but to Benvenuto Cellini and Leonardo. He is celebrated as a patron of the arts in Castiglione's *Book of the Courtier.*

l. 157. *You.* Corrected in later editions to 'I', although it is just possible to imagine 'you' as Lucrezia.

l. 161. *this face beyond.* The face of his wife who remained in Italy awaiting his return.

l. 177. *the Roman's.* Raphael's, who produced his principal works in Rome. Vasari suggests that Andrea was deterred from settling in Rome by the fear that he might be unable to emulate the achievements of Raphael and his followers (3. 232).

ll. 183–92. The anecdote is given in a footnote to Vasari: 'the estimation in which the powers of Andrea were held by Michael Angelo likewise, may be inferred from a remark of that master to Raphael, which we find cited in Bocchi, *Bellezze di Firenze.* "There is a bit of a manikin in Florence," observes Michael Angelo, "who, if he had chanced to be employed in great undertakings as you have happened to be, would compel you to look well about you"' (3. 232).

l. 188. *scrub.* A mean or insignificant fellow.

ll. 193–6. Andrea makes the alteration to the copy from Raphael sent him by Vasari. See 103–5.

l. 209. *cue-owls.* The scops owl is called 'chui' in Italy after its call.

ll. 212–13. Vasari suggests that the house was built with the money embezzled from Francis I.

l. 219. *Cousin.* The implication is that this is Lucrezia's lover. Compare the Prior's 'niece' in *Fra Lippo Lippi.*

ll. 220–1. The wife uses Andrea's money to fund her lover's debts.

l. 233. *friend.* It seems that the friend is a man to whom Lucrezia's lover is indebted. Andrea has been persuaded to repay the debt by providing paintings and a portrait for his 'corridor' or gallery.

l. 240. *scudi.* A scudo was an Italian coin worth about four shillings. Vasari mentions that Andrea's prices were contemptibly low.

l. 249. Vasari reports that Andrea's 'immoderate love' for his wife led him 'in great measure to discontinue the assistance which he had given to his parents' (3. 194, note).

l. 261. *the angel's reed.* The reed with which the angel measures the walls of the New Jerusalem in Revelation 21: 16.

In a Year

The woman speaker of the poem laments the coldness of the man who had once loved her. She recalls in stanza 5 how she acknowledged that she was not able fully to reciprocate his love, and goes on to trace the unfortunate consequence of her honesty. She darkly imagines that the proof of love men demand of women is that they die for it, an outcome that satisfyingly demonstrates their feminine fragility: 'Can't we touch these bubbles then | But they break?' (71–2). The short lines are cretics (two stressed interrupted by an unstressed syllable) as in 'Love Among the Ruins'. The eight-line stanza is syntactically divided into two quatrains, but the rhyme scheme knits the quatrains together, so that, like the lovers in 7–8, in each stanza the two quatrains at once embrace and remain single.

ll. 22–4. He responds to the sound of the voice even before registering the import of the words.

l. 29. The expression seems to reverse the thought that she was brimful of love to suggest that love (his love) was brimful of her.

l. 35. Trust that your love for me is a true indication of what my love for you will become.

l. 52. *content.* Satisfy.

l. 54. Exchange the gold of his love for dust because she did not yet love him as he loved her, but could only offer him material things in return, her 'wealth and ease, | Beauty, youth' (45–6). Compare Shakespeare, *Cymbeline*, IV. ii. 263–4, 'Golden lads and girls all must, | As chimney-sweepers, come to dust.'

l. 70. *White and pink!* The defining colours of young womanhood, as when Half-Rome describes Pompilia 'Recumbent upstairs in her pink and white' (*The Ring and the Book*, II. 1004).

ll. 77–8. Compare EBB, 'Bianca Among the Nightingales' (1862), 100–1, in which a faithless woman is described as 'mere cold clay | As all false things are'. The man's heart is deadened because it no longer feels love. Its gold has become dust (see 54).

Old Pictures in Florence

The poem, a remarkable hybrid, functions at once as a self-caricature rather like Walter Scott's caricature of himself as Jonathan Oldbuck in *The Antiquary*, a history of aesthetics, and a political prophecy. The speaker of the poem admits a devotion to early Italian art that is fuelled, like RB's own, at least in part by the hope of picking up for a trifle some unrecognized masterpiece such as the Giotto recently discovered by a more fortunate rival (233–40). The defence of a Christian aesthetic of imperfection restates a position RB frequently maintained, for example in 'Andrea del Sarto', and yet in this poem it is an imperfection secured in part by the decay of the pictures that the speaker values. The frescoes are not unfinished, but many of them are peeling off the wall. The speaker is aware that his taste for early Italian art is not shared by the Italians, who are content to whitewash over the frescoes in their churches. His taste identifies him as an outsider, as one of the 'dealers and stealers, Jews and the English!' (228), as well as revealing him as a man whose business is confined to the 'empty cells of the human hive' (36). Yet somehow this speaker emerges in the poem's final lines as a man whose gaze is turned rapturously to the future, where he sees Florence re-born on 'the day that vindicates Giotto | And Florence together' (287–8). He imagines Giotto's campanile, left unfinished by his successors, at last completed by the spire that Giotto had planned. It is a vision that ratifies his conviction that his interest in the dusty past of Florence authenticates rather than counters his concern for the city's future. As Julia Markus has pointed out, RB's poem is closely related to EBB's *Casa Guidi Windows* (1851), the poem, explicitly referred to by RB in 260, in which EBB had first advanced the claim that neither her gender nor her nationality disqualified her from engaging directly with the Italian politics of her day (see Julia Markus, '"Old Pictures in Florence" through "Casa Guidi Windows"', *Browning Institute Studies*, 6 (1978), 43–61), but RB seems at least as interested in exploring the difference between his and his wife's way of writing poems as in their shared political sentiments. The proximity of EBB to the speaker of her poem is one of the premises from which she writes: the relationship between RB and his speaker is a problem that his poem investigates.

ll. 1–2. Eels are supposed to be startled by thunder out of the mud at the bottom of the pond. See Shakespeare, *Pericles*, IV. ii. 143–5: 'I warrant you, mistress, thunder shall not so awake the bed of eels as my giving out her beauty sirs up the lewdly inclin'd,' and John Marston, *Scourge of Villainy*, II. vii. 78–80: 'They are naught but Eeles, that never will appeare, | Till that tempestuous winds or thunder teare | Their slimy beds.'

l. 3. *aloed*. The aloe is not usually a climbing plant.

l. 5. *flash snapt*. Compare *The Ring and the Book*, X. 290: 'Two names now snap and flash from mouth to mouth'; *dumb thunder*. The epithet is transferred: thunder strikes dumb, as in *Aurora Leigh*, 6. 765.

l. 7. Water-gold is the liquid amalgam used in gilding: compare Alfred Domett, 'Flowers' (1833), Part the Second, 11–12: 'And sweet the Sun-set to behold— | The crimson and the water-gold.'

l. 15. The campanile of Florence Cathedral was designed by Giotto, although the building was incomplete at his death, and has remained uncompleted ever since.

l. 22. That is, Giotto's contemporaries are deservedly forgotten.

l. 33. *chaffer*. Buy and sell.

l. 37. The chapter-room or chapterhouse is a room attached to a church where meetings are held.

l. 38. *apsis*. Apse, the recess, often domed, at the eastern end of the nave behind the altar.

l. 40. The façade of the church faces the sun directly, but the speaker neglects it in favour of the dark, unfrequented inner spaces of the church.

l. 47. 'His mother used to read Croxall's Fables to his little sister and him. The story contained in them of a lion who was kicked to death by an ass affected him so painfully that he could no longer endure the sight of the book' (Orr, *Life*, 28).

l. 51. *Michaels*. Michelangelos.

l. 54. Compare 1 Corinthians 13: 12: 'For now we see through a glass; but then face to face.'

l. 55. Michelangelo wrote poetry in the intervals of his work as a painter, sculptor, and architect. RB believed that Raphael, too, had written a sequence of sonnets. See 'One Word More', 5. The thought is that in Heaven they will have the opportunity to master the art.

l. 58. *wronged great souls*. Those, as Shelley puts it in *Adonais*, 'whose names on Earth are dark' (406).

l. 61. The reference is to ways of referring to painters whose names remain unknown, whether by a periphrasis, as the Master of the Osservanza Triptych, or some such expression as early Sienese school.

ll. 62–4. The point is that the work of the great masters of the Renaissance was possible only because of the work of their unremembered predecessors.

l. 64. *Dellos*. Dello di Niccolo Delli (*c*.1403–*c*.1470), a little-known Florentine painter and sculptor, some fifty years Leonardo's senior.

ll. 67–8. RB leans on the traditional association between critics and dogs, as in Thomas Moore's comic opera *M.P., Or the Bluestocking*, I. iv, in which the poet 'dreams all the night about critics and dogs'. The association possibly derives from a belief that a cynic is etymologically dog-like.

l. 67. *girns*. Snarls.

ll. 69–72. Stefano, the pupil of Giotto claimed by Vasari to have 'not only surpassed all those who had preceded him in the art, but left even his master, Giotto himself, far behind' (1. 133). His fellow artists called him 'the ape of nature' (1. 135).

l. 76. *There's its transit*. Changed in later editions to *sic transit* as in the well-known Latin tag *sic transit gloria mundi*. But the 1855 version makes sense as signifying the short-lived prominence of a comet in the night sky.

ll. 77–80. Unlike the blind who can work while keeping their gaze turned upwards (towards God), unappreciated artists of the past are imagined as looking downwards from Heaven, irritated by their neglect.

l. 81. *deal your dole*. Give your alms.

l. 84. *in fructu*. As profit.

ll. 85–8. The classical Greek sculptors re-created the ideal human form, in which soul and body perfectly express one another, an ideal that actual human beings misrepresent ('actual generations garble').

ll. 89–96. Because the ideal beauty of Greek art is unattainable by its admirers it serves only to reconcile them to their lack of the power, beauty, and ability to transcend time that the statues embody.

l. 98. RB is probably thinking of the recumbent Theseus on the Parthenon pediment in the British Museum, which was sketched by RB's American painter friend William Page.

ll. 99–100. Paris is the most frequently sculpted of Priam's sons. Thomas suggests that the reference is to 'the Paris of the Aegina sculptures, kneeling and drawing a bow, now in the Munich Glyptothek' (C. F. Thomas, *Art and*

Architecture in the Poetry of Robert Browning, 1991, 186). Perhaps a more likely reference is to a statue such as the Lansdowne Paris unearthed by Gavin Hamilton in 1769 from the Emperor Hadrian's villa in Tivoli, a Roman copy of a Greek fourth-century BC original now in the Louvre.

l. 101. The Apollo Belvedere in the Vatican, also known as the Pythian Apollo, because Apollo is represented after having just released an arrow, as in his killing of the Python.

l. 102. Probably the figure of Niobe sheltering one of her daughters in the Uffizi. Niobe's fourteen children were killed by Apollo and Artemis.

l. 103. The horse race on the Parthenon frieze in the British Museum.

l. 104. A Greek bust in the Uffizi, commonly known as 'the dying Alexander'.

l. 108. *worsted.* Punning on two senses of the word, defeated, and the common woollen material that, in contrast with marble, exemplifies ordinary life.

l. 111. Modern life is lived collectively, and hence a single individual only lives that life partially.

ll. 113–20. The stanza identifies modernity with a turn towards the inward that establishes at once the insignificance of the outward world in comparison with the world of thought and feeling, and a radical equality, because in the inner world social distinctions are erased. For a similar thought see the extract from *The Recluse* that Wordsworth prefixed to *The Excursion.*

l. 118. *types.* The word is used in its biological sense, as in Tennyson, *In Memoriam*, LVI. 1.

ll. 121–8. The contrast is between static classical art that inhabits an eternal present and dynamic Christian art, the imperfection of which in itself implies a future towards which it strives.

l. 127. *They stand for our copy.* They offer us a model for imitation.

l. 129. Leaven is fermented dough. Compare Galatians 5: 9: 'A little leaven leaveneth the whole lump.'

ll. 134–5. Vasari records that when asked by the Pope to provide a preliminary drawing for a proposed painting, 'Giotto, who was very courteous, took a sheet of paper, and a pencil dipped in a red colour, then, resting his elbow on his side, to form a sort of compass, with one turn of the hand he drew a circle, so perfect and exact that it was a marvel to behold. This done, he turned smiling to the courtier, saying, "Here is your drawing"' (1. 103).

l. 136. See note to l. 15.

l. 140. *gulf.* The gulf of Hell.

l. 147. That is, the role of the artist is to teach human beings who they really are.

l. 156. *quiddit.* Quiddity, here meaning simply argument or saying.

l. 157. *The worthies.* The early painters.

l. 159. *allocution.* Exhortation.

l. 160. Do not withhold your honour until the process that they began has been completed.

l. 165. *this world's congeries*. The groups into which this world is divided.

l. 179. *Nicolo the Pisan*. Niccolo Pisano (*c*.1220–*c*.1284), often identified as the father of Italian sculpture. He carved the pulpit in the Baptistery in Pisa. According to Anna Jameson, 'He was the first to leave the stiff monotony of the traditional forms for the study of nature and the antique' (Jameson, 16).

l. 180. Cimabue (*c*.1240–1302), according to Anna Jameson the 'Father of Modern Painting' (Jameson, 1).

l. 182. Lorenzo Ghiberti (1378–1455), best known for his casting of the bronze doors of the Baptistery of Florence Cathedral; Domenico Ghirlandaio (1449–94), Florentine painter who was the master of Michelangelo.

l. 190. The opposition to removing paintings and other artefacts from Italy was strong and growing in the 19th century despite Anna Jameson's opposition in *Visits and Sketches at Home and Abroad* (1837) to the notion that 'fresco-painting is unfitted for our climate, damp and sea-coal fires being equally injurious' (94).

l. 192. *quick-lime*. Whitewash.

ll. 193–200. The early masters are imagined walking the back streets of Florence mourning the fate of their pictures.

l. 199. *captive*. A painting imprisoned in obscurity waiting to be searched out.

l. 201. *Bigordi*. Ghirlandaio's family name.

l. 202. *Sandro*. Botticelli (*c*.1455–1510), a pupil of Fra Lippo Lippi, whose reputation was only beginning to revive in 1855.

l. 203. *Lippino*. Filippino Lippi, the son of Fra Lippo Lippi and the pupil of Botticelli, who is wronged either because of what Vasari calls 'the stain' of illegitimacy 'left to him by his father', a monk (2. 283), or more probably because his reputation has been overshadowed by that of his father.

l. 204. Fra Angelico (*c*.1395–1455) was known as 'il beato Angelico' because of the purity of his life and his paintings.

l. 205. Taddeo Gaddi (*c*.1290–1366) was the most celebrated of Giotto's pupils. A painting by him might be easier to acquire because, according to Jameson, 'His pictures are numerous' (Jameson, 53). He thinks himself fine because, according to Vasari, he so increased his social status by the exercise of his talent that he conferred 'riches and nobility' on his descendants (1. 191–2).

l. 206. *intonaco*. The thin plaster surface to which in a fresco the paint is applied.

l. 207. St Jerome is a common subject for Renaissance painters. A painting of Jerome in the Wilderness or Jerome in Penitence is suggested.

l. 208. Lorenzo Monaco (*c*.1370–*c*.1425) was a monk as his name suggests; all of his subjects are religious.

ll. 209–10. *Pollajolo*. Antonio Pollaiuolo (*c*.1429–1498) had studied anatomy, and was celebrated for his depictions of the male nude. A fresco in the Brancacci Chapel traditionally identified as *St Peter and St Paul before the Proconsul*, completed by Filippino Lippi, includes a figure in a red cap reputed to be Pollaiuolo. He was 'twice a craftsman' because he was apprenticed as a goldsmith before he trained to become a painter. The RBs owned a 'Christ at the Column' that they believed to be by Pollaiuolo (see Kelley and Coley, *The Browning Collections*, H20 and plate 16).

ll. 213–16. Baldovinetti (1425–99), was 'petty, | Of finical touch' because, according to Vasari, he was 'extremely careful and exact in his works, and of all the minutiae which mother nature is capable of presenting, he took pains to be the close imitator' (2. 66). His 'tempera' or fresco painting is 'crumbly' because, according to Vasari, he tempered his colours with a preparation designed to 'defend his work from the effects of damp, but it was so exceedingly strong, that where it has been laid on too thickly the work has in several places peeled off' (2. 65).

ll. 217–20. According to Vasari, Margaritone of Arezzo lived 1236–1313. Turner suggests that the description of him is modelled on the portrait reproduced in the edition of Vasari that RB owned, the Le Monnier edition published in Florence in 13 volumes, 1846–57. He is 'in a pet' because, according to Vasari, he recognized that the work of Cimabue and Giotto 'must well-nigh extinguish his fame' (1. 88).

l. 218. *barret*. Biretta, the cap worn by Italian clerics.

l. 225. *thrill*. Be pierced by holes (as the wooden panels are attacked by woodworm).

l. 226. The fresco paint is attacked by fungal cultures; *tinglish* is a coinage.

l. 230. Zeno of Citium, founder of the Stoic School and hence a type of imperturbability, which explains his calmness when confronted by nudes.

232 *Carlino*. Carlo Dolci (1616–86), disapproved because representative of what the speaker thinks of as the decadence of 17th-century Italian art. RB shared his disapproval, and in his essay on Shelley notes with an exclamation mark Shelley's admiration of the painter.

ll. 233–40. Oxford quotes a letter from RB to John Kenyon of 17 March 1853, reporting that the art-dealer Metzger had recently discovered a famous lost painting by Giotto, *The Death of the Virgin*, 'of which Vasari says so much, and how he heard Michaelangelo admire it to heart's content'.

l. 241. San Spirito was built after his death in 1446 from designs by Brunelleschi. It has frescoes by Filippino Lippi.

l. 242. *Ognissanti*. All Saints is a 17th-century baroque church, but frescoes by Ghirlandaio and Botticelli have been preserved.

l. 244. *detur amanti*. May it be given to the one who loves it.

l. 245. The Koh-i-noor, then the largest known diamond in the world, arrived in Britain from India in 1850.

l. 246. When he referred to an eye 'Bright as the jewel of Giamschid' (*The Giaour*, 479), Byron added a note explaining his reference to the 'celebrated fabulous ruby of Sultan Giamschid'; *Sofi*. The Shah.

l. 251. That is, the Swiss side of the mountain that divides Italy from Switzerland.

l. 253. EBB, in a letter to Arabella from Florence of March 1849, complains of 'the stupid habit of expressing joy here by firing into the air . . . gunpowder without balls! so stupid!' (*EBB to Arabella*, i. 229).

l. 255. *Radetsky*. Count Joseph Radetzky was appointed the Austrian Viceroy of Lombardy-Venetia in 1848, when he was 82 (hence a dotard).

l. 258. The stone in the Piazza del Duomo marking the place where Dante was reputed to have preferred to sit, described by EBB in *Casa Guidi Windows*, i. 602–6, as 'the plain flat stone scarce discerned | From others in the pavement,—whereupon | He used to bring his quiet chair out, turned | To Brunelleschi's church, and pour alone | The lava of his spirit when it burned.'

l. 259. *Witan-agemot*. Witenagemot, Parliament (the name of the Anglo-Saxon Parliament presumably indicates that the speaker favours a constitution for Tuscany modelled on the British).

l. 260. The reference is not to the Brownings' house in Florence, but to EBB's poem *Casa Guidi Windows*, which laments the failure of the 1849 Florentine Republic and the restoration of the rule of the Grand Duke Leopold II under Austrian protection; *quod videas ante*. For which see above.

l. 263. Leopold II claimed to rule Tuscany as the descendant of Francis Stephen of Lorraine to whom Tuscany was ceded in the Treaty of Vienna (1738).

l. 264. Andrea Orcagna is the representative of the high point of the Florentine Republic because he was the architect reputed (falsely) to have built the Loggia (1376–82).

l. 269. *fructuous*. Fertile.

ll. 270–1. Bears are popularly reputed to lick into shape their cubs that are born unformed; a chimaera is a monster, compounded from a lion, a goat, and a serpent.

l. 272. The purity of art and the purity of politics being mutually dependent.

l. 274. *spare of an "issimo"*. Sparing in the use of superlatives.

l. 275. Chaucer's Squire left the tale of Cambuscan unfinished, like Giotto's campanile.

l. 276. *alt altissimo*. High to highest. Corrected from 1855's 'altaltissimo'.

l. 277. *beccacia*. The woodcock which has an elegant long thin beak; *fifty briaccia*. The Italian braccio (pl. braccia) is a unit of length of about two feet, but RB uses the term only loosely. Giotto had designed the Campanile to be 400 feet high with its spire. In its unfinished state it is 280 feet high.

l. 285. *God and the People*. Translating the motto of Mazzini, the Italian Republican leader, 'Dio e popolo'.

l. 286. Italian Republicans first adopted their tricolour (equal bands of green, white, and red) in 1797 in imitation of the French.

In a Balcony

This dramatic sketch, or 'suggestion of a drama', as George Eliot described it in her review of *Men and Women* (*Westminster Review*, 65 (January 1856), 295), shows that RB retained his youthful interest both in the fragment (its three scenes allude to events such as the Queen's marriage that remain unexplained) and in the drama. 'In a Balcony' engages the question of the relationship between art and life that always preoccupied RB. Constance describes the Queen's life in her palace as a life spent in a picture gallery, surrounded by representations rather than realities (103–23), and Norbert argues that for an artist the love of the art always compromises the love of the mistress (661–77). It is in the drama, RB seems to feel, that the artist's life and the life of action that Norbert leads approach each other most nearly. It is probably the most limpid poem in the collection, which makes it interesting that it should hinge on a misunderstanding, when Norbert, on advice from Constance that seems astute enough but turns out to be misguided as well as disastrous, phrases his confession of love for Constance in a way that allows the Queen to take it as an expression of love for herself. The date at which the action takes place is not defined (though the reference to Rubens who died in 1640 may suggest that the painter is still alive). Constance represents the Queen as sharing Elizabeth I's hostility to the marriage of her favourite courtiers, but at least until the moment when Constance hears the approach of a 'measured heavy tread' (915), RB's Queen seems less intimidating. The whole play explores the relationship between the private and the public and the relative value to be attached to each; in the Queen's acknowledgement that power offers no compensation for the lack of love; in Constance's generous attempt to sacrifice her own happiness to the public weal, and most searchingly in Norbert's perception (695–713) of how his love for Constance has exalted his sense of what a statesman might accomplish, although, by a sad irony, it is also what loses him the regard of the Queen that allows him to act as her minister. The title may invite a comparison with the earlier 'In a Gondola', both fragments of love tragedies, both operatic in their construction. A dramatic reading of the play was arranged by the RB Society at the Prince's Hall on the evening of Friday, 28 November 1884.

l. 14. *One heaven, one hell.* Compare Shelley on love, *Epipisychidion*, 584–7: 'One hope within two wills, one will beneath | Two overshadowing minds, one life, one death, | One Heaven, one Hell, one immortality, | And one annihilation.'

ll. 24–8. She has, in loving him, become him so completely that she feels a masculine carelessness about her reputation.

l. 61. Norbert presumably appealed to reason in defiance of sentiment.

l. 101. That is, she believes that his service to her ought to have been its own reward.

l. 106. *magic dome*. Compare the 'mystic dome' of Tennyson's 'The Palace of Art' (1832), in which the Soul lives like the Queen amidst representations of reality rather than reality itself.

l. 117. Compare Aesop's fable 'The King's Son and the Painted Lion', in which a King, warned that his son will be killed by a lion, confines him within a palace in which only a representation of a lion is available to him. The stratagem proves unavailing.

l. 123. *mediate*. At a distance, in antithesis to immediate.

l. 130. *Rubens*. Peter Paul Rubens (1577–1640), chosen presumably as the representative court painter, acting in this capacity for Philip IV of Spain, for Marie de' Medici, widow of Henri IV of France, and for Charles I of England. The reference may suggest that RB's poem is set in the earlier 17th century.

l. 165. *white star*. Compare Tennyson's reference in 'The Gardener's Daughter' (1842), 161, to Venus as 'Love's white star'.

l. 192. *telegraphs*. Signals designed to be interpreted at a distance, as, for example, semaphore.

l. 195. *compression's*. Constraint's.

l. 203. *her*. The cousin, Constance.

l. 208. *ring the falcon's foot*. That is, to domesticate the falcon, to train it rather than leave it in the wild.

l. 211. He never legitimately hunted until he did so at the falconer's bidding.

l. 239. *revulsion*. Reaction (against politics).

l. 245. *yon first trembling star*. The evening star, Venus.

l. 256. *Silence to her rose*. Compare *Aurora Leigh*, 6. 596–7 : 'As red and still indeed as any rose, | That blows in all the silence of its leaves.'

l. 284. Compare Burns's schoolmaster in 'The Vowels', 5–8: 'Sir A B C the great, | In all his pedagogic powers elate, | His awful chair of state resolves to mount, | And call the trembling Vowels to account.'

l. 324. *disertate*. Normally 'dissertate', discourse.

l. 342. *Mercifullest Mother*. That is, Mary, as in 350.

l. 358. *Egypt*. The country of the palm's origin.

ll. 373–4. Compare Byron, *Don Juan*, I. 194. 1–2: 'Man's love is of man's life a thing apart, | 'Tis woman's whole existence.'

l. 401. *dear extremes that long to touch*. Unlike poles attract.

l. 412. *baladine*. Dancer (the word is borrowed from the French).

l. 418. *broke rank*. Disregarded his (inferior) rank.

l. 422. *halbert*. A weapon that combines an axehead and a spearhead.

l. 426. *this one who did*. That is, Norbert.

l. 445. *in intelligence*. In confidential communication.

ll. 516–20. Fountains are valued for the flow of water rather than for the figures from whom the water gushes, so that it is immaterial whether it gushes from a Triton, a sea god commonly represented as an old man, or a nymph.

The Queen's hope is that the quality of her love will render immaterial the decay of her person.

ll. 521–2. The reference seems to be to a fairy story, but we cannot identify it, although Cooke suggests a reference to Madame de Maintenon whose first husband was the crippled poet Paul Scarron, and who subsequently secretly married Louis XIV (*A Guide-Book to the Poetic and Dramatic Works of Robert Browning*, 1894, 172).

l. 529. *phantasy*. The image as it is impressed on the mind, as opposed to its material reality.

l. 538. *favourite*. The implication is lover, as in references to Catherine the Great's 'favourites'.

l. 545. *curdling*. Thickening (because in the light of the moon the mist becomes visible).

l. 558. *cuts the knot*. Challenged to untie the Gordian knot, Alexander cut it through with his sword.

l. 585. *current coin*. Compare Aurora Leigh's paraphrase of her cousin, Romney's, proposal to her, *Aurora Leigh*, 2. 539–41: 'Come, sweep my barns and keep my hospitals, | And I will pay thee with a current coin | Which men give women.'

l. 595. Compare RB's description of EBB's tribute to his love, *Sonnets from the Portuguese*, as 'a strange, heavy crown' (*Wedgwood*, 99).

l. 605. *God's moon*. Human love that reflects God's love as the moon reflects the light of the sun.

l. 630. *lay all to the first glow*. Think of this day's heat as the point from which all the rest of your life originates.

l. 669. *pale dictatress*. The woman as muse rather than the flesh and blood woman.

l. 677. A Rubens is presumably hanging on the wall. Rubens's paintings of his second wife, Hélène Fourment, are among his most celebrated.

l. 686. *due tithe*. Proper share (strictly, a tenth).

l. 687. It is the people who assign the means by which he directs them.

ll. 688–9. *They see no star*. The founder of the Dominican Order is often represented with a star on his forehead. His godmother is said to have seen the star at his baptism. The contrast is between a secular and spiritual leader.

l. 701. *this mass of men*. Oxford compares Carlyle's definition in the first of his lectures, *On Heroes and Hero-Worship*, of 'Great Men' as 'the modellers, patterns, and in a wide sense creators, of whatsoever the general mass of men contrived to do or to attain'.

l. 703. *plastic*. Capable of moulding.

l. 705. Just as my first life is crowned by my love for you, the second will be crowned by my moulding the people I govern as a potter throws a vase.

ll. 710–13. The state he will fashion is compared to a pot that meets the needs at once of the highest nature, the god, and lower natures, and is at once perfectly functional and perfectly beautiful.

l. 712. *Graces*. The three Graces, often represented interlinked in a dance.

l. 718. *gratitude's true decency*. The appropriate expression of your gratitude (reacting to the Queen's entry Constance pretends that Norbert's kiss is a belated acknowledgement of his gratitude rather than passionate).

l. 732. *stalking-horse*. Suggesting that Norbert has used Constance to disguise the fact that his love is really directed towards the Queen, and that, in kissing her, he has courteously refused abruptly to terminate the relationship when it is no longer useful to him.

ll. 777–9. Norbert believes that Constance and the Queen are playing a joke on him, and asks which of the two instigated it. She loses by it, perhaps, because the joke requires her to break off the embrace.

l. 795. *overcharge her part*. Overact.

l. 827. Norbert believes that the Queen's declaration is designed to test the sincerity of the love he has professed for Constance.

l. 837. *small eyeflower*. The daisy, etymologically day's eye.

"De Gustibus—"

There has been speculation as to the identity of the 'old fellow of mine' (17) to whom the poem is addressed, but it seems likely that it is an address from one side to the other of a divided self. The poem concludes when the speaker compares his love of Italy with a celebrated expression of English patriotism (note, too, the aggressively English pronunciation of 'Calais'), that may itself have been brought to mind by lines in Byron's 'Beppo': '"England! with all thy faults I love thee still," | I said at Calais, and have not forgot it' (369–70). The division between home and abroad is marked by the division between the poem's two, unequal stanzas, but running across them is the strongly marked, idiosyncratic character of the verse that seems to be alluded to in the poem's title. It is a character that RB implicitly claims for himself by accommodating details from earlier poems (the sprawling 'scorpion' (38), for example, recalls the 'scorpion with wide angry nippers' (285) that falls from the wall in 'The Englishman in Italy'). The idiosyncrasy is still more strongly marked in the metre and the rhyme scheme than in the natural description. The title is a truncated version of a well-known Latin maxim, 'de gustibus non est disputandum', meaning, there is no arguing over questions of taste.

l. 2. That is, if the capacity to love survives death.

l. 22. *cicalas*. Cicadas.

l. 24. The Italian cypress, or 'cupressus sempervirens', is, as its name implies, famous for its longevity. Specimens are said to have lived for a thousand years. The bark of the mature tree is reddish.

l. 25. Iron spikes are driven into trees that exhibit symptoms of chlorophyll deficiency: the fruits of the cypress, small cones, become brown on maturity.

ll. 35–7. Ferdinand II of the Two Sicilies, notorious for his suppression of the revolutionary outbursts in Naples in 1848 that instigated similar revolutionary attempts throughout Europe, and in particular for the shelling of the city of Messina that earned him the nickname King Bomba. British opposition to his reign was led, after 1850, by Gladstone. The assassination attempt is a baseless rumour, though there was an assassination attempt in 1856, by a soldier with a bayonet, that left the king wounded.

l. 36. *liver-wing*. A jocular reference to the king's right arm, from the right wing of the fowl, which, when dressed, traditionally has the liver tucked under it.

ll. 40–4. The saying on the loss of Calais to the French famously attributed to Mary Tudor, 'When I am dead and opened, you shall find Calais lying in my heart', derives from Holinshed.

ll. 41–2. The rhyme is jocular in its aggressive Englishness. Compare Coleridge, 'The Delinquent Travellers', 22–3: 'If you but perch, where Dover tallies, | So strangely with the coast of Calais.'

Cleon

'Cleon' has always been compared with 'An Epistle . . . of Karshish' because both monologues take the form of letters, both are set in the early Christian era, and both conjure a dramatic irony produced by the speakers' ignorance of a Christian revelation with which the reader is assumed to be familiar. The parallels between the two poems underline the differences between their two speakers. The contrast with Karshish calls attention to the suave vanity with which Cleon cloaks his inner despair. Cleon and Karshish are both mirror images, images in reverse, of figures contemporary with RB. Cleon admits, and tries to discount, the sense of the belated, secondary character of his own achievement that few Victorian poets were able wholly to repress, and Cleon's lofty confidence that Christian doctrines 'could be held by no sane man' (353) was a posture that was beginning to be adopted by those of RB's contemporaries who, like Cleon, prided themselves on their intellectual sophistication. Much has been made of the relationship between 'Cleon' and Arnold's *Empedocles on Etna*. Arnold withdrew the poem, after its first publication in 1852, and re-published it in 1867 'at the request of a man of genius', RB, and a letter from EBB of 2 May 1853 suggests that she had already read *Empedocles on Etna, and Other Poems* (*George Barrett*, 184). The two poems have little in common, and the discussion is perhaps best understood as a covert acknowledgement that Arnold is the leading exemplar of the Victorian type that RB's Cleon reflects. It is possible to read RB's epigraph as covertly admitting as much.

"As certain also of your own poets have said"—. Acts 17: 28, in which Paul preaches to 'certain philosophers of the Epicureans, and of the Stoicks' (17: 18), arguing that the Christian truths have been glimpsed by pagan poets, and that the Christian dispensation is not confined to the Jews because God 'hath

made of one blood all nations of men' (17: 26). He goes on to promise 'the resurrection of the dead', at which 'some mocked: and others said. We will hear thee again of this matter' (17: 32).

l. 1. *the sprinkled isles.* The Sporades, literally, scattered islands.

l. 4. *Protos in his Tyranny.* Protos is appropriately named because the word means, first. Tyranny, like tyrant, is not necessarily a pejorative term in ancient Greece: it signifies simply the rule of a city-state by a single individual.

l. 13. The pavement is a gift to Cleon from the nation whose workmanship it exemplifies.

l. 14. *settle-down.* The *OED* identifies this as RB's coinage to describe a flock of birds coming to ground.

l. 15. *one lyric woman.* A woman singer.

ll. 15–16. The crocus vest ought, the Greek etymology of the word suggests, to be yellow, but it is easiest to explain the 'sea-wools' from which it is woven as wool dyed 'sea-purple', that is, purple from the dye extracted from the shellfish murex.

l. 17. *strainers* (some surviving ancient Greek examples are gold-plated) prevented the herbs and spices with which the wine was flavoured from being poured into the cup.

l. 24. *straight.* Punning on strait, in the sense of narrow.

ll. 26–36. Cleon's metaphor exemplifies the perception that RB uses as his epigraph. Unwittingly, Cleon convicts Protos of the presumption that the Bible recognizes in the building of the Tower of Babel and classical mythology in the attempt of the Giants to scale heaven by piling Pelion on Ossa.

l. 37. *thy festival.* The phrase suggests how in the 1st century CE, when Julius Caesar and Augustus Caesar were declared gods immediately after their deaths, and Augustus, because Julius Caesar had adopted him, could style himself, 'divi filius', son of a god, ideas of secular and heavenly kingship merged.

l. 38. *libation.* The spilling of wine in honour of a god.

ll. 39–40. The lines may remind the reader by contrast of the slave at the triumph of a Roman general who held above the general's head a gold crown, but continuously repeated in his ear, 'Remember you are mortal.'

l. 42. As an Epicurean Cleon holds that the end of life is to achieve the state of calm tranquillity termed 'ataraxia'.

l. 47. *epos.* Possibly an epic, but in the late poem, 'Imperante Augusto Natus Est' (1889), the word is used to describe a 'Panegyric on the Emperor' (10).

l. 51. *phare.* Lighthouse; some descriptions suggest that the great Pharos of Alexandria was surmounted by a colossal statue of the sun god, Helios.

l. 53. *Poecile.* The name of a portico decorated with paintings in ancient Athens; RB's friend William Wetmore Story in 'Blue Beard's Cabinets' in *Graffiti d'Italia*, 1848, 62–3, has 'ebon cabinets | With ivory intarsia storied o'er'.

ll. 55–6. RB's friend, the sculptor William Page, believed that he had made a discovery about the proportions of the human body that he communicated to RB. The most famous such discovery is associated with Vitruvius and embodied in the sketch by Leonardo known as 'Vitruvian Man'.

ll. 57–9. The most celebrated Greek book on the soul is Aristotle's *De Anima*. Epicurus held that the soul is material, and like all other things composed of atoms, into which it disperses at death.

ll. 60–1. The Greeks distinguished between several musical modes or moods, such as the Dorian and Phrygian, associating each with a particular emotional effect.

ll. 64–72. The distinction between ancient simplicity and modern complexity is commonplace in the period, as, for example, in Schiller's distinction between naive and sentimental poetry. The distinction achieved new currency when Arnold explained in the Preface to his *Poems* (1853) that he had rejected from the volume his own *Empedocles on Etna* as representing a period when Greek culture had been infected by modernity: 'the dialogue of the mind with itself has commenced' and the 'noble simplicity' of earlier Greek art has been sacrificed.

ll. 73–80. If the history of the human race is designed to be contemplated ultimately as a whole, then no achievement of the past can be effaced by a present achievement.

ll. 83–4. A lozenge is a kind of rhomb or rhombus, usually a diamond-shaped rhombus; a trapezoid has four sides no two of which are parallel.

ll. 89–92. Darwin's predecessors such as Lamarck and Robert Chambers characteristically explained evolution as a development from simple to more complex forms.

ll. 99–111. The men of old time are compared to water, modern men to air. Even a small amount of water will touch every point in a sphere if swirled around, but air completely fills the sphere, although it remains invisible. The point is that modern achievements, because they are subtler, are less noticeable although they are greater.

l. 112. *misknown*. Compare Carlyle, *Sartor Resartus*, 1. 3: 'great men are too often unknown, or what is worse, misknown.'

ll. 115–26. The point is that Cleon imagines as fictions or fables ideas that with the birth of Christ became historical.

l. 126. In his translation of the *Iliad* (24. 529), Pope describes the disguised Hermes as 'the latent God'.

l. 132. *suave*. Sweet; *savage-tasted*. Tasted by savages; a drupe is any fleshy fruit with a stone: RB is referring to an uncultivated plum.

l. 140. *Terpander*. The father of Greek music.

l. 141. Phidias is the most celebrated of ancient Greek sculptors and painters. The 'friend' may be one of Phidias' pupils, who, according to Pausanias, also served as his lovers, or more likely a contemporary imagined to excel in painting as Phidias excelled in sculpture.

l. 160. *varicoloured*. Diverse, but referring back to the analogy he draws between his works and cultivated flowers.

l. 164. *crown and proper end of life*. Playing against the Christian sense, as in Bunyan, *Pilgrim's Progress*, Second Part: 'but be you faithful unto death, and the King will give you a Crown of Life.'

l. 175. *brazen statue*. Compare Shakespeare, Sonnet 55, 1–2: 'Not marble, nor the gilded monuments | Of princes, shall outlive this powerful rhyme.' RB also has in mind statues such as that in Shelley's 'Ozymandias', or Nero's colossal statue of himself that a successor modified into the statue of a sun god.

l. 198. Cleon holds to the Kantian view, widely shared by the mid-19th century, that what distinguishes man from other animals is self-consciousness, by virtue of which man becomes a rational animal. Longman appositely quotes Milton's explanation of why God's creation of the world was completed only by the creation of man. Before that, 'There wanted yet the master work, the end | Of all yet done; a creature who not prone | And brute as other creatures, but endued | With sanctity of reason, might erect | His stature, and upright with front serene | Govern the rest, self-knowing', *Paradise Lost*, VII. 505–10.

l. 204. RB perhaps recalls the finger of God that imparts the divine spark to Adam in Michelangelo's representation of the creation in the Sistine Chapel.

l. 205. Compare Wordsworth on 'How exquisitely the individual Mind... to the external World is fitted:—and how exquisitely, too... The external World is fitted to the Mind' (lines from *The Recluse* prefixed to *The Excursion*, 63–8).

l. 212. *intro-active*. Itself the source of its own activity.

l. 224. *the sense of sense*. *Love's Labour's Lost*, V. ii. 258, but here the phrase seems to refer to self-consciousness.

l. 229. *lore*. Doctrine. Cleon unwittingly hints at the relationship between the Old and New Testaments.

l. 231. *pleasure-house*. Tennyson describes 'The Palace of Art' as 'a lordly pleasurehouse' (1), and it too towers over a flat landscape.

l. 232. *Watch-tower*. Compare the 'speculum or watch-tower' from which Teufelsdröckh surveys the city in Carlyle's *Sartor Resartus*, chapter 3.

l. 241. *the soul craves all*. Compare 'Pauline', 278, in which the speaker confesses that he would 'would be all, have, see, know, taste, feel, all'.

ll. 251–60. Carlyle uses a similar metaphor to a different end in *Sartor Resartus*, chapter 3, to describe Teufelsdröckh's 'memorable utterances', which he would let fall 'not more conscious of them, than is the sculptured stone head of some public fountain, which through its brass mouth-tube emits water to the worthy and the unworthy; careless whether it be for cooking victuals or quenching conflagrations; indeed, maintains the same earnest assiduous look, whether any water be flowing or not.'

l. 252. *Naiad*. Water nymph. RB would have seen the naiad fountain at Peterhof in St Petersburg.

ll. 273–300. Compare Norbert's insistence that to love is better than to paint or write of love, 'In a Balcony', 661–78.

ll. 304–5. Sappho, the most celebrated of women poets, survives only in fragments: only seven of Aeschylus' many plays are extant.

l. 319. The sense is that the survival of his works after he had died constitutes a mockery rather than an achievement.

ll. 332–3. The traditional analogy between life after death and the metamorphosis of the caterpillar into a butterfly is supported by the Greek word, psyche, which signifies both a butterfly and a soul.

l. 334. *revealed.* The word is chosen to suggest the Christian revelation of which Cleon is ignorant.

l. 340. *his fame.* What people say of him.

l. 341. Again, in his ignorance of whether or not Paul and Christ are one and the same person, Cleon unwittingly stumbles over a Christian truth. As Paul puts it, 'ye are all one in Christ Jesus', Galatians 3: 28.

l. 344. *As Paulus proves to be.* Paul proves to be a Jew despite the fact that he is a Roman citizen, Acts 23: 26–7.

Two in the Campagna

Like 'Love Among the Ruins', the poem seems to have been inspired by excursions into the Roman Campagna in the spring of 1854, in which RB was sometimes accompanied by EBB, and still more often by Fanny Kemble, the actress, and her sister Adelaide Sartoris, the singer. RB parodies a 17th-century seduction poem in which, reclining in an appropriate landscape ('Such primal naked forms of flowers', 28), the poet asks his mistress to consummate their love, but RB's lover suggests that he and his mistress be 'unashamed of soul' (32), rather than of body, and instead of protesting that his love is absolute, he acknowledges its limitations: 'I would that you were all to me, | You that are just so much, no more' (36–7). By the end of the poem the gruffly comic tone has disappeared in a plangent recognition that the capacity to love infinitely must always be frustrated in a world in which all possible objects of love are finite. Shelley explores the thought in his essay 'On Love' and in a series of poems from *Alastor* to *Epipsychidion*. RB seems less happy than Shelley to admit that satisfaction in love would be equivalent to death, and yet, like Shelley, he suggests an analogy with the perfect poem, that, like the perfect love, always eludes the grasp, so that the poet, like the lover, makes attempts that because they never quite succeed must always be renewed.

l. 12. *seed.* Caraway seeds.

l. 15. *weft.* The thread that runs from one side to another of a web, meshing with the warp which run up and down.

l. 17. *blind.* Beetles are proverbially blind. Mr Sludge describes his auditor, who is insensitive to the spirit world, as 'Blind as a beetle that way' (1250).

l. 18. *honey-meal*. Pollen, the powdery substance collected by bees and thus essential to the production of honey.

l. 21. *champaign*. For the Italian 'campagna'.

l. 24. *wash*. Possibly suggesting the application of a thin layer of colour in watercolour painting. The Campagna was a popular subject for painters.

l. 25. The Campagna had been abandoned for centuries because it was malarial and because it lacked the irrigation to support agriculture, but the ruined structures that remained evoked its former life.

l. 53. *like the thistle-ball*. Like thistle-down, which, because it is blown by the wind, exemplifies capricious lack of purpose. John Wilson describes himself as 'wafted like the thistle-down, | Yet not so wholly aimless, not so moved | By impulse from without' ('An Evening in Furness Abbey', ll. 214–16); *no bar*. Compare 'Pictor Ignotus', 2–3: 'No bar | Stayed me'.

l. 55. The reference is probably to the star by which the mariner fixes his position, as in Shakespeare's 'Let me not to the marriage of true minds admit impediments', in which love is 'an ever-fixed mark', 'the star to every wandering bark' (Sonnet 116).

A Grammarian's Funeral

Commentary on the poem has focused on the question of whether RB shares the admiration of the grammarian expressed by his students, or whether he is the object of RB's contemptuous satire. Proponents of the former view stress RB's respect for classical scholarship, proponents of the latter stress his contempt for merely bookish learning. But it may be that RB's interest is focused on the relationship between the grammarian, who seems to be a 15th-century European scholar (his nationality is not identified) associated with the revival of learning, and the students who carry his body to the mountain summit that they have chosen as its appropriate resting place. It is a relationship played out in the contrast between the poem's often crabbed pentameters and the jaunty swing of the shorter two-beat lines with which they alternate, and it carries the implication that however much the students may admire their master they remain themselves creatures of the valleys rather than the solitary mountain heights, unlikely to be contented with a life lived 'Dead from the waist down' (132).

l. 3. *vulgar*. Ordinary, but the word supports the metaphor associating the mountains with classical learning, because it may also signify the vernacular; *thorpes*. More commonly thorps, villages.

l. 4. *Each in its tether*. The farms and villages are compared to tethered farm animals, that have only a restricted range of movement.

l. 8. *Rimming the rock-row*. Fringing the line of mountains that forms the horizon.

l. 11. *Self-gathered*. Compare the 'self-gather'd laurels' that the warrior strews on a 'self-sought grave' in Byron's 'Elegy on Newstead Abbey', 70.

l. 12. *Chafes in the censer!* Is heated in the thurible, the vessel in which incense is burnt.

l. 15. *citied.* Compare 'the citied earth', Keats, *Lamia*, 2. 90.

l. 16. The students leave one kind of culture for another, the agriculture of the plains for the intellectual culture that they associate with the mountains.

ll. 38–41. When he began to feel the effects of age, he did not, like most people, concede that his dancing days were over.

l. 48. *their shaping.* What they imagined or predicted.

l. 50. *he gowned him.* He took up the academic life.

l. 55. *"Up with the curtain!"* A theatrical metaphor signifying, 'let the show begin!'

l. 68. *Sooner, he spurned it!* He disdained to live life before he had completed his studies.

l. 71. *ere steel strike fire from quartz.* Before the blocks of stone from which the building will be constructed are hewn.

l. 86. *Calculus.* The stone, for example, kidney stone.

l. 87. *dross.* The residue or scum produced when a metal is refined.

l. 88. *Tussis.* Cough (Latin).

l. 95. *hydroptic.* Morbidly or extravagantly thirsty. In his life of Donne, Izaak Walton quotes the letter in which Donne describes himself as succumbing in his youth to 'the worst voluptuousness, *an hydroptique immoderate* desire of human leaning and languages'.

l. 97. *draw a circle.* Bring to completion.

l. 103. *period.* Conclusion, although the term may also signify a perfectly achieved cadence or a completed unit of sense that will repair what is left incomplete in life.

ll. 107–8. He would not sacrifice long-term profit to immediate needs by discounting bills, that is, by accepting for the bills a sum less than the bills would secure if kept for their full term.

l. 109. *He ventured neck or nothing.* A sporting expression, signifying that he risked everything on one attempt.

l. 122. *Let the world mind him*! Let this world, rather than the future world, supply him.

l. 124. Compare Matthew 7: 7: 'Ask, and it shall be given you; seek, and ye shall find; knock, and it shall be opened unto you.'

l. 127. *the rattle.* The death rattle.

l. 129. *Hoti's business.* 'στι' may be a conjunction meaning because, or a pronoun meaning whatever.

l. 130. *Oun.* 'συη' is a conjunction meaning 'therefore'.

l. 131. *the enclitic De.* The unaccented 'δϵ' meaning 'towards', as opposed to the accented 'δϵ' meaning 'but', as RB explained in a letter published in the *Daily News* on 21 November 1874. In a letter to Tennyson published by Ricks, *TLS*, 3 June 1965, 464, RB cited as his authority Buttman's *Greek Grammar*, which also comments on 'στι' and 'συη'.

"*Transcendentalism*"

Sutherland Orr explains that '"Transcendentalism" is addressed to a young poet, who is accused of presenting his ideas "naked," instead of draping them, in poetic fashion, in sights and sounds' (*Handbook*, 212–13). As Oxford points out, RB's own earlier works had often been categorized as 'transcendental', a term commonly used to categorize writing deemed metaphysical and obscure, hence the poem has been persuasively presented as an address by the poet of *Men and Women*, a collection that includes many lyrics, to the younger RB, the author of *Paracelsus*, 1835. But the poem engages more general Victorian disputes. In preferring the poetry of sensation to a poetry of reflection in which sentiments that might be expressed in prose are translated into poetry, it repeats a distinction made by Arthur Hallam in his review of Tennyson's *Poems, Chiefly Lyrical.* The title parodies the epic ambitions evident in so many 19th-century poems such as Robert Pollok's *The Course of Time: A Poem, in Ten Books*, 1828, or two poems directly influenced by *Paracelsus*, Philip Bailey's *Festus. A Poem*, 1839, and Richard Henry Horne's *Orion: An Epic Poem in Three Books*, 1843. Its fifty-one lines mock their diffuseness. At its centre is the celebration of the poet as magician, who can work miracles in just 'a brace of rhymes' (39). But in its final six lines, the poem concludes by transferring attention from the poem to the poet, whose genius is best signalled by the inadequacy of his achievements to his conceptions, an aesthetic position more closely associated with RB, although it follows Shelley's contention in his *Defence of Poetry* that 'the most glorious poetry that has ever been communicated to the world is probably a feeble shadow of the original conception of the poet'. It is a notion that reclaims RB's title from parody through its insistence that the truest poem transcends its own imperfections because, like the cherub, it 'points to God' (51).

l. 6. *prolusion.* Preliminaries.

l. 10. *Stark-naked thought.* In *Sordello*, RB contrasts 'Bocafoli's stark-naked psalms' with 'Plara's sonnets spoilt by toying with' (2. 768–9).

l. 12. The alpenhorn, which may be from four to six feet in length, is commonly made of birchwood and covered with bark, and is sometimes supposed to have been used for communicating between alpine villages.

l. 22. *Swedish Boehme.* Jakob Boehme (1575–1624), who apprehended in an experience of mystical illumination the doctrine of signatures that he set out in his *De Signatura Rerum*, that is, the notion that natural forms speak to us because their outward appearance communicates spiritual truth. RB was embarrassed when it was pointed out to him that Boehme was German rather than Swedish, and corrected the mistake in subsequent editions.

ll. 23–7. The following account of Boehme's second 'illumination' is given in the life that prefaces the 1764 edition of *The Works of Jacob Behmen*: 'about the year 1600, in the twenty-fifth Year of his Age, he was again surrounded by the divine Light and replenished with the heavenly Knowledge; insomuch, as going abroad in the Fields, to a Green before *Neys-Gate*, at *Görlitz*, he there sat down and, viewing the Herbs and Grass of the Field in his inward Light, he saw into their Essences, Use and Properties, which were discovered to him by their Lineaments, Figures and Signatures.

In like Manner he beheld the whole Creation, and from that Foundation of Revelation he afterwards wrote his Book, *De Signatura Rerum*', xiii–xiv.

l. 26. *daisy*. Daisy derives etymologically from day's eye.

l. 27. *Colloquised*. Conversed.

ll. 37–45. According to Cooke, who does not give his source, 'Johann Semeca, known as Teutonicus, was a canonist and ecclesiastical dignitary of Halberstadt, who wrote a commentary on the *Decretum Gratiani*. He was also a magician and astrologer, and caused flowers to appear in winter,' G. W. Cooke, *A Guide-book to the Poetic and Dramatic Works of Robert Browning*, 1891, 422.

l. 46. Resume the posture in which you may play the harp.

l. 47. *You are a poem*. Compare 'but I never have begun, even, what I hope I was born to begin and end,—"R.B. a poem"' (*Correspondence*, x. 69).

l. 49. *finer chords*. The thinner strings that play the higher notes.

ll. 50–1. The harp is decorated at the top of its pillar with a cherub.

One Word More: To E.B.B.

The title of the poem, 'A Last Word' in the manuscript sent to the printer, was changed, it may be, to accommodate a private allusion. On 31 August 1845, EBB had responded to RB's declaration of love by writing, 'What could I give you, which it would not be ungenerous to give?—Therefore we must leave this subject—& I must trust you to leave it without one word more' (*Correspondence*, xi. 54). In the poem RB represents himself as speaking 'this once in my true person' (137), an exercise as foreign to his professional character as a poet as it was for Raphael to write poems and Dante to draw pictures. He offers his adoption of a lyric voice as a double proof of sincerity. It is not just that the voice is his own but that the adoption of an unfamiliar and unpractised poetic manner is itself testament to his willingness 'to be the man and leave the artist' (71). The poem ends in a celebration of the privacy to which RB so fiercely asserts his right in poems such as 'The Householder'. Each individual, like the moon, has a dark side unknown to all onlookers except the one privileged individual who finds through love magical access to it. But it is also the poem in *Men and Women* in which RB acknowledges most forcefully his painful sensitivity to the hostile reception that his poems had received, and a poem that insistently compares the poet to Moses, who is at once separated from the Israelites, granted a direct access to God that is denied them, and the leader who confers on them their identity as a people. The poem is an appropriate epilogue to a volume of dramatic monologues, despite its claim to lyric status, because dramatic monologues are, like this lyric, centrally concerned with the fraught relationship between private identity and public speech.

l. 5. As Frederick Page first noted (*TLS*, 25 May 1940, 255), in his *Notizie dei professori del disegno* Filippo Baldinucci claims that a celebrated book of a hundred sonnets written by Raphael in the possession of Guido Reni went missing after his death.

l. 7. *silver-pointed pencil.* A silverpoint drawing is made by dragging a silver rod across a prepared surface.

ll. 9–17. Early 19th-century accounts of Raphael often offer a romanticized account of his relationship with the baker's daughter, Margherita Luti, *La Fornarina*.

ll. 19–21. RB follows a Romantic convention that the sonnet offers transparent access to the inner life of a poet, as in Wordsworth, 'Scorn not the sonnet', 2–3: 'with this key | Shakespeare unlocked his heart.' The tradition had been strengthened by EBB's 'Sonnets from the Portuguese', in *Poems*, 1850.

ll. 22. *Her, San Sisto names.* The Sistine Madonna or La Madonna di San Sisto, Raphael's last Madonna, praised by Vasari as 'a truly admirable production' (3, 4): the painting had been in Dresden since the mid-18th century; *Her, Foligno.* The Madonna of Foligno, looted by Napoleon but returned to the Vatican after Waterloo.

ll. 23–4. In a letter to William Rolfe RB identified the first painting as the *Madonna del Granduca* in the Pitti Palace in Florence, 'which represents her as "appearing to a votary in a vision"—so say the describers; it is in the earlier manner, and very beautiful', and the second, more tentatively, as 'La Belle Jardinière, which is in the Louvre, but does not feature lilies', cited by C. F. Thomas, *Art and Architecture in the Poetry of Robert Browning*, 1991, 206.

l. 25. *in circle.* A metaphor from the theatre, indicating that the paintings are on public display.

l. 27. *Guido Reni.* Guido Reni (1575–1642), the painter, died in Bologna: *eye's apple.* Literally the pupil of the eye, although commonly used to designate an especially cherished object.

ll. 32–3. Dante records in *La Vita Nuova* that on the anniversary of Beatrice's death, 'remembering of her as I sat alone, I betook myself to draw the resemblance of an angel upon certain tablets' (D. G. Rossetti's translation).

ll. 37–8. In Canto xxxii of the *Inferno* Dante seizes the hair of the traitor, Bocca degli Abati, to force him to reveal his name, and then promises to publish his fate.

ll. 38–9. The ink in which Dante writes the *Inferno* is represented as an acid that eats into the flesh of those he denounces, branding them with a stigma, as God branded Cain.

ll. 45–9. In *La Vita Nuova* Dante records that he was interrupted in drawing the angel by important visitors, but he writes that he resumed the drawing as soon as they left.

l. 57. *Bice.* Familiar form of Beatrice.

ll. 63–4. The use of an artistic medium (poetry for Raphael, drawing for Dante) that has not been mastered is represented as a more authentic expression of the love to which it testifies. Compare Jules's decision to give up sculpture for painting in *Pippa Passes.*

ll. 74–8. The artist is compared to Moses, who in Exodus 17: 1–7 is chided by the Israelites for bringing them to a place without water, until, on God's advice, he produces water by striking the rock with his rod.

ll. 88–9. God's command is besmirched for the poet who has been the victim of his readership's importunate demands, so that even an achievement as miraculous as Moses striking the rock to produce water is marred by being performed either carelessly or self-consciously.

l. 90. *an ancient wrong.* The public's ingratitude to artists.

l. 91. *phalanxed.* Closely packed, like a phalanx of Roman soldiers.

l. 95. *Egypt's flesh-pots.* See Exodus 16: 3: 'Would to God we had died by the hand of the Lord in the land of Egypt, when we sat by the flesh pots.'

l. 97. *Sinai-forehead's cloven brilliance.* The phrase conflates Jerome's celebrated mistranslation of Exodus 34: 29, which represented Moses as horned when he descends from Sinai with the tablets of the Lord (a mistake reproduced in Michelangelo's statue), and the accurate translation of the King James version which records that 'the skin of his face shone'.

l. 98. *fiat.* A decree, especially one with divine authority, as in Genesis 1: 3: 'fiat lux', 'Let there be light.'

l. 101. *Jethro's daughter.* Zipporah, Moses's wife, See Exodus 2: 21, and 3: 1.

l. 102. *Aethiopian bondslave.* See Numbers 12: 1, which records that Moses also 'married an Ethiopian woman'.

ll. 115–16. The references to 'heights' recall Mount Sinai.

l. 121. *hair-brush.* The fine hair brush used by the miniature painter as opposed to the bristle brush used by the fresco painter.

l. 125. *missal-marge.* The margins of missals or mass-books are often splendidly decorated with miniatures.

l. 126. The contrast is between a brass instrument such as the trumpet, and instruments such as the flute.

l. 136. *Karshook.* Evidently an error for Karshish; *Norbert* appears in 'In a Balcony'.

l. 145. The Brownings arrived in London from Florence in July 1855.

l. 146. *thrice-transfigured.* The three states of the moon as described in the following lines.

l. 150. *Samminiato.* San Miniato al Monte, the Romanesque church that overlooks Florence from one of the city's highest hills.

l. 160. *the old sweet mythos.* The love of Endymion for the goddess of the moon, an ancient legend re-worked in 1818 by John Keats. See line 166.

l. 163. *Zoroaster.* The Persian sage who understood the world as the site of a contest between the powers of light and darkness.

l. 164. Galileo (1564–1642) extended knowledge of the moon by viewing it through a telescope.

l. 165. *Dumb to Homer.* 'Homer's Hymn to the Moon', a poem no longer regarded as Homeric, was translated by Shelley.

l. 166. *moonstruck mortal.* Here the mortal, like Endymion, stricken by love for the moon.

ll. 172–9. See Exodus 24: 9–11: 'Then went up Moses, and Aaron, Nadab, and Abihu, and seventy of the elders of Israel: And they saw the God of Israel: and there was under his feet as it were a paved work of a sapphire stone, and as it were the body of heaven in his clearness. And upon the nobles of the children of Israel he laid not his hand: also they saw God, and did eat and drink.'

l. 182. Only one side of the moon is visible from earth.

LETTER TO JOHN RUSKIN, 10 DECEMBER 1855

RB replies to a letter from Ruskin acknowledging the volumes of *Men and Women* that RB had presented to him. Ruskin's letter is published in full in David J. De Laura, 'Ruskin and the Brownings: Twenty-Five Unpublished Letters', *Bulletin of the John Rylands Library*, 54 (1972), 314–56. RB's reply (published in W. G. Collingwood, *Life and Work of John Ruskin*, 2 vols., 1893, i. 199–202) registers his gratitude and answers Ruskin's objections to the metrical roughness of RB's verse, and, more significantly, to the excessive demands that the poems make on their readers. In 1856, in volume iv of *Modern Painters*, Ruskin was to acknowledge that 'The Bishop Orders his Tomb' expresses 'nearly all that I have said of the central Renaissance in thirty pages of the *Stones of Venice* put into as many lines, Browning's being also the antecedent work.' But even here Ruskin repeated his misgivings: 'The worst of it is that this kind of concentrated writing needs so much *solution* before the reader can fairly get the good of it, that people's patience fails them, and they give the thing up as insoluble.' RB's reply to Ruskin's letter is sharpened by the opportunity it afforded him to respond to all those critics who, since the publication of *Sordello*, had maintained that his work was unreadably obscure. RB's insistence that the poet's primary duty is not to his readership but to God seems unpersuasive, since a poet intent only on addressing God might forgo publication, or even the translation of his conception into language, but it is a position that RB adopts repeatedly, in several of the letters to EBB, for example, and he seems to explore it in one of the poems in *Men and Women*, 'How It Strikes a Contemporary'. RB goes on to offer his most forceful and condensed defence of his own compositional methods. All poems are fragmentary because execution never matches conception, a notion that RB derived from Shelley and had first expressed in the note to his first published poem: Pauline asserts that even in Shakespeare, Raphael, and Beethoven 'la concentration des idées est due bien plus à leur conception qu'à leur mise en exécution'. It is a predicament that requires the reader to become the poet's active accomplice, willing to respond to a poem with an imaginative energy of which RB believes the passive readership of the mid-19th century incapable.

Our text is from Collingwood.

l. 25. *sprang over there?* Ruskin had written: 'your Ellipses are quite Unconscionable: before one can get through ten lines, one has to patch you up in twenty places, wrong or right, and if one hasn't much stuff of one's own to spare to patch with! You are worse than the worst Alpine Glacier I ever crossed. Bright, & deep enough truly, but so full of Clefts that half the journey has to be done with ladder & hatchet.'

l. 31. *My little song*. The song is 'Popularity'. Ruskin had chosen the poem to illustrate the objectionable obscurity he thought characteristic of the volumes.

l. 31. 'Hobbs or Nobbs', used by RB as representative nondescript names in 'Popularity', 58.

l. 32. *devisings*. Legacies of property.

l. 34. *'Stand still'*. 'Stand still, true poet that you are! | I know you; let me try to draw you.' 'Popularity', 1–2. Ruskin had asked, 'Does this mean: literally—stand still? or where was the poet figuratively going—and why couldn't he be drawn as he went?'

l. 37. *'going on'*. Railing, a sense that *OED* first records in 1863.

l. 39. *Authentic astronomical records*. In his star catalogue, published in 1846, Jean-François Biot refers to Chinese records of the disappearance of stars.

l. 41. *I. xv. 16*. 'Then Samuel said unto Saul, Stay, and I will tell thee what the Lord hath said to me this night.'

l. 51. *Foldskirts*. 'Saul', 20 and 21. Ruskin had written, 'I entirely deny & refuse the right of any poet to require me to pronounce words short and long, exactly as he likes—to require me to read a plain & harsh & straightforward piece of prose. 'Till I felt where the fold-skirt (*fly*, redundant) open. Then, once more, I prayed, as a dactylic verse with skirts! for a short syllable.'

l. 52. *A spondee possible in English?* In his *History of English Rhythms* (1838) Edwin Guest quotes the view that 'Egypt' is the only spondee in English before insisting that the word is, in fact, trochaic (p. 76).

l. 55. *Long time he bore*. An exemplary epitaph, quoted by RB in 'Epitaph: The Householder', 30.

l. 61. *Once more I prayed*. 'Saul', 20. Ruskin had claimed that metre requires the phrase to be pronounce, 'Wunce-mur-y.'

l. 62. *'I stand here for law'*. Shylock's contention in *The Merchant of Venice*, IV. i. 142.

l. 66. *peccavi*. I have sinned. Ruskin had written, 'I entirely deny that a poet of your real dramatic power ought to let *himself* come up, as you constantly do, through all manner of characters, so that every now and then poor Pippa herself [in *Pippa Passes*] shall speak a long piece of Robert Browning.'

l. 74. *worshipped.* According to Clement of Alexandria in his *Exhortation to the Greeks*, Orpheus, by inspiring stocks and stones to follow him, led men to idol worship.

l. 81. *flourished it hither and thither.* The reference is to Macready's Hamlet first presented in London in 1845, in which many noted an excessive use of a handkerchief. G. H. Lewes, for example, thought him 'too fond of a cambric pocket-handkerchief to be really affecting'.

l. 86. *Pleased to be kind.* Oliver Goldsmith, 'The Haunch of Venison', 43–4.

ll. 93–5. *orris-root . . . Good savour.* 'Fra Lippo Lippi', 351. In that poem Ruskin had failed to understand 'the grated orris-root, which I looked for in the Encyclopaedia and couldn't find'; the Florentine lily, iris florentina, or, in Italian, *giaggolo*, was cultivated because of the aromatic qualities of the rhizome.

LETTER TO EUPHRASIA HAWORTH, 20 JULY 1861

RB wrote this letter to Fanny Haworth three weeks after the death of EBB on 29 June 1861. Fanny Haworth had been a literary friend of his youth, addressed in *Sordello* as his 'English Eyebright' after her first name, Euphrasia. She had become a friend of EBB during their visit to England in 1851. Our text is from *Wise*, 64–5.

l. 2. *Isa Blagden.* The Brownings' closest friend in the expatriate community of Florence.

l. 10. *the week's illness.* The Brownings had spent the winter at Rome, where, shortly before their return to Florence on 5 June, EBB had suffered an alarming illness.

l. 27. *Annunziata.* Properly Annunciata, who had been employed as nurse to the new baby in 1846 and remained in service as EBB's maid.

l. 30. *Peni.* The son of RB and EBB, known as Pen, Peni, or Penini.

l. 55. *St Germ[n].* St Germain: RB planned to stay in Paris for some time with his father before returning to England.

FROM *DRAMATIS PERSONÆ*, (1864)

[*James Lee's Wife*] *James Lee*

The poem is a monodrama, a form to which Tennyson had drawn attention through the publication of *Maud* (1854), in which, as Tennyson explained it, 'different phases of passion in one person take the place of different characters'. The microscopic focus on the cricket and the butterfly wings in section V of the poem might even recall Tennyson's focus on the shell in Part II, section II of *Maud*, which is also set in Brittany. Just as *Maud* had its origin in a lyric 'Oh! that 'twere possible' that had been previously published in *The Tribute* as 'Stanzas', so RB's poem originated in stanzas (152–81) that had been previously published in the *Monthly Repository* 10.112 (April 1836), 270–1, as

'Lines'. In 1857 RB had offered another section of the poem, 244–69, for publication in *The Keepsake* under the title 'Study of a Hand, by Lionardo', but in the event, the poem was received only after *The Keepsake* had ceased publication. In later collections, RB twice offered extracts as independent poems, in partial fulfilment of a plan he confided to Julia Wedgwood: 'I have expressed it all insufficiently, and will break the chain up one day, and leave so many separate round rings to roll each its way, if it can' (*Wedgwood*, 123). When he re-printed the full poem he changed its title from 'James Lee' to 'James Lee's Wife', under which title it is now usually known, and added a passage of 63 lines after line 269. All this suggests that RB was unusually anxious about the poem, unsure even whether it was a single poem or several poems loosely linked, an anxiety that nicely coincides with the wife's uncertainty as to the nature of her marital union. In the same letter to Julia Wedgwood RB explained that his poem concerned 'people newly-married, trying to realize a dream of being sufficient to each other, in a foreign land (where you can try such an experiment) and finding it break up—the man being tired *first*,—and tired precisely of the love' (*Wedgwood*, 123). This is puzzling on two counts; first, because it suggests that the poem traces the husband's change of heart, which in the poem is known only as refracted through the wife's voice, and second, because it suggests that the love of the wife, like the love of the husband, is mutable, a suggestion that the whole of the poem seems to resist. The wife's moving attempt to preserve in the face of her husband's desertion a sense of the value of the love that they shared raises issues central to RB's aesthetics: whether beauty is located in time, like the beauty of the landscape (closely modelled on the Brittany where RB holidayed in the early 1860s), or whether like the beauty of the drawing (in 'James Lee' drawn by the wife, but originally one of Leonardo's studies of hands) it transcends time; and what is the relationship between the wife's love and the 'weak earth' (98) of the man who is its object, and between the beauty of the drawing and the 'poor coarse hand' (270) that prompted it?

l. 4. *the bird's estranged.* The bird has migrated.

l. 23. *oak and pine.* The hull of wooden ships was commonly made of oak while pine supplied the masts.

l. 33. *stark.* Stiff with cold.

l. 51. (*now, gnash your teeth!*). The implication is that the sailors, were they aware of the true state of the home they look at from the dangerous sea, would have no reason to envy its occupants.

l. 58. *the weather-side.* The windward side.

l. 62. *five fingers.* The fig leaf is commonly divided into five sections.

l. 72. *bent.* Coarse grass.

l. 74. *rebuff.* Possibly signifying here a gust of wind as in Milton, *Paradise Lost*, II. 936.

l. 81. *let Winter estrange!* The exclamation mark registers outrage, implying 'why let Winter estrange?'

l. 90. *God's aglow*. Compare *Aurora Leigh*, 7. 840–3, in which EBB argues that every 'natural flower which grows on earth' has as its counterpart a spiritual flower 'all aglow'. For EBB it is poetry rather than love that reveals the second flower.

l. 92. The name Adam was commonly derived from the Hebrew for earth.

ll. 104–6. In the Bible, oil and wine commonly represent material prosperity.

ll. 117–18. Longman compares Pope, *Eloisa to Abelard*, 75–6: 'Love, free as air, at sight of human ties, | Spreads his light wings, and in a moment flies.'

l. 120. That is, in the eye of another woman.

l. 135. *films*. Probably referring to the insect's wings.

ll. 136–9. The cricket is re-imagined as a fairy charger given by an eccentric wizard to a minuscule knight.

l. 137. *barded and chanfroned*. Armoured on its body and head (the horse armour is suggested by the cricket's protective outer casing).

l. 143. *fans*. Wings, as in Keats, *Endymion*, 1. 764–5, 'the fans | Of careless butterflies'.

l. 191. The phrasing suggests that the young man's confidence that the failures of others serve only to underline his own invulnerability is all but blasphemous.

ll. 227–9. Ohio compares Isaiah 49: 16, in which the Lord promises Zion, 'Behold, I have graven thee upon the palms of my hands'. The wish is that something once grasped should make a permanent impression, like the lines on the palm of the hand.

l. 230. The point is that the real 'sting' is not death, but the thought that even before death all those things will be obliterated that he would have died to save.

l. 237. *sealark*. A name given to a number of birds. The references to the white breast and the sweet twitter suggest the ringed plover.

l. 243. *Give earth yourself.* Give yourself to the earth.

l. 247. God's counsels are advisory rather than mandatory, suggestions to improve the moral life.

ll. 251–2. That is, she finds in the beauty of the hand an expression of God's love, which would be equally evident if she were to study its skill or its power.

l. 257. Compare 209–10, the hand is so beautiful as to imperil the knowledge that all beauty is circumscribed.

ll. 262–9. The fancy is that by repudiating manual dexterity, and drawing with the chalk held not in the hand but the mouth, the drawing, however clumsy, would better reproduce her sense of the hand's beauty. Compare the thought in 'One Word More' that Dante might best express his love in a drawing and Raphael in a poem.

l. 278. *mutual flame*. It may be intended that the reader recognize the expression as a poetic commonplace used amongst many others by Shakespeare, Pope, Goldsmith, Chatterton, Burns, Byron, and L.E.L.

l. 284. Compare l. 244.

Gold Hair: A Legend of Pornic

The poem rehearses an anecdote that RB found in François-Jean Carou's *Histoire de Pornic*, 1859, 67–9. Its title, as Longman notes, recalls the title of several of Barham's *Ingoldsby Legends* (1840), for example, 'The Lay of St Aloys: A Legend of Blois'. RB added three stanzas to the second impression of *Dramatis Personae* after stanza 20, in response, it is said, to George Eliot's complaint that the girl's motivation remained unclear (RB inscribed the stanzas in pencil in George Eliot's copy). The addition is not an improvement, because the girl's act is irrational, and irrational acts cannot in any ordinary sense be explained. The poem offers itself as an illustration of a familiar biblical text, Matthew 6: 19–21: 'Lay not up for yourselves treasures upon earth, where moth and rust doth corrupt, and where thieves break through and steal: But lay up for yourselves treasures in heaven, where neither moth nor rust doth corrupt, and where thieves do not break through nor steal: For where your treasure is, there will your heart be also.' More interestingly it interrogates the basis on which the reader's indulgence of the girl's vanity in wishing to take with her into the grave her gold hair (a Bishop in Coventry Patmore's *The Angel in the House* (1854) responds smilingly when a young woman asks whether 'women *should* be vain') gives way to stern disapproval when she wishes to take her gold coins. In the poem's conclusion RB's *faux naïf* response to the liberal Anglican theology of *Essays and Studies* and Bishop Colenso (as he shows in *A Death in the Desert* he had a sophisticated understanding of the new biblical criticism) introduces a strangely emphatic assertion of the doctrine of original sin, but RB's point is that it is a doctrine that at least breeds tolerance for human imperfection. It excludes the ideal of purity that permits the parents of the young woman to think of her body simply as a screen behind which her soul can remain uncontaminated by the world.

l. 2. *Pornic.* A port town in Brittany near which RB holidayed in 1862 and 1863, south of the Loire estuary.

ll. 3–4. The girl is named in RB's source as Mlle Beaulon des Roussières.

l. 16. *flix and floss.* Fur and silk.

l. 18. *dross.* The waste produced when a metal such as gold is refined.

ll. 53–5. As RB's source pointed out, it was an unusual distinction for a lay person to be buried in the church itself rather than the churchyard.

l. 58. *both robe and pall.* The hair that was her chief adornment in life serves as her shroud in death.

l. 73. *in the lurch.* In the lurking place, concealed.

ll. 86–7. *O cor | Humanum, pectora caeca.* O human heart, blind breasts, adapted from Lucretius, *De Rerum Natura*, 2. 14: 'O miseras hominum mentes, pectora caeca', 'O miserable minds of men, blind breasts.'

l. 90. *double louis d'or.* A gold coin, the most valuable in circulation in pre-revolutionary France.

ll. 91–2. *heard,* | *Marked, inwardly digested*. Parodying the Book of Common Prayer: 'Read, mark, learn, and inwardly digest.'

l. 99. *for the nonce*. Expressly.

l. 107. *praise, gold-like*. Compare *Luria*, III. 89: 'pure gold that praise must be!'

l. 109. *true*. Literal, though playing on other senses of the word.

ll. 112–15. In Matthew 27: 6–7, when Judas returns the thirty pieces of silver that he had accepted to betray Christ, 'the chief priests took the silver pieces, and said, it is not lawful for to put them into the treasury, because it is the price of blood. And they took counsel, and bought with them the potter's field, to bury strangers in.'

ll. 116–20. The priest refers to the common saying, 'there's no use crying over spilt milk', signifying that it is pointless to be distressed by events that cannot be undone.

l. 117. *Watch and pray*! Compare Matthew 26: 41: 'Watch and pray, that ye enter not into temptation: the spirit indeed is willing, but the flesh is weak.'

ll. 126–30. *Essays and Reviews* (1860) was a collection of seven essays by liberal Anglicans, amongst them Benjamin Jowett, some of which gently introduced to the volume's readers the tenets of German Higher Criticism. The book caused a scandal, and its authors were described as 'The Seven against Christ'. John Colenso, Bishop of Natal, wrote *The Pentateuch and the Book of Joshua Critically Examined* (1862), which cast doubt on the historical accuracy of the early books of the Old Testament. Colenso was convicted of heresy, a verdict that was later overturned on a technicality.

ll. 133–4. *launched point-blank her dart* | *At the head of a lie*. Compare Ithuriel, the touch of whose spear penetrates Satan's disguise as a toad, 'for no falsehood can endure | Touch of celestial temper', *Paradise Lost*, IV. 811–12.

l. 134. *Original Sin*. The doctrine compactly stated by Paul in Romans 5: 12: 'as by one man sin entered into the world, and death by sin; and so death passed upon all men, for that all have sinned.'

Dîs Aliter Visum; or, Le Byron de nos Jours

A woman speaks at a Parisian evening party to an ageing poet, at least twenty-five years her senior, and recalls their first meeting, ten years before, on the Brittany coast, when, as she imagines, the poet had contemplated proposing to her, before wiser, or at least more cautious, counsels prevailed. The poem, in which the young woman recreates the poet's thought processes ten years before, even imagining in one passage (81–5) how he had imagined hers, is remarkable for its formal narrative complexity. The octosyllabic five-line stanza includes a daring second line, in which the sixth and eighth syllables rhyme, an effect that allows surprisingly various results: pathos in a line such as 'Perfect the hour would pass, alas!' (67), energy in 'No feat which done, would make time break' (117), and even a waspish mockery of the old poet as a mawkish rhymester, when she imagines him admiring her beauty 'round and sound', and her 'youth and truth | With loves and doves' (61–3). Like 'The Statue and the Bust' it is a poem of missed opportunity, but unlike the earlier poem, the opportunity comes in the form of a marriage between a young woman and an older man, a match in which his fame purchases her youth and beauty (although she has money too), that one might expect would be pronounced regrettably worldly, but the woman imagines it allowing exactly that futile attempt to transcend the mortal condition in which RB so often locates the value of human experience. The poet has continued even in his old age to indulge in the 'love-freaks' (60) that contributed to his celebrity when he was young. His latest mistress, Stephanie, is a dancer, who, if the speaker is to be believed, is not quite the catch she once was: 'her vogue has had its day' (149). The woman has made a depressingly conventional match, crisply epitomized in the poem's bleakly casual final line; 'Here comes my husband from his whist.'

Dîs Aliter Visum; or Le Byron de nos Jours. The gods have judged otherwise (Virgil, *Aeneid*, II. 428); or the Byron of our age.

ll. 7–8. *A mass of brass | That sea looks.* Compare William Motherwell, 'Hollo My Fancy' (1849): 'while the sea | Of molten brass appears to be' (63–4).

l. 19. *Bath-house.* Here, a facility that offers sea-water baths, as 106 indicates.

l. 30. *garlands.* Presumably decorative architectural features of the church.

ll. 36–40. Robert Schumannn (1810–56), Dominique Ingres (1780–1867), and Heinrich Heine (1797–1856) are chosen to exemplify an advanced taste in the arts. Schumann often has march movements, as, for example, in his Piano Quintet. Ingres first secured his reputation with a religious painting, but he is not most celebrated for his saints. EBB's 'Paraphrases on Heine' appeared in her *Last Poems* (1862), seen through the press by RB, and Arnold's essay on him appeared in the *Cornhill Magazine* in 1863.

l. 37. *mouth.* Vehemence or vigour.

l. 39. Compare D. G. Rossetti, 'The Blessed Damozel' (1850), 1–2: 'The blessed damozel leaned out | From the gold bar of Heaven.'

ll. 41–5. It was a Breton custom for sailors who had survived danger to present a model boat to be hung in the local church.

l. 42. *votive.* Presented in obedience to a vow.

l. 45. The suggestion is that the boat might have been understood as preaching a sermon against risk, and hence deterred the man from proposing.

l. 57. *verse and worse.* Compare Thomas Hood, 'Literary and Literal', 23: 'Think of your prose and verse, and worse.'

l. 58. The Acadèmie Française is limited to forty members. A 'fauteuil' (arm-chair) becomes vacant only on the death of a member.

l. 64. *Three per Cents.* Government bonds offering a secure but modest return (notionally 3 per cent).

l. 85. The thought is that her heart's blood is needed to oil his wheels.

l. 100. *for best or worst.* In the marriage service in the Book of Common Prayer, the bride and groom promise 'to have and to hold . . . for better for worse'.

ll. 128–9. *sure of range above* | *The limits here.* Confident that in Heaven the limits of earthly experience may be transcended.

l. 130. Despair would be an appropriate response to the failure of God but not to the failure of earthly love (which may be repaired in Heaven).

l. 134. *faculties to seek.* Aptitudes still undiscovered.

l. 138. *Rose-jacinth.* The jacinth is a rose-red variety of zircon, used as a gemstone.

Abt Vogler

Georg Joseph Vogler (1749–1814), a performer, composer, and musical theorist, as well as an ordained priest, invented his own version of the organ that he named the orchestrion and exhibited in London in 1790. Vogler had distinguished pupils, Weber and Meyerbeer, but by the 1860s he was best known for Mozart's lively ridicule of him in letters to his father. Mozart was particularly exercised by Vogler's disdain of Bach. There is a wide and potentially comic disparity between Vogler's Victorian reputation and the lofty sense of his own achievement with which RB credits him, but its primary function is to underline the discrepancy between conception and execution that, for RB, characterizes all true art. It is still more apparent in the piece that Vogler plays, which, because it is improvised, has a beauty that cannot survive his performance. Vogler's religious vocation underwrites his faith that the 'broken arcs', the fragments of a heavenly architecture that are all that can be accomplished on earth, will become in Heaven a 'perfect round' (72). The poem's six-beat, frequently dactylic line deftly approximates the 'manifold music' that Vogler's orchestrion produces.

l. 4. In the pseudepigraphical *Testament of Solomon*, Solomon gains control of the demons by means of a ring inscribed with the name of God given him by Michael. With the assistance of the demons he is able to build the Temple of Jerusalem.

l. 5. *brute*, *reptile*, *fly*. By tradition Solomon's ring also conferred on him the power to talk with animals.

l. 7. *ineffable Name.* The name of God.

l. 8. See 1 Kings 3: 1: 'And Solomon made affinity with Pharaoh king of Egypt, and took Pharaoh's daughter, and brought her into the city of David, until he had made an end of building his own house, and the house of the Lord, until those days.'

ll. 13–24. Vogler's music builds two cities, an infernal city like the city that Milton in *Paradise Lost* calls Pandemonium, and a celestial city like the new Jersusalem of Revelation.

l. 16. *nether springs*. See Judges 1: 13: 'And Caleb gave her the upper springs and the nether springs.'

l. 19. *rampired*. Ramparted; *walls of gold as transparent as glass*. Compare Revelation 21: 21: 'and the street of the city was pure gold, as it were transparent glass.'

ll. 21–3. On the feast of St Peter, 29 June, St Peter's was illuminated.

l. 25. *Not half!* Not nearly!; *to match man's birth*. Vogler compares his creation to the creation of man.

l. 30. *wandering star*. Planet.

l. 31. *Meteor-moons*. Shining or blazing moons, as in Shelley, 'The Cloud', 31, in which he refers to the 'meteor eyes' of the sunrise.

l. 35. *the Protoplast*. The Creator, a word used on several occasions by RB, who perhaps took it from Coleridge, *The Destiny of Nations*, 290.

ll. 59–61. Vogler's music is improvised and hence does not survive its performance.

l. 66. Compare 2 Corinthians 5: 1: 'For we know that if our earthly house of this tabernacle were dissolved, we have a building of God, and house not made with hands, eternal in the heavens.'

l. 91. *the common chord*. The basic three-note chord. Charles Dibdin explains in *The Harmonic Preceptor*, 1804, Part Third, 121–2: 'The *bass* shall be C, and, the *common-chord* played, | Which, we know, by the *third, fifth*, and *octave*, is made.' In *Fifine at the Fair*, RB speaks of 'life's common chord' (968).

l. 93. *ninth*. Ninth chords are characteristically dissonant.

l. 96. *C Major*. The simplest and commonest of keys, and hence the key of common life.

Rabbi Ben Ezra

The failure of more recent readers to share the widespread admiration of this poem by RB's contemporaries marks a shift of attention from RB as ethical and religious teacher to the psychological insight and formal daring of the poems. RB's Rabbi is based on the historical Abraham ibn Ezra, a 12th-century scholar, but there seems little doubt that the Rabbi is a mouthpiece through which RB voices his own opinions. The poem attempts the fullest resolution of two positions that RB repeats in many poems but may seem inconsistent one with another; the notion that human experience aspires to transcendence and the insistence on the value of the body, the 'rose-mesh' container of the soul. Longman persuasively argues that the poem is directed against the philosophical pessimism that became fashionable in mid-century in such poems as FitzGerald's translation of the *Rubáiyát* (1850), which

D. G. Rossetti may well have brought to RB's attention, and Arnold's *Empedocles on Etna* (1852), which Arnold re-printed, after withdrawing the poem, in response to RB's urging. The metaphor central to the poem of God as a potter and man as the wine pot that is turned on his wheel seems in particular designed as a combative response to FitzGerald. RB's stanza with its rousing concluding alexandrine might itself be thought of as responding to the elegiac cadence of FitzGerald's quatrains.

l. 4. Compare Psalm 31: 15: 'My times are in thy hand.'

l. 5. *A whole I planned.* Longman contrasts Arnold, *Empedocles on Etna*, I. ii. 82–5: 'Hither and thither spins | The wind-borne, mirroring soul, | A thousand glimpses wins, | And never sees a whole.'

l. 6. *trust God: see all, nor be afraid!* Compare Isaiah 12: 2: 'Behold, God is my salvation; I will trust, and not be afraid.'

ll. 8–9. Youth regrets having to choose between the lily and the rose.

l. 11. Youth is content neither with Jove nor Jupiter, associated astrologically with stable, prosperous rule, nor with Mars, associated astrologically with conflict.

l. 12. *Mine be some figured flame.* A star that has a particular shape, and also perhaps a figurative star, that is, a star that accommodates the astrological significances of all the planets.

ll. 13–18. The sense and movement of the lines may recall Wordsworth's 'Ode: Intimations of Immortality', especially Wordsworth's contention that his 'song of thanks and praise' celebrates 'obstinate questionings' (141–2).

l. 18. Compare the hymn by the Wesleys: 'Father, see this living clod, | This spark of heavenly fire!'

l. 30. *tribes.* Divisions in the classification of animals.

l. 62. *rose-mesh.* The body imagined as a pink net in which the soul is held.

l. 105. Longman contrasts Edward FitzGerald's preface to his translation of the *Rubáiyát* in which he represents Omar Khayyám as one who 'after vainly endeavouring to unshackle his Steps from Destiny, and to catch some authentic glimpse of TOMORROW, falls back upon TODAY (what has outlasted so many Tomorrows!) as the only Ground he has got to stand on, however momentarily slipping from under his Feet'.

ll. 150–6. Longman persuasively suggests a corrective reference to the 'Kuza-Nama' stanzas of the *Rubáiyát* in which various pots mock and bewail the notion that they are God's handiwork. The proposition of the 'fools' in line 156 certainly echoes a moral that is repeatedly articulated in FitzGerald's poem.

l. 164. *plastic circumstance.* Charles Mackay writes of an imagined perfect human being, 'Him would all plastic circumstance obey', *Egeria* (1850), 3. 121. Plastic here means susceptible to being shaped.

ll. 169–74. The metaphor compares human life to a pot, the base of which (youth) is engraved with cherubs, and the rim of which (age) is engraved with skulls.

l. 186. The thought is that in Heaven man will be the wine that slakes God's thirst, just as on earth in the Eucharist God is the wine for which man thirsts.

A Death in the Desert

The poem is commonly represented as RB's response to Renan's *Vie de Jésus* (1863), and RB's John certainly comes close to confessing, as Renan charged, that he had not been present at the Crucifixion: 'And it is written, "I forsook and fled" | There was my trial, and it ended thus' (311–12). More generally, the poem addresses the biblical scholarship of RB's own day, which derived from the work of German scholars such as Karl Gottlieb Bretschneider, David Friedrich Strauss, and Ferdinand Christian Baur. John, the fourth evangelist, assumed author of the late Gospel, the authorship of which was doubted even by those who admitted the authenticity of the synoptic Gospels, defends himself against a 19th century in which 'unborn people in strange lands' (194) will say, 'Was John at all and did he say he saw?' (196). John's Gospel with its insistent emphasis on the fact of the Incarnation, on how 'the Word was made flesh' (John 1: 14) was written, John explains, in defiance of Cerinthus, an all but forgotten figure from the early Church who, because he doubted the divinity of Christ, anticipates (and also, RB suggests, anticipates the fate of) his modern-day counterparts. RB offers a robust and idiosyncratic statement of his own Trinitarianism, in which the guarantee that God is at once a God who is, a God who acts, and a God who loves is the coincidence in his creature, man, of power, will, and love. But the poem makes its point formally as much as through argument. A bibliophile of the 3rd or 4th century begins the poem by describing a prized item in his library, a parchment in which a follower of John, one Pamphylax, records the last words John delivered before he died. The parchment includes a passage (82–104) in which a later commentator, Theotypas, glosses esoterically a homely remark by John, and it ends with a coda in which an unnamed commentator celebrates the discomfiture that the manuscript inflicted on Cerinthus. It is a text in which John imagines and answers critics of his own major text, his Gospel. The poem insists on the materiality of the text ('it is a parchment of my rolls the fifth, | Hath three skins glued together', 2–3); it raises questions of attribution that cannot be certainly resolved (it is only 'Supposed of Pamphylax the Antiochene' (1), and it is unknown who gives 'the glossa of Theotypas' (104), or who 'added' (666) the coda); it accommodates paratextual and supplementary material, and the text is itself fragmentary (it only 'goeth from *epsilon* down to *Mu*'). In all this it recalls an early, experimental poem by RB such as *Pauline*, but in 'A Death in the Desert' the experimentation is strictly functional. RB's concern is to construct a text as unstable as the Gospel the authenticity of which it defends, because RB wishes to offer instability as the guarantee of authenticity. No text is written on stone, a truth that RB wittily illustrates (626–30) by instancing the stone tablets that Moses brought down from Sinai, broke to pieces, and then re-wrote. It is only because texts are unstable that they can be truthful, for truth itself is constantly evolving. As RB puts it, man may 'learn a thousand things, not twice the same' (452). The poem drives toward a rich paradox, central both to RB's theology and to his aesthetics; the biblical scholarship of the 19th century, the Higher Criticism as it was known, has demonstrated the textuality of the scriptures, and in doing so it has shown conclusively that it is proper to accept them as the Word of God.

l. 1. *Pamphylax* is an invention of RB's, a phylax is a guard or sentinel, so that the word might be translated all-guarding or all-watching; Antioch was one of the most important centres of the Early Church, visited by both Peter and Paul, the city in which the followers of Christ were first called Christians, and the city of the first Gentile church.

ll. 2–3. *parchment*. Parchment is prepared from animal skins; *rolls*. Scrolls.

l. 4. Greek manuscripts were numbered using a letter system in which Epsilon represented 5, and Mu represented 40, so the parchment is a fragment, its first four sections missing.

l. 5. *surnamed*. A surname is an additional name: hence the chest referred to as the chosen chest.

l. 6. *juice of terebinth*. Turpentine.

l. 8. *Xanthus*. In *Sordello* RB has Paul spend his last night before leaving Antioch at the house of Xanthus. Most of the household, the poem notes, will subsequently be martyred. See *Sordello*, 3. 991–1021. Xanthus can be named because he is dead, but the writer conceals his own identity under a cipher.

l. 14. *plantain*. A broad-leaved plant with medicinal properties. See *Romeo and Juliet*, I. ii. 51.

l. 15. *lappet*. Fold.

l. 30. *Valens*. A common Roman name, meaning strong or healthy.

l. 36. *Bactrian*. Bactria is an area in modern-day Afghanistan that had been a Greek colony since its conquest by Alexander.

l. 39. *quitch*. Couch grass.

l. 41. The sense is that the persecution of the Christians was so much common knowledge that even a thief or a soldier would have known how to profit from it.

l. 50. *nard*. The spikenard of the Bible, an ointment produced from the plant of the same name, that might be used as a perfume or medicinally.

l. 57. Suggesting that the writer has taken on himself the task of recording John's last hours that Xanthus was prevented from carrying out by his martyrdom.

l. 59. Compare Keats, *Eve of St Agnes*, 136: 'Sudden a thought came like a full-blown rose.'

l. 60. *plate of graven lead*. Greek writing survives on lead sheets as well as on parchment.

l. 64. Jesus's words recorded in John 11: 25.

l. 69. Probably a variety of vulture, a bird that J. A. Heraud nominates 'the strong-beaked Vulture-King | With ruff of ashy grey', *The Judgement of the Flood* (1857), 6. 302–3.

ll. 82–104. Theotypas' gloss on the manuscript illustrates the process by which, according to David Friedrich Strauss, a historical narrative such as that preserved in John's Gospel might become contaminated by what Strauss terms Alexandrian metaphysics. The gloss expands John's classic statement of Trinitarianism in his First Epistle 5: 7–8: 'For there are three that bear record in heaven, the Father, the Word, and the Holy Ghost: and these three are one. And there are three that bear witness in earth, the spirit, and the water, and the blood: and these three agree in one.' Theotypas reads body, 'what Does', mind, 'what Knows', and spirit, 'what Is', as echoing in each individual the divine trinity of Father, Son, and Holy Ghost. It may be that RB is parodying the manner of an influential 19th-century Trinitarian such as Coleridge.

l. 101. *that dread point of intercourse*. The point at which the human and divine converge.

l. 104. *glossa*. The Latin for gloss.

l. 115. Acts 12: 2 records that Herod 'killed James, the brother of John with the sword', which places his death in or before 44 CE, and Peter is said traditionally to have suffered inverted crucifixion under Nero, which places his death in or before 68 CE.

ll. 122–3. John remembers the vision he records in Revelation 1: 14–16: 'His head and his hairs were white like wool, as white as snow; and his eyes were as a flame of fire; And his feet like unto fine brass, as if they burned in a furnace; and his voice as the sound of many waters. And he had in his right hand seven stars: and out of his mouth went a sharp twoedged sword.'

l. 130. John is traditionally believed to have lived to a great age and died around 100 CE.

ll. 131–2. Compare 1 John 1: 1–2: 'That which was from the beginning, which we have heard, which we have seen with our eyes, which we have looked upon, and our hands have handled, of the Word of life; (for the life was manifested, and we have seen it, and bear witness, and shew unto you that eternal life, which was with the Father, and was manifested unto us).'

l. 140. *Patmos*. By tradition, John was exiled by the Roman authorities to the Greek isle of Patmos, where he had the vision that he records in Revelation.

l. 143. *to my arbitrament*. To decide for myself. Compare Raphael to Adam, *Paradise Lost*, VIII. 640–1: 'to stand or fall | Free in thine own arbitrament it lies.'

l. 149. *a letter*. It may be that the simile suggests that RB follows the contemporary biblical scholars who ascribed only the first of John's three epistles to the Evangelist.

l. 155. *the mighty things*. In her 1833 translation of *Prometheus Bound*, EBB has 'the mighty things of former years', 10.

l. 158. *Antichrist.* This term for a false religious leader first appears in I John 2: 18: 'ye have heard that antichrist shall come, even now there are many antichrists; whereby we know that it is the last time.'

l. 160. *Jasper.* An invented character, but the exchange recalls Matthew 13: 55, in which Jesus's fellow townsmen ask, 'Is not this the carpenter's son? is not his mother called Mary? and his brethren, James, and Joseph, and Simon, and Judas.'

l. 163. In Luke 9: 54–6, John and his brother ask Jesus whether they should 'command fire to come down from heaven, and consume' a Samaritan village, and Jesus rebukes them: 'the Son of man is not come to destroy men's lives, but to save them.'

l. 165. Compare Luke 10: 19: 'Behold, I give unto you power to tread on serpents and scorpions.'

l. 177. See 2 Peter 3: 3–4: 'there shall come in the last day scoffers . . . saying, Where is the promise of his coming?'

l. 193. *blank profound.* A. H. Clough has 'the primal peaceful blank profound', 'Uranus' (1862), 1.

ll. 195–6. A visionary glimpse of the scepticism as to the authorship of John's Gospel common amongst Victorian biblical scholars.

l. 213. This whole line was omitted in later editions.

ll. 228–35. John seems anachronistically to compare the detachment given by age to the view of the world through a telescope, but a telescope with a concave rather than a convex lens, a lens that clarifies by placing at a distance things too near to be seen distinctly.

l. 241. *that Life and Death.* That is Christ's.

l. 242. In *Sordello* it is Sordello's verses rather than Christ's life that 'spring, dispread | Dispart, disperse' (3. 593–4).

l. 271. *barriers.* The palisades enclosing the ground where a tournament is held (in which the soul's prowess is tested).

l. 280. *the fable.* According to which Prometheus stole fire from the gods and gave it to man, on which Aeschylus founded his Promethean trilogy.

ll. 285–8. Recalling the last satyr play that accompanied the Promethean trilogy, through the quotation from it that Plutarch introduces into his *Moralia*:

'The Satyr, when he saw fire for the first time, wished to kiss it and embrace it, but Prometheus warned him, "Goat, thou wilt surely mourn thy loss of beard". For fire burns whoever touches it, but it also gives light and warmth, and is an instrument of art to all those who know how to use it' (translated by A. R. Shilleto).

l. 305. *transfigured.* See Matthew 17: 2.

l. 306. *trod the sea.* See John 6: 19; for the raising of Lazarus, see John 11: 1–45.

l. 311. *I forsook and fled.* See Matthew 26: 56: when Jesus is taken at Gethsemane, 'Then all the disciples forsook him, and fled.'

l. 318. Nero, Emperor 54–68 CE, was notorious for having Christians burned alive.

ll. 327–9. Just as John was obstructed from his pursuit of truth by the military might of Rome, people now are obstructed by specious reasoners.

l. 329. *glozing*. Specious argument.

l. 330. *Cerinthus*. An opponent of John who did not maintain the divinity of Christ. Ebion is sometimes named as his successor. Theirs is the heresy that John is represented as having written his Gospel and Epistles in order to refute.

ll. 341–50. A Christianized version of Plato's Allegory of the Cave in Book VII of *The Republic*.

l. 362. *Ephesus*. In 1863 J. T. Wood was granted a permit by the British Museum for the excavation of ancient Ephesus.

l. 373. *Wonders, that would prove doctrine*. Miracles that would prove a tenet of the Church (here, the divinity of Christ).

ll. 375–9. John entertains the notion that the idea of Christ's divinity might have been generated by the human need to imagine a perfect reconciliation of power and love.

l. 384. *projection*. The *OED* quotes from the *North American Review* (April 1864): 'His Deity is an inference from himself,—a projection of his own image on the walls of the universe.' The thought is common in Blake and Shelley, for example, in *The Marriage of Heaven and Hell* (plate 11): 'All deities reside in the human breast.'

ll. 393–4. Robert Inglesfield, 'Two Interpolated Speeches in RB's "A Death in the Desert"', *VP* 41–3 (2003), 333–47, compares Herbert Spencer, *First Principles* (1862): 'Of old the sun was regarded as the chariot of a god, drawn by horses' (p. 103).

l. 399. *OED* ascribes to G. H. Lewes in 1858 the first use of the word anthropomorphism to denote the attribution of human qualities to the impersonal.

l. 406. *Or else stood still*. See Joshua 10: 13, 'And the sun stood still.' Note also the darkening of the sun at the Crucifixion.

ll. 436–44. Alluding to the gardener's practice of identifying newly planted seeds on a label attached to a stake, a 19th-century rather than a 1st-century practice.

ll. 446–8. Miracles acted like the gardener's labels to preserve Christ's teachings from being trampled underfoot and destroyed.

l. 449. *Was man made a wheelwork to wind up*. Compare *Sordello*, 3. 843–54:

ll. 460–1. See Acts 5: 12: 'And by the hands of the apostles were many signs and wonders wrought among the people.'

l. 493. *the written word*. The Bible, although it is unclear what John would have understood by that.

ll. 495–500. When man argues that power need not imply agency, neglecting that he has in his own human nature a demonstration in little of how the two qualities are combined in God, he refuses knowledge that he has already been given, which, John suggests, is a kind of death.

ll. 515–20. The sceptic's point is that the discrepancies between John and the synoptic Gospels as to historical fact, the 'prior truth', endanger the spiritual truth that it was John's purpose to convey, the secondary truth.

l. 524. Longman suggests that the phrase is coined in antithesis to the German 'Aberglaube' or after-belief, meaning superstition.

l. 533. *ephemerals.* Transient beings, mortals.

l. 534. *in a cane.* Prometheus, when he stole fire from the gods, concealed it in a hollow stalk of fennel.

l. 552. Compare Revelation 22: 13: 'I am Alpha and Omega, the beginning and the end, the first and the last.'

l. 566. *Atlas.* The mountain.

l. 593. *wait.* Be reserved for.

l. 609. *statuary.* Sculptor.

l. 624. *at a jet.* In one go.

ll. 626–30. Just as Moses broke the tablets of the law that God gave him on Sinai, and God then re-wrote them differently, so the teaching of Christ must be repeatedly renewed to meet changing needs.

l. 630. *the type.* The ideal to which the individual instance aspires.

l. 632. *angels' law.* Compare Acts 7: 53: 'Who have received the law by the disposition of angels, and have not kept it.'

l. 653. Paul imagines having 'fought with beasts at Ephesus', 1 Corinthians 15: 32.

l. 656. *Beloved John.* John is commonly referred to as the Beloved Disciple, because he is identified with the 'disciple, whom Jesus loved', John 20: 2.

l. 658. *mistaking what was darkly spoke.* When Peter asks Jesus what will befall 'the disciple whom Jesus loved', he is told, 'If I will that he tarry till I come, what is that to thee?' which is mistakenly interpreted by some to mean 'that that disciple should not die', John 21: 20–3.

l. 665. *breast to breast.* Compare John 13: 25, in which the disciple whom Jesus loved is represented 'lying on Jesus' breast'.

l. 666. *Cerinthus.* See note to line 330.

Caliban upon Setebos; or, Natural Theology in the Island

The poem may be a delayed outcome of RB's relationship with William Charles Macready whose 1838 production of *The Tempest* at Covent Garden restored Shakespeare's text, and featured George John Bennett as Caliban in a performance that restored dignity to Shakespeare's character. Joseph Phelan has persuasively argued that the poem may also have been prompted by the American poet R. H. Stoddard's 'The Witch's Whelp' included in his *Poems*, 1852 ('Richard Henry Stoddard and the Brownings', *BSN* 33 (2008), 58–68); Stoddard was known to several members of the RBs' Roman circle. In

Stoddard's monologue, as in RB's, Caliban wallows in the rich swamp of sensual experience that the island affords him, and his Caliban, like RB's, is terrified by a thunderstorm. Stoddard's poem ends when Caliban acknowledges that the life of the senses is the only life he craves, which may itself have provoked RB to endow his own primitive man with aspirations, however deformed, towards the life of the mind. The poem has often been understood as a response to Darwin's *Origin of Species* (1859), but, as RB's subtitle indicates, he is most engaged by the implications of Darwin's work for natural theologians. The argument that the benevolence of the Christian God could be demonstrated by examining his Creation, an argument given its classic expression in William Paley's *Natural Theology: or, Evidences of the Existence and Attributes of the Deity, Collected from the Appearances of Nature* (1802), had become difficult to reconcile with the findings of Victorian science even before the publication of *Origin of Species*. As Tennyson puts it in *In Memoriam* (1850): 'I found Him not in world or sun, | Or eagle's wing, or insect's eye' (CXXIV. 5–6). The quotation from Psalm 50 that RB chooses as his epigraph mocks Caliban's attempt to understand the nature of God by reference to his own brutish nature, but it functions more searchingly to question the grounds on which the poem's readers might disclaim their own kinship with the poem's speaker. RB, it may be, invites his reader to reach the same conclusion as Shakespeare's Prospero: 'this thing of darkness I | Acknowledge mine' (*The Tempest*, V. i. 275–6). Caliban refers to himsef in the third person (with the pronoun commonly omitted), to signify that he has not yet learned to separate himself from his world, but interspersed are passages in which he uses a first person, indicating that he is on the verge of self-consciousness. Caliban is a primitive creature but capable of groping towards thoughts that anticipate Plato, and St Paul, and Lucretius, thinkers who continued in the 19th century to inform even the most sophisticated thinking about man's place in the universe. There is also an uncomfortable sense in which Caliban acts as the prototype of the Victorian poet. He begins, as he wallows in his mud-bath, with the life of the body, the sensual life, before he goes on to entertain his more abstract speculations, and that is the pattern followed in very many Victorian poems, including RB's own, as RB came close to acknowledging when he accepted the parallel between the structure of Caliban's thinking in this poem and his own in *La Saisiaz* (Furnivall, 95).

"Thou thoughtest that I was altogether such an one as thyself". Psalm 50: 21.

l. 5. *eft-things*. Creatures like newts.

l. 7. *pompion-plant*. Pumpkin.

l. 16. Shakespeare's Caliban speaks of 'my dam's god, Setebos', *The Tempest*, I. ii. 375.

ll. 26–7. Compare Genesis 1: 16: 'And God made two great lights; the greater light to rule the day, and the lesser night to rule the night: he made the stars also.'

l. 27. Possibly because the stars, unlike the sun and moon, seem exempt from mutability.

l. 28. *meteors*. Atmospheric or meteorological phenomena.

l. 41. *Flounced back*. Flung back.

l. 45. *creeping thing*. Genesis 1: 24.

l. 47. *Yon auk*. Probably the Great Auk, which became extinct in the mid-19th century. The 'fire-eye' may refer to the dramatic white circle just above its bill.

l. 50. *pie*. The description suggests the greater spotted woodpecker rather than the magpie.

l. 51. *oakwarts*. Oak galls (protuberances on the bark produced by various insects).

ll. 53–4. Probably describing the mounds made by wood ants.

ll. 57–8. Compare Milton's Adam to God, *Paradise Lost*, VIII. 419–21: 'No need that thou | Shouldst propagate, already infinite; | And through all numbers absolute, though one.'

ll. 68–74. Caliban describes how he ferments fruit to produce an alcoholic drink, which makes him drunk.

l. 68. *mash*. In brewing, the mash is the liquid to be fermented.

l. 72. To have maggots in the brain is to be mad.

l. 76. Compare the myth in which man is fashioned from clay by Prometheus, and life breathed into him by Athena.

l. 83. *grigs*. Crickets that make their chirping by rubbing their wings together.

l. 117. The pith of the elder can be removed to form a pipe.

l. 120. Jays plunder chicks from the nests of other birds.

ll. 130–1. As, for example, Zeus or Jupiter ousted his father Chronos or Saturn.

l. 135. Compare the arrival of quails in Exodus 16: 13, and Numbers 11: 31–2.

l. 138. *outposts of its couch*. The stars are thought of as guards protecting the Quiet as it sleeps.

l. 147. *bauble-world*. Toy world, as in *Red Cotton Night-Cap Country*, 706.

ll. 150–3. In *The Tempest*, Caliban advises Stefano, 'Remember | First to possess his books; for without them | He's but a sot as I am', III. ii. 89–91.

l. 154. *wand*. Imitating the 'staff' with which Prospero performs his magic. See *The Tempest*, V. i. 54.

l. 155. *enchanter's robe*. Prospero's mantle, his 'magic garment', *The Tempest*, I. ii. 24.

l. 156. *oncelot*. Apparently RB's misspelling of ocelot, a kind of wild cat.

l. 157. *ounce*. Lynx.

l. 159. *mind his eye*. 'Mind your eye' is a colloquial expression meaning, be careful.

ll. 161–2. The appearance of the crane suggests a pelican, and the behaviour a cormorant.

l. 177. *orc.* Used by RB in *The Ring and the Book*, IX. 972, to mean sea monster.

l. 211. *a ball.* A meteorite.

ll. 214–15. Presumably referring to a fossil, but note also the legendary ability for toads to survive encased in solid stone.

l. 229. *urchin.* Hedgehog.

ll. 246–7. That is, if Setebos were not to make a surprise attack on the Quiet of the kind that Caliban proposes to Stefano in *The Tempest*, III. ii. 85–9.

l. 259. *pompion-bell.* The bell-shaped flower of the pumpkin.

ll. 276–8. Caliban's rough song is probably modelled on the song of Shakespeare's Caliban in *The Tempest*, II. ii. 170–5.

l. 286. *His raven.* Compare Norse mythology in which two ravens serve as Odin's eyes and ears.

ll. 290–1. In *The Tempest*, it is Trinculo not Caliban who says, 'If it should thunder as it did before, I know not where to hide my head,' II. ii. 23–4.

Confessions

The poem echoes EBB's 'Confessions' (1850), in which a woman, urged by her confessor to speak 'as if the angels of judgment stood over' her, acknowledges herself a sinner, but adds, 'I have *loved*', and insists to the confessor's horror, 'I have not sinned in this!' RB makes the same point, but infuses it with a dry social comedy. In his last illness the dying man, freed by his illness from the conventional reticence that he would ordinarily assume before his social superiors, relates to the clergyman who is attending him his fondest memory, of a summer's liaison with a young woman in service (her room is in the attic) that the two of them successfully concealed from her employers.

l. 7. *suburb.* Outside the city, as in *Sordello*, 3. 881–6, in which Plara explains that, because he was raised in 'a grim town', 'The brighter shone the suburb.'

l. 11. *the curtain.* The curtain of his sick room that reminds him of the summer sky.

l. 15. *Ether.* Spirit of ether, ether mixed with alcohol, was commonly used as an analgesic.

l. 17. *terrace.* Balcony.

l. 23. *two eyes except.* Except the two eyes of the young woman.

l. 28. *stretch themselves to Oes.* Open wide, but possible remembering Tennyson's poet 'rolling out his hollow oes and aes', 'The Epic', 50.

l. 35. *sad and bad and mad.* DeVane points out that EBB may be echoing this line in a letter to Anna Jameson of 22 February 1860, in which she writes of her volume *Poems Before Congress*, 'Say it's mad, and bad, and sad; but *add* that somebody did it who meant it, thought it, felt it, throbbed it out with heart and brain, and that she holds it for truth in conscience and not in partisanship' (DeVane, *Handbook*, 266–7).

Prospice

The poem begins dramatically as the speaker rebuts the suggestion that he is afraid of death, but the final lines of the poem in which he anticipates a reunion after death with the soul of his soul have always been understood as personal, and can only have been so intended in a poem published so soon after EBB's death in 1861. The metaphor which compares the approach to death to the ascent of a mountain and as an assault on an enemy encourages a stalwart embrace of death, a posture that Victorian readers admired, and some more recent readers have found embarrassing. Even DeVane is concerned that the poem's 'primitive love of battle conflicts a little with the Christian spirit of the ending' (DeVane, *Handbook*, 268).

Prospice. The word is most often encountered in the Latin motto 'Respice Prospice', which might be rendered, 'Learn from the past, look to the future.' Here, the omission of the first word underlines the poem's refusal of retrospection and commitment to the future, indeed to the afterlife.

l. 7. *Arch Fear*. Death, although the phrase may recall Milton's references to Satan as 'th'Arch-Enemy', 'th'Arch-fiend', 'th'arch-fellon', 'the arch foe'.

l. 15. *death bandaged my eyes*. As the eyes of those facing execution are often bandaged.

l. 17. *my peers*. Compare the reference in 'Childe Roland', 195 to 'all the lost adventurers my peers.'

Youth and Art

Like 'The Statue and the Bust' and 'Dîs Aliter Visum' this is a poem of missed opportunity. In its nostalgia for the bohemian life of the artist it is also a London counterpart to 'Respectability', which is set in Paris. The woman, a singer, imagines that she might have married ('joined hands with', 50) the sculptor who lodged opposite her, when they were both struggling young artists, but to him the move seemed 'rash', and to her it seemed 'rasher and something over' (54), it being harder for a woman to reconcile a career as an artist with a settled domestic life. They have both found fame and respectability but she regrets the youth that, when she had the opportunity, she failed to misspend.

l. 4. *of his feather*. Of the same species as him.

l. 5. *sticks and clay*. That is, he sculpts maquettes, preliminary models, made from clay on a wooden frame, not having the money to buy marble.

l. 8. *Gibson*. John Gibson (1790–1866), the sculptor, leader of the British art colony in Rome, and an acquaintance of the Brownings. His humble origins (he was the son of a gardener) and the royal patronage that he succeeded in winning make him an appropriate role model for the young man.

l. 12. *Grisi*. Giulia Grisi (1810?–1869), the Italian soprano, who dominated London opera from her first appearance in 1842 until her first retirement in 1854.

l. 18. *Hindoos*. They eat like Hindoos because they cannot afford meat.

l. 22. He dresses in a self-consciously bohemian manner: note that in *Pippa Passes* RB's sculptor, Jules, is said to have married in 'the same old blouse that he murders the marble in'.

l. 26. *flower-fence*. Hedge.

l. 31. *E in alt*. The equivalent for sopranos of the tenor's high C, which is why she as yet sings it insecurely.

l. 32. *chromatic scale*. The chromatic scale divides the octave into its twelve semitones.

l. 36. The appearance of watercress for sale in the London streets would have marked the arrival of spring. The bulrushes may simply be an appropriate decoration for a watercress stall.

l. 57. *the Prince at the Board*. Possibly the Fine Arts Commission established in 1841 and chaired by Prince Albert to commission the decoration of the new Houses of Parliament. Distinguished artists served on the Commission, amongst them Charles Lock Eastlake as Secretary.

l. 58. *bals-paré*. Balls where evening dress is worn, grand balls.

l. 60. An RA is a fellow of the Royal Academy. Its president from 1850 until his death in 1865 was Charles Lock Eastlake, who was knighted on his election as president in 1850. Other artists also won honours, such as the sculptor Sir Francis Chantrey, who was knighted in 1835.

A Face

The sheet on which the poem was copied by RB in Emily Patmore's album is preserved in the Armstrong Baylor Library, signed and dated 11 October 1852. Emily Patmore, the poet Coventry Patmore's first wife, was celebrated by her husband in *The Angel in the House* (1854), a poem anticipated in Patmore's 'Tamerton Church-Tower', published in 1853, that the Brownings had read in manuscript. RB's poem, in which the woman is regarded with a strained, aesthetic intensity at once sensuous and idolatrous, seems as much a response to her husband's poetry as to Emily Patmore's beauty.

ll. 2–3. The speaker is thinking of 14th-century Tuscan panel painting in which the head is painted on a background of gold leaf, a technique borrowed from Byzantine art.

l. 14. Antonio da Correggio, 1489–1534. The allusion seems specific to his fresco of the Assumption of the Virgin that decorates the cupola of Parma Cathedral, which was greatly admired by RB. Massed ranks of angels gaze as the Virgin ascends into a gold sky and Christ descends to welcome her.

Mr. Sludge, "the Medium"

The 19th-century vogue for spiritualism had its origin in 1848, in the claims of Kate and Margaret Fox, two sisters on the eastern seaboard of the United States, to be in contact with a spirit who communicated with them through raps. Daniel Dunglas Home (1833–86) was the most celebrated of the American mediums who followed in their footsteps. Home embarked in 1855 on the voyage to Europe that Sludge is planning at the end of the poem. On 23 July 1855, the Brownings attended a séance given by Home in Ealing, in the house of Mr and Mrs Rymer, who were put in contact with their dead child. RB did not voice his scepticism at the time out of concern for the feelings of the Rymers, and he seems not to have detected Home cheating, but he was unimpressed, and a few days later, when Home called on the Brownings at their lodgings, RB insulted him. EBB by contrast was inclined to accept Home's claims. It was one of two major differences of opinion that they encountered in their married life, the other being their disagreement over the character of Napoleon III. Both differences prompted poems that RB seems to have felt free to write and publish only after EBB's death, *Prince Hohenstiel-Schwangau, Saviour of Society* (1871), and 'Mr. Sludge, "the Medium"' (1864). A more immediate spur to RB's composition of 'Mr. Sludge' may have been Home's publication in 1863 of an autobiography, *Incidents in my Life*. Sludge and the Prince are modelled on Home and Napoleon III in a manner quite different from the much looser sense in which one might claim that the Duke in 'My Last Duchess' is modelled on the fifth Duke of Ferrara. In both cases the reader is expected to recognize RB's original.

They are both exceptionally long monologues, as if RB were unable to vent his hatred and contempt in any more abbreviated form. The intensity of his aversion is more marked in 'Mr. Sludge' than in *Prince Hohenstiel-Schwangau*. It had its origin, no doubt, in his conviction that Home was exploiting his wife's most painful susceptibilities, in particular her feelings for her dead brother, but it has to be admitted that the strongest argument that Sludge advances is that his admirers are complicit in his dishonesties, and hence share a responsibility for them. RB seems also to have been dismayed that in resorting to crude trickery Home and his ilk threatened the integrity of the belief in personal immortality that was central to RB's own religious faith. But it may also be that RB's contempt was sharpened into hatred by his recognition that Sludge's practices constituted, as Sludge himself more than once claims, a kind of bastard poetry. Poets, too, as RB acknowledges (most forcefully in *The Ring and the Book*), bring the dead back to life, and the achievement of poets is as dependent on their deployment of rhetorical skills as is Sludge's on his own, more disreputable stratagems. The violence with which RB repudiates Sludge may itself be a measure of the extent to which RB recognizes Sludge's profession as a grotesque version of his own.

Title. The *OED* dates the word 'medium' in its spiritualist sense to 1851, and cites its first use as American.

l. 9. Sludge had mistaken the French champagne for the sparkling wine made in Ohio by Nicholas Longworth from the Catawba grape in imitation of champagne.

l. 16. *rowdy*. A quarrelsome troublemaker; an Americanism.

l. 23. *shirt-studs*. EBB mentions the 'splendid presents' given to Home by his admirers, amongst which she specifies 'a most magnificent set of studs in black pearl & diamonds, by the Empress Eugenie' (*EBB to Arabella*, ii. 340).

l. 31. *undeveloped*. Compare EBB, *Aurora Leigh*, 7. 1151, in which mortal life is described as a grave 'undeveloped yet to life'.

ll. 32–3. The mass Catholic emigration from Ireland to the United States from the 1840s prompted comparisons in America between negroes and the Irish.

ll. 35–6. Sludge refers, it may be, to shares in the Magnetic Telegraph Company established by Samuel Morse in 1845. The advice of Benjamin Franklin (1706–90) would have been sought no doubt because of Franklin's own electrical experiments.

l. 37. *Tom Paine*. Thomas Paine (1737–1809), the English radical, resident in America 1774–87, during which period he played a prominent role in the American Revolution.

l. 47. *A rap or tip!* Table-rapping and table-tilting or tipping were two of the best-known means through which spirits made contact at Victorian séances.

l. 48. The reference is to automatic writing, in which the spirit guides a pen held by the medium.

l. 54. Horace Greely founded the *New York Tribune* in 1841, and remained editor until his death in 1872.

l. 65. *Vs*. Five-dollar bills, an Americanism.

l. 72. 'The smallest worm will turn being trodden on,' *3 Henry VI*, II. ii. 17.

l. 77. *egg-nogg*. A drink usually made in America from rum, cream, sugar, and beaten eggs.

l. 79. *sympathetic sideboards*. Food and drink would be set out on the sideboard.

l. 81. Sludge's ascription of so well worn a cliché to Francis Bacon comically exposes his ignorance.

ll. 87–94. Sludge makes clear in line 155 that the bird to which he compares Horsfall is the peacock.

l. 98. *help*. Domestic servant, an American usage.

l. 112. *trucked*. Exchanged.

l. 117. *cow-hide*. A whip, an Americanism.

l. 122. Books of alchemy.

l. 136. Boswell quotes Johnson, 'It is wonderful that five thousand years have now elapsed since the creation of the world, and still it is undecided whether or not there has ever been an instance of the spirit of any person appearing after death. All argument is against it; but all belief is for it'; in 1716–17 the vicarage of the father of John Wesley was troubled by a ghost that Wesley's sister named Jeffrey. The incident was much discussed.

l. 152. *phenomena*. A word often used to describe supernatural events.

l. 153. *heart of grace*. Courage.

l. 158. 'There are more things in heaven and earth, Horatio, | Than are dreamt of in your philosophy' (*Hamlet*, I. v. 166–7).

l. 168. *Porson*. Richard Porson (1759–1808), regius professor of Greek at Cambridge and the leading classical scholar of the later 18th century. Sludge's mistake is another indication of his ignorance.

l. 218. *the stranger in your gates*. 'thy stranger that is within thy gates', Exodus 20: 10; *guest without the wedding garb*. See Jesus's parable, Matthew 22: 11–13, in which a king punishes a wedding guest who has come to the wedding without 'a wedding garment' by casting him into outer darkness.

l. 221. *doubting Thomas*. The disciple known as Doubting Thomas because he refused to believe in Jesus's resurrection without seeing 'in his hands the print of the nails'. See John 20: 25.

l. 233. *Mexican War*. The war of 1846–7 between Mexico and the United States.

ll. 240–2. The image is of a snowball.

ll. 246–7. *gulling | You to the top of your bent*. Compare *Hamlet*, III. ii. 374: 'They fool me to the top of my bent.'

l. 265. *canvass-backs*. The canvasback is the largest of the American ducks.

l. 269. *dizened*. Dressed.

l. 280. The First Association of Spiritualists of Philadelphia first met in 1852.

l. 284. *illy-oh-yo*. Compare Hamlet's call to Horatio: 'Hillo, ho, ho, boy!', *Hamlet*, I. iv. 119.

l. 286. The Horseshoe or Canadian Falls is the principal waterfall in Niagara Falls.

l. 305. The religious ecstasies sought by religious mystics such as the dervishes and the religious trances of mediums were sometimes explained by 19th-century rationalists as symptoms of epilepsy.

l. 307. *lovers, friends and countrymen*. Compare *Henry V*, IV, Chorus, 34, 'brothers, friends and countrymen'.

ll. 309–12. Francis Bacon, Lord Verulam (naming him Francis Verulam again exposes Sludge's ignorance), was born in London, and died there in 1626.

l. 328. A kibe is a chilblain on the heel. Compare *Hamlet*, V. i. 134–6: 'the age is grown so picked that the toe of the peasant comes so near the heel of the courtier he galls his kibe.'

l. 330. *Barnum*. Phineas Taylor Barnum (1810–91), the American showman best known for his travelling circus.

l. 343. Beethoven did in fact compose thirty-two piano sonatas.

l. 345. The Shakers are a Protestant sect, the members of which emigrated to America in 1774. The best known of the Shaker Hymns, 'Simple Gifts' written by Joseph Brackett in 1848, is in G Major, a key in which F is sharp rather than natural.

l. 346. *'Stars and Stripes'*. Probably 'The Star-Spangled Banner', which, set to consecutive fourths, would be discordant.

l. 353. *gamboge*. A bright yellow gum resin.

l. 361. *puddled*. Muddied.

l. 370. *double-shotted*. A broadside using a double quantity of shot.

l. 387. *cockered*. Pampered.

l. 388. *coddled*. Petted.

l. 393. *kennel*. Gutter.

l. 412. *Flowers we might touch*. At the séance given by Home and attended by the Brownings in Ealing on 23 July 1855, a spirit hand placed a garland on EBB's head.

l. 432. Has decided how you would like the tea (souchong) to taste.

l. 441. *Pipes pierced*. The reference is to the craft of the pipe turner; *chip*. Snap.

l. 453. Longman suggest a reference to Judge John Worth Edmonds, a member of the United States Supreme Court, who in *Spiritualism*, 2 vols., 1853 and 1855, brought his legal skills to an examination of the evidence and pronounced it convincing, and later wrote an introduction to the American edition, 1863, of Home's *Incidents in my Life*. Judge Edmunds became a medium himself and one of his principal spirits was Francis Bacon. See lines 81 and 309–12.

l. 461. *Very like a whale*. *Hamlet*, III. ii. 372 (Polonius is humouring Hamlet).

l. 479. Compare RB on the Ealing séance, at which his hosts, the Rymers, witnessed a manifestation of the hands of their dead child: 'one could no more presume to catch at the hands (for instance) of what they believed the spirit of their child, than one could have committed any other outrage on their feelings.' Quoted in Daniel Karlin, *Browning's Hatreds*, 1993, 49–53.

l. 500. *blacks*. Smuts, flecks of soot.

l. 523. *fall West*. The expression is probably intended as an Americanism.

l. 526. *their Broadway*. Probably the Corso.

l. 528. *lapstone*. A stone that cobblers lay on their laps to beat leather upon.

l. 541. *impassible*. Immune to sentiment.

ll. 559–61. Cat's fur is notorious as a conductor of static electricity.

l. 567. *half-and-halfs*. An American expression for those of mixed race, used for example by James Fenimore Cooper in *The Prairie* (1827).

l. 576. *prairie-dog*. A mistake: RB evidently means a coyote rather than the rodent.

ll. 591–2. Traditionally it was Asaph who set David's Psalms to music, but he would not have known modern musical notation.

l. 595. *pothooks*. Scrawls.

ll. 626–7. The combination of nude women and clothed men is in fact rare in Italian art. The two most famous examples are Giorgione's *Tempesta* and the painting known as the *Fête Champêtre* that RB would also have ascribed to Giorgione.

l. 630. To go for wool and go home shorn is proverbial.

ll. 636–7. Sludge's argument is that if he proves not to be a smoked glass through which the sun can be looked at without damage but a red-hot plate that blinds the eye, the responsibility lies not with him but with the person who chooses to look through him.

l. 643. The goose that laid the golden egg is the subject of one of Aesop's fables.

l. 651. Sludge compares himself with Macbeth presumably because of Macbeth's dealings with the spirit world.

l. 655. *spawl*. Spit; *target*. Shield.

l. 658. *fustian*. Bombastic speech.

l. 659. Like a jester wearing his motley costume of red and yellow.

l. 667. Emanuel Swedenborg (1688–1772), the Swedish religious mystic admired by EBB.

l. 678. Rahab, the prostitute from Jericho who became a Jewish heroine by betraying her country to Joshua in order to safeguard her family. See Joshua 2: 6. Sludge's point is that deeds that seem nefarious might secure a good reputation.

ll. 682–3. Compare Isaiah 6: 6–7, in which the prophet's sin is purged when one of the seraphim lays a live coal on his mouth.

ll. 684–5. Sludge is thinking of works such as Aristotle's treatise on the soul.

l. 688. *fondling*. A term that expresses both affectionate regard and inferiority, like pet.

ll. 691–3. Nelson famously secured his victory in the Battle of Copenhagen by refusing to see the order given him to withdraw, holding his telescope to his blind eye.

ll. 741–5. The reference is to Paul's encounter with 'certain philosophers of the Epicureans and of the Stoicks' in Athens. The Athenians are said to be ever anxious 'to hear some new thing'. Paul stands 'in the midst of Mars' hill' (that is, the Areopagus) to address them, after which 'some mocked' while others 'clave unto him, and believed'. See Acts 17.

l. 772. Umber and bistre are both brown pigments.

l. 775. *fribble*. Trifler.

l. 784. *greenhorn*. Novice (an Americanism); *bully*. Pimp.

l. 788. *Pasiphae*. The wife of King Minos of Greece whose lust for a white bull made her a type of unnatural female desire.

l. 797. *with sugar*. Accepting presumably another 'egg-nogg'.

l. 802. The ink was sympathetic in allowing the name he had written to be read variously.

l. 803. *odic lights.* Carl Reichenbach (1788–1869) had postulated that all living matter emits an odic force, which mediums apprehended or made visible as light emanating from the body, usually the fingers.

ll. 814–33. The beliefs that Sludge holds to be general resemble those of the Swedenborgian church, which was well established in America.

l. 832. *delf.* Earthenware.

l. 840. Compare Genesis 2: 23.

l. 846. In 1 Samuel 28, the Witch of Endor summons the dead Samuel to appear before Saul.

l. 887. Santa Claus was a figure imported to Britain from America, where it was introduced by the Dutch: in Britain gift-giving was associated with New Year rather than with Christmas.

l. 910. *raree-show.* A vulgar exhibition, often a freak show.

ll. 916–19. Compare Genesis 1: 14 in which God says of the stars, 'let them be for signs, and for seasons, and for days, and years.'

l. 921. Charles's Wain is otherwise known as the Plough.

ll. 929–30. James I ascribed his survival of the Gunpowder Plot to miraculous divine intervention rather than to the good offices of an informant.

l. 986. Sludge holds that grace does not come from merit. Compare Isaiah 64: 6: 'all our righteousnesses are as filthy rags.'

l. 1002. *top of toe.* Walking rapidly, a phrase RB also uses in *Aristophanes' Apology*, l. 2395.

ll. 1024–5. Gold-bearing quartz was common in California.

l. 1035. *canthus.* The corner of the eye nearer the nose.

l. 1044. *wiseacre.* A pretender to wisdom (a term more commonly used in America than Britain).

l. 1046. *dew-point.* The temperature at which dew appears, commonly noted in meteorological reports.

l. 1050. *cent. per cent.* A hundred per cent profit.

l. 1052. *brindled.* Streaked.

l. 1056. *kissing goes by favour.* A proverb signifying that reward is not determined by merit.

l. 1065. *break egg-shell.* In fact, the fly emerges from the egg as a larva.

l. 1074. *Great and Terrible Name.* Psalm 99: 3; *Heaven of Heavens.* Biblical, as in Deuteronomy 10: 14: 'Behold the heaven, and the heaven of heavens is the Lord's thy God.'

l. 1077. *Magnum et terribile.* A literal translation of 'Great and Terrible', but as Longman points out the Vulgate has 'terribile, et sanctum'.

l. 1086–8. Referring to the belief that the Hebrew name of God, the Tetragrammaton, the Ineffable or Unutterable Name, may not be spoken.

l. 1098. Compare Exodus 24: 17: 'And the sight of the glory of the Lord was like devouring fire on the top of the mount in the eyes of the children of Israel.'

l. 1110. Sludge's point is that scientific advance in the 19th century owes more to the microscope than the telescope.

l. 1117. *stomach-cyst*. Stomach-sac. Sludge seems to be thinking of a one-celled organism, some of which such as the amoeba and bacterium were first named in the mid-19th century.

ll. 1124–6. Sludge seems to be describing a Victorian electrical experiment, such as the 'Illuminated Vacuum', in which electricity passed through a jar from which the air has been removed produces flashes of light.

ll. 1131–2. Sludge is thinking of the role of lightning in the nitrogen cycle: it returns nitrates to the soil, conserving its fertility.

l. 1140. *Bridgewater Book*. The eight Bridgewater treatises 'On the Power, Wisdom, and Goodness of God, as manifested in the Creation' were published between 1833 and 1840.

ll. 1157–8. Compare Romans 8: 16–17: 'we are the children of God: And if children, then heirs; heirs of God, and joint-heirs with Christ.'

l. 1170. *boblink*. An American songbird, according to Washington Irving, the American lark, the 'happiest bird of our spring', 'The Birds of Spring' (1855).

l. 1180. Possibly a reference to George Washington's Vision at Valley Forge, first reported in 1859, in which he was shown in a vision the three great perils over which the new nation would triumph.

l. 1224. Bach's fugues for the solo violin require virtuoso skills of the soloist.

l. 1225. Time the thrust while fencing (carte is a kind of thrust).

l. 1226. *a five*. As opposed to the commoner and easier figure of eight.

l. 1227. In billiards, potting the red ball or winning hazard on the red, secures the highest score, three points.

l. 1244. *outside the veil*. Compare Tennyson, *In Memoriam*, LVI. 27–8: 'What hope of answer, or redress? | Behind the veil, behind the veil.'

l. 1247. cranes are celebrated for their courtship dances.

l. 1268. Jenny Lind (1820–87), known as the Swedish Nightingale, toured America 1850–2.

l. 1269. *Emerson*. Ralph Waldo Emerson (1803–82), who in the 1850s became enormously successful as a lecturer. Several series were offered in Boston; *the Benicia Boy*. John C. Heenan (1834–73), a bare-knuckle prize fighter, best known for his contest with the British champion, Tom Sayers, in Hampshire in 1860 that ended in a draw.

ll. 1281–2. *enough | To make an apostle swear*. A variant of the American proverb 'Enough to make an angel swear.'

l. 1299. *Beacon Street*. An important thoroughfare in Boston, laid out in 1850–1.

ll. 1305–6. Compare Galatians 5: 9: 'A little leaven leaveneth the whole lump', where the sense is that to commit a single error may corrupt the whole person.

l. 1307. *chalk egg*. The 'nest egg' introduced to encourage the hen to lay.

ll. 1330–7. 'The most disgraceful of the Babylonian customs is this: every native woman must, once in her life, sit down in the holy precinct of Venus, and have communication with some stranger . . . After surrendering her person, the goddess being satisfied, she returns home, and from that time however great a sum you may give her, you will not obtain her favours,' Herodotus, trans. P. E. Laurent, 1837.

l. 1381. *cresset.* Torch.

l. 1392. *harlequin's pasteboard sceptre.* The magic wand, in fact a slapstick, with which Harlequin is equipped in pantomime.

ll. 1439–41. Sludge invokes three of the most celebrated American men of letters, the poets James Russell Lowell (1819–91) and Henry Wadsworth Longfellow (1807–82), and Nathaniel Hawthorne (1804–64), the novelist.

l. 1450. *Lizard Age.* The age of the dinosaurs.

l. 1451. *Old Country War.* Presumably the War of Independence.

l. 1452. *Jerome Bonaparte.* Possibly the brother of Napoleon, but more likely his son by his American wife, or even his grandson, both of whom served in the American army.

l. 1457. Theseus marked his way through the Cretan labyrinth by unwinding a thread.

l. 1466. *"Bliss in the Golden City".* An imaginary title, but perhaps recalling Shelley's *Laon and Cythna; or the Revolution of the Golden City.*

l. 1478. *cock-tail.* At this time a distinctively American name for a spirit-based drink.

l. 1479. *arnica.* A plant that yields an anti-inflammatory used to treat bruises.

l. 1493. *V-notes.* See note to l. 65.

l. 1494. *Greely.* See note to l. 54.

l. 1511. *cuss.* An Americanism, a term applied to a person held in contempt.

l. 1523. *herring-pond.* A jocular term for the North Atlantic Ocean that divides Britain from America.

FROM *HELEN'S TOWER, CLANDEBOYE* (1870)

Helen's Tower

A Petrarchan sonnet written for inclusion in the second issue in 1870 of the Marquis of Dufferin's pamphlet, *Helen's Tower, Clandeboye*, in which he explains that the tower is dedicated to his mother, Lady Dufferin, and encloses, inscribed on a golden tablet, the poem she had written for her son on his coming of age. The first issue of the pamphlet had included a commendatory poem by Tennyson, also called 'Helen's Tower'. RB's own poem, it may be, was written in a spirit of competition. Lady Dufferin, who had died in 1867, had been famously beautiful, one of the three granddaughters of Richard Brinsley Sheridan who were known collectively as the Three Graces. The sonnet represents her as the antithesis of the still more famously beautiful

Helen of Troy, the maternal love of the one contrasting with the adulterous love of the other, the tower of the one Helen still standing, the tower on which the other stood having long disappeared into the Trojan plain. RB's poem was subsequently published with very minor changes in the *Pall Mall Gazette*, 28 December 1883.

'Ελενη επι πυργω. *Iliad*, 3. 154, 'Helen on the tower'.

l. 2. *Scœan Gate*. More commonly, and in the *Pall Mall Gazette*, the Scaean gate, the gate in the walls of Troy to which Helen repairs in Book 3 of the *Iliad*, when she feels a longing to see her countrymen who are besieging the city.

l. 3. *unanimous*. Of one mind.

l. 11. Possibly recalling the fate of the statue in Shelley's 'Ozymandias': 'Round the decay | Of that colossal wreck, boundless and bare | The lone and level sands stretch far away' (12–14).

l. 12. *Love's rock-built tower*. Compare Jesus choosing Peter as the rock upon which he will build his church, Matthew 16: 18.

l. 13. Compare 1 Chronicles 16: 30: 'Fear before him, all the earth: the world also shall be stable, that it be not moved,' and Job 38: 4, 'Where wast thou when I laid the foundations of the earth?'

l. 14. Compare Job 38: 7: 'When the morning stars sang together, and all the sons of God shouted for joy.'

FROM *FIFINE AT THE FAIR* (1872)

Prologue: Amphibian

The poem was published in 1872 as the Prologue to *Fifine at the Fair*. It has its origin in the death of EBB and in the enthusiasm for swimming that RB developed in the long holidays in Brittany that he took in the 1860s. The poem accommodates both the desire to fly that swimming half assuages, and the recalcitrant fear that persuades the swimmer not to venture out of sight of land. Poetry, as well as the swimmer, is represented as amphibian, poised as it is between heaven and earth, between the life of the soul and the life of the body.

l. 16. *Like soul*. In Greek the same word, psyche, signifies butterfly and soul.

l. 23. *it*. The butterfly.

l. 28. *clay*. The designation of flesh as clay is biblical, as, for example, Job 10: 9: 'thou hast made me as the clay.'

ll. 31–2. That is, when the butterfly was a caterpillar.

l. 53. Compare Coleridge, 'The Picture, or the Lover's Resolution', 118–19: 'emancipate | From passion's dreams'.

Epilogue: The Householder

Like 'Amphibian' this is a lyric of widowhood, in which RB represents himself as the tenant of a house that is at once 19 Warwick Crescent, the house that was RB's London base for twenty-five years, and the tenement of clay that RB's spirit continues to inhabit. The poem is at once revealing and protective of RB's privacy. RB shelters within the well-used clichés in which so much of the poem is written much in the way that he sheltered within the 'embrowned' bricks of the house on Warwick Crescent. It was evidently paranoid of D. G. Rossetti to find in the two lyrics, and in the poem that they introduced and concluded, a mordant commentary on his own relationship with Elizabeth Siddal, but it may have been that RB's interest in the relationship between lovers separated by death was stimulated by Rossetti's treatment of the theme in poems such as 'The Blessed Damozel' and paintings such as *Beata Beatrix* and most pertinently the earliest versions of *The House of Life*.

l. 4. *blaspheming like a Turk*. To swear like a Turk is proverbial in English and in Italian, 'bestemmiare come un Turco'.

ll. 21–2. Possibly a recollection of offers by spiritualists to make contact with the dead EBB.

l. 25. *reunited to his wife*. A common form in notices of deaths in newspapers.

l. 27. *M., or N.* In the marriage service as laid out in the Book of Common Prayer, 'M.' stands for the name of the groom, and 'N.' for the bride.

ll. 30–1. Fragments of a homely epitaph commonly found in British churchyards. One version is as follows:

Afflictions sore, long time we bore
Physicians were in vain
Till God did please to give us ease
And free us of our pain.

THE INN ALBUM (1875)

The Inn Album

In the early 1870s RB busied himself with his Euripidean poems *Balaustion's Adventure* (1871) and *Aristophanes' Apology* (1875), and, in stark contrast to them, a series of poems that emphatically take up EBB's challenge that poets should address 'their age, not Charlemagne's', *Aurora Leigh*, 1857, Book 5, 203. Of the four major modern poems, *Prince Hohenstiel-Schwangau* (1871), *Fifine at the Fair* (1872), *Red Cotton Night-Cap Country* (1873), and *The Inn Album* (1875), we print the last and most uncompromisingly modern of all. As RB wrote on 22 April 1875, to his publisher, George Smith, it is a poem 'on so very modern a subject that it concerns last Whitsuntide' (quoted in Walter Kendrick, '*The Inn Album*, Browning's Marginal Poem', *Browning Institute Studies*, 11 (1983), 113–25). *The Inn Album* demands a literary reader but a reader who is just as conversant with the newspapers, who knows what horse won the Derby in 1875, that Psidium is the fragrance of the season, and that the recent fashion for roller-skating has made 'rink' one of the words of the year. The unfinished verses in the Inn Album that punctuate the poem, functioning as an ironic chorus, 'Hail, calm acclivity, salubrious spot,' mock amateur verse-making but carry also, perhaps, a suggestion that the verse produced by most of RB's contemporaries is a variety of pastoral that evades rather than engages with the social world to which it is addressed. *The Inn Album* is made from material that one might more readily expect to find in a novel than a poem, but, RB suggests, a novel that was far more likely to have been written in France than England. The bizarre parody of novel language that RB inserts into the poem (1. 310–25) seems intended to indicate through its archaic fustian that the English novel of the period, for all its claims, is as unwilling to engage with the contemporary world as poetry. Just a few months after the publication of the poem F. J. Furnivall revealed in *Notes and Queries* (25 March 1876, 244–5) that RB's plot, like that of *Red Cotton Night-Cap Country*, was founded on a true story, one that had 'made a great sensation in London, over thirty years ago'. The 'original story', 'too repulsive to be reproduced in all its details', had 'the gambling lord producing the portrait of the lady he had seduced and abandoned, and offering his expected dupe, but real beater, an introduction to the lady, as a bribe to induce him to wait for payment of the money he had won; secondly, the eager acceptance of the bribe by the young gambler, and the suicide of the lady from horror at the base proposal of her old seducer.' Furnivall does not name the lord in question but RB's reference to the card cheat known as *sauter la coupe* confirms the opinion of commentators that he has in mind Lord Henry de Ros (1793–1839), who in 1837 was involved in a notorious court case when he brought suit against those who had accused him of cheating in this manner. But RB is less concerned to drag up an old scandal than to use it as a means of representing England in the 1870s. It is a tawdry, venial world from which the reader is invited to flinch (like its two predecessors, *Fifine at the Fair* and *Red Cotton Night-Cap Country,* the poem is infected by the sexual disgust that seems to have been precipitated in RB by the unfortunate and mysterious crisis in his relationship with Lady Ashburton). The disgust extends from sexual to social relations. The older man, brother to a duke, asserts his social superiority over the younger man, son of a father who wears a 'warehouse-apron' (1. 242), but it is a superiority that no longer has any basis. The Tichborne Claimant is the representative figure of the age, Arthur Orton, a butcher's son from Wapping, sentenced to fourteen years' imprisonment in 1874 for his false claim to be the long-lost heir to the Tichborne baronetcy (RB refers to the case in 2. 344–6). His claim was supported by the heir's mother, and by so large a proportion of the electorate that in 1875 his defence lawyer was triumphantly elected to Parliament. The point is that there was no longer any clear means of distinguishing between the son of a baronet and the son of a butcher. The social disorganization is only the sign of a more fatal moral dislocation. RB agrees with Shelley that the 'devil is a gentleman'. The older man, brother to a duke, is 'the Adversary', but even he seems capable, if unavailingly, of love. The young man is rewarded at the end of the poem with a bride, but only after he has committed a murder, and the older woman who acts as fairy godmother to him is a woman who has been seduced, has given herself in marriage to a clergyman for whom she feels only contempt, and at the last poisons herself. In this poem written when RB was in his sixties, he is still conducting restless generic experiments. The poem is, like most of his poems, dramatic: the speeches of its four unnamed characters are punctuated by laconic third-person interruptions, and regularly disregard the limits that even the most tolerant audience would set to the speeches of characters on stage. RB compares his poem with a sensation novel, with a tragedy (it does after all end in a murder and suicide), with a comedy (it also ends in a marriage), with an opera (in its closing lines it invokes *Lohengrin* and *La clemenza di Tito*), and to a Shakespearian problem play. 'All's well that ends well!' says the older man (4. 544) in a poem that concludes with a marriage that makes the match between Bertram and Helena seem innocently idealistic. The poem represents a world so fractured that no single genre can contain it. RB announced it to George Smith as a tragedy, but a 'tragedy in a new style'. In the final lines even chronology crumples. The younger woman speaks, 'half song though meant for speech' (8. 31), as she prepares to enter a room occupied by the young man and two corpses, and spoken or sung too in the immediate aftermath of the young man's acquittal on a charge of murder. Furnivall described *The Inn Album* as 'the most profoundly touching and most powerful poem of modern times'. It may be an eccentric judgement, but it is not a judgement that can be dismissed out of hand.

It is certainly a poem that RB worried over: most of the manuscript RB prepared for the printer (Balliol College, Oxford, Archives, Browning Collection, MS 388) is reasonably clean but some revisions in the MS indicate problems at the end of section VII with the murder of the older man and to a lesser extent with the ending of the whole poem. RB also significantly decided to alter, between the printer's MS and the printed text, the length of time that the young man has been under the tutelage of the older man from two years in the MS to one year and, even more tellingly, the length of time since both men have seen the older woman from four years to two.

l. 9. *cipher-work*. Sums, here financial calculations.

l. 11. *acclivity*. Ascending slope.

l. 12. *we burn daylight*. We waste candles by burning them when it is light. Compare Mercutio in *Romeo and Juliet*, I. iv. 43: 'Come, we burn daylight.'

ll. 17–18. An ironic self-reference that reviewers failed to heed. The *Saturday Review* concluded its review of the poem by observing that RB's 'works will live, not in any way by reason of the gnarled form which snatches rather than attracts attention, but by the strong imagination and thought which overcome their uncouth clothing' (4 December 1875, xl. 717).

l. 23. Écarte, Blind Hookey, and Cutting-the-Pack are card games, all generally played for stakes, of an ascending order of simplicity, a sequence suggesting that the interest comes to focus on the gamble rather than the game.

l. 31. *coign of vantage*. A situation affording a pleasant view, from *Macbeth*, I. vi. 7.

ll. 35–7. The references are to Landseer's *The Monarch of the Glen* (1851), and his *A Distinguished Member of the Humane Society* (1831), a portrait of a Newfoundland dog reputed to have saved from drowning twenty-three people in fourteen years; Millais's *A Huguenot, on St Bartholomew's Day, Refusing to Shield Himself from Danger by Wearing the Roman Catholic Badge* (1852), in which a young Catholic woman is unable to persuade her lover to adopt the disguise that would save his life; and Holman Hunt's *The Light of the World* (1853), a portrait of Christ in which he supports the description offered of him in the poem's title by carrying a lantern. All four paintings were extremely popular, engravings of them were very widely distributed, and all would by 1875 have been regarded with amusement by those who prided themselves on the sophistication of their taste.

l. 39. *Salmo ferox*. A Victorian designation for an unusually large brown trout: the specimen is stuffed and displayed in a glass case.

l. 72. John Guillim's *Display of Heraldrie* (1610) is the first comprehensive work on the topic.

l. 77. Jean-Baptiste-Camille Corot (1796–1875), whose landscapes in which topography is subordinated to mood would have seemed by 1875 modern in comparison with the work of Landseer, Millais, and Holman Hunt. Corot's death in February 1875 focused attention on his work. The *Athenaeum* for 27 February 1875 praised his originality, and noted that his work had become celebrated only within the last fifteen years (p. 297).

l. 79. *handsweep*. A RB coinage probably referring to broad brushstrokes in contrast to the brushstrokes favoured by the Pre-Raphaelites in the 1850s.

l. 108. *Colenso*. John William Colenso, Bishop of Natal (1814–83). The reference is not to his controversial theological writings but to his popular textbook *Arithmetic*, first published in 1843.

l. 111. *what's the damage?* A colloquial expression meaning, 'what do I owe you?'

l. 120. *Apollinaris*. Apollinaris Natural Mineral Water, imported from Germany and widely advertised in *The Times* in 1874–5 for its purity and efficacy in the treatment of conditions such as gout.

l. 127. *fool's fortune*. Alluding to the proverb, a fool and his money are soon parted.

ll. 132–7. The repeated references to the figure five refer to écarte, in which five points wins the game.

l. 139. *Simpkin*. Or Simkin, a generic name for a simpleton.

l. 143. *snob*. Vulgarian.

ll. 157–60. The young man plays on lines from Scott's *Marmion* already proverbial: 'Oh what a tangled web we weave | When first we practise to deceive.'

l. 163. In 1875 the Paris Opera moved to its new home at the Palais Garnier, a theatre 'the most perfect specimen of its kind that exists', *All the Year Round*, 28 November 1874, p. 150.

l. 164. *the Salon*. The biannual exhibition of the Académie des Beaux-Arts at the Louvre.

l. 165. Chantilly, 50 kilometres north of the city, established itself as the race-track for Paris in the 1830s.

l. 189. *crow-nest*. The crow's nest is the look-out position at the top of a mast, hence the phrase refers to the views that the inn affords.

l. 194. *Pisgah- view*. Pisgah is the mountain from which Moses glimpsed the Promised Land.

l. 206. *runs to earth*. Disappears like a hunted fox into its earth or burrow.

l. 210. *pass-book*. An account book issued by the bank that records the sum a depositor is in credit.

l. 217. *firework-nosegay!* Conflating the firework display that ends a celebration with the bouquet given to a performer at the end of a performance.

l. 227. He is remembering a duel.

ll. 234–5. *chaff* | *Covers the corn*. Husks cover the grain, but accommodating the sense in which chaff refers to raillery.

l. 240. *doit*. The type of a coin of little value.

l. 242. Acknowledging that the young man's father gained his wealth from trade.

l. 272. *sort*. Lot or fortune.

l. 282. Possibly recalling Coleridge's rook 'vanishing in light', 'This Lime-Tree Bower my Prison', 71.

ll. 283–4. Recalling Aesop's fable in which a jackdaw attempts to pass as a peacock by putting on some peacock feathers only to be rejected by both the peacocks that he aspired to join and the jackdaws that he had scorned.

l. 302. In 1871 Ruskin formed the organization that was to become the Guild of St George, the aims of which were to be financed by the donations of the wealthy.

l. 305. *Timon*. In Shakespeare's *Timon of Athens* Timon becomes a misanthrope when his generosity is met with ingratitude.

ll. 310–25. The archaic forms identify the passage as parodying literary English.

l. 318. *Rothschild*. The name of the banking family functioned in the 19th century as the type of a phenomenally wealthy individual.

l. 321. Presumably the father called himself a commission-agent to distance his connection with manufacture, the shame of which is one factor that drives his son abroad.

l. 325. *one more asteroid*. The *Annual of Scientific Discovery for 1871* (p. 315) records the award to Professor J. Watson of an astronomy prize for the discovery of eight asteroids in one year.

l. 327. *Alfred's*. A London club with premises in Albemarle Street, which merged with the Oriental Club in 1854: Istria is the peninsula to the north-west of the Dalmatian coast.

l. 333. *Polo*. A game imported from India: the first polo club in Britain was founded in 1872; *Tent-pegging*. A cavalry exercise originating in India in which a cantering horseman spears with his lance the metal ring on a tent peg pressed into the turf: *Once a Week* for 26 June 1875 notes that most of the spectators that gathered at Hurlingham Park had gathered to see 'the novel tent-pegging' (2: 43, p. 213); the Hurlingham Club was founded in 1867 and polo was introduced in 1874; an article in *London Society* for July 1875 reports that within the past year 'rink' has become 'almost a household word' and that 'rinks and roller-skating have become quite a new British institution' (28: 163: p. 24).

ll. 348–9. That is, the deposit of the ten thousand pounds will be recorded in his pass-book.

l. 353. *Galopin*. In his career of two seasons Galopin won eight of his nine races including the 1875 Derby, his final race; Thomas Gainsborough (1727–88), who was by 1875 as celebrated a landscape painter as he was a portraitist.

l. 359. *phoenix*. The mythological bird figures in an extended sense a person of unique excellence.

ll. 362–3. The Book of Common Prayer stipulates that at the end of a reading from the Bible the reader may say, 'Here endeth the lesson'.

l. 379. *kennel flush*. Gutter full to overflowing.

l. 388. Edmund Yates founded *The World: A Journal for Men and Women* in 1874: it was a society magazine notorious for the circulation of scandalous gossip.

l. 393. *Coreggio's long-lost Leda*. When Correggio's *Leda and the Swan* was in the collection of the Duke of Orleans, the Duke's son, unnerved by Leda's sensuality, ordered it to be cut up, but the painting was in fact restored and sold to Frederick the Great of Prussia.

l. 395. *I . . . aristocrat*. I polished a vulgar man until he could be taken for an aristocrat.

l. 397. *court-vesture*. The court dress, archaic and made from velvet, that was worn by those officially presented to the monarch at court.

ll. 397–8. An elaboration of the proverb 'you can't make a silk purse of a sow's ear'.

l. 413. *scotch-pebble*. A semi-precious stone such as agate.

l. 418. *brilliant*. A diamond of the finest.

l. 439. *coupons*. Certificates attached to a bond that are detached and presented successively as interest payments become due to the holder.

l. 443. *wind-egg*. An egg with a soft shell that is unlikely to hatch.

II.

l. 13. RB acknowledged the grammatical error when it was pointed out by a reviewer.

l. 28. *strychnine*. A metonym for suicide.

l. 29. *Unlimited Loo*. A variation of the card game loo, in which, because the stakes are variable, large sums may be won or lost quickly.

l. 37. Gladstone, Carlyle, and Tennyson, who had been Poet Laureate since 1850, represent statesmanship, philosophy, and art. Gladstone was Prime Minister 1868–74, when he called a general election and was unexpectedly defeated by Disraeli; in 1875 Carlyle was honoured by the presentation of a medal accompanied by a testimonial letter signed by 119 distinguished Victorian intellectuals.

l. 46. *pearl*. Inlaid with mother-of-pearl.

l. 61. *Rule Britannia*. A rousing patriotic song: the words by James Thomson were set to music by Thomas Arne in 1740.

l. 72. The player would probably have been taught not to play black keys with the thumb, but doing so makes certain chords and passages a good deal easier.

l. 73. *fatality*. Decree of fate.

l. 75. The sharp is a black key.

l. 81. *Dizzy*. Benjamin Disraeli (1804–81), in 1875 the Prime Minister, and for RB the type of the political opportunist.

ll. 85–6. The young man is recalling the French saying 'cherchez la femme', popularized by Alexandre Dumas in *Les Mohicans de Paris* (1854) and suggesting that women are behind otherwise inexplicable behaviour.

l. 93–4. That is, teach me by rapping me over the knuckles.

l. 103. *'Twixt you, me and the gate-post*. Proverbial.

l. 161. *the wood of life*. The figure, as in lines 116–36, may owe something to Dante's representation of the pilgrimage of life as a journey through a dark wood at the opening of the *Inferno*.

l. 169. *Ess or Psidium*. Perfumes. A paper on perfumes in *All the Year Round* notes 'the luxurious lusciousness of the Ess bouquet' (9. 229, 19 April 1873, 538); Psidium, a perfume extracted from pomegranate flowers, is described in an advertisement in the *Saturday Review*, 39.1008, 20 February 1875, as 'The Fashion for the Season of 1875'.

l. 203. *Leporello-list*. Refers to the aria 'Madamina il catologo e questa' in Mozart's *Don Giovanni* in which Leporello lists the conquests made by his master.

l. 225. *the world would grow one eye*. Compare ‘A Face’, 21–2: ‘All heaven, meanwhile, condensed into one eye | Which fears to lose the wonder, should it wink.’

l. 230. *with ‘a head reposed’*. Translates the French phrase *avec tête reposée*, meaning with a clear head.

l. 238. *Long Vacation*. The summer vacation for students at Oxford or Cambridge.

l. 251. field-flower-foolishness, possibly a blasphemous reference to ‘the lilies of the field’ (Matthew 6: 28), who take no thought for their life.

l. 265. *conjurers*. Street magicians, tricksters.

l. 309. *packthread’s pith*. Strength of the twine used for tying parcels or bundles.

l. 310. *thaw*. Loosen.

l. 321. *intermediate*. Adolescent.

ll. 325–6. Playing on the proverbial expression ‘a storm in a teacup’.

l. 340. *Magdalen*. Fallen woman, after Mary Magdalen.

l. 341. *evangelically*. Both in the manner of evangelical Christians, and in the manner exemplified in the Gospels, as in John 8: 1–11, in which Jesus refuses to condemn the woman taken in adultery.

l. 342. In ‘Epistle to a Lady’, 12, Pope refers to ‘Magdalen’s loose hair and lifted eye’.

l. 345. *Finsbury*. A London borough which became a parliamentary constituency after the 1832 reform bill, electing two members. The young man’s suggestion is ironic because the Finsbury electorate was famously radical. Arthur Orton was the Tichbourne Claimant, whose defence lawyer, Edward Kenealy, was elected MP for Stoke in 1875 on a wave of radical support, radicals believing that Orton’s imprisonment for perjury revealed that the system of justice served only the interests of the rich. For the Tichbourne Claimant see the headnote.

ll. 369–70. *cock-and-bull | Adventure*. Idle, desultory story.

l. 373. *the swart sign*. The black smoke that signifies that the older man has missed the train.

ll. 429–30. In chapter 47, Sancho Panza remarks, ‘being a man I may come to be pope, not to say governor of an island’.

l. 440. *maiden-speech*. The first speech given by an MP after his election to the House of Commons.

l. 446. *Commemoration-week*. The week after teaching ends in the summer term when Oxford colleges hold balls, and students give parties. An attempt by the university in 1875 to moderate the festivities was ineffective. See *The Examiner*, 12 June 1875, 658–9.

l. 477. Cherub and seraph are paired by Milton, as in *Paradise Lost*, I. 324.

l. 484. *Apollo Ball*. The annual ball given in Commemoration Week by the Apollo University Lodge (the university’s own Masonic lodge). The ball in 1863 was attended by the Prince and Princess of Wales.

l. 485. *wine and oil.* The Good Samaritan pours 'oil and wine' into the wounds of the man who fell among thieves, Luke 10: 34.

l. 495. Translating the French expression *succès avec le sexe.*

l. 559. *Badger-like.* Badgers are commonly unearthed using dogs, traditionally dachshunds.

l. 584. *Flaunt the blazon.* The older man relies on his aristocratic lineage to intimidate as the younger man should have relied on his physique.

l. 593. By probing the wound the older man has shown that the younger retains his sensitiveness.

l. 599. *the spur.* Spurs are attached to fighting cocks.

ll. 604–5. A reference to a fable attributed to Aesop: a cock scratches up a jewel in a dungheap and laments that he would rather have discovered a grain of corn.

III.

l. 7. *Barry.* Either Edward Middleton Barry (1830–80) or his father Sir Charles Barry (1795–1860), both celebrated architects who worked in association until the father's death.

l. 19. *forewent him.* Passed him by.

l. 46. A jocular reference to the widely reported Arctic Expedition led by Captain George Nares that sailed from Portsmouth on 29 May 1875.

l. 115. *changeling.* The child left in exchange by fairies for the child taken.

l. 130. *'drop' the elm-tree.* Drop the question, propose, the elm-tree representing marriage.

l. 153. *cat beneath the counterpane.* An expression that seems to be modelled on 'pig in a poke'.

l. 159. *rough-smooth.* Compare 'Pisgah-Sights', 23–4, 'Rough-smooth let globe be, | Mixed—man's existence.'

ll. 161–2. *'Ach, mein Gott! | Sagen Sie "easy"?'* 'Oh, my God, do you say it's easy?'

l. 163. *mit.* With.

l. 164. *Raff.* Joachim Raff (1822–82), according to *The Athenaeum*, the 'most prolific composer in Germany': four of his symphonies were performed in London in 1875. See *The Athenaeum*, 21 November 1874, 685, and 13 November 1875, 647–8.

l. 165. *Czerny.* Carl Czerny (1791–1857), who wrote a number of popular text books used by piano teachers.

ll. 166–7. Presumably she asks whether she should prepare herself by reading Trollope's novels of love and marriage before venturing on the real thing.

l. 231. *dispenses.* Exempts.

l. 256. *ferny feet.* Compare Tennyson, 'The Talking Oak' (1842), 29, which has the tree 'hidden to the knees in fern'.

l. 281. See note to l. 256.

l. 283. The expression, 'time and tide wait for no man', is proverbial.

IV.

l. 12. *toils*. Nets.

l. 20. *black-blooded*. An epithet used three times in Act III, scene i of Tennyson's *Queen Mary*, published June 1875.

l. 24. *silly-sooth*. Simple truth, as in *Twelfth Night*, II. iv. 45.

l. 45. *snuffs*. Compare Sin sensing the success of Satan's plot against Adam and Eve: 'So saying, with delight he snuffed the smell | Of mortal change on earth', *Paradise Lost*, X. 272–3.

l. 47. *perdue*. Hidden.

l. 77. *Babies*. Pupils, from the miniaturized image of the onlooker reflected in the pupils. To 'look babies' is to look into each other's eyes.

ll. 98–9. *some fine fifth act | Of tragedy*. That is, that the 'play' should end with her suicide.

l. 110. *fulsome*. Plump.

ll. 114–15. He recalls how he had foolishly stood against his brother the Duke's candidate, in a parliamentary election for a constituency controlled by the Duke's interest.

l. 144. *flamboyant*. Used in the French sense, flaming.

l. 160. *in petto*. Secretly or privately.

l. 170. Australia was a refuge for debtors, most famously for Mr Micawber in Dickens's *David Copperfield*.

l. 195. *That self-display made absolute*. When he had decisively revealed himself as the wickedest of men.

l. 228. See Ephesians 2: 2: 'in time past ye walked according to the course of this world, according to the prince of the power of the air.'

l. 230. *true Lord Byron!* He accuses the woman of being melodramatic, inflating her sentiments in the manner of Byron.

l. 236. Mockingly comparing the parson to St Peter. See Matthew 16: 18: 'thou art Peter, and upon this rock I will build my church.'

l. 237. *bloodstone*. A type of chalcedony, but playing on the proverb that one cannot get blood from a stone.

ll. 237–8. The Evangelicals and Ritualists are at either wing of the Church of England, the Ritualists often favouring as Anglo-Catholics the celibacy of the clergy.

l. 257. The cleric is compared to a mill horse or donkey that powers the mill wheel by unceasingly circling it.

ll. 261–2. Perhaps an allusion to Chaucer's *Merchant's Tale*, which describes the marriage between the aged January and his young bride, May.

ll. 277–8. Another reference to the fable of the cock and the jewel (see 2. 604–5) in which the cleric figures as the cock.

l. 283. A reference to the servant who wasted his talent by burying it in the ground instead of using it and is cast into outer darkness. See Matthew 25: 25–30.

ll. 287–8. See note to III. l. 46.

l. 301. *earth sown with salt.* Compare Judges 9: 45, in which Abimelech 'beat down the city, and sowed it with salt', a ritual curse, but commonly understood as a means of rendering the land infertile.

l. 311. *root of bitterness.* See Hebrews 12: 15.

ll. 316–17. A reference to the 'bistre method' of underpainting, in which the design is painted onto the canvas in bistre, a transparent brown pigment, which is then painted over.

l. 359. The husband is the spiritual equivalent of a Brownite (follower of John Brown) in medicine, believing that all ailments may be treated either by the application of a stimulant or a depressant.

l. 361. *drenched.* Dosed.

l. 362. *dub.* Pound.

l. 405. *eye-cast.* Glance.

l. 414. Dickens's Christianity is of a Broad Church rather than a dogmatic character, but the reference is also to novel-reading, which the husband would now condemn.

l. 415. *Bach and Brahms.* An indication of the woman's (and RB's) advanced tastes. The *Musical Times* for 1 June 1874, 507, notes, 'Only a few years ago the number of admirers in this country of Johann Sebastian Bach was but small', and *The Athenaeum* for 27 February 1875, 300, remarks of Brahms that it is 'only within the last three years that his productions have been gaining ground here'.

ll. 428–9. *house* | *Of bondage.* Exodus 20: 2.

l. 471. *Potter's Field.* Bought with Judas's thirty pieces of silver. See Matthew 27: 10.

l. 483. *Obeah-man.* Witch doctor.

l. 487. *Fetish.* An inanimate object worshipped by primitive people who believe it to have magical powers.

l. 493. *pasteboard.* The material from which stage scenery is made, hence theatrical rather than real.

l. 523. *faith moves mountains.* See Matthew 17: 20.

l. 544. In Shakespeare's play Bertram and Helena resolve their differences despite Bertram's treachery, but the ending is full of conditionals.

l. 560. *bubble scheme.* A deceptive or fraudulent financial scheme, after the South Sea Bubble.

l. 577. *strike work.* Refuse to work.

l. 590. *his shrine.* The object of his veneration.

l. 608. *Quicken me!* Bring me to life!

ll. 633–4. He continues to treasure the memory of how her beauty blossomed, like a lily bursting from its green bud or glove, in response to him.

ll. 669–71. Compare 1 Peter 5: 8: 'your adversary the devil, as a roaring lion, walketh about, seeking whom he may devour,' and *Paradise Lost*, II. 629–39, 'the adversary of God and man, | Satan'.

l. 686. *Bismarck*. Otto von Bismarck (1815–98), Chancellor of Prussia, known as the 'Iron Chancellor' because of his intransigence in diplomacy.

V.

l. 14. *palsy-fixed*. Paralysed.

ll. 23–4. A baggage is also a strumpet.

l. 38. *tip-top swells*. Current slang for people of the most elevated social position.

l. 51. The appearances of the celebrated Italian actor Tommaso Salvini on the London stage in 1875 produced what *The Academy* described on 8 May, 491, as 'Salvini fever'. Othello was one of his roles.

l. 60. Translating the apothegm 'ars est celare artem'.

ll. 89–90. Contrasting the young man, pure at heart, with the older man, whose heart within his polished exterior is like a spider enclosed in amber.

l. 136. *rag-and-feather*. In *The Ring and the Book*, IV. 1287, 'rag-and-feather trim' refers to theatrical costume.

ll. 157–8. In Genesis 3: 15 God says to the serpent, 'I will put enmity between thee and the woman, and between thy seed and her seed; it shall bruise thy head, and thou shalt bruise his heel.'

l. 274. *sauter la coupe*. Translated in a court report of Lord de Ros's suit, in *The Times* for 14 February 1837, 5, as 'changing the turn-up card', but the statements of witnesses reported in the account of the trial on 11 February suggest that the trick consisted in dealing to the dealer's advantage a card exposed by the cut and placed at the bottom of the deck. In *The Times* for 14 February Sir William Ingilby is reported to have testified that he had seen the trick performed by Lord de Ros 'fifty or a hundred times'. The punning on the word 'cut' in lines 275–6 refers to the cheat.

ll. 278–9. As Ohio notes, there were rumours concerning the defeat of Macgregor, who started the race as an overwhelming favourite at 9–4 on, in the 1870 Derby. A historian of the race recollects that 'all sorts of ugly stories were circulated regarding the untoward event', that 'no true reason' for Macgregor's defeat had ever been arrived at, and that 'many suppositions, some of them ugly enough, have from time to time been made' (Louis Henry Curzon, *The Blue Ribbon of the Turf*, 1890, 346–7).

l. 308. *post*. Shame by publishing a statement of an individual's dishonourable conduct, most often a refusal to accept a challenge to a duel.

l. 316. *wheal*. Variant spelling of weal.

l. 318. *scorpion-scourge!* See 1 Kings 12: 11 and 2 Chronicles 10: 14: 'my father hath chastised you with whips, but I will chastise you with scorpions.'

l. 329. *launch*. Rush.

l. 335. *ready rhymer.* As in the rhyming riddles with which he entertains Desdemona in *Othello*, II. i.

l. 337. *boltsprit.* Bowsprit.

VI.

l. 3. See note to IV, ll. 669–71.

l. 21. *kennel.* Gutter.

l. 31. *phyz.* Jocular abbreviation of physiognomy.

l. 32. *couched it.* Removed the cataract from it.

l. 61. Byron's Childe Harold takes his wounded heart into exile, as did the young man when he exiled himself to Dalmatia.

l. 110. Anglo-Catholics were 'clean-shaven, whereas Protestants favoured side-whiskers or beards without moustaches'. *Encyclopaedia of Protestantism*, ed. H. J. Hillerbrand, i. 118.

l. 111. The placing of six candles on the altar commonly denoted a clergyman's High Church principles.

l. 114. Referring to the fable by Aesop in which the ass claims to relish a thistle as much as he would the fine provisions he is carrying for others to dine on.

l. 134. *Roman punch.* Punch served semi-frozen.

l. 137. *spooniness.* Sentimental infatuation.

l. 147. *catastrophe.* The turn that leads to the conclusion of a play.

l. 173. *hulls.* Wrappings.

l. 205. Hercules' eleventh labour is to secure the golden apples guarded by the Hesperides.

l. 212. *Consols.* Consolidated Annuities, government bonds.

VII.

ll. 13–17. See Exodus 7: 9–12, in which Aaron casts his rod before Pharaoh and it becomes a serpent which swallows up the rods cast by the Egyptian sorcerers.

l. 19. *The Adversary!* See note to IV, ll. 669–71.

l. 43. *chapman.* Merchant.

l. 51. Merton College had a celebrated lime-tree avenue in the 19th century that no longer survives.

l. 63. 1 Corinthians 8: 5.

l. 65. *burned.* Fired in the kiln.

ll. 96–7. As Satan in the form of a toad seeks to corrupt the dreams of Eve, *Paradise Lost*, IV. 800–9.

l. 225. *Till us death do part.* In the marriage service in the Book of Common Prayer bride and groom make their vows to each other 'till death us do part'.

l. 245. Playing on the term Honeymoon, which referred originally to the first month of marriage.

l. 248. *duffel.* A coarse woollen cloth.

l. 249. *Christmas-come-never.* An expression for a day that never comes.

l. 251. Compare 'springtime, the only pretty ringtime', *As You Like It*, V. iii. 16.

l. 255. *Stand for the county.* Stand for election as a member of parliament.

l. 258. *Christ Church.* The most fashionable of the Oxford colleges, at which RB's son Pen was briefly an unsuccessful student.

l. 294. The douche suggests scandalous information concerning the woman, the horsewhip scandalous information concerning the man.

l. 298. *monomania.* A technical term in the period. A brief notice in *Reynolds's Miscellany* , 3.71, 17 November 1849, 263, argues that the condition might be hereditary, citing the case of seven wealthy French brothers all of whom committed suicide.

l. 314. *place aux dames!* Ladies first!

l. 348. *buttoned foil.* A foil used for fencing practice in which the sword's point is protected.

ll. 358–9. *Flat* | *Cards lie on table.* To put one's cards on the table is a proverbial expression signifying to acknowledge frankly what one is really thinking.

ll. 381–2. Horace's rule in the *Ars Poetica*, 185, forbids the representation of murderous violence on stage: 'ne pueros coram populo Medea trucidet', let not Medea kill her boys in the face of the people. RB modifies the sentiment, 'let not the young man kill the old man in the face of the people.'

VIII.

l. 38. When she gives judgement in *The Merchant of Venice*, IV. i, Portia dressed as 'a doctor of laws' is described as a Daniel, first by Shylock, 219, and then when he recognizes her true purpose by Gratiano, who describes her as a 'second Daniel, a Daniel' (328). The allusion is to the story of Susannah and the Elders in the Apocrypha, in which Daniel convicts the Elders 'by their own mouths'.

ll. 42–3. love is a cultivated rather than a wild flower.

ll. 46–7. *Cigno fedel, cigno fedel,* | *Addio.* Faithful song, faithful swan, farewell, an Italian translation of the Swan-Song from the third act of Wagner's *Lohengrin*.The first British performances of *Lohengrin* at Covent Garden and at Drury Lane in 1875 were in an Italian translation.

l. 48. The omen is ugly because the song is sung after Elsa has asked Lohengrin his name, which, when he reveals it, prevents him from marrying her.

ll. 49–50. *Amo te solo, te* | *Solo amai.* 'I love you only, I have only loved you', from Servilia's aria in the first act of Mozart's *La clemenza di Tito*, 1791, in which she proclaims her love for Annio rather than the Emperor Tito, who seeks her hand. When he learns of her attachment Tito renounces his own claim in favour of the younger man. *La clemenza di Tito* was the first Mozart opera to be performed in London, in 1806, but there seem to have been no further performances before 1875. Metastasio's libretto, which was arranged for Mozart by Caterino Mazzola, had been set to music by many other composers, most notably by Gluck.

FROM *PACCHIAROTTO AND HOW HE WORKED IN DISTEMPER: WITH OTHER POEMS* (1876)

House

The poem is often understood as a rebuke aimed specifically at D. G. Rossetti who had in his *Poems* of 1870 included a sequence of fifty sonnets followed by songs entitled, 'SONNETS AND SONGS *Towards a Work to be called* "THE HOUSE OF LIFE"'. The sonnets, which candidly explore Rossetti's relationships with Elizabeth Siddal and Jane Morris, are clearly examples of the kind of poetry that RB disapproves of, but he is at least as concerned with the threat to his own privacy posed by his new-found celebrity and the established celebrity of his late wife, and by the misreading of his own poetry that had resulted from an assumption that all poems were first-person statements that allowed direct access to the poet's most private emotions.

l. 3. *gear*. Stuff, household goods; *pelf*. May refer to money, or more generally to material possessions.

l. 4. In 'Scorn not the sonnet' (1827), Wordsworth claims, 'with this key | Shakespeare unlocked his heart.'

ll. 6–9. Mimicking the small advertisements in newspapers advising of houses for rent or lease.

l. 24. RB took to smoking cigarettes after his return to England. Smoking was widely believed to damage the health. See, for example, 'The Tobacco Question', *Dublin University Magazine* (September 1871), 279–89.

l. 26. He burned, that is, aromatic pastilles.

l. 29. *goodman*. Head of the household.

l. 35. *the spirit-sense*. That is, clairvoyance, compare *Aurora Leigh*, 7. 844.

l. 37. *Hoity toity!*, a disparaging description of someone felt to be putting on airs.

ll. 38–9. See note to l. 4.

Bifurcation

Like 'The Statue and the Bust' and 'Dîs Aliter Visum', 'Bifurcation' is a poem of missed opportunity, and like them it questions the immorality of surrendering to desire. The poem hinges on the conventional distinction between, as Shakespeare puts it, 'the steep and thorny way to heaven' and 'the primrose path' to hell (*Hamlet*, I. iii. 48–50), but to the man it is love's road that is 'rock-rough', whereas to the woman (as she is represented by the man, for it is the man who supplies her epitaph), it is the road of duty that is paved with stone rather than planted with flowers. It is just possible that RB would have been familiar, through the Rossettis, with the 'Argument' of Blake's *The Marriage of Heaven and Hell*, in which he points out that the 'perilous path' that once led to heaven, because it has become the path preferred by the worldly wise, has changed its character: 'Roses are planted where thorns grew' (6).

Bifurcation. Division into two branches, used most often in technical contexts.

l. 8. *causeway*. Highway.

l. 31. *the star*. The pole star or north star by which ships navigate. Compare Shakespeare on love: 'It is the star to every wand'ring bark' (*Sonnets*, 116. 7).

l. 39. Recalling the myth recounted by Aristophanes in Plato's *Symposium* according to which lovers are the divided halves of what were once hermaphroditic wholes.

Numpholeptos

RB explained the poem to Furnivall as an 'allegory . . . of an impossible ideal object of love, accepted conventionally as such by a man who, all the while, cannot blind himself to the demonstrable fact that the possessor of knowledge and purity obtained without the natural consequences of obtaining them by achievement—not inheritance,—such a being is imaginary, not real, a nymph and no woman: and such an one would be ignorant of and surprised at the results of a lover's endeavour to emulate the qualities which the beloved is entitled to consider as pre-existent to earthly experience and independent of its inevitable results' (W. R. Nicholl and T. J. Wise, *Literary Anecdotes of the Nineteenth Century*, 1895, 497). He suggested too that the clue to the poem was in its title, 'Numpholeptos' (RB's practice in transliterating from the Greek was thought eccentric even by his contemporaries), 'caught or entranst by a Nymph'. The poem may recall the relationship between Numa, the second king of Rome, and the nymph Egeria, as recounted by Plutarch. But Byron's recapitulation of the tale and the meditation that it prompts in *Childe Harold*, IV, stanzas 114–25, seem more germane, especially since Byron identifies Numa's passion as the 'nympholepsy of some fond despair' (115. 5). The speaker describes himself as a 'pilgrim' (120), and in this he recalls not only Childe Harold but the speaker of 'Childe Roland', who seems also to be engaged in a futile, self-defeating quest. RB explores the contrast between white light and fragmented light that always figured for him the difference between his own kind of dramatic poetry and a poetry of self-expression. As he wrote in an early letter to EBB, 13 January 1845, 'You speak out, *you*,—I only make men and women speak,—give you truth broken into prismatic hues, and fear the pure white light, even if it is in me' (*Correspondence*, x. 22). 'Numpholeptos' may imply RB's recognition that dramatic poetry is in some sense dependent on the lyric poetry that it repudiates. The speaker's confrontation with the nymph is a confrontation with his muse: it recalls the confrontation of the poet-dreamer with Moneta in Keats's *The Fall of Hyperion*, and even has something of the same asperity. The moon-like beloved in 'Numpholeptos' has often and properly reminded readers of the 'cold, chaste moon' in Shelley's *Epipsychidion* (281), who burns, like RB's nymph, with a 'soft yet icy flame (283)', and few have doubted that Shelley's moon-woman who 'warms not but illumines' (285) is offered as a characterization of, even a rebuke to, his wife. But it seems more likely that the poem expresses RB's frustration at being separated from the woman that he loves by her death rather than recalls any estrangement between them. In his note to Furnivall RB seems to stress the unreasonableness of the woman, but RB found beguiling the notion of love that Shelley expressed most clearly in his 'Essay on Love', in which the failure of the lover to find his ideal love object is presented as redemptive, because it impels the lover to find a shadow of that ideal in the imperfect objects which are all that mortal experience affords. It may be that in being impelled to follow one coloured ray after another, the speaker is driven to experience the full spectrum of beauty that the world affords, and, did he but see it, he might respond with gratitude rather than querulously. RB would also have been aware of EBB's characterization of the poet in the preface to her *Poems* of 1844: 'it is no new form of the nympholepsy of poetry, that my ideal should fly before me:—and if I cry out too hopefully at sight of the white vesture receding between the cypresses, let me be blamed gently if justly.'

l. 3. Compare with the 'soft and sweet' moonbeam, Arnold, *Tristram and Iseult*, 1853, 286: 'At this soft hour, under this sweet moon.'

l. 11. *prime*. The time just after sunrise.

l. 12. *blood-streaked*. Compare Revelation 6: 12, where, on the opening of the sixth seal, 'the moon became as blood'.

l. 20. *the Spirit-Seven*. Compare the 'seven angels' in Revelation 15 and 16, and EBB, 'The Poet's Vow', 214–15: 'where the spirits seven do show in heaven | A *Man* upon the throne.'

l. 30. *redundant bliss*. Compare Edward Young, *Night Thoughts*, Night IX, 580–1: 'Heaven's King, whose face unveil'd consummates bliss | Redundant bliss!'

l. 51. *unembued*. Unmoistened

ll. 59–60. The hall is compared to a cut jewel with a hundred faces surmounting a crown: the jewel acts as a prism refracting the light emanating from the moon-like woman.

l. 71. *irradiation*. Compare Shelley, 'Letter to Maria Gisborne', 203–4, 'the exceeding lustre, and the pure | Intense irradiation of a mind' (Coleridge's).

l. 77. *the topaz tint*. Dark yellow, but luminous, like the stone.

ll. 78–9. Sulphur is associated with hell and with volcanoes.

l. 101. *bickers*. Flashes or gleams.

l. 106. *protruding*. Shooting out.

l. 116. *course*. Chase.

l. 121. *smatch*. Suggestion, but perhaps influenced by smutch.

ll. 127–8. A yellow tunic signifies an impenitent heretic who is to die by burning: it is represented by RB as parodying the gold robes worn by priests at Christian festivals.

A Forgiveness

This is another in the long succession of monologues by RB in which he chooses a psychopath as his speaker. The manuscript title 'Komm Spanisch! (Flemish for 'How Spanish!'), to the right of which appears the name Egmont, has been explained by J. H. Baker as a reference to a rumour reported in Motley's *Rise of the Dutch Republic* that William the Silent, leader of the Dutch revolt against Spain, had stabbed to death his first wife, Anne of Egmont (*Notes and Queries*, 44.3 (September 1997), 339). The suggestion is striking because a poem that seems on the face of it to insist on the difference between its Spanish speaker, who has so icily accomplished his revenge against his wife and her priestly lover, and the English reader, may end by suggesting that the difference may be more apparent than real. Ohio suggests the influence on the poem of D. G. Rossetti's 'A Last Confession' (1870). Rossetti's speaker is divided between his love for the woman he had adopted as a young girl and his commitment to the Italian nationalist cause just as RB's speaker is divided between his statecraft and his married life. But however disconcerting the relationship represented by Rossetti may be, his speaker commits murder simply and passionately in comparison with RB's. A closer parallel may be with Meredith's *Modern Love* (1862), in which husband and wife as in RB's poem perform their marital happiness, long after it has been wrecked, so skilfully that they are the envy of their friends. The poem may lead its reader to question the contrast between the English and the foreign, the native and the exotic. After all, the most exotic item in the poem, the dagger tipped with poison with which the Spanish husband kills his wife, is closely modelled on a weapon in RB's own collection.

l. 6. *confession-grate*. The grill through which the confession is spoken to the confessor.

ll. 10–11. *gains | Of good*. Achievements.

l. 23. *postern-gate*. Back or sidegate.

l. 28. *ensconce*. Shelter or hide.

l. 74. *toils*. Nets.

l. 76. *bell-flower*. Campanula.

ll. 97–100. In chapter XXI of *Don Quixote*, the Don mistakes a barber's brass basin (used for letting blood) that he is wearing on his head to protect a new hat from the rain for the legendary helmet of Mambrino, a solid gold helmet that confers invulnerability on its wearer.

l. 101. *sacramental cup*. The chalice that holds the communion wine.

ll. 105–6. Don Quixote acknowledges his delusions only on his deathbed.

l. 126. *enarming*. Embracing.

l. 163. *saloon*. Translating the French, 'salon', a room for the reception of guests.

l. 181. *sepulchred*. Compare *Aurora Leigh*, 5. 1040: 'We are sepulchred alive in this close world.'

l. 201. *arquebuss*. Musket.

l. 242. *fresh serpent's tooth*. Compare *King Lear*, I. iv. 288–9: 'How sharper than a serpent's tooth it is | To have a thankless child!'

l. 250. *Yataghan*. An Arab sword; *kandjar*. An eastern dagger. The description is founded on the collection of oriental weaponry bequeathed to RB by the steel magnate Ernest Benzon. Sutherland Orr comments: 'he values it, perhaps, for the reason he imputes to its imagined owner: that those who are accustomed to the slower processes of thought, like to play with the suggestions of prompt (if murderous) action; as the soldier, tired of wielding the sword, will play with paper and pen' (Orr, *Handbook*, 254).

l. 256. *bicker*. Flicker.

l. 265. *diapered*. Patterned.

ll. 271–4. One weapon in RB's collection, a 'peskkabz', a variety of dagger from Sind, has a 'green jade hilt carved as a bird pecking at fruit' (Kelley and Coley, *The Browning Collections*, lot 1297).

ll. 295. *the firework and the goad*. The reference is to bullfighting in which the bull may be infuriated by lighting fireworks attached to its horns, and by barbed darts which are driven into its shoulders.

ll. 334–6. The lines play with the phrase *A Blot in the 'Scutcheon*, the title of one of RB's plays, meaning a stain on a person's reputation. Since his wife has lost her reputation, her scutcheon has been removed leaving a hole in the wall that the speaker disguises with a tapestry or wall-hanging, 'broidered stuff'.

l. 348. *weave ropes of sand*. An expression signifying an impossible task, often a task given to the devil. In Ben Jonson's *The Devil is an Ass*, I. i. 118–19, Pug tells Satan, 'Get you e'en back, sir, | To making of your rope of sand again.'

l. 370. *minion*. Court favourite.

l. 393. *cuirass*. Breastplate.

FROM *LA SAISIAZ* AND *THE TWO POETS OF CROISIC* (1878)

On 14 September 1877, RB returned from his morning swim to find that the old friend with whom he was holidaying, Anne Egerton Smith, had died. The poem is his response to that sudden and wholly unexpected event. RB described it as the only poem 'relating to a personal experience (at least, directly) in all my books' (letter of 30 January 1880 to J. D. Williams, *Browning Institute Studies*, 4 (1976), 14). It is also RB's contribution to a series of papers debating 'The Soul and Future Life' that appeared in the monthly periodical

The Nineteenth Century in 1877. The debate featured a paper published in June and July by the Comtean Frederic Harrison, which argued that it was nonsensical to suppose that the soul might exist independently of the body, and that consequently the only immortality that might properly be anticipated is a participation in the progress of humanity to which each individual contributes, an immortality that he defines as 'an eternity of spiritual influence' (July, 840). In September and October a number of well-known intellectuals responded to Harrison, all of them except Thomas Huxley and W. R. Greg arguing the case for personal immortality. RB recalls that he had discussed Harrison's essay and the responses to it with Miss Smith in lines 162–6. It is also a more distant response to another poem written after a sudden and unexpected death more than twenty-five years earlier, Tennyson's *In Memoriam.* Harrison had Tennyson specifically in mind when he observed that the question of a future life was 'too great a thing to be trusted to poetic ejaculations', quoting from the poem (LVI. 28) in his mockery of those who 'assume the question closed, when they have murmured triumphantly, "Behind the veil, behind the veil"' (June 1877, 623). The lyric with which RB introduces the poem seems rather emphatically to distinguish body and soul, the one belonging to the earth and the other to the sky, by replacing argument with a figure of speech in precisely the manner that had prompted Harrison's scorn, except that RB's metaphor does not quite perform the task that RB sets it, the bird to which the soul is compared being a creature of earth as much as of sky (the grave is even described as if it were a kind of nest), and it introduces a poem that begins with a rhapsodic account of RB's ascent of La Salève five days after Miss Smith's death in which mountain beauty is understood as a result of the interpenetration of earth and sky, 'Earth's most exquisite disclosure, heaven's own God in evidence!' (6). Most readers will, like Watts Dunton in his review of the volume in *The Athenæum* (28 May 1878, 662), regret that the dazzling account of the climb in which RB notices, for example, 'the pink perfection of the cyclamen', and the moving account of Miss Smith's death, should be 'merely used as an occasion for ratiocinative writing' in the second half of the poem, in which RB seems so intent on arguing his case that the eight-beat trochaic line that had so winningly expressed the breathless enthusiasm of the climb and the urgency of a death so wholly unexpected becomes almost inaudible. A line such as 'So much gain or loss for that next life which on this life depends' (478) seems almost to have dispensed with metre. It is as if RB has set himself to evacuate from his writing all those elements that might provoke Harrison's distrust. The argument for the soul's immortality seems at first improbably confident, and then rather unexpectedly collapses, as RB reaches a conclusion that in 'A Modern "Symposium"' seems most closely anticipated by W. R. Greg: 'To that more solid certainty I am obliged to confess, sorrowfully and with bitter disappointment, that I can contribute nothing—nothing, I mean, that resembles evidence, or that I can hope will be received as even the barest confirmation' (October, 508).

La Saisiaz was the name of the villa near Geneva where RB holidayed in the summer of 1877. Sutherland Orr reports that the name is 'Savoyard for "The Sun"' (Orr, *Handbook*, 188) which may report RB's belief, though it seems that he was mistaken and the name of the villa refers more probably to its rocky location.

Good to forgive

ll. 1–3. Compare *Oedipus at Colonus*, 'Not to be born is, past all prizing, best; but, when a man hath seen the light, this is next best by far, that with all speed he should go thither, whence he hath come' (trans. Richard C. Jebb, 1225).

l. 16. Soul-flight, the American poet William Gilmore Simms has a poem entitled 'Soul-Flight' (1853), similar in theme to RB's lyric.

l. 22. *Ferns of all feather*. An expression modelled on and reversing the sense of the proverbial expression, birds of a feather, meaning birds of a single species.

La Saisiaz

l. 1. *Dared and done*. Compare the final lines of Christopher Smart's *Song to David*, 'And now the matchless deed's atchiev'd | DETERMINED, DARED, and DONE' (515–16).

l. 11. *Infinitude*. Compare Wordsworth, *The Prelude* (1850), 6. 538–9 on crossing the Alps: 'Our destiny, our nature, and our home | Is with infinitude and only there.'

l. 16. The cyclamen is a rock plant sometimes known as the Alpine violet.

l. 17. *the sloe-tree*. The blackthorn.

l. 18. The mountain ash or rowan has bright red berries.

l. 22. *the four low walls*. The walls of La Saisiaz, the house where RB and Anne Egerton Smith were staying.

l. 24. *Collonge*. The village near La Saisiaz where Egerton Smith was buried.

l. 29. *the mountain*. La Salève, at the foot of which La Saisiaz was built.

l. 34. The plan had been to ascend the mountain the next day by carriage.

l. 37. The Jura mountains are visible to the south of Mont Salève.

l. 45. Mont Salève overlooks Geneva, and is sometimes called Geneva's mountain.

l. 54. RB's sister Sarianna and their French friend Gustave Dourlans.

l. 56. *prepotency*. Predominance; in 1877 Mars was particularly close to the earth. It was the year in which its two moons were first observed.

l. 62. *our travelled friend*. Dourlans.

l. 75. There is a fine view of Mont Blanc from the summit of La Salève.

l. 80. The French President and Marshal of France, the Royalist, Patrice MacMahon, precipitated a constitutional crisis on 16 May 1877, when he dismissed the National Assembly that had a Republican majority. That majority was confirmed in the elections that followed, prompting the Republican leader Léon Gambetta to demand that the President either accept the sovereign will of the French people or resign. The crisis established the constitutional authority of the National Assembly over the President.

l. 85. *transmutation.* The alchemic term for the transformation of a base metal into gold.

l. 88. *overflowing ardours.* The rising temperature.

l. 96. In fact the Arve joins with the Rhone below Lake Leman.

l. 104. Calvin, who lived in Geneva from 1541 until his death in 1564, established it as the centre of the Calvinist faith.

l. 124. The butterfly may figuratively represent a showy, trivial person.

l. 130. The alpine rose and edelweiss are (with the blue gentian) the representative plants of the Swiss alps. The alpine rose, a variety of rhododendron, has a red, and the edeleweiss a white flower.

l. 151. His answers, because they are weak, can be expressed in human language.

ll. 163–4. Referring to a series entitled 'A Modern "Symposium"', launched in the monthly *The Nineteenth Century* in April 1877.

l. 171. *palter.* Prevaricate: Frederic Harrison accuses churchmen of 'paltering with the greatest of all things', in his contribution to the debate, July 1877, 833.

ll. 187–8. This is the afterlife anticipated by Frederic Harrison, a participation in human progress that he describes as 'an eternity of spiritual influence' (July 1877, 840).

l. 193. *timed.* Established the time of.

l. 200. *groundlings.* Animals that cannot fly and are confined to the ground.

l. 210. *that controverted doctrine.* Roden Noel refers ironically to the present as a time when established 'theologies and philosophies' are 'now exploded' (September 1877, 350).

l. 212. *the solemn Tuscan.* Dante.

ll. 213–15. Translating the final sentence of Dante's *Il convivio*, *The Banquet.*

ll. 217–22. Lord Blachford founds his argument for the possibility that the soul may exist independently of the body on the distinction between the 'percipient' and the 'perceptible' (September 1877, 334), though for him the perceptible is the sensible world rather than God.

l. 247. Lord Blachford explains the difference between body and soul by analogy with the difference between words that signify things and words that signify 'qualities, relations, consequences, processes or occurrences', a distinction that he clinches by pointing to the distinction 'between a fiddle and a tune' (September 1877, 341–2).

ll. 263–4. Compare Lord Blachford arguing that there can be no direct knowledge of percipients other than the self: 'Are they perceptible? Not to my knowledge. Their existence is to me a matter of inference from their perceptible appendages. Them—their very selves—I certainly cannot perceive' (September 1877, 344).

l. 318. *fineless.* Unlimited.

l. 353. Compare Job 2: 7–8: 'So went Satan forth from the presence of the Lord, and smote Job with sore boils from the sole of his foot unto his crown. And he took him a potsherd to scrape himself withal; and he sat down among the ashes.' The substitution of dung for ashes may suggest a recollection of Job 20: 7: 'Yet he shall perish for ever like his own dung.'

l. 354. Compare Job 38: 1: 'Then the Lord answered Job out of the whirlwind.'

l. 355. Pope announces his ambition to 'vindicate the ways of God to man', *Essay on Man*, 16, but he is echoing Milton's ambition to 'justify the ways of God to men' *Paradise Lost*, I. 26.

l. 356. *traversing.* Piercing, running through (as with a sword).

l. 371. *Barked the bole.* Stripped the bark from the trunk.

l. 372. Death is represented as an alchemic apparatus that converts the sorrows of life into an 'elixir', that is, both a remedy for all diseases and the alchemic substance that confers eternal life on whoever imbibes it.

l. 377. *narrow ways are well to tread.* Compare Matthew 7: 13–14: 'Enter ye in at the strait gate for wide is the gate, and broad is the way, that leadeth to destruction, and many there be which go in thereat: Because strait is the gate, and narrow the way, which leadeth unto life, and few there be that find it.'

ll. 384–5. The allusions may be specific, to the storm in Beethoven's sixth symphony, the Pastoral, and to Sarastro quelling the storm summoned by the Queen of the Night in Act II of *The Magic Flute*, but they may make a more general distinction between the music of the two composers.

l. 386. *Yonder precinct.* That is, the grave.

l. 419. A reference to the tendency of Greek gods to punish human aspiration, as exemplified, for example, in the story of Prometheus' punishment for stealing fire from Olympus.

l. 421. The suggestion is that evolution progressively removes the more baneful species. Dragons probably refers to dinosaurs, as in Tennyson, *In Memoriam*, LVI. 22: blindworms or slow-worms are not venomous.

l. 422. *Python.* The creature killed by Apollo rather than the species of snake.

l. 430. *mingled measure.* Coleridge, 'Kubla Khan', 33.

l. 446. *the provided room.* Compare John 14: 2: 'I go to prepare a place for you.'

l. 479. *amerced.* Penalized.

l. 480. *Six facts now.* RB may be recalling (and parodying) the Catholic contributor to 'A Modern "Symposium"', W. G. Ward, who enumerates six 'premisses' which demonstrate conclusively the immortality of the soul (October, 521).

l. 546. *Athanasius contra mundum*. A phrase celebrating the doctrinal intransigence of the 4th-century Bishop of Alexandria that became a proverb signalling a willingness to back one's own judgement against the world.

l. 553. *Bossex*. Bossey, the village to the south of Geneva in which for two years as a boy Rousseau was tutored by the Protestant minister.

l. 554. *like a fiery flying serpent*. Rousseau is compared to the cockatrice with which, Isaiah prophesies, the Lord will destroy the enemies of Israel. See Isaiah 14: 29.

l. 555. *Diodati*. The villa on Lake Leman in which Byron stayed in the summer of 1816, while the Shelley household stayed in a neighbouring house.

l. 558. *till putridity looked flame*. Phosphorescence may be produced by bacteria associated with putrefaction.

l. 560. *cynosure*. Guiding star.

ll. 561–3. A disapproving summary of Byronic pessimism.

l. 564. *Dying day with dolphin hues!* Compare *Childe Harold*, IV. 258–61: 'Parting day | Dies like the dolphin, whom each pang imbues | With a new colour as it gasps away, | The last still loveliest.'

l. 565. *Storm, for loveliness and darkness like a woman's eye*. Compare *Childe Harold*, III. 860–3: 'Oh night | And storm, and darkness, ye are wondrous strong, | Yet lovely in your strength, as is the light | Of a dark eye in woman!'

ll. 565–7. Loosely paraphrasing *Childe Harold*, II. 219, in which the flood, the forest, and the mountain are 'things that own not man's dominion'.

l. 570. *let him go a-howling to his gods*. Compare *Childe Harold*, IV. 1617–19, where the ocean send man 'shivering in [its] playful spray | And howling, to his Gods, where haply lies | His petty hope'.

l. 579. Referring to the passage in Aeschylus' *Agamemnon*, that RB himself had translated, in which Makistos is one of the mountains on which a beacon fire is lit signalling the Greek victory over Troy. For RB the flame represents fame. For RB's translation of the passage, see *The Agamemnon of Aeschylus* (1877), 302–37.

l. 580. *architrave*. Here the beam that rests on a pillar.

l. 582. *Lausanne*. Representing Gibbon because of his residence there, first as a young man, and then again 1783–7, the period during which he completed *The Decline and Fall of the Roman Empire*.

l. 586. *Ferney*. Associated with Voltaire because of his residence there from 1758 until just before his death in 1778. RB no doubt has in mind Byron, *Childe Harold*, III. 976–7: 'Lausanne! and Ferney! ye have been the abodes | Of Names which unto you bequeathed a name.'

l. 588. *Bossex*. Associated with Rousseau. See note to l. 553: the terebinth tree is particularly inflammable because its resin is turpentine. Compare Byron on Rousseau in *Childe Harold*, III. 733–5: 'His love was Passion's essence—as a tree | On fire by lightning; with ethereal flame | Kindled he was, and blasted.'

l. 590. *monkeys and macaques*. RB's contempt for Byron's admirers centred on the poet Alfred Austin, referred to in 'Of Pacchiarotto, and How He Worked in Distemper', 530, as 'Banjo-Byron'. Austin's public attacks on RB had succeeded in provoking him into an uncharacteristic fury.

l. 591. Referring to the leaf of ivy RB picked at the Villa Diodati (see l. 556), and also perhaps to Byron in *Childe Harold*, IV. 985, 'Crown me with ivy'.

l. 603. *bauble*. The stick carried by a jester as a mock-emblem of office.

l. 604. RB contrasts his fame with that of Gibbon, Voltaire, Rousseau, and Byron, all of whom were associated with scepticism in matters of religion.

ll. 615–18. The point is presumably that RB can put into question the survival after death of Miss Smith, whereas it would be unbearable for him to put the same question in respect of EBB.

FROM *DRAMATIC IDYLS: SECOND SERIES* (1880)

Pan and Luna

RB founded his tale of the rape of Luna, goddess of the moon, by Pan on three enigmatic lines in Virgil's *Georgics*. Luna is herself the origin of the light that she flees, because it reveals so flagrantly her nakedness, but she flees into the rough arms of Pan, who has disguised himself as a sheltering cloud. Luna, fleeing from her own light, resembles in her reflexiveness one of Shelley's beauties, like the Mediterranean island that 'Blushes and trembles at its own excess' (*Epipsychidion*, 476), but the chalice filled 'to the brim' with 'fresh-squeezed yet fast-thickening poppy-juice' (9–10) more nearly recalls the Keats of 'Ode to a Nightingale' and 'Ode on Melancholy'. RB glances quizzically at Victorian rationalist responses to myth when he asks whether his story might be explained as a primitive account of a lunar eclipse (89–91). He might have responded more violently to critical attempts (thinly justified by RB's tendency to associate EBB with the moon) to offer a biographical reading of the poem. The 'verse of five words' with which the poem ends seems designed as a brusque rebuttal of the notion that poems might yield to such interpretative stratagems. Pan's assault on Luna disconcertingly recalls the violent marital embraces to which Guido subjects Pompilia in *The Ring and the Book*. It might be best to read the poem as a stringent testing of the Keatsian notion that poetry has the capacity of 'making all disagreeables evaporate, from their being in close relationship with Beauty and Truth'.

Si credere dignum est. If it is worthy of belief.

l. 2. *Strange three lines*: *Georgics* III. 391–3

> Munere sic niveo lanae, si credere dignum est,
> Pan deus Arcadiae captam te, Luna, fefellit,
> In nemora alta vocans; nec tu aspernata vocantem.

Dryden translates:

> 'Twas thus, with fleeces milky-white (if we
> May trust report), Pan, god of Arcady,
> Did bribe thee, Cynthia: nor didst thou disdain,
> When called in woody shades, to cure a lover's pain.

l. 42. *rounds on rounds.* Compare 'Andrea del Sarto', 26, 'My serpentining beauty, rounds on rounds!'

l. 50. *Conglobe.* Form into a globe.

l. 53. *dented.* Vertebral.

l. 55. *constringe.* Compress.

l. 59. *Amphitrite.* Consort of Poseidon, the sea god.

l. 60. *bladdery.* Bubbly, compare 'Caliban upon Setebos', 71; 'when froth rises bladdery'.

l. 61. *elf from gnome.* Elves are commonly ethereal, gnomes earthy.

l. 68. *earth-breath.* Because the water vapour of which clouds are formed is produced by evaporation.

ll. 70–6. *the fact | As learned Virgil gives it.* In the passage immediately before the three lines on which RB founds his poem Virgil advises that only the whitest sheep should be used for breeding, and a ram rejected, no matter how white its fleece, if it have a black tongue, which might 'darken all the flock' (Dryden).

l. 84. *boar-sward.* Boar skin: the word sward is commonly used to refer to the rind of pork.

FROM *JOCOSERIA* (1883)

Never the Time and the Place

Clearly a lyric in which RB stills his doubts of reunion in death with EBB. The poem's conclusion rebuts, perhaps consciously, Marvell's contention in 'To his Coy Mistress': 'The grave's a fine and private place, | But none I think do there embrace' (31–2).

l. 7. *the house is narrow.* The grave is 'the house appointed for all living' (Job 30: 23), and 'the narrow room' ('The Statue and the Bust', 216).

ll. 12–13. The enemy is Satan, who, by tempting mankind to disobedience, contrived it that 'He with his whole posterity must die' (*Paradise Lost*, III. 209), a sentence from which Christ offered redemption.

ll. 19–21. A reference to 'Soul Sleep', the waiting period between death and resurrection at the Second Coming.

FROM *FERISHTAH'S FANCIES* (1884)

Epilogue

Another lyric evidently addressed to EBB. It seems to offer one of RB's most boisterous celebrations of life as process rather than product. The exhortations not to shirk the fight seem schoolboyishly Kiplingesque: 'not sneaks to lag behind!' (16), 'no care for cowards' (20). But when the cloud rift widens and life is seen for a moment not as a blind struggle but as the 'perfection' that God sees, a sudden terror 'disencharms' the scene, the thought that the glory with which the speaker feels himself crowned might all be an illusion, and the poem ends when the disenchantment produces a charm more potent than the charm that had been dispelled, the thought that the rainbow around his head might not be a mark of his own achievement but produced by the embrace of the woman that he loves.

l. 7. *Iridescent splendours.* Compare the double 'moon-rainbow' of *Christmas-Eve*, 385–404, a vision the granting of which seems to the speaker a mark of special dispensation.

l. 8. *bright-edged the blackest shroud.* Varying the proverb that every cloud has a silver lining.

ll. 9–12. Compare the 'lost adventurers' who stand 'ranged along the hill-sides' to view the last of the speaker in "Childe Roland to the Dark Tower Came", 194–202.

l. 13. *mumming.* Empty show, with the further implication that life is a mummer's play, a coarse entertainment in which we each perform our parts.

FROM ANDREW REID, ED., *WHY I AM A LIBERAL* (1885)

Why I am a Liberal

The poem was written at the invitation of Andrew Reid and published by him in 1885 in *Why I Am a Liberal: Being Definitions of Faith by the Best Minds of the Liberal Party*, a volume clearly designed as a contribution to the general election campaign of that year. RB's poem appears immediately after the preface and is followed by a contribution by Gladstone. It is unusual because RB, unlike EBB, was reluctant directly to espouse political causes in his poems. As a young man, introducing *Paracelsus* to W. J. Fox, he was eager to assert his political daring: 'there are precious bold bits here & there, & the drift & scope are awfully radical' (*Correspondence*, iii. 134). As he grew older he became more reticent. Even his support for Italian nationalism often seems oddly ambivalent. This is his only party political poem, but even here the label liberal is construed etymologically to mean freeman rather than in party terms. The vocabulary suggests that the alternative to a nation of freemen is not a Conservative government, but a nation in which one section of the population enslaves the other. Hence the use of an abolitionist diction; 'fetters', 'emancipated', even 'brother', that might in this context recall the celebrated Wedgwood medallion, 'Am I not a man and a brother?' The central tenet of RB's liberalism, revealed in the references to 'fortune' and 'degree', is the duty of the privileged to extend the advantages that they enjoy to those less fortunate. The use of the Petrarchan sonnet form in itself repels any notion that the freedom RB celebrates is at all anarchic.

l. 3. *fortune*. The word suggests both luck and wealth.

l. 9. Compare 'The Last Ride Together', 52–3: 'Contrast | The petty Done, the Undone vast.'

l. 13. *live*, *love*, *labour*. Compare Alice Cary, 'The Living Present', 24, 'Live, love, and labour' (Cary's poem is so Browningesque that it may have caught his attention).

FROM *PARLEYINGS WITH CERTAIN PEOPLE OF IMPORTANCE IN THEIR DAY* (1887)

VI. With Gerard de Lairesse

RB wrote in his copy of Gerard de Lairesse's *The Art of Painting*, 'I read this book more often and with greater delight, when I was a child, than any other: and still remember the main of it most gratefully for the good I seem to have got by the prints, and wondrous text' (Kelley and Coley, *The Browning Collections*, A1379). The poem has its origin in the adult's bemusement at his childhood predilections, but it gives rise to an exploration of a number of themes important to RB. First, there is the contention, placed years earlier in the mouth of Sordello, that poets justify their claim to have outdone their predecessors by showing themselves able to assume their predecessors' manner. Second, there is the assertion that the modern poet has disproved Lairesse's assumption that the real world is unworthy of the painter's or poet's attention except as a background to mythological fables. Third, there is an argument that the modern poet can accept the world as it is, divested of the fabulous, because of a Christian faith in the immortality of the soul. It is this that distinguishes RB from Homer, for whom, as becomes evident in Book 11 of the *Odyssey*, the afterlife is only a ghostly half-existence, and distinguishes him, too, from several significant predecessors and contemporaries. He has in mind particularly Shelley (the Promethean landscape of section VIII recalls *Prometheus Unbound*), Keats (the Artemis of section IX recalls the moon goddess of *Endymion*), Byron (the interrupted night scene may recall 'Darkness'), and Arnold, all of whom continue to weight their poetry with mythological reference, because, as RB would have it, they have repudiated a faith in Christian immortality. The poem ends with one of RB's most condensed celebrations of natural vitality in lines that had first been published as an independent lyric in *The New Amphion*, a collection published in 1886 by the students of Edinburgh University. The lines express a joy in the dancing tulips that is confirmed rather than invalidated by the grave that the flower bed neighbours.

l. 1. De Lairesse was struck suddenly blind in 1690, a consequence of hereditary syphilis.

l. 15. *the severe serene*. That is, the calmly composed attitudes in which divinities are represented in classical sculpture: EBB has God 'in His serene of might', *Casa Guidi Windows*, II. 335.

l. 18. Sutherland Orr observes that the poem addresses 'a question: the poet's fancy no longer peoples the earth with gods and goddesses; has his insight become less vivid? has the poetic spirit gone back?' (Orr, *Handbook*, 356).

l. 20. *Are not the pictures extant?* RB had known from boyhood two paintings in Dulwich Art Gallery then attributed to Gerard de Lairesse but since reattributed to Gerard Hoet. *Pan and Syrinx* and *Apollo and Daphne* are landscapes that accommodate in their foregrounds a representation of mythological assaults. In the first Pan clutches Syrinx, caught in the moment of her transformation into an oddly naturalistic clump of reeds. Neither of them attends to the tomb in the right foreground. In the second, Apollo reaches out to a fleeing Daphne whose hands have already metamorphosed into laurel leaves.

l. 33. *that prodigious book*. The book that RB knew in the translation of J. R. Fritsch as *The Art of Painting, in All its Branches* (1778).

ll. 40–2. De Lairesse was the most celebrated painter in Amsterdam after the death of Rembrandt, and known, because of his classicizing style, as the Dutch Poussin.

l. 46. *that memorable "Walk"*. In Book VI of *The Art of Painting*, trans. Fritsch, 253–62, de Lairesse invites the reader to accompany him on an imaginary walk during which he advises on the different ways in which landscape subjects may be treated.

l. 50. *Faustus' robe*. In Marlowe's *Doctor Faustus* the robe that Mephistopheles bestows on Faustus confers invisibility, A text, III. i. 58.

l. 51. Fortunatus' cap transports him immediately to wherever he wishes to go.

l. 80. *Consult the tome*. RB is drawing on de Lairesse's description of 'an ancient tomb or sepulcher' on which is a bas-relief that 'exhibited a flying eagle, with thunder in its bill; whence I conjectured it might be *Phaeton*'s grave'. The conjecture is confirmed when he unearths 'a piece of a chariot, and half a wheel in the shape of a star' which, he thought, 'must be the chariot of the sun, as being not much unlike it' (*Art of Painting*, 255).

l. 100. *antique song*. Shakespeare in Sonnet 17, 'Who will believe my verse in time to come,' speaks of the 'stretched metre of an antique song' (12), a line that Keats chose as the epigraph for *Endymion*.

l. 101. *Fancy's rainbow-birth*. A conventional trope, as in Byron, *The Prophecy of Dante*, III. 112: 'His fancy like a rainbow.'

ll. 105–6. De Lairesse mocks the painter who claims to 'discover a thousand things, both delightful and useful, whenever I cast my eyes' (p. 259).

l. 120. *Dryope*. De Lairesse's chapter XIII is entitled 'The Fable of Dryope, for the Embellishment of Landscapes'. He describes Dryope walking with her child: 'Near the lake stood a tree, called Lotos, bearing red blossoms; of which she rashly broke a twig to pleasure her child; but perceiving blood to issue from it, and that the whole tree was thereby violently agitated, she was much affrighted; and the more that in going thence, she felt her feet to fasten into the earth: for she was transformed into a tree' (239).

l. 162. *human shape divine*. Compare William Blake, 'human form divine', 'The Divine Image', 11 and 15.

ll. 163–5. De Lairesse describes an elaborate composition in which Venus discovers the dead Adonis (236–8), but it does not accommodate roses.

l. 165. *retrogression*. A term given new currency by Darwin.

l. 170. *the Protoplast*. The first maker or mover, God, a word used several times by RB. Compare, for example, 'Abt Vogler', 35.

l. 189. *erect*. Compare the chained Prometheus in EBB's translation of Aeschylus, 'Erect, unslumbering, bending not the knee' (*Prometheus Bound*, 36).

l. 193. *deprecation*. Possibly used in a sense that *OED* describes as rare to mean imprecation or curse.

l. 200. *Fate's secret*. Prometheus' knowledge that if Zeus has a son by Thetis, that son will overthrow him.

l. 202. *patronage of men*. Not only the gift of fire, but all the arts of civilization.

l. 204. *pallid brow*. Compare the 'white and quivering brow' of Shelley's Prometheus, *Prometheus Unbound*, I. 565.

l. 208. *laughters manifold*. A phrase used by Edward Bulwer Lytton, *Croesus and Adrastus* (1868), 308.

l. 215. *Prone the runnels*. Headlong the streams.

ll. 230–1. Artemis or Diana.

l. 231. *succinct*. Girded up.

l. 237. *brow's crescent*. The crescent moon with which Artemis or Diana is conventionally crowned.

ll. 255–61. Artemis's arrows are sometimes represented as killing women in childbirth.

l. 256. *Hymen*. Goddess of marriage.

ll. 272–4. Possibly suggesting a comparison with Otus and Ephialtes, punished for attempting to scale Olympus by piling mountains one on top of the other.

l. 280. *service-tree*. A variety of sorb, bearing a pear-like fruit.

l. 281. *barberry*. A shrub bearing edible red berries.

l. 294. Mary Shelley had published Shelley's translation from Moschus, 'Pan loved his neighbour Echo', describing the love triangle in which Pan loved Echo who loved the satyr who loved Lyda, in the *Posthumous Poems* of 1824.

ll. 302–7. Oxford persuasively suggests that the description is modelled on Correggio's *Venus and Cupid with a Satyr* in the Louvre. As Oxford also notes, the diction is Keatsian (couches, slumberous, supine, heaped), and the situation recalls Porphyro gazing on Madeline's unclothed body in 'The Eve of St Agnes'.

l. 311. Tennyson's brother Charles has 'sapphirine' for the sky in 'The stars of yon blue placid sky', 10, in *Poems by Two Brothers* (1827).

ll. 332–3. The reference is to Alexander the Great's defeat of Darius III's Persian army at the Battle of Issus in 333 BC. RB may recall Tennyson's account of the battle, 'Warrior of God, whose strong right arm debased', not published until 1872 but written decades earlier. The battle is often cited as exemplifying the defeat of the east by the west.

l. 334. *fillet-folds his brow*. Winds a band of cloth around his forehead.

l. 381. *glozed*. Commented, with the implication that the comment is specious.

ll. 397–8. Referring to Horace, *Odes*, 1. 28, in which Archytas begs for the three sprinkles of dust that will allow his soul to rest.

ll. 398–9. In Book 11 of the *Odyssey*, the dead can speak only if they drink the blood of a sacrificed ram.

ll. 405–8. In Book 11 of the *Odyssey*, Achilles, when questioned by Ulysses, asserts that he would rather be the wretchedest man alive than a king amongst the dead.

ll. 423–5. The sentiment with which the *Lament for Bion* commonly attributed to Moschus ends, and a sentiment common in poets writing in an anti-Christian classical tradition, such as Gray in his sonnet on the death of Richard West, Shelley in *Adonais*, and Matthew Arnold in *Empedocles on Etna*.

FROM *THE ATHENAEUM*, NO. 3220, 13 JULY 1889

To Edward FitzGerald

As RB explains in the poem, he had chanced upon W. A. Wright's *Letters and Literary Remains of Edward FitzGerald* soon after its publication in 1889 (FitzGerald had died in 1883). He claims, unpersuasively, to have read only six or seven words. The full passage to which RB objects appears in a letter of 7 December 1861 to FitzGerald's Cambridge friend W. H. Thompson: 'Mrs Browning's Death is rather a relief to me, I must say: no more Aurora Leighs, thank God! A woman of real Genius, I know: but what is the upshot of it all? She and her Sex had better mind the Kitchen and their Children; and perhaps the Poor: except in such things as little Novels, they only devote themselves to what Men do much better, leaving that which Men do worse or not at all' (1. 280). RB tried to withdraw the poem he wrote in response, but too late. It was published in *The Athenaeum* for 13 July 1889, 64. The next issue (20 July, 94) carried a letter from W. A. Wright regretting 'how great an injustice' he had done 'to FitzGerald in making public what was but the careless outburst of a passing mood, and thus investing it with a significance which was never designed. That I should have allowed a passage to remain which has so wronged the dead and pained the living causes me, I need not say, extreme vexation, and I can only beg publicly to express my sincere regret.' The poem is a memorial to an embarrassing literary misadventure and a fine expression of the genius for hatred that Daniel Karlin has explored in his *Browning's Hatreds* (Oxford: Clarendon Press, 1993).

FROM *ASOLANDO: FANCIES AND FACTS* (1889)

Development

RB had first visited Asolo and been struck by its beauty in 1838. Two years later, in *Pippa Passes*, he had made his heroine a resident of the town. In 1889 he returned for what he knew would be the last time, and found the town as beautiful as he had found it fifty years before. It was here that he received the proofs and made his final revisions to his last volume. The title, *Asolando*, commemorates the town. It derives, as he explains in his dedication, from a verb coined at the end of the 15th century by the town's most famous resident, Queen Cornaro, the dispossessed Queen of Cyprus: 'Asolare—"*to disport in the open air, amuse oneself at random*".' In 'Development' RB recalls a time still earlier than his first visit to Asolo, when he was a boy living with his parents at Hanover Cottage in Camberwell. The Troy game with which the poem begins is, according to RB's sister Sarianna, imagined rather than recalled (Maynard, *Browning's Youth*, 138), and the suggestion that the Browning family included amongst their servants a 'page-boy' who might be enlisted to act the part of Hector (15) is surely fanciful. RB may have recalled a passage cited by Maynard in a poem by his benefactor, John Kenyon, an old schoolfriend of his father, in which he had described playing games based on the *Iliad* at school:

> Next he, the lord of each upgrowing mind,
> Poet and legislator of mankind,
> Next Homer came—as yet, not He of Greek,
> But Homer, such as Pope had made him speak.
> What vows were straight for every hero sped,
> The while, as temper willed, or fancy led,
> We parted, like Scamander's branching tide,
> This to the Grecian, this the Trojan side;
> Then with mock sword, and slate, our mimic shield,
> Hector or Ajax, overfought each field!

('Prefatory Dialogue', 392–401 in *Rhymed Plea for Tolerance in Two Dialogues*, 1839).

In blank verse as delightfully easy as any he ever wrote, very different from Kenyon's stiff Popean couplets, RB maps his development from youth to age by tracing the changes in his understanding of Homer. The robust preference for adult realities over childish dreams ('But then "No dream's worth waking"—Browning says', 84) is complicated by his insistence that his youthful response to the poem, before he ever knew of Wolf or any modern Homeric scholarship, retains its own truth. The poem ends with finely judged lines in which RB contrives fondly to remember the boyhood he has outgrown:

> At least I soil no page with bread and milk,
> Nor crumple, dogsear and deface—boys' way. (114–15)

Robert Browning died at his son's home, Ca' Rezzonico in Venice, on 12 December, 1889; the volume, *Asolando*, was published on the same day.

l. 11. *Atreidae*. Sons of Atreus, that is, the Greek leaders, Menelaus, Helen's husband, and Agamemnon.

l. 13. *Achilles ceased to sulk*. Achilles withdrew to his tent when forced to cede to Agamemnon the beautiful Trojan captive Briseis, and only joined battle again when enraged by the death of his friend Patroclus.

l. 22. *sand-blind*. Half-blind.

ll. 33–5. The reference is to the Homeric Hymn to Apollo, which ends by instructing the audience when they are asked who is 'the sweetest singer' to reply, 'He is a blind man, and lives in rocky Chios.'

l. 38. *Pope*. Alexander Pope's translation of the *Iliad* appeared 1715–20. The poet's father wisely ignores the conventional insistence that Pope, for all his virtues, is not Homer.

l. 40. *Primer*. An elementary introduction to Greek grammar.

l. 43. *Buttman*. Philipp Carl Buttman was a German scholar whose grammar, translated into English as *Intermediate or Larger Greek Grammar*, went through many editions in the 19th century.

l. 46. *Heine*. C. G. Heyne's was the standard edition of Homer in the first half of the 19th century. The Brownings had a copy in Italy.

l. 47. *Lexicon*. Liddell and Scott's *Greek–English Lexicon* was first published in 1843.

l. 58. *Thinks Byron*. Byron refers to Homer as 'The blind old man of Scio's rocky isle!', *The Bride of Abydos*, 509: 'Those Hymns', a collection of thirty-three hymns to various gods, attributed to Homer by Thucydides.

l. 59. *"Battle of the Frogs and Mice"*. *Batrachomyomachia*, a comic parody of the *Iliad* once attributed to Homer.

l. 60. *Margites*. The lost comic epic attributed to Homer by Aristotle.

l. 67. *Prolegomena*. Friedrich August Wolf's *Prolegomena ad Homerum* (1795) decisively challenged the assumption of single authorship of the *Iliad* by showing that it had its origin in poems that had at first been transmitted orally, and were written down and assembled into a single poem only by later editors.

ll. 70–1. Schliemann's claim to have discovered the historical Troy, published in 1874, did not at once persuade sceptics, and did not establish the historicity of the Trojan War, which remained in dispute.

ll. 76–7. Homer and the Trojan War may be fanciful, neither of them historical, but the acceptance of their historical reality has worked to preserve a poem the imaginative truth of which might otherwise have been lost.

l. 81. *his Spouse*. Andromache.

l. 84. *'No dream's worth waking'*. No dream is delightful enough to compensate for the pain of awakening to the realization that it is untrue.

l. 88. *nonage*. Youth or minority.

l. 99. *forthrights not meanderings*. Compare *The Tempest*, III. iii. 2–3: 'Here's a maze trod indeed | Through forthrights and meanders.'

ll. 100–1. *Peleus' son*. Achilles: compare Pope's *Iliad*, 9. 412–13: 'Who dares think one thing, and another tell, | My Heart detests him as the Gates of Hell.'

ll. 101–2. *love my wedded wife | Like Hector*. EBB had translated the meeting of Hector and Andromache from Book 6 of the *Iliad*.

l. 106. *The 'Ethics'*. Aristotle's *Nicomachean Ethics*.

l. 113. *growing double*. Compare Wordsworth, 'The Tables Turned', 3–4: 'Up', up, my friend, and quit your books, | Or surely you'll grow double'; *the Stagirite*. Aristotle, from his birthplace, Stagira.

Epilogue ['At the midnight']

The poem imagines how RB will be thought of after he is dead, self-consciously taking its place as his final published poem. It seems to be addressed to RB's hostess Mrs Arthur Bronson, the American who kept houses in Venice and Asolo, to whom RB's final volume is dedicated. The poem expresses deeper feelings than those due from a grateful houseguest. Mrs Bronson had separated from her husband shortly before RB met her, and since Mr Bronson's death in 1885 she had been a single woman. The complaint that she had taken him to be slothful, mawkish, and unmanly suggests that she had mistaken the nature of his affection for her, possibly accepting the picture of the poet (a picture that he had himself been complicit in painting) as a widower still, after more than a quarter of a century, in mourning for his dead wife. The demand that he be remembered at noon rather than at midnight, that he be recognized as a fact rather than a fancy, is suggestive. The vociferous assertions of stalwartness, the military metaphors, and the insistence that the afterlife, just as much as this, will be a life given over to energetic striving recall poems such as 'Rabbi Ben Ezra' and 'Prospice', but here they are still more emphatic, as if RB were increasingly sensitive to the charge levelled years earlier by RB's bête noire Alfred Austin that contemporary poets are 'women, or men with womanly deficiencies, steeped in the feminine temper of the times'.

l. 9. *helpless*. Hopeless, compare the 'helpless, hopeless scorn' of Romney Leigh's laughter when he learns that Aurora believes him to be married to Lady Waldemar, *Aurora Leigh*, 8. 1208.

l. 19. *Strive and thrive*. The title of an uplifting tale published in 1840 by Mary Howitt.

INDEX OF TITLES AND FIRST LINES

The manufacturer's authorised representative in the EU for product safety is Oxford University Press España S.A. of el Parque Empresarial San Fernando de Henares, Avenida de Castilla, 2 – 28830 Madrid (www.oup.es/en or product.safety@oup.com). OUP España S.A. also acts as importer into Spain of products made by the manufacturer.

www.ingramcontent.com/pod-product-compliance
Lightning Source LLC
Chambersburg PA
CBHW071834110726
47971CB00017B/122

* 9 7 8 0 1 9 8 7 9 7 6 2 3 *

La Saisiaz.

A. E. S. September 14, 1877.

Dared and done: at last I stand upon the summit, Dear and True!
Singly dared and done, the climbing both of us were bound to do.
Petty feat and yet prodigious: every side my glance was bent,
For the grandeur and the beauty lavished through the whole ascent.
Ledge by ledge, out broke new marvels, now minute and now immense:
Earth's most exquisite disclosure, heaven's own God in evidence!
And no berry in its hiding, no blue space in its outspread,
Pleaded to escape my footstep, challenged my emerging head
(As I climbed or paused from climbing, now o'erbranched by shrub and tree,
Now built round by rock and boulder, now at just a turn set free,
Stationed face to face with—Nature? rather with Infinitude)
—No revealment of them all, as singly I my ~~upward~~ path pursued,
But a bitter touched its sweetness, for the thought stung "Even so
Both of us had loved and wondered just the same, five days ago!"
Five short days, sufficient hardly to entice, from out its den
Splintered in the slab, this pink perfection of the cyclamen,—
Scarce enough to heal and coat with amber gum the sloe-tree's gash,
Bronze the clustered wilding apple, redden ripe the mountain-ash,—
Yet of might to place between us—Oh the barrier! Yon Profound
Shrinks beside it, proves a pin-point: barrier this, without a bound!
Boundless though it be, I reach you—somehow seem to have you here
—Who are there: yes, there you dwell now, plain the four low walls appear;
Those are vineyards they enclose from, and the little spire which points
—That's Collonge, henceforth your dwelling! All the same, whate'er disjoints
Past from present, no less certain you are here, not there—have dared,
Done the feat of mountain-climbing,—five days since, we both prepared
Daring, doing, arm in arm, if other help should haply fail.
For you asked, as forth we sallied to see sunset from the vale,

FIG. 10 MS in Browning's hand of opening lines of *La Saisiaz* (1878), Balliol College Library.

FROM *HOOD'S MAGAZINE*, vol. 1, June 1844; vol. 2, July 1844; vol. 3, March 1845; vol. 3, April 1845

FIRST LETTER TO ELIZABETH BARRETT, 10 JANUARY 1845

FROM *BELLS AND POMEGRANATES, NO. VII, DRAMATIC ROMANCES AND LYRICS* (1845)

FROM *LETTERS OF PERCY BYSSHE SHELLEY* (1852)

FROM *MEN AND WOMEN, I AND II* (1855)